"DOCTORED"
New Testament

The King James New Testament

"Doctored" by B. F. Westcott, D.D. & F. J. A. Hort, D.D. 1881
Documented by F. H. A. Scrivener, M.A., D.C.L., L.L.D. 1881

With Westcott & Hort's *Departures*
from Scrivener's Greek Text
***
Highlighted & Coded **in the *KJV***
and
Translated **from the Greek and**
Explained **in English Footnotes**
(with letter **differences bolded** in English
and in Transliterated Greek)

by D. A. Waite, Jr., M.A., M.L.A.

i

Published by

THE BIBLE FOR TODAY PRESS
900 Park Avenue
Collingswood, New Jersey 08108
U.S.A.

Phone: 856-854-4452
Orders: 1-800-John 10:9
e-mail: BFT@BibleForToday.org
website: www.BibleForToday.org
fax: 856-854-2464

September, 2003
B.F.T. #3138

Preface

Did the <u>title</u> of the *"Doctored" New Testament* catch your
attention? If so, you are probably wondering just how the term
doctored" applies to this particular New Testament. As the
title page suggests, the *"Doctored" New Testament* began with
the work of three learned "doctors"—Dr. Westcott (D.D.), Dr.
Hort, (D.D.), and Dr. Scrivener, (D.C.L, LL.D.) It has,
therefore, been "doctored" in that way.

But this New Testament was "doctored" in another, more
significant way. Previous revisions of the traditional English
New Testament primarily focused on improving the English
text and not on changing its Greek basis. But with the 1881
English Revised Version, a new wind began to blow. Doctors
Westcott and Hort (together with the *majority[1]* of the Revision
Committee) made thousands of New Testament changes based
on their new Greek Testament. This new Greek Testament had
been significantly "doctored"[2] with thousands of "various[3]
readings" from their two favorite Greek manuscripts—*Codex
Vaticanus* (B) and *Codex Sinaiticus* (א).

Even though most of the "various readings" from *Codex
Vaticanus* (B) and *Codex Sinaiticus* (א) are almost entirely
unsupported by the vast majority of surviving Greek
manuscripts, Doctors Westcott and Hort included thousands of
these "various readings" in their new 1881 Greek Testament
and in the 1881 *English Revised Version*.

These changes were made over the repeated objections of Dr. Scrivener.
"The text of Westcott & Hort is practically the text of אB," wrote Dr. F.C.
Burkitt (as quoted by Herman Hoskier on p. vi of *Codex B and Its Allies*, 1914).
Hoskier wrote: "Now in the following pages I submit a vast number of other
instances where B has a doctored text, plainly indubitably doctored." [p. vi]
Dean John William Burgon noted on page 35 of his *Traditional Text of the
Holy Gospels* that so-called "Various Readings" are readings that "possess
really strong attestation [verification or support]." He estimated that "more
than nineteen-twentieths [over 95%] of the 'Various Readings' commonly
quoted are only the vagaries [quirks or eccentricities, i.e. mistakes or errors]
of scribes, and ought not to be called 'Readings' at all."

Codex Vaticanus (B) and *Codex Sinaiticus* (א), indeed may be some of the "oldest" surviving manuscripts of the New Testament. As ancient curiosities, therefore, they deserve secure place in a museum of ancient artifacts. But oldness—all by itself—does not of necessity make a witness "best." In textual criticism--just as in a court of law—it is best to take witnesses one at a time. And it is best to judge each witness' veracity by direct examination and by cross examination.

Just as in a court of law, a judge and a jury must strive to be as impartial and unbiased as is humanly possible. So should it be when evaluating Greek manuscripts. There should be no respect of persons (or manuscripts) in judgment. No one should favor the rich, elegant-looking vellum manuscript and distain the poor, tattered papyrus one—based on appearance alone. Each manuscript deserves its "day in court." And any judgment should be based on solid evidence—not on preconceived theories.

If we were to give *Codex Vaticanus* (B) and *Codex Sinaiticus* (א) their own "day in court," scribal tradition would respectfully testify against their integrity. A *trusted* copy of New Testament Greek manuscript was copied again and again until it finally wore out from use. When this *trusted* manuscript became hard to read because of use, it was destroyed. A faithful copy of that *trusted* (now destroyed) manuscript carried on the tradition until it too was worn out and was replaced by another *trusted* copy.

If the ancient scribes[1] who copied *Codex Vaticanus* (B) and *Codex Sinaiticus* (א) had really trusted the textual integrity of these codices, they (or their contemporaries) would have copied their text over and over again until these ancient documents were worn out from use and destroyed. The existence and condition of these ancient curiosities suggest that

---

[1] According to Dr. Scrivener (on page 116 of his *A Plain Introduction to New Testament Textual Criticism*, 4*[th]* Edition 1894), Tischendorf concluded that *Codex Sinaiticus* (א) and *Codex Vaticanus* (B) are "documents of the same age." and that "the scribe who wrote the latter [B] is one of the four to whose diligence we owe the former [א]."

they were not copied over and over again as a *trusted* manuscript would have been copied. Instead of being <u>copied</u> over and over again, however, they were <u>corrected</u> by several scribes over a period of centuries.

One of the difficulties in determining the true testimony of *Codex Vaticanus* (B) is the presence of four different sets of handwriting. The "early scribes" included the "original writer" and "his διορθωτής" or corrector. Both of these scribes "supplied words or letters here and there in the margin or between the lines." Another "ancient scribe" also made corrections to the Codex. Finally, a fourth "person"—trying either to clarify or to obscure—"retraced the faded writing at a later period."[1]

But if each[2] letter has been "retraced" or overwritten, how can anyone know <u>with certainty</u> what the original letters of this Codex were? It would seem that this "person" who "retraced the faded writing" of *Codex Vaticanus* (B) destroyed whatever credibility this ancient curiosity had ever had.

The text of *Codex Sinaiticus* (א) has also seen significant corruption over the centuries. From the fourth to the twelfth centuries "at least ten" different "revisers" saw fit to correct the text of this venerable curiosity.[3] If the text was "oldest and best" to begin with, then why did at least ten different "revisers" feel the need to correct it? How does anyone know for sure when or why each revision occurred? Instead of <u>copying</u> this codex again and again, scribes <u>corrected</u> it again and again. Did they know something that we don't know?

Because of the large number of obvious scribal errors in his two favorite manuscripts, even Dr. Hort had to admit that the copyist of *Codex Vaticanus* (B) "reached by no means a high standard of accuracy."[4] He further conceded that

---

[1] Dr. Scrivener provided these details on page 116 of his *A Plain Introduction to New Testament Textual Criticism*, 4th Edition, 1894.

[2] Kenyon indicated in his *Text of the Greek Bible* that the scribe "went over every letter, except those which he thought incorrect." (This quote was found on p. 115 of Jack Mooreman's *Forever Settled*, 1985 [DBS 1999].)

[3] These ideas were found on page 113 of *Forever Settled*.

[4] This is another way of saying that the copyist was careless and inaccurate.

"[*Codex*] *Sinaiticus* [א] is acknowledged on every side to be worse than [*Codex Vaticanus*] B in every way."[1] These words hardly sound like a ringing defense of the textual integrity of these venerable codices. If a "various reading" from *Codex Vaticanus* (B) or *Codex Sinaiticus* (א) had no significant support from other Greek manuscripts, how did Dr. Hort distinguish readings that were "scribal errors" from readings that were the "true text?"

Of *Codex Vaticanus* (B) and *Codex Sinaiticus* (א), Dean John William Burgon wrote that "the text of these two Codexes is very nearly the foulest in existence."[2] In *Revision Revised* Burgon compared *Codex Vaticanus* (B) to the Received Text of the Gospels. According to his count, it <u>omitted</u> 2,877 or more words, <u>added</u> 536 words, <u>substituted</u> 935 words, <u>transposed</u> 2,098 words, and <u>modified</u> 1,132 words. More than 7,578 words were affected by these changes to the Gospels.

Burgon also compared *Codex Sinaiticus* (א) to the Received Text of the Gospels. According to his count, it <u>omitted</u> 3,455 words, <u>added</u> 839 words, <u>substituted</u> 1,114 words, <u>transposed</u> 2,299 words, and <u>modified</u> 1,265 words. These changes to the Gospels affected 8,972 total words.

But these "oldest and best" manuscripts do not just differ with the Received Text in thousands of places. They also differ with **themselves** in thousands of places as well. Having compared both *Codex Vaticanus* (B) and *Codex Sinaiticus* (א), Burgon concluded: "It is in fact easier to find two consecutive verses in which these two MSS differ, than two consecutive verses in which they entirely agree."[3] In his 924-paged *Codex B and its Allies*, Herman Hoskier demonstrated that "over 3,000 real differences between [*Codex Sinaiticus* א] Aleph and [*Codex Vaticanus*] B are recorded in the Gospels alone!"[4]

---

[1] These quotes were found on p. 113 of Jack Mooreman's *Forever Settled*, DBS 1999 ed. He quoted from *INTT* [*Integrity of the New Testament Text*].
[2] page 75 of *The Traditional Text of the Holy Gospels,* 1896 (DBS 1998)
[3] This quotation and the counts from the previous two paragraphs all come from page 12 of Burgon's *Revision Revised*, 1883 (DBS 2nd Printing, 2000).
[4] The quote is from Volume I, page vi of *Codex B and Its Allies*, 1914.

Please note that Burgon and Hoskier were counting changes in the Gospels[1] only. This includes Matthew, Mark, Luke, and John—but NOT Acts through Revelation. If we approximate the New Testament's total length by doubling Burgon's and Hoskier's totals, *Codex Vaticanus* (B) could have differed[2] with the Received Text in about 15,156 words; *Codex Sinaiticus* (‪א‬) could have differed with the Received Text in about 17,994 words; and the two codices could have differed with **themselves** in about 6,000 places.

In a court of law, how many discrepancies are necessary before a witness is successfully impeached? Are two or three enough? How about 7,000 or 20,000 or more? Would you trust a pair of witnesses who were caught lying over 15,000 times to their neighbors and who were caught lying over 6,000 times to each other?

As a member of a jury, would you place any confidence in the accuracy of a court stenographer who had made over 15,000 known mistakes in recording the testimony of just one witness? And if that witness were now dead, how could you determine exactly what that witness had really said? How would you know which part of the transcript you could trust and which part you could not trust?

Whether you share Westcott and Hort's confidence in *Codex Vaticanus* (B) and *Codex Sinaiticus* (‪א‬) or not, one fact still remains. They <u>did</u> introduce thousands of changes into the existing text of the Greek New Testament (and into the text of the traditional English Bible). The *"Doctored" New Testament* is designed to help you discover and to understand in English the number and nature of these changes.

But what about F. H. A. Scrivener--did he not also "doctor" the Greek New Testament? Yes, he did. But he "doctored" it for a very important reason--he "doctored" it for <u>comparison</u> purposes only. He did not claim that he was making his Greek text closer to the original.

---

[1] The Gospels contain about one-half of the New Testament.

[2] The reader must understand that Codex Vaticanus is missing Hebrews (9:15 to the end), the Pastoral Epistles, and the book of Revelation.

The 1881 *English Revised Version* did not simply revise the English of the *KJV*. Under Westcott and Hort's leadership, it revised the Greek basis as well. When Westcott and Hort's new Greek Testament was published in 1881, people could compare the *ERV* with its Greek textual basis. They could compare the English of the *KJV* with the English of the *ERV*. But they could NOT effectively compare the *KJV* with its Greek textual basis or compare the Greek textual basis of the *ERV* with the Greek textual basis of the *KJV*.

Why was this so? On page vii of his "Preface," Dr. Scrivener answered this question: "The Authorised Version was not a translation of any one Greek text then in existence, and no Greek text intended to reproduce in any way the original of the Authorised Version has ever been printed." He explained that "the composite nature of the Authorised Version" was caused by "successive revisions of Tyndales's translation." Although "Tyndale himself followed the second and third editions of Erasmus's Greek text (1519, 1522)[,]" later revisers of his translation before 1611 made "a partial use of other texts ."

Dr. Scrivener chose to begin his task with Beza's 1598 Greek edition. This slightly reduced the number of required changes (compared to starting with other Greek editions of Erasmus, Stephanus, Beza, or Elzevir). He also reasoned that "between 1598 and 1611 no important edition appeared; so that Beza's fifth and last text of 1598 was more likely than any other to be in the hands of King James's revisers, and to be accepted by them as the best standard within their reach."

Where the English of the *KJV* differed from Beza's 1598 Greek edition, Dr. Scrivener (in about 162 places) used readings from previous Greek editions of the Received Text. He kept Beza's 1598 reading in about 59 places where the *KJV* had only Latin support. He listed these c. 221 deviations from Beza's 1598 Greek edition in his "Appendix" (pages 648-656).

D. A. Waite, Jr., M.A., M.L.A.
Chesapeake Beach, MD
July 21, 2003

Table of Contents

Transliteration Chart

Name	Capital / Small		Eng Equivalent	Doc NT Char
A alpha	A	α	A as in hat	a
Ata[1]	H	η	A as in hate	A
B beta	B	β	B as in boy	b
C chi	X	χ	Ch as in chasm	c
D delta	Δ	δ	D as in dog	d
E epsilon	E	ε	E as in pet	e
F phi	Φ	φ	Ph as in phase	f
G gamma	Γ	γ	G as in goat	g
H	[Rough Breathing Mark]'		H as in hit	h
I iota	I	ι	I as in fit	i
J	[The J sound is approximated by using iota.]			----
K kappa	K	κ	K as in king	k
L lambda	Λ	λ	L as in lion	l
M mu	M	μ	M as in mouse	m
N nu	N	ν	N as in nose	n
O omikron	O	o	O as in ox	o
Omega	Ω	ω	O as in over	O
P pi	Π	π	P as in pig	p
Q	[There is no Q sound in Greek.]			----
R ro	P	ρ	R as in rat	r
S sigma	Σ	σ /s[2]	S as in sit	s
psi	Ψ	ψ	pS as in psych	s̬
T tau	T	τ	T as in top	t
theta	Θ	θ	Th as in thing	th
U upsilon	Υ	υ	U as in cupid	u
V	[There is no V sound in Greek.]			----
W	[There is no W sound in Greek.]			----
X Xi	Ξ	ξ	Ks as in box	x
Y	[The Y sound is approximated by using iota.]			----
Z Zeta	Z	ζ	Dz as in zest	z

[1] The usual spelling of this letter is *Eta*. Since I was taught to pronounce *Eta* as the long *A* sound, I spelled it *Ata*. (There are many who pronounce *Eta* as the long *E* sound.)

[2] Sigma is written as σ except at the end of words where it is written as *s*.

Transliterations Used in the *"Doctored" New Testament.*

by D. A. Waite, Jr., M.A., M.L.A.

In the chart on the previous page, I have arranged the Greek letters in the order of the English alphabet. The first column displays the English letter together with the name of the Greek letter that most closely approximates it. The second column lists the upper-case and lower-case form of that Greek letter. The third column lists a traditional example of how the letter may have been pronounced. And the fourth (and final) column lists the character that I used to represent that Greek letter throughout the *"Doctored" New Testament.*

Except for using th for *theta* (θ) and ş for *psi* (ψ), I maintained a letter-for-letter correspondence in transliterating from Greek to English. The th is a single computer-character that looks like a *t* linked to an *h* with a horizontal line. The ş combination is my attempt at transliterating the Greek *psi* (ψ). The *psi* is pronounced like the *ps* in ***psychology*** or ***psychosomatic***. The *p* sound is only slightly pronounced, while the *S* sound dominates. Please note that the ş and the th each represent just <u>one</u> Greek letter.

I transliterated *omicron* ("short" *o* as in *ox*) as a lower case *o*, and I transliterated *Omega* ("long" *O* as in *Over*) as an Upper Case *O*. To distinguish the "short" *alpha* sound (*a* as in *hat*) from the "long" *Ata* sound (*A* as in *hAte*), I used the lower-case *a* and the Upper-Case *A* respectively.

I used *c* for *chi*, *f* for *phi*, *x* for *xi*, and *z* for *zeta*. I represented the rough breathing mark as a superscript [h]. The exact koine Greek pronunciation of the First Century A.D. is not certain. These approximations, however, correspond to the sounds I was taught in my New Testament Greek classes in the 1960's and 1970's.

An Introduction
to the
"Doctored" New Testament
by D. A. Waite, Jr., M.A., M.L.A.

The purpose of this work is simple—to communicate **in English** the changes that Doctors Westcott and Hort (WH)[1] made to the Greek text that approximates (as far as possible) the English of the *KJV*.

My primary source for Westcott and Hort's changes is a work by Dr. Frederick. H. A. Scrivener, M.A., D.C.L., LL. D., first published in 1881 by the Cambridge University Press.[2] Dr. Scrivener called this work *The New Testament in Greek According to the Text Followed in the Authorised Version Together with the Variations Adopted in the Revised Version.*

This Greek New Testament (based <u>primarily</u> on Beza's 1598 Greek edition) was specifically designed to reconstruct— as far as possible—a Greek text that underlies the English of the Authorized Version.[3] Its footnoted annotations faithfully represented the Greek basis for the changes made to the New Testament of the 1881 *English Revised Version*. Careful comparison reveals that this Greek basis corresponds almost exactly[4] with the wording of Westcott & Hort's 1881 Greek New Testament.

---

[1] Throughout the *"Doctored" NT*, I abbreviated Westcott & Hort as "WH."

[2] I used the edition of this work reprinted by the Dean Burgon Society in December of 1999. This reprinted edition has these words on the title page: "*Scrivener's Annotated Greek New Testament Being the Exact Greek Textus Receptus that Underlies the King James Bible* by the late Dr. Frederick H. A. Scrivener Showing the E.R.V. 1881 / Westcott and Hort Erroneous Departures from the Textus Receptus Dean Burgon Society Press Box 354 Collingswood, New Jersey 08108, U.S.A. December, 1999 DBS1670 ISBN 1-888328-05-3[.]" This DBS reprint also includes original title pages identifying this copy as a 1908 reprint (8th printing) of the 1881 edition.

[3] The Cambridge University Press commissioned Dr. Scrivener to use this format as the most effective way of displaying the Greek changes that were adopted as the basis of the 1881 *English Revised New Testament*.

[4] I noted a few minor differences. Some of these differences seem to have been corrections of errors no longer perpetuated in subsequent printings.

Scrivener's invaluable work contains a 7-paged "Preface" (pp. v-xi), a 647-paged Greek New Testament with footnoted annotations containing all *ERV* readings whose Greek basis is **"at variance with the readings 'presumed to underlie the Authorised Version'"** (pp. 1-647), and a 9-paged "Appendix" (pp. 648-656). The "Appendix" contains a list of about 162 places where the *KJV* seems to differ from the 1598 edition of Beza's Greek New Testament. It also contains a list of about 59 places[1] where the *KJV* is based on the Latin and not on any known Greek authority[2]. Dr. Scrivener bolded the Greek words affected by Dr. Westcott and Dr. Hort's changes and used footnotes to document those Greek changes.

This is an excellent work edited by one of history's few legitimate, NT Greek textual scholars. Unfortunately—except for its introduction—this work is all in Greek. The *"Doctored" New Testament* is an attempt to take the Greek changes of Westcott & Hort (as documented by Scrivener) and make them understandable to the English reader.

Explanations and Examples of Methods and Markings Used in the *"Doctored" New Testament*

<u>NOTE</u>: In a work of this kind, a **rigidly literal translation is absolutely necessary to demonstrate the fine distinctions represented by most of the changes that Westcott and Hort introduced** into their 1881 Greek New Testament. In order to demonstrate the word-for-word and letter-by-letter changes, I have used modern translation formulas—especially when distinguishing tenses in English. In the 1500's (when the bulk of the traditional English Bible's text was established) such modern distinctions were seldom made. I trust that each reader of the *"Doctored" New Testament* will

---

[1] On page 656, Dr. Scrivener writes that "the present list is probably quite incomplete, and a few cases seems precarious." (These are my own counts.)

[2] In those *KJV* portions with no known Greek support, Scrivener let the readings of Beza's 1598 Greek NT stand (page 655, last paragraph). He did not backwards-translate from Latin to Greek!

appreciate the challenges involved in trying to make these difficult distinctions. I have tried vigorously to avoid errors in this very technical work. Unfortunately, errors—inevitably linked to all human endeavors—may still lurk in the shadows.

I began with the computerized copy of the King James New Testament that I had prepared for the *Defined King James Bible*. After removing all *DKJB* footnotes and bolding, I began to BOLD all words in the New Testament that were affected by Dr. Westcott and Dr. Hort's 1881 changes. Next, I subdivided all changes into two basic categories: **I. Changes WH <u>MADE</u> in their <u>Text</u>** and **II. Changes WH <u>PROPOSED</u> in their <u>Margin</u>**.

I then further subdivided each of these two basic categories into four subcategories: (A) <u>Omission,</u> (B) <u>Addition,</u> (C) <u>Transposition,</u> and (D) <u>Substitution.</u>

I. CHANGES WH <u>MADE</u> IN THEIR <u>TEXT</u>

A. Examples of Text OMISSION

When there was an OMISSION in the text, I crossed out the words affected by that omission [~~like this~~].

Example 1--In Matthew 1:6 we find these words: "And Jesse begat David the king; and David ~~the king~~[1] begat Solomon of her *that had been the wife* of Urias;" // The footnote reads as follows: "[1]WH omitted <u>the</u> <u>king</u> ([h]o basileus)." [For transliteration information, see pages xi-xii.]

In this example, notice that **the king** is in bold type and is crossed out. In the OMISSION footnotes of the *"Doctored" NT*, I first cite an English translation of the Greek words omitted. Then in parentheses, I cite the transliteration of those Greek words. For example, the transliteration [h]o basileus is how we would write and pronounce the two Greek words ὁ βασιλεὺς. Footnote 1 tells us that Doctors Westcott and Hort omitted two Greek words—the transliterated words in parentheses ([h]o basileus). This footnote also tells us that the two Greek words that WH (my abbreviation for Doctors Westcott and Hort throughout) omitted can be translated <u>the</u> <u>king</u>. (When two English words have two separate underlinings, they are translations of two separate Greek words. Because WH omitted two Greek words translated into English as <u>the</u> <u>king</u>, I underlined each individual English word. I also transliterated the two Greek words WH omitted and underlined each Greek word individually.) Throughout the *"Doctored" NT*, I used a superscript ^h to indicate the Greek rough breathing mark. The rough breathing marks and smooth breathing marks were added in printed Greek texts to help in pronunciation.

Example 2--In Matthew 5:22 we find these words: "But I say unto you, That whosoever is angry with his brother ~~without a cause~~[2] shall be in danger of the judgment: and whosoever shall say to his brother, Raca, shall be in danger of the council: but whosoever shall say, Thou fool, shall be in danger of hell fire." // The footnote reads as follows : "[2] WH omitted <u>without a cause</u> (<u>eikA</u>) in their text, but retained <u>eikA</u> in their margin."

The English words **without a cause** are in bold type and are crossed out. Since WH only omitted one Greek word here (transliterated as <u>eikA</u>), the English translation of that one word—**<u>without a cause</u>**—shows only one term with one separate underlining (NOT three separate words with three separate underlinings like this—**<u>without</u> <u>a</u> <u>cause</u>**.)

Example 3—In Matthew 6:13 we find these words: "And lead us not into temptation, but deliver us from evil**: ~~For thine is the kingdom, and the power, and the glory, for ever. Amen~~**[3]." // The footnote reads as follows: "[3] WH omitted <u>for thine</u> <u>is</u> <u>the</u> <u>kingdom</u> <u>and</u> <u>the</u> <u>power</u> <u>and</u> <u>the</u> <u>glory</u> <u>unto</u> <u>the</u> <u>ages</u> <u>Amen</u> (^h<u>oti</u> <u>sou</u> <u>estin</u> ^h<u>A</u> <u>basileia</u> <u>kai</u> ^h<u>a</u> <u>dunamis</u> <u>kai</u> ^h<u>A</u> <u>doxa</u> <u>eis</u> <u>tous</u> <u>aiOnas</u> <u>amAn</u>) in their text. In their margin, WH included these words"

Notice again that the omitted words are bolded and crossed out in the *KJV* text. In the footnote, each underlined English word represents an underlined Greek word. The translation unto the ages is a literal rendering that shows the word-for-word translation of eis tous aiOnas.

Example 4—In Matthew 6:10 we find these words: "Thy kingdom come. Thy will be done in [the][4] earth, as *it is* in heaven." // The footnote reads as follows: "[4]WH omitted the untranslated the (tAs) before earth."

The *KJV* frequently does not translate a definite article [the] contained in Scrivener's Greek NT. Whenever WH omitted an untranslated definite article, I added that the in brackets and cross it out to show the change. Notice here that the is single underlined since it represents a Greek word in Scrivener's Greek NT transliterated as tAs.

Example 5—In Matthew 6:18 we find these words: "That thou appear not unto men to fast, but unto thy Father which is in secret: and thy Father, which seeth in secret, shall reward thee openly[5]. // The footnote reads as follows: "[5]WH omitted in the open (en tO fanerO)."

In this example, WH omitted three Greek words transliterated en tO fanerO. The literal word-for-word translation of these words is in the open.

B. Examples of Text ADDITION

When there was an ADDITION in the text, I used a carrot [ʌ] and entered the words in brackets where WH wanted the addition to go [ʌlike this].

Example 1--In Matthew 3:6 we find these words: "And were baptized of him in Jordan [ʌriver][1], confessing their sins." // The footnote reads as follows: "[1]WH added *river* (*potamO*) after Jordan."

To show additions to the text, I used square brackets [ ] to enclose words that were not present in the English of the *KJV*. I inserted a carrot [ʌ] together with a bolded English translation of the addition to show where WH inserted Greek words into their text. In this example, WH added the single Greek word *potamO* after <u>Jordan</u>. Since *river* is a good translation of that Greek addition, I added *river* in brackets with a carrot before the word. To highlight the change, I also bolded **river**. Throughout the footnotes of the *"Doctored" NT*, I have used italic type [*like this*] to indicate English or Greek words that are based on *Westcott and Hort's Greek New Testament.* In like manner, I have used single underlining [<u>like</u> <u>this</u>] to indicate English or Greek words that are based on <u>Scrivener's Greek New Testament</u>. Notice that both *river* and the Greek transliteration *potamO* are in italics. They represent words in *Westcott and Hort's Greek New Testament.* Also notice that <u>Jordan</u> is single underlined because I am referring to a word based on <u>Scrivener's Greek New Testament</u>.

Example 2—In Matthew 7:29 we find these words: "For he taught them as *one* having authority, and not as the scribes [∧**of them**][2]." // The footnote reads as follows: "[2]WH added *of them* (*autOn*) after <u>scribes</u>."

According to the footnote, WH added one Greek word *autOn*. This Greek word and its translation are both in italic type because they represent words in WH's Greek New Testament. Although WH only added one Greek word, that word is translated as *them*, and its genitive case ending is translated as *of*.

Example 3—In Matthew 19:21 we find these words: "Jesus said unto him, If thou wilt be perfect, go *and* sell that thou hast, and give to ∧**the**[3] poor, and thou shalt have treasure in heaven: and come *and* follow me." // The footnote reads as follows: "[3]WH added *the* (*tois*) as the KJV supplied.

The *KJV* frequently supplied a definite article [the] where none existed in the Greek text. Whenever WH added a *the* that was already supplied by the *KJV*, I bolded the supplied **the** and used a carrot to show the place of the WH addition. I did not use brackets since the *KJV* had already introduced the WH addition into the English text.

Example 4—In Matthew 21:15 we find these words: "And when the chief priests and scribes saw the wonderful things that he did, and the children [ʌ**the** {ones}][4] crying in the temple, and saying, Hosanna to the Son of David; they were sore displeased," // The footnote reads as follows: "[4]WH added *the* {ones} (*tous*)."

In this example, WH added only one Greek word. I transliterated it as *tous* and translated it as *the*. Since this word was plural, I supplied {ones} in braces. If *the* had been singular, I would have supplied {one} instead of {ones}.

Example 5—In Mark 12:8 we read these words: "And they took him, and killed *him*, and cast ʌ*him*[5] out of the vineyard." // The footnote reads as follows: "[5]WH added the *him* (*auton*) that the KJV supplied in italics."

Occasionally the *KJV* supplied in italics words that are not contained in the Greek text. Whenever WH added a Greek word already supplied by the *KJV* in italics, I bolded the supplied word and used a carrot to show the place of the WH addition. I did not use brackets since the *KJV* had already introduced the WH addition into the English text.

C. Examples of Text TRANSPOSITION

When WH made a text change in Word-Order (or text TRANSPOSITION), I bolded and single-underlined the fewest words necessary to make the change in word order [**like this**].

Example 1—In Mark 3:27 we read these words: "No man can enter **into a** strong man's **house**, and spoil his **goods**[1], except he will first bind the strong man; and then he will spoil his house." // The footnote reads as follows: "[1]WH changed the word order from THE GOODS of the strong man enter INTO THE HOUSE to *INTO THE HOUSE of the strong man enter THE GOODS*."

In the *"Doctored" NT* footnotes, the most effective way to show the word order differences (in most cases) was for me to translate the <u>Scrivener's Greek Text</u> (<u>underlined</u>) and the *WH Greek Text* (*italicized*) very literally, following the Greek word order almost slavishly. I placed the actual words that were transposed in Small Capital letters [LIKE THIS]. Following my usual pattern, I gave the literal translation of <u>Scrivener's Greek NT</u> first followed by the literal translation of *WH's Greek NT.*

Notice in this example that WH moved the two Greek words translated <u>THE GOODS</u> from the <u>beginning</u> of the portion (<u>Scrivener</u>) to the *end* of the portion (*WH*). Notice also that WH moved the three Greek words translated <u>INTO THE HOUSE</u> from the <u>end</u> of the portion (<u>Scrivener</u>) to the *beginning* of the portion (*WH*). <u>Of the</u> and <u>strong man</u> are two examples of one Greek word translated by two English words.

Example 2—In Mark 4:11 we find these words: "And he said unto them, Unto you it is given to know **the mystery**[2] of the kingdom of God: but unto them that are without, all *these* things are done in parables:" // The footnote reads as follows: "[2]WH changed the word order from **it** <u>is given</u> **to know** <u>THE MYSTERY</u> to *THE MYSTERY is given.*"

In this example, WH moved two Greek words (translated <u>THE MYSTERY</u>) from the end of the passage to the beginning of the passage. (The words **it to know** [in the footnote] are in bold because they were changed in some way, as noted in another footnote.)

Example 3—In John 5:37 we find these words: "And the Father himself, which hath sent me, hath borne witness of me. Ye have neither heard his voice **at any time**[3], nor seen his shape." // The footnote reads as follows: "[3]WH changed the word order from <u>ye have heard</u> <u>AT ANY TIME</u> to *AT ANY TIME ye have heard.*"

Notice that **at any time** is underlined together as one term. This term represents one Greek word. WH moved this single Greek word from the end of the passage to the beginning.

Example 4—In John 10:42 we find these words: "And **many believed on him there**[4]." // The footnote reads as follows: "[4]WH changed the word order from BELIEVED MANY THERE ON HIM to *MANY BELIEVED ON THERE HIM*."

In this example, WH completely scrambled the order of these five Greek words. MANY and BELIEVED change places; and THERE moved from before ON HIM to between ON and HIM.

Example 5—In John 18:33 we read these words: "Then Pilate entered into the judgment hall **again**[5], and called Jesus, and said unto him, Art thou the King of the Jews?" // The footnote reads as follows: "[5]WH changed the word order from into the judgment hall AGAIN to *AGAIN into the judgment hall*."

In this example, WH moved the single Greek word (translated AGAIN) from the last word in the passage to the first word in the passage. Five separate Greek words correspond to the five separately underlined English words in this portion.

D. Examples of Text SUBSTITUTION

When there was SUBSTITUTION in the text , I double underlined the words affected by that change [**like this**].

(1) SIMPLE Substitutions—Whenever WH made a change of *one* kind only, I called that a "Simple" Substitution. The most common "Simple" Substitutions were in Tense, Case, Number, Spelling, Mood, Gender, Person, and Voice.

a. TENSE Examples

Present to *Aorist* Tense
In Matthew 4:5, we read these words: "Then the devil taketh him up into the holy city, and **setteth**[1] him on a pinnacle of the temple." // The footnote reads as follows: "[1]WH changed sets ([h]istAsin) to *set* (*estAsen*). **Pres** Act Ind to *Aor* Act Ind. [tense]"

Please note that I classified each simple substitution by putting a word or two in brackets at (or near the end) of the footnote. In this case, I put *tense* in brackets because the verb tense is all that changed. In English, notice that I modernized <u>setteth</u> to <u>sets</u> to avoid exaggerating the change from <u>sets</u> to *set*. In Greek, notice also that the changes involved two letters and a breathing mark—WH changed $^h\underline{i}$ to *e*; and <u>i</u> to *e*.

<u>Future</u> to *Present* Tense

In Matthew 5:39, we read these words: "But I say unto you, That ye resist not evil: but whosoever **shall smite**[2] thee on thy right cheek, turn to him the other also."// The footnote reads as follows: "[2]WH changed **shall** smite (^{h}rapisei) to *is smiting* (^{h}rapizei). **Fut** Act Ind to *Pres* Act Ind. [tense]"

In English, notice that **shall** became *is* and the last letter in <u>smite</u> (<u>e</u>) became the last three letters in *smiting* (*ing*). In Greek, however, WH changed just one letter—the <u>s</u> became a *z*. Again notice that I classifed the change by bracketing *tense*.

<u>Present</u> to *Imperfect* Tense

In Matthew 9:24, we read these words: "**He said**[3], Give place: for the maid is not dead, but sleepeth. And they laughed him to scorn." // The footnote reads as follows: "[3]WH changed <u>he says</u> (<u>legei</u>) to *he was saying* (*elegen*). **Pres** Act Ind to *Impf* Act Ind. [tense]"

The traditional English Bible frequently did not distinguish tenses as we would do so today[1]. This practice can exaggerate or confuse tense differences—especially when dealing with Greek technicalities. In English, notice that I have avoided *overstating* the English differences by literally translating the present tense as <u>he says</u> (and not as <u>he said</u>). The English change here involves adding *was* after <u>he</u> and changing the <u>s</u> in <u>says</u> to the *ing* in *saying*. In Greek, notice that WH added the prefix *e* before the root and changed the last letter from <u>i</u> to *n*.

---

[1] In Mark 9:24, the 1611 revisers wisely modernized the spelling of *sayd* (as the *Bishops' Bible* had it) to *said*. They corrected the spelling, but kept the past tense.

Aorist to *Present* Tense

In Matthew 21:13, we read these words: "And said unto them, It is written, My house shall be called the house of prayer; but ye **have made**[4] it a den of thieves." // The footnote reads as follows: "[4]WH changed made (**epoiAsate**) to *are making* (*poieite*). **Aor** Act Ind to *Pres* Act Ind. [tense]"

In English, notice that I avoided *overstating* the differences by literally translating the Aorist tense as made (instead of **have** made). The change required adding an *are* and changing the **de** in made to a *king* in *making*. In Greek, WH added the prefix *e* before the root and changed **Asa** to *ei* before the *te* at the end of the word.

Aorist to *Perfect* Tense

In Matthew 22:4, we read these words: "Again, he sent forth other servants, saying, Tell them which are bidden, Behold, **I have prepared**[5] my dinner: my oxen and *my* fatlings *are* killed, and all things *are* ready: come unto the marriage." // The footnote reads as follows: "[5]WH changed I prepared ([h]Atoimasa) *to I have prepared* ([h]Atoimaka). **Aor** Act to a *Pf* Act. [tense]"

In English, I avoided the confusion that would have resulted if I had failed to distinguish the tenses[1]. The *KJV* English here is a literal translation of the WH Greek text[2]. Taking care to distinguish the tenses, I translated the Aorist tense as I prepared (not I **have** prepared). I prepared then became *I have prepared*. In English, the change required the adding of a *have* after the I. In Greek, WH simply changed one letter—an **s** became a *k*.

---

[1] Some may criticize me for deviating from the *KJV* wording. The vast majority of the differences between the WH Greek text and the Scrivener's Greek text, however, can not be distinguished in English without rigidly literal translations.

[2] This phenomenon occurs numerous times in the New Testament. A rigidly literal translation of the Scrivener's Greek NT, however, delivers the *KJV* from such textual "heresy."

Present to *Aorist* Tense

In Matthew 26:43, we read these words: "And he came and **found**[6] them asleep again: for their eyes were heavy." // The footnote reads as follows: "[6]They changed finds (eu**riskei**) to *found* (*euren*). **Pres** Act Ind to *Aor* Act Ind. [tense]"

In English, I avoided the confusion that would have resulted if I had failed to distinguish the tenses. Here again the *KJV* English is a literal translation of the WH Greek text. Taking care to distinguish the tenses, I translated the Present tense as finds (instead of found[1]). In English, Finds then became *found*. In Greek, WH changed the **iskei** to *en* at the end of the word.

Perfect to *Aorist* Tense

In Mark 1:38, we find these words: "And he said unto them, Let us go into the next towns, that I may preach there also: for therefore **came I forth**[7]." // The footnote reads as follows: "[7]WH changed I **have** come out (ex-el**Alutha**) to *I came out* (*ex-Althon*). **Pf** Act Ind to *Aor Act Ind.* [tense]"

In English, I avoided the confusion that would have resulted if I had failed to distinguish the tenses. I translated the Perfect tense as I **have** come **out**[2] (instead of came I **forth**). I **have** come out became *I came out*. In Greek, WH removed *el* after ex and removed *u* after Al.

b. CASE Examples
Dative to *Genitive* Case

In Mark 2:9, we read these words: "Whether is it easier to say to the sick of the palsy, *Thy* sins be forgiven **thee**[1]; or to say, Arise, and take up thy bed, and walk?" // The footnote

---

[1] In Matthew 26:43, the 1611 revisers modernized the *Bishops' Bible* spelling of *founde* to *found*. They changed the spelling but retained the past tense.

[2] Although I have come **forth** was possible, I wanted to stress the root meaning of the prefix eks (which is **out**).

reads as follows: "[1]WH changed {**to**} <u>thee</u> (<u>so</u>*i*) to {**of**} *thee* (*sou*). **Dat** to ***Gen***. [case]"

In Greek, this case change involved just one letter—WH changed the <u>i</u> to a *u*. In English, one preposition supplied by the Dative (<u>to</u>) changed into a different preposition supplied by the genitive (*of*).

Genitive to *Accusative* Case

In Mark 6:43, we read these words: "And they took up twelve baskets full **<u>of the fragments</u>**[2], and of the fishes." // The footnote reads as follows: "[2]WH changed *of* <u>fragments</u> (<u>klasmat**On**</u>) to *fragments* (*klasmata*). **<u>Gen</u>** Neut Plur to ***Acc*** Neut Plur. [case]"

In Greek, WH changed two letters (<u>On</u>) into one letter (*a*). This case change is made in English by dropping the <u>of</u> (supplied by the genitive case) before <u>fragments</u>.

Accusative to *Nominative* Case

In Mark 8:2, we read these words: "I have compassion on the multitude, because they have now been with me three **<u>days</u>**[3], and have nothing to eat:" // The footnote reads as follows: "[3]WH changed *days* ([h]<u>Ameras</u>) to *days* ([h]*Amerai*). **<u>Acc</u>** to ***Nom***. [case]"

In Greek, this case change involved one letter--<u>s</u> became *i*. In English, however, there was no translatable difference.

Accusative to *Genitive* Case

In Mark 9:28, we read these words: "And **<u>when he was come</u>**[4] into the house, his disciples asked him privately, Why could not we cast him out?" // The footnote reads as follows: "[4]WH changed <u>having come him</u> (<u>eiselth̶onta auton</u>) to *having come him* (*eiselth̶ontos autou*). Both Aor Act Part. **<u>Acc</u>** Masc Sing to ***Gen*** Masc Sing. [case]"

In Greek, all that changed was the case ending of both words—**<u>a</u>** became *os* in word one, and **<u>n</u>** became *u* in word two. In English, there was no translatable difference.

c. NUMBER Examples

Singular to *Plural* Number

In Mark 12:2, we read these words: "And at the season he sent to the husbandmen a servant, that he might receive from the husbandmen of **the fruit**[1] of the vineyard." // The footnote reads as follows: "[1]WH changed <u>the</u> <u>fruit</u> (**tou** <u>kar**pou**</u>) to *the fruits* (*tOn karpOn*). Gen **Sing** Masc to Gen *Plur* Masc. [number]"

Plural to *Singular* Number

In Mark 13:3, we read these words: "And as he sat upon the mount of Olives over against the temple, Peter and James and John and Andrew **asked**[2] him privately." // The footnote reads as follows: "[2]WH changed [**they**] <u>asked</u> (<u>epArOt**On**</u>) to [**he**] asked (*epArOta*). Both Impf Act Ind. 3rd **Plur** to 3rd *Sing*. [number]"

d. SPELLING Examples

lamma to *lama*

In Mark 15:34, we read these words: "And at the ninth hour Jesus cried with a loud voice, saying, Eloi, Eloi, **lama**[1] sabachthani? which is, being interpreted, My God, my God, why hast thou forsaken me?" // The footnote reads as follows: "[1]WH changed <u>lama</u> (<u>lam**m**a</u>) to *lama* (*lama*). [spell]"

Joses to *Joseph*

In Matthew 13:55, we read these words: "Is not this the carpenter's son? is not his mother called Mary? and his brethren, James, and **Joses**[2], and Simon, and Judas?" // The footnote reads as follows: "[2]WH changed <u>Joses</u> (<u>iOsAs</u>) to *Joseph* (*iOsAph*). [spell]

Fourtunatus to *Fortunatus*

In 1 Corinthians 16:17, we read these words: "I am glad of the coming of Stephanas and **Fortunatus**[3] and Achaicus: for that which was lacking on your part they have supplied." // The footnote reads as follows: "[3]WH changed Fortunatus (**fou**rtounatou) to *Fortunatus (fortounatou)*. [spell]]"

Priscilla to *Priska*

In 1 Corinthians 16:19, we read these words: "The churches of Asia salute you. Aquila and **Priscilla**[4] salute you much in the Lord, with the church that is in their house." // The footnote reads as follows: "[4]WH changed Pris**cill**a (pris**kill**a) to *Priska (priska)*. [spell]]"

was sacrificed to *was sacrificed*

In 1 Corinthians 5:7, we read these words: "Purge out therefore the old leaven, that ye may be a new lump, as ye are unleavened. For even Christ our passover **is sacrificed**[5] for us." // The footnote reads as follows: "[5]WH changed was sacrificed (e~~th~~uthAn) to *was sacrificed (etu~~th~~A)*. Both Aor **Pass** Ind *3rd* **Sing**. [spell]]"

e. MOOD Examples

Indicative to *Subjunctive*

In 2 Corinthians 3:15, we read these words: "But even unto this day, when Moses **is read**[1], the vail is upon their heart." // The footnote reads as follows: "[1]WH changed is being read (anaginOsketai) to *may be being read (anaginOskAtai)*. Pres Pass **Ind** to Pres Pass *Sub*. [mood]]"

Indicative to *Participle*

In 2 Corinthians 12:1, we read these words: "**It is** not **expedient**[2] for me doubtless to glory. I will come to visions and revelations of the Lord." // The footnote reads as follows: "[2]WH changed it is expedient (sumferei) to *being expedient (sumferon)*. Pres Act **Ind** to Pres Act *Part*. [mood]]"

Participle to *Indicative*

In 2 Corinthians 12:15, we read these words: "And I will very gladly spend and be spent for you; though the more abundantly **I love**[3] you, the less I be loved." // The footnote reads as follows: "[3]WH changed loving (agapOn) to *I love* (*agapO*). Pres Act **Part** to Pres Act *Ind*. [mood]"

Participle to *Imperative*

In Ephesians 5:17, we read these words: "Wherefore be ye not unwise, but **understanding**[4] what the will of the Lord *is*." // The footnote reads as follows: "[4]WH changed understand**ing** (sunientes) to *understand ye* (*suniete*). Pres Act **Part** to Pres Act *Imp*. [mood]"

Optative to *Subjunctive*

In Ephesians 6:19, we read these words: "And for me, that utterance **may be given**[5] unto me, that I may open my mouth boldly, to make known the mystery of the gospel." // The footnote reads as follows: "[5]WH changed **should** be given (dotheiA) to *might* be given (*dothA*). Aor Pass **Opt** to Aor Pass *Sub*. [mood]"

Imperative to *Participle*

In Philippians 2:4, we read these words: : "**Look** not every man **on**[6] his own things, but every man also on the things of others." // The footnote reads as follows: "[6]WH changed look on (skop**eite**) to *looking on* (*skopountes*). Pres Act **Imp** to Pres Act *Part*. [mood]"

Imperative to *Infinitive*

In 2 Thessalonians 3:14, we read these words: "And if any man obey not our word by this epistle, note that man, and **have** no **company with**[7] with him, that he may be ashamed." // The footnote reads as follows: "[7]WH changed have company with (sunanamignus**the**) to *to have company with* (*sunanamignus**thai***). Pres Mid **Imp** to Pres M/P *Inf*. [mood]"

Subjunctive to *Optative*

In 2 Timothy 2:25, we read these words: "In meekness instructing those that oppose themselves; if God peradventure **will give**[8] them repentance to the acknowledging of the truth;" // The footnote reads as follows: "[8]WH changed **might** give (dO) to *should give* (*dOA*). Aor Act **Sub** to Aor Act *Opt.* [mood]"

f. GENDER Examples

Masculine to *Neuter*

In Ephesians 1:14, we read these words: "**Which**[2] is the earnest of our inheritance until the redemption of the purchased possession, unto the praise of his glory." // The footnote reads as follows: "[2]WH change who ([h]os) to *which* ([h]o). **Masc** to *Neut.* [gender]"

Masculine to *Feminine*

In Hebrews 9:9, we read these words: "Which *was* a figure for the time then present, **in which**[3] were offered both gifts and sacrifices, that could not make him that did the service perfect, as pertaining to the conscience." // The footnote reads as follows: "[3]WH changed in which ([h]on) to *in whom* ([h]An). Acc **Masc** Sing to Acc *Fem* Sing. [gender]"

Neuter to *Masculine*

In 1 Peter 2:25, we read these words: "For ye were as sheep **going astray**[4]; but are now returned unto the Shepherd and bishop of your souls." // The footnote reads as follows: "[4]WH changed going astray (planOmena) to *going astray* (*planOmenoi*). Both Pres Pass Part. Nom **Neut** Plur to Nom *Masc* Plur. [gender]"

Feminine to *Masculine*

In 1 Peter 3:20, we read these words: "Which sometime were disobedient, when once the longsuffering of God waited in the days of Noah, while the ark was a preparing, wherein **few**[5], that is, eight souls were saved by water." // The footnote reads as follows: "[5]WH changed few (^{h}oligai) to *few* (^{h}oligoi). Nom **Fem** Plur to Nom *Masc* Plur. [gender]"

Feminine to *Masculine*

In 2 Peter 2:4, we read these words: "For if God spared not the angels that sinned, but cast *them* down to hell, and delivered *them* into **chains**[6] of darkness, to be reserved unto judgment[.]" // The footnote reads as follows: "[6]WH changed chains (seirais) to *chains* (*seirois*). Dat **Fem** Plur to Dat *Masc* Plur. [gender]"

Neuter to *Masculine*

In Revelation 4:7, we read these words: "And the first beast *was* like a lion, and the second beast like a calf, and the third beast **had**[7] a face as a man, and the fourth beast *was* like a flying eagle." // The footnote reads as follows: "[7]WH changed **it** had (econ) to *he had* (*ecOn*). Both Pres Act Part. Nom **Neut** Sing to Nom *Masc* Sing. [gender]"

g. **PERSON Examples**

Second to *First*

In Galatians 4:6, we read these words: "And because ye are sons, God hath sent forth the Spirit of his Son into **your**[1] hearts, crying, Abba, Father." // The footnote reads as follows: "[1]WH changed of **you** (^{h}**umOn**) to *of us* (^{h}*AmOn*) in the hearts of you. [person]"

First to *Second*

In Ephesians 5:2, we read these words: "And walk in love, as Christ also hath loved **us**[2], and hath given himself for us an offering and a sacrifice to God for a sweetsmelling savour." // The footnote reads as follows: "[2]WH changed **us** (^{h}**Amas**) to *you* (^{h}*umas*). [person]"

First to *Second*

In 2 John 1:8, we read these words: "Look to yourselves, that **we lose**[3] not those things which we have wrought, but that **we receive**[4] a full reward." // The first footnote reads as follows: "[3]WH changed **we might lose** (apoles**Omen**) to *ye might lose* (apoles**Ate**). Both Aor Act Sub. **1**[rs] Plur to *2*[nd] Plur. [person]" The second footnote reads as follows: "[4]WH changed **we might receive** (apolab**Omen**) to *ye might receive* (apolab**Ate**). Both Aor Act Sub. **1**[rst] Plur to *2*[nd] Plur. [person]"

First to *Third*

In Revelation 5:10, we read these words: "And hast made us unto our God kings and priests: and **we shall reign**[5] on the earth." // The footnote reads as follows: "[5]WH changed **we shall reign** (basileuso**men**) to *they shall reign* (basileuousin). Both Fut Act Ind. **1**[rst] Plur to *3*[rd] Plur. [person]"

Third to *Second*

In Mark 8:23, we read these words: "And he took the blind man by the hand, and led him out of the town; and when he had spit on his eyes, and put his hands upon him, he asked him if **he saw**[7] ought." // The footnote reads as follows: "[7]WH changed **he sees** (blepei) to **you**[s] see (blepeis). Both Pres Act Ind. **3**[rd] Pers Sing to *2*[nd] Pers Sing. [person]"

First to *Third*

In Luke 23:15, we read these words: "No, nor yet Herod: for **I sent**[8] you to him; and, lo, nothing worthy of death is done unto him." // The footnote reads as follows: "[8]WH changed **I sent** (anepem$a) to *he sent* (anepem$e). Aor Act Ind **1**[rst] Sing to Aor Act Ind *3*[rd] Sing. [person]"

Third to *First*

In Acts 20:8, we read these words: "And there were many lights in the upper chamber, where **they were**[9] gathered together." // The footnote reads as follows: "[9]WH changed **they were** (Asan) to *we were* (Amen). **3rd** Plur to *1^{rst}* Plur. [person]"

Second to *Third*

In Acts 25:18, we read these words: "Against whom when the accusers stood up, **they brought**[10] none accusation of such things as I supposed:" // The footnote reads as follows: "[10]WH changed **you** were bringing (**ep**eferon) to *they were bringing* (*eferon*). Both Impf Act Ind. **2nd** person Pl to *3rd* person Pl. [person]"

h. **VOICE Examples**

Passive to *Active*

In 2 Corinthians 11:6, we read these words: "But though *I be* rude in speech, yet not in knowledge; but **we have been throughly made manifest**[1] among you in all things." // The footnote reads as follows: "[1]WH changed we **were** throughly made manifest (fanerOthentes) to *we throughly made manifest* (*fanerOsantes*). Aor **Pass** Part to Aor *Act* Part. [voice]"

Active to *Passive*

In Ephesians 3:3, we read these words: "How that by revelation **he made known**[2] unto me the mystery; (as I wrote afore in few words." // The footnote reads as follows: "[2]WH changed he made known (egnOrise) to *he was made known* (*egnOristhA*). Aor **Act** Ind to Aor *Pass* Ind. [voice]"

(2) Complex Substitutions—Whenever WH made a change of two or more different kinds, I called that a "Complex" Substitution.

Sometimes W&H made a change of Tense, Voice, and Mood all at once. Other times they changed Gender, Number, and Case all at one time. On other occasions, they added a Prefix and changed the Case. The reader will notice these kinds of Complex Substitutions (and many others) as he reads through the *"Doctored" New Testament.*

II. CHANGES WH <u>PROPOSED</u> IN THEIR <u>MARGIN</u>

All Changes that Westcott and Hort proposed in their margin are bolded and underlined with dotted underlining [**like this**]. Since these changes were only proposed in the margin and not actually made in the text, I did not show additional distinctions in the *KJV* text.

A. Example of Marginal OMISSION
In Matthew 1:18, we read these words: "Now the **birth** of **Jesus**[1] Christ was on this wise." // The footnote reads as follows: "[1]In their margin, WH omitted <u>Jesus</u>.

B. Example of Marginal ADDITION
In Matthew 3:16, we read these words: "and, lo, the heavens were opened **unto him**[2]." // The footnote reads as follows: "[2]In their margin, WH omitted <u>unto him</u> (*autO*)."

C. Example of Marginal TRANSPOSITION
In Matthew 5:4-5, we read these words: "4 **Blessed *are* they that mourn: for they shall be comforted.** 5 **Blessed *are* the meek: for they shall inherit the earth**.[3]" // [3]The footnote reads as follows: "In their margin, WH changed the word order and put verse five <u>before</u> verse four."

D. Example of Marginal SUBSTITUTION
In Matthew 5:37, we read these words: But **let** your communication **be**[4], Yea, yea; Nay, nay." // The footnote reads as follows: "[4]In their margin, WH changed <u>be **letting**</u> (*estO*) to *will be* (*estai*). **Pres Imp** to *Fut Ind*. [tense & mood]"

Quotes from Scrivener's "Preface"
To his Annotated Greek New Testament

Since this present work is so heavily dependent on Dr. F. H. A. Scrivener's work, it is extremely important to understand the purpose and premises of that work. Some quotations from the 1880 Christmas "Preface" to *The New Testament in Greek According to the Text Followed in the Authorised Version Together With the Variations Adopted in the Revised Version* edited by F. H. A. Scrivener, M.A., D.C. L., LL.D. are in order.

[01]¹ "The special design of this volume [i.e. *Scrivener's Annotated Greek NT*] is to **place clearly** before the reader the **variations from** the Greek Text represented by the **Authorised** Version of the New Testament which have been **embodied in the Revised Version**." [p. v]

[02] "They [i.e. the Revisers of the 1881 *ERV*] therefore communicated to the Oxford and Cambridge University Presses a full and carefully corrected **list of the readings adopted** which are **at variance with the readings 'presumed to underlie the Authorised Version,'** in order that they might be published independently in some shape or other." [pp. v-vi]

[03]²"The Cambridge Press has therefore judged it **best to set the readings** actually **adopted by** the **Revisers at the foot of the page, and** to **keep** the continuous **text** consistent throughout by making it **so far as was possible** uniformly **representative of** the Authorised Version." [p. vii]

[04] "The publication of an edition formed on this plan appeared to be all the more desirable, inasmuch as **the Authorised Version was not a translation of any one Greek text then in existence**, and no Greek text intended to reproduce in any way the original of the Authorised Version has ever been printed." [p. vii]

---

¹ I have added the underlining & bold emphasis and the bracketed numbers.
² Citations [3] through [18] are one continuous quotation and can be found on "Preface" pages vii-ix.

[05] "In considering what text had the best right to be regarded as 'the text presumed to underlie the Authorised Version,' **it was necessary to take into account the composite nature of the Authorised Version, as due to successive <u>revisions</u> <u>of Tyndale's translation</u>**." [p. vii]

[06] "**Tyndale** himself **followed the second and third editions of Erasmus's Greek text** (1519, 1522)." [p. vii]

[07] "**In the <u>revisions</u>** of his [i.e. Tyndale's] translation **<u>previous to 1611</u> a partial use was made of other texts**; of which ultimately the most influential were the various editions of Beza from 1560 to 1598, if indeed his Latin version of 1556 should not be included." [p. vii]

[08] "Between 1598 and 1611 no important edition appeared; so that **Beza's fifth and last text of 1598 was <u>more likely</u>** than any other to be in the hands of <u>King James's revisers</u>, **and to be accepted by them as the best standard within their reach**." [p. vii]

[09] "It [Beza's 1598 edition] is moreover found on comparison to agree more closely with the Authorised Version than any other Greek text; and accordingly it has been adopted by the Cambridge Press as the primary authority." [pp. vii-viii]

[10] "There are however **many places** in which the Authorised Version is **at variance with Beza's text**; chiefly **because it retains language inherited from Tyndale or his successors**, which had been **founded on the text of other Greek editions**." [p. viii]

[11] "In these cases **it is** often **doubtful how far the <u>revisers of 1611</u> deliberately preferred a different Greek reading; for their attention was not specially directed to textual variations**, and they might not have thought it necessary to weed out every rendering inconsistent with Beza's text, which might linger among the <u>older and unchanged portions</u> of the version[1]." [p. viii]

---

[1] A careful comparison of the *Bishops Bible* (the version upon which King James insisted that the 1611 revision be based) with the *1611 KJV*

[12] "On the other hand some of the readings followed, though discrepant [i.e. different] from Beza's text, may have seemed to be in a manner sanctioned by him, as he had spoken favourably of them in his notes; and others may have been adopted on independent grounds." [p. viii]

[13] "These uncertainties do not however affect the present edition, in which the different elements that actually make up the Greek basis of the Authorised Version have an equal right to find a place." [p. viii]

[14] "**Wherever** therefore the **Authorised renderings agree with other Greek readings** which might naturally be **known** through printed editions **to the <u>revisers of 1611</u>** or their predecessors, **Beza's reading has been displaced** from the text in favour of the more truly representative reading, the **variation from Beza** being **indicated by** *." [pp. viii-ix]

[15] "It was manifestly necessary to accept only Greek authority, though **in some places the Authorised Version <u>corresponds but loosely</u> with any form of the Greek** original, while it <u>exactly follows</u> the <u>Latin Vulgate</u>.**" [p. ix]

[16] **"All variations from Beza's text of 1598**, in number **about 190 are set down in an Appendix** at the end of the volume, **together with the authorities** on which they respectively rest." [p. ix]

[17] "**Whenever a Greek reading** adopted for the Revised Version **differs from the <u>presumed</u> Greek original** of the Authorised Version, **the reading** which it is intended to **displace** is printed in the text **in a thicker type**, **with a numerical reference to** the **reading substituted by the Revisers**, which bears the same numeral at the foot of the pages." [p. ix]

---

demonstrates that—except for spelling and punctuation changes—most of the *Bishops Bible* New Testament remained untouched by King James' 1611 revisers.

[18] "Alternative readings are given in the margin by the Revisers in places 'in which, for the present, it would not' in their judgement 'be safe to accept one reading to the absolute exclusion of others,'[1] provided that the differences seemed to be of sufficient interest or importance to deserve notice. These **alternative readings**, which are **more than 400** in number, are **distinguished by** the notation *Marg.* or *marg.*" [p. ix]

Quotation from Scrivener's "Appendix"
to his Annotated Greek NT

"APPENDIX (See Preface, pp. viii, ix) Containing a list of the passages (marked *) in the Greek text of this volume, wherein the readings of Beza's N. T. 1598 are departed from, to agree with those adopted by the Authorised Version on the authority of certain earlier Greek editions." [p. 648]

"N.B. The readings of the Greek Text of this volume are placed first, followed by the authorities on which they rest: next come the readings of Beza 1598, and the authorities (if any) which support them. If no numerals follow Er. St. Bez., the reading given is the same in all the editions of their respective works." [p. 648]

"The **text of Beza 1598** has been **left <u>unchanged</u>** when the variation from it made in the **Authorised Version** is **not countenanced by** [i.e. supported, sanctioned, condoned, or approved by] any **earlier edition of** the **<u>Greek</u>**. In the following places the **Latin Vulgate** appears to have been the **authority** adopted in preference to Beza. The **present list** is probably **<u>quite incomplete</u>**, and a few cases seem precarious [i.e. uncertain]. It is possible that some of the readings for which Compl. Vulg. [Complutensian Vulgate N.T. (1514)] have been cited above, were derived from Vulg. rather than from Compl. The same may be said of Col. [Colinaeus' (1534)] Vulg. In 1 Cor xiv. 10; 1 John i. 5." [pp. 655-656]

---

[1] I have corrected typographical errors in the use of quotation marks.

Author's Note

On page 648 of the "Appendix" to his annotated Greek New Testament, Dr. Scrivener identified the Greek New Testaments that he used when the Greek text of Beza's 1598 edition differed with the English of the KJV. Here is the list in chronological order: 1514 Complutensian Polyglot New Testament; 1516 Erasmus, 1519 Erasmus, 1522 Erasmus; 1527 Erasmus, 1535 Erasmus; 1546 Stephanus, 1549 Stephanus, 1550 Stephanus, 1551 Stephanus; 1560 Beza, 1565 Beza, 1582 Beza, and 1589 Beza.

Note: Since 1624 Elzevir and 1633 Elzevir were published after King James's 1611 revisers did their work, Scrivener did not use any of their distinctive readings. Elzevir's 1633 edition of his Greek New Testament gave rise to the term "*textus receptus*" [text received]. In the "*Typographi Lectorius de haec editione*" portion [p. 2], we find these Latin words: "*Textum ergo habes, nuc ab omnibus receptum*" [Text therefore we have now, by all received].

***

As anyone who has written a page of text knows, repeated proof-readings do NOT produce perfection; they only produce more-refined imperfection. It is my prayer, however, that the "*Doctored*" *New Testament* become as perfect as is humanly possible. Please send the publisher a written note with any proposed corrections or suggestions. I plan to review each of these written notes prior to any future reprints.

It is my hope and prayer that all those who use the "*Doctored*" *New Testament* will be characterized both by accuracy and charitableness. May the Lord use this work to add more "light" than "heat" to a polarizing subject.

To God be the Glory!

D. A. Waite, Jr., M.A., M.L.A.
Chesapeake Beach, MD
July 21, 2003

List of Abbreviations
(with tense, voice, mood, case, person, & number distinguished)

Verb Tenses

Pres = present tense
  He *runs*. He *is running*.
Aor = aorist tense
  He *ran* [at one point].
Fut = future tense
  He *will run*. I *shall run*.
Pf = present perfect tense
  He *has run*. They *have run*.
PastPf = past perfect tense
  He *had run*.
FutPf = future perfect tense
  He *will have* run. I *shall have* run.
Impf = imperfect tense
  He *was running*. They *were running*.

Verb Voices

Act = active voice
  Jill hit Joe. (Subject performs verb action.)
Pass = passive voice
  Joe *was* {being} *hit* by Jill. They *were* {being} *hit*. (Subject receives verb action.)
Mid = middle voice
M/P = middle/passive voice
D = deponent--m/p form, active use

Verb Moods

Ind = indicative mood
  reality, fact—usual mood
Sub = subjunctive mood
  possibility or probability
Opt = optative mood
  improbability, impossibility
Imp = imperative mood
  command or polite request

Verbals

Inf = infinitive
  to be running, to run
Part = participle
  running, having run

Gender

Masc = masculine gender (*he*)
Fem = feminine gender (*she*)
Neut = neuter gender (*it*)

Number

Sing = singular number (*1*)
Plur = plural number (*2+*)

Cases

Nom = nominative case
  subjects & predicate nom
Gen = genitive case (*of*)
Dat = dative case (*to* or *for*)
Acc = accusative case
  Objects: direct/indirect/prep
Voc = vocative case
  case of direct address (*O Death, where is thy sting?*)

Parts of Speech

Verb =verb (*shows* action or being)
Noun = noun (*names* person/thing)
Pro =pronoun (*replaces* a noun)
  Dem = demonstrative
  Pers = personal
Adj = adjective (*modifies* n/pro)
Adv = adverb (*modifies* v/adj/adv)
Prep =preposition (*relates* n/pro)
Conj =conjunction (*joins* words)
Int= interjection (*shows* emotion)

Miscellaneous

syn = synonym | ^{p} = plural
spell = spelling | ^{s} = singular

The "Doctored" New Testament

MATTHEW

CHAPTER 1

1　The book of the generation of Jesus Christ, the son of David, the son of Abraham.

2　Abraham begat Isaac; and Isaac begat Jacob; and Jacob begat Judas and his brethren;

3　And Judas begat Phares and Zara of Thamar; and Phares begat Esrom; and Esrom begat Aram;

4　And Aram begat Aminadab; and Aminadab begat Naasson; and Naasson begat Salmon;

5　And Salmon begat Booz of Rachab; and Booz begat Obed of Ruth; and Obed begat Jesse;

6　And Jesse begat David the king; and David ~~the king~~[1] begat Solomon of her *that had been the wife* of Urias;

7　And Solomon begat Roboam; and Roboam begat Abia; and Abia begat **Asa**[2];

8　And **Asa**[2] begat Josaphat; and Josaphat begat Joram; and Joram begat Ozias;

9　And Ozias begat Joatham; and Joatham begat Achaz; and Achaz begat Ezekias;

10　And Ezekias begat Manasses; and Manasses begat **Amon**[3]; and **Amon**[3] begat Josias;

11　And Josias begat Jechonias and his brethren, about the time they were carried away to Babylon:

12　And after they were brought to Babylon, Jechonias begat Salathiel; and Salathiel begat Zorobabel;

13　And Zorobabel begat Abiud; and Abiud begat Eliakim; and Eliakim begat Azor;

14　And Azor begat Sadoc; and Sadoc begat Achim; and Achim begat Eliud;

15　And Eliud begat Eleazar; and Eleazar begat Matthan; and Matthan begat Jacob;

16　And Jacob begat Joseph the husband of Mary, of whom was born Jesus, who is called Christ.

17　So all the generations from Abraham to David *are* fourteen generations; and from David until the carrying

---

[1] WH omitted <u>the king</u> (<u>ho basileus</u>).

[2] WH changed <u>Asa</u> (<u>asa</u>) to *Asaf* (*asaf*). [spell]

[3] WH changed <u>Amon</u> (<u>amOn</u>) to *Amos* (*amOs*). [spell]

1

away into Babylon *are* fourteen generations; and from the carrying away into Babylon unto Christ *are* fourteen generations.

18 Now the **birth**[1] of **Jesus**[2] Christ was on this wise: ~~When as~~[3] his mother Mary was espoused to Joseph, before they came together, she was found with child of the Holy Ghost.

19 Then Joseph her husband, being a just *man*, and not willing to make her a publick example, was minded to put her away privily.

20 But while he thought on these things, behold, the angel of the Lord appeared unto him in a dream, saying, Joseph, thou son of David, fear not to take unto thee Mary thy wife: for that which is conceived in her is of the Holy Ghost.

21 And she shall bring forth a son, and thou shalt call his name JESUS: for he shall save his people from their sins.

22 Now all this was done, that it might be fulfilled which was spoken of the Lord by the prophet, saying,

23 Behold, a virgin shall be with child, and shall bring forth a son, and they shall call his name Emmanuel, which being interpreted is, God with us.

24 Then Joseph **being raised**[4] from sleep did as the angel of the Lord had bidden him, and took unto him his wife:

25 And knew her not till she had brought forth **her**[5] **firstborn**[6] son: and he called his name JESUS.

CHAPTER 2

1 Now when Jesus was born in Bethlehem of Judaea in the days of Herod the king, behold, there came wise men from the east to Jerusalem,

2 Saying, Where is he that is born King of the Jews? for we have seen his star in

---

[1] WH changed **birth** (*genA-sis*) to **beginning** (*genesis*) .

[2] In their margin, WH omitted Jesus.

[3] WH omitted when as (*gar*).

[4] WH changed being raised {**up** or fully} (**di**-egertheis) to *being raised* (*egertheis*). [prefix dropped]

[5] WH omitted the (ton) from the son of her.

[6] WH omitted of her the firstborn (autAs ton prOtotokon) from the son of her the firstborn.

the east, and are come to worship him.

3   When Herod the king had heard *these things*, he was troubled, and all Jerusalem with him.

4   And when he had gathered all the chief priests and scribes of the people together, he demanded of them where Christ should be born.

5   And they said unto him, In Bethlehem of Judaea: for thus it is written by the prophet,

6   And thou Bethlehem, *in* the land of Juda, art not the least among the princes of Juda: for out of thee shall come a Governor, that shall rule my people Israel.

7   Then Herod, when he had privily called the wise men, enquired of them diligently what time the star appeared.

8   And he sent them to Bethlehem, and said, Go and search diligently for the young child; and when ye have found *him*, bring me word again, that I may come and worship him also.

9   When they had heard the king, they departed; and, lo, the star, which they saw in the east, went before them, till it came and stood over where the young child was.

10 When they saw the star, they rejoiced with exceeding great joy.

11 And when they were come into the house, they saw the young child with Mary his mother, and fell down, and worshipped him: and when they had opened their treasures, they presented unto him gifts; gold, and frankincense, and myrrh.

12 And being warned of God in a dream that they should not return to Herod, they departed into their own country another way.

13 And when they were departed, behold, the angel of the Lord appeareth to Joseph in a dream, saying, Arise, and take the young child and his mother, and flee into Egypt, and be thou there until I bring thee word: for Herod will seek the young child to destroy him.

14 When he arose, he took the young child and his mother by night, and departed into Egypt:

15 And was there until the death of Herod: that it might be fulfilled which was spoken of the Lord by the prophet, saying, Out of Egypt have I called my son.

16 Then Herod, when he saw that he was mocked of the wise men, was exceeding wroth, and sent forth, and

slew all the children that were in Bethlehem, and in all the coasts thereof, from two years old and under, according to the time which he had diligently enquired of the wise men.

17 Then was fulfilled that which was spoken **by**[1] Jeremy the prophet, saying,

18 In Rama was there a voice heard, ~~lamentation~~, ~~and~~[2] weeping, and great mourning, Rachel weeping *for* her children, and would not be comforted, because they are not

19 But when Herod was dead, behold, an angel of the Lord appeareth in a dream to Joseph in Egypt,

20 Saying, Arise, and take the young child and his mother, and go into the land of Israel: for they are dead which sought the young child's life.

21 And he arose, and took the young child and his mother, and came into the land of Israel.

22 But when he heard that Archelaus did reign in Judaea in the room of his father Herod, he was afraid to go thither: notwithstanding, being warned of God in a dream, he turned aside into the parts of Galilee:

23 And he came and dwelt in a city called Nazareth: that it might be fulfilled which was spoken by the prophets, He shall be called a Nazarene.

CHAPTER 3

1 In those days came John the Baptist, preaching in the wilderness of Judaea,

2 ~~And~~[3] saying, Repent ye: for the kingdom of heaven is at hand.

3 For this is he that was spoken of **by**[4] the prophet Esaias, saying, The voice of one crying in the wilderness, Prepare ye the way of the Lord, make his paths straight.

4 And the same John had his raiment of camel's hair, and a leathern girdle about his loins; and his meat was locusts and wild honey.

5 Then went out to him Jerusalem, and all Judaea, and all the region round about Jordan,

---

[1] WH changed **by** (^h**upo**) to *through* (*dia*).
[2] WH omitted lamentation and (~~thr~~Anos kai).

---

[3] WH omitted and (kai).
[4] WH changed **by** (^h**upo**) to *through* (*dia*).

6   And were baptized of him in Jordan [∧**river**][1], confessing their sins.

7   But when he saw many of the Pharisees and Sadducees come to his baptism, he said unto them, O generation of vipers, who hath warned you to flee from the wrath to come?

8   Bring forth therefore **fruits** **meet**[2] for repentance:

9   And think not to say within yourselves, We have Abraham to *our* father: for I say unto you, that God is able of these stones to raise up children unto Abraham.

10 And now ~~also~~[3] the axe is laid unto the root of the trees: therefore every tree which bringeth not forth good fruit is hewn down, and cast into the fire.

11 I indeed baptize you with water unto repentance: but he that cometh after me is mightier than I, whose shoes I am not worthy to bear: he shall baptize you with the Holy Ghost, and *with* fire:

12 Whose fan *is* in his hand, and he will throughly purge his floor, and gather his wheat into the garner; but he will burn up the chaff with unquenchable fire.

13 Then cometh Jesus from Galilee to Jordan unto John, to be baptized of him.

14 But John forbad him, saying, I have need to be baptized of thee, and comest thou to me?

15 And Jesus answering said unto him, Suffer *it to be so* now: for thus it becometh us to fulfil all righteousness. Then he suffered him.

16 And Jesus, when he was baptized, went up straightway out of the water: and, lo, the heavens were opened **unto him**[4], and he saw the Spirit of God descending like a dove, and lighting upon him:

17 And lo a voice from heaven, saying, This is my beloved Son, in whom I am well pleased.

CHAPTER 4

1   Then was Jesus led up of the Spirit into the wilderness to be tempted of the devil.

2   And when he had

---

[1] WH added *river* (*potamO*) after Jordan.
[2] WH changed fruits meet (*karpous axious*) to *fruit meet* (*karpon axion*) [number]
[3] WH omitted also (*kai*).

[4] In their margin, WH omitted unto him (*autO*).

fasted forty days and forty nights, he was afterward an hungred.

3 And when the tempter came **to him**[1], he said, If thou be the Son of God, command that these stones be made bread.

4 But he answered and said, It is written, [∧**the**][2] Man shall not live by bread alone, but by every word that proceedeth out of the mouth of God.

5 Then the devil taketh him up into the holy city, and **setteth**[3] him on a pinnacle of the temple,

6 And saith unto him, If thou be the Son of God, cast thyself down: for it is written, He shall give his angels charge concerning thee: and in *their* hands they shall bear thee up, lest at any time thou dash thy foot against a stone.

7 Jesus said unto him, It is written again, Thou shalt not tempt the Lord thy God.

8 Again, the devil taketh him up into an exceeding high mountain, and sheweth him all the kingdoms of the world, and the glory of them;

9 And **saith**[4] unto him, All these things will I give thee, if thou wilt fall down and worship me.

10 Then saith Jesus unto him, Get thee hence, Satan: for it is written, Thou shalt worship the Lord thy God, and him only shalt thou serve.

11 Then the devil leaveth him, and, behold, angels came and ministered unto him.

12 Now when ~~**Jesus**~~[5] had heard that John was cast into prison, he departed into Galilee;

13 And leaving Nazareth, he came and dwelt in Capernaum, which is upon the sea coast, in the borders of Zabulon and Nephthalim:

14 That it might be fulfilled which was spoken by Esaias the prophet, saying,

15 The land of Zabulon, and the land of Nephthalim, *by* the way of the sea, beyond

---

[1] WH changed the word order from <u>and when the tempter came TO HIM he said</u> to *and when the tempter came he said TO HIM.*

[2] WH added *the* (*ʰo*) before <u>Man.</u>

[3] WH changed <u>sets</u> (*ʰistAsin*) to *set* (*estAsen*). **Pres** Act Ind to *Aor* Act Ind. [tense]

---

[4] WH changed <u>says</u> (**legei**) to *said* (*eipen*). **Pres** Act Ind to *Aor* Act Ind. [tense]

[5] WH omitted <u>the Jesus</u> (*ʰo iAsous*).

Jordan, Galilee of the Gentiles;

16 The people which sat in darkness saw great light; and to them which sat in the region and shadow of death light is sprung up.

17 From that time Jesus began to preach, and to say, Repent: for the kingdom of heaven is at hand.

18 And ~~Jesus~~[1], walking by the sea of Galilee, saw two brethren, Simon called Peter, and Andrew his brother, casting a net into the sea: for they were fishers.

19 And he saith unto them, Follow me, and I will make you fishers of men.

20 And they straightway left *their* nets, and followed him.

21 And going on from thence, he saw other two brethren, James *the son* of Zebedee, and John his brother, in a ship with Zebedee their father, mending their nets; and he called them.

22 And they immediately left the ship and their father, and followed him.

23 And **Jesus**[2] went about

ʌ**in**[3] **all Galilee**[4], teaching in their synagogues, and preaching the gospel of the kingdom, and healing all manner of sickness and all manner of disease among the people.

24 And his fame went throughout all Syria: and they brought unto him all sick people that were taken with divers diseases and torments, **and**[5] those which were possessed with devils, and those which were lunatick, and those that had the palsy; and he healed them.

25 And there followed him great multitudes of people from Galilee, and *from* Decapolis, and *from* Jerusalem, and *from* Judaea, and *from* beyond Jordan.

CHAPTER 5

1 And seeing the multitudes, he went up into a mountain: and when he was set, his disciples came unto him:

---

forced the verb to supply the subject *he*.

[3] WH added in (*en*).

[4] WH changed all the Galilee (ʰol**An** t**An** Galilaian) to *all the Galilee* (ʰolA tA Galilaia). **Acc** to *Dat*. [case]

[5] WH omitted and (kai).

---

[1] WH omitted the Jesus (ʰo iAsous).

[2] In their margin, WH omitted the Jesus (ʰo iAsous) and

2 And he opened his mouth, and taught them, saying,

3 Blessed *are* the poor in spirit: for theirs is the kingdom of heaven.

4 **Blessed *are* they that mourn: for they shall be comforted.**

5 **Blessed *are* the meek: for they shall inherit the earth.**[1]

6 Blessed *are* they which do hunger and thirst after righteousness: for they shall be filled.

7 Blessed *are* the merciful: for they shall obtain mercy.

8 Blessed *are* the pure in heart: for they shall see God.

9 Blessed *are* the peacemakers: for they shall be called the children of God.

10 Blessed *are* they which are persecuted for righteousness' sake: for theirs is the kingdom of heaven.

11 Blessed are ye, when *men* shall revile you, and persecute *you*, and shall say all manner of evil **[~~words~~]**[2]

against you falsely, for my sake.

12 Rejoice, and be exceeding glad: for great *is* your reward in heaven: for so persecuted they the prophets which were before you.

13 Ye are the salt of the earth: but if the salt have lost his savour, wherewith shall it be salted? it is thenceforth good for nothing, but **to be cast**[3] out, **~~and~~**[4] to be trodden under foot of men.

14 Ye are the light of the world. A city that is set on an hill cannot be hid.

15 Neither do men light a candle, and put it under a bushel, but on a candlestick; and it giveth light unto all that are in the house.

16 Let your light so shine before men, that they may see your good works, and glorify your Father which is in heaven.

17 Think not that I am come to destroy the law, or the prophets: I am not come to destroy, but to fulfil.

18 For verily I say unto you, Till heaven and earth

---

[1] In their margin, WH changed the word order and put verse five before verse four.
[2] WH omitted the untranslated words ([h]rAma).

---

[3] WH changed **to be cast** (bl**Ath**Anai) to *having been cast* (bl*A **th**en*). Aor Pass **Inf** to Aor Pass *Part* [mood]
[4] WH omitted *and* (kai).

pass, one jot or one tittle shall in no wise pass from the law, till all be fulfilled.

19 Whosoever therefore shall break one of these least commandments, and shall teach men so, he shall be called the least in the kingdom of heaven: but whosoever shall do and teach _them_, the same shall be called great in the kingdom of heaven.

20 For I say unto you, That except your righteousness shall exceed _the righteousness_ of the scribes and Pharisees, ye shall in no case enter into the kingdom of heaven.

21 Ye have heard that it was said by them of old time, Thou shalt not kill; and whosoever shall kill shall be in danger of the judgment:

22 But I say unto you, That whosoever is angry with his brother ~~without a cause~~[1] shall be in danger of the judgment: and whosoever shall say to his brother, Raca, shall be in danger of the council: but whosoever shall say, Thou fool, shall be in danger of hell fire.

23 Therefore if thou bring thy gift to the altar, and there rememberest that thy brother hath ought against thee;

24 Leave there thy gift before the altar, and go thy way; first be reconciled to thy brother, and then come and offer thy gift.

25 Agree with thine adversary quickly, whiles thou art in the way **with him**[2]; lest at any time the adversary deliver thee to the judge, and the judge **deliver thee**[3] to the officer, and thou be cast into prison.

26 Verily I say unto thee, Thou shalt by no means come out thence, till thou hast paid the uttermost farthing.

27 Ye have heard that it was said ~~by them of old time~~[4], Thou shalt not commit adultery:

28 But I say unto you, That whosoever looketh on a woman to lust after her hath committed adultery with her already in his heart.

29 And if thy right eye offend thee, pluck it out, and

---

[1] WH omitted <u>without a cause</u> (<u>eikA</u>) in their text, but retained <u>eikA</u> in their margin.

[2] WH changed the word order from <u>in</u> <u>the</u> <u>way</u> WITH HIM to _WITH HIM in the way._

[3] In their margin, WH omitted <u>deliver</u> <u>thee</u> (<u>se parado</u>).

[4] WH omitted <u>by them</u> <u>of old time</u> (<u>tois arcaiois</u>).

cast *it* from thee: for it is profitable for thee that one of thy members should perish, and not *that* thy whole body should be cast into hell.

30 And if thy right hand offend thee, cut it off, and cast *it* from thee: for it is profitable for thee that one of thy members should perish, and not *that* thy whole body **should be cast**[1] **into hell**[2].

31 It hath been said, Whosoever shall put away his wife, let him give her a writing of divorcement:

32 But I say unto you, That **whosoever**[3] **shall put away**[4] his wife, saving for the cause of fornication, causeth

---

[1] WH changed might **be cast** (**blAthA**) to *might go away* (*apelthA*). Aor **Pass** Sub of **ballO** to Aor **Act** Sub of *apercomai*. [voice & msc]

[2] WH changed the word order from might **be cast** INTO HELL to INTO HELL *might go away*.

[3] WH changed **whoso ever** ([h]os **an**) to *all the* {*ones*} (*pas* [h]*o*).

[4] WH changed **shall** put away (apo-lusA) to *putting away* (*apoluOn*). **Fut** Act **Ind** to *Pres* Act *Part*. [tense & mood]

her **to commit adultery**[5]: and whosoever shall marry her that is divorced committeth adultery.

33 Again, ye have heard that it hath been said by them of old time, Thou shalt not forswear thyself, but shalt perform unto the Lord thine oaths:

34 But I say unto you, Swear not at all; neither by heaven; for it is God's throne:

35 Nor by the earth; for it is his footstool: neither by Jerusalem; for it is the city of the great King.

36 Neither shalt thou swear by thy head, because thou canst not make one hair white or black.

37 But **let** your communication **be**[6], Yea, yea; Nay, nay: for whatsoever is more than these cometh of evil.

38 Ye have heard that it

---

[5] WH changed to commit adultery {as a continuing practice} (moicasthai) to *to commit adultery* {at a point in time} (*moiceuthAnai*). **Pres** M/P Inf of *moicaO* to *Aor* Pass Inf of *moiceuO*). [tense & syn]

[6] In their margin, WH changed be **letting** (estO) to *will be* (*estai*). **Pres** **Imp** to *Fut Ind*. [tense & mood]

hath been said, An eye for an eye, and a tooth for a tooth:

39 But I say unto you, That ye resist not evil: but whosoever **shall smite**[1] thee **on**[2] thy right cheek, turn to him the other also.

40 And if any man will sue thee at the law, and take away thy coat, let him have *thy* cloke also.

41 And whosoever shall compel thee to go a mile, go with him twain.

42 Give to him that asketh thee, and from him that would borrow of thee turn not thou away.

43 Ye have heard that it hath been said, Thou shalt love thy neighbour, and hate thine enemy.

44 But I say unto you, Love your enemies, ~~bless them that curse you, do good to them that hate you~~[3], and pray for them which ~~despitefully use you, and~~[4] persecute you;

45 That ye may be the children of your Father which is in heaven: for he maketh his sun to rise on the evil and on the good, and sendeth rain on the just and on the unjust.

46 For if ye love them which love you, what reward have ye? do not even the publicans the same?

47 And if ye salute your brethren only, what do ye more *than others*? do not even the **publicans so**[5]?

48 Be ye therefore perfect, **even as**[6] your Father which is **in heaven**[7] is perfect.

CHAPTER 6

1 Take heed that ye do not your **alms**[8] before men,

---

[1] WH changed **shall** smite (^hrapisei) to *is smiting* (^hrapizei). **Fut** Act Ind to **Pres** Act Ind. [tense]

[2] WH changed **upon** (epi) to *into* (eis). [prep]

[3] WH omitted bless the {ones} cursing you well do to the {ones} hating you (eulogeite tous katarOmenous ^humas kalOs poieite tous misountas ^hu-mas).

[4] WH omitted despitefully use you and (epAreazontOn ^humas kai).

[5] WH changed **publicans so** (**telOnai** ^h**outO**) to *gentiles the same* (e*th*nikoi to auto).

[6] WH changed **even** as (^h**Os-per**) to *as* (^h*Os*).

[7] WH changed **in the** heavens (**en tois ouranois**) to *heavenly* (*ouranios*).

[8] WH changed **alms** (**eleA-mosunAn**); to *righteousness* (*dikaiosunAn*).

to be seen of them: otherwise ye have no reward of your Father which is in heaven.

2   Therefore when thou doest *thine* alms, do not sound a trumpet before thee, as the hypocrites do in the synagogues and in the streets, that they may have glory of men. Verily I say unto you, They have their reward.

3   But when thou doest alms, let not thy left hand know what thy right hand doeth:

4   That thine alms may be in secret: and thy Father which seeth in secret **himself**[1] shall reward thee ~~openly~~[2].

5   And when **thou prayest**[3], **thou shalt not be**[4] **as**[6]

the hypocrites *are*: for they love to pray standing in the synagogues and in the corners of the streets, that they may be seen of men. Verily I say unto you, They have their reward.

6   But thou, when thou prayest, enter into thy closet, and when thou hast shut thy door, pray to thy Father which is in secret; and thy Father which seeth in secret shall reward thee ~~openly~~[7].

7   But when ye pray, use not vain repetitions, as the heathen *do*: for they think that they shall be heard for their much speaking.

8   Be not ye therefore like unto them: for **[the God]**[8] your Father knoweth what things ye have need of, before ye ask him.

9   After this manner therefore pray ye: Our Father which art in heaven, hallowed be thy name.

10 Thy kingdom come. Thy will be done in **[the]**[9] earth, as *it is* in heaven.

---

[1] WH omitted <u>himself</u> (<u>autos</u>).
[2] WH omitted <u>in</u> <u>the</u> <u>open</u> (<u>en tO fanerO</u>).
[3] WH changed **thou** <u>pray<u>est</u></u> (<u>proseucA</u>) to *ye pray* (*proseucАs**the***). **Sing** to **Plur**. [Number]
[4] WH changed, <u>not</u> **thou** <u>shalt be</u> (<u>ouk esA</u>) to *not ye shall be* (*ouk eses**the***). **Sing** to **Plur**. [number]
[5] WH changed the word order from **JUST AS you**[s] pray not **you**[s] shall be to *you*[p] *pray not you*[p] *shall be AS*.
[6] WH changed **just** <u>as</u> (^h*Os*-

per) to *as* (^h*Os*)
[7] WH omitted <u>in</u> <u>the</u> <u>open</u> (<u>en tO fanerO</u>).
[8] In their margin, WH added *the God* (*^ho **the**os*).
[9] WH omitted the untranslated <u>the</u> (<u>tAs</u>) before <u>earth</u>.

11 Give us this day our daily bread.

12 And forgive us our debts, as we **forgive**[1] our debtors.

13 And lead us not into temptation, but deliver us from evil**: ~~For thine is the kingdom, and the power, and the glory, for ever. Amen~~**[2].

14 For if ye forgive men their trespasses, your heavenly Father will also forgive you:

15 But if ye forgive not men their trespasses, neither will your Father forgive your trespasses.

16 Moreover when ye fast, be not, **as**[3] the hypocrites, of a sad countenance: for they disfigure their faces, that they may appear unto men to fast.

Verily I say unto you, They have their reward.

17 But thou, when thou fastest, anoint thine head, and wash thy face;

18 That thou appear not unto men to fast, but unto thy Father which is in secret: and thy Father, which seeth in secret, shall reward thee **~~openly~~**[4].

19 Lay not up for yourselves treasures upon earth, where moth and rust doth corrupt, and where thieves break through and steal:

20 But lay up for yourselves treasures in heaven, where neither moth nor rust doth corrupt, and where thieves do not break through nor steal:

21 For where **your**[5] treasure is, there will **your**[6] heart be also.

22 The light of the body is the eye: if therefore thine eye be single, thy whole body shall be full of light.

23 But if thine eye be evil,

---

[1] WH changed <u>forgive</u> (<u>afie-men</u>) to *forgave* (*afAkamen*). **Pres** Act Ind to **Aor** Act Ind. [tense]

[2] WH omitted <u>for</u> <u>thine</u> <u>is</u> <u>the</u> <u>kingdom</u> <u>and</u> <u>the</u> <u>power</u> <u>and</u> <u>the</u> <u>glory</u> <u>unto</u> <u>the</u> <u>ages</u> <u>Amen</u> (^h<u>oti</u> <u>sou</u> <u>estin</u> ^h<u>A</u> <u>basileia</u> <u>kai</u> ^h<u>a</u> <u>dunamis</u> <u>kai</u> ^h<u>A</u> <u>doxa</u> <u>eis</u> <u>tous</u> <u>aiOnas</u> <u>amAn</u>) in their text. In their margin, WH included these words.

[3] WH changed **just** <u>as</u> (^h**Os-per**) to *as* (^h*Os*).

---

[4] WH omitted <u>in</u> <u>the</u> <u>open</u> (en tO fanerO).

[5] WH changed **your**[p] (^h<u>u-mOn</u>) to *your*[s] (*sou*). **Plur** to ***Sing***. [number]

[6] WH changed **your**[p] (^h<u>u-mOn</u>) to *your*[s] (*sou*). **Plur** to ***Sing***. [number]

thy whole body shall be full of darkness. If therefore the light that is in thee be darkness, how great *is* that darkness!

24 No man can serve two masters: for either he will hate the one, and love the other; or else he will hold to the one, and despise the other. Ye cannot serve God and mammon.

25 Therefore I say unto you, Take no thought for your life, what ye shall eat, **or**[1] what ye shall drink; nor yet for your body, what ye shall put on. Is not the life more than meat, and the body than raiment?

26 Behold the fowls of the air: for they sow not, neither do they reap, nor gather into barns; yet your heavenly Father feedeth them. Are ye not much better than they?

27 Which of you by taking thought can add one cubit unto his stature?

28 And why take ye thought for raiment? Consider the lilies of the field, how they grow; they toil not, neither do they spin:

29 And yet I say unto you, That even Solomon in all his glory was not arrayed like one of these.

30 Wherefore, if God so clothe the grass of the field, which to day is, and to morrow is cast into the oven, *shall he* not much more *clothe* you, O ye of little faith?

31 Therefore take no thought, saying, What shall we eat? or, What shall we drink? or, Wherewithal shall we be clothed?

32 (For after all these things do the Gentiles seek:) for your heavenly Father knoweth that ye have need of all these things.

33 But seek ye first the kingdom ~~of God~~[2], and his righteousness; and all these things shall be added unto you.

34 Take therefore no thought for the morrow: for the morrow shall take thought for ~~the things~~[3] of itself. Sufficient unto the day *is* the evil thereof.

CHAPTER 7

1 Judge not, that ye be

---

[1] WH changed <u>or</u> (**kai**) to *or* (*A*).

[2] WH omitted <u>of the</u> <u>God</u> (tou ~~theou~~).

[3] WH omitted <u>the</u> {things} (<u>ta</u>).

not judged.

2   For with what judgment ye judge, ye shall be judged: and with what measure ye mete, **it shall be measured** to you **again**[1].

3   And why beholdest thou the mote that is in thy brother's eye, but considerest not the beam that is in thine own eye?

4   Or how wilt thou say to thy brother, Let me pull out the mote **out of**[2] thine eye; and, behold, a beam *is* in thine own eye?

5   Thou hypocrite, first cast out the beam out of thine own eye; and then shalt thou see clearly to cast out the mote out of thy brother's eye.

6   Give not that which is holy unto the dogs, neither cast ye your pearls before swine, lest they trample them under their feet, and turn again and rend you.

7   Ask, and it shall be given you; seek, and ye shall find; knock, and it shall be opened unto you:

8   For every one that asketh receiveth; and he that seeketh findeth; and to him that knocketh it shall be opened.

9   Or what man is there of you, whom **if**[3] his son **ask**[4] bread, will he give him a stone?

10   **Or if**[5] **he ask**[6] a fish, will he give him a serpent?

11   If ye then, being evil, know how to give good gifts unto your children, how much more shall your Father which is in heaven give good things to them that ask him?

12   Therefore all things whatsoever ye would that men should do to you, do ye even so to them: for this is the law and the prophets.

13   Enter ye in at the strait gate: for wide *is* **the gate**[7], and broad *is* the way, that

---

[1] WH changed it shall be measured **again** (**anti-**metrA**th**Asetai) to *it shall be measured* (*metrA th Asetai*). [prefix dropped]

[2] WH changed **from** (**apo**) to *out of* (*ek*).

[3] WH omitted if (ean).

[4] WH changed **may** ask (ai-tAsA) to *shall ask* (*aitAsei*). *Aor* Act *Sub* to **Fut** Act **Ind**. [tense & mood]

[5] WH changed also if (kai ean) to *or also* (*A kai*).

[6] WH changed he **might** ask (aitAsA) to *he will ask* (*aitAsei*). **Aor** Act **Sub** to *Fut Act Ind*. [tense & mood]

[7] In their margin, WH omitted the gate (ʰA pulA).

leadeth to destruction, and many there be which go in thereat:

14 **Because**[1] strait *is* the gate, and narrow *is* the way, which leadeth unto life, and few there be that find it.

15 Beware [~~then~~][2] of false prophets, which come to you in sheep's clothing, but inwardly they are ravening wolves.

16 Ye shall know them by their fruits. Do men gather grapes of thorns, or figs of thistles?

17 Even so every good tree bringeth forth good fruit; but a corrupt tree bringeth forth evil fruit.

18 A good tree cannot bring forth evil fruit, neither *can* a corrupt tree bring forth good fruit.

19 Every tree that bringeth not forth good fruit is hewn down, and cast into the fire.

20 Wherefore by their fruits ye shall know them.

21 Not every one that saith unto me, Lord, Lord, shall enter into the kingdom of heaven; but he that doeth the will of my Father which is in heaven.

22 Many will say to me in that day, Lord, Lord, have we not prophesied in thy name? and in thy name have cast out devils? and in thy name done many wonderful works?

23 And then will I profess unto them, I never knew you: depart from me, ye that work iniquity.

24 Therefore whosoever heareth these sayings of mine, and doeth them, **I will liken**[3] **him**[4] unto a wise man, which built his house upon a rock:

25 And the rain descended, and the floods came, and the winds blew, and beat upon that house; and it fell not: for it was founded upon a rock.

26 And every one that heareth these sayings of mine, and doeth them not, shall be likened unto a foolish man, which built his house upon the sand:

27 And the rain descended, and the floods came, and the winds blew, and beat upon that house;

---

[1] In their margin, WH changed **because** (*^{h}oti*) to *who, which, what* (*ti*).

[2] WH omitted the untranslated then (*de*).

[3] WH changed **I will liken** (*^{h}omoiOsO*) to *he will be likened* (*^{h}omoiOthAsetai*). Fut **Act** Ind **1st** Sing to Fut *Pass* Ind *3rd Sing.* [voice & person]

[4] WH omitted him (*auton*).

and it fell: and great was the fall of it.

28 And it came to pass, when Jesus **had ended**[1] these sayings, the people were astonished at his doctrine:

29 For he taught them as *one* having authority, and not as the scribes [∧**of them**][2].

CHAPTER 8

1 When he was come down from the mountain, great multitudes followed him.

2 And, behold, **there came**[3] a leper and worshipped him, saying, Lord, if thou wilt, thou canst make me clean.

3 And ~~Jesus~~[4] put forth *his* hand, and touched him, saying, I will; be thou clean. And immediately his leprosy was cleansed.

4 And Jesus saith unto him, See thou tell no man; but go thy way, shew thyself to the priest, and offer the gift that Moses commanded, for a testimony unto them.

5 And **when Jesus was entered**[5] into Capernaum, there came unto him a centurion, beseeching him,

6 And saying, Lord, my servant lieth at home sick of the palsy, grievously tormented.

7 And ~~Jesus~~[6] saith unto him, I will come and heal him.

8 The centurion answered and said, Lord, I am not worthy that thou shouldest come under my roof: but speak the **word**[7] only, and my servant shall be healed.

9 For I am a man under authority **[having been ranked]**[8], having soldiers under me: and I say to this *man*,

---

[1] WH changed had ended {**together**} (**sun**-etelesen) to *had ended* (*etelesen*). [prefix dropped]

[2] WH added *of them* (*autOn*) after scribes.

[3] WH changed there came (el**th**On) to *there came **forward*** (***pros**-el**th**On*). [prefix added]

[4] WH omitted the Jesus (ʰo iAsous).

[5] WH changed when **Jesus** was entered (eis-el**th**onti **tO iAsou**) to *when **he** was entered* (*eis-el**th**ontos autou*).

[6] WH omitted the Jesus (ʰo iAsous).

[7] WH changed word (log**os**) to *word* (*log**O***). **Acc** Masc Sing to ***Dat*** Masc Sing. [case]

[8] In their margin, WH added *having been ranked* (*tassomenos*).

Go, and he goeth; and to another, Come, and he cometh; and to my servant, Do this, and he doeth *it*.

10 When Jesus heard *it*, he marvelled, and said to them that followed, Verily I say unto you, I have not found so great faith, [1]**no**, **not**[2] in Israel.

11 And I say unto you, That many shall come from the east and west, and shall sit down with Abraham, and Isaac, and Jacob, in the kingdom of heaven.

12 But the children of the kingdom shall be cast out into outer darkness: there shall be weeping and gnashing of teeth.

13 And Jesus said unto the centurion, Go thy way; ~~and~~[3] as thou hast believed, *so* be it done unto thee. And ~~his~~[4] servant was healed in the selfsame hour.

14 And when Jesus was

come into Peter's house, he saw his wife's mother laid, and sick of a fever.

15 And he touched her hand, and the fever left her: and she arose, and ministered **unto them**[5].

16 When the even was come, they brought unto him many that were possessed with devils: and he cast out the spirits with *his* word, and healed all that were sick:

17 That it might be fulfilled which was spoken by Esaias the prophet, saying, Himself took our infirmities, and bare *our* sicknesses.

18 Now when Jesus saw great multitudes about him, he gave commandment to depart unto the other side.

19 And a certain scribe came, and said unto him, Master, I will follow thee whithersoever thou goest.

20 And Jesus saith unto him, The foxes have holes, and the birds of the air *have* nests; but the Son of man hath not where to lay *his* head.

21 And another of ~~his~~[6]

---

[1] In their margin, WH changed the word order from **not** **even** in the Israel so GREAT FAITH to *beside nothing* SO GREAT FAITH *in the Israel*.

[2] In their margin, WH changed **no** **not** (oude) to *beside nothing* (*par oudeni*).

[3] WH omitted and (kai).

[4] WH omitted of him (autou) from the of him servant.

[5] WH changed unto **them** (autois) to *unto* **him** (autO). [number]

[6] WH omitted of him (autou) from the disciples of him.

disciples said unto him, Lord, suffer me first to go and bury my father.

22 But Jesus **said**[1] unto him, Follow me; and let the dead bury their dead.

23 And when he was entered into a **[the]**[2] ship, his disciples followed him.

24 And, behold, there arose a great tempest in the sea, insomuch that the ship was covered with the waves: but he was asleep.

25 And ~~his disciples~~[3] came to *him*, and awoke him, saying, Lord, save ~~us~~[4]: we perish.

26 And he saith unto them, Why are ye fearful, O ye of little faith? Then he arose, and rebuked the winds and the sea; and there was a great calm.

27 But the men marvelled, saying, What manner of man is this, that even the winds and the sea obey him!

28 And when he was come to the other side into the country of the **Gergesenes**[5], there met him two possessed with devils, coming out of the tombs, exceeding fierce, so that no man might pass by that way.

29 And, behold, they cried out, saying, What have we to do with thee, ~~Jesus~~[6], thou Son of God? art thou come hither to torment us before the time?

30 And there was a good way off from them an herd of many swine feeding.

31 So the devils besought him, saying, If thou cast us out, **suffer us to go away**[7] into the herd of swine.

32 And he said unto them, Go. And when they were come out, they went into ~~the herd~~[8] of swine: and, behold, the whole herd ~~of swine~~[9] ran violently down a steep place

---

[5] WH changed <u>Gerges</u>enes (**gerges**AnOn) to *Gadarenes* (*gadarAnOn*). [spell]

[6] WH omitted <u>Jesus</u> (<u>iAsou</u>).

[7] WH changed **suffer** us **to go** away (**epitre**şon [h]Amin apel~~th~~ein) to *send us away* (*aposteilon* [h]*Amas*).

[8] WH omitted <u>the herd</u> (<u>tOn</u> <u>coirOn</u>) and changed <u>the herd of the</u> swine to *the swine*.

[9] WH omitted <u>of the</u> swine (<u>tOn</u> <u>coirOn</u>).

---

[1] WH changed <u>said</u> (**eipen**) to *says* (*legei*). **Aor** Act Ind to *Pres* Act Ind [tense]

[2] WH omitted the untranslated *the* (to).

[3] WH omitted <u>his</u> <u>disciples</u> ([h]<u>oi</u> ma~~th~~Atai <u>autou</u>).

[4] WH omitted <u>us</u> ([h]<u>Amas</u>).

into the sea, and perished in the waters.

33 And they that kept them fled, and went their ways into the city, and told every thing, and what was befallen to the possessed of the devils.

34 And, behold, the whole city came out to meet Jesus: and when they saw him, they besought *him* that he would depart out of their coasts.

CHAPTER 9

1   And he entered into a [the][1] ship, and passed over, and came into his own city.

2   And, behold, they brought to him a man sick of the palsy, lying on a bed: and Jesus seeing their faith said unto the sick of the palsy; Son, be of good cheer; **thy**[2] sins be forgiven **thee**[3].

3   And, behold, certain of the scribes said within themselves, This *man* blasphemeth.

4   And Jesus **knowing**[4] their thoughts said, Wherefore think ye [**yourselves**][5] evil in your hearts?

5   For whether is easier, to say, *Thy* sins be forgiven **thee**[6]; or to say, Arise, and walk?

6   But that ye may know that the Son of man hath power on earth to forgive sins, (then saith he to the sick of the palsy,) Arise, take up thy bed, and go unto thine house.

7   And he arose, and departed to his house.

8   But when the multitudes

---

[1] WH omitted the untranslated the (to).

[2] WH changed the word order from be forgiven the sins OF THEE to *be forgiven OF THEE the sins*.

[3] WH omitted thee (soi).

[4] WH changed having known {**at one point**} (idOn) to *having known* {**and continuing to know**} (*eidOs*) in their text. **Aor** Act Part to *Pf* Act Part. [tense] They retained having known (idOn) in their margin.

[5] WH omitted the untranslated intensive pronoun yourselves ([h]umeis). They changed from why are ye **yourselves** thinking to *why are ye thinking*.

[6] WH changed **to thee** (so**i**) to *of thee* (so**u**). They changed be forgiven **to thee** the sins to *be forgiven the sins of thee*. **Dat** to **Gen**. [case]

saw *it*, they **marvelled**[1], and glorified God, which had given such power unto men.

9 And as Jesus passed forth from thence, he saw a man, named Matthew, sitting at the receipt of custom: and he saith unto him, Follow me. And he arose, and followed him.

10 And it came to pass, as Jesus sat at meat in the house, behold, many publicans and sinners came and sat down with him and his disciples.

11 And when the Pharisees saw *it*, they said unto his disciples, Why eateth your master with publicans and sinners?

12 But when ~~Jesus~~[2] heard *that*, he said ~~unto them~~[3], They that be whole need not a physician, but they that are sick.

13 But go ye and learn what *that* meaneth, I will have mercy, and not sacrifice: for I am not come to call the righteous, but sinners ~~to repentance~~[4].

14 Then came to him the disciples of John, saying, Why do we and the Pharisees fast **oft**[5], but thy disciples fast not?

15 And Jesus said unto them, Can the children of the bridechamber mourn, as long as the bridegroom is with them? but the days will come, when the bridegroom shall be taken from them, and then shall they fast.

16 No man putteth a piece of new cloth unto an old garment, for that which is put in to fill it up taketh from the garment, and the rent is made worse.

17 Neither do men put new wine into old bottles: else the bottles break, and the wine runneth out, and the bottles **perish**[6]: but they put new wine into new bottles, and both are preserved.

18 While he spake these

---

[1] WH changed **marvelled** (e~~th~~auma~~san~~) to *were afraid* (*efobА*~~th~~*Аsan*).
[2] WH omitted Jesus (iAsous) and forced the verb to supply the subject *he*.
[3] WH omitted unto them (autois).
[4] WH omitted to repentance (eis metanoian).
[5] In their margin, WH omitted oft (polla).
[6] WH changed **will be** destroyed (apolountai) to *are being* destroyed (apoll*u*ntai). **Fut** **Mid** Ind to *Pres Pass* Ind. [tense & voice]

things unto them, behold, there came a certain ruler, and worshipped him, saying, My daughter is even now dead: but come and lay thy hand upon her, and she shall live.

19 And Jesus arose, and followed him, and *so did* his disciples.

20 And, behold, a woman, which was diseased with an issue of blood twelve years, came behind *him*, and touched the hem of his garment:

21 For she said within herself, If I may but touch his garment, I shall be whole.

22 But Jesus **turned him about**[1], and when he saw her, he said, Daughter, be of good comfort; thy faith hath made thee whole. And the woman was made whole from that hour.

23 And when Jesus came into the ruler's house, and saw the minstrels and the people making a noise,

24 **He said**[2] ~~unto them~~[3],

Give place: for the maid is not dead, but sleepeth. And they laughed him to scorn.

25 But when the people were put forth, he went in, and took her by the hand, and the maid arose.

26 And the fame hereof went abroad into all that land.

27 And when Jesus departed thence, two blind men followed him, crying, and saying, *Thou* Son of David, have mercy on us.

28 And when he was come into the house, the blind men came to him: and Jesus saith unto them, Believe ye that I am able to do this? They said unto him, Yea, Lord.

29 Then touched he their eyes, saying, According to your faith be it unto you.

30 And their eyes were opened; and Jesus straitly charged them, saying, See *that* no man know *it*.

31 But they, when they were departed, spread abroad his fame in all that country.

32 As they went out, behold, they brought to him a dumb ~~man~~[4] possessed with a devil.

---

[1] WH changed <u>having turned **around**</u> (**epi-**<u>strafeis</u>) to *having turned* (*strafeis*). Both Aor Pas Part. [prefix dropped]

[2] WH changed <u>he says</u> (<u>legei</u>) to *he **was** saying* (*elegen*). **Pres** Act Ind to *Impf* Act Ind. [tense]

[3] WH omitted <u>unto them</u> (<u>autois</u>).

[4] WH omitted <u>man</u> (an~~th~~rOpon).

33 And when the devil was cast out, the dumb spake: and the multitudes marvelled, saying, It was never so seen in Israel.

34 But the Pharisees said, He casteth out devils through the prince of the devils.

35 And Jesus went about all the cities and villages, teaching in their synagogues, and preaching the gospel of the kingdom, and healing every sickness and every disease ~~among the people~~[1].

36 But when he saw the multitudes, he was moved with compassion on them, because they **fainted**[2], and were scattered abroad, as sheep having no shepherd.

37 Then saith he unto his disciples, The harvest truly *is* plenteous, but the labourers *are* few;

38 Pray ye therefore the Lord of the harvest, that he will send forth labourers into his harvest.

---

[1] WH omitted among the people (en tO laO).

[2] WH changed were being **exhausted** (ʰAsan **eklelu**menoi) to *were being harrassed* (ʰAsan *eskul*menoi). [verb root & prefix changed]

CHAPTER 10

1 And when he had called unto *him* his twelve disciples, he gave them power *against* unclean spirits, to cast them out, and to heal all manner of sickness and all manner of disease.

2 Now the names of the twelve apostles are these; The first, Simon, who is called Peter, and Andrew his brother; James *the son* of Zebedee, and John his brother;

3 Philip, and Bartholomew; Thomas, and Matthew the publican; James *the son* of Alphaeus, and ~~Lebbaeus, whose surname was~~[3] Thaddaeus;

4 Simon the **Canaanite**[4], and Judas Iscariot, who also betrayed him.

5 These twelve Jesus sent forth, and commanded them, saying, Go not into the way of the Gentiles, and into *any* city of the Samaritans enter ye not:

6 But go rather to the lost sheep of the house of Israel.

---

[3] WH omitted Lebbaeus whose surname was (lebbaios ʰo epiklAtheis).

[4] WH changed Canaanite (kananitAs) to *Cananai* (*kananaios*). [spell]

7   And as ye go, preach, saying, The kingdom of heaven is at hand.

8   Heal the sick, cleanse the lepers, **raise the dead**[1], cast out devils: freely ye have received, freely give.

9   Provide neither gold, nor silver, nor brass in your purses,

10   Nor scrip for *your* journey, neither two coats, neither shoes, nor yet **staves**[2]: for the workman is worthy of his meat.

11   And into whatsoever city or town ye shall enter, enquire who in it is worthy; and there abide till ye go thence.

12   And when ye come into an house, salute it.

13   And if the house be worthy, let your peace come upon it: but if it be not worthy, let your peace return to you.

14   And whosoever shall not receive you, nor hear your words, when ye depart out [ᴧ**outside**][3] of that house or city, shake off the dust of your feet.

15   Verily I say unto you, It shall be more tolerable for the land of Sodom and Gomorrha in the day of judgment, than for that city.

16   Behold, I send you forth as sheep in the midst of wolves: be ye therefore wise as serpents, and harmless as doves.

17   But beware of men: for they will deliver you up to the councils, and they will scourge you in their synagogues;

18   And ye shall be brought before governors and kings for my sake, for a testimony against them and the Gentiles.

19   But when they deliver you up, take no thought how or what ye shall speak: for it shall be given you in that same hour what ye shall speak.

20   For it is not ye that speak, but the Spirit of your Father which speaketh in you.

21   And the brother shall deliver up the brother to death, and the father the child: and the children shall

---

[1] WH changed the word order from <u>cleanse</u> <u>the</u> <u>lepers,</u> <u>RAISE</u> <u>THE</u> <u>DEAD</u> to *RAISE THE DEAD, cleanse the lepers.*

[2] WH changed from <u>staff**s**</u> ([h]rabdo**us**) to *staff* ([h]*rabdon*). **<u>Plur</u>** to ***Sing***. [number]

[3] WH added *outside* (*exO*) after <u>depart out</u>.

rise up against *their* parents, and cause them to be put to death.

22 And ye shall be hated of all *men* for my name's sake: but he that endureth to the end shall be saved.

23 But when they persecute you in this city, flee ye into **another**[1]: for verily I say unto you, Ye shall not have gone over the cities of Israel, till the Son of man be come.

24 The disciple is not above *his* master, nor the servant above his lord.

25 It is enough for the disciple that he be as his master, and the servant as his lord. If **they have called**[2] the master of the house Beelzebub, how much more *shall they call* them of his household?

26 Fear them not therefore: for there is nothing covered, that shall not be revealed; and hid, that shall not be known.

27 What I tell you in darkness, *that* speak ye in light:

---

[1] WH changed another {of the **same** kind} (**allAn**) to *another* {of a *different* kind} (*[h]eteran*).
[2] WH changed they called (ekalesan) to *they called* **upon** (*epekalesan*). Both Aor. [prefix added]

and what ye hear in the ear, *that* preach ye upon the housetops.

28 And fear not them which kill the body, but are not able to kill the soul: but rather fear him which is able to destroy both soul and body in hell.

29 Are not two sparrows sold for a farthing? and one of them shall not fall on the ground without your Father.

30 But the very hairs of your head are all numbered.

31 Fear ye not therefore, ye are of more value than many sparrows.

32 Whosoever therefore shall confess me before men, him will I confess also before my Father which is in heaven.

33 But whosoever shall deny me before men, him will I also deny before my Father which is in heaven.

34 Think not that I am come to send peace on earth: I came not to send peace, but a sword.

35 For I am come to set a man at variance against his father, and the daughter against her mother, and the daughter in law against her mother in law.

36 And a man's foes *shall be* they of his own household.

37 He that loveth father or

mother more than me is not worthy of me: and he that loveth son or daughter more than me is not worthy of me.

38 And he that taketh not his cross, and followeth after me, is not worthy of me.

39 He that findeth his life shall lose it: and he that loseth his life for my sake shall find it.

40 He that receiveth you receiveth me, and he that receiveth me receiveth him that sent me.

41 He that receiveth a prophet in the name of a prophet shall receive a prophet's reward; and he that receiveth a righteous man in the name of a righteous man shall receive a righteous man's reward.

42 And whosoever shall give to drink unto one of these little ones a cup of cold *water* only in the name of a disciple, verily I say unto you, he shall in no wise lose his reward.

CHAPTER 11

1 And it came to pass, when Jesus had made an end of commanding his twelve disciples, he departed thence to teach and to preach in their cities.

2 Now when John had heard in the prison the works of Christ, he sent **two**[1] of his disciples,

3 And said unto him, Art thou he that should come, or do we look for another?

4 Jesus answered and said unto them, Go and shew John again those things which ye do hear and see:

5 The blind receive their sight, and the lame walk, [∧**and**][2] the lepers are cleansed, and the deaf hear, the dead are raised up, and the poor have the gospel preached to them.

6 And blessed is *he*, whosoever shall not be offended in me.

7 And as they departed, Jesus began to say unto the multitudes concerning John, What went ye out into the wilderness to see? A reed shaken with the wind?

8 But what went ye out for to see? A man clothed in soft ~~raiment~~[3]? behold, they that wear soft *clothing* are in kings' houses.

---

[1] WH changed **two** (**duo**) to *through* (*dia*). The result is *he sent **through** his disciples.*

[2] WH added *and* (*kai*) before the lepers.

[3] WH omitted raiment ([h] imatiois).

9   But what went ye out for to see? A prophet? yea, I say unto you, and more than a prophet.

10   ~~For~~[1] this is *he*, of whom it is written, Behold, I send my messenger before thy face, which shall prepare thy way before thee.

11   Verily I say unto you, Among them that are born of women there hath not risen a greater than John the Baptist: notwithstanding he that is least in the kingdom of heaven is greater than he.

12   And from the days of John the Baptist until now the kingdom of heaven suffereth violence, and the violent take it by force.

13   For all the prophets and the law prophesied until John.

14   And if ye will receive *it*, this is Elias, which was for to come.

15   He that hath ears **to hear**[2], let him hear.

16   But whereunto shall I liken this generation? It is like unto **children**[3] sitting in the markets, ~~and~~[4] [∧who][5] **call-**

ing[6] unto ~~their~~[7] fellows,

17   ~~And~~[8] saying[9], We have piped unto you, and ye have not danced; we have mourned ~~unto you~~,[10] and ye have not lamented.

18   For John came neither eating nor drinking, and they say, He hath a devil.

19   The Son of man came eating and drinking, and they say, Behold a man gluttonous, and a winebibber, a friend of publicans and sinners. But wisdom is justified of her **children**[11].

20   Then began he to upbraid the cities wherein most of his mighty works were done, because they repented

---

[5] WH added *who* (*ʰa*).

[6] WH changed calling (pros-fOnousi{**n**}) to *calling* (pros-fOnounta). Both Pres Act Part. **Dat Masc** Plur to *Nom Neut* Plur. [case & gender]

[7] WH omitted of them (autOn) from the fellows of them.

[8] WH omitted and (kai).

[9] Instead of **and** calling unto **their** fellows, **and** saying, WH has *who are calling unto the fellows, saying*.

[10] WH omitted unto youᵖ (ʰumin).

[11] In their margin, WH changed **children** (teknOn) to *works* (ergOn).

---

[1] WH omitted for (gar).

[2] In their margin, WH omitted to hear (akouein).

[3] WH changed **lads** (paidariois) to *children* (*paidiois*).

[4] WH omitted and (kai).

not:

21 Woe unto thee, Chorazin! woe unto thee, Bethsaida! for if the mighty works, which were done in you, had been done in Tyre and Sidon, they would have repented long ago in sackcloth and ashes.

22 But I say unto you, It shall be more tolerable for Tyre and Sidon at the day of judgment, than for you.

23 And thou, Capernaum, **which**[1] **art exalted**[2] unto heaven, **shalt be brought down**[3] to hell: for if the mighty works, which have been done in thee, had been done in Sodom, it would have remained until this day.

24 But I say unto you, That it shall be more tolerable

---

[1] WH changed **which** (^{h}A) to *not* (*mA*).
[2] WH changed **having been** exalted (^{h}u$_s$Otheisa) to *you*^{s} *will be exalted* (^{h}u$_s$OthAsA). **Aor** Pass **Part** to *Fut* Pass *Ind*. [tense & mood]
[3] WH changed you^s will **be brought** down (kata-bi-**basth**AsA) to *you*^{s} *will go down* (*kata-bAsA*). Fut **Pass** Ind of kata**bibaz**O to Fut *Mid* Ind of *katabainO*. [verb root] WH retained kata-bi-**basth**AsA in their margin.

for the land of Sodom in the day of judgment, than for thee.

25 At that time Jesus answered and said, I thank thee, O Father, Lord of heaven and earth, because thou hast hid these things from the wise and prudent, and hast revealed them unto babes.

26 Even so, Father: for so it seemed good in thy sight.

27 All things are delivered unto me of my Father: and no man knoweth the Son, but the Father; neither knoweth any man the Father, save the Son, and *he* to whomsoever the Son will reveal *him*.

28 Come unto me, all *ye* that labour and are heavy laden, and I will give you rest.

29 Take my yoke upon you, and learn of me; for I am meek and lowly in heart: and ye shall find rest unto your souls.

30 For my yoke *is* easy, and my burden is light.

CHAPTER 12

1 At that time Jesus went on the sabbath day through the corn; and his disciples were an hungred, and began to pluck the ears of corn, and to eat.

2 But when the Pharisees

saw *it*, they said unto him, Behold, thy disciples do that which is not lawful to do upon the sabbath day.

3   But he said unto them, Have ye not read what David did, when he [~~himself~~][1] was an hungred, and they that were with him;

4   How he entered into the house of God, and <u>did eat</u>[2] the shewbread, which was not lawful for him to eat, neither for them which were with him, but only for the priests?

5   Or have ye not read in the law, how that on the sabbath days the priests in the temple profane the sabbath, and are blameless?

6   But I say unto you, That in this place is <u>*one*</u> **greater** <u>than</u>[3] the temple.

7   But if ye had known what *this* meaneth, I will have mercy, and not sacrifice, ye would not have condemned the guiltless.

8   For the Son of man is Lord **even**[4] of the sabbath day.

9   And when he was departed thence, he went into their synagogue:

10   And, behold, ~~there was~~[5] a man which had ***his***[6] hand withered. And they asked him, saying, Is it lawful to heal on the sabbath days? that they might accuse him.

11   And he said unto them, What man shall there be among you, that shall have one sheep, and if it fall into a pit on the sabbath day, will he not lay hold on it, and lift *it* out?

12   How much then is a man better than a sheep? Wherefore it is lawful to do well on the sabbath days.

13   Then saith he to the man, Stretch forth thine hand. And he stretched *it* forth; and it was restored whole, like as the other.

14   Then   the   Pharisees

---

[1] WH omitted the untranslated intensive pronoun <u>himself</u> (<u>autos</u>).

[2] In their margin, WH changed **he** <u>did eat</u> (<u>efagen</u>) to ***they*** *did eat* (*efagon*). Both Aor Act Ind. 3rd **Sing** to 3rd *Plur*. [number]

[3] WH changed {some**one**} <u>greater than</u> (<u>meizOn</u>) to {some**thing**} *greater than* (*meizon*). Nom **Masc** Sing to Nom *Neut* Sing. [gender]

[4] WH omitted <u>even</u> (<u>kai</u>).

[5] WH omitted <u>there was</u> (<u>An</u>).

[6] WH omitted <u>the</u> (<u>tAn</u>) where the KJV supplied *his*.

went out[1], and held a council against him, how they might destroy him.

15 But when Jesus knew *it*, he withdrew himself from thence: and great ~~multitudes~~[2] followed him, and he healed them all;

16 And charged them that they should not make him known:

17 That it might be fulfilled which was spoken by Esaias the prophet, saying,

18 Behold my servant, whom I have chosen; my beloved, in whom my soul is well pleased: I will put my spirit upon him, and he shall shew judgment to the Gentiles.

19 He shall not strive, nor cry; neither shall any man hear his voice in the streets.

20 A bruised reed shall he not break, and smoking flax shall he not quench, till he send forth judgment unto victory.

21 And ~~in~~[3] his name shall the Gentiles trust.

22 Then was brought unto him one possessed with a devil, ~~blind~~[4], ~~and~~[5] dumb: ~~and~~[6] he healed him, insomuch that the blind and dumb both spake and saw.

23 And all the people were amazed, and said, Is not this the son of David?

24 But when the Pharisees heard *it*, they said, This *fellow* doth not cast out devils, but by Beelzebub the prince of the devils.

25 And ~~Jesus~~[7] knew their thoughts, and said unto them, Every kingdom divided against itself is brought to desolation; and every city or house divided against itself shall not stand:

26 And if Satan cast out Satan, he is divided against himself; how shall then his kingdom stand?

27 And if I by Beelzebub cast out devils, by whom do

---

[1] WH changed the word order from then the Pharisees a council held against him HAVING GONE OUT to *then the Pharisees HAVING GONE OUT a council held against him.*
[2] WH omitted multitudes (ocloi).

[3] WH omitted in (en) and forced the case of name to provide the prepositon.
[4] WH omitted blind (tuflon).
[5] WH omitted and (kai).
[6] WH omitted and (kai).
[7] WH omitted the Jesus ([h]o iAsous) and forced the verb to supply the subject *he.*

your children cast *them* out? therefore they shall be your judges.

28 But if I cast out devils by the Spirit of God, then the kingdom of God is come unto you.

29 Or else how can one enter into a strong man's house, and spoil his goods, except he first bind the strong man? and then he will spoil his house.

30 He that is not with me is against me; and he that gathereth not with me scattereth abroad.

31 Wherefore I say unto you, All manner of sin and blasphemy shall be forgiven [you]¹ unto men: but the blasphemy *against* the *Holy* Ghost shall not be forgiven unto men².

32 And whosoever speaketh a word against the Son of man, it shall be forgiven him: but whosoever speaketh against the Holy Ghost, it shall not be forgiven him, neither in this world, neither in the *world* to come.

33 Either make the tree good, and his fruit good; or

else make the tree corrupt, and his fruit corrupt: for the tree is known by *his* fruit.

34 O generation of vipers, how can ye, being evil, speak good things? for out of the abundance of the heart the mouth speaketh.

35 A good man out of the good treasure of the heart³ bringeth forth [the]⁴ good things: and an evil man out of the evil treasure bringeth forth evil things.

36 But I say unto you, That every idle word that men shall speak, they shall give account thereof in the day of judgment.

37 For by thy words thou shalt be justified, and by thy words thou shalt be condemned.

38 Then certain of the scribes and of the Pharisees answered [ʌhim]⁵, saying, Master, we would see a sign from thee.

39 But he answered and said unto them, An evil and adulterous generation seeketh after a sign; and there shall no

---

¹ In their margin, WH added *you* (ʰ*umin*).
² WH omitted unto the men (tois anthrOpois)

³ WH omitted of the heart (tAs kardias).
⁴ WH omitted the untranslated *the* (*ta*).
⁵ WH added *him* (*autO*) after answered.

sign be given to it, but the sign of the prophet Jonas:

40 For as Jonas was three days and three nights in the whale's belly; so shall the Son of man be three days and three nights in the heart of the earth.

41 The men of Nineveh shall rise in judgment with this generation, and shall condemn it: because they repented at the preaching of Jonas; and, behold, a greater than Jonas *is* here.

42 The queen of the south shall rise up in the judgment with this generation, and shall condemn it: for she came from the uttermost parts of the earth to hear the wisdom of Solomon; and, behold, a greater than Solomon *is* here.

43 When the unclean spirit is gone out of a man, he walketh through dry places, seeking rest, and findeth none.

44 Then he saith, I will return into my house from whence I came out; and when he is come, he findeth *it* empty, swept, and garnished.

45 Then goeth he, and taketh with himself seven other spirits more wicked than himself, and they enter in and dwell there: and the last *state* of that man is worse than the first. Even so shall it be also unto this wicked generation.

46 [~~but~~][1] While he yet talked to the people, behold, *his* mother and ~~his~~[2] brethren stood without, desiring to speak with him.

47 **Then one said unto him, Behold, thy mother and thy brethren stand without, desiring to speak with thee**[3].

48 But he answered and said unto him that told him, Who is my mother? and who are my brethren?

49 And he stretched forth his hand toward his disciples, and said, Behold my mother and my brethren!

50 For whosoever shall do the will of my Father which is in heaven, the same is my brother, and sister, and mother.

---

[1] WH omitted the untranslated but (de).

[2] WH omitted of him (autou) from the of him and left *the mother and the brothers stood.*

[3] In their margin, WH omitted all of Mt.12:47—then one said unto him behold thy mother and thy brethren stand outside desiring to speak with thee (eipe de tis autO idou [h]A mAtAr sou kai [h]oi adelfoi sou exO [h]estAkasi zAtountes soi lalasai).

CHAPTER 13

1 [but]¹ The same day went Jesus out of the house, and sat by the sea side.

2 And great multitudes were gathered together unto him, so that he went into [the]² a ship, and sat; and the whole multitude stood on the shore.

3 And he spake many things unto them in parables, saying, Behold, a sower went forth to sow;

4 And when he sowed, some *seeds* fell by the way side, and the fowls came and devoured them up:

5 Some fell upon stony places, where they had not much earth: and forthwith they sprung up, because they had no deepness of earth:

6 And when the sun was up, they were scorched; and because they had no root, they withered away.

7 And some fell among thorns; and the thorns sprung up, and choked them:

8 But other fell into good ground, and brought forth fruit, some an hundredfold, some sixtyfold, some thirty-fold.

9 Who hath ears ~~to hear~~³, let him hear.

10 And the disciples came, and said unto him, Why speakest thou unto them in parables?

11 He answered and said unto them, Because it is given unto you to know the mysteries of the kingdom of heaven, but to them it is not given.

12 For whosoever hath, to him shall be given, and he shall have more abundance: but whosoever hath not, from him shall be taken away even that he hath.

13 Therefore speak I to them in parables: because they seeing see not; and hearing they hear not, neither do they understand.

14 And ~~in~~⁴ them is fulfilled the prophecy of Esaias, which saith, By hearing ye shall hear, and shall not understand; and seeing ye shall see, and shall not perceive:

15 For this people's heart is waxed gross, and *their* ears

---

¹ WH omitted the untranslated <u>but</u> (<u>de</u>).
² WH omitted <u>the</u> (<u>to</u>) before <u>ship</u>.

³ WH omitted <u>to hear</u> (<u>ak-ouein</u>) in their text, but retained it in their margin.
⁴ WH omitted <u>in</u> (<u>epi</u>--upon) and forced the case of <u>them</u> to supply the preposition.

are dull of hearing, and their eyes they have closed; lest at any time they should see with *their* eyes, and hear with *their* ears, and should understand with *their* heart, and should be converted, and **I should heal**[1] them.

16 But blessed *are* your eyes, for they see: and your ears, for they hear.

17 For verily I say unto you, That many prophets and righteous *men* have desired to see *those things* which ye see, and have not seen *them*; and to hear *those things* which ye hear, and have not heard *them*.

18 Hear ye therefore the parable of the sower.

19 When any one heareth the word of the kingdom, and understandeth *it* not, then cometh the wicked *one*, and catcheth away that which was sown in his heart. This is he which received seed by the way side.

20 But he that received the seed into stony places, the same is he that heareth the word, and anon with joy re-ceiveth it;

21 Yet hath he not root in himself, but dureth for a while: for when tribulation or persecution ariseth because of the word, by and by he is offended.

22 He also that received seed among the thorns is he that heareth the word; and the care of **this**[2] world, and the deceitfulness of riches, choke the word, and he be-cometh unfruitful.

23 But he that received seed into the good ground is he that heareth the word, and understandeth *it*; which also beareth fruit, and bringeth forth, some an hundredfold, some sixty, some thirty.

24 Another parable put he forth unto them, saying, The kingdom of heaven is likened unto a man which sowed good seed in his field:

25 But while men slept, his enemy came and **sowed**[3] tares among the wheat, and

---

[2] WH omitted this (toutou) from the world {age} this (one).
[3] WH changed sow**ed** (espeire) to *were sowing* (*ep-espeire*). **Aor** Act Ind of speirO to an *Impf* Act Ind of *epi-speirO*. [tense & prefix added]

---

[1] WH changed I **might** heal (iasOmai) to *I will heal* (*iasomai*). **Aor** Mid-D **Sub** to *Fut* Mid *Ind*. [tense & mood]

went his way.

26 But when the blade was sprung up, and brought forth fruit, then appeared the tares also.

27 So the servants of the householder came and said unto him, Sir, didst not thou sow good seed in thy field? from whence then hath it [~~the~~]¹ tares?

28 He said unto them, An enemy hath done this. The servants **said**² **unto him**³, Wilt thou then that we go and gather them up?

29 But he **said**⁴, Nay; lest while ye gather up the tares, ye root up also the wheat with them.

30 Let both grow together until the harvest: and in the time of harvest I will say to the reapers, Gather ye together first the tares, and bind them in bundles to burn them: but gather the wheat into my barn.

31 Another parable put he forth unto them, saying, The kingdom of heaven is like to a grain of mustard seed, which a man took, and sowed in his field:

32 Which indeed is the least of all seeds: but when it is grown, it is the greatest among herbs, and becometh a tree, so that the birds of the air come and lodge in the branches thereof.

33 Another parable spake he unto them; The kingdom of heaven is like unto leaven, which a woman took, and hid in three measures of meal, till the whole was leavened.

34 All these things spake Jesus unto the multitude in parables; and without a parable spake he **not**⁵ unto them:

35 That it might be fulfilled which was spoken by the prophet, saying, I will open my mouth in parables; I will utter things which have been kept secret from the foundation **of the world**⁶.

---

¹ WH omitted the untranslated <u>the</u> (<u>ta</u>).
² WH changed <u>said</u> (**eipon**) to *say* (*legousi*). **Aor** Act Ind to ***Pres*** Act Ind. [tense & syn]
³ WH changed the word order from **said** UNTO HIM to *UNTO HIM* **say**.
⁴ WH changed **were** <u>saying</u> (**efA**) to *says* (*fAsin*). **Impf** NV Ind to ***Pres*** Act Ind (*says*). [tense]

⁵ WH changed <u>not</u> (<u>ouk</u>) to *nothing* (*ouden*).
⁶ In their margin, WH omitted <u>of the world</u> (<u>kosmou</u>).

36 Then ~~Jesus~~[1] sent the multitude away, and went into the house: and his disciples came unto him, saying, **Declare**[2] unto us the parable of the tares of the field.

37 He answered and said ~~unto them~~[3], He that soweth the good seed is the Son of man;

38 The field is the world; the good seed are the children of the kingdom; but the tares are the children of the wicked *one*;

39 The enemy that sowed them is the devil; the harvest is the end of ~~the~~[4] world; and the reapers are the angels.

40 As therefore the tares are gathered and burned in the fire; so shall it be in the end of ~~this~~[5] world.

41 The Son of man shall send forth his angels, and they shall gather out of his kingdom all things that offend, and them which do iniquity;

42 And shall cast them into a furnace of fire: there shall be wailing and gnashing of teeth.

43 Then shall the righteous shine forth as the sun in the kingdom of their Father. Who hath ears ~~to hear~~[6], let him hear.

44 ~~Again~~[7], the kingdom of heaven is like unto treasure hid in a field; the which when a man hath found, he hideth, and for joy thereof goeth and selleth all that he hath, and buyeth that field.

45 Again, the kingdom of heaven is like unto a merchant man, seeking goodly pearls:

46 **Who**[8], when he had found one pearl of great price, went and sold all that he had, and bought it.

47 Again, the kingdom of heaven is like unto a net, that was cast into the sea, and gathered of every kind:

---

[1] WH omitted the Jesus (^{h}o iAsous) and forced the verb to supply the subject *he*.

[2] WH changed **declare** (frason) to *explain* (*diasafAson*). Aor Act Imp of frazO to Aor Act Imp of *dia-safeO*. [syn]

[3] WH omitted unto them (autois).

[4] WH omitted the (tou) before world (aiOnos).

[5] WH omitted this (toutou) from the world this {one}.

[6] WH omitted to hear (ak-ouein) in their text, but retained it in their margin.

[7] WH omitted again (palin).

[8] WH changed **who** (^{h}os) to *but* (*de*).

48 Which, when it was full, they drew to shore, and sat down, and gathered the good into vessels, but cast the bad away.

49 So shall it be at the end of the world: the angels shall come forth, and sever the wicked from among the just,

50 And shall cast them into the furnace of fire: there shall be wailing and gnashing of teeth.

51 ~~Jesus saith unto them~~[1], Have ye understood all these things? They say unto him, Yea, ~~Lord~~[2].

52 Then said he unto them, Therefore every scribe _which is_ instructed **unto**[3] **the kingdom**[4] of heaven is like unto a man _that is_ an householder, which bringeth forth out of his treasure _things_ new and old.

53 And it came to pass, _that_ when Jesus had finished these parables, he departed thence.

54 And when he was come into his own country, he taught them in their synagogue, insomuch that they were astonished, and said, Whence hath this _man_ this wisdom, and _these_ mighty works?

55 Is not this the carpenter's son? is not his mother called Mary? and his brethren, James, and **Joses**[5], and Simon, and Judas?

56 And his sisters, are they not all with us? Whence then hath this _man_ all these things?

57 And they were offended in him. But Jesus said unto them, A prophet is not without honour, save in his own country, and in his own house.

58 And he did not many mighty works there because of their unbelief.

CHAPTER 14

1 At that time Herod the tetrarch heard of the fame of Jesus,

2 And said unto his servants, This is John the Baptist; he is risen from the dead; and therefore mighty works

---

[1] WH omitted <u>says</u> <u>to</u> <u>them</u> <u>the</u> <u>Jesus</u> (<u>legei</u> <u>autois</u> [h]<u>o</u> <u>iasous</u>).

[2] WH omitted <u>Lord</u> (<u>kurie</u>).

[3] WH omitted <u>unto</u> (<u>eis</u>) and forced the case of <u>the</u> <u>king-dom</u> to supply the preposition.

[4] WH changed <u>the</u> <u>kingdom</u> (<u>tAn</u> <u>Basileian</u>) to _the king-dom_ (_tA Basileia_). **Acc** Fem Sing to **_Dat_** Fem Sing. [case]

---

[5] WH changed <u>Joses</u> (<u>iOsAs</u>) to Jose**ph** (iOsA**f**). [spell]

do shew forth themselves in him.

3 For Herod had laid hold on John, and bound **him**[1], and put *him* in prison for Herodias' sake, his brother Philip's wife.

4 For John said unto him, It is not lawful for thee to have her.

5 And when he would have put him to death, he feared the multitude, because they counted him as a prophet.

6 But **when** Herod's **birthday** **was kept**[2], the daughter of Herodias danced before them, and pleased Herod.

7 Whereupon he promised with an oath to give her whatsoever she would ask.

8 And she, being before instructed of her mother, said, Give me here John Baptist's head in a charger.

9 And the king was sorry: nevertheless for the oath's sake, and them which sat with him at meat, he commanded *it* to be given *her*.

10 And he sent, and beheaded John in the prison.

11 And his head was brought in a charger, and given to the damsel: and she brought *it* to her mother.

12 And his disciples came, and took up the **body**[3], and buried **it**[4], and went and told Jesus.

13 **[and]**[5] When Jesus heard *of it*, he departed thence by ship into a desert place apart: and when the people had heard *thereof*, they followed him on foot out of the cities.

14 And **Jesus**[6] went forth, and saw a great multitude, and was moved with compassion toward them, and he healed their sick.

15 And when it was evening, his disciples came **to him**[7], saying, This is a desert

---

[1] WH omitted <u>him</u> (*auton*).
[2] WH changed birthday **being observed** (*genesOn* de **agomenOn**) to birthday *having come* (*genesiois genomenois*). **Pres Pass** Part of **agO** to an *Aor Mid* Part of *ginomai*. [tense, voice, & verb]

[3] WH changed **body** (*sOma*) to *corpse* (*ptOma*). [syn]
[4] WH changed **it** (<u>auto</u>) to *him* (*auton*). **Acc Neut** Sing to *Acc Masc* Sing. [case & gender]
[5] WH changed the untranslated **and** (**kai**) to *but* (*de*).
[6] WH omitted <u>the</u> Jesus (^h<u>o</u> iAsous).
[7] WH omitted <u>to him</u> (<u>autou</u>).

place, and the time is now past; send the multitude away, that they may go into the villages, and buy themselves victuals.

16 But Jesus said unto them, They need not depart; give ye them to eat.

17 And they say unto him, We have here but five loaves, and two fishes.

18 He said, Bring them hither to me.

19 And he commanded the multitude to sit down on the grass, and took the five loaves, and the two fishes, and looking up to heaven, he blessed, and brake, and gave the loaves to *his* disciples, and the disciples to the multitude.

20 And they did all eat, and were filled: and they took up of the fragments that remained twelve baskets full.

21 And they that had eaten were about five thousand men, beside women and children.

22 And straightway ~~Jesus~~[1] constrained ~~his~~[2] disciples to get into a ship, and to go before him unto the other side, while he sent the multitudes

away.

23 And when he had sent the multitudes away, he went up into a mountain apart to pray: and when the evening was come, he was there alone.

24 But the ship **was now in the midst of the sea**[3], tossed with waves: for the wind was contrary.

25 And in the fourth watch of the night ~~Jesus~~[4] **went**[5] unto them, walking on **the sea**[6].

26 And when the disciples saw him walking on **the sea**[7],

---

[1] WH omitted the Jesus ([h]o iAsous).

[2] WH omitted of him (autou) from the disciples of him.

---

[3] In their margin, WH completely changed was **now in the midst** of the **sea** (**meson tAs** ~~th~~**alassAn An**) to *was **already many stadia away from** the **land** (**stadious pollous apo tAs gAs apeice**).

[4] WH omitted the Jesus ([h]o iAsous) and forced the verb to supply the subject *he*.

[5] WH changed went {away}(**apAl**~~th~~**e**) to *went* (*Al*~~th~~*e*). [prefix dropped]

[6] WH changed the sea (tAs ~~th~~**alassAs**) to *the sea* (*tAn* ~~th~~*alassan*). **Gen** to *Acc*. [case]

[7] In their margin, WH changed the sea (tAn ~~th~~**alassan**) to *the sea* (*tAs* ~~th~~*alassAs*). **Acc** to *Gen*. [case]

they were troubled, saying, It is a spirit; and they cried out for fear.

27 But straightway Jesus spake unto them, saying, Be of good cheer; it is I; be not afraid.

28 And Peter answered him and said, Lord, if it be thou, bid me come unto thee on the water.

29 And he said, Come. And when Peter was come down out of the ship, he walked on the water, **to go**[1] to Jesus.

30 But when he saw the wind ~~boisterous~~[2], he was afraid; and beginning to sink, he cried, saying, Lord, save me.

31 And immediately Jesus stretched forth *his* hand, and caught him, and said unto him, O thou of little faith, wherefore didst thou doubt?

32 And **when** they **were come**[3] into the ship, the wind ceased.

33 Then they that were in the ship ~~came and~~[4] worshipped him, saying, Of a truth thou art the Son of God.

34 And when they were gone over, they came **into**[5] the land [∧**into**][6] of Gennesaret.

35 And when the men of that place had knowledge of him, they sent out into all that country round about, and brought unto him all that were diseased;

36 And besought him that they might only touch the hem of his garment: and as many as touched were made perfectly whole.

CHAPTER 15

1 Then came to Jesus scribes and **Pharisees**[7], ~~which were~~[8] of Jerusalem,

---

[1] In their margin, WH changed **to go** (el~~th~~ein) to *went* (Al~~the~~) Aor **Inf** to Aor **Ind**. [mood]
[2] WH omitted boisterous (is-curon) in their text, but retained it in their margin.
[3] WH changed when were come {**in**}(**em**bantOn) to *when were come {up} (anabantOn)*. [prefix changed]

[4] WH omitted came {and} (el~~th~~ontes).
[5] WH changed **into** (eis) to *upon* (epi).
[6] WH added *into* (eis).
[7] WH changed the word order from scribes and PHARISEES to *PHARISEES and scribes*.
[8] WH omitted which ([h]oi--the) together with the supplied were.

saying,

2   Why do thy disciples transgress the tradition of the elders? for they wash not **their**[1] hands when they eat bread.

3   But he answered and said unto them, Why do ye also transgress the commandment of God by your tradition?

4 For God **commanded**[2], **saying**[3], Honour **thy**[4] father and mother: and, He that curseth father or mother, let him die the death.

5   But ye say, Whosoever shall say to *his* father or *his* mother, *It is* a gift, by whatsoever thou mightest be profited by me;

6   **And**[5] **honour**[6] not his father **or his mother**[7], *he shall be free*. Thus have ye made **the commandment**[8] of God of none effect by your tradition.

7   *Ye* hypocrites, well did Esaias prophesy of you, saying,

8   This people **draweth nigh unto me with their mouth, and**[9] honoureth me with *their* lips; but their heart is far from me.

9   But in vain they do worship me, teaching *for* doctrines the commandments of men.

10   And he called the multitude, and said unto them, Hear, and understand:

11   Not that which goeth into the mouth defileth a man; but that which cometh out of the mouth, this defileth a man.

---

[1] WH omitted of them (autOn) from the hands of them.

[2] WH omitted commanded (eneteilato).

[3] WH changed saying (legOn) to *said* (*eipe*). **Pres** Act **Part** to *Aor* Act *Ind*. [tense & mood]

[4] WH omitted of thee (sou) from the father of thee.

[5] WH omitted and (kai).

[6] WH changed honour (timAsA) to *will honour* (*timAsei*). **Aor** Act **Sub** to a *Fut Act Ind*. [tense & mood]

[7] WH omitted or the mother of him (A tAn mAtera autou) in their text, but retained these words in their margin.

[8] WH changed the **commandment** (tAn **entolAn**) to *the word* (*ton logon*). In their margin, they changed to *the law* (*ton nomon*).

[9] WH omitted draws near to me with the mouth of them and (eggizei moi tO stomati autOn kai).

12 Then came **his**[1] disciples, and said unto him, knowest thou that the Pharisees were offended, after they heard this saying?

13 But he answered and said, Every plant, which my heavenly Father hath not planted, shall be rooted up.

14 Let them alone: they be blind leaders **of the blind**[2]. And if the blind lead the blind, both shall fall into the ditch.

15 Then answered Peter and said unto him, Declare unto us **this**[3] parable.

16 And **Jesus**[4] said, Are ye also yet without understanding?

17 Do **not** ye **yet**[5] understand, that whatsoever entereth in at the mouth goeth into the belly, and is cast out into the draught?

18 But those things which proceed out of the mouth come forth from the heart; and they defile the man.

19 For out of the heart proceed evil thoughts, murders, adulteries, fornications, thefts, false witness, blasphemies:

20 These are *the things* which defile a man: but to eat with unwashen hands defileth not a man.

21 Then Jesus went thence, and departed into the coasts of Tyre and Sidon.

22 And, behold, a woman of Canaan came out of the same coasts, and cried **unto him**[6], saying, Have mercy on me, O Lord, *thou* Son of David; my daughter is grievously vexed with a devil.

23 But he answered her not a word. And his disciples came and besought him, saying, Send her away; for she crieth after us.

24 But he answered and said, I am not sent but unto the lost sheep of the house of Israel.

25 Then came she and worshipped him, saying, Lord, help me.

26 But he answered and said, It is not meet to take the children's bread, and to cast *it*

---

[1] WH omitted of him (autou) from the disciples of him.

[2] WH omitted of the blind (tuflOn).

[3] WH omitted this (tautAn) from the parable this (one).

[4] WH omitted the Jesus (^ho iAsous) and forced the verb to supply the subject he.

[5] WH omitted not yet (oupO).

[6] WH omitted unto him (autO).

to dogs.

27 And she said, Truth, Lord: yet the dogs eat of the crumbs which fall from their masters' table.

28 Then Jesus answered and said unto her, O woman, great *is* thy faith: be it unto thee even as thou wilt. And her daughter was made whole from that very hour.

29 And Jesus departed from thence, and came nigh unto the sea of Galilee; and went up into a mountain, and sat down there.

30 And great multitudes came unto him, having with them *those that were* lame, blind, dumb, maimed, and many others, and cast them down at **Jesus'**[1] feet; and he healed them:

31 Insomuch that **the multitude**[2] wondered, when they saw the dumb to speak, the maimed to be whole, [∧**and**][3] the lame to walk, and the blind to see: and they glorified the God of Israel.

32 Then Jesus called his disciples *unto him,* and said, I have compassion on the multitude, because they continue with me now three **days**[4], and have nothing to eat: and I will not send them away fasting, lest they faint in the way.

33 And ~~his~~[5] disciples say unto him, Whence should we have so much bread in the wilderness, as to fill so great a multitude?

34 And Jesus saith unto them, How many loaves have ye? And they said, Seven, and a few little fishes.

35 And **he commanded**[6] **the multitude**[7] to sit down on the ground.

36 ~~And~~[8] **he took**[9] the

---

[1] WH changed **the of Jesus'** (**tou iAsou**) to *his* (*autou*).

[2] WH changed the multitudes (to**us** oclo**us**) to *the multitude* (*ton oclon*). **Plur** to *Sing.* [number]

[3] WH added *and* (*kai*).

[4] WH changed days ([h]Am-eras) to *days* ([h]*Amerai*). **Acc** to ***Nom.*** [case]

[5] WH omitted of him (autou) from the disciples of him.

[6] WH changed he com-manded (**ekeleuse**) to *having commanded* (*paraggeilas*). Aor Act **Ind** of keleuO to and Aor Act *Part* of par-aggellO. [mood & syn]

[7] WH changed the multitudes (**tois** oclois) to *the multitude* (*tO oclO*). Dat Masc **Plur** to Dat Masc *Sing.* [number]

[8] WH omitted and (kai).

[9] WH changed **having ta**ken (labOn) to *he took* (*elabe*). Aor Act **Part** to Aor Act ***Ind.*** [mood]

seven loaves and the fishes,
∧**and**[1] gave thanks, and brake
them, and **gave**[2] to ~~his~~[3] disciples, and the disciples to **the
multitude**[4].

37 And they did all eat,
and were filled: and they took
up of the broken *meat* that
was left seven baskets full.

38 And they that did eat
were four thousand men, beside women and children.

39 And he sent away the
multitude, and took ship, and
came into the coasts **of Mag-
dala**[5].

CHAPTER 16

1 The Pharisees also with
the Sadducees came, and
tempting desired him that he
would shew them a sign from
heaven.

2 He answered and said
unto them, **When it is evening, ye say,** *It will be* **fair
weather: for the sky is red.**
3 **And in the morning,**
It will be **foul weather to
day: for the sky is red and
lowring.** ~~O ye hypocrites~~[6],
**ye can discern the face of
the sky; but can ye not** *discern* **the signs of the times?**[7]
4 A wicked and adulter-
ous generation seeketh after a

---

[1] WH added <u>and</u> (kai) as it is
supplied in the KJV.
[2] WH changed g<u>ave</u> (ed**O**ke)
to *were giving* (*edidou*). **Aor**
Act Ind to *Impf* Act Ind.
[tense]
[3] WH omitted <u>of him</u> (autou)
from <u>the disciples of him</u>.
[4] WH changed from <u>the mul-
titude</u> (t**O** ocl**O**) to *the multitudes* (*tois oclois*). **Sing** to
Plur. [number]
[5] WH changed <u>Mag**dala**</u>
(<u>mag**dala**</u>) to *Magadan* (*magadan*). ND to ND.

[6] WH omitted <u>O</u> [ye] <u>hypo-
crites</u> (^h<u>upocritai</u>).
[7] In their margin, WH omit-
ted <u>when</u> it <u>is</u> <u>evening</u> <u>ye say</u>
[it will be] <u>fair</u> <u>weather</u> <u>for</u>
<u>the</u> <u>sky</u> <u>is</u> <u>red</u> <u>and</u> <u>in</u> <u>the</u>
<u>morning</u> [It will be] <u>foul</u>
<u>weather</u> <u>to day</u> <u>for</u> <u>the</u> <u>sky</u> <u>is</u>
<u>red</u> <u>and</u> <u>lowring</u> <u>O</u> [ye] <u>hypo-
crites</u> <u>ye can discern</u> <u>the</u> <u>face</u>
<u>of the</u> <u>sky</u> <u>but</u> <u>can ye</u> <u>not</u>
[discern] <u>the</u> <u>signs</u> <u>of the</u>
<u>times</u> (o<u>s</u>ias <u>genomenAs</u>
<u>legete</u> <u>eudia</u> <u>purrazei</u> <u>gar</u> ^h<u>o</u>
<u>ouranos</u> <u>kai</u> <u>prOti</u> <u>sAmeron</u>
<u>keirOn</u> <u>purrazei</u> <u>gar</u> <u>stugna-
zOn</u> ^h<u>o</u> <u>ouranos</u> ^h<u>upocritai</u> <u>to</u>
<u>men</u> <u>prosOpon</u> <u>tou</u> <u>ouranou</u>
<u>ginOskete</u> <u>diakrinein</u> <u>ta</u> <u>de</u>
<u>sAmeia</u> <u>tOn</u> <u>kairOn</u> <u>ou</u> <u>du-
nas</u>~~the~~ <u>genea</u> <u>ponAra</u> <u>kai</u> <u>moi-
calis</u> <u>sAmeion</u> <u>epizAtei</u> <u>kai</u>
<u>sAmeion</u> <u>ou</u> <u>do</u>~~th~~<u>Asetai</u> <u>autA</u>
<u>ei</u> <u>me</u> <u>to</u> <u>sAmeion</u> <u>Iova</u> <u>tou</u>
<u>profAtou</u> <u>kai</u> <u>katalipOn</u> <u>aut-
ous</u> <u>apAl</u>~~the~~).

sign; and there shall no sign be given unto it, but the sign of ~~the prophet~~[1] Jonas. And he left them, and departed.

5   And when ~~his~~[2] disciples were come to the other side, they had forgotten to take bread.

6   Then Jesus said unto them, Take heed and beware of the leaven of the Pharisees and of the Sadducees.

7   And they reasoned among themselves, saying, *It is* because we have taken no bread.

8   *Which* when Jesus perceived, he said ~~unto them~~[3], O ye of little faith, why reason ye among yourselves, because **ye have brought**[4] no bread?

9   Do ye not yet understand, neither remember the five loaves of the five thousand, and how many baskets ye took up?

10 Neither   the   seven loaves of the four thousand, and how many baskets ye took up?

11 How is it that ye do not understand that I spake *it* not to you concerning bread, [∧but][5] **that ye should beware**[6] of the leaven of the Pharisees and of the Sadducees?

12 Then understood they how that he bade *them* not beware of the leaven **of bread**[7], but of the doctrine of the Pharisees and of the Sadducees.

13 When Jesus came into the coasts of Caesarea Philippi, he asked his disciples, saying, Whom do men say that **I**[8] the Son of man am?

14 And they said, Some *say that thou art* John the Baptist: some, Elias; and others, Jeremias, or one of the prophets.

---

[1] WH omitted the profet (tou profAtou).

[2] WH omitted of him from the disciples of him.

[3] WH omitted unto them (autois).

[4] WH changed ye **brought** (elabete) to ye *are having* (ecete). **Aor** Act Ind of **lambanO** to *Pres* Act Ind of *ecO*. [tense & verb]

[5] WH added *but* (*de*).

[6] WH changed **to be being** aware (prosecein) to *be being aware* (*prosecete*). Pres Act **Inf** to a Pres Act *Imp*. [mood]

[7] WH changed of bread (**tou artou**) to *of breads* (*tOn artOn*). **Sing** to *Plur*. [number]

[8] WH omitted I (me) in their text, but retained it in their margin.

15 He saith unto them, But whom say ye that I am?

16 And Simon Peter answered and said, Thou art the Christ, the Son of the living God.

17 **And**[1] Jesus answered and said unto him, Blessed art thou, Simon Barjona: for flesh and blood hath not revealed *it* unto thee, but my Father which is in heaven.

18 And I say also unto thee, That thou art Peter, and upon this rock I will build my church; and the gates of hell shall not prevail against it.

19 **And**[2] I will give unto thee the keys of the kingdom of heaven: and whatsoever thou shalt bind on earth shall be bound in heaven: and whatsoever thou shalt loose on earth shall be loosed in heaven.

20 Then charged he **his**[3] disciples that they should tell no man that he was **Jesus**[4] the Christ.

21 From that time forth began **Jesus**[5] to shew unto

his disciples, how that he must go unto Jerusalem, and suffer many things of the elders and chief priests and scribes, and be killed, and be raised again the third day.

22 Then Peter took him, and began to rebuke him, saying, Be it far from thee, Lord: this shall not be unto thee.

23 But he turned, and said unto Peter, Get thee behind me, Satan: thou art an offence **unto me**[6]: for thou savourest not the things that be of God, but those that be of men.

24 Then said Jesus unto his disciples, If any *man* will come after me, let him deny himself, and take up his cross, and follow me.

25 For whosoever will save his life shall lose it: and whosoever will lose his life for my sake shall find it.

26 For what **is** a man **profited**[7], if he shall gain the

---

[1] WH changed **and** (**kai**) to *but* (*de*).
[2] WH omitted and (kai).
[3] WH omited of him (autou) from the disciples of him.
[4] WH omitted Jesus (iAsous).
[5] In their margin, WH changed the Jesus (**ʰo** iAsous)

to *Jesus* **Christ** (*iAsous* **cristos**).
[6] WH changed unto me (mou) to *unto me* (*emou*). [mou is simpler than emou.]
[7] WH changed *is being* profited (Ofeleitai) to **will be** profited (OfelAthAsetai). **Pres** Pass Ind to *Fut* Pass Ind. [tense]

whole world, and lose his own soul? or what shall a man give in exchange for his soul?

27 For the Son of man shall come in the glory of his Father with his angels; and then he shall reward every man according to his works.

28 Verily I say unto you, There be some standing here, which shall not taste of death, till they see the Son of man coming in his kingdom.

CHAPTER 17

1 And after six days Jesus taketh Peter, James, and John his brother, and bringeth them up into an high mountain apart,

2 And was transfigured before them: and his face did shine as the sun, and his raiment was white as the light.

3 And, behold, there appeared unto them Moses and Elias talking with him.

4 Then answered Peter, and said unto Jesus, Lord, it is good for us to be here: if thou wilt, **let us make**[1] here

three tabernacles; one for thee, and one for Moses, and **one**[2] for Elias.

5 While he yet spake, behold, a bright cloud overshadowed them: and behold a voice out of the cloud, which said, This is my beloved Son, in whom I am well pleased; hear ye him.

6 And when the disciples heard _it_, they fell on their face, and were sore afraid.

7 And Jesus came and touched them, and said, Arise, and be not afraid.

8 And when they had lifted up their eyes, they saw no man, save Jesus only.

9 And as they came down **from**[3] the mountain, Jesus charged them, saying, Tell the vision to no man, until the Son of man be risen again from the dead.

10 And his disciples asked him, saying, Why then say the scribes that Elias must first come?

11 And ~~Jesus~~[4] answered

---

[1] WH changed **let us** make (_poiAsOmen_) to _I will make_ (_poiAsO_). **Aor** Act **Sub** 1^{rst} **Plur** to _Fut_ Act _Ind_ 1^{rst} _Sing_. [tense, mood, number]

[2] WH changed the word order from ONE for Elias to _for Elias_ ONE.

[3] WH changed **from** (**apo**) to _out of_ (**ek**).

[4] WH omitted the Jesus (^{h}o iAsous) and forced the verb to supply the subject _he_.

and said ~~unto them~~[1], Elias truly shall ~~first~~[2] come, and restore all things.

12 But I say unto you, That Elias is come already, and they knew him not, but have done unto him whatsoever they listed. Likewise shall also the Son of man suffer of them.

13 Then the disciples understood that he spake unto them of John the Baptist.And when ~~they~~[3] were come to the multitude, there came to him a *certain* man, kneeling down **to him**[4], and saying,

15 Lord, have mercy on my son: for he is lunatick, and sore vexed: for ofttimes he falleth into the fire, and oft into the water.

16 And I brought him to thy disciples, and they could not cure him.

17 Then Jesus answered and said, O faithless and perverse generation, how long shall I be with you? how long shall I suffer you? bring him hither to me.

18 And Jesus rebuked the devil; and he departed out of him: and the child was cured from that very hour.

19 Then came the disciples to Jesus apart, and said, Why could not we cast him out?

20 And ~~Jesus~~[5] **said**[6] unto them, Because of your **unbelief**[7]: for verily I say unto you, If ye have faith as a grain of mustard seed, ye shall say unto this mountain, Remove hence to yonder place; and it shall remove; and nothing shall be impossible unto you.

21 ~~Howbeit this kind goeth not out but by prayer and fasting~~[8].

---

[1] WH omitted <u>unto them</u> (<u>autois</u>).
[2] WH omitted <u>first</u> (<u>prOton</u>).
[3] WH omitted <u>they</u> (<u>autOn</u>).
[4] WH changed **to** <u>him</u> (<u>aut**O**</u>) to {*to*} *him* (*auton*). **Dat** to *Acc.* [case]

[5] WH omitted <u>the Jesus</u> (^h<u>o iAsous</u>) and forced the verb to supply the subject *he.*
[6] WH changed <u>said</u> (**eipen**) to *says* (*legei*). **Aor** Act Ind to *Pres* Act Ind. [tense]
[7] WH changed **no**-<u>faith</u> (<u>a</u>-pistian) to *little-faith* (*oligo-pistian*). [prefix changed]
[8] WH omitted all of Mat 7:21—<u>howbeit</u> <u>this</u> <u>kind</u> <u>goeth</u> <u>not</u> <u>out</u> <u>but</u> <u>by</u> <u>prayer</u> <u>and</u> <u>fasting</u> (<u>touto de to ginos ouk ekporeuetai ei mA en proseucA</u>). In their margin, WH included the entire verse.

22 And **while** they **abode**[1] in Galilee, Jesus said unto them, The Son of man shall be betrayed into the hands of men:

23 And they shall kill him, and the third day he shall be raised again. And they were exceeding sorry.

24 And when they were come to Capernaum, they that received tribute *money* came to Peter, and said, Doth not your master pay tribute?

25 He saith, Yes. And when he was come into the house, Jesus prevented him, saying, What thinkest thou, Simon? of whom do the kings of the earth take custom or tribute? of their own children, or of strangers?

26 ~~Peter~~[2] [∧and][3] **saith**[4] ~~unto him~~[5], Of strangers. Je-sus saith unto him, Then are the children free.

27 Notwithstanding, lest we should offend them, go thou to the sea, and cast an hook, and take up the fish that first cometh up; and when thou hast opened his mouth, thou shalt find a piece of money: that take, and give unto them for me and thee.

CHAPTER 18

1 At the same time came the disciples unto Jesus, saying, Who is the greatest in the kingdom of heaven?

2 And ~~Jesus~~[6] called a little child unto him, and set him in the midst of them,

3 And said, Verily I say unto you, Except ye be converted, and become as little children, ye shall not enter into the kingdom of heaven.

4 Whosoever therefore shall humble himself as this little child, the same is greatest in the kingdom of heaven.

5 And whoso shall receive one such little child in my name receiveth me.

---

[1] In their margin, WH changed abiding {**again**} (**ana**strefomenOn) to abiding {**together**} (*su*strefomenOn). [prefix changed]

[2] WH omitted the Peter (ʰo petros).

[3] WH added *and* (*de*).

[4] WH changed says (**legei**) to *having said* (*eipontos*). **Pres** Act **Ind** to *Aor* Act *Part.* [tense & mood]

[5] WH omitted unto him (autO). They changed **Peter**

saith unto him (legei autO ʰo petros) to *and having said* (*eipontos de*).

[6] WH omitted the Jesus (ʰo iAsous) and forced the verb to supply the subject *he*.

6   But whoso shall offend one of these little ones which believe in me, it were better for him that a millstone were hanged **about**[1] his neck, and *that* he were drowned in the depth of the sea.

7   Woe unto the world because of offences! for it must needs be that offences come; but woe to that man by whom the offence cometh!

8   Wherefore if thy hand or thy foot offend thee, cut **them**[2] off, and cast *them* from thee: it is better for thee to enter into life **halt**[3] or maimed, rather than having two hands or two feet to be cast into everlasting fire.

9   And if thine eye offend thee, pluck it out, and cast *it* from thee: it is better for thee to enter into life with one eye, rather than having two eyes to be cast into hell fire.

10   Take heed that ye despise not one of these little ones; for I say unto you, That in heaven their angels do always behold the face of my Father which is in heaven.

11   ~~For the Son of man is come to save that which was lost.~~[4]

12   How think ye? if a man have an hundred sheep, and one of them be gone astray, doth he not leave the ninety and nine, and goeth into the mountains, and seeketh that which is gone astray?

13   And if so be that he find it, verily I say unto you, he rejoiceth more of that *sheep*, than of the ninety and nine which went not astray.

14   Even so it is not the will of **your**[5] Father which is in heaven, that one of these little ones should perish.

15   Moreover if thy brother shall trespass **against thee**[6], go **and**[7] tell him his fault between thee and him alone: if he shall hear thee, thou hast

---

[1] WH changed **upon** (**epi**) to *around* (*peri*).

[2] WH changed **them** (*auta*) to *him* (*auton*). Acc **Neut Plur** to Acc **Masc** *Sing*. [gender & number]

[3] WH changed the word order from HALT or maimed to *maimed or HALT*.

[4] WH omitted all of Mat. 18:11—for came the son of the man to save the lost (Al~~the~~ gar [h]o [h]uios tou an~~thr~~Opou sOsai to apolOlos.) In their margin, WH included this entire verse.

[5] In their margin, WH changed **your**[p] (**[h]umOn**) to *my* (*mou*).

[6] In their margin, WH omitted *against* thee (eis se).

[7] WH omitted and (kai).

gained thy brother.

16 But if he will not hear *thee, then* take with thee one or two more, that in the mouth of two or three witnesses every word may be established.

17 And if he shall neglect to hear them, tell *it* unto the church: but if he neglect to hear the church, let him be unto thee as an heathen man and a publican.

18 Verily I say unto you, whatsoever ye shall bind on earth shall be bound in heaven: and whatsoever ye shall loose on earth shall be loosed in heaven.

19 Again I say unto you, That if two of you shall agree on earth as touching any thing that they shall ask, it shall be done for them of my Father which is in heaven.

20 For where two or three are gathered together in my name, there am I in the midst of them.

21 Then came Peter to him, and **said**[1], Lord, how oft shall my brother sin against me, and I forgive him? till seven times?

22 Jesus saith unto him, I say not unto thee, Until seven times: but, Until seventy times seven.

23 Therefore is the kingdom of heaven likened unto a certain king, which would take account of his servants.

24 And when he had begun to reckon, one was brought unto him, which owed him ten thousand talents.

25 But forasmuch as he had not to pay, his lord commanded him to be sold, and his wife, and children, and all that he had, and payment to be made.

26 The servant therefore fell down, and worshipped him, saying, Lord, have patience with me, and I will pay thee all.

27 Then the lord of that servant was moved with compassion, and loosed him, and forgave him the debt.

28 But the same servant went out, and found one of his fellowservants, which owed him an hundred pence: and he laid hands on him, and took *him* by the throat, saying, Pay ~~me~~[2] **that**[3] thou owest.

---

[1] WH changed the word order from to him the Peter SAID to *the Peter SAID to him.*

[2] WH omitted me (*moi*).

[3] WH changed **that** what (ᴴo ti) to *if what* (*ei ti*).

29 And his fellowservant fell down ~~at his feet~~[1], and besought him, saying, Have patience with me, and I will pay thee ~~all~~[2].

30 And he would not: but went and cast him into prison, till he should pay the debt.

31 **So**[3] when his fellowservants saw what was done, they were very sorry, and came and told unto their lord all that was done.

32 Then his lord, after that he had called him, said unto him, O thou wicked servant, I forgave thee all that debt, because thou desiredst me:

33 Shouldest not thou also have had compassion on thy fellowservant, even as I had pity on thee?

34 And his lord was wroth, and delivered him to the tormentors, till he should pay all that was due ~~unto him~~[4].

35 So likewise shall my heavenly Father do also unto you, if ye from your hearts forgive not every one his

brother ~~their trespasses~~[5].

CHAPTER 19

1 And it came to pass, *that* when Jesus had finished these sayings, he departed from Galilee, and came into the coasts of Judaea beyond Jordan;

2 And great multitudes followed him; and he healed them there.

3 ~~The~~[6] Pharisees also came unto him, tempting him, and saying ~~unto him~~[7], Is it lawful ~~for a man~~[8] to put away his wife for every cause?

4 And he answered and said ~~unto them~~[9], Have ye not read, that he <u>which made</u>[10]

---

[1] WH omitted <u>at the feet of him</u> (eis tous podas autou).

[2] WH omitted <u>all</u> (panta).

[3] WH changed <u>so</u> (**de**) to *therefore* (**oun**).

[4] WH omitted <u>unto him</u> (autO).

[5] WH omitted <u>the tresspasses of them</u> (ta paraptOmata autOn).

[6] WH omitted <u>the</u> ([h]oi) from their text, but retained it in their margin.

[7] WH omitted <u>unto him</u> (autO).

[8] WH omitted <u>for a man</u> (anthrOpO).

[9] WH omitted <u>unto them</u> (autois).

[10] In their margin, WH changed <u>having **made**</u> (**poi-Asas**) to *having **created*** (*kti-sas*) Both Aor Act Part. [verb root]

them at the beginning made them male and female,

5 And said, For this cause shall a man leave father and mother, and shall cleave to his wife: and they twain shall be one flesh?

6 Wherefore they are no more twain, but one flesh. What therefore God hath joined together, let not man put asunder.

7 They say unto him, Why did Moses then command to give a writing of divorcement, and to put her away?

8 He saith unto them, Moses because of the hardness of your hearts suffered you to put away your wives: but from the beginning it was not so.

9 And I say unto you, Whosoever shall put away his wife, **except** *it be* **for fornication**[1], **and shall marry another, committeth adultery**[2]**: and whoso marrieth her which is put away doth commit adultery**[3].

10 His disciples say **unto him**[4], If the case of the man be so with *his* wife, it is not good to marry.

11 But he said unto them, All *men* cannot receive this saying, save *they* to whom it is given.

12 For there are some eunuchs, which were so born from *their* mother's womb: and there are some eunuchs, which were made eunuchs of men: and there be eunuchs, which have made themselves eunuchs for the kingdom of heaven's sake. He that is able to receive *it*, let him receive *it*.

13 Then were there brought unto him little children, that he should put *his* hands on them, and pray: and the disciples rebuked them.

14 But Jesus said, Suffer

---

[1] In their margin, WH changed **if not upon** fornication (**ei mA epi** porneia) to *apart from word of fornication* (*parektos logou porneias*).

[2] In their margin, WH changed **and shall marry another committeth adultery** (**kai gamAsA allAn**, moicatai) to *makes her to be "adulteried"* (*poiei autAn moiceuthAnai*).

[3] In their margin, WH omitted and whoso marrieth her which is put away doth commit adultery (kai ho apolelumenAn gamAsas moicatai).

[4] In their margin, WH omitted unto him (autou).

little children, and forbid them not, to come unto me: for of such is the kingdom of heaven.

15 And he laid *his* hands on them, and departed thence.

16 And, behold, one came and **said**[1] unto him, ~~Good~~[2] Master, what good thing shall I do, that I may have eternal life?

17 And he said unto him, Why **callest thou**[3] me [∧about the][4] **good**[5]? *there is* ~~none~~ **good** ~~but~~[6] one [∧is][7],

---

[1] WH changed the word order from SAID to him to *to him* SAID.

[2] WH omitted good (ag~~at~~he) in their text, but retained it in their margin.

[3] WH changed do you **call** (**legeis**) to *do you ask* (**erO-tas**).

[4] WH added *about the* (*peri tou*).

[5] WH changed good (agath~~on~~) to *good* (aga~~th~~ou). **Acc** to *Gen*. [case] (They changed why do you[s] **call** me good to *why do you[s] ask me about the good*.)

[6] WH omitted none (oudeis), but (ei mA), and God (~~th~~eos).

[7] WH added *is* (estin)

that is, [**the**][8] ~~God~~[9]: but if thou wilt enter into life, keep the commandments.

18 He saith unto him, Which? Jesus said, Thou shalt do no murder, Thou shalt not commit adultery, Thou shalt not steal, Thou shalt not bear false witness,

19 Honour thy father and *thy* mother: and, Thou shalt love thy neighbour as thyself.

20 The young man saith unto him, All these things have I kept ~~from my youth up~~[10]: what lack I yet?

21 Jesus said unto him, If thou wilt be perfect, go *and* sell that thou hast, and give to ∧the[11] poor, and thou shalt have treasure in heaven: and come *and* follow me.

22 But when the young

---

[8] WH changed the word order from **none** GOOD **but** one THE **God** to *one is THE GOOD*.

[9] WH omitted God (~~th~~eos). They changed **none** good **but** one, the **God** (**oudeis** agathos, **ei mA** [h]eis [h]o ~~th~~eos) to *one is the good* ([h]eis **estin** [h]o aga~~th~~os) In their margin, WH did not make these changes.

[10] WH omitted out of youth of me (ek neotAtos mou).

[11] WH added *the* (tois) as the KJV supplied.

man heard that saying, he went away sorrowful: for he had great possessions.

23 Then said Jesus unto his disciples, Verily I say unto you, That a rich man shall hardly enter into the kingdom of heaven.

24 And again I say unto you, It is easier for a camel to go through the eye of a needle, than for a rich man to enter into the kingdom of God.

25 When ~~his~~[1] disciples heard *it*, they were exceedingly amazed, saying, Who then can be saved?

26 But Jesus beheld *them*, and said unto them, With men this is impossible; but with God all things are possible.

27 Then answered Peter and said unto him, Behold, we have forsaken all, and followed thee; what shall we have therefore?

28 And Jesus said unto them, Verily I say unto you, That ye which have followed me, in the regeneration when the Son of man shall sit in the throne of his glory, ye also shall sit upon twelve thrones, judging the twelve tribes of Israel.

29 And every one that hath forsaken houses, or brethren, or sisters, or father, or mother, ~~or wife~~[2], or children, or lands, for my name's sake, shall receive **an hundredfold**[3], and shall inherit everlasting life.

30 But many *that are* first shall be last; and the last *shall be* first.

CHAPTER 20

1 For the kingdom of heaven is like unto a man *that is* an householder, which went out early in the morning to hire labourers into his vineyard.

2 And when he had agreed with the labourers for a penny a day, he sent them into his vineyard.

3 And he went out about the third hour, and saw others standing idle in the marketplace,

4 And said unto them; Go ye also into the vineyard,

---

[1] WH omitted of him (autou) from the disciples of him.

[2] WH omitted or wife (A gunaika) in their text, but retained it in their margin.
[3] In their margin, WH changed **an hundredfold** (**ekatonta-**plasiona) to ***much more*** (***polla-**plasiona*). [prefix changed]

and whatsoever is right I will give you. And they went their way.

5 Again he went out about the sixth and ninth hour, and did likewise.

6 And about the eleventh ~~hour~~[1] he went out, and found others standing ~~idle~~[2], and saith unto them, Why stand ye here all the day idle?

7 They say unto him, Because no man hath hired us. He saith unto them, Go ye also into the vineyard; ~~and whatsoever is right, *that* shall ye receive~~[3].

8 So when even was come, the lord of the vineyard saith unto his steward, Call the labourers, and give them *their* hire, beginning from the last unto the first.

9 And when they came that *were hired* about the eleventh hour, they received every man a penny.

10 **But**[4] when the first came, they supposed that they should have received more; and they likewise received every man a penny.

11 And when they had received *it*, they murmured against the goodman of the house,

12 Saying, These last have wrought *but* one hour, and thou hast made them equal unto us, which have borne the burden and heat of the day.

13 But he answered one of them, and said, Friend, I do thee no wrong: didst not thou agree with me for a penny?

14 Take *that* thine *is*, and go thy way: I will give unto this last, even as unto thee.

15 [~~or~~][5] Is it not lawful for me to do what I will with mine own? [<u>or</u>][6] Is thine eye evil, because I am good?

16 So the last shall be first, and the first last: ~~for many be called, but few chosen~~[7].

17 And Jesus going up to Jerusalem took the twelve disciples apart in the way, **and**[8] said unto them,

---

[1] WH omitted <u>hour</u> (^h<u>Oran</u>).

[2] WH omitted <u>idle</u> (<u>argous</u>).

[3] WH omitted <u>and what ever is right shall ye receive</u> (<u>kai</u> ^h<u>o ean</u> <u>A</u> <u>dikaion</u> <u>lApesthe</u>).

[4] WH changed **but** (**de**) to *and* (*kai*).

[5] WH omitted the untranslated <u>or</u> (<u>A</u>).

[6] WH changed the untranslated <u>or</u> (<u>ei</u>) to *or* (*A*).

[7] WH omitted <u>for many be called but few chosen</u> (<u>polloi gar eisi klAtoi</u> ^h<u>oligoi de eklektoi</u>).

[8] WH changed the word order from <u>in the way</u> AND to *AND in the way*.

18 Behold, we go up to Jerusalem; and the Son of man shall be betrayed unto the chief priests and unto the scribes, and they shall condemn him to death,

19 And shall deliver him to the Gentiles to mock, and to scourge, and to crucify *him*: and the third day **he shall rise again**[1].

20 Then came to him the mother of Zebedee's children with her sons, worshipping *him*, and desiring a certain thing of him.

21 And he said unto her, What wilt thou? She saith unto him, Grant that these my two sons may sit, the one on thy right hand, and the other on the left [ʌ**of thee]**[2], in thy kingdom.

22 But Jesus answered and said, Ye know not what ye ask. Are ye able to drink of the cup that I shall drink of, **and to be baptized with the baptism that I am baptized with**[3]? They say unto him,

We are able.

23 And he saith unto them, Ye shall drink indeed of my cup, **and be baptized with the baptism that I am baptized with**[4]: but to sit on my right hand, and on **my**[5] left, is not mine to give, but *it shall be given to them* for whom it is prepared of my Father.

24 And when the ten heard *it*, they were moved with indignation against the two brethren.

25 But Jesus called them *unto him*, and said, Ye know that the princes of the Gentiles exercise dominion over them, and they that are great exercise authority upon them.

26 **But**[6] it shall not be so among you: but whosoever will be great among you, **let him be**[7] your minister;

---

[1] WH changed he shall **rise again** (**an-ast**Asetai) to *he shall **be raised** (egert*Asetai*)*. Fut **Mid** Ind of an-istAmi to *Fut **Pas** Ind of egeirO*. [voice & syn]
[2] WH added *of thee (sou)*.
[3] WH omitted and to be baptized with the baptism that I

am baptized with (kai to baptisma ᵇo ego baptizomai baptisthAnai).
[4] WH omitted and to be baptized with the baptism that I am baptized with (kai to baptisma ᵇo ego baptizomai baptisthAnai).
[5] WH omitted my (mou).
[6] WH omitted but (de).
[7] WH changed **be letting him** be (estO) to *he will be (estai)*. **Pres Imp** to *Fut Ind*. [tense & mood]

27 And whosoever will be chief among you, **let him be**[1] your servant:

28 Even as the Son of man came not to be ministered unto, but to minister, and to give his life a ransom for many.

29 And as they departed from Jericho, a great multitude followed him.

30 And, behold, two blind men sitting by the way side, when they heard that Jesus passed by, cried out, saying, Have mercy on us, **O Lord**[2], *thou* Son of David.

31 And the multitude rebuked them, because they should hold their peace: but they cried the more, saying, Have mercy on us, **O Lord**[3], *thou* Son of David.

32 And Jesus stood still, and called them, and said, What will ye that I shall do unto you?

33 They say unto him, Lord, that our eyes may be opened.

34 So Jesus had compassion *on them*, and touched their eyes: and immediately ~~their eyes~~[4] received sight, and they followed him.

CHAPTER 21

1 And when they drew nigh unto Jerusalem, and were come to Bethphage, **unto**[5] the mount of Olives, then sent Jesus two disciples,

2 Saying unto them, Go into the village over against you, and straightway ye shall find an ass tied, and a colt with her: loose *them*, and bring *them* unto me.

3 And if any *man* say ought unto you, ye shall say, The Lord hath need of them; and straightway he will send them.

4 ~~All~~[6] this was done, that it might be fulfilled which was spoken by the prophet,

---

[1] WH changed **be letting him** be (est**O**) to *he will be* (*estai*). **Pres Imp** to *Fut Ind*. [tense & mood]

[2] WH changed the word order from have mercy on us, O LORD to *O LORD, have mercy on us*.

[3] WH changed the word order from have mercy on us, O LORD to *O LORD, have mercy on us*.

[4] WH omitted their eyes (aut**O**n [h]oi ofthalmoi) and forced the verb to supply the subject *they*.

[5] WH changed **unto** (**pros** {toward}) to *into* (*eis*).

[6] WH omitted ([h]olon).

saying,

5   Tell ye the daughter of Sion, Behold, thy King cometh unto thee, meek, and sitting upon an ass, and [ʌon]¹ a colt the foal of an ass.

6   And the disciples went, and did as Jesus **commanded**² them,

7   And brought the ass, and the colt, and put on them their clothes, and **they set**³ *him* thereon.

8   And a very great multitude spread their garments in the way; others cut down branches from the trees, and strawed *them* in the way.

9   And the multitudes that went before [ʌhim]⁴, and that followed, cried, saying, Hosanna to the Son of David: Blessed *is* he that cometh in the name of the Lord; Hosanna in the highest.

10   And when he was come into Jerusalem, all the city was moved, saying, Who is this?

11   And the multitude said, This is **Jesus**⁵ the prophet of Nazareth of Galilee.

12   And Jesus went into the temple **of God**⁶, and cast out all them that sold and bought in the temple, and overthrew the tables of the moneychangers, and the seats of them that sold doves,

13   And said unto them, It is written, My house shall be called the house of prayer; but ye **have made**⁷ it a den of thieves.

14   And the blind and the lame came to him in the temple; and he healed them.

15   And when the chief priests and scribes saw the wonderful things that he did, and the children [ʌthe {ones}]⁸ crying in the temple, and saying, Hosanna to the

---

¹ WH added *on* (*epi*).
² WH changed **command**ed (**pros**-etazen) to *appointed* (*sun-etazen*). [prefix changed]
³ WH changed **they** set (epekathisan) to *he set* (*epekathisen*). Both Aor Act Ind. 3ʳᵈ **Plur** to 3ʳᵈ *Sing*. [number]
⁴ WH added *him* (*auton*).

⁵ WH changed the word order from JESUS the prophet to *the prophet JESUS*.
⁶ In their margin, WH omitted of God (*tou theou*).
⁷ WH changed made (epoi-Asate) to *are making* (*poieite*). **Aor** Act Ind to *Pres* Act Ind. [tense]
⁸ WH added *the* {ones} (*tous*).

Son of David; they were sore displeased,

16 And said unto him, Hearest thou what these say? And Jesus saith unto them, Yea; have ye never read, Out of the mouth of babes and sucklings thou hast perfected praise?

17 And he left them, and went out of the city into Bethany; and he lodged there.

18 Now in the morning as he returned into the city, he hungered.

19 And when he saw a fig tree in the way, he came to it, and found nothing thereon, but leaves only, and said unto it, Let no fruit grow on thee henceforward for ever. And presently the fig tree withered away.

20 And when the disciples saw *it*, they marvelled, saying, How soon is the fig tree withered away!

21 Jesus answered and said unto them, Verily I say unto you, If ye have faith, and doubt not, ye shall not only do this *which is done* to the fig tree, but also if ye shall say unto this mountain, Be thou removed, and be thou cast into the sea; it shall be done.

22 And all things, whatsoever ye shall ask in prayer, believing, ye shall receive.

23 And **when he was come**[1] into the temple, the chief priests and the elders of the people came unto him as he was teaching, and said, By what authority doest thou these things? and who gave thee this authority?

24 And Jesus answered and said unto them, I also will ask you one thing, which if ye tell me, I in like wise will tell you by what authority I do these things.

25 The baptism of John, whence was it? from heaven, or of men? And they reasoned with themselves, saying, If we shall say, From heaven; he will say unto us, Why did ye not then believe him?

26 But if we shall say, Of men; we fear the people; for all hold John as a prophet.

27 And they answered Jesus, and said, We cannot tell. And he said unto them, Neither tell I you by what authority I do these things.

28 But what think ye? A *certain* man had two sons; and he came to the first, and

---

[1] WH changed <u>he having come</u> (elthonti autO) to <u>he having come</u> (*elthontos autou*). Both Aor Act Part. **Dat** to *Gen*. [case]

said, Son, go work to day in ~~my~~[1] vineyard.

29 He answered and said, I will not: but afterward he repented, and went.

30 And he came to the second, and said likewise. And he answered and said, I *go*, sir: and went not.

31 Whether of them twain did the will of *his* father? They say ~~unto him~~[2], The first. Jesus saith unto them, Verily I say unto you, That the publicans and the harlots go into the kingdom of God before you.

32 For John came unto you in the way of righteousness, and ye believed him not: but the publicans and the harlots believed him: and ye, when ye had seen *it*, repented **not**[3] afterward, that ye might believe him.

33 Hear another parable: There was ~~a certain~~[4] householder, which planted a vineyard, and hedged it round about, and digged a winepress in it, and built a tower,

and let it out to husbandmen, and went into a far country:

34 And when the time of the fruit drew near, he sent his servants to the husbandmen, that they might receive the fruits of it.

35 And the husbandmen took his servants, and beat one, and killed another, and stoned another.

36 Again, he sent other servants more than the first: and they did unto them likewise.

37 But last of all he sent unto them his son, saying, They will reverence my son.

38 But when the husbandmen saw the son, they said among themselves, This is the heir; come, let us kill him, **and let us seize on**[5] his inheritance.

39 And they caught him, and cast *him* out of the vineyard, and slew *him*.

40 When the lord therefore of the vineyard cometh, what will he do unto those husbandmen?

41 They say unto him, He will miserably destroy those wicked men, and will let out

---

[1] WH omitted of me (<u>mou</u>) from <u>the</u> <u>vineyard</u> <u>of me</u>.
[2] WH omitted <u>unto him</u> (<u>autO</u>).
[3] WH changed <u>not</u> (<u>ou</u>) to *not* **even** (*oude*).
[4] WH omitted <u>a certain</u> (<u>tis</u>).

[5] WH changed <u>let us hold</u> **down** (**kata**-<u>scOmen</u>) to *let us* **hold** (*scOmen*). [prefix droppped]

his vineyard unto other husbandmen, which shall render him the fruits in their seasons.

42 Jesus saith unto them, Did ye never read in the scriptures, The stone which the builders rejected, the same is become the head of the corner: this is the Lord's doing, and it is marvellous in our eyes?

43 Therefore say I unto you, The kingdom of God shall be taken from you, and given to a nation bringing forth the fruits thereof.

44 **And whosoever shall fall on this stone shall be broken: but on whomsoever it shall fall, it will grind him to powder**[1].

45 And when the chief priests and Pharisees had heard his parables, they perceived that he spake of them.

46 But when they sought to lay hands on him, they feared the multitude, because they took him **for**[2] a prophet.

CHAPTER 22

1 And Jesus answered and spake **unto them**[3] again by parables, and said,

2 The kingdom of heaven is like unto a certain king, which made a marriage for his son,

3 And sent forth his servants to call them that were bidden to the wedding: and they would not come.

4 Again, he sent forth other servants, saying, Tell them which are bidden, Behold, **I have prepared**[4] my dinner: my oxen and *my* fatlings *are* killed, and all things *are* ready: come unto the marriage.

5 But they made light of *it*, and went their ways, one to his farm, another **to**[5] his merchandise:

6 And the remnant took his servants, and entreated

---

[1] In their margin, WH omitted all of 21:44—and whosoever shall fall on this stone shall be broken but on whomsoever it shall fall it will grind him to powder (kai ⁿo pesOn epi ton lithon touton sunthlasthAsetai ef' ⁿon d' an pesA likmAsei auton).

[2] WH changed **as** (ⁿOs) to

into (*eis*).

[3] WH changed the word order from UNTO THEM by parables to *by parables* UNTO THEM.

[4] WH changed I prepared (ⁿAtoimasa) to *I have prepared* (ⁿAtoimaka). **Aor** Act to a *Pf* Act. [tense]

[5] WH changed **to** (*eis*) to *upon* (*epi*).

them spitefully, and slew *them*.

7 **But**[1] ~~when~~ the king ~~heard thereof~~, **he**[2] was wroth: and he sent forth his armies, and destroyed those murderers, and burned up their city.

8 Then saith he to his servants, The wedding is ready, but they which were bidden were not worthy.

9 Go ye therefore into the highways, and as many as ye shall find, bid to the marriage.

10 So those servants went out into the highways, and gathered together all as many as they found, both bad and good: and the wedding was furnished with guests.

11 And when the king came in to see the guests, he saw there a man which had not on a wedding garment:

12 And he saith unto him, Friend, how camest thou in hither not having a wedding garment? And he was speechless.

13 Then **said**[3] the king to the servants, Bind him hand and foot, ~~and take him away~~[4], and cast [∧*him*][5] *him* into outer darkness; there shall be weeping and gnashing of teeth.

14 For many are called, but few *are* chosen.

15 Then went the Pharisees, and took counsel how they might entangle him in *his* talk.

16 And they sent out unto him their disciples with the Herodians, **saying**[6], Master, we know that thou art true, and teachest the way of God in truth, neither carest thou for any *man*: for thou regardest not the person of men.

17 Tell us therefore, What thinkest thou? Is it lawful to give tribute unto Caesar, or not?

---

[1] When WH omitted when he heard [thereof] (akousas), they forced the but (de) to follow the ([h]o) instead of ak-ousas. [word order]

[2] WH omitted when heard *thereof* he (akousas).

[3] WH changed the word order from SAID the king to *the king SAID*.

[4] WH omitted and take him away (arate auton kai).

[5] WH added *him* (*auton*) where the KJV supplied the word in italics.

[6] WH changed saying (legon-tes) to *saying* (legontas). Both Pres Act Part. **Nom** Masc Plur to *Acc* Masc Plur. [case]

18 But Jesus perceived their wickedness, and said, Why tempt ye me, *ye* hypocrites?

19 Shew me the tribute money. And they brought unto him a penny.

20 And he saith unto them, Whose *is* this image and superscription?

21 They say unto him, Caesar's. Then saith he unto them, Render therefore unto Caesar the things which are Caesar's; and unto God the things that are God's.

22 When they had heard *these words*, they marvelled, and left him, and went their way.

23 The same day came to him the Sadducees, ~~which~~[1] say that there is no resurrection, and asked him,

24 Saying, Master, Moses said, If a man die, having no children, his brother shall marry his wife, and raise up seed unto his brother.

25 Now there were with us seven brethren: and the first, when he had married a wife, deceased, and, having no issue, left his wife unto his brother:

26 Likewise the second also, and the third, unto the seventh.

27 And last of all the woman died ~~also~~[2].

28 **Therefore**[3] in the resurrection whose wife shall she be of the seven? for they all had her.

29 Jesus answered and said unto them, Ye do err, not knowing the scriptures, nor the power of God.

30 For in the resurrection they neither marry, nor are given in marriage, but are as the angels ~~of God~~[4] in heaven.

31 But as touching the resurrection of the dead, have ye not read that which was spoken unto you by God, saying,

32 I am the God of Abraham, and the God of Isaac, and the God of Jacob? ~~God~~[5]

---

[1] WH omitted <u>which</u> (^h<u>oi</u>) and changed **the {ones}** <u>saying</u> (^h<u>oi</u> <u>legontes</u>) to *saying* (*le-gontes*).

[2] WH omitted <u>also</u> (<u>kai</u>).

[3] WH changed the word order from <u>in the</u> THEREFORE <u>resurrection</u> to *in the resurrection THEREFORE.*

[4] WH omitted <u>of the God</u> (<u>tou</u> <u>theou</u>) in their text, but included these words in their margin.

[5] WH omitted <u>the God</u> (^h<u>o</u> <u>theos</u>) and made the verb supply the subject *he.*

is not the God of the dead, but of the living.

33 And when the multitude heard *this*, they were astonished at his doctrine.

34 But when the Pharisees had heard that he had put the Sadducees to silence, they were gathered together.

35 Then one of them, *which was* a lawyer, asked *him a question*, tempting him, ~~and saying~~¹,

36 Master, which *is* the great commandment in the law?

37 ~~Jesus~~² said unto him, Thou shalt love the Lord thy God with all thy heart, and with all thy soul, and with all thy mind.

38 This is ∧**the**³ first and **great**⁴ commandment.

39 And the second *is* like ~~unto it~~⁵, Thou shalt love thy

neighbour as thyself.

40 On these two commandments **hang**⁶ all the law and the prophets.

41 While the Pharisees were gathered together, Jesus asked them,

42 Saying, What think ye of Christ? whose son is he? They say unto him, *The Son* of David.

43 He saith unto them, How then doth David in spirit call him Lord, saying,

44 The LORD said unto my Lord, Sit thou on my right hand, till I make thine enemies **thy footstool**⁷?

45 If David then call him Lord, how is he his son?

46 And no man was able to answer him a word, neither durst any *man* from that day forth ask him any more *questions*.

CHAPTER 23

1   Then spake Jesus to the

---

¹ WH omitted <u>and</u> <u>saying</u> (<u>kai legOn</u>).
² WH omitted <u>the</u> <u>Jesus</u> (^{h}o iAsous) and forced the verb to supply the subject *he*.
³ WH added the supplied *the* (^hA).
⁴ WH changed the word order from <u>is</u> <u>first</u> <u>and</u> GREAT to *is* **the** GREAT *and first*.
⁵ WH omitted <u>unto it</u> (<u>autA</u>) in their text, but retained <u>autA</u> in their margin.

⁶ WH changed the word order from <u>all</u> <u>the</u> <u>law</u> <u>and</u> <u>the</u> <u>prophets</u> HANG to *all the law* HANG *and the prophets*.
⁷ WH changed **footstool of the** <u>feet</u> of thee (^{h}upo-**podion** tOn podOn sou) to **under** *the feet of thee* (^{h}upo-**katO** *tOn podOn sou*).

multitude, and to his disciples,

2   Saying, The scribes and the Pharisees sit in Moses' seat:

3   All therefore whatsoever they bid you ~~observe~~[1], *that* **observe**[2] and **do**[3]; but do not ye after their works: for they say, and do not.

4   **For**[4] they bind heavy burdens **and grievous to be borne**[5], and lay *them* on men's shoulders; but they ˄*themselves*[6] will not move them with one of their fingers.

5   But all their works they do for to be seen of men: **[for]**[7] they make broad their

phylacteries, and enlarge the borders ~~of their garments~~[8],

6   **And**[9] love the uppermost rooms at feasts, and the chief seats in the synagogues,

7   And greetings in the markets, and to be called of men, Rabbi, **Rabbi**[10].

8   But be not ye called Rabbi: for one is your **master**[11], ~~even Christ~~[12]; and all ye are brethren.

9   And call no *man* your father upon the earth: for one is your Father, which is ~~in~~[13] **heaven**[14].

10   Neither be ye called masters: for one is your master, *even* Christ.

11   But he that is greatest among you shall be your servant.

12   And whosoever shall

---

[1] WH omitted <u>observe</u> (<u>tArein</u>).

[2] WH changed the word order from <u>OBSERVE</u> <u>and</u> <u>do</u> to *do and OBSERVE.*

[3] They changed **be** **do**<u>ing</u> {**continually**} (<u>poieite</u>) to *do* {*at one point in time*} (*poi-Asatai*). **Pres** Act Imp to *Aor* Act Imp. [tense]

[4] WH changed **for** (**gar**) to *but* (*de*).

[5] In their margin, WH omitted <u>and grievous to be bourne</u> (<u>kai dusbastakta</u>).

[6] WH added *themselves* (*autoi*), a word that the KJV supplied in italics.

[7] WH changed the untrans-

lated <u>for</u> (**de**) to *for* (*gar*).

[8] WH omitted <u>of their garments</u> (<u>tOn ʰimatiOn autO</u>).

[9] WH changed <u>and</u> (**te**) to *and* (*de*).

[10] WH omitted <u>Rabbi</u> (ʰrabbi).

[11] WH changed <u>master</u> (**kathAgAtAs**) to *master* (*didaskalos*).

[12] WH omitted <u>the Christ</u> (ʰo cristos).

[13] WH omitted <u>in the</u> (<u>en tois</u>).

[14] WH changed <u>heavens</u> (<u>ouranois</u>) to *heavenly* (*ouranios*).

exalt himself shall be abased; and he that shall humble himself shall be exalted.

13 But woe unto you, scribes and Pharisees, hypocrites! for ye shut up the kingdom of heaven against men: for ye neither go in *yourselves*, neither suffer ye them that are entering to go in.

14 ~~Woe unto you, scribes and Pharisees, hypocrites! for ye devour widows' houses, and for a pretence make long prayer: therefore ye shall receive the greater damnation.~~ [1]

15 Woe unto you, scribes and Pharisees, hypocrites! for ye compass sea and land to make one proselyte, and when he is made, ye make

him twofold more the child of hell than yourselves.

16 Woe unto you, *ye* blind guides, which say, Whosoever shall swear by the temple, it is nothing; but whosoever shall swear by the gold of the temple, he is a debtor!

17 *Ye* fools and blind: for whether is greater, the gold, or the temple that **sanctifieth** [2] the gold?

18 And, whosoever shall swear by the altar, it is nothing; but whosoever sweareth by the gift that is upon it, he is guilty.

19 *Ye* **fools and** [3] blind: for whether *is* greater, the gift, or the altar that sanctifieth the gift?

20 Whoso therefore shall swear by the altar, sweareth by it, and by all things thereon.

21 And whoso shall swear by the temple, sweareth by it, and by him that dwelleth therein.

22 And he that shall swear by heaven, sweareth by the throne of God, and by him

---

[1] WH omitted woe unto you scribes and pharisees hypocrites for ye devour the houses of the widows and for a pretence make long prayer because of this ye shall receive the greater damnation (ouai ʰumin grammateis kai parisaioi ʰupokritai ʰoti katestiete tas oikias tOn cArOn kai profasei makra proseucomenoi dia touto lAʃesthe perissoteron krima) from their text. In their margin, WH included Mat. 23:14.

---

[2] WH changed sanctifies (ʰagiazOn) to *sanctified* (ʰagiasas). **Pres** Act Part to *Aor* Act Part. [tense]

[3] WH omitted fools and (mOroi kai).

that sitteth thereon.

23 Woe unto you, scribes and Pharisees, hypocrites! for ye pay tithe of mint and anise and cummin, and have omitted the weightier *matters* of the law, judgment, mercy, and faith: these [∧**then**]¹ ought ye to have done, and not **to leave** the other **undone**².

24 *Ye* blind guides, which strain at a gnat, and swallow a camel.

25 Woe unto you, scribes and Pharisees, hypocrites! for ye make clean the outside of the cup and of the platter, but within they are full of extortion and excess.

26 *Thou* blind Pharisee, cleanse first that *which is* within the cup and platter, that the outside **of them**³ may be clean also.

27 Woe unto you, scribes and Pharisees, hypocrites! for ye are like unto whited sepulchres, which indeed appear beautiful outward, but are within full of dead *men's*

bones, and of all uncleanness.

28 Even so ye also outwardly appear righteous unto men, but within ye are full of hypocrisy and iniquity.

29 Woe unto you, scribes and Pharisees, hypocrites! because ye build the tombs of the prophets, and garnish the sepulchres of the righteous,

30 And say, If we had been in the days of our fathers, we would not have been partakers with them in the blood of the prophets.

31 Wherefore ye be witnesses unto yourselves, that ye are the children of them which killed the prophets.

32 Fill ye up then the measure of your fathers.

33 *Ye* serpents, *ye* generation of vipers, how can ye escape the damnation of hell?

34 Wherefore, behold, I send unto you prophets, and wise men, and scribes: **and**⁴ *some* of them ye shall kill and crucify; and *some* of them shall ye scourge in your synagogues, and persecute *them* from city to city:

35 That upon you may come all the righteous blood shed upon the earth, from the blood of righteous Abel unto the blood of Zacharias son of

---

¹ WH added *then* (*de*).
² WH changed to leave undone (afienai) to *to leave undone* (*afeinai*). [spell]
³ WH changed of **them** (aut**On**) to *of it* (*autou*). **Plur** to *Sing*. [number]

---

⁴ WH omitted and (kai).

Barachias, whom ye slew between the temple and the altar.

36 Verily I say unto you, All these things shall come upon this generation.

37 O Jerusalem, Jerusalem, *thou* that killest the prophets, and stonest them which are sent unto thee, how often would I have gathered thy children together, even as a hen gathereth her chickens under *her* wings, and ye would not!

38 Behold, your house is left unto you **desolate**[1].

39 For I say unto you, Ye shall not see me henceforth, till ye shall say, Blessed *is* he that cometh in the name of the Lord.

CHAPTER 24

1 And Jesus went out, and **departed**[2] from the temple: and his disciples came to *him* for to shew him the buildings of the temple.

2 And **Jesus**[3] said unto

them, See ye not all these things? verily I say unto you, There shall not be left here one stone upon another, that shall not [~~not~~][4] be thrown down.

3 And as he sat upon the mount of Olives, the disciples came unto him privately, saying, Tell us, when shall these things be? and what *shall be* the sign of thy coming, and of the end of the world?

4 And Jesus answered and said unto them, Take heed that no man deceive you.

5 For many shall come in my name, saying, I am Christ; and shall deceive many.

6 And ye shall hear of wars and rumours of wars: see that ye be not troubled: for ~~all these things~~[5] must come to pass, but the end is not yet.

7 For nation shall rise against nation, and kingdom against kingdom: and there

---

[1] In their margin, WH omitted <u>desolate</u> (<u>erAmos</u>).

[2] WH changed the word order from <u>DEPARTED</u> <u>from the temple</u> to *from the temple DEPARTED*.

[3] WH changed <u>the</u> **Jesus** (^h<u>o</u>

iAsous) *to this* {*one*} ***having been answered*** (^h*o apo-cri~~th~~eis*). Noun to Aor Pass Part.

[4] WH omitted the untranslated <u>not</u> (<u>mA</u>) from <u>that</u> <u>not</u> <u>not</u> <u>shall be thrown down.</u>

[5] WH omitted <u>all</u> {these things} (<u>panta</u>).

shall be famines, ~~and pesti-lences~~[1], and earthquakes, in divers places.

8   All these *are* the beginning of sorrows.

9   Then shall they deliver you up to be afflicted, and shall kill you: and ye shall be hated of all nations for my name's sake.

10   And then shall many be offended, and shall betray one another, and shall hate one another.

11   And many false prophets shall rise, and shall deceive many.

12   And because iniquity shall a-bound, the love of many shall wax cold.

13   But he that shall endure unto the end, the same shall be saved.

14   And this gospel of the kingdom shall be preached in all the world for a witness unto all nations; and then shall the end come.

15   When ye therefore shall see the abomination of desolation, spoken of by Daniel the prophet, stand in the holy place, (whoso readeth, let him understand:)

16   Then let them which be in Judaea flee into the mountains:

17   Let him which is on the housetop not come down to take **any thing**[2] out of his house:

18   Neither let him which is in the field return back to take his **clothes**[3].

19   And woe unto them that are with child, and to them that give suck in those days!

20   But pray ye that your flight be not in the winter, neither ~~on~~[4] the sabbath day:

21   For then shall be great tribulation, such as was not since the beginning of the world to this time, no, nor ever shall be.

22   And except those days should be shortened, there should no flesh be saved: but for the elect 's sake those days shall be shortened.

23   Then if any man shall say unto you, Lo, here *is* Christ, or there; believe *it* not.

---

[2] WH changed **any** thing (**ti**) to *these* {*things*} (*ta*). **Sing** to *Plur*. [number]
[3] WH changed garments (**ta** [h]imatia) to *garment* (*to* [h]*imation*). **Plur** to *Sing*. [number]
[4] WH omitted on (en) and forced the case of sabbath to supply the preposition.

---

[1] WH omitted and pestilences (kai loimoi).

24 For there shall arise false Christs, and false prophets, and shall shew great signs and wonders; insomuch that, if *it were* possible, they shall deceive the very elect.

25 Behold, I have told you before.

26 Wherefore if they shall say unto you, Behold, he is in the desert; go not forth: behold, *he is* in the secret chambers; believe *it* not.

27 For as the lightning cometh out of the east, and shineth even unto the west; so shall ~~also~~[1] the coming of the Son of man be.

28 ~~For~~[2] wheresoever the carcase is, there will the eagles be gathered together.

29 Immediately after the tribulation of those days shall the sun be darkened, and the moon shall not give her light, and the stars shall fall from heaven, and the powers of the heavens shall be shaken:

30 And then shall appear the sign of the Son of man in heaven: and then shall all the tribes of the earth mourn, and they shall see the Son of man coming in the clouds of heaven with power and great glory.

31 And he shall send his angels with a great **sound**[3] of a trumpet, and they shall gather together his elect from the four winds, from one end of heaven to the other.

32 Now learn a parable of the fig tree; When his branch is yet tender, and putteth forth leaves, ye know that summer *is* nigh:

33 So likewise ye, when ye shall see all these things, know that it is near, *even* at the doors.

34 Verily I say unto you, This generation shall not pass, till all these things be fulfilled.

35 Heaven and earth shall pass away, but my words shall not pass away.

36 But of that day and [~~the~~][4] hour knoweth no *man*, no, not the angels of heaven, [ʌ**not even the son**][5] but ~~my~~[6] Father only.

---

[1] WH omitted <u>also</u> (kai).
[2] WH omitted for (gar).

[3] In their margin, WH omitted <u>sound</u> (fOnAs). [The supplied words <u>of a</u> would drop out also.]
[4] WH omitted the untranslated <u>the</u> (tAs).
[5] WH added *not even the son* (*oude* [h]*o* [h]*uios*) in their text, but not in their margin.
[6] WH omitted <u>of me</u> (mou) from <u>the</u> <u>father</u> <u>of me</u>.

37 But as the days of Noe *were*, so shall ~~also~~[1] the coming of the Son of man be.

38 For as in the days [∧those][2] that were before the flood they were eating and drinking, marrying and giving in marriage, until the day that Noe entered into the ark,

39 And knew not until the flood came, and took them all away; so shall ~~also~~[3] the coming of the Son of man be.

40 Then shall two be in the field; ~~the~~[4] one shall be taken, and the other left.

41 Two *women shall be* grinding at the **mill**[5]; the one shall be taken, and the other left.

42 Watch therefore: for ye know not what **hour**[6] your Lord doth come.

43 But know this, that if the goodman of the house had known in what watch the thief would come, he would have watched, and would not have suffered his house to be broken up.

44 Therefore be ye also ready: for in such an hour as ye think not the Son of man cometh.

45 Who then is a faithful and wise servant, whom **his**[7] lord hath made ruler over his **household**[8], to give them meat in due season?

46 Blessed *is* that servant, whom his lord when he cometh shall find so doing.

47 Verily I say unto you, That he shall make him ruler over all his goods.

48 But and if that evil servant shall say in his heart, My lord delayeth ~~his coming~~[9];

49 And shall begin to smite *his* fellowservants [∧**of him**][10], and **to eat**[11] and

---

[1] WH omitted <u>also</u> (<u>kai</u>).
[2] WH added *those* (*ekeinais*).
[3] WH omitted <u>also</u> (<u>kai</u>).
[4] WH omitted <u>the</u> (^h<u>o</u>).
[5] WH changed <u>mill</u> (<u>mulOni</u>) to *mill* (*mulO*). Both Dat Masc Sing. [spell]
[6] WH changed **hour** (^h<u>Ora</u>) to *day* (^h*Amera*).

[7] WH omitted <u>of him</u> (<u>autou</u>) from <u>the</u> <u>lord</u> <u>of him</u>.
[8] WH changed <u>household</u> (~~therap~~eias {of servants}) to *household* (*oiketeias*{of slaves}).
[9] WH omitted <u>his coming</u> (<u>el</u>~~th~~<u>ein</u>).
[10] WH added *of him* (*autou*) and thereby changed <u>the</u> <u>fel</u><u>lowservants</u> to *the fellowservants of him*.
[11] WH changed **to be eating** (<u>es</u>~~th~~<u>iein</u>) to *may be eating* (*es*~~th~~*iA*). Pres Act **Inf** to Pres Act ***Sub***. [mood]

drink[1] with the drunken;

50 The lord of that servant shall come in a day when he looketh not for *him*, and in an hour that he is not aware of,

51 And shall cut him asunder, and appoint *him* his portion with the hypocrites: there shall be weeping and gnashing of teeth.

CHAPTER 25

1 Then shall the kingdom of heaven be likened unto ten virgins, which took their lamps, and went forth to meet the bridegroom.

2 And five of them were **wise**, and [~~the~~][2] five *were* **foolish**[3].

3 **They that**[4] *were* foolish took their lamps, and took no oil with them:

4 But the wise took oil in their vessels with their lamps.

5 While the bridegroom tarried, they all slumbered and slept.

6 And at midnight there was a cry made, Behold, the bridegroom **~~cometh~~**[5]; go ye out to meet him.

7 Then all those virgins arose, and trimmed their lamps.

8 And the foolish said unto the wise, Give us of your oil; for our lamps are gone out.

9 But the wise answered, saying, *Not so*; lest there be **not**[6] enough for us and you: **~~but~~**[7] go ye rather to them that sell, and buy for yourselves.

10 And while they went to buy, the bridegroom came; and they that were ready went in with him to the marriage: and the door was shut.

11 Afterward came also the other virgins, saying, Lord, Lord, open to us.

12 But he answered and said, Verily I say unto you, I know you not.

---

[1] WH changed **to** be drinking (**pinein**) to *may be drinking* (*pinA*). Pres Act **Inf** to Pres Act *Sub*. [mood]

[2] WH omitted the untranslated the (ai).

[3] WH changed the word order from five of them were WISE, and five were FOOLISH to *five of them were FOOLISH, and five were WISE*.

[4] WH changed they that (**aitines**--some that) to *for these* (*ai gar*).

[5] WH omitted cometh (ercetai).

[6] WH changed not (ouk) to *not* (*ou mA*).

[7] WH omitted but (de).

13 Watch therefore, for ye know neither the day nor the hour ~~wherein the Son of man cometh~~[1].

14 For *the kingdom of heaven is* as a man travelling into a far country, *who* called his own servants, and delivered unto them his goods.

15 And unto one he gave five talents, to another two, and to another one; to every man according to his several ability; and straightway took his journey.

16 ~~Then~~[2] he that had received the five talents went and traded with the same, and made *them* other five talents.

17 And likewise he that *had received* two, ~~he also~~[3] gained other two.

18 But he that had received one went and digged ~~in~~[4] the **earth**[5], and hid his lord's money.

19 After a long time the lord of those servants cometh, and reckoneth with them.

20 And so he that had received five talents came and brought other five talents, saying, Lord, thou deliveredst unto me five talents: behold, I have gained ~~beside them~~[6] five talents more.

21 **[but]**[7] His lord said unto him, Well done, *thou* good and faithful servant: thou hast been faithful over a few things, I will make thee ruler over many things: enter thou into the joy of thy lord.

22 **He** also that ~~had received~~[8] two talents came and said, Lord, thou deliveredst unto me two talents: behold, I have gained two other talents ~~beside them~~[9].

---

[1] WH omitted in which the son of the man cometh (en ^hA ^ho ^huios tou an~~th~~rOpou ercetai).

[2] WH omitted then (de).

[3] WH omitted he also (kai autos).

[4] WH omitted in (en) and changed digged **in** the earth to digged the earth.

[5] WH changed earth (gA) to *earth* (gA*n*). **Dat** to *Acc*. [case]

[6] WH omitted beside them (ep' autois).

[7] WH omitted the untranslated but (de).

[8] WH omitted he had received (labOn). WH changed then having come also the (one) **having received** the two talents said to *then having come also the* (*one*) **[with]** *two talents said.*

[9] WH omitted beside them (ep' autois).

23 His lord said unto him, Well done, good and faithful servant; thou hast been faithful over a few things, I will make thee ruler over many things: enter thou into the joy of thy lord.

24 Then he which had received the one talent came and said, Lord, I knew thee that thou art an hard man, reaping where thou hast not sown, and gathering where thou hast not strawed:

25 And I was afraid, and went and hid thy talent in the earth: lo, *there* thou hast *that is* thine.

26 His lord answered and said unto him, *Thou* wicked and slothful servant, thou knewest that I reap where I sowed not, and gather where I have not strawed:

27 Thou oughtest therefore to have put my money to the exchangers, and *then* at my coming I should have received mine own with usury.

28 Take therefore the talent from him, and give *it* unto him which hath ten talents.

29 For unto every one that hath shall be given, and he shall have abundance: but **from**[1] **him**[2] that hath not

shall be taken away even that which he hath.

30 And cast ye the unprofitable servant into outer darkness: there shall be weeping and gnashing of teeth.

31 When the Son of man shall come in his glory, and all the **holy**[3] angels with him, then shall he sit upon the throne of his glory:

32 And before him shall be gathered all nations: and he shall separate them one from another, as a shepherd divideth *his* sheep from the goats:

33 And he shall set the sheep on his right hand, but the goats on the left.

34 Then shall the King say unto them on his right hand, Come, ye blessed of my Father, inherit the kingdom prepared for you from the foundation of the world:

35 For I was an hungred, and ye gave me meat: I was thirsty, and ye gave me drink: I was a stranger, and ye took me in:

36 Naked, and ye clothed me: I was sick, and ye visited me: I was in prison, and ye came unto me.

---

[1] WH omitted from (apo).
[2] WH changed the word order from but HIM to *HIM but*.
[3] WH omitted holy ([h]agioi).

37 Then shall the righteous answer him, saying, Lord, when saw we thee an hungred, and fed *thee*? or thirsty, and gave *thee* drink?

38 When saw we thee a stranger, and took *thee* in? or naked, and clothed *thee*?

39 Or when saw we thee sick, or in prison, and came unto thee?

40 And the King shall answer and say unto them, Verily I say unto you, Inasmuch as ye have done *it* unto one of the least of these my brethren, ye have done *it* unto me.

41 Then shall he say also unto them on the left hand, Depart from me, **[the]**[1] ye cursed, into everlasting fire, prepared for the devil and his angels:

42 For I was an hungred, and ye gave me no meat: I was thirsty, and ye gave me no drink:

43 I was a stranger, and ye took me not in: naked, and ye clothed me not: sick, and in prison, and ye visited me not.

44 Then shall they also answer **him**[2], saying, Lord, when saw we thee an hun-

gred, or athirst, or a stranger, or naked, or sick, or in prison, and did not minister unto thee?

45 Then shall he answer them, saying, Verily I say unto you, Inasmuch as ye did *it* not to one of the least of these, ye did *it* not to me.

46 And these shall go away into everlasting punishment: but the righteous into life eternal.

CHAPTER 26

1 And it came to pass, when Jesus had finished all these sayings, he said unto his disciples,

2 Ye know that after two days is *the feast of* the passover, and the Son of man is betrayed to be crucified.

3 Then assembled together the chief priests, **and the scribes**[3], and the elders of the people, unto the palace of the high priest, who was called Caiaphas,

4 And consulted that they might take Jesus by subtilty, and kill *him*.

5 But they said, Not on the feast *day*, lest there be an uproar among the people.

---

[1] WH omitted the untranslated the (^hoi) before ye cursed {ones}.

[2] WH omitted him (autO).

---

[3] WH omitted and the scribes (kai ^hoi grammateis).

6   Now when Jesus was in Bethany, in the house of Simon the leper,

7   There came unto him a woman having an alabaster box of very precious ointment, and poured it on his <u>head</u>[1], as he sat *at meat.*

8   But when ~~his~~[2] disciples saw *it,* they had indignation, saying, To what purpose *is* this waste?

9   For this ~~ointment~~[3] might have been sold for much, and given to the poor.

10   When Jesus understood *it,* he said unto them, Why trouble ye the woman? for she hath wrought a good work upon me.

11   For ye have the poor always with you; but me ye have not always.

12   For in that she hath poured this ointment on my body, she did *it* for my burial.

13   Verily I say unto you, wheresoever this gospel shall be preached in the whole world, *there* shall also this,

that this woman hath done, be told for a memorial of her.

14   Then one of the twelve, called Judas Iscariot, went unto the chief priests,

15   And said *unto them,* What will ye give me, and I will deliver him unto you? And they covenanted with him for thirty pieces of silver.

16   And from that time he sought opportunity to betray him.

17   Now the first *day* of the *feast of* unleavened bread the disciples came to Jesus, saying ~~unto him~~[4], Where wilt thou that we prepare for thee to eat the passover?

18   And he said, Go into the city to such a man, and say unto him, The Master saith, My time is at hand; I will keep the passover at thy house with my disciples.

19   And the disciples did as Jesus had appointed them; and they made ready the passover.

20   Now when the even was come, he sat down with the twelve [∧ **disciples**][5].

---

[1] WH changed <u>the head</u> (tAn kepfhalAn) to *the head* (tAs kefalAs) in <u>upon</u> the <u>head</u> of him. **Acc** to *Gen.* [case]

[2] WH omitted <u>of him</u> (autou) from <u>the disciples</u> **of him**.

[3] WH omitted <u>the ointment</u> (<u>to</u> muron).

[4] WH omitted <u>unto him</u> (autO).

[5] WH added *disciples* (*mathAton*). In their margin, however, they did not make this addition.

21 And as they did eat, he said, Verily I say unto you, that one of you shall betray me.

22 And they were exceeding sorrowful, and began [∧**unto**][1] every one ~~of them~~[2] to say unto him, Lord, is it I?

23 And he answered and said, He that dippeth *his hand*[3] with me in the dish, the same shall betray me.

24 The Son of man goeth as it is written of him: but woe unto that man by whom the Son of man is betrayed! it had been good for that man if he had not been born.

25 Then Judas, which betrayed him, answered and said, Master, is it I? He said unto him, Thou hast said.

26 And as they were eating, Jesus took [~~the~~][4] bread, and blessed *it*, and brake *it*, and **gave**[5] *it* to the disciples,

~~and~~[6] said, Take, eat; this is my body.

27 And he took ~~the~~[7] cup, and gave thanks, and gave *it* to them, saying, Drink ye all of it;

28 For this is my blood of the ~~new~~[8] testament, which is shed for many for the remission of sins.

29 But I say unto you, I will not drink henceforth of this fruit of the vine, until that day when I drink it new with you in my Father's kingdom.

30 And when they had sung an hymn, they went out into the mount of Olives.

31 Then saith Jesus unto them, All ye shall be offended because of me this night: for it is written, I will smite the shepherd, and the sheep of the flock shall be scattered abroad.

32 But after I am risen again, I will go before you into Galilee.

33 Peter answered and

---

[1] WH added *unto* (*eis*).

[2] WH omitted of them (autOn).

[3] WH changed the word order from with me in the dish THE HAND to *with me THE HAND in the dish.*

[4] WH omitted the untranslated the (ton).

[5] WH changed **was giving** (**edi**dou) to *having given* (*dous*). **Impf** Act **Ind** to an

Aor Act Part. [tense & mood]

[6] WH omitted and (kai).

[7] WH omitted the (to) in their text, but retained it in their margin.

[8] WH omitted new (kainAs) in their text, but retained it in their margin.

said unto him, **Though**[1] all *men* shall be offended because of thee, *yet* will I never be offended.

34 Jesus said unto him, Verily I say unto thee, That this night, before the cock crow, thou shalt deny me thrice.

35 Peter said unto him, Though I should die with thee, yet will I not deny thee. Likewise also said all the disciples.

36 Then cometh Jesus with them unto a place called Gethsemane, and saith unto the disciples [∧**of him**][2], Sit ye here, while I go and pray **yonder**[3].

37 And he took with him Peter and the two sons of Zebedee, and began to be sorrowful and very heavy.

38 Then saith he unto them, My soul is exceeding sorrowful, even unto death: tarry ye here, and watch with me.

39 And he went a little further, and fell on his face,

and prayed, saying, O my Father, if it be possible, let this cup pass from me: nevertheless not as I will, but as thou *wilt*.

40 And he cometh unto the disciples, and findeth them asleep, and saith unto Peter, What, could ye not watch with me one hour?

41 Watch and pray, that ye enter not into temptation: the spirit indeed *is* willing, but the flesh *is* weak.

42 He went away again the second time, and prayed, saying, O my Father, if this **cup**[4] may not pass away **from me**[5], except I drink it, thy will be done.

43 And he came and **found**[6] them asleep **again**[7]: for their eyes were heavy.

44 And he left them, and went away **again**[8], and

---

[1] By omitting <u>also</u> (<u>kai</u>), WH changed <u>though</u> (<u>ei</u> **kai** {if **also**}) to *if* (*ei*).

[2] WH added *of him* (*autou*) after <u>the</u> <u>disciples</u>.

[3] WH changed the word order from <u>pray</u> YONDER to *YONDER pray.*

[4] WH omitted <u>the</u> <u>cup</u> (<u>to po-tArion</u>).

[5] WH omitted <u>from me</u> (<u>ap' emou</u>).

[6] They changed <u>finds</u> (<u>euriskei</u>) to *found* (*euren*). **Pres** Act Ind to *Aor* Act Ind. [tense]

[7] WH changed the word order from <u>finds</u> <u>them</u> AGAIN to *AGAIN found them.*

[8] WH changed the word order from <u>went away</u> AGAIN to *AGAIN went away.*

prayed the third time, saying the same words [∧**again**]¹.

45 Then cometh he to ~~his~~² disciples, and saith unto them, Sleep on now, and take *your* rest: behold, the hour is at hand, and the Son of man is betrayed into the hands of sinners.

46 Rise, let us be going: behold, he is at hand that doth betray me.

47 And while he yet spake, lo, Judas, one of the twelve, came, and with him a great multitude with swords and staves, from the chief priests and elders of the people.

48 Now he that betrayed him gave them a sign, saying, Whomsoever I shall kiss, that same is he: hold him fast.

49 And forthwith he came to Jesus, and said, Hail, Master; and kissed him.

50 And Jesus said unto him, Friend, **wherefore**³ art thou come? Then came they, and laid hands on Jesus, and took him.

51 And, behold, one of them which were with Jesus stretched out *his* hand, and drew his sword, and struck a servant of the high priest's, and smote off his ear.

52 Then said Jesus unto him, Put up again thy sword into his place: for all they that take the sword shall perish with the sword.

53 Thinkest thou that I cannot ~~now~~⁴ pray to my Father, and he shall presently give me [∧**now**]⁵ more than twelve legions of angels?

54 But how then shall the scriptures be fulfilled, that thus it must be?

55 In that same hour said Jesus to the multitudes, Are ye come out as against a thief with swords and staves for to take me? I sat daily ~~with you~~⁶ teaching **in the temple**⁷, and ye laid no hold on me.

56 But all this was done, that the scriptures of the prophets might be fulfilled. Then all the disciples forsook him, and fled.

---

¹ WH added *again* (*palin*).

² WH omitted of him (autou) from the disciples of him.

³ WH changed upon what (ef' ʰ**O**) to *upon what* (*ef' ʰo*). **Dat** Neut Sing to *Acc* Neut Sing. [case]

⁴ WH omitted now (arti).

⁵ WH added *now* (*arti*) here.

⁶ WH omitted with you (pros ʰumas).

⁷ WH changed the word order from I sat teaching IN THE TEMPLE to *IN THE TEMPLE I sat teaching.*

57 And they that had laid hold on Jesus led *him* away to Caiaphas the high priest, where the scribes and the elders were assembled.

58 But Peter followed him afar off unto the high priest's palace, and went in, and sat with the servants, to see the end.

59 Now the chief priests, ~~and elders~~[1], and all the council, sought false witness against Jesus, to put him to death;

60 But found none: ~~yea~~[2], though many false witnesses __came__[3], ~~yet found they none~~[4]. At the last came two ~~false witnesses~~[5],

61 And said, This *fellow* said, I am able to destroy the temple of God, and to build it in three days.

62 And the high priest arose, and said unto him, Answerest thou nothing? what *is*
it which these witness against thee?

63 But Jesus held his peace. And the high priest ~~answered and~~[6] said unto him, I adjure thee by the living God, that thou tell us whether thou be the Christ, the Son of God.

64 Jesus saith unto him, Thou hast said: nevertheless I say unto you, Hereafter shall ye see the Son of man sitting on the right hand of power, and coming in the clouds of heaven.

65 Then the high priest rent his clothes, saying, He hath spoken blasphemy; what further need have we of witnesses? behold, now ye have heard ~~his~~[7] blasphemy.

66 What think ye? They answered and said, He is guilty of death.

67 Then did they spit in his face, and buffeted him; and others smote *him* with the palms of their hands,

68 Saying, Prophesy unto us, thou Christ, Who is he that smote thee?

69 Now Peter sat without in the palace: and a damsel

---

[1] WH omitted <u>and the elders</u> (<u>kai</u> <u>hoi presbuteroi</u>).

[2] WH omitted <u>yea</u> (<u>kai</u>).

[3] WH changed the word order from <u>false witnesses</u> <u>CAME</u> to *CAME fase witnesses.*

[4] WH omitted {yet} <u>found</u> <u>they</u> <u>none</u> (<u>ouc</u> <u>euron</u>).

[5] WH omitted <u>false witnesses</u> (<u>seudomartures</u>).

[6] WH omitted <u>answered</u> {and} (<u>apokritheis</u>).

[7] WH omitted <u>of him</u> (<u>autou</u>) from <u>the</u> <u>blasphemy</u> <u>of him</u>.

came unto him, saying, Thou also wast with Jesus of Galilee.

70 But he denied before *them* all, saying, I know not what thou sayest.

71 And when he was gone out into the porch, another *maid* saw him, and said unto them that were there, This *fellow* was also with Jesus of Nazareth.

72 And again he denied with an oath, I do not know the man.

73 And after a while came unto *him* they that stood by, and said to Peter, Surely thou also art *one* of them; for thy speech bewrayeth thee.

74 Then began he **to curse**[1] and to swear, *saying*, I know not the man. And immediately the cock crew.

75 And Peter remembered the word of Jesus, which said **unto him**[2], Before the cock crow, thou shalt deny me thrice. And he went out, and wept bitterly.

CHAPTER 27

1 When the morning was come, all the chief priests and elders of the people took counsel against Jesus to put him to death:

2 And when they had bound him, they led *him* away, and delivered **him**[3] to **Pontius**[4] Pilate the governor.

3 Then Judas, which had betrayed him, when he saw that he was condemned, repented himself, and **brought again**[5] the thirty pieces of silver to the chief priests and [**to the**][6] elders,

4 Saying, I have sinned in that I have betrayed the **innocent**[7] blood. And they said, What *is that* to us? see thou *to that*.

5 And he cast down the pieces of silver **in the temple**[8], and departed, and went and hanged himself.

---

[1] WH changed to curse (kat-anathematizein) to *to curse* (*kat-athematizein*). [spell]

[2] WH omitted unto him (autO).

[3] WH omitted him (auton).

[4] WH omitted Pontius (pontiO).

[5] WH changed brought **again** (**ape-stre,se**) to *brought* (*stre,se*). [prefix dropped]

[6] WH omitted the untranslated to the (tois).

[7] In their margin, WH changed **innocent** (**athOon**) to *righteous* (*dikaion*).

[8] WH changed in the temple (**in tO naO**) to *into the temple* (*eis ton naon*). [prep & case]

6　And the chief priests took the silver pieces, and said, It is not lawful for to put them into the treasury, because it is the price of blood.

7　And they took counsel, and bought with them the potter's field, to bury strangers in.

8　Wherefore that field was called, The field of blood, unto this day.

9　Then was fulfilled that which was spoken by Jeremy the prophet, saying, And they took the thirty pieces of silver, the price of him that was valued, whom they of the children of Israel did value;

10　And **gave**[1] them for the potter's field, as the Lord appointed me.

11　And Jesus stood before the governor: and the governor asked him, saying, Art thou the King of the Jews? And Jesus said unto him, Thou sayest.

12　And when he was accused of the chief priests and [the][2] elders, he answered nothing.

13　Then said Pilate unto him, Hearest thou not how many things they witness against thee?

14　And he answered him to never a word; insomuch that the governor marvelled greatly.

15　Now at *that* feast the governor was wont to release unto the people a prisoner, whom they would.

16　And they had then a notable prisoner, called Barabbas.

17　Therefore when they were gathered together, Pilate said unto them, Whom will ye that I release unto you? Barabbas, or Jesus which is called Christ?

18　For he knew that for envy they had delivered him.

19　When he was set down on the judgment seat, his wife sent unto him, saying, Have thou nothing to do with that just man: for I have suffered many things this day in a dream because of him.

20　But the chief priests and elders persuaded the multitude that they should ask Barabbas, and destroy Jesus.

21　The governor answered and said unto them, Whether of the twain will ye that I release unto you? They said, Barabbas.

---

[1] In their margin, WH changed gave (*edOkan*) to gave (*edOka*). Both Aor Act Ind. [spell]

[2] WH omitted the untranslated the (*tOn*).

83

22 Pilate saith unto them, What shall I do then with Jesus which is called Christ? *They* all say **unto him**[1], Let him be crucified.

23 And the **governor**[2] said, Why, what evil hath he done? But they cried out the more, saying, Let him be crucified.

24 When Pilate saw that he could prevail nothing, but *that* rather a tumult was made, he took water, and washed *his* hands before the multitude, saying, I am innocent of the blood of this **just person**[3]: see ye *to it*.

25 Then answered all the people, and said, His blood *be* on us, and on our children.

26 Then released he Barabbas unto them: and when he had scourged Jesus, he delivered *him* to be crucified.

27 Then the soldiers of the governor took Jesus into the common hall, and gathered unto him the whole band *of soldiers*.

28 And **they stripped**[4] him, and put on him a scarlet robe.

29 And when they had platted a crown of thorns, they put *it* upon his **head**[5], and a reed **in** his **right hand**[6]: and they bowed the knee before him, and mocked him, saying, Hail, King of the Jews!

30 And they spit upon him, and took the reed, and smote him on the head.

31 And after that they had mocked him, they took the robe off from him, and put his own raiment on him, and led him away to crucify *him*.

32 And as they came out, they found a man of Cyrene, Simon by name: him they compelled to bear his cross.

33 And when they were come unto a place called Golgotha, that is to say, a place of a skull,

---

[1] WH omitted unto him (autO).
[2] WH omitted governor ([h]AgemOn).
[3] In their margin, WH omitted just person (tou dikaiou {the righteous [one]}).

[4] WH changed they stripped (ek-dusantes) to *they clothed* (*en-dusantes*). [prefix changed]
[5] WH changed head (tAn kefalAn) to *head* (*tAs kefalAs*). **Acc** to **Gen**. [case]
[6] WH changed **upon** the right hand (**epi** tAn dexian) to *in the right hand* (*en tA dexia*). [prep & case]

34 They gave him **vine-gar**[1] to drink mingled with gall: and when he had tasted *thereof*, he would not drink.

35 And they crucified him, and parted his garments, casting lots: ~~that it might be fulfilled which was spoken by the prophet, They parted my garments among them, and upon my vesture did they cast lots~~[2].

36 And sitting down they watched him there;

37 And set up over his head his accusation written, THIS IS JESUS THE KING OF THE JEWS.

38 Then were there two thieves crucified with him, one on the right hand, and another on the left.

39 And they that passed by reviled him, wagging their heads,

40 And saying, Thou that destroyest the temple, and buildest *it* in three days, save thyself. If thou be the Son of God, come down from the cross.

41 Likewise **also**[3] the chief priests mocking *him*, with the scribes and elders, said,

42 He saved others; himself he cannot save. **If**[4] he be the King of Israel, let him now come down from the cross, and we will believe [ᴧ**upon**][5] **him**[6].

43 He trusted in God; let him deliver him now, if he will have him: for he said, I am the Son of God.

44 The thieves also, which were crucified with him, cast the same in his teeth.

45 Now from the sixth hour there was darkness over all the land unto the ninth hour.

46 And about the ninth hour Jesus cried with a loud voice, saying, Eli, Eli, lama sabachthani? that is to say, My God, my God, why hast thou forsaken me?

---

[1] WH changed **vinegar** (oxos—sour wine or wine vinegar) to *wine* (*oinon*).

[2] WH omitted that it might be fulfilled which was spoken by the prophet they parted my garments among them and upon my vesture did they cast lots (ʰina plArOᵗʰA to ʰrAᵗʰen ʰupo tou profAtou diemerisanto ta ʰimatia mou ʰeautois kai epi ton ʰima-tismon mou ebalon klAron).

[3] WH omitted also (de).

[4] WH omitted if (ei).

[5] WH added upon (epi).

[6] WH changed him (autO) to *him* (*auton*) **Dat** to *Acc*. [case]

47 Some of them that stood there, when they heard *that*, said, This *man* calleth for Elias.

48 And straightway one of them ran, and took a spunge, and filled *it* with vinegar, and put *it* on a reed, and gave him to drink.

49 The rest said, Let be, let us see whether Elias will come to save him. [But another, having taken a spear, pierced his side and blood and water came out.][1]

50 Jesus, when he had cried again with a loud voice, yielded up the ghost.

51 And, behold, the veil of the temple was rent in twain from the top to the bottom; and the earth did quake, and the rocks rent;

52 And the graves were opened; and many bodies of the saints which slept arose,

53 And came out of the graves after his resurrection, and went into the holy city, and appeared unto many.

54 Now when the centurion, and they that were with him, watching Jesus, saw the earthquake, and those things that were done, they feared greatly, saying, Truly this was the Son of God.

55 And many women were there beholding afar off, which followed Jesus from Galilee, ministering unto him:

56 Among which was Mary Magdalene, and Mary the mother of James and Joses, and the mother of Zebedee's children.

57 When the even was come, there came a rich man of Arimathaea, named Joseph, who also himself was Jesus' disciple:

58 He went to Pilate, and begged the body of Jesus. Then Pilate commanded ~~the body~~[2] to be delivered.

59 And when Joseph had taken the body, he wrapped it in a clean linen cloth,

60 And laid it in his own new tomb, which he had hewn out in the rock: and he rolled a great stone to the door of the sepulchre, and departed.

61 And there was Mary

---

[1] In their margin, WH added: *But another, having taken a spear, pierced his side and blood and water came out.* (*allos de labOn logcAn enuxen autou tAn pleuran, kai exAl then [h]udOr kai [h]aima.*)

[2] WH omitted the body (to sOma).

Magdalene, and the other Mary, sitting over against the sepulchre.

62 Now the next day, that followed the day of the preparation, the chief priests and Pharisees came together unto Pilate,

63 Saying, Sir, we remember that that deceiver said, while he was yet alive, After three days I will rise again.

64 Command therefore that the sepulchre be made sure until the third day, lest his disciples come ~~by night~~[1], and steal him away, and say unto the people, He is risen from the dead: so the last error shall be worse than the first.

65 Pilate [~~then~~][2] said unto them, Ye have a watch: go your way, make *it* as sure as ye can.

66 So they went, and made the sepulchre sure, sealing the stone, and setting a watch.

CHAPTER 28

1   In the end of the sabbath, as it began to dawn to-ward the first *day* of the week, came Mary Magdalene and the other Mary to see the sepulchre.

2   And, behold, there was a great earthquake: for the angel of the Lord descended from heaven, ʌand[3] came and rolled back the stone ~~from the door~~[4], and sat upon it.

3   His countenance was like lightning, and his raiment white as snow:

4   And for fear of him the keepers did shake, and became as dead *men*.

5   And the angel answered and said unto the women, Fear not ye: for I know that ye seek Jesus, which was crucified.

6   He is not here: for he is risen, as he said. Come, see the place where **the Lord**[5] lay.

7   And go quickly, and tell his disciples that he is risen from the dead; and, behold, he goeth before you

---

[1] WH omitted by night (nuktos).

[2] WH omitted the untranslated then (de).

[3] WH added *and* (*kai*) as did the KJV.

[4] WH omitted from the door (apo tAs thuras).

[5] In their margin, WH omitted the Lord ([h]o kurios). This forced the verb to supply the subject *he*.

into Galilee; there shall ye see him: lo, I have told you.

8 And **they departed**[1] quickly from the sepulchre with fear and great joy; and did run to bring his disciples word.

9 ~~And as they went to tell his disciples~~[2], behold, Jesus met them, saying, All hail. And they came and held him by the feet, and worshipped him.

10 Then said Jesus unto them, Be not afraid: go tell my brethren that they go into Galilee, and there shall they see me.

11 Now when they were going, behold, some of the watch came into the city, and shewed unto the chief priests all the things that were done.

12 And when they were assembled with the elders, and had taken counsel, they gave large money unto the soldiers,

13 Saying, Say ye, His disciples came by night, and stole him *away* while we slept.

14 And if this come to the governor's ears, we will persuade him, and secure you.

15 So they took the money, and did as they were taught: and this saying is commonly reported among the Jews until this day.

16 Then the eleven disciples went away into Galilee, into a mountain where Jesus had appointed them.

17 And when they saw him, they worshipped **him**[3]: but some doubted.

18 And Jesus came and spake unto them, saying, All power is given unto me in heaven and in earth.

19 Go ye therefore, and teach all nations, baptizing them in the name of the Father, and of the Son, and of the Holy Ghost:

20 Teaching them to observe all things whatsoever I have commanded you: and, lo, I am with you alway, *even* unto the end of the world. ~~Amen~~.[4]

---

[1] WH changed <u>they went **out**</u> (**ex**-el~~th~~housai) to *they went away* (**ap**-el~~th~~housai). [prefix changed]

[2] WH omitted <u>and</u> <u>as</u> <u>they</u> <u>went</u> <u>to</u> <u>tell</u> <u>his</u> <u>disciples</u> (^h<u>Os</u> <u>de</u> <u>eporeuonta</u> <u>apaggeilai</u> <u>tois</u> <u>math</u>~~h~~<u>Atais</u> <u>autou</u>).

[3] WH omitted <u>him</u> (<u>autO</u>).

[4] WH omitted <u>amen</u> (<u>amAn</u>).

MARK

CHAPTER 1

1 The beginning of the gospel of Jesus Christ, <u>**the Son of God**</u>[1];

2 <u>**As**</u>[2] it is written in <u>**the prophets**</u>[3], Behold, I send my messenger before thy face, which shall prepare thy way <s>**before thee**</s>[4].

3 The voice of one crying in the wilderness, Prepare ye the way of the Lord, make his paths straight.

4 John did [∧**the**][5] baptize in the wilderness, and preach the baptism of repentance for the remission of sins.

5 And there went out unto him all the land of Judaea, and they of Jerusalem, and were <u>**all**</u>[6] baptized of him in the river of Jordan, confessing their sins.

6 And John was clothed with camel's hair, and with a girdle of a skin about his loins; and he did eat locusts and wild honey;

7 And preached, saying, There cometh one mightier than I after me, the latchet of whose shoes I am not worthy to stoop down and unloose.

8 I <s>**indeed**</s>[7] have baptized you with water: but he shall baptize you with the Holy Ghost.

9 And it came to pass in those days, that Jesus came from Nazareth of Galilee, and was baptized of John in Jordan.

10 And straightway coming up <u>**out of**</u>[8] the water, he saw the heavens opened, and the Spirit <u>**like**</u>[9] a dove descending upon him:

---

[1] In their margin, WH omitted [the] <u>Son of the God</u> (^huiou tou theou).

[2] WH changed <u>as</u> (^hOs) to *just as* (ka*th*Os). [prefix added]

[3] WH changed <u>the prophets</u> (<u>tois</u> prof*A*tais) to *the Hosea the prophet* (*tO Asaia tO profAtA*) in their text, but retained <u>the prophets</u> (<u>tois</u> prof*A*t<u>ais</u>) in their margin.

[4] WH omitted <u>before thee</u> (empros*th*en <u>sou</u>).

[5] WH added *the* (^ho) before the participle translated <u>baptize</u>.

[6] WH changed the word order from <u>and were baptized ALL</u> to *ALL and were baptized.*

[7] WH omitted <u>indeed</u> (<u>men</u>).

[8] WH changed <u>**from**</u> (**apo**) to *out of* (*ek*).

[9] WH changed <u>like</u> {**as**}(<u>Osei</u>) to *like* (*Os*).

11 And there came a voice from heaven, *saying*, Thou art my beloved Son, in **whom**[1] I am well pleased.

12 And immediately the Spirit driveth him into the wilderness.

13 And he was ~~there~~[2] in the wilderness forty days, tempted of Satan; and was with the wild beasts; and the angels ministered unto him.

14 Now after that John was put in prison, Jesus came into Galilee, preaching the gospel ~~of the kingdom~~[3] of God,

15 And saying, The time is fulfilled, and the kingdom of God is at hand: repent ye, and believe the gospel.

16 **Now** [4] **as he walked**[5] by the sea of Galilee, he saw Simon and Andrew **his**[6]

brother **casting**[7] ~~a net~~[8] into the sea: for they were fishers.

17 And Jesus said unto them, Come ye after me, and I will make you to become fishers of men.

18 And straightway they forsook ~~their~~[9] nets, and followed him.

19 And when he had gone a little further ~~thence~~[10], he saw James the *son* of Zebedee, and John his brother, who also were in the ship mending their nets.

20 And straightway he called them: and they left their father Zebedee in the ship with the hired servants, and went after him.

21 And they went into Capernaum; and straightway on the sabbath day he entered into the synagogue, and taught.

22 And they were astonished at his doctrine: for he

---

[1] WH changed **whom** (**ʰO**) to *you* (*soi*).

[2] WH omitted there (ekei).

[3] WH omitted of the kingdom (tAs basileias).

[4] WH changed **now** (**de**) to *and* (*kai*).

[5] WH changed as he **walked** (**peripat**On) to *as he passed by* (*parag*On). [syn]

[6] WH changed **his** brother (ton adelfon **autou**) to *Simon's brother* (*ton adelfon tou simOnos*).

[7] WH changed casting (ballontas) to *casting a net* (*amfi*-ballontas). [prefix added]

[8] WH omtted a net (amfiblAstron).

[9] WH omitted of them (autOn) from the nets of them.

[10] WH omitted thence (ekeithen).

taught them as one that had authority, and not as the scribes.

23 And [∧**immediately**]¹ there was in their synagogue a man with an unclean spirit; and he cried out,

24 Saying, ~~Let *us* alone~~²; what have we to do with thee, thou Jesus of Nazareth? art thou come to destroy us? I know thee who thou art, the Holy One of God.

25 And Jesus rebuked him, saying, Hold thy peace, and come out of him.

26 And when the unclean spirit had torn him, and **cried**³ with a loud voice, he came out of him.

27 And they were all amazed, insomuch that they questioned among **themselves**⁴, saying, What thing is this? **what**⁵ [**the**]⁶ new [**the**]⁷

doctrine ~~*is* **this**~~⁸? ~~**for**~~⁹ with authority commandeth he even the unclean spirits, and they do obey him.

28 And immediately [∧**everywhere**]¹⁰ his fame spread abroad throughout all the region round about Galilee.

29 And forthwith, w̲h̲e̲n̲ t̲h̲e̲y̲ w̲e̲r̲e̲ c̲o̲m̲e̲¹¹ out of the synagogue, t̲h̲e̲y̲ e̲n̲t̲e̲r̲e̲d̲¹² into the house of Simon and Andrew, with James and John.

30 But Simon's wife's mother lay sick of a fever, and anon they tell him of her.

31 And he came and took her by the hand, and lifted her

---

¹ WH added *immediately* (*eu**th**us*).
² WH omitted the interjection Let *us* alone (*ea*).
³ WH changed **cried** (**kraz**an) to *called* (*f**On**Asan*) [syn]
⁴ WH changed themselves (autous) to *themselves* (*ʰeautous*). [prefix added]
⁵ WH omitted what (tis).
⁶ WH omitted the untranslated the (ʰA) before new.
⁷ WH omitted the untrans-

lated the (ʰA) before doctrine.
⁸ WH omitted this (autA).
⁹ WH omitted for (ʰoti).
¹⁰ WH added *everywhere* (*pantacou*).
¹¹ In their margin, WH changed when **they** came (exel**th**ontes) to *when he came* (*exel**th**On*). Both Aor Part. 3ʳᵈ **Plur** Masc to 3ʳᵈ *Sing* Masc. [number]
¹² In their margin, WH changed **they** entered (Al**th**on) *he entered* (*Al**th**en*). Both Aor Ind. 3ʳᵈ **Plur** Masc to 3ʳᵈ *Sing* Masc. [number]

up; and ~~immediately~~[1] the fever left her, and she ministered unto them.

32 And at even, when the sun did set, they brought unto him all that were diseased, and them that were possessed with devils.

33 And all the city was gathered together at the door.

34 And he healed many that were sick of divers diseases, and cast out many devils; and suffered not the devils to speak, because they knew him [∧**to be Christ**][2].

35 And in the morning, rising up a great while **before day**[3], he went out, and departed into a solitary place, and there prayed.

36 And Simon and they that were with him followed after him.

37 **And**[4] **when they had found**[5] him, they said unto him, All *men* seek for thee.

38 And he said unto them, Let us go [∧**elsewhere**][6] into the next towns, that I may preach there also: for therefore **came I forth**[7].

39 And **he preached**[8] **in**[9] **their synagogues**[10] throughout all Galilee, and cast out devils.

40 And there came a leper to him, beseeching him, **and kneeling down to him**[11], and saying unto him, If thou wilt, thou canst make me clean.

([h]**eurontes**) to *they found* ([h]*euron*). Aor Act **Part** to *Aor Act Ind.* [mood]

[6] WH added *elsewhere* (*allacou*).

[7] WH changed I **have** come out (ex-**elAlutha**) to *I came out* (*ex-Althon*). **Pf** Act Ind to *Aor Act Ind.* [tense]

[8] WH changed he **was** preaching (**An** kArussOn to *he went preaching* (*Althe kArussOn*). [prefix changed]

[9] WH changed **in** (**en**) to *into* (*eis*). [prep]

[10] WH changed their synogogues (ta**is** sunagOga**is** autOn) to their synogogues (*tas sunagOgas autOn*). **Dat** to *Acc.* [case]

[11] In their margin, WH omitted and kneeling down to him (kai gonupetOn auton).

---

[1] WH omitted immediately (eu**the**Os).

[2] WH added *to be Christ* (*criston einai*).

[3] WH changed before day (ennu**con**) to *before day* (*ennuca*). [(mis)spell]

[4] WH changed the word order from AND **having found** him to *they found* him AND.

[5] WH changed **having** found

41 **And**[1] ~~Jesus~~[2], moved with compassion, put forth *his* hand, and touched him, and saith unto him, I will; be thou clean.

42 And ~~as soon as he had spoken~~[3], immediately the leprosy departed from him, and he was cleansed.

43 And he straitly charged him, and forthwith sent him away;

44 And saith unto him, See thou say nothing to any man: but go thy way, shew thyself to the priest, and offer for thy cleansing those things which Moses commanded, for a testimony unto them.

45 But he went out, and began to publish *it* much, and to blaze abroad the matter, insomuch that Jesus could no more openly enter into the city, but was without in desert places: and they came to him **from every quarter**[4].

---

[1] WH changed and (**de**) to *and* (**kai**).
[2] WH omitted the Jesus (ʰo iAsous) and forced the verb to supply the subject *he*.
[3] WH omitted he having spoken (eipontos autou).
[4] WH changed from every quarter (pant**a**co**th**en) to *from every quarter* (pant**o**ᵗʰen). [spell]

CHAPTER 2

1 And **again**[5] **he entered**[6] into Capernaum after *some* days; **and**[7] it was noised that he was in the house.

2 And **straightway**[8] many were gathered together, insomuch that there was no room to receive *them*, no, not so much as about the door: and he preached the word unto them.

3 And they come unto him, **bringing**[9] one sick of the palsy, which was borne of four.

4 And when they could not **come nigh**[10] unto him for

---

[5] WH changed the word order from AGAIN **he** entered to *having entered* AGAIN.
[6] WH changed **he** entered (eisAltʰen) to *having entered* (eiselᵗʰOn). Aor Act **Ind** to *Aor Act* **Part**. [mood]
[7] WH omitted and (kai).
[8] WH omitted straightway (euᵗʰeOs).
[9] WH changed the word order from to him one sick of the palsy BRINGING to *BRINGING to him one sick of the palsy*.
[10] In their margin, WH changed **come nigh** (proseggisai) to **bring** (prosenegkai).

the press, they uncovered the roof where he was: and when they had broken *it* up, they let down the bed wherein the sick of the palsy lay.

5   **[but]**[1] When Jesus saw their faith, he said unto the sick of the palsy, Son, **thy**[2] sins be forgiven ~~thee~~[3].

6   But there were certain of the scribes sitting there, and reasoning in their hearts,

7   Why doth this *man* thus speak **blasphemies**[4]? who can forgive sins but God only?

8   And immediately when Jesus perceived in his spirit that they so reasoned within themselves, **he said**[5] unto them, Why reason ye these things in your hearts?

9   Whether is it easier to say to the sick of the palsy, *Thy* sins be forgiven **thee**[6]; or to say, Arise, and take up thy bed, and walk?

10 But that ye may know that the Son of man hath power on earth **to forgive**[7] sins, (he saith to the sick of the palsy,)

11 I say unto thee, Arise, **and**[8] take up thy bed, and go thy way into thine house.

12 And immediately he arose **[and]**[9], took up the bed, and went forth before them all; insomuch that they were all amazed, and glorified God, saying, We never saw it on this fashion.

13 And he went forth again by the sea side; and all the multitude resorted unto him, and he taught them.

14 And as he passed by, he

---

[1] WH changed the untranslated **but** (**de**) to *and* (*kai*) and put it before idOn (having seen).

[2] WH changed the word order from the sins OF THOU to *OF THOU the sins.*

[3] WH omitted thee (sou).

[4] WH changed blasphemies (blasfAmias) to *he blasphemes* (*blasfAmei*). They changed a plural **noun** to a Pres Act Ind *verb*. [noun to verb]

[5] WH changed he said (**eipen**) to *he says* (*legei*). **Aor** to *Pres*. [tense]

---

[6] WH changed {**to**} thee (soi) to {**of**} *thee* (*sou*). **Dat** to *Gen*. [case]

[7] WH changed the word order from TO FORGIVE on the earth to *on the earth TO FORGIVE.*

[8] WH omitted and (kai).

[9] WH changed the word order from and he arose immediately AND to *and he arose AND immediately.*

saw Levi the *son* of Alphaeus sitting at the receipt of custom, and said unto him, Follow me. And he arose and followed him.

15 And it came to pass, **that**[1], as Jesus sat at meat in his house, many publicans and sinners sat also together with Jesus and his disciples: for there were many, and **they followed**[2] him.

16 And when the scribes **and**[3] **Pharisees**[4] saw **him**[5] **eat**[6] with publicans and **sinners**[7], they said unto his disciples, **How is it**[8] that he eateth **and drinketh**[9] with publicans and sinners?

17 When Jesus heard *it*, he saith unto them, They that are whole have no need of the physician, but they that are sick: I came not to call the righteous, but sinners **to repentance**[10].

18 And the disciples of John and [**the**] **of the**[11] Pharisees[12] used to fast: and they come and say unto him, Why do the disciples of John and [**the**] [∧**disciples**][13] of the Pharisees fast, but thy disciples fast not?

19 And Jesus said unto them, Can the children of the bridechamber fast, while the bridegroom is with them? as long as they have the bridegroom with them, they cannot fast.

---

[1] WH omitted that (en tO {in the}).

[2] WH changed they follow**ed** (Akolou**th**Asan) to *they **were** following* (Akolou**th**oun). **Aor** Act Ind to *Impf* Act Ind. [tense]

[3] WH omitted and (kai).

[4] WH changed the Pharisees (ʰoi farisaioi) to *of the Pharisees* (tOn farisaiOn) in their text, but not in their margin. **Nom** to *Gen*. [case]

[5] WH changed **him** (**auton**) to *that* (ʰoti). **Personal** Pronoun to *Relative* Pronoun.

[6] WH changed eat**ing** (es**th**ionta) to *he eats* (es**th**iei). Pres Act **Part** to Pres Act *Ind*. [mood]

[7] WH changed the word order from publicans and SINNERS to *SINNERS and pub-*

licans.

[8] WH omitted how {is it} (ti).

[9] In their margin, WH omitted and drink (kai pinei).

[10] WH omitted to repentance (eis metanoian).

[11] WH omitted of the (tOn).

[12] WH changed the **of the** Pharisees (ʰoi **tOn** farisaiOn) to *the Pharisees* (ʰoi farisaioi). **Gen** to *Nom*. [case]

[13] WH added *disciples* (ma**th**Atai) following the plural untranslated the (ʰoi).

20 But the days will come, when the bridegroom shall be taken away from them, and then shall they fast in **those days**[1].

21 No man ~~also~~[2] seweth a piece of new cloth on **an old garment**[3]: else the new piece that filled [∧**from**][4] it up taketh away from the old, and the rent is made worse.

22 And no man putteth new wine into old bottles: else the ~~new~~[5] wine **doth burst**[6] the bottles, and the wine ~~is spilled~~[7], and the bottles **will be marred**[8]: but new wine ~~must be put~~[9] into new bottles.

23 And it came to pass, **that he**[10] **went**[11] through the corn fields ~~on~~[12] the sabbath day; and his disciples began, as they went, to pluck the ears of corn.

24 And the Pharisees said unto him, Behold, why do they on the sabbath day that which is not lawful?

25 And he [**himself**][13] said unto them, Have ye never read what David did, when he had need, and was an hungred, he, and they that were with him?

---

[1] WH changed **those** days (ekeinais tais ᴴAmerais) to *that* day (ekeinA tA ᴴAmera). **Plur** to *Sing* [number]

[2] WH omitted <u>also</u> (kai).

[3] WH changed <u>an old gar</u>ment (ᴴimatiO palaiO) to *an old garment* (ᴴimation palaion). **Dat** to *Acc.* [case]

[4] WH added *from* (af') after <u>filled up</u> (plArOma) and before <u>it</u> (autou).

[5] WH omitted <u>the new</u> (ᴴo neos).

[6] WH changed **does** burst (ᴴrAssei) to *will burst* (ᴴrAxei). **Pres** Act Ind to *Fut* Act Inc. [tense]

[7] WH omitted <u>is spilled</u> (ek-ceitai).

[8] WH changed the word order from <u>and the bottles</u> WILL

BE MARRED to *WILL BE MARRED and the bottles.*

[9] WH omitted <u>must be put</u> (blAteon).

[10] WH changed the word order from <u>that went</u> HE <u>on the sabbath</u> <u>through the corn-fields</u> to *that* HE *on the sabbath went through the corn-fields.*

[11] WH changed <u>that went</u> {beside} (**para**-poreuestʰai) to *that went* {through} (*dia-poreuestʰai*). [prefix changed]

[12] WH omitted <u>on</u> (en) and forced the case endings of <u>the Sabbath</u> to provide the implied preposition.

[13] WH omitted the untranslated <u>himself</u> (autos).

26 How he went into the house of God in the days of Abiathar ~~the~~[1] high priest, and did eat the shewbread, which is not lawful to eat but for the priests, and gave also to them which were with him?

27 And he said unto them, The sabbath was made for man, ∧**and**[2] not man for the sabbath:

28 Therefore the Son of man is Lord also of the sabbath.

CHAPTER 3

1 And he entered again into the synagogue; and there was a man there which had a withered hand.

2 And they watched him, whether he would heal him on the sabbath day; that they might accuse him.

3 And he saith unto the man which **had**[3] the **withered**[4] hand, Stand forth.

4 And he saith unto them, Is it lawful to do good on the sabbath days, or to do evil? to save life, or to kill? But they held their peace.

5 And when he had looked round about on them with anger, being grieved for the hardness of their hearts, he saith unto the man, Stretch forth thine hand. And he stretched *it* out: and his hand was restored ~~whole as the other~~[5].

6 And the Pharisees went forth, and straightway took counsel with the Herodians against him, how they might destroy him.

7 But Jesus **withdrew himself**[6] with his disciples to the sea: and a great multitude from Galilee followed ~~him~~[7], and from Judaea,

8 And from Jerusalem, and from Idumaea, and *from*

---

[1] WH omitted the (tou) from their text but included it in their margin.
[2] WH added *and* (kai) as did the KJV.
[3] WH changed the word order from **withered** HAVING the hand to *the hand HAVING withered*.
[4] WH changed **having been**

withered {and continuing to be so} (**exAra**mmen**An**) to *withered* (*xAran*). **Pf Pass Part** to *Adj.*
[5] WH omitted whole as the other (ʰugiAs ʰOs ʰA allA).
[6] WH changed the word order from WITHDREW HIMSELF with his disciples to *with his disciples* WITHDREW HIMSELF.
[7] WH omitted him (autO).

beyond Jordan; and ~~they~~[1] about Tyre and Sidon, a great multitude, **when they had heard**[2] what great things he did, came unto him.

9 And he spake to his disciples, that a small ship should wait on him because of the multitude, lest they should throng him.

10 For he had healed many; insomuch that they pressed upon him for to touch him, as many as had plagues.

11 And unclean spirits, when they saw him, fell down before him, and cried, saying, Thou art the Son of God.

12 And he straitly charged them that they should not make him known.

13 And he goeth up into a mountain, and calleth *unto him* whom he would: and they came unto him.

14 And he ordained twelve, **[whom also he named apostles]**[3] that they should be with him, and that he might send them forth to preach,

15 And to have power ~~to heal sicknesses, and~~[4] to cast out devils:

16 **[and he ordained the twelve]**[5] And Simon he surnamed Peter;

17 And James the *son* of Zebedee, and John the brother of James; and he surnamed them Boanerges, which is, The sons of thunder:

18 And Andrew, and Philip, and Bartholomew, and Matthew, and Thomas, and James the *son* of Alphaeus, and Thaddaeus, and Simon the **Canaanite**[6],

19 And Judas Iscariot, which also betrayed him: and **they went**[7] into an house.

---

[1] WH omitted they (^hoi—the {ones}).

[2] WH changed **having** heard (akousantes) to *hearing* (akouontes). **Aor** Act Part to *Pres* Act Part. [tense]

[3] In their margin, WH added *whom also he named apostles* (*ous kai apostolous Ono-* *masen*).

[4] WH omitted to heal sicknesses and (~~t~~herapeuein tas nosous kai).

[5] In their margin, WH added *and he ordained the twelve* (*kai epoiAse tous dOdeka*).

[6] WH changed Canaan**ite** (kananit**An**) to Canan**ean** (kanan**aion** {zealot, revolutionary}).

[7] WH changed they went (er-**con**tai) to *they went* (ercetai). [spell]

20 And ∧the¹ multitude cometh together again, so that they could **not so much as**² eat bread.

21 And when his friends heard *of it*, they went out to lay hold on him: for they said, He is beside himself.

22 And the scribes which came down from Jerusalem said, He hath Beelzebub, and by the prince of the devils casteth he out devils.

23 And he called them *unto him*, and said unto them in parables, How can Satan cast out Satan?

24 And if a kingdom be divided against itself, that kingdom cannot stand.

25 And if a house be divided against itself, that house **cannot**³ stand.

26 And if Satan rise up against himself, and **be divided**⁴, he cannot stand, but

hath an end.

27 [∧but]⁵ No man can enter **into a** strong man's **house**, and spoil his **goods**⁶, except he will first bind the strong man; and then he will spoil his house.

28 Verily I say unto you, All **sins**⁷ shall be forgiven unto the sons of men, and [∧the]⁸ blasphemies **wherewith**⁹ soever they shall blaspheme:

29 But he that shall blaspheme against the Holy Ghost hath never forgiveness, but is in danger of eternal

---

(**memeristai**) to *was divided* {at one point} (*emeris**th**A*). **Pf** Pass Ind to *Aor* Pass Ind [tense]

⁵ WH added *but* (*alla*).

⁶ WH changed the word order from THE GOODS of the strong man enter INTO THE HOUSE to *INTO THE HOUSE of the strong man enter THE GOODS.*

⁷ WH changed the word order from THE SINS unto the sons of men to *unto the sons of men THE SINS.*

⁸ WH added *the* (*ʰai*).

⁹ WH changed wherewith (*ʰosas*) to *wherewith* (*ʰosa*). **Masc** Nom **Sing** to *Neut* Nom/Acc *Plur* [number & gender]

---

¹ WH added *the* (*ʰo*) as the KJV did.

² WH changed not **so much as** (*mAte*) to *not even* (*mAde*).

³ WH changed not **is being** able (*ou dunatai*) to *not will be able* (*ou dunAsetai*). **Pres** M/P Ind to *Fut* Mid Ind. [tense]

⁴ WH changed **has been** divided {and continues to be}

damnation[1]:

30 Because they said, He hath an unclean spirit.

31 **There came then**[2] his **brethren [ʌof him]**[3] and his **mother**[4], and, standing without, sent unto him, calling him.

32 And the multitude sat about him, **and they said**[5] unto him, Behold, thy mother and thy brethren without seek for thee.

33 And **he answered**[6]

them, **saying**[7], Who is my mother, **or**[8] my brethren?

34 And he looked **round about**[9] on them which sat about him, and said, Behold my mother and my brethren!

35 For whosoever shall do the will of God, the same is my brother, and ~~my~~[10] sister, and mother.

CHAPTER 4

1 And he began again to teach by the sea side: and **there was gathered**[11] unto him **a great**[12] multitude, so

---

[1] WH changed **damnation** (**krisis** {judgment}) to *sin* (*ʰamartAmatos*).

[2] WH changed **then** (**oun**) to *and* (*kai*).

[3] WH added *of him* (*autou*) after brethren [as the KJV did].

[4] WH changed the word order from COMING **then** the BROTHERS and the MOTHER of him to *and* COMING *the MOTHER of him and the BROTHERS* **of him**.

[5] WH changed and they said (**eipon de**) to *and they are say*ing (*kai legousi*). **Aor** Act Ind to a *Pres* Act Ind. [tense]

[6] WH changed **he** answered (apekrithA) to *having been answered* (*apekritheis*) Aor **Act Ind** to Aor *Pass Part.* [voice & mood]

[7] WH changed saying (le-gOn) to *he says* (*legei*). Pres Act **Part** to Pres Act *Ind.* [mood]

[8] WH changed **or** (**A**) to *and* (*kai*).

[9] WH changed the word order from ROUND ABOUT on them about him to *on them about him ROUND ABOUT.*

[10] WH omitted of me (mou) from the sister of me.

[11] WH changed **having been** gathered (sunAcĦA) to *being gathered* (*sunagetai*). **Aor** Pass Ind to *Pres* Pass Ind. [tense]

[12] WH changed **a great** (**po-lus**) to *the greatest* (*pleistos* {superlative of polus}).

that he **entered**[1] into a [**the**][2] ship, and sat in the sea; and the whole multitude **was**[3] by the sea on the land.

2   And he taught them many things by parables, and said unto them in his doctrine,

3   Hearken; Behold, there went out a sower to sow:

4   And it came to pass, as he sowed, some fell by the way side, and the fowls ~~of the air~~[4] came and devoured it up.

5   **And some**[5] fell on stony ground, where it had not much earth; and immediately it sprang up, because it had no depth of earth:

6   **But**[6] ∧**when**[7] ∧**the**[8]

sun[9] **was up**[10], it was scorched; and because it had no root, it withered away.

7   And some fell among thorns, and the thorns grew up, and choked it, and it yielded no fruit.

8   And **other**[11] fell on good ground, and did yield fruit that sprang up and **increased**[12]; and brought forth, **some**[13] thirty, and **some**[14] sixty, and **some**[15] an hundred.

---

[1] WH changed the word order from he HAVING ENTERED into **the** ship to *he into a ship HAVING ENTERED*.

[2] WH omitted the untranslated the (to) before ship.

[3] WH changed {**it**}was (An) to {**they**}*were* (*Asan*). 3rd **Sing** to 3rd *Plur*. [number]

[4] WH omitted of the air (tou ouranou).

[5] WH changed and some (allo de) to *and some* (*kai allo*). [syn word order]

[6] WH changed **but** (**de**) to *and* (*kai*).

[7] WH added *when* (ʰoti) [supplied by KJV from the partici-

particle].

[8] WH added *the* (ʰo) [supplied by KJV].

[9] WH changed the word order from **but** SUN **having risen up** (ʰAliou de anateilantos) to **and when rose up the** SUN (*kai* ʰoti ʰo ʰAlios*).

[10] WH changed **having risen up** (anateilantos) to *rose up* (*aneteilen*) Aor Act **Part** to Aor Act *Ind*. [mood]

[11] WH changed **other** (allo) to *but* (*alla*).

[12] WH changed having increased (auxanonta) to *having been increased* (*auxanomena*). Pres **Act** Part to Pres *Pass* Part. [voice]

[13] WH changed **some** (ʰen) to *into* (*eis*).

[14] WH changed **some** (ʰen) to *into* (*eis*).

[15] WH changed **some** (ʰen) to *into* (*eis*).

9   And   he   said   ~~unto~~
~~them~~[1],   **He that**[2]   hath[3]   ears to
hear, let him hear.

10   **And   when**[4]   he   was
alone, they that were about
him with the twelve **asked**[5]
of him **the parable**[6].

11   And he said unto them,
Unto   you   ~~it~~[7]   is   given   ~~to~~
~~know~~[8]   **the   mystery**[9]   of the
kingdom of God: but unto
them   that   are   without,   all
these things are done in parables:

12   That seeing they may
see, and not perceive; and
hearing they may hear, and
not   understand;   lest   at   any
time   they   should   be   converted,   and   *their   sins*[10]
should be forgiven them.

13   And he said unto them,
Know ye not this parable?
and how then will ye know all
parables?

14   The sower soweth the
word.

15   And these are they by
the way side, where the word
is sown; but when they have
heard, Satan cometh immediately, and taketh away the
word   that   was   sown   **in**[11]
their[12] [the] ~~hearts~~[13].

16   And these are they likewise   which   are   sown   on

---

[1] WH omitted unto them
(autois).
[2] WH changed **the** [one] (^ho)
to *whoever* (^hos). **Definite
Article** to *Relative Pronoun*.
[3] WH changed having
(ecOn) to *has* (^hos ecei). Pres
Act **Part** to Pres Act *Ind*.
[mood]
[4] WH changed and when
(^hote **de**) to *and when* (*kai*
^hote). [syn]
[5] WH changed asked (ArO-
tAsan) to *was asking* (*ArO-
tOn*). **Aor** Act Ind to an *Impf*
Act Ind. [tense]
[6] WH changed the parable
(tAn parabolAn) to *the parables* (*ta parabolas*). Acc
Sing to Acc *Plur*. [number]
[7] WH omitted the supplied
subject it.
[8] WH omitted to know
(gnOnai).
[9] WH changed the word order from **it is given to know
THE MYSTERY** to *THE MYSTERY
is given.*

---

[10] WH omitted the sins (ta
^hamartAmata).
[11] WH changed in (en) to
into (*eis*).
[12] WH changed of them
(autOn) to *them* (*autous*).
[case]
[13] WH omitted the hearts
(tais kardiais). They replaced
in **the hearts of** them with
into them.

stony ground; who, when they have heard the word, immediately receive it with gladness;

17 And have no root in themselves, and so endure but for a time: afterward, when affliction or persecution ariseth for the word's sake, immediately they are offended.

18 And **these**¹ are they which are sown among thorns; [ₐ**these are]**² such as **hear**³ the word,

19 And the cares of ~~this~~⁴ world, and the deceitfulness of riches, and the lusts of other things entering in, choke the word, and it becometh unfruitful.

20 And **these**⁵ are they which are sown on good ground; such as hear the

word, and receive _it_, and bring forth fruit, **some**⁶ thirtyfold, **some**⁷ sixty, and **some**⁸ an hundred.

21 And he said unto them, Is a candle brought to be put under a bushel, or under a bed? and not **to be set**⁹ on a candlestick?

22 For there is nothing hid, ~~which~~¹⁰ [ₐ**that]**¹¹ shall not be manifested; neither was any thing kept secret, but that it should come abroad.

23 If any man have ears to hear, let him hear.

24 And he said unto them, Take heed what ye hear: with what measure ye mete, it shall be measured to you: and unto you ~~that hear~~¹² shall more be given.

25 For he that **hath**¹³, to

---

¹ WH changed **these** (ᴴ**outo**i) to _others_ (_alloi_).

² WH added _these are_ (ᴴ_outoi eisin_).

³ WH changed hear**ing** (ak-ouon**tes**) to _having heard_ (_akousantes_). **Pres** Act Part to _Aor_ Act Part. [tense]

⁴ WH omitted this (toutou) and changed from the world **this** {one} (tou aiOnos **tou-tou**) to _the world_ (_tou aiOnos_).

⁵ WH changed these (ᴴ**outo**i) to _those_ (_ekeinoi_).

⁶ WH changed **some** (ᴴ_en) to _in_ (_en_).

⁷ WH changed **some** (ᴴ_en) to _in_ (_en_).

⁸ WH changed **some** (ᴴ_en) to _in_ (_en_).

⁹ WH changed to be set {**upon**}(**epi**te_th_A) to _to be set_ (_te_~~th~~_A_). [prefix added]

¹⁰ WH omitted which (ᴴ_o).

¹¹ WH added _that_ (ᴴ_ina_).

¹² WH omitted that hear (tois akouousin).

¹³ WH changed **may** have (ec_A) to _having_ (_ecei_). Both Pres Act. **Sub** to _Part_. [mood]

him shall be given: and he that hath not, from him shall be taken even that which he hath.

26 And he said, So is the kingdom of God, as ~~if~~[1] a man should cast seed into the ground;

27 And should sleep, and rise night and day, and the seed should spring and grow up, he knoweth not how.

28 ~~For~~[2] the earth bringeth forth fruit of herself; first the blade, then the ear, after that the full corn in the ear.

29 But when the fruit is brought forth, immediately he putteth in the sickle, because the harvest is come.

30 And he said, **Whereunto**[3] shall we liken the kingdom of God? or with **what**[4] comparison **shall we compare**[5] **it**[6]?

31 *It is* like a grain of mustard seed, which, when it is sown in the earth, is[7] **less than**[8] all the seeds that be in the earth:

32 But when it is sown, it groweth up, and becometh **greater than**[9] **all herbs**[10], and shooteth out great branches; so that the fowls of the air may lodge under the shadow of it.

33 And with many such parables spake he the word unto them, as they were able to hear *it*.

34 But without a parable spake he not unto them: and when they were alone, he expounded all things to **his**[11]

IT comparison might we make.

[7] WH changed **is** (**esti**) to *being* (*on*). Pres NV **Ind** to Pres Act *Part*. [mood]

[8] WH changed is less than (*mikroteros*) *to is less than* (*mikroteron*). **Masc** to *Neut*. [gender]

[9] WH changed greater than (*meizOn*) to *greater than* (*meizon*). Nom **Masc** Sing to Nom *Neut* Sing. [gender]

[10] WH changed the word order from ALL THE HERBS greater than *to greater than ALL THE HERBS*.

[11] WH changed of him (**autou**) to *his own* (*idiois*). [Pro to Adj]

---

[1] WH omitted if (ean).

[2] WH omitted for (gar).

[3] WH changed **to whom** (**tini**) to *how* (*pOs*) [**Rel Pro** to *Sub Con*].

[4] WH changed what (**poia**) to *what* (*tini*). Both Dat Fem Sing. [Inter **Pro** to Inter *Adj*]

[5] WH changed might we **compare** (**parabalOmen**) to *might we make (thOmen)*. Both Aor Act Sub 2 Plur.

[6] WH changed the word order from what comparison might we **compare** IT to *what*

disciples¹.

35 And the same day, when the even was come, he saith unto them, Let us pass over unto the other side.

36 And when they had sent away the multitude, they took him even as he was in the ship. And there were ~~also~~² with him other **little ships**³.

37 And there arose a great storm of wind, **and**⁴ **the**⁵ waves beat into the ship, so that **it**⁶ was **now**⁷ full.

38 And **he**⁸ was **in**⁹ the hinder part of the ship, asleep on a pillow: and they **awake**¹⁰ him, and say unto him, Master, carest thou not that we perish?

39 And he arose, and rebuked the wind, and said unto the sea, Peace, be still. And the wind ceased, and there was a great calm.

40 And he said unto them, Why are ye **so**¹¹ fearful? ~~how is it that~~¹² ye have ~~no~~¹³ faith?

41 And they feared exceedingly, and said one to another, What manner of man is this, that even the wind and the sea obey him?

CHAPTER 5

1 And they came over unto the other side of the sea, into the country of the

---

¹ WH changed the word order from DISCIPLES **of him** to _his own_ DISCIPLES.

² WH omitted <u>also</u> (<u>de</u>).

³ WH changed <u>little ships</u> (<u>ploiaria</u>) to _ships_ (_ploia_). [syn]

⁴ WH changed <u>and</u> (<u>de</u>) to _and_ (_kai_).

⁵ WH changed the word order from <u>THE</u> <u>and</u> (<u>ta de</u>) to _and_ THE (_kai_ ta).

⁶ WH change <u>it</u> (**auto**) to _the ship_ (_to ploion_).

⁷ WH changed the word order from **it** NOW <u>was full</u> to _NOW was full_ **the ship**.

⁸ WH changed the word order from <u>HE</u> <u>was</u> {HIMSELF} **upon** to {HIMSELF} HE was _in_.

⁹ WH changed **upon** (<u>epi</u>) to _in_ (_en_).

¹⁰ WH changed <u>awaken</u> (**di-egeirousin**--are [**completely**] waking) to _waken_ (_egeirousin_--are waking). [prefix dropped]

¹¹ WH changed **so** (^h<u>outO</u>) to _not yet_ (^h_oupO_).

¹² WH omitted <u>how</u> (<u>pos</u>) and the implied <u>is it that</u>. [WH then read: And he said unto them, Why are ye fearful? not yet ye have faith?]

¹³ WH omitted <u>no</u> (<u>ouk</u>).

<u>**Gadarenes**</u>[1].

2   And   **<u>when he was come</u>**[2]   out   of   the   ship, immediately   there   met   him out of the **<u>tombs</u>**[3] a man with an unclean spirit,

3   Who had *his* dwelling among the tombs; and [ʌ**no longer**][4] no man could bind him, **<u>no</u>, <u>not</u>**[5] **<u>with chains</u>**[6]:

4   Because that he had been often bound with fetters and chains, and the chains had been plucked asunder by him, and the fetters broken in pieces: neither could any *man* tame him.

5   And always, night and day, he was in the **<u>mountains</u>**, and in the **<u>tombs</u>**[7], crying, and cutting himself with stones.

6   **<u>But</u>**[8] **<u>when he saw</u>**[9] Jesus afar off, he ran and worshipped him,

7   And cried with a loud voice, and **<u>said</u>**[10], What have I to do with thee, Jesus, *thou* Son of the most high God? I adjure thee by God, that thou torment me not.

8   For he said unto him, Come out of the man, *thou* unclean spirit.

9   And he asked him, What *is* thy name? And **<u>he answered</u>, <u>saying</u>**[11], My name *is* Legion: for we are many.

---

[1] WH changed <u>Gadarenes</u> (<u>Gadar</u>AnOn) to *Gerasenes* (*Geras*AnOn).

[2] WH changed <u>he having come out</u> (ex-el<del>th</del>onti <u>aut</u>O) to *he having come out* (*ex-el<del>th</del>ontos autou*). Both Aor Act Part. **<u>Dat</u>** to *Gen.* [case]

[3] WH changed <u>tombs</u> (mn<u>A</u>meiois) to *tombs* (*mnA-masi*). WH changed from the noun <u>mnemeion</u> to the noun *mnema*.

[4] WH added *no longer* (*ouketi*).

[5] WH changed **no not** (<u>oute</u>) to *neither* (*oude*).

[6] WH changed <u>with chains</u> ([h]aluse<u>sin</u>) to *with chain* (*[h]a-lusei*). **Dat** <u>Fem</u> **Plur** to *Dat Fem* **Sing**. [number]

[7] WH changed the word order from <u>MOUNTAINS, and in the TOMBS</u> to *TOMBS, and in the MOUNTAINS*.

[8] WH changed **<u>but</u> (<u>de</u>)** to *and (kai)*.

[9] WH changed the word order from <u>SEEING</u> **but** to *and SEEING*.

[10] WH changed <u>said</u> (**<u>eipe</u>**) to *says* (*legei*). **<u>Aor</u>** Act Ind to *Pres* Act Ind. [tense]

[11] WH changed <u>he **answered**, saying</u> (**apekri**<del>th</del>**A**, leg**On**) to *he says **to him** (legei autO)*.

10 And he besought him much that he would not send them away out of the country.

11 Now there was there nigh unto **the mountains**[1] a great herd of swine feeding.

12 And ~~all the devils~~[2] besought him, saying, Send us into the swine, that we may enter into them.

13 And ~~forthwith Jesus~~[3] gave them leave. And the unclean spirits went out, and entered into the swine: and the herd ran violently down a steep place into the sea, (~~[but] they were~~[4] about two thousand;) and were choked in the sea.

14 **And**[5] **they that**[6] fed

the swine[7] fled, and **told**[8] *it* in the city, and in the country. And they **went out**[9] to see what it was that was done.

15 And they come to Jesus, and see him that was possessed with the devil, and had the legion, sitting, **and**[10] clothed, and in his right mind: and they were afraid.

16 And they that saw *it* told them how it befell to him that was possessed with the devil, and *also* concerning the swine.

17 And they began to pray him to depart out of their coasts.

18 And **when he was come**[11] into the ship, he that had been possessed with the devil prayed him that he

---

[1] WH changed <u>the</u> <u>mountains</u> (**ta** or**A**) to *the mountain* (*tO orei*). **Acc** Neut **Plur** to *Dat* Neut *Sing*. [case & number]

[2] WH omitted <u>all</u> <u>the</u> <u>devils</u> (pantes [h]<u>oi</u> <u>daimones</u>) and supplied the less specific *they* contained in the verb <u>besought</u>.

[3] WH omitted <u>immediately</u> <u>the</u> <u>Jesus</u> (eut<del>h</del>eOs [h]<u>o</u> iAsous) and supplied the less specific *he* contained in the verb.

[4] WH omitted <u>they were</u> (Asan) and the untranslated <u>but</u> (<u>de</u>).

[5] WH changed **but** (**de**) to *and* (*kai*).

[6] WH changed the word order from <u>THE</u> {ones} <u>but</u> to *and THE* {ones}).

[7] WH changed **the** **swine** (<u>tous</u> **coirous**) to *them* (*autous*).

[8] WH changed <u>told</u> (an-Aggeilan) to told (*ap-Aggeilan*). [prefix changed]

[9] WH changed <u>went</u> **out** (<u>ex-</u>Al<del>th</del>on) to *went* (*Al<del>th</del>on*). [prefix dropped]

[10] WH omitted <u>and</u> (<u>kai</u>).

[11] WH changed **having** <u>come</u> (<u>embantos</u>) to *coming* (*embainontos*). **Aor** Act Part to *Pres* Act Part. [tense]

might be with him.

19 **Howbeit**[1] ~~Jesus~~[2] suffered him not, but saith unto him, Go home to thy friends, and **tell**[3] them how great things the Lord **hath done**[4] for thee, and hath had compassion on thee.

20 And he departed, and began to publish in Decapolis how great things Jesus had done for him: and all *men* did marvel.

21 And when Jesus was passed over again by ship unto the other side, much people gathered unto him: and he was nigh unto the sea.

22 And, ~~behold~~[5], there cometh one of the rulers of the synagogue, Jairus by name; and when he saw him, he fell at his feet,

23 And **besought**[6] him

greatly, saying, My little daughter lieth at the point of death: *I pray thee*, come and lay thy hands on her, **that**[7] she may be healed; and **she shall live**[8].

24 And *Jesus* went with him; and much people followed him, and thronged him.

25 And a ~~certain~~[9] woman, which had an issue of blood twelve years,

26 And had suffered many things of many physicians, and had spent all that she had, and was nothing bettered, but rather grew worse,

27 When she had heard of Jesus, came in the press behind, and touched his garment.

28 For she said, [ʌ**if**][10] **If I may touch**[11]_but his clothes, I shall be whole.

---

[1] WH changed **but** (**de**) to *and* (**kai**).

[2] WH omitted the Jesus (ʰ**o** iAsous).

[3] WH changed tell {**again**} (**an**-aggeilon) to *tell* {**from**} *(ap-aggeilon)*. [prefix changed]

[4] WH changed **did** (e-poiAse) to *has done* (pe-poiAke). **Aor** Act Ind to *Pf* Act Ind of *poieO*. [tense]

[5] WH omitted behold (idou).

[6] WH changed **was** beseeching (pare-kalei) to *is beseech-*

ing (para-kalei). **Impf** Act Ind to *Pres* Act *Ind*. [tense]

[7] WH changed that (ʰ**opOs**) to *that* (ʰ**ina**).

[8] WH changed she shall live (zAsetai) to *she shall live* (zAsA). They changed a Fut **Mid-D** Ind to a Fut *Act* Ind. [voice]

[9] WH omitted certain (tis).

[10] WH added *if (ean)*.

[11] WH changed the word order from IF [kan] the garments of him I MAY TOUCH to *If* [ean] *I MAY TOUCH BUT* [kan] *the garments of him.*

29 And straightway the fountain of her blood was dried up; and she felt in *her* body that she was healed of that plague.

30 And Jesus, immediately knowing in himself that virtue had gone out of him, turned him about in the press, and said, Who touched my clothes?

31 And his disciples said unto him, Thou seest the multitude thronging thee, and sayest thou, Who touched me?

32 And he looked round about to see her that had done this thing.

33 But the woman fearing and trembling, knowing what was done ~~in~~[1] her, came and fell down before him, and told him all the truth.

34 And he said unto her, Daughter, thy faith hath made thee whole; go in peace, and be whole of thy plague.

35 While he yet spake, there came from the ruler of the synagogue's *house certain* which said, Thy daughter is dead: why troublest thou the Master any further?

36 ~~As soon as~~[2] Jesus **heard**[3] the word that was spoken, he saith unto the ruler of the synagogue, Be not afraid, only believe.

37 And he suffered no man to follow [∧**with**][4] **him**[5], save Peter, and James, and John the brother of James.

38 And **he cometh**[6] to the house of the ruler of the synagogue, and seeth the tumult, and them that wept and wailed greatly.

39 And when he was come in, he saith unto them, Why make ye this ado, and weep? the damsel is not dead, but sleepeth.

40 And they laughed him

---

[2] WH kept the <u>de</u> (<u>but</u>) but omitted the <u>eu~~the~~Os</u> (<u>immediately</u>) in the word combination translated <u>as soon as</u>.

[3] WH changed <u>having **heard**</u> (<u>akousas</u>) to *having **ignored*** (***par-**akousas*). Both Aor Act Part. [prefix added]

[4] WH added the preposition *with* (*met'*).

[5] WH changed <u>him</u> (<u>aut**O**</u>) to *him* (*autou*). **Dat** to **Gen**. [case]

[6] WH changed **he** comes (<u>ercetai</u>) to ***they** come* (*er-contai*). Pres <u>M/P-D</u> 3rd **Sing** to *Pres Mid Ind 3rd* **Plur**. [number]

---

[1] WH omitted <u>in</u> (<u>epi</u>--upon) and let the case of <u>her</u> supply the preposition.

to scorn. But when **he**[1] had put **them all**[2] out, he taketh the father and the mother of the damsel, and them that were with him, and entereth in where the damsel was ~~lying~~[3].

41 And he took the damsel by the hand, and said unto her, Talitha cumi; which is, being interpreted, Damsel, I say unto thee, arise.

42 And straightway the damsel arose, and walked; for she was *of the age* of twelve years. And they were astonished [∧**immediately**][4] with a great astonishment.

43 And he charged them straitly that no man should know it; and commanded that something should be given her to eat.

CHAPTER 6

1 And he went out from thence, and **came**[5] into his own country; and his disciples follow him.

2 And when the sabbath day was come, he began to teach in the synagogue: and [**the**][6] many hearing *him* were astonished, saying, From whence hath this *man* these things? and what wisdom *is* this which is given **unto him**[7], ~~that~~[8] even such [∧**the**][9] mighty works **are wrought**[10] by his hands?

3 Is not this the carpenter, the son of Mary, [**but**][11] the brother of James, and Joses, and of Juda, and Simon? and are not his sisters

---

[1] WH changed he (*ʰo*) to *himself* (*autos*) as the subject of the Aor Act Part. **Personal** Pro to *Intensive* Pro.

[2] WH changed all {of them} (**apantas**) to *all* {of them} (*pantas*). [prefix dropped]

[3] WH omitted lying (anakeimenon).

[4] WH added *immediately* (eu~~th~~hus).

[5] WH changed came (**Al~~th~~hen**) to *is coming* (*ercetai*). **Aor Act** Ind to a *Pres Mid/Pas* Ind. [tense & voice]

[6] In their margin, WH added *the* (*ʰoi*).

[7] WH changed unto **him** (autO) to *unto* **this** {one} (*toutO*).

[8] WH omitted that (*ʰoti*).

[9] WH added *the* (*ʰai*).

[10] WH changed **are** being wrought (**ginon**tai) to *being wrought* (*ginomenai*). Pres M/P-D **Ind** to a Pres Mid *Part*. [mood]

[11] WH changed the untranslated **but** (**de**) to *and* (*kai*).

here with us? And they were offended at him.

4   **But**[1] Jesus **said**[2] unto them, A prophet is not without honour, but in his own country, and among his own kin [ʌof him][3], and in his own house.

5   And he could there do no mighty work, save that he laid his hands upon a few sick folk, and healed *them*.

6   And he marvelled because of their unbelief. And he went round about the villages, teaching.

7   And he called *unto him* the twelve, and began to send them forth by two and two; and gave them power over unclean spirits;

8   And commanded them that they should take nothing for *their* journey, save a staff only; no **scrip**, no **bread**[4], no

money in *their* purse:

9   But *be* shod with sandals; and not **put on**[5] two coats.

10   And he said unto them, In what place soever ye enter into an house, there abide till ye depart from that place.

11   And   **whosoever**[6] [ʌplace][7] **shall** not **receive**[8] you, nor hear you, when ye depart thence, shake off the dust under your feet for a testimony against them. ~~Verily I say unto you, It shall be more tolerable for Sodom and Gomorrha in the day of judgment, than for that~~

---

[1] WH changed **and** (**kai**) to *but* (*de*).

[2] WH added the re-movable *nu* so that said (elege) became *said* (elege**n**). [Not a significant change.]

[3] WH added *of him* (*autou*) in harmony with the KJV interpretation of the definite article. [The KJV translated **the** kin (tois suggenesi) as **his own** kin.]

[4] WH changed the word or-

der from SCRIP, no BREAD to *BREAD, no SCRIP.*

[5] WH changed **to** put on (en-dusas~~thai~~) to *might put on* (*endusAs~~the~~*) Aor Mid **Inf** to Aor Mid *Sub*. [mood]

[6] WH changed whoever ([h]o-soi an) to *whoever* (*[h]os an*). Both Nom Masc. **Plur** to *Sing*. **Correlative** Pro to *Relative* Pro. [number]

[7] WH added *place* (*topos*).

[8] WH changed **might** not receive (mA dexOntai) to *is not receiving* (*mA dexAtai*). **Aor** Mid **Sub** to *Pres* Mid/Pass **Ind**. [tense & mood]

~~eity.~~ [1]

12 And they went out, and **preached**[2] that men should repent.

13 And they cast out many devils, and anointed with oil many that were sick, and healed _them_.

14 And king Herod heard _of him_; (for his name was spread abroad:) and **he said**[3], That John the Baptist **was risen**[4] **from the dead**[5], and

therefore mighty works do shew forth themselves in him.

15 [∧**but**][6] Others said, That it is Elias. And others said, That ~~it is~~[7] a prophet, ~~or~~[8] as one of the prophets.

16 But when Herod heard _thereof_, he **said**[9], [~~that~~][10] It ~~is~~ John, whom I beheaded: ~~he~~[11] is risen ~~from the dead~~[12].

17 For Herod himself had sent forth and laid hold upon John, and bound him in [~~the~~][13] prison for Herodias' sake, his brother Philip's wife: for he had married her.

18 For John had said unto Herod, It is not lawful for thee to have thy brother's wife.

19 Therefore Herodias had a quarrel against him, and

---

[1] WH omitted <u>verily</u> <u>I say unto you</u> <u>it shall be</u> <u>more tolerable</u> <u>for Sodom</u> <u>and</u> <u>Gomorrha</u> <u>in</u> <u>the day</u> <u>of judgment</u> <u>than</u> <u>for that</u> <u>city</u> (amAn legO ʰumin anektoteron estai sodomois <u>A</u> gomorrois en ʰAmera kriseOs <u>A</u> <u>tA</u> polei ekeina).

[2] WH changed **were preaching** (ekArussan) to _preached_ (_ekAruxan_). **Impf** Act Ind to _Aor_ Act Ind. [tense]

[3] In their margin, WH changed <u>he said</u> (elegen) to _he was saying_ (elegon). **Aor Mid** Ind to _Impf Act_ Ind. [tense & voice]

[4] WH changed **was risen** (**Ager~~thA~~**) to _has risen_ (_egAgertai_). **Aor** Pass Ind to a _Pf_ Pass Ind. [tense]

[5] WH changed the word order from <u>FROM</u> <u>THE DEAD</u> **was** <u>risen</u> to _has_ risen _FROM_

THE DEAD.

[6] WH added _but_ (_de_).

[7] WH omitted <u>it is</u> (estin).

[8] WH omitted <u>or</u> (A).

[9] WH changed <u>said</u> (eipen) to _was saying_ (elegen). **Aor** Act Ind changed to _Impf_ Act Ind. [tense]

[10] WH omitted the untranslated <u>that</u> (ʰoti).

[11] WH omitted the intensive <u>he</u> {himself} (autos).

[12] WH omitted <u>from</u> <u>the dead</u> (ek nekrOn).

[13] WH omitted the untranslated <u>the</u> (tA).

would have killed him; but she could not:

20 For Herod feared John, knowing that he was a just man and an holy, and observed him; and when he heard him, **he did**[1] many things, and heard him gladly.

21 And when a convenient day was come, that Herod on his birthday **made**[2] a supper to his lords, high captains, and chief *estates* of Galilee;

22 And when the daughter **of the said**[3] [the][4] Herodias came in, and danced, and **pleased**[5] Herod and them

that sat with him, [ʌbut][6] the king **said**[7] unto the damsel, Ask of me whatsoever thou wilt, and I will give *it* thee.

23 And he sware unto her, Whatsoever thou shalt ask of me, I will give *it* thee, unto the half of my kingdom.

24 **And**[8] [the][9] she went forth, and said unto her mother, What **shall I ask**[10]? And she said, The head of John the **Baptist**[11].

25 And she came in straightway with haste unto the king, and asked, saying, I will that thou give **me**[12] by

---

[1] Although they retained it in their margin, WH changed he **did** (epoiei) to he *was uncertain of* (Aporei). Both Impf Act Ind. **poieO** to *aporeO*.

[2] WH changed **having** made (epoiei) to *made* (*epoiAse*). Aor Act **Part** to Aor Act **Ind.** [mood]

[3] In their margin, WH changed of her (autAs) to *of him* (*autou*). Gen **Fem** Sing to Gen *Masc* Sing. [gender].

[4] In their margin, WH omitted the untranslated the (tAs). [These changes in of the said [the] are now made in the WH text.]

[5] WH changed **having** pleased (aresasAs) to *pleased* (*Arese*). Aor Act

Part to Aor Act **Ind**. [mood]

[6] WH added *but* (*de*).

[7] WH changed the word order from SAID the king to *the king SAID*.

[8] WH changed **but** (**de**) to *and* (*kai*).

[9] WH omitted the untranslated the ([h]A).

[10] WH changed **shall** I ask (aitAsomai) to *might I ask* (*aitAsOmai*). **Fut** Mid **Ind** to *Aor* Mid *Sub*. [tense & mood]

[11] WH changed Baptist (baptistou) to *Baptist* (*baptizontos*).

[12] WH changed the word order from TO ME thou give right now to *right now thou give TO ME*.

and by in a charger the head of John the Baptist.

26 And the king was exceeding sorry; *yet* for his oath's sake, and for their sakes which **sat with him**[1], he would not reject her.

27 **And**[2] **[the]**[3] immediately the king sent an executioner, and commanded his head **to be brought**[4]: and he went and beheaded him in the prison,

28 And brought his head in a charger, and gave it to the damsel: and the damsel gave it to her mother.

29 And when his disciples heard *of it*, they came and took up his corpse, and laid it in a tomb.

30 And the apostles gathered themselves together unto Jesus, and told him all things, **both**[5] what they had done, and what they had taught.

31 And **he said**[6] unto them, Come ye yourselves apart into a desert place, and **rest**[7] a while: for there were many coming and going, and they had no leisure so much as to eat.

32 And they departed into a desert place [∧**in**][8] **by ship**[9] privately.

33 And **the people**[10] saw them departing, and many knew him, and ran afoot thither out of all cities, and outwent them, **and came together unto him**[11].

34 And Jesus, when he came out, saw much people,

---

[1] WH changed feasting **together** (**sus**-ana-keimenous) to *feasting* (*ana-keimenous*). Both Pres M/P Part. [prefix dropped]

[2] WH changed and (**de**) to *and* (*kai*).

[3] WH omitted the untranslated the (ᵸo).

[4] WH changed to **be brought** (enec**th**Anai) to *to bring* (*enegkai*). Aor **Pass** Inf to Aor *Act* Inf. [voice]

[5] WH omitted both (kai).

[6] WH changed he said (**eipen**) to *he says* (*legei*). **Aor** Act Ind to *Pres* Act. [tense]

[7] WH changed **be rest**ing (ana-pauest**he**) to *rest* (*ana-pausas*t*he*). **Pres** Mid Imp to *Aor* Mid Imp. [tense]

[8] WH added in (en).

[9] WH changed the word order from into a desert place {in} THE SHIP to *IN THE SHIP into a desert place.*

[10] WH omitted the people (ᵸoi ocloi) and forced the verb to supply the subject *they.*

[11] WH omitted and came together unto him (kai su-nAl**th**on pros auton).

and was moved with compassion toward them, because they were as sheep not having a shepherd: and he began to teach them many things.

35 And when the day was now far spent, his disciples came unto him, and **said**[1], This is a desert place, and now the time *is* far passed:

36 Send them away, that they may go into the country round about, and into the villages, and buy themselves ~~bread: for they have nothing~~[2] to eat.

37 He answered and said unto them, Give ye them to eat. And they say unto him, Shall we go and buy two hundred pennyworth of bread, and **give**[3] them to eat?

38 He saith unto them, How many loaves have ye? go **and**[4] see. And when they knew, they say, Five, and two

fishes.

39 And he commanded them **to make** all **sit down**[5] by companies upon the green grass.

40 And they sat down in ranks, by hundreds, and by fifties.

41 And when he had taken the five loaves and the two fishes, he looked up to heaven, and blessed, and brake the loaves, and gave *them* to ~~his~~[6] disciples to set before them; and the two fishes divided he among them all.

42 And they did all eat, and were filled.

43 And they took up twelve **baskets**[7] **full**[8] **of the**

---

[1] WH changed **say** (<u>legousin</u>) to *were saying* (*elegon*). **Pres** Act Ind to *Impf* Act Ind. [tense]

[2] WH omitted <u>bread</u> <u>for</u> <u>they</u> <u>have</u> <u>nothing</u> (<u>artous</u> <u>gar</u> <u>ouk</u> <u>ecousin</u>).

[3] WH changed **might** <u>give</u> (<u>dOmen</u>) to *will* <u>give</u> (*dOsomen*). **Aor** Act **Sub** to *Fut* Act *Ind*. [tense & mood]

[4] WH omitted <u>and</u> (<u>kai</u>).

[5] WH changed <u>to make</u> <u>sit</u> <u>down</u> (<u>ana-klinai</u>) to *to be made to sit down* (*ana-klithAnai*). Aor **Act** Inf to Aor *Pass* Inf. [voice]

[6] WH omitted <u>of him</u> (<u>autou</u>) from the words <u>the</u> <u>disciples</u> <u>of him</u>.

[7] WH changed <u>baskets</u> (<u>kofinous</u>) to *of baskets* (*kofinOn*). **Acc** Masc Plur to *Gen* Masc Plur. [case]

[8] WH changed <u>full</u> (<u>plAreis</u>) to *full* (*plArOmata*). Acc **Masc** Plur to Acc *Neut* Plur. [gender]

fragments[1], and of the fishes.

44 And they that did eat of the loaves were ~~about~~[2] five thousand men.

45 And straightway he constrained his disciples to get into the ship, and to go to the other side before unto Bethsaida, while he **sent away**[3] the people.

46 And when he had sent them away, he departed into a mountain to pray.

47 And when even was come, the ship was in the midst of the sea, and he alone on the land.

48 And he **saw**[4] them toiling in rowing; for the wind was contrary unto them: ~~and~~[5] about the fourth watch of the night he cometh unto them, walking upon the sea, and would have passed by them.

49 But when they saw him **walking**[6] upon the sea, they supposed [ʌthat][7] **it had been**[8] a spirit, and cried out:

50 For they all saw him, and were troubled. [ʌthe][9] **And**[10] **immediately**[11] he talked with them, and saith unto them, Be of good cheer: it is I; be not afraid.

51 And he went up unto them into the ship; and the wind ceased: and they were sore amazed in themselves ~~beyond measure~~[12], ~~and wondered~~[13].

52 For they considered not *the miracle* of the loaves:

---

[1] WH changed **of** fragments (klasmat**On**) to *fragments* (*klasmata*). **Gen** Neut Plur to *Acc* Neut Plur. [case]

[2] WH omitted about (ʰOsei).

[3] WH changed sent away (apo-lus**A**) to *sends away* (*apo-lusei*). **Aor** Act **Sub** to *Pres* Act *Ind*. [tense & mood]

[4] WH changed saw (**eiden**) to *having seen* (*idOn*). Aor Act **Ind** of to Aor Act *Part*. [mood]

[5] WH omitted and (kai).

[6] WH changed the word order from WALKING upon the sea to *upon the sea WALKING*.

[7] WH added *that* (ʰoti).

[8] WH changed **to be** being (**einai**) to *it is being* (*esti*). Pres NV *Inf* to Pres Act *Ind*. [mood]

[9] WH added *the* (ʰo).

[10] WH changed **and** (**kai**) to *but* (*de*).

[11] WH changed **immediately** (eu~~th~~e**Os**) to *suddenly* (*eu~~th~~us*).

[12] WH omitted beyond measure (ek perissou).

[13] WH omitted and wondered (kai e~~th~~aumazon).

for[1] their heart **was**[2] hardened.

53 And when they had passed over, **they came**[3] into the land [∧**into**][4] of Gennesaret, and drew to the shore.

54 And when they were come out of the ship, straightway they knew him,

55 **And ran through**[5] that whole **region round about**[6], ∧**and**[7] began to carry about in beds those that were sick, where they heard he was [there][8].

---

56 And whithersoever he entered, into villages, or [∧**into**][9] cities, [∧**into**][10] or country, they laid the sick in the streets, and besought him that they might touch if it were but the border of his garment: and as many as **touched**[11] him were made whole.

CHAPTER 7

1 Then came together unto him the Pharisees, and certain of the scribes, which came from Jerusalem.

2 And when they saw [∧**that**][12] some of his disciples **eat**[13] [∧**the**][14] bread with defiled, that is to say, with unwashen, hands, ~~they found fault~~[15].

---

[1] WH changed **for** (**gar**) to *but* (*alla*).
[2] WH changed the word order from WAS **for** to *but WAS*.
[3] WH changed the word order from THEY CAME upon the land to *upon the land THEY CAME into*.
[4] WH added *into* (*eis*).
[5] WH changed **having run** through (**peri-dramontes**) to *they ran through* (*peri-edramon*). Aor Act **Part** to Aor Act **Ind**. [mood]
[6] WH changed region **round about** (**peri-cOron**) to *region* (*cOran*). [prefix dropped & Adj to Noun]
[7] WH added *and* (*kai*) as the KJV supplied.
[8] WH omitted the untranslated there (ekei) in the phrase that there he is (ʰoti

---

ekei esti).
[9] WH added *into* (*eis*).
[10] WH added *into* (*eis*).
[11] WH changed **were** touch**ing** (ʰAₚ̱stonto) to *touched* (ʰAₚ̱s anto). **Impf** M/P Ind to *Aor* Mid Ind. [tense]
[12] WH added *that* (ʰoti).
[13] WH changed eating (esthiontas) to *they eat* (esthiousi). Pres Act **Part** to Pres Act **Ind**. [mood]
[14] WH added *the* (*tous*).
[15] WH omitted they found fault (ememṣanto).

3 For the Pharisees, and all the Jews, except they wash *their* hands oft, eat not, holding the tradition of the elders.

4 And *when they come* from the market, except **they wash**[1], they eat not. And many other things there be, which they have received to hold, *as* the washing of cups, and pots, brasen vessels, ~~and of tables~~[2].

5 **Then**[3] the Pharisees and scribes asked him, Why walk not thy disciples according to the tradition of the elders, but eat bread with **unwashen**[4] hands?

6 He ~~answered and~~[5] said unto them, Well hath Esaias prophesied of you hypocrites, as it is written, This people honoureth me with *their* lips, but their heart is far from me.

7 Howbeit in vain do they worship me, teaching *for* doctrines the commandments of men.

8 ~~For~~[6] laying aside the commandment of God, ye hold the tradition of men, ~~*as* the washing of pots and cups: and many other such like things ye do~~[7].

9 And he said unto them, Full well ye reject the commandment of God, that ye may keep your own tradition.

10 For Moses said, Honour thy father and thy mother; and, whoso curseth father or mother, let him die the death:

11 But ye say, If a man shall say to his father or mother, *It is* Corban, that is to say, a gift, by whatsoever thou mightest be profited by me; *he shall be free.*

12 ~~And~~[8] ye suffer him no more to do ought for his father or his mother;

---

[1] In their margin, WH changed they **wash** (**baptisOntai**) to *they sprinkle* (*ʰrantisOntai*).

[2] WH omitted and of tables (kai klinOn) in their text, but retained them in their margin.

[3] WH changed **then** (**epeita**) to *and* (*kai*).

[4] WH changed **unwashen** (**aniptois**) to *common* (*koinais*).

[5] WH omitted answered and the supplied and (apokritheis).

[6] WH omitted for (gar).

[7] WH omitted as the washing of pots and cups and many other such like things ye do (baptismous xestOn kai potAriOn kai alla paromoia toiauta polla poieite).

[8] WH omitted and (kai).

13 Making the word of God of none effect through your tradition, which ye have delivered: and many such like things do ye.

14 And when he had called **all**[1] the people *unto him*, he said unto them, Hearken unto me every one *of you*, and understand:

15 There is nothing from without a man, that entering into him can defile him: but the things **which come out**[2] **of**[3] **him**[4], ~~those~~[5] are they that defile the man.

16 ~~If any man have ears to hear, let him hear~~[6].

17 And when he was entered into the house from the people, his disciples asked him ~~concerning~~[7] **the parable**[8].

18 And he saith unto them, Are ye so without understanding also? Do ye not perceive, that whatsoever thing from without entereth into the man, *it* cannot defile him;

19 Because it entereth not into his heart, but into the belly, and goeth out into the draught, **purging**[9] all meats?

20 And he said, That which cometh out of the man, that defileth the man.

21 For from within, out of the heart of men, proceed evil thoughts, **adulteries**[10], fornications, murders,

22 Thefts, covetousness, wickedness, deceit, lasciviousness, an evil eye, blasphemy, pride, foolishness:

---

[1] WH changed all (<u>panta</u>) to *again* (*palin*).

[2] WH changed the word order from <u>the</u> [things] COMING OUT **from** **him** to *the* [things] *out of the man* COMING OUT.

[3] WH changed **of** (**ap'**) to *out of* (*ek*).

[4] WH changed **him** (<u>autou</u>) to *the man* (*tou anthrOpou*), and placed the verb last. [wo]

[5] WH omited <u>those</u> (<u>ekeina</u>)

[6] WH omitted <u>if anyone has ears to hear let him hear</u> (<u>ei tis ecei Ota akouein akouetO</u>) in their text, but retained the words in their margin.

---

[7] WH omitted <u>concerning</u> (<u>peri</u>).

[8] WH changed <u>the parable</u> (<u>tAs parabolAs</u>) to *the parable* (*tAn parabolAs*). **Gen** to *Acc.* [case]

[9] WH changed <u>purging</u> (<u>katharizon</u>) to *purging* (*katharizOn*). Both Pres Act Part. Nom **Neut** Sing to Nom *Masc* Sing. [gender]

[10] WH changed the word order from ADULTERIES, fornications, murders, thefts to *fornications, murders, thefts, ADULTERIES.*

23 All these evil things come from within, and defile the man.

24 **And**[1] from thence he arose, and went into the borders of Tyre and **Sidon**[2], and entered into [~~the~~][3] an house, and would have no man know *it*: but he could not be hid.

25 **For**[4] [∧**immediately**][5] a *certain* woman, whose young daughter had an unclean spirit, **heard**[6] of him, and came and fell at his feet:

26 The woman was a Greek, a Syrophenician by nation; and she besought him that he would cast forth the devil out of her daughter.

27 **But**[7] ~~Jesus~~[8] **said**[9] unto her, Let the children first be filled: for it is not meet to take the children's bread, and to cast *it* unto the dogs.

28 And she answered and said unto him, Yes, Lord: ~~yet~~[10] the dogs under the table eat of the children's crumbs.

29 And he said unto her, For this saying go thy way; the devil is gone out of thy daughter.

30 And when she was come to her house, she found **the devil gone out, and**[11] **her daughter**[12] **laid**[13] upon

[1] WH changed **and** (**kai**) to *but* (*de*).
[2] WH omitted and Sidon (kai sidOnos) in their margin.
[3] WH omitted the untranslated the (tAn).
[4] WH changed for (gar) to *but* (*alla*).
[5] WH added *immediately* (eu~~th~~us).
[6] WH changed the word order from HAVING HEARD **for** woman to *but immediately* HAVING HEARD woman.
[7] WH changed **but** (**de**) to *and* (*kai*).
[8] WH omitted the Jesus ([h]o iAsous) and forced the verb

to supply the subject *he*.
[9] WH changed **said** (**eipen**) to *was saying* (*elegen*). **Aor** Act Ind to *Impf* Act Ind. [tense]
[10] WH omitted for (gar) the second word in a two word compound translated yet (kai gar).
[11] WH changed the word order from THE DEMON HAVING GONE OUT AND the **daughter** laid upon the bed to *the child laid upon the bed* AND THE DEMON HAVING GONE OUT.
[12] WH changed the **daughter** (tAn ~~th~~ugatera) to *the child* (*to paidion*).
[13] WH changed laid (beblAmenAn) to *laid* (*beblAmenon*). Both Pf Pass Part. Acc **Fem** Sing to Acc *Neut* Sing. [gender]

the bed.[1]

31 And again, departing from the coasts of Tyre **and**[2] [∧**through**][3] Sidon, **he came**[4] **unto**[5] the sea of Galilee, through the midst of the coasts of Decapolis.

32 And they bring unto him one that was deaf, ∧**and**[6] had an impediment in his speech; and they beseech him to put his hand upon him.

33 And he took him aside from the multitude, and put his fingers into his ears, and he spit, and touched his tongue;

34 And looking up to heaven, he sighed, and saith unto him, Ephphatha, that is, Be opened.

35 And ~~straightway~~[7] his ears were opened, and the string of his tongue was loosed, and he spake plain.

36 And he charged them that they should tell no man: but the more he charged them, so much the more a great deal they published *it*;

37 And were beyond measure astonished, saying, He hath done all things well: he maketh both the deaf to hear, and ~~the~~[8] dumb to speak.

CHAPTER 8

1 In those days the multitude being **very great**[9], and having nothing to eat, ~~Jesus~~[10] called his disciples *unto him*, and saith unto them,

2 I have compassion on the multitude, because they have now been with me three **days**[11], and have nothing to eat:

3 And if I send them away fasting to their own houses, they will faint by the

---

[1] WH changed <u>the bed</u> (tAs klinAs) to *the bed* (*tАn linАn*). **Gen** to *Acc.* [case]

[2] WH omitted <u>and</u> (<u>kai</u>).

[3] WH added *through* (*dia*).

[4] WH changed the word order from **and** Sidon HE CAME **toward** to *HE CAME* **through** *Sidon* **into**

[5] WH changed <u>unto</u> (**pros**) to *into* (**eis**).

[6] WH added *and* (*kai*) as the KJV supplied.

[7] WH omitted <u>straightway</u> (eu~~th~~eОs).

[8] WH omitted <u>the</u> (<u>tous</u>).

[9] WH changed **very great** (<u>pampollou</u>) to *again many* (*palin pollou*).

[10] WH omitted <u>the</u> Jesus (^h<u>o</u> <u>iAsous</u>).

[11] WH changed *days* (^hAm-<u>eras</u>) to *days* (^h*Amerai*). **Acc** to *Nom.* [case]

way: **for**[1] **divers**[2] of them came **[ˆfrom]**[3] from far.

4 And his disciples answered him, From whence can a man satisfy these *men* with bread here in the wilderness?

5 And he asked them, How many loaves have ye? And they said, Seven.

6 And **he commanded**[4] the people to sit down on the ground: and he took the seven loaves, and gave thanks, and brake, and gave to his disciples to set before *them*; and they did set *them* before the people.

7 And they had a few small fishes: and he blessed **[ˆthem]**[5], and commanded **to set them**[6] **also**[7] **before**[8] *them*.

8 **So**[9] **they did eat**[10], and were filled: and they took up of the broken *meat* that was left seven baskets.

9 And ~~they that had eaten~~[11] were about four thousand: and he sent them away.

10 And straightway he entered into a ship with his disciples, and came into the parts of Dalmanutha.

11 And the Pharisees came forth, and began to question with him, seeking of him a sign from heaven, tempting him.

12 And he sighed deeply in his spirit, and saith, Why

---

[1] WH changed **for** (**gar**) to *and* (*kai*).

[2] WH changed the word order from SOME **for** to *and SOME*.

[3] WH added *from* (*apo*) just before from afar (makrothen--from afar or afar).

[4] WH changed he commanded (parAggeile) *to he commands* (*paraggellei*). **Aor** Act Ind to *Pres* Act Ind. [tense]

[5] WH added *them* (*auta*).

[6] WH changed them (auta) to *these* (*tauta*). **Personal** Pro

to *Demonstrative* Pro.

[7] WH changed the word order from commanded TO SET BEFORE ALSO **them** to *commanded ALSO these TO BE SETTING BEFORE*.

[8] WH changed to set before (paratheinai) to *to be setting before* (*paratithenai*). **Aor** Act Inf to *Pres* Act Inf. [tense]

[9] WH changed **so** (**de**) to *and* (*kai*).

[10] WH changed the word order from THEY ATE **but** to *and THEY ATE*.

[11] WH omitted they that had eaten (ʰoi fagontes).

doth this generation **seek af-**
ter[1] **a sign**[2]? verily I say unto
you, There shall no sign be
given unto this generation.

13 And he left them, and
entering ~~into the ship~~[3]
again[4] departed to the other
side.

14 Now *the disciples*[5] had
forgotten to take bread, neither had they in the ship with
them more than one loaf.

15 And he charged them,
saying, Take heed, beware of
the leaven of the Pharisees,
and *of* the leaven of Herod.

16 And they reasoned
among themselves, saying, *It*
is because **we have**[6] no
bread.

---

[1] WH changed <u>doth seek **af-**
ter</u> (**epi**-zAtei) to *doth seek*
(*zAtei*). [prefix dropped]

[2] WH changed the word or-
der from <u>SIGN</u> <u>doth seek **af-**</u>
ter to *doth seek SIGN*.

[3] WH omitted <u>into the ship</u>
(<u>eis to ploion</u>).

[4] WH changed the word or-
der from <u>entering AGAIN **into**</u>
the ship to *AGAIN entering*.

[5] WH omitted <u>the disciples</u>
(<u>hoi mathAtai</u>), words that
the KJV put in italics.

[6] In their margin, WH
changed **we** have (<u>ecomen</u>)
to *they have* (*ecousi*). [per-
son]

---

17 And when Jesus knew
it, he saith unto them, Why
reason ye, because ye have
no bread? perceive ye not
yet, neither understand? have
ye your heart ~~yet~~[7] hardened?

18 Having eyes, see ye
not? and having ears, hear ye
not? and do ye not remem-
ber?

19 When I brake the five
loaves among five thousand,
how many baskets full of
fragments took ye up? They
say unto him, Twelve.

20 And when the seven
among four thousand, how
many baskets full of fragments took ye up? **And they**
said[8] [∧**to him**][9], Seven.

21 And he said unto them,
How is it that ye do **not**[10]
understand?

22 And **he cometh**[11] to
Bethsaida; and they bring a
blind man unto him, and besought him to touch him.

---

[7] WH omitted <u>yet</u> (<u>eti</u>).

[8] WH changed **but** <u>they</u> <u>said</u>
(<u>ho de eipon</u>) to *and they say*
(<u>kai legousin</u>).

[9] WH added *to him* (*autO*).

[10] WH changed **how** <u>NOT</u>
(<u>pOs ou</u>) to *NOT yet* (*oupO*).

[11] WH changed **he** comes
(<u>ercetai</u>) to *they come* (*er-*
contai). Both Pres M/P Ind.
3rd **Sing** to 3rd **Plur**. [number]

23 And he took the blind man by the hand, and **led**[1] him out of the town; and when he had spit on his eyes, and put his hands upon him, he asked him if **he saw**[2] ought.

24 And he looked up, and said, I see men [ᴧ**that**][3] as trees, walking.

25 After that he put *his* hands again upon his eyes, and ~~made him~~[4] **look up**[5]: and he was restored, and **saw**[6] **every man**[7] clearly.

---

[1] WH changed **led** out (ex-Agagen) to *carried* out (*ex-Anegken*).

[2] WH changed **he sees** (blepei) to **you** see (*blepeis*). Both Pres Act Ind. **3**ʳᵈ Pers Sing to **2**ⁿᵈ Pers Sing. [person]

[3] WH added *that* (ʰoti).

[4] WH omitted made him (epoiAsen auton).

[5] WH changed **to look up** (**ana**-blesai) to *opened his eyes wide* (*di-eblese*). Aor Act **Inf** to Aor Act **Ind**. [mood]

[6] WH changed saw (aneblese) to *was seeing* (eneblepe). **Aor** Act Ind to *Impf* Act Ind. [tense]

[7] WH changed every man (ʰapantas) to *every man* (ʰa-panta). Acc **Masc** Plur to

26 And he sent him away to [~~the~~][8] his house, saying, Neither go into the town, ~~nor tell *it* to any in the town~~[9].

27 And Jesus went out, and his disciples, into the towns of Caesarea Philippi: and by the way he asked his disciples, saying unto them, Whom do men say that I am?

28 And they **answered**[10] [ᴧ**to him saying**][11], John the Baptist: but some *say*, Elias; and others, One of the prophets.

29 And **he saith**[12] **unto them**[13], But whom say ye

Acc *Neut* Plur. [gender]

[8] WH omitted the (ton) from into the house of him (eis ton oikon autou).

[9] WH omitted nor tell [it] to any in the town (mAde eipAs tini en takOmA).

[10] WH changed **answered** (**apekrithAsan**) to *said* (*eipon*). [syn]

[11] WH added *to him saying* (*autO legontes*).

[12] WH changed he says (**legei**) to *he was saying* (*epArOta*). **Pres** Act Ind of **legO** to *Impf* Act Ind of *epe-rotaO*. [syn]

[13] WH changed unto them (auto**is**) to *unto them* (*aut-ous*). **Dat** to *Acc*. [case]

that I am? ~~And~~[1] Peter answereth and saith unto him,
Thou art the Christ.

30 And he charged them
that they should tell no man
of him.

31 And he began to teach
them, that the Son of man
must suffer many things, and
be rejected **of**[2] the elders, and
of ∧**the**[3] chief priests, and
[∧**the**][4] scribes, and be killed,
and after three days rise
again.

32 And he spake that say-
ing openly. And Peter took
him, and began to rebuke
him.

33 But when he had
turned about and looked on
his disciples, he rebuked Peter, [∧**and**][5] **saying**[6], Get
thee behind me, Satan: for
thou savourest not the things
that be of God, but the things
that be of men.

34 And when he had called
the people *unto him* with his
disciples also, he said unto
them, **Whosoever**[7] will come
after me, let him deny himself, and take up his cross,
and follow me.

35 For whosoever will
save his life shall lose it; but
whosoever shall lose his life
for my sake and the gospel's,
~~the same~~[8] shall save it.

36 For what **shall it
profit**[9] a man, ~~if~~[10] **he shall
gain**[11] the whole world, and
lose[12] his own soul?

37 **Or**[13] **what**[14] shall a

---

[1] WH omitted <u>and</u> (<u>de</u>).

[2] WH changed **of** (<u>apo</u>) to *by*
(**ʰupo**).

[3] WH added *the* (*ton*) as the
KJV supplied it.

[4] WH added *the* (*ton*).

[5] WH added *and* (*kai*).

[6] WH changed <u>say</u>**ing** (<u>le-
gOn</u>) to *he says* (*legei*). Pres
Act **Part** to Pres Act *Ind.*
[mood]

[7] WH changed **whosoever**
(**ʰ**<u>ostis</u>) to *if anyone* (*ei tis*).

[8] WH omitted <u>the same</u> (ʰ<u>ou-
tos</u>).

[9] WH changed **shall** it profit
(Ofel**A**sei) to *is it profiting*
(*Ofelei*). **Fut** Act Ind to *Pres*
Act Ind.

[10] WH omitted <u>if</u> (<u>ean</u>).

[11] WH changed **he might**
<u>gain</u> (<u>kerdAsA</u>) to *to gain*
(*kerdAsai*). Aor Act **Sub** to
Aor Act *Inf.* [mood]

[12] WH changed <u>lose</u>
(<u>zAmiOťhA</u>) to *to lose*
(*zAmiOťhAnai*). Aor Pass
Sub to Aor Pass *Inf.* [mood]

[13] WH changed <u>or</u> (**A**) to *for*
(*gar*).

[14] WH changed the word or-
der from **OR** <u>what</u> **shall** <u>he</u>
<u>give</u> to *what FOR might he
give*.

man **give**[1] in exchange for his soul?

38 Whosoever therefore shall be ashamed of me and of my words in this adulterous and sinful generation; of him also shall the Son of man be ashamed, when he cometh in the glory of his Father with the holy angels.

CHAPTER 9

1 And he said unto them, Verily I say unto you, That there be some of them that stand **here**[2], which shall not taste of death, till they have seen the kingdom of God come with power.

2 And after six days Jesus taketh *with him* Peter, and James, and John, and leadeth them up into an high mountain apart by themselves: and he was transfigured before them.

3 And his raiment became shining, exceeding white ~~as snow~~[3]; so as no

fuller on earth [ᴧ**in this manner**][4] can white them.

4 And there appeared unto them Elias with Moses: and they were talking with Jesus.

5 And Peter answered and said to Jesus, Master, it is good for us to be here: and let us make three tabernacles; one for thee, and one for Moses, and one for Elias.

6 For he wist not what **to say**[5]; **for**[6] **they were**[7] sore afraid.

7 And there was a cloud that overshadowed them: and a voice **came**[8] out of the

---

[4] WH added *in this manner* (*[h]utO*).
[5] WH changed he might **say** (**lalAsA**) to he might **reply** (*apokrithA*). Aor **Act** Sub of **laleO** to Aor **Pass** Sub of *apo-krinomai*. [voice & syn]
[6] WH changed the word order from they **were** FOR terrified to *terrified FOR they became*.
[7] WH changed they **were** (**Asan**) to *they became* (*egenonto*) **Impf** NV Ind of *An* to *Aor* Mid Ind of *ginomai* [tense & syn]
[8] WH changed came (**Alt̶h̶e**) to *became* (*egeneto*). Aor **Act** Ind of **erc̶omai** to Aor *Mid* Ind of *ginomai*. [voice & syn]

---

[1] WH changed **shall** give (**dOsei**) to *might give* (*doi*). **Fut** Act **Ind** to *Aor* Act *Sub*. [tense & mood]
[2] WH changed the word order from of them HERE to *HERE of them*.
[3] WH omitted as snow (*[h]Os ciOn*).

cloud, ~~saying~~[1], This is my beloved Son: hear him.

8 And suddenly, when they had looked round about, they saw no man any more, **save**[2] Jesus only with themselves.

9 **And**[3] as they came down from the mountain, he charged them that they should tell no man what things they had seen, till the Son of man were risen from the dead.

10 And they kept that saying with themselves, questioning one with another what the rising from the dead should mean.

11 And they asked him, saying, **Why say**[4] the scribes that Elias must first come?

12 And he ~~answered and~~[5]

told[6] them, Elias verily cometh first, and restoreth all things; and how it is written of the Son of man, that he must suffer many things, and be set at nought.

13 But I say unto you, That Elias is indeed come, and they have done unto him whatsoever they listed, as it is written of him.

14 And **when he came**[7] to *his* disciples, **he saw**[8] a great multitude about them, and the scribes questioning with [∧**towards**][9] **them**[10].

15 And straightway all the people, when they beheld him, were greatly amazed, and running to *him* saluted

---

[1] WH omitted saying (legousa).

[2] WH changed save (**alla--but**) to *except* (**ei mA--if not**).

[3] WH changed **but** (**de**) to *and* (**kai**) and changed the word order from as came down **BUT** to *AND as came down*.

[4] In their margin, WH put why say (ʰoti legousin) in parentheses.

[5] WH omitted answered (apokriˍtheˍs). This would

cause the and supplied by attendant circumstances to drop also.

[6] WH changed **told** (**eipen**) to *was saying* (**efA**). **Aor** Act Ind of **apokrinomai** to *Impf* Ind of *fAmi*. [tense & syn]

[7] WH changed when **he** came (elthˍOˍn) to *when **they** came* (*elˍthˍontes*). Both Aor Act Part. Nom **Sing** Masc to Nom *Plur* Masc. [number]

[8] WH changed **he** saw (**eiden**) to *they saw* (*eidon*). [number]

[9] WH added *towards* (*pros*).

[10] WH changed them (aut**ois**) to *them* (aut**ous**). **Dat** to *Acc*. [case]

him.

16 And he asked **the scribes**[1], What question ye with them?

17 And one of the multitude **answered**[2] ~~and said~~[3] [˄to him][4], Master, I have brought unto thee my son, which hath a dumb spirit;

18 And wheresoever he taketh him, he teareth him: and he foameth, and gnasheth with ~~his~~[5] teeth, and pineth away: and I spake to thy disciples that they should cast him out; and they could not.

19 He answereth **him**[6], and saith, O faithless generation, how long shall I be with you? how long shall I suffer you? bring him unto me.

20 And they brought him unto him: and when he saw him, **straightway**[7] **the spirit**[8] **tare**[9] him; and he fell on the ground, and wallowed foaming.

21 And he asked his father, How long is it ago since this came unto him? And he said, Of a child.

22 And ofttimes it hath cast **him**[10] into the fire, and into the waters, to destroy him: but if thou canst do any thing, have compassion on us, and help us.

23 Jesus said unto him, If thou canst ~~believe~~[11], all things *are* possible to him that believeth.

24 ~~And~~[12] straightway the father of the child cried out,

---

[1] WH changed **the scribes** (tous **grammateis**) to *them* (*autous*).

[2] WH changed **having** answered (apokri~~th~~eis) to answered (apekri~~th~~A). Aor Pass-D **Part** to Aor Pass *Ind*. [mood]

[3] WH omitted and said (eipe). The and would drop out with the omission of said.

[4] WH added *to him* (*autO*).

[5] WH omitted of him (autou) from the words the teeth of him (tous odontas autou).

[6] WH changed **him** (autO) to *them* (*autois*). [number]

[7] WH changed **straightway** (eu~~the~~Os) to *suddenly* (*eu~~th~~us*). [syn]

[8] WH changed the word order from **immediately** THE SPIRIT tore to *THE SPIRIT suddenly completely tore.*

[9] changed tore (esparaxen) to **completely** tore (*sunesparaxen*). [prefix added]

[10] WH changed the word order from HIM also into fire to *also into fire HIM.*

[11] WH omitted believe (pisteusai).

[12] WH omitted and (kai).

and said ~~with tears~~[1], ~~Lord~~[2], I believe; help thou mine unbelief.

25 When Jesus saw that the people came running together, he rebuked the foul spirit, saying unto him, *Thou* dumb and deaf spirit, I charge thee, come out of him, and enter no more into him.

26 And *the spirit* **cried**[3], and **rent**[4] ~~him~~[5] sore, and came out of him: and he was as one dead; insomuch that [ʌ**the**][6] many said, He is dead.

27 But Jesus took **him**[7] by the hand, and lifted him up; and he arose.

28 And **when he was come**[8] into the house, his disciples asked him **privately**[9], Why could not we cast him out?

29 And he said unto them, This kind can come forth by nothing, but by prayer ~~and fasting~~[10].

30 And they departed thence, and passed through Galilee; and he would not that any man should know *it.*

31 For he taught his disciples, and said unto them, The Son of man is delivered into the hands of men, and they shall kill him; and after that he is killed, he shall rise **the third day**[11].

---

[1] WH omitted with tears (meta dakruOn) in their text, but retained them in their margin.
[2] WH omitted Lord (kurie).
[3] WH canged {**he**} cried (kraxan) to {*it*} *cried* (*kraxas*). Both Aor Act Part. Nom Sing **Neut** to Nom Sing *Masc*. [gender]
[4] WH changed {*it*} rent (sparaxan) to {*he*} *rent* (*sparaxas*). Both Aor Act Part. Nom Sing **Neut** to Nom Sing *Masc*. [gender]
[5] WH omitted him (auton).
[6] WH added *the* (*tous*).
[7] WH changed him (auto**n**) to *of him* (*autou*) and changed the word order from HIM by the hand to *by the hand OF HIM*.

[8] WH changed having come him (eis-elͭhonta auto**n**) to *having come him* (*eis-elͭhontos autou*). Both Aor Act Part. **Acc** Masc Sing to *Gen* Masc Sing. [case]
[9] WH changed the word order from asked him PRIVATELY to *PRIVATELY asked him.*
[10] WH omitted and fasting (kai nAsteia) in their text, but retained them in their margin.
[11] WH changed **the** third day (t**A** trit**A** ͪAmera) to *after three days* (*meta treis* ͪAmeras*).

32 But they understood not that saying, and were afraid to ask him.

33 And **he came**[1] to Capernaum: and being in the house he asked them, What was it that ye disputed ~~among yourselves~~[2] by the way?

34 But they held their peace: for by the way they had disputed among themselves, who *should be* the greatest.

35 And he sat down, and called the twelve, and saith unto them, If any man desire to be first, *the same* shall be last of all, and servant of all.

36 And he took a child, and set him in the midst of them: and when he had taken him in his arms, he said unto them,

37 Whosoever shall receive one of such children in my name, receiveth me: and whosoever **shall receive**[3] me, receiveth not me, but him that sent me.

38 ~~And~~[4] John **answered**[5] him, ~~saying~~[6], Master, we saw one casting out devils in thy name, and ~~he followeth not us~~[7]: and **we forbad**[8] him, because **he followeth**[9] not us.

39 But Jesus said, Forbid him not: for there is no man which shall do a miracle in my name, that can lightly speak evil of me.

40 For he that is not against us is on our part.

41 For whosoever shall give you a cup of water to drink in ~~my~~[10] name, because

---

[1] WH changed **he** came (Alt̄hen) to *they came* (Alt̄hon). [number]

[2] WH omitted among yourselves (pros ʰeautous).

[3] WH changed **might** receive (dexAtai) to *receives* (decAtai). **Aor** Mid **Sub** to *Pres* M/P ***Ind***. [tense & mood]

[4] WH omitted and (de).

[5] WH changed answered (**apekrith̄**A) to *was answering* (efA). **Aor** Mid-D Ind to *Impf Act* Ind. [tense voice & syn]

[6] WH omitted saying (legOn).

[7] WH omitted he followeth not us (ʰos ouk akolouth̄ei ʰAmin).

[8] WH changed we forbade (ekOlusamen) to we *were fobidding* (ekOluomen). **Aor** Act Ind to *Impf* Act Ind. [tense]

[9] WH changed he followeth (akolouth̄ei) to *he was following* (Akolouth̄ei). **Pres** Act Ind to *Impf* Act Ind. [tense]

[10] WH omitted the (tO) and of me (mou) in the phrase the name of me (tO onomati mou).

ye belong to Christ, verily I say unto you, [ʌ**that**]¹ he shall not lose his reward.

42 And whosoever shall offend one of _these_ little ones that believe <u>in me</u>², it is better for him that <u>**a millstone**</u>³ were hanged about his neck, and he were cast into the sea.

43 And if thy hand <u>**offend**</u>⁴ thee, cut it off: <u>**it is**</u>⁵ better <u>**for thee**</u>⁶ to enter into life maimed, than having two hands to go into hell, into the fire that never shall be quenched:

44 ~~Where their worm dieth not, and the fire is not quenched.~~⁷

45 And if thy foot offend thee, cut it off: it is better for thee to enter halt into life, than having two feet to be cast into hell, ~~into the fire that never shall be quenched~~⁸:

46 ~~Where their worm dieth not, and the fire is not quenched.~~⁹

47 And if thine eye offend thee, pluck it out: it is better <u>**for thee**</u>¹⁰ to enter into the kingdom of God with one eye, than having two eyes to be cast into hell **fire**¹¹:

48 Where their worm dieth

---

¹ WH added _that_ (ʰ_oti_).

² In their margin, WH omitted <u>in</u> <u>me</u> (<u>eis</u> <u>eme</u>).

³ WH changed <u>a millstone</u> (**lith**os <u>mulikos</u>--**stone made of** millstone) to _millstone_ (_mulos onikos_--millstone **turned by an ass**).

⁴ WH changed **may be** offending (<u>skandalizA</u>) to _might_ offend (_scandalisA_). **Pres** Act Sub to _Aor_ Act Sub. [tense]

⁵ WH changed the word order from <u>for thee</u> IT IS to _IT IS for thee._

⁶ WH changed <u>for thee</u> (<u>**soi**</u>) to _for thee_ (_se_). **Dative** to _Acc._ [case]

⁷ WH omitted <u>where</u> <u>their</u> <u>worm</u> <u>dieth</u> <u>not</u> <u>and</u> <u>the</u> <u>fire</u> <u>is</u> <u>not</u> <u>quenched</u> (ʰ<u>opou</u> ʰ<u>o</u> <u>skO-lAx</u> <u>autOn</u> <u>ou</u> <u>teleuta</u> <u>kai</u> <u>to</u> <u>pur</u> <u>ou</u> <u>sbennutai</u>).

⁸ WH omitted <u>into</u> <u>the</u> <u>fire</u> <u>that</u> <u>shall</u> <u>never</u> <u>be</u> <u>quenched</u> (<u>eis</u> <u>to</u> <u>pur</u> <u>to</u> <u>asbeston</u>).

⁹ WH omitted <u>Where</u> <u>their</u> <u>worm</u> <u>dieth</u> <u>not</u> <u>and</u> <u>the</u> <u>fire</u> <u>is</u> <u>not</u> <u>quenched</u> (ʰ<u>opou</u> ʰ<u>o</u> <u>skO-lAx</u> <u>autOn</u> <u>ou</u> <u>teleuta</u> <u>kai</u> <u>to</u> <u>pur</u> <u>ou</u> <u>sbennutai</u>).

¹⁰ WH changed <u>for thee</u> (<u>**soi**</u>) to _for thee_ (_se_). **Dat** to _Acc._ [case]

¹¹ WH omitted <u>of</u> <u>the</u> <u>fire</u> (<u>tou</u> <u>puros</u>) in the phrase <u>into</u> <u>the</u> <u>gehenna</u> <u>of</u> <u>the</u> <u>fire</u> (<u>eis</u> <u>tAn</u> <u>geennan</u> <u>tou</u> <u>puros</u>).

not, and the fire is not quenched.

49 For every one shall be salted with fire, ~~and every sacrifice shall be salted with salt~~[1].

50 Salt *is* good: but if the salt have lost his saltness, wherewith will ye season it? Have salt in yourselves, and have peace one with another.

CHAPTER 10

1 And he arose from thence, and cometh into the coasts of Judaea **by the**[2] farther side of Jordan: and the people resort unto him again; and, as he was wont, he taught them again.

2 And ~~the~~[3] Pharisees came to him, **and asked**[4] him, Is it lawful for a man to put away *his* wife? tempting him.

3 And he answered and said unto them, What did Moses command you?

4 And they said, Moses suffered to write a bill of divorcement, and to put *her* away.

5 **And**[5] Jesus ~~answered and~~[6] said unto them, For the hardness of your heart he wrote you this precept.

6 But from the beginning of the creation ~~God~~[7] made them male and female.

7 For this cause shall a man leave his father and mother, **and cleave to his wife**[8];

8 And they twain shall be one flesh: so then they are no more twain, but one flesh.

9 What therefore God hath joined together, let not man put asunder.

---

[1] WH omitted and every sacrifice will be salted with salt (kai pasa thusia ʰali ʰalisthAsetai) in their text, but retained these words in their margin.

[2] WH changed **by the** (**dia tou**) to *and* (*kai*).

[3] WH omitted the (ʰoi).

[4] WH changed {and} ask**ed** (epArOt**Asan**) to {and} *were asking* (epArOt**On**). **Aor** Act Ind to *Impf* Act Ind. [tense]

[5] WH changed **and** the (**kai** ʰo) to *the* **but** (ʰo de).

[6] WH omitted answered (apokritheis). The and supplied by attendant circumstances dropped also.

[7] WH omitted the God (ʰo theos).

[8] In their margin, WH omitted and cleave to his wife (kai proskollAtAsetai pros tAn gunaika autou).

10 And __in__[1] __the house__[2]
__his__[3] disciples __asked__[4] him
again of ~~the same *matter*~~[5].

11 And he saith unto
them, Whosoever shall put
away his wife, and marry another, committeth adultery
against her.

12 And if __a woman__[6] __shall
put away__[7] her husband, ~~and~~[8]
__be married__[9] __to another__[10],

---

[1] WH changed __in__ (__en__) to *into*
(*eis*).
[2] WH changed __the__ house (tA
oikia) to *the house* (*tAn
oikian*). __Dat__ to *Acc.* [case]
[3] WH omitted __of him__ (autou)
in __the__ __disciples__ __of him__ ("oi
ma†hAtai autou).
[4] WH changed ask__ed__ (epA-
rOt**Asan**) to *was asking*
(*epArOt**On***). __Aor__ Act Ind to
Impf Act Ind.
[5] WH omitted __the__ __same__ [mat-
ter] (__tou__ autou) but retained
the __of__ (peri).
[6] WH changed __a woman__
(__gun__A) to *she* (*aut**A***).
[7] WH changed __might__ put
away (apolus**A**) to *having
put away* (*apolusasa*). Aor
Act __Sub__ to Aor Act *Part.*
[mood]
[8] WH omitted __and__ (kai).
[9] WH changed __may be__ mar-
__ried__ (gamA†hA) to *might
marry* (*gamAsA*). Aor __Pass__
Sub to Aor *Act* Sub. [voice]

she committeth adultery.

13 And they brought
young children to him, that
he should touch them: and
his disciples rebuked __those
that brought *them*__[11].

14 But when Jesus saw *it*,
he was much displeased, and
said unto them, Suffer the little children to come unto me,
~~and~~[12] forbid them not: for of
such is the kingdom of God.

15 Verily I say unto you,
Whosoever shall not receive
the kingdom of God as a little
child, he shall not enter
therein.

16 And he took them up in
his arms, __put *his* hands
upon them__, ~~and~~[13] __blessed__[14]

---

[10] WH changed {__to__} __another__
(all__O__) to *another* (*allon*).
__Dat__ to *Acc.* [case]
[11] WH changed __those that
brought__ [them] (__tois pros-
ferousin__) to *them* (*autois*).
[12] WH omitted __and__ (kai).
[13] WH changed the word order from PUT THE HANDS
UPON THEM {AND} was blessing __them__ to *blesses* {AND}
PUT THE HANDS UPON THEM.
[14] WH changed {and} __was__
bless__ing__ (Aulogei) to *blesses*
(*katAulogei*). __Impf__ Act Ind
to *Pres* Act Ind [tense & prefix added]

them[1].

17 And when he was gone forth into the way, there came one running, and kneeled to him, and asked him, Good Master, what shall I do that I may inherit eternal life?

18 And Jesus said unto him, Why callest thou me good? *there is* none good but one, *that is*, God.

19 Thou knowest the commandments, Do not commit adultery, **Do not kill**[2], Do not steal, Do not bear false witness, Defraud not, Honour thy father and mother.

20 And he **answered and**[3] **said**[4] unto him, Master, all these have I observed from my youth.

21 Then Jesus beholding him loved him, and said unto him, One thing **thou**[5] lackest: go thy way, sell whatsoever thou hast, and give to **the**[6] poor, and thou shalt have treasure in heaven: and come, **take up the cross**[7], and follow me.

22 And he was sad at that saying, and went away grieved: for he had great possessions.

23 And Jesus looked round about, and saith unto his disciples, How hardly shall they that have riches enter into the kingdom of God!

24 And the disciples were astonished at his words. But Jesus answereth again, and saith unto them, Children, how hard is it **for them that trust in [the]**[8] **riches**[9] to enter into the kingdom of God!

25 It is easier for a camel to go through **the**[10] eye of **a**[11]

---

[1] WH omitted them (auta).
[2] WH changed the word order from do not commit adultery, DO NOT KILL to *DO NOT KILL, do not commit adultery*.
[3] WH omitted answered (apokritheis). The and, supplied because of attendant circumstances, dropped out also.
[4] WH changed said (eipen) to *was saying (efA)*. **Aor** Pass **Part** to *Impf Ind*.
[5] WH changed thou (soi) to thou (se). **Dat** to *Acc.* [case]
[6] WH omitted the (tois).
[7] WH omitted take up the cross (aras ton stauron).
[8] WH omitted the untranslated the (tois).
[9] In their margin, WH omitted for them that trust in riches (tous pepoithontas epi crAmasin).
[10] WH omitted the (tAs).
[11] WH omitted the definite article the (tAs) before needle.

needle, than for a rich man to enter into the kingdom of God.

26 And they were astonished out of measure, saying among ~~themselves~~[1], Who then can be saved?

27 ~~And~~[2] Jesus looking upon them saith, With men *it is* impossible, but not with God: for with God all things are possible.

28 ~~Then~~[3] Peter began to say unto him, Lo, we have left all, and **have followed**[4] thee.

29 ~~And~~[5] **Jesus**[6] ~~answered and~~[7] **said**[8], Verily I say unto you, There is no man that

hath left house, or brethren, or sisters, or **father**, or **mother**[9], ~~or wife~~[10], or children, or lands, for my sake, and [∧**for the sake of**][11] the gospel's,

30 But he shall receive an hundredfold now in this time, houses, and brethren, and sisters, and mothers, and children, and lands, with persecutions; and in the world to come eternal life.

31 But many *that are* first shall be last; and the last first.

32 And they were in the way going up to Jerusalem; and Jesus went before them: and they were amazed; **and**[12] as they [∧**the**][13] followed, they were afraid. And he took again the twelve, and began

---

[1] WH omitted themselves (^heautous) in their text, but retained it in their margin.

[2] WH omitted and (de).

[3] WH omitted then (kai).

[4] WH changed followed (AkolouthAsamen) to *have followed* (*AkolouthAkamen*). **Aor** Act Ind to *Pf* Act Ind. [tense]

[5] WH omitted and (de).

[6] WH changed the word order from THE JESUS **said** to *was saying* THE JESUS.

[7] WH omitted answered and (apokritheis de).

[8] WH changed said (eipen) to *was saying* (efA). **Aor** Act Ind to *Impf* Act Ind. [tense]

[9] WH changed the word order from or FATHER or MOTHER to or MOTHER or FATHER.

[10] WH omitted or wife (A gunaika).

[11] WH added *for the sake of* (eneken).

[12] WH changed **and** (**kai**) to *but* (*de*).

[13] WH added *the* {ones} (^hoi) before the participle following. They changed from **and** following **they** were afraid to *but the* {ones} *following were afraid.*

to tell them what things should happen unto him,

33 *Saying*, Behold, we go up to Jerusalem; and the Son of man shall be delivered unto the chief priests, and unto the scribes; and they shall condemn him to death, and shall deliver him to the Gentiles:

34 And they shall mock him, and shall **scourge** him, and shall **spit upon**[1] him, and shall kill ~~him~~[2]: and **the third day**[3] he shall rise again.

35 And James and John, the sons of Zebedee, come unto him, saying **[ʌto him]**[4], Master, we would that thou shouldest do for us whatsoever we shall desire **[ʌyou]**[5].

36 And he said unto them, What would ye that I should do for you?

37 They said unto him, Grant unto us that we may sit, one on thy right hand, and

the other on ~~thy~~[6] left hand, in thy glory.

38 But Jesus said unto them, ye know not what ye ask: can ye drink of the cup that I drink of? **and**[7] be baptized with the baptism that I am baptized with?

39 And they said unto him, We can. And Jesus said unto them, Ye shall ~~indeed~~[8] drink of the cup that I drink of; and with the baptism that I am baptized withal shall ye be baptized:

40 But to sit on my right hand **and**[9] on ~~my~~[10] left hand is not mine to give; but *it shall be given to them* for whom it is prepared.

41 And when the ten heard *it*, they began to be much displeased with James and John.

42 **But**[11] **Jesus**[12] called

---

[1] WH changed the word order from and shall SCOURGE him, and shall SPIT UPON him to *and shall SPIT UPON him, and shall SCOURGE him*.

[2] WH omitted him (auton).

[3] WH changed **the** third day (**tA** trit**A** ʰAmera) to *after three days* (*meta treis* ʰ*Ameras*).

[4] WH added to him (autO).

[5] WH added *you* (*se*).

[6] WH omitted thy (sou).

[7] WH changed and (**kai**) to *or* (ʰ*A*).

[8] WH omitted indeed (men).

[9] WH changed and (**kai**) to *or* (ʰ*A*).

[10] WH omitted my (mou).

[11] WH changed **but** (**de**) to *and* (*kai*).

[12] WH changed the word order from **but** THE JESUS having called them [to him] to *and having called them* [to him] THE JESUS.

them *to him*, and saith unto them, Ye know that they which are accounted to rule over the Gentiles exercise lordship over them; and their great ones exercise authority upon them.

43 But so **shall it** not **be**[1] among you: but whosoever will be great among you, shall be your minister:

44 And whosoever [**∧in**][2] **of you**[3] **will be**[4] the chiefest, shall be servant of all.

45 For even the Son of man came not to be ministered unto, but to minister, and to give his life a ransom for many.

46 And they came to Jericho: and as he went out of Jericho with his disciples and a great number of people,

[**the**][5] blind [**∧beggar**][6] Bartimaeus, **∧the**[7] son of Timaeus, sat by the highway side **begging**[8].

47 And when he heard that it was Jesus **of Nazareth**[9], he began to cry out, and say, Jesus, *thou* Son of David, have mercy on me.

48 And many charged him that he should hold his peace: but he cried the more a great deal, *Thou* Son of David, have mercy on me.

49 And Jesus stood still, and commanded **him**[10] **to be called**[11]. And they call the blind man, saying unto him, Be of good comfort, rise; he calleth thee.

---

[1] WH changed **shall it be** (est**ai**) to *it is* (*esti*). **Fut** Ind to *Pres* Ind. [tense]

[2] WH added *in* (*en*) before the single Greek word translated of you.

[3] WH changed **of you** (^hu**mOn**) to *you* (^h*umin*). **Gen** Plur to *Dat* Plur. [case]

[4] WH changed **to become** (**genesthai**) to *to be being* (*einai*). **Aor** Mid Inf of *ginomai* to *Pres* Inf of *eimi*. [tense & syn]

---

[5] WH omitted the untranslated the (^ho).

[6] WH added *beggar* (*prosaitAs*).

[7] WH added the *the* (^ho) that the KJV supplied.

[8] WH omitted begging (*prosaitOn*).

[9] WH changed the Nazarite (^ho naz**Oraio**s) to *the Nazarine* (^ho *nazarAnos*).

[10] WH changed the word order from HIM **to be called** to *call HIM*.

[11] WH changed **to be called** (*fOnAthAnai*) to *call* (*fOnAsate*). Aor **Pass Inf** to Aor *Act Imp*. [voice & mood]

50 And he, casting away his garment, **rose**[1], and came to Jesus.

51 And Jesus answered and **said**[2] **unto him**,[3] What wilt thou that I should do unto thee? The blind man said unto him, Lord, that I might receive my sight.

52 And Jesus said unto him, Go thy way; thy faith hath made thee whole. And immediately he received his sight, and followed **Jesus**[4] in the way.

CHAPTER 11

1 And when they came nigh to Jerusalem, unto Bethphage and Bethany, at the mount of Olives, he sendeth forth two of his disciples,

2 And saith unto them, Go your way into the village over against you: and as soon as ye be entered into it, ye shall find a colt tied, whereon never [∧**not yet**][5] man **sat**[6]; **loose**[7] him, ∧**and**[8] **bring him**[9].

3 And if any man say unto you, Why do ye this? say ye **that**[10] the Lord hath need of him; and straightway **he will send**[11] ∧**again**[12] him hither.

4 **And**[13] they went their

---

[1] WH changed having **stood** up (anastas) to *having* **jumped** *up* (*anapAdAsas*). Both Aor Act Part. [syn]

[2] WH changed says (**legei**) to *said* (*eipe*). **Pres** Act Ind of legO to **Aor** Act Ind of *erO*. [tense & syn]

[3] WH changed the word order from says TO HIM the Jesus to TO HIM the Jesus said.

[4] WH changed **the Jesus** (tO iAsou) to *him* (*autO*).

[5] WH added *not yet* (*[h]upO*).

[6] WH changed had sat (**kekathike**) to *sat* (*ekathise*). **Pf** Act Ind to **Aor** Act Ind. [tense]

[7] WH changed **having** loosed (lusantes) to *loose* (*lusate*). Aor Act **Part** to Aor Act **Imp**. [mood]

[8] WH added the *and* (*kai*) that the KJV supplied.

[9] WH changed bring [him] (**agagete**) to *be bringing* [him] (*ferete*). **Aor** Act Imp of **agO** to **Pres** Act Imp of **ferO**. [tense & syn]

[10] WH omitted that ([h]oti).

[11] WH changed he **will send** (apostelei) to *he sends* (*apostellei*). **Fut** Act Ind to **Pres** Act Ind. [tense]

[12] WH added *again* (*palin*) after send.

[13] WH changed **but (de)** to *and (kai)*. [syn]

way, and found ~~the~~[1] colt tied by the door without in a place where two ways met; and they loose him.

5   And certain of them that stood there said unto them, What do ye, loosing the colt?

6   And they said unto them even as Jesus **had commanded**[2]: and they let them go.

7   And **they brought**[3] the colt to Jesus, and **cast** their garments **on**[4] him; and he sat upon **him**[5].

8   And many spread their garments in the way: and others **cut down**[6] **branches**[7] off

off the **trees**[8], ~~and strawed~~ ***them* in the way**[9].

9   And they that went before, and they that followed, cried, ~~saying~~[10], Hosanna; Blessed *is* he that cometh in the name of the Lord:

10   Blessed *be* the kingdom of our father David, that cometh ~~in the name of the Lord~~[11]: Hosanna in the highest.

11   And ~~Jesus~~[12] entered into Jerusalem, ~~and~~[13] into the temple: and when he had looked round about upon all things, and now the eventide was come, he went out unto

---

[1] WH omitted the (ton).
[2] WH changed **commanded** (**eneteilato**) to *said* (*eipen*). Aor **Mid** Ind of **entellomai** to Aor *Act* Ind of *legO*. [voice & syn]
[3] WH changed they **led** (**Agagon**) to *they are bringing* (*ferousi*). **Aor** Act Ind of **agO** to *Pres* Act Ind of *ferO*. [tense & syn]
[4] WH changed cast on (epebalon) to *are casting on* (*epiballousin*). **Aor** Act Ind to *Pres* Act Ind. [tense]
[5] WH changed him (autO) to *him* (*auton*). **Dat** Sing Masc to *Acc* Sing Masc. [case]
[6] WH changed (**were cut**ting

down (**ekopton**) *to having cut down* (*ko$antes*). **Impf** Act **Ind** to *Aor* Act *Part*. [tense & mood]
[7] WH changed branches (**stoibadas**) to *branches* (*stibadas*). [Only WH example of this spell]
[8] WH changed **trees** (**dendrOn**) to *fields* (*agrOn*).
[9] WH omitted and strawed [them] in the way (kai estrOnnuon eis tAn [h]odon).
[10] WH omitted saying (legontes).
[11] WH omitted in name of Lord (en onomati kuriou).
[12] WH omitted the Jesus ([h]o iAsous).
[13] WH omitted and (kai).

Bethany with the twelve.

12 And on the morrow, when they were come from Bethany, he was hungry:

13 And seeing a fig tree [∧**from**]¹ afar off having leaves, he came, if haply he might find any thing thereon: and when he came to it, he found nothing but leaves; for ∧**the**² time of figs **was**³ **not**⁴ *yet*.

14 And ~~Jesus~~⁵ answered and said unto it, No man eat fruit of thee hereafter for ever. And his disciples heard *it*.

15 And they come to Jerusalem: and ~~Jesus~~⁶ went into the temple, and began to cast out them that sold and [∧**them that**]⁷ bought in the temple, and overthrew the tables of the moneychangers, and the seats of them that

sold doves;

16 And would not suffer that any man should carry *any* vessel through the temple.

17 And he taught, [∧**and**]⁸ **saying**⁹ unto them, Is it not written, My house shall be called of all nations the house of prayer? but ye **have made**¹⁰ it a den of thieves.

18 And the **scribes** and **chief priests**¹¹ heard *it*, and sought how they might destroy him: for they feared him, **because**¹² **all**¹³ the people was astonished at his doctrine.

---

¹ WH added *from* (*apo*).
² WH added *the* (*ʰo*) as supplied by the KJV.
³ WH changed the word order from **NOT** for WAS time to *the for time NOT WAS*.
⁴ WH changed not (ou) to *not* (*ouk*). [spell]
⁵ WH omitted the Jesus (ʰo iAsous).
⁶ WH omitted the Jesus (ʰo iAsous).
⁷ WH added *them that* (*tous*).

⁸ WH added *and* (*kai*).
⁹ WH changed saying (le-g**On**) to *he was saying* (*elegen*). **Pres** Act **Part** to *Impf* Act *Ind*. [tense & mood]
¹⁰ WH changed made (epoi-Asate) to *have made* (*pepoi-Akate*). **Aor** Act Ind to *Pf* Act Ind. [tense]
¹¹ WH changed the word order from SCRIBES and the CHIEF-PRIESTS to CHIEF-PRIESTS and the SCRIBES.
¹² WH changed **because** (ʰ**oti**) to *for* (*gar*)
¹³ WH changed the word order from **because** ALL to *ALL for*.

19 And **when**[1] even was come, **he went**[2] out of the city.

20 And **in the morning**[3], as they passed by, they saw the fig tree dried up from the roots.

21 And Peter calling to remembrance saith unto him, Master, behold, the fig tree which thou cursedst is withered away.

22 And Jesus answering saith unto them, Have faith in God.

23 ~~For~~[4] verily I say unto you, That whosoever shall say unto this mountain, Be thou removed, and be thou cast into the sea; and shall not doubt in his heart, but **shall believe**[5] that **those**

things which he saith[6] shall come to pass; he shall have ~~whatsoever he saith~~[7].

24 Therefore I say unto you, What things soever ye desire, **when**[8] **ye pray**[9] [∧**also**][10], believe that **ye receive**[11] *them*, and ye shall have *them*.

25 And when ye stand praying, forgive, if ye have ought against any: that your Father also which is in heaven may forgive you your trespasses.

26 ~~But if ye do not forgive, neither will your Father which is in heaven for~~

---

[1] WH changed when (^hote) to *when* (^h*otan*).

[2] In their margin, WH changed he went (exeporeueto) to *he went* (*exeporeuonto*). Only time WH used this spelling. [spell]

[3] WH changed the word order from IN THE MORNING as they passed by to *as they passed by IN THE MORNING*.

[4] WH omitted for (gar).

[5] WH changed **might** believe (pisteusA) to *may believe* (*pisteuA*). **Aor** Act Sub to *Pres* Act Sub.

[6] WH changed those things which he sayeth (^h**a** legei) to *that thing which he speaketh* (^h*o lalei*). **Nom Pl** Neut to *Acc Sing* Neut. [case number & syn]

[7] WH omitted what soever he saith (^ho ean eipA).

[8] WH changed **when** (**an**) to *also* (*kai*).

[9] WH changed praying (proseuco**menoi**) to *you*^p *pray* (*proseuces**the***). Pres M/P **Part** to Pres M/P *Imp*. [mood]

[10] WH added *also* (*kai*).

[11] WH changed ye receive (lambane**te**) to *ye received* (*elabet*). **Pres** Act Ind to *Aor* Act Ind. [tense]

~~give your trespasses~~.[1]

27 And they come again to Jerusalem: and as he was walking in the temple, there come to him the chief priests, and the scribes, and the elders,

28 And **say**[2] unto him, By what authority doest thou these things? **and**[3] who gave thee this authority to do these things?

29 And Jesus ~~answered and~~[4] said unto them, I will ~~also~~[5] ask of you one question, and answer me, and I will tell you by what authority I do these things.

30 The baptism [∧**the**][6] of John, was *it* from heaven, or of men? answer me.

31 And **they reasoned**[7] with themselves, saying, If we shall say, From heaven; he will say, Why then did ye not believe him?

32 **But**[8] ~~if~~[9] we shall say, Of men; they feared the people: for all *men* counted John, **that**[10] he was a prophet indeed.

33 And they answered and **said**[11] unto Jesus, We cannot tell. And Jesus ~~answering~~[12] saith unto them, Neither do I tell you by what authority I do these things.

CHAPTER 12

1 And he began **to**

---

[1] WH omitted but if ye do not forgive neither will your Father which is in heaven forgive your trespasses (ei de ͪumeis ouk afiete oude ͪo patAr ͪumOn ͪo en tois ouranois afAsei ta paraptOmata ͪumOn). In their margin, WH included all of the words in verse 26.

[2] WH changed say (lego**usin**) to *were saying* (*elegon*). **Pres** Act Ind to *Impf* Act Ind. [tense]

[3] WH changed **and** (**kai**) to *or* (*A*).

[4] WH omitted answered (apokritheis) and the supplied and.

[5] WH omitted also (kagO).

[6] WH added *the* (to).

[7] WH changed they reasoned (elogizonto) to *they reasoned again* (*dielogizonto*). [prefix added]

[8] WH changed but (all') to *but* (*alla*). [spell]

[9] WH omitted if (ean).

[10] WH changed the word order from THAT indeed to *indeed THAT*.

[11] WH changed the word order from SAID to Jesus to *to Jesus SAID*.

[12] WH omitted answering (apokritheis).

speak[1] unto them by parables. A *certain* man planted a vineyard, and set an hedge about *it*, and digged *a place for* the winefat, and built a tower, and let it out to husbandmen, and went into a far country.

2 And at the season he sent to the husbandmen a servant, that he might receive from the husbandmen of **the fruit**[2] of the vineyard.

3 **And they**[3] caught *him*, and beat *him*, and sent *him* away empty.

4 And again he sent unto them another servant; and at him ~~they cast stones~~[4], **and wounded** *him* **in the head**[5], and ~~sent~~ *him* ~~away~~[6] shame-**fully handled**[7].

5 And **again**[8] he sent another; and him they killed, and many others; beating some, and killing some.

6 **Having**[9] yet ~~therefore~~[10] one **son**[11], **his**[12] wellbeloved, he sent him **also**[13] **last**[14] unto them, saying, They will reverence my son.

7 But those husbandmen said among themselves, This is the heir; come, let us kill him, and the inheritance shall be ours.

---

[1] WH changed to be **say**ing (**leg**ein) to *to be speaking* (*lalein*). Both Pres Act Inf. [syn].

[2] WH changed the fruit (**tou** kar**pou**) to *the fruits* (*tOn karpOn*). Gen **Sing** Masc to Gen **Plur** Masc. [number]

[3] WH changed but they ([h]oi de) to *and* (*kai*).

[4] WH omitted they cast stones (lit[h]obolAsantes).

[5] WH changed and wounded [him] in the head (ekefalaiO-san) to *and wounded* [*him*] *in the head* (ekefaliOsan). [spell]

[6] WH omitted sent [him]

away (apesteilan).

[7] WH changed **having been** shamefully handled (AtimO-menon) to *they shamefully handled* [*him*] (*AtimAsan*). **Pf Pass Par** to *Aor Act Ind.* [tense voice & mood]

[8] WH omitted again (palin).

[9] WH changed having (ec**On**) to *he was having* (*eicen*). **Pres** Act **Part** to *Impf Act Ind.* [tense & mood]

[10] WH omitted therefore (oun).

[11] WH changed the word order from SON **having** to *he was having* SON.

[12] WH omitted his (autou).

[13] WH omitted also (kai).

[14] WH changed the word order from unto them LAST to *LAST unto them.*

8 And they took **him**[1], and killed *him*, and cast ˄*him*[2] out of the vineyard.

9 What shall therefore the lord of the vineyard do? he will come and destroy the husbandmen, and will give the vineyard unto others.

10 And have ye not read this scripture; The stone which the builders rejected is become the head of the corner:

11 This was the Lord's doing, and it is marvellous in our eyes?

12 And they sought to lay hold on him, but feared the people: for they knew that he had spoken the parable against them: and they left him, and went their way.

13 And they send unto him certain of the Pharisees and of the Herodians, to catch him in *his* words.

14 **And**[3] when they were come, they say unto him, Master, we know that thou art true, and carest for no man: for thou regardest not the person of men, but teachest the way of God in truth: Is it lawful to give tribute to Caesar, or not?

15 Shall we give, or shall we not give? But he, knowing their hypocrisy, said unto them, Why tempt ye me? bring me a penny, that I may see *it*.

16 And they brought *it*. And he saith unto them, Whose *is* this image and superscription? And they said unto him, Caesar's.

17 And Jesus answering [˄**also**][4] said unto them, **Render**[5] to Caesar the things that are Caesar's, and to God the things that are God's. And **they marvelled**[6] at him.

18 Then come unto him the Sadducees, which say there is no resurrection; and **they asked**[7] him, saying,

19 Master, Moses wrote

---

[1] WH changed the word order from HIM and killed to *and killed HIM.*

[2] WH added the *him* (*auton*) that the KJV supplied in italics.

[3] WH changed **but the** (ʰ**oi de**) to *and* (*kai*).

[4] WH added *also* (*de*).

[5] WH changed the word order from RENDER to Caesar to *to Caesar* RENDER.

[6] WH changed they marvelled (e**th**aumasan) to *they* **were** *marvelling* **out** (*exe**th**aumazon*). **Aor** Act Ind to *Impf* Act Ind. [prefix added & tense]

[7] WH changed they asked (epArOAsan) *to they* **were** *asking* (*epArOtOn*). **Aor** Act Ind to *Impf* Act Ind. [tense]

unto us, If a man's brother die, and leave *his* wife *behind him*, and leave no **children**[1], that his brother should take his wife, and raise up seed unto his brother.

20 ~~Now~~[2] there were seven brethren: and the first took a wife, and dying left no seed.

21 And the second took her, and died, [∧**and**][3] **nei-ther**[4] [~~himself~~][5] **left he any**[6] seed: and the third likewise.

22 And the seven ~~had her~~[7], ~~and~~[8] left no seed: **last**[9] of all the woman **died**[10] also.

23 In   the   resurrection **therefore**[11], ~~when they shall rise~~[12], whose wife shall she be of them? for the seven had her to wife.

24 ~~And~~[13] Jesus ~~answer-ing~~[14] **said**[15] **unto them**[16], Do ye not therefore err, because ye know not the scriptures, neither the power of God?

25 For when they shall rise from the dead, they neither marry, nor are given in marriage; but are as the angels ~~which are~~[17] in heaven.

26 And as touching the dead, that they rise: have ye not read in the book of

---

[1] WH changed the word order from CHILDREN no leave to *no leave* CHILDREN.
[2] WH omitted now (oun).
[3] WH omitted the untranslated and (kai).
[4] WH changed not **even** (oude) to *not* (*mA*).
[5] WH omitted the untranslated himself (autos).
[6] WH changed **he** left (afAke) to *having left behind* (*katalipOn*). Aor Act **Ind** to Aor Act *Part*. [mood & syn]
[7] WH omitted had her (elabon autAn).
[8] WH omitted and (kai).
[9] WH changed last (escatA) to (escaton). **Nom** Fem Sing to *Acc* Neut Sing. [case]
[10] WH changed the word or-

der from DIED also the woman to *also the woman DIED*.
[11] WH omitted therefore (oun).
[12] WH omitted when they shall rise ([h]otan anastOsi).
[13] WH omitted and (kai).
[14] WH omitted answering (apokritheis).
[15] WH changed said (**eipen**) to *said* (*efA*). Both Aor Act Ind. {*efA* could also be *Impf* Act Ind (*was saying*).} [syn]
[16] WH changed the word order from and answering the Jesus said TO THEM to *said TO THEM the Jesus*.
[17] WH omited the {ones}([h]oi).

Moses, **how**[1] in the bush God spake unto him, saying, I *am* the God of Abraham, and the God of Isaac, and ~~the~~[2] God of Jacob?

27 He is not ~~the~~[3] God of the dead, but ~~the God~~[4] of the living: ye **[~~yourselves~~]**[5] ~~therefore~~[6] do greatly err.

28 And one of the scribes came, and having heard them reasoning together, and perceiving that he had answered them well, asked him, Which is the first **commandment**[7] of all?

29 ~~And~~[8] **Jesus**[9] answered

---

[1] WH changed how (ʰOs--**as**) to *how* (*pOs*--**how**).
[2] WH omitted the (ʰo).
[3] WH omitted the (ʰo).
[4] WH omitted the God (~~th~~eos).
[5] WH omitted the untranslated yourselves (ʰumeis). The ye supplied by the verb remained.
[6] WH omitted therefore (oun).
[7] WH changed the word order from first of all COMMANDEMENT to *COMMANDMENT first of all.*
[8] WH omitted and (de).
[9] WH changed the word order from **and** JESUS answered **him** to *answered JESUS.*

him[10] , The first ~~of all the commandments~~[11] ‸*is*[12], Hear, O Israel; The Lord our God is one Lord:

30 And thou shalt love the Lord thy God with all thy heart, and with all thy soul, and with all thy mind, and with all thy strength: ~~this *is* the first commandment~~[13].

31 ~~And~~[14] the second *is* ~~like~~[15], *namely* this, Thou shalt love thy neighbour as thyself. There is none other commandment greater than these.

32 And the scribe said unto him, Well, Master, thou hast said the truth: for there is one ~~God~~[16]; and there is none other but he:

33 And to love him with all the heart, and with all the understanding, ~~and with all~~

---

[10] WH omitted him (autO).
[11] WH omitted of all the commandments (pasOn tOn entolOn).
[12] WH added *is* (*estin*) as the KJV supplied in italics.
[13] WH omitted this [is] the first commandment (autA prOta entolA).
[14] WH omitted and (kai).
[15] WH omitted like (ʰomoia).
[16] WH omitted God (~~th~~eos).

~~the soul~~[1], and with all the strength, and to love *his* neighbour as himself, is **more**[2] than all whole burnt offerings and sacrifices.

34 And when Jesus saw that he answered discreetly, he said unto him, Thou art not far from the kingdom of God. And no man after that durst ask him *any question.*

35 And Jesus answered and said, while he taught in the temple, How say the scribes that Christ is the Son of David?

36 ~~For~~[3] David himself said by the Holy Ghost, The LORD said to my Lord, Sit thou on my right hand, till I make thine enemies thy **footstool**[4].

37 David ~~therefore~~[5] himself calleth him Lord; and whence is he *then* his son? And the common people

heard him gladly.

38 And **he said**[6] ~~unto them~~[7] in his doctrine, Beware of the scribes, which love to go in long clothing, and *love* salutations in the marketplaces,

39 And the chief seats in the synagogues, and the uppermost rooms at feasts:

40 Which devour widows' houses, and for a pretence make long prayers: these shall receive greater damnation.

41 And ~~Jesus~~[8] sat over against the treasury, and beheld how the people cast money into the treasury: and many that were rich cast in much.

42 And there came a certain poor widow, and she threw in two mites, which make a farthing.

43 And he called *unto him* his disciples, and **saith**[9] unto

---

[1] WH omitted <u>and with all the soul</u> (<u>kai ex ^holAs tA ŝucAs</u>).
[2] WH changed <u>more</u> (**pleion**) to *far more* (**perissoteron**).
[3] WH omitted <u>for</u> (<u>gar</u>).
[4] In their margin, WH changed **footstool** (^h**upopodion**) to *underneath* (^h**upo-katO**). [They changed **footstool** <u>of the feet of you</u> to *underneath the feet of you.*]
[5] WH omitted <u>therefore</u> (<u>oun</u>).

---

[6] WH changed the word order from <u>HE SAID</u> **unto them** <u>in the teaching of him</u> to *in the teaching of him HE SAID.*
[7] WH omitted <u>unto them</u> (<u>autois</u>).
[8] WH omitted <u>the Jesus</u> (^ho iasous).
[9] WH changed <u>says</u> (**legei**) to *said* (**eipen**). **Pres** Act Ind to *Aor* Act Ind. (tense)

them, Verily I say unto you, That this poor widow **hath cast** more **in**[1], than all they which **have cast**[2] into the treasury:

44 For all *they* did cast in of their abundance; but she of her want did cast in all that she had, *even* all her living.

CHAPTER 13

1 And as he went out of the temple, one of his disciples saith unto him, Master, see what manner of stones and what buildings *are here!*

2 And Jesus **answering**[3] said unto him, seest thou these great buildings? there shall not be left [ʌ**here**][4] one stone upon **another**[5], that shall not be thrown down.

3 And as he sat upon the mount of Olives over against the temple, Peter and James and John and Andrew **asked**[6] him privately,

4 Tell us, when shall these things be? and what *shall be* the sign when **all**[7] these things shall be fulfilled?

5 And Jesus **answering**[8] them began to say, Take heed lest any *man* deceive you:

6 ~~For~~[9] many shall come in my name, saying, I am *Christ*; and shall deceive many.

7 And when ye shall hear of wars and rumours of wars, be ye not troubled: ~~for~~[10] *such things* must needs be; but the end *shall* not *be* yet.

8 For nation shall rise against nation, and kingdom against kingdom: ~~and~~[11] there

---

[1] WH changed **has** cast in (**beblAke**) to *cast in* (*ebale*). **Pf** Act Ind to *Aor* Act Ind. [tense]

[2] WH changed have cast (ba-lontOn) to *have cast* (*ballon-tOn*). [spell]

[3] WH omitted answering (apokritheis).

[4] WH added *here* (^hOde).

[5] WH changed another (lithO--stone) to *another* (lithon--stone). **Dat** Sing Masc to *Acc* Sing Masc. [case]

[6] WH changed [**they**] asked (epArOtOn) to [**he**] *asked* (*epArOta*). Both Impf Act Ind. 3rd **Plur** to 3rd *Sing*. [number]

[7] WH changed the word order from ALL these things shall be fulfilled to *these things shall be fulfilled* ALL.

[8] WH omitted answering (apokritheis).

[9] WH omitted for (gar).

[10] WH omitted for (gar).

[11] WH omitted and (kai).

shall be earthquakes in divers places, ~~and~~[1] there shall be famines ~~and troubles~~[2]: these *are* the **beginnings**[3] of sorrows.

9 But take heed to yourselves: for they shall deliver you up to councils; and in the synagogues ye shall be beaten: and **ye shall be brought**[4] before rulers and kings for my sake, for a testimony against them.

10 And the gospel must first be published among all nations.

11 **But**[5] **when**[6] **they shall lead**[7] *you*, and deliver you up, take no thought before-

hand what ye shall speak, ~~neither do ye premeditate~~[8]: but whatsoever shall be given you in that hour, that speak ye: for it is not ye that speak, but the Holy Ghost.

12 **Now**[9] the brother **shall betray**[10] the brother to death, and the father the son; and children shall rise up against *their* parents, and shall cause them to be put to death.

13 And ye shall be hated of all *men* for my name's sake: but he that shall endure unto the end, the same shall be saved.

14 But when ye shall see the abomination of desolation, ~~spoken of by Daniel the prophet~~[11], **standing**[12] where it ought not, (let him

---

[1] WH omitted <u>and</u> (<u>kai</u>).

[2] WH omitted <u>and</u> troubles (<u>kai</u> <u>taracai</u>).

[3] WH changed <u>beginnings</u> (<u>arcai</u>) to *beginning* (*arcA*). **Plur** to *Sing*. [number]

[4] WH changed <u>ye shall be</u> **brought** (ac<u>th</u>Ases<u>the</u>) to *ye shall be* **stood** (sta<u>th</u>Ases<u>the</u>). Fut Pass Ind of **agO** to Fut Pass Ind of [h]*istAmi*. (*)

[5] WH changed **but** (<u>de</u>) to *and* (*kai*).

[6] WH moved <u>when</u> ([h]<u>otan</u>) first.

[7] They changed <u>they</u> **might** <u>lead</u> (ag<u>ag</u>Osin) to *they may lead* (*agOsin*) **Aor** Act Sub to *Pres* Act Sub. [tense]

[8] WH omitted <u>neither</u> do ye premeditate (<u>mAde</u> <u>meletate</u>).

[9] WH changed **now** (<u>de</u>) to *and* (*kai*).

[10] WH changed the word order from SHALL BETRAY **but** to *and* SHALL BETRAY.

[11] WH omitted <u>spoken of</u> by Daniel <u>the prophet</u> (<u>to</u> [h]<u>rAthen</u> [h]<u>upo</u> <u>daniAl</u> <u>tou</u> profAtou).

[12] WH changed [**it**] <u>having stood</u> (est<u>Os</u>) to [**he**] *having stood* (est**Akota**). Both Pf Act Part Acc Sing. **Neut** to *Masc*. [gender]

that readeth understand,) then let them that be in Judaea flee to the mountains:

15 And let him that is on the housetop not go down ~~into the house~~[1], neither enter *therein*, to take any thing out of his house:

16 And let him ~~that is~~[2] in the field not turn back again for to take up his garment.

17 But woe to them that are with child, and to them that give suck in those days!

18 And pray ye that ~~your flight~~[3] be not in the winter.

19 For *in* those days shall be affliction, such as was not from the beginning of the creation which God created unto this time, neither shall be.

20 And except that the Lord had shortened those days, no flesh should be saved: but for the elect 's sake, whom he hath chosen, he hath shortened the days.

21 And then if any man shall say to you, Lo, here *is* Christ; or, lo, *he is* there; believe *him* not:

22 For false Christs and false prophets shall rise, and shall shew signs and wonders, to seduce, if *it were* possible, **even**[4] the elect.

23 But take ye heed: behold, I have foretold you all things.

24 But in those days, after that tribulation, the sun shall be darkened, and the moon shall not give her light,

25 And the stars [∧**out of**][5] **of heaven**[6] shall **fall**[7], and the powers that are in heaven shall be shaken.

26 And then shall they see the Son of man coming in the clouds with great power and glory.

27 And then shall he send **his**[8] angels, and shall gather together his elect from the four winds, from the uttermost part of the earth to the

---

[1] WH omitted <u>into the house</u> (<u>eis</u> <u>tan</u> <u>oikian</u>).

[2] WH omitted <u>that is</u> (<u>On--</u> being).

[3] WH omitted <u>the flight</u> of <u>you</u> (^h<u>A</u> <u>fugA</u> ^h<u>umOn</u>).

[4] WH omitted <u>even</u> (<u>kai</u>).

[5] WH added *out of* (<u>ek</u>).

[6] WH changed the word order from <u>OF THE HEAVEN</u> <u>shall be</u> <u>falling</u> **OUT** to *shall be* ***OUT OF*** *THE HEAVEN fal-ling.*

[7] WH changed <u>falling</u> {**out**} (**ek**-<u>piptontes</u>) to *falling* (*piptontes*). Both Pres Act Part. [prefix dropped]

[8] WH omitted <u>of him</u> (<u>autou</u>) from <u>the</u> <u>angels</u> of <u>him</u>.

uttermost part of heaven.

28 Now learn a parable of the fig tree; When her branch is yet tender, and putteth forth leaves, ye know that summer is near:

29 So ye in like manner, when ye shall see these things come to pass, know that it is nigh, *even* at the doors.

30 Verily I say unto you, that this generation shall not pass, till **all**[1] these things be done.

31 Heaven and earth shall pass away: but my words shall not pass away.

32 But of that day **and**[2] *that* hour knoweth no man, no, not the angels ~~which are~~[3] in heaven, neither the Son, but the Father.

33 Take ye heed, watch **and pray**[4]: for ye know not when the time is.

34 *For the Son of man is* as a man taking a far journey, who left his house, and gave authority to his servants,

~~and~~[5] to every man his work, and commanded the porter to watch.

35 Watch ye therefore: for ye know not when the master of the house cometh, [∧**or**][6] at even, or at midnight, or at the cockcrowing, or in the morning:

36 Lest coming suddenly he find you sleeping.

37 And **what**[7] I say unto you I say unto all, Watch.

CHAPTER 14

1 After two days was *the feast of* the passover, and of unleavened bread: and the chief priests and the scribes sought how they might take him by craft, and put *him* to death.

2 **But**[8] they said, Not on the feast *day*, lest there be an uproar of the people.

3 And being in Bethany in the house of Simon the leper, as he sat at meat, there came a woman having an alabaster

---

[1] WH changed the word order from ALL these things to *these things* ALL.

[2] WH changed **and** (**kai**) to *or* (*A*).

[3] WH omitted which {are} (ʰ**oi**—the {ones}).

[4] In their margin, WH omitted and pray.

---

[5] WH omitted and (kai).

[6] WH added or (*A*).

[7] WH changed what {thing**s**} (ʰ**a**) to *what* {*thing*} (ʰ*o*). Acc Neut **Plur** to Acc Neut *Sing*. [number]

[8] WH changed **but** (**de**) to *for* (*gar*).

box of ointment of spikenard very precious; ~~and~~[1] she brake the box, and poured *it* ~~on~~[2] his head.

4 And there were some that had indignation within themselves, ~~and said~~[3], Why was this waste of the ointment made?

5 For it [∧the ointment][4] might have been sold for more than three hundred pence, and have been given to the poor. And they murmured against her.

6 And Jesus said, Let her alone; why trouble ye her? she hath wrought a good work **on me**[5].

7 For ye have the poor with you always, and whensoever ye will ye may do them good: but me ye have not always.

8 She hath done what **she** [~~herself~~][6] **could**[7]: she is come

aforehand to anoint my body to the burying.

9 [∧but][8] Verily I say unto you, Wheresoever **this**[9] gospel shall be preached throughout the whole world, *this* also that she hath done shall be spoken of for a memorial of her.

10 And Judas Iscariot, [∧the][10] one of the twelve, went unto the chief priests, to betray him unto them.

11 And when they heard *it*, they were glad, and promised to give him money. And he sought how he might conveniently betray him.

12 And the first day of unleavened bread, when they killed the passover, his disciples said unto him, Where wilt thou that we go and prepare that thou mayest eat the passover?

13 And he sendeth forth two of his disciples, and saith unto them, Go ye into the city, and there shall meet you a man bearing a pitcher of water: follow him.

---

[1] WH omitted <u>and</u> (<u>kai</u>).

[2] WH omitted <u>on</u> (<u>kata</u>).

[3] WH omitted <u>and</u> <u>said</u> (<u>kai legontes</u>).

[4] WH added *the ointment* (*to muron*) after <u>it</u> (<u>touto</u>-this).

[5] WH changed **on** <u>me</u> (<u>eis eme</u>) to *in me* (*en emoi*). **Acc** to *Dat*. [case]

[6] WH omitted the untranslated <u>herself</u> (^{h}<u>autA</u>).

[7] WH changed <u>she</u> **was** hav-

ing (<u>eicen</u>) to *she had* (*escen*). **Impf** Act Ind to *Aor* Act Ind. [tense]

[8] WH added *but* (*de*).

[9] WH omitted <u>this</u> (<u>touto</u>) from <u>the</u> <u>gospel</u> this.

[10] WH added *the* (^{h}*o*).

14 And wheresoever he shall go in, say ye to the goodman of the house, The Master saith, Where is the guestchamber [∧of me][1], where I shall eat the passover with my disciples?

15 And he will shew you a large upper room furnished *and* prepared: there make ready for us.

16 And ~~his~~[2] disciples went forth, and came into the city, and found as he had said unto them: and they made ready the passover.

17 And in the evening he cometh with the twelve.

18 And as they sat and did eat, Jesus said, Verily I say unto you, One of you which eateth with me shall betray me.

19 ~~And~~[3] they began to be sorrowful, and to say unto him one by one, *Is* it I? ~~and another *said, Is* it I~~?[4]

20 And he ~~answered~~[5] and said unto them, *It is* one of the twelve, that dippeth with me in the dish.

21 [∧that][6] The Son of man indeed goeth, as it is written of him: but woe to that man by whom the Son of man is betrayed! good were it for that man if he had never been born.

22 And as they did eat, ~~Jesus~~[7] took bread, and blessed, and brake *it*, and gave to them, and said, Take, ~~eat~~[8]: this is my body.

23 And he took ~~the~~[9] cup, and when he had given thanks, he gave *it* to them: and they all drank of it.

24 And he said unto them, This is my blood [~~the~~][10] of the ~~new~~[11] testament, which is shed **for**[12] many.

25 Verily I say unto you, I will drink no more of the fruit of the vine, until that day that

---

[1] WH added *of me* (*mou*).
[2] WH omitted *of him* (autou) from the disciples of him.
[3] WH omitted the compound translated and (oi de).
[4] WH omitted and another not it I (kai allos mA ti egO).
[5] WH omitted answered (apokri~~th~~eis).

[6] WH added *that* ([h]*oti*) to begin the verse.
[7] WH omitted the Jesus ([h]o iasous).
[8] WH omitted eat (fagete).
[9] WH omitted the (to).
[10] WH omitted the untranslated the (to).
[11] WH omitted new (kainAs) in their text, but retained it in their margin.
[12] WH changed for (**peri**) to *for* ([h]***uper***).

I drink it new in the kingdom of God.

26 And when they had sung an hymn, they went out into the mount of Olives.

27 And Jesus saith unto them, All ye shall be offended ~~because of me this night~~[1]: for it is written, I will smite the shepherd, and the sheep shall be scattered.

28 But after that I am risen, I will go before you into Galilee.

29 But Peter said unto him, **Although**[2] all shall be offended, yet *will* not I.

30 And Jesus saith unto him, Verily I say unto thee, That [ʌ**thou**][3] this day, *even* ~~in~~[4] **this**[5] night, before the cock crow twice, thou shalt deny me thrice.

31 But **he spake**[6] ~~the~~

more[7] **vehemently**[8], If I should die with thee, I will not deny thee in any wise. Likewise also said they all.

32 And they came to a place which was named Gethsemane: and he saith to his disciples, Sit ye here, while I shall pray.

33 And he taketh with him Peter and James and John, and began to be sore amazed, and to be very heavy;

34 And saith unto them, My soul is exceeding sorrowful unto death: tarry ye here, and watch.

35 And he went forward a little, and **fell**[9] on the ground, and prayed that, if it were possible, the hour might pass from him.

36 And he said, Abba, Father, all things *are* possible unto thee; take away this cup

---

[1] WH omitted <u>because of me this night</u> (<u>in moi en tA nukti tautA</u>).

[2] In the word-combination translated <u>although</u>, WH changed the word order from <u>and IF</u> to *IF not*.

[3] WH added the intensive *thou* (*su*).

[4] WH omitted <u>in</u> (<u>en</u>).

[5] WH changed the word order from **in** the night THIS to {*in*} THIS *the night*.

[6] WH changed <u>he was saying</u>

(el<u>ege</u>) to *he was speaking* (el<u>alei</u>). Impf Act Ind of **legO** to Impf Act Ind of *laleO*. [syn]

[7] WH omitted <u>the more</u> (<u>mallon</u>).

[8] WH changed <u>vehemently</u> (**ek** <u>perissou</u>) to *vehemently* (*ekperissOs*).

[9] WH changed <u>fell</u> (epesen) to *was falling* (epipten). **Aor** Act Ind to *Impf* Act Ind. [tense]

from me: nevertheless not what I will, but what thou wilt.

37 And he cometh, and findeth them sleeping, and saith unto Peter, Simon, sleepest thou? couldest not thou watch one hour?

38 Watch ye and pray, lest ye enter into temptation. The spirit truly *is* ready, but the flesh *is* weak.

39 And again he went away, and prayed, and spake the same words.

40 And **when he returned**[1], he found them asleep **again**[2], (for their eyes **were heavy**[3],) neither wist they what to answer him.

41 And he cometh the third time, and saith unto them, Sleep on now, and take *your* rest: it is enough, the hour is come; behold, the Son of man is betrayed into the hands of sinners.

42 Rise up, let us go; lo, he that betrayeth me is at hand.

43 And immediately, while he yet spake, cometh Judas, **[being]**[4] one of the twelve, and with him a **great**[5] multitude with swords and staves, from the chief priests and the scribes and the elders.

44 And he that betrayed him had given them a token, saying, Whomsoever I shall kiss, that same is he; take him, and lead *him* away safely.

45 And as soon as he was come, he goeth straightway to him, and saith, Master, **master**[6]; and kissed him.

46 And they laid their hands on him, and took him.

47 And one of them that stood by drew a sword, and smote a servant of the high priest, and cut off his ear.

48 And Jesus answered and said unto them, Are ye come out, as against a thief, with swords and *with* staves to take me?

49 I was daily with you in the temple teaching, and ye

---

[1] WH changed <u>having</u> **returned** (ʰ**upostreṣas**) to *having* **come again** (*palin elthOn*). Both Aor Act Part. [syn]

[2] WH omitted <u>again</u> (*palin*).

[3] WH changed **having been made heavy** (**bebarAmenoi**) to **being** *made heavy* (*katabarunomenoi*). **Pf** Pass Part to **Pres** Pass Part. [tense]

[4] WH omitted the untranslated <u>being</u> (On),

[5] WH omitted <u>great</u> (*polus*).

[6] WH omitted the second <u>master</u> (ʰ<u>rabbi</u>).

took me not: but the scriptures must be fulfilled.

50 And they all forsook him, and fled.

51 And, **there followed**[1] him [one][2] **a certain**[3] young man, having a linen cloth cast about *his* naked *body*; and the young men[4] laid hold on him:

52 And he left the linen cloth, and fled from them naked.

53 And they led Jesus away to the high priest: and with him were assembled all the chief priests and the elders and the scribes.

54 And Peter followed him afar off, even into the palace of the high priest: and he sat with the servants, and warmed himself at the fire.

55 And the chief priests and all the council sought for witness against Jesus to put him to death; and found none.

56 For many bare false witness against him, but their witness agreed not together.

57 And there arose certain, and bare false witness against him, saying,

58 We heard him say, I will destroy this temple that is made with hands, and within three days I will build another made without hands.

59 But neither so did their witness agree together.

60 And the high priest stood up in the midst, and asked Jesus, saying, Answerest thou nothing? what *is it which* these witness against thee?

61 But he held his peace, and [∧not][5] answered **nothing**[6]. Again the high priest asked him, and said unto him, Art thou the Christ, the Son of the Blessed?

62 And Jesus said, I am: and ye shall see the Son of man sitting on the right hand of power, and coming in the clouds of heaven.

---

[1] WH changed there followed (Akolouthei) to *there followed **with** (sunAkolouthei).* Impf Act Ind. [prefix added]

[2] WH omitted the untranslated one (eis).

[3] WH changed the word order from A CERTAIN young man to *young man A CERTAIN.*

[4] WH omitted the young men ([h]oi neaniskoi) and forced the verb to supply the subject *they.*

[5] WH added *not* (*ouk*).

[6] WH changed the word order from NOTHING he answered to ***not** he answered NOTHING.*

63 Then the high priest rent his clothes, and saith, What need we any further witnesses?

64 Ye have heard the blasphemy: what think ye? And they all condemned him to be guilty of death.

65 And some began to spit on him, and to cover his face, and to buffet him, and to say unto him, Prophesy: and the servants **did strike**[1] him with the palms of their hands.

66 And as Peter was **beneath**[2] in the palace, there cometh one of the maids of the high priest:

67 And when she saw Peter warming himself, she looked upon him, and said, And thou also **wast**[3] with [∧**the**][4] Jesus of Nazareth.

68 But he denied, saying, I know **not**[5], **neither**[6] under-stand I what thou sayest. And he went out into the porch; **and the cock crew**[7].

69 And a maid saw him **again**[8], and began to say to them that stood by, This is *one* of them.

70 And he denied it again. And a little after, they that stood by said again to Peter, Surely thou art *one* of them: for thou art a Galilaean, ~~and thy speech agreeth *thereto*~~[9].

71 But he began to curse and to swear, *saying*, I know not this man of whom ye speak.

72 And [∧**suddenly**][10] the second time the cock crew. And Peter called to mind **the word**[11] **that**[12] Jesus said unto

---

[1] WH changed **were** striking (**eballon**) to *struck* (*elabon*). **Impf** Act Ind to *Aor* Act Ind. [tense]

[2] WH changed the word order from in the palace BELOW to *BELOW in the palace*.

[3] WH changed the word order from with the Nazarene Jesus WAS to *with the Nazarene WAS the Jesus*.

[4] WH added *the* (*tou*) before Jesus

[5] WH changed not (ouk) to and not (*oute*).

[6] WH changed **nothing** (oude) to *and not* (*oute*).

[7] In their margin, WH omitted and the cock crew.

[8] WH changed the word order from AGAIN saw to *saw AGAIN*.

[9] WH omitted and thy speech agreeth [thereto] (kai [h]A lalia sou [h]omoiazei).

[10] WH added *suddenly* (*euthus*).

[11] WH changed the word (tou [h]rAmatos) to *the word* (*to [h]rAma*). **Gen** to *Acc*. [case]

[12] WH changed **that** ([h]ou) to *as* ([h]Os).

him, Before the cock crow twice, thou shalt deny **me thrice**[1]. And when he thought thereon, he wept.

CHAPTER 15

1 And straightway ~~in the~~[2] morning the chief priests held a consultation with the elders and scribes and the whole council, and bound Jesus, and carried *him* away, and delivered *him* to Pilate.

2 And Pilate asked him, Art thou the King of the Jews? And he answering **said**[3] **unto him**[4], Thou sayest *it*.

3 And the chief priests accused him of many things: ~~but he answered nothing~~[5].

4 And Pilate asked him again, saying, Answerest thou nothing? behold how many things **they witness against**[6] thee.

5 But Jesus yet answered nothing; so that Pilate marvelled.

6 Now at *that* feast he released unto them one prisoner, **whomsoever**[7] **they desired**[8].

7 And there was *one* named Barabbas, *which lay* bound with **them that had made insurrection**[9] with him, who had committed murder in the insurrection.

8 And the multitude **crying aloud**[10] began to desire

---

[1] WH changed the word order from thou shalt deny ME THRICE to *THRICE ME thou shalt deny.*

[2] WH omitted in the (epi to).

[3] WH changed said (**eipen**) to say**s** (*legei*). **Aor** Act Ind to *Pres* Act Ind. [tense]

[4] WH changed the word order from said UNTO HIM to *UNTO HIM says.*

[5] WH omitted but he answered nothing (autos de ouden apekrinato).

[6] WH changed they **witness against** (kata-marturousin) to *they accuse* (*katAgorousin*). Both Pres Act Ind. kata-martureO to *kat-AgoreO*.

[7] WH changed whomsoever (ʰonper) to *whom* (ʰon). [root added]

[8] WH changed they desired (ʰAtounto) to *they desired* (*parAtounto*). Both Impf Act Ind. [prefix added]

[9] WH changed them that had made insurrection **with him** (tOn **sustasiastOn**) to *them that had made insurrection* (*tOn stasiastOn*). [prefix dropped]

[10] WH changed having **cried aloud** (anaboAsas) to *having gone up* (*anabas*). Both Aor Act Part. anaboaO to *anabainO*.

him to do as he had **ever**[1] done unto them.

9 But Pilate answered them, saying, Will ye that I release unto you the King of the Jews?

10 For he knew that the chief priests had delivered him for envy.

11 But the chief priests moved the people, that he should rather release Barabbas unto them.

12 And Pilate answered and said **again**[2] unto them, What ~~will ye~~[3] then that I shall do *unto him* whom ye call ∧**the**[4] King of the Jews?

13 And they cried out again, Crucify him.

14 Then Pilate said unto them, Why, what evil hath he done? And they cried out **the more exceedingly**[5], Crucify him.

15 And *so* Pilate, willing to content the people, released Barabbas unto them,

and delivered Jesus, when he had scourged *him*, to be crucified.

16 And the soldiers led him away into the hall, called Praetorium; and they call together the whole band.

17 And they clothed him with purple, and platted a crown of thorns, and put it about his *head*,

18 And began to salute him, Hail, King of the Jews!

19 And they smote him on the head with a reed, and did spit upon him, and bowing *their* knees worshipped him.

20 And when they had mocked him, they took off the purple from him, and put **his own**[6] clothes on him, and led him out to crucify him.

21 And they compel one Simon a Cyrenian, who passed by, coming out of the country, the father of Alexander and Rufus, to bear his cross.

22 And they bring him unto the place Golgotha, which is, being interpreted, The place of a skull.

23 And they gave him ~~to drink~~[7] wine mingled with myrrh: but he received *it* not.

---

[1] WH omitted <u>ever</u> (<u>aei</u>).

[2] WH changed the word order from <u>answered</u> AGAIN to *AGAIN answered.*

[3] WH omitted <u>will ye</u> (~~th~~<u>elete</u>).

[4] WH added a *the* (*ton*) where the KJV supplied it.

[5] WH changed **the more** ex-ceedingly (<u>perissoterOs</u>) to *exceedingly* (*perissOs*).

---

[6] WH changed <u>his</u> **own** (**ta idia**) to *his* (*autou*).

[7] WH omitted <u>to drink</u> (<u>pien</u>).

24 And **when they had crucified**[1] him, [ʌ**and**][2] **they parted**[3] his garments, casting lots upon them, what every man should take.

25 And it was the third hour, and they crucified him.

26 And the superscription of his accusation was written over, THE KING OF THE JEWS.

27 And with him they crucify two thieves; the one on his right hand, and the other on his left.

28 ~~And the scripture was fulfilled, which saith, And he was numbered with the transgressors.~~[4]

29 And they that passed by railed on him, wagging their heads, and saying, Ah, thou that destroyest the temple, and **buildest**[5] it in three days,

30 Save thyself, **and**[6] **come down**[7] from the cross.

31 [~~but~~][8] Likewise also the chief priests mocking said among themselves with the scribes, He saved others; himself he cannot save.

32 Let Christ the King of Israel descend now from the cross, that we may see and believe. And they that were crucified with him reviled him.

33 **And**[9] when the sixth hour was come, there was darkness over the whole land until the ninth hour.

---

[1] WH changed **having** crucified (staur**O**santes) to **they are** *crucifying* (staur*ousi*). **Aor** Act **Part** to *Pres* Act *Ind*. [tense & mood]

[2] WH added *and* (*kai*).

[3] WH changed they **were** parting (diemerizon) to *they are* parting {**for themselves**} (*diamerizontai*). **Impf Act** Ind to *Pres Mid* Ind. [tense & voice]

[4] WH omitted and the scripture was fulfilled which saith and he was numbered with the transgressors (kai epl**A**roth**A** ʰ**A** graf**A** ʰ**A** legousa kai meta anom**O**n elogist~~h~~a) in their text. In their margin, WH included verse 28.

[5] WH changed the word order of in three days BUILDEST [it] to BUILDEST [it] in three days.

[6] WH omitted and (kai).

[7] WH changed come down (kataba) to *having* come down (*katabas*). Aor Act **Imp** to Aor Act *Part*. [mood]

[8] WH omitted the untranslated but (de).

[9] WH changed and (de) to *and* (*kai*) and moved it to the beginning of the verse.

34 And at the ninth hour Jesus cried with a loud voice, **saying**[1], Eloi, Eloi, **lama**[2] sabachthani? which is, being interpreted, My God, my God, why hast thou forsaken me?

35 And some of them that stood by, when they heard *it*, said, Behold, he calleth Elias.

36 And **one**[3] ran **and**[4] filled a spunge full of vinegar, and put *it* on a reed, **and**[5] gave him to drink, saying, Let alone; let us see whether Elias will come to take him down.

37 And Jesus cried with a loud voice, and gave up the ghost.

38 And the veil of the temple was rent in twain from the top to the bottom.

39 And when the centurion, which stood over against him, saw that he so **cried out**[6], **and**[7] gave up the

ghost, he said, Truly this man was the Son of God.

40 There were also women looking on afar off: among whom was Mary Magdalene, and Mary the mother of James the less and of Joses, and Salome;

41 (Who also, when he was in Galilee, followed him, and ministered unto him;) and many other women which came up with him unto Jerusalem.

42 And now when the even was come, because it was the preparation, that is, the day before the sabbath,

43 Joseph of Arimathaea, an honourable counsellor, which also waited for the kingdom of God, **came**[8], and went in boldly unto Pilate, and craved the body of Jesus.

44 And Pilate marvelled if he were already dead: and calling *unto him* the centurion, he asked him whether he had been **any while**[9] dead.

---

[1] WH omitted <u>saying</u> (<u>legOn</u>).
[2] WH changed <u>lama</u> (<u>lamma</u>) to *lama* (*lama*). [spell]
[3] WH changed <u>one</u> (^h<u>eis</u>) to *a certain one* (*tis*).
[4] WH omitted <u>and</u> (<u>kai</u>).
[5] WH omitted <u>and</u> (<u>te</u>).
[6] WH omitted <u>cried out</u> (<u>kraxas</u>) in their text, but retained it in their margin.
[7] When WH omitted <u>cried out</u> from their text, the sup-

plied <u>and</u> dropped out.
[8] WH changed <u>came</u> (**AlthEn**) to *having come* (*elthOn*). Aor Act **Ind** to Aor Act *Part*. [mood]
[9] In their margin, WH changed **any while** (**palai**) to *already* (*AdA*).

45 And when he knew *it* of the centurion, he gave the **body**[1] to Joseph.

46 And he bought fine linen, **and**[2] took him down, and wrapped him in the linen, and **laid**[3] him in a sepulchre which was hewn out of a rock, and rolled a stone unto the door of the sepulchre.

47 And Mary Magdalene and Mary *the mother* of [ᴧthe][4] Joses beheld where he was laid.

CHAPTER 16

1 And when the sabbath was past, Mary Magdalene, and Mary the *mother* of James, and Salome, had bought sweet spices, that they might come and anoint him.

2 And very early in the morning **the first**[5] *day* of ᴧthe[6] week, they came unto the sepulchre at the rising of the sun.

3 And they said among themselves, Who shall roll us away the stone from the door of the sepulchre?

4 And when they looked, they saw that the stone **was rolled away**[7]: for it was very great.

5 And entering into the sepulchre, they saw a young man sitting on the right side, clothed in a long white garment; and they were affrighted.

6 And he saith unto them, Be not affrighted: ye seek Jesus of Nazareth, which was crucified: he is risen; he is not here: behold the place where they laid him.

7 But go your way, tell his disciples and Peter that he goeth before you into Galilee: there shall ye see him, as he said unto you.

8 And they went out

---

[1] WH changed **body** (sOma) to *corpse* (*ptOma*).

[2] WH omitted and (kai).

[3] WH changed having laid {**down**} (kate̶t̶hAken) to *having laid* (e̶t̶hAken). Both Aor Act Part. [prefix dropped]

[4] WH added *the* (ʰA) before Joses.

[5] WH changed the first (tAs mias) to *the first* (tA mia).

Gen to **Dat**. [case]

[6] WH added *the* (ton) before week (sabbatOn) as the KJV supplied.

[7] WH changed having been rolled **away** (apokekulistai) to *having been rolled again* (*anakekulistai*). Aor Act Part. [prefix changed]

~~quickly~~,[1] and fled from the sepulchre; **for**[2] they trembled and were amazed: neither said they any thing to any *man*; for they were afraid.

9 //[3] Now when *Jesus* was risen early the first *day* of the week, he appeared first to Mary Magdalene, **out of**[4] whom he had cast seven devils.

10 *And* she went and told them that had been with him, as they mourned and wept.

11 And they, when they had heard that he was alive, and had been seen of her, believed not.

12 After that he appeared in another form unto two of them, as they walked, and went into the country.

13 And they went and told *it* unto the residue: neither believed they them.

14 [∧**but**][5] Afterward he appeared unto the eleven as they sat at meat, and upbraided them with their unbelief and hardness of heart, because they believed not them which had seen him after he was risen.

15 And he said unto them, Go ye into all the world, and preach the gospel to every creature.

16 He that believeth and is baptized shall be saved; but he that believeth not shall be damned.

17 And these signs shall follow them that believe; In my name shall they cast out devils; they shall speak with **new**[6] tongues;

18 They shall take up serpents; and if they drink any deadly thing, it **shall** not **hurt**[7] them; they shall lay hands on the sick, and they shall recover.

19 So then after the Lord [∧*Jesus*][8] had spoken unto them, he was received up into heaven, and sat on the right

---

[1] WH omitted quickly (tacu).

[2] WH changed for (**de**) to *for* (*gar*).

[3] In their margin, WH indicated that verses 9-20 are missing in certain ancient authorities and that some have a different ending to Mark's Gospel.

[4] WH changed **out of** (**ap'**) to *from* (*par'*).

[5] WH added *but* (*de*).

[6] In their margin, WH omitted new (kainais).

[7] WH changed **shall** hurt (blašei) to *might* hurt (blaš A). **Fut** Act **Ind** to *Aor* Act *Sub*. [tense & mood]

[8] WH added *Jesus* (iAsous) after Lord (kurios).

hand of God.

20 And they went forth, and preached every where, the Lord working with *them*, and confirming the word with signs following. Amen. //[1]

---

[1] In their margin, WH indicated that verses 9-20 are missing in certain ancient authorities and that some have a different ending to Mark's Gospel.

LUKE

CHAPTER 1

1 Forasmuch as many have taken in hand to set forth in order a declaration of those things which are most surely believed among us,

2 Even as they delivered them unto us, which from the beginning were eyewitnesses, and ministers of the word;

3 It seemed good to me also, having had perfect understanding of all things from the very first, to write unto thee in order, most excellent Theophilus,

4 That thou mightest know the certainty of those things, wherein thou hast been instructed.

5 There was in the days of Herod, **the**[1] king of Judaea, a certain priest named Zacharias, of the course of Abia: and **[the]**[2] **his**[3] wife *was* of the daughters of Aaron, and her name *was* Elisabeth.

6 And they were both righteous **before**[4] God, walking in all the commandments and ordinances of the Lord blameless.

7 And they had no child, because that Elisabeth was barren, and they both were *now* well stricken in years.

8 And it came to pass, that while he executed the priest's office before God in the order of his course,

9 According to the custom of the priest's office, his lot was to burn incense when he went into the temple of the Lord.

10 And the whole multitude of the people were praying without at the time of incense.

11 And there appeared unto him an angel of the Lord standing on the right side of the altar of incense.

12 And when Zacharias saw *him*, he was troubled, and fear fell upon him.

13 But the angel said unto him, Fear not, Zacharias: for thy prayer is heard; and thy wife Elisabeth shall bear thee a son, and thou shalt call his name John.

14 And thou shalt have joy

---

[1] WH omitted the (tou).

[2] WH omitted the untranslated the (^{h}A).

[3] WH changed wife **of** him (aut**ou**) to *wife to him* (aut*O*). **Gen** to *Dat.* [case]

[4] WH changed **before** (enO-pion) to *opposite to* (*enantion*).

and gladness; and many shall rejoice at his **birth**[1].

15 For he shall be great in the sight of the Lord, and shall drink neither wine nor strong drink; and he shall be filled with the Holy Ghost, even from his mother's womb.

16 And many of the children of Israel shall he turn to the Lord their God.

17 And he **shall go before**[2] him in the spirit and power of Elias, to turn the hearts of the fathers to the children, and the disobedient to the wisdom of the just; to make ready a people prepared for the Lord.

18 And Zacharias said unto the angel, Whereby shall I know this? for I am an old man, and my wife well stricken in years.

19 And the angel answering said unto him, I am Gabriel, that stand in the presence of God; and am sent to speak unto thee, and to shew thee these glad tidings.

20 And, behold, thou shalt be dumb, and not able to speak, until the day that these things shall be performed, because thou believest not my words, which shall be fulfilled in their season.

21 And the people waited for Zacharias, and marvelled that he tarried so long in the temple.

22 And when he came out, he could not speak unto them: and they perceived that he had seen a vision in the temple: for he beckoned unto them, and remained speechless.

23 And it came to pass, that, as soon as the days of his ministration were accomplished, he departed to his own house.

24 And after those days his wife Elisabeth conceived, and hid herself five months, saying,

25 Thus hath the Lord dealt with me in the days wherein he looked on *me*, to take away my reproach among men.

26 And in the sixth month the angel Gabriel was sent **from**[3] God unto a city of Galilee, named Nazareth,

27 To a virgin espoused to

---

[1] WH changed **birth** (gen-**n**Asei) to *origin* (genesei).

[2] In their margin, WH changed shall go before (proeleusetai) to *shall go before* (*proseleusetai*). [spell]

[3] WH changed **by** (**h**u**po**) to *from* (*apo*).

a man whose name was Joseph, of the house of David; and the virgin's name *was* Mary.

28 And ~~the angel~~[1] came in unto her, and said, Hail, *thou that art* highly favoured, the Lord *is* with thee: ~~blessed *art* thou among women~~[2].

29 And ~~when she saw *him*~~[3], **she was troubled at his**[4] **saying**[5], and cast in her mind what manner of salutation this should be.

30 And the angel said unto her, Fear not, Mary: for thou hast found favour with God.

31 And, behold, thou shalt conceive in thy womb, and bring forth a son, and shalt call his name JESUS.

32 He shall be great, and shall be called the Son of the Highest: and the Lord God shall give unto him the throne of his father David:

33 And he shall reign over the house of Jacob for ever; and of his kingdom there shall be no end.

34 Then said Mary unto the angel, How shall this be, seeing I know not a man?

35 And the angel answered and said unto her, The Holy Ghost shall come upon thee, and the power of the Highest shall overshadow thee: therefore also that holy thing which shall be born ~~of thee~~[6] shall be called the Son of God.

36 And, behold, thy **cousin**[7] Elisabeth, she **hath** also **conceived**[8] a son in her old age: and this is the sixth month with her, who was called barren.

---

[1] WH omitted the angel (^ho aggelos).

[2] WH omitted blessed [art] thou among women (eulogAmenA su en gunaixin) in their text, but retained these words in their margin.

[3] WH omitted when she saw [him] (idousa).

[4] WH omitted of him (autou) from the saying of him.

[5] WH changed the word order from she was troubled at THE SAYING **of him** to *at THE SAYING she was troubled.*

---

[6] WH omitted of thee (ek sou) from their text, but retained them in their margin.

[7] WH changed cousin (suggenAs) to cousin (*suggenis*). Both Nom Fem Sing. **Adj** to *Noun*.

[8] WH changed having conceived (suneilAfuia) to *has conceived* (*suneilAfen*). Pf Act **Part** to Pf Act **Ind**. [mood]

37 For with **God**[1] nothing shall be impossible.

38 And Mary said, Behold the handmaid of the Lord; be it unto me according to thy word. And the angel departed from her.

39 And Mary arose in those days, and went into the hill country with haste, into a city of Juda;

40 And entered into the house of Zacharias, and saluted Elisabeth.

41 And it came to pass, that, when Elisabeth heard the salutation of Mary, the babe leaped in her womb; and Elisabeth was filled with the Holy Ghost:

42 And she spake out with a loud **voice**[2], and said, Blessed *art* thou among women, and blessed *is* the fruit of thy womb.

43 And whence *is* this to me, that the mother of my Lord should come to me?

44 For, lo, as soon as the voice of thy salutation sounded in mine ears, the babe leaped in my womb for joy.

45 And blessed *is* she that believed: for there shall be a performance of those things which were told her from the Lord.

46 And Mary said, My soul doth magnify the Lord,

47 And my spirit hath rejoiced in God my Saviour.

48 For he hath regarded the low estate of his handmaiden: for, behold, from henceforth all generations shall call me blessed.

49 For he that is mighty hath done to me **great things**[3]; and holy *is* his name.

50 And his mercy *is* on them that fear him from generation to [∧the][4] **generation**[5].

51 He hath shewed strength with his arm; he hath scattered the proud in the imagination of their hearts.

52 He hath put down the mighty from *their* seats, and exalted them of low degree.

53 He hath filled the hungry with good things; and the

---

[3] WH changed great {things} (megaleia) to *great* {things} (*megala*). Both Acc Neut Plur.

[4] WH added *the* (kai).

[5] WH changed to generation (geneOn) to *to generation* (*geneas*). **Gen** to *Acc.* [case]

---

[1] WH changed the God (tO theO) to *the God* (*tou theou*). Dat to Gen. [case]

[2] WH changed **voice** (fOnA) to **outcry** (*kraugA*).

rich he hath sent empty away.

54 He hath holpen his servant Israel, in remembrance of *his* mercy;

55 As he spake to our fathers, to Abraham, and to his seed for ever.

56 And Mary abode with her **about**[1] three months, and returned to her own house.

57 Now Elisabeth's full time came that she should be delivered; and she brought forth a son.

58 And her neighbours and her cousins heard how the Lord had shewed great mercy upon her; and they rejoiced with her.

59 And it came to pass, that on the eighth day they came to circumcise the child; and they called him Zacharias, after the name of his father.

60 And his mother answered and said, Not *so*; but he shall be called John.

61 And they said unto her, There is none **of**[2] **thy kindred**[3] that is called by this name.

62 And they made signs to his father, how he would have him called.

63 And he asked for a writing table, and wrote, saying, His name is John. And they marvelled all.

64 And his mouth was opened immediately, and his tongue *loosed*, and he spake, and praised God.

65 And fear came on all that dwelt round about them: and all these sayings were noised abroad throughout all the hill country of Judaea.

66 And all they that heard *them* laid *them* up in their hearts, saying, What manner of child shall this be! [ᴧfor][4] And the hand of the Lord was with him.

67 And his father Zacharias was filled with the Holy Ghost, and prophesied, saying,

68 Blessed *be* the Lord God of Israel; for he hath visited and redeemed his people,

69 And hath raised up an horn of salvation for us in the house of his servant David;

70 As he spake by the mouth of his holy prophets,

---

[1] WH changed <u>as **if**</u> (^h**Osei**) to *as* (^h*Os*).
[2] WH changed **in** (<u>en</u>) to *out of* (e**k**).
[3] WH changed <u>thy kindred</u> (t**A** <u>suggeneia</u> <u>sou</u>) to *thy kindred* (t**As** suggeneia**s** *sou*).

Dat to *Gen*. [case]
[4] WH added *for* (*gar*).

~~which have been~~[1] since the world began:

71 That we should be saved from our enemies, and from the hand of all that hate us;

72 To perform the mercy *promised* to our fathers, and to remember his holy covenant;

73 The oath which he sware to our father Abraham,

74 That he would grant unto us, that we being delivered out of the hand of our enemies might serve him without fear,

75 In holiness and righteousness before him, all the days ~~of~~ our ~~life~~[2].

76 And thou, child, shalt be called the prophet of the Highest: for thou shalt go before the face of the Lord to prepare his ways;

77 To give knowledge of salvation unto his people by the remission of their sins,

78 Through the tender mercy of our God; whereby the dayspring from on high ~~hath visited~~[3] us,

79 To give light to them that sit in darkness and *in* the shadow of death, to guide our feet into the way of peace.

80 And the child grew, and waxed strong in spirit, and was in the deserts till the day of his shewing unto Israel.

CHAPTER 2

1 And it came to pass in those days, that there went out a decree from Caesar Augustus, that all the world should be taxed.

2 (*And* this **[the]**[4] taxing was first made when Cyrenius was governor of Syria.)

3 And all went to be taxed, every one into **his own**[5] city.

4 And Joseph also went up from Galilee, out of the city of Nazareth, into Judaea, unto the city of David, which is called Bethlehem; (because he was of the house and lineage of David:)

---

[1] WH omitted which have been (tOn--the).

[2] WH omitted of the life (tAs zOAs) from the days of the life of us.

[3] WH omitted hath visited

(episkesetai) from their text, but retained it in their margin.

[4] WH omitted the untranslated the (hA).

[5] WH changed **his own** (**idian**) to *of himself* (heautou).

5   To be taxed with Mary his espoused wife, being great with child.

6   And so it was, that, while they were there, the days were accomplished that she should be delivered.

7   And she brought forth her firstborn son, and wrapped him in swaddling clothes, and laid him in [the]¹ a manger; because there was no room for them in the inn.

8   And there were in the same country shepherds abiding in the field, keeping watch over their flock by night.

9   And, lo², the angel of the Lord came upon them, and the glory of the Lord shone round about them: and they were sore afraid.

10   And the angel said unto them, Fear not: for, behold, I bring you good tidings of great joy, which shall be to all people.

11   For unto you is born this day in the city of David a Saviour, which is Christ the Lord.

12   And this *shall be* a sign unto you; ye shall find the babe wrapped in swaddling clothes, [∧and]³ lying in [the]⁴ a manger.

13   And suddenly there was with the angel a multitude of the heavenly host praising God, and saying,

14   Glory to God in the highest, and on earth peace, **good will**⁵ toward men⁶.

15   And it came to pass, as the angels were gone away from them into heaven, [and the men]⁷ the shepherds said one to another, Let us now go even unto Bethlehem, and see this thing which is come to pass, which the Lord hath made known unto us.

16   And they came with haste, and found Mary, and Joseph, and the babe lying in a manger.

---

¹ WH omitted the untranslated the (tA).
² WH omitted lo (idou).

³ WH added *and* (*kai*).
⁴ WH omitted the untranslated the (tA).
⁵ WH changed good will (eudokia) to *of good will* (*eudokias*). **Nom** Sing Fem to *Gen* Sing Fem. [case] In their margin, however, WH retained good will (eudokia).
⁶ WH changed from upon the earth peace in men good will to *upon the earth peace in men of good will*.
⁷ WH omitted the untranslated and the men (kai ʰoi anthrOpoi).

17 And when they had seen *it*, **they made known abroad**[1] the saying which was told them concerning this child.

18 And all they that heard *it* wondered at those things which were told them by the shepherds.

19 But Mary kept all these things, and pondered *them* in her heart.

20 And the shepherds **returned**[2], glorifying and praising God for all the things that they had heard and seen, as it was told unto them.

21 And when eight days were accomplished for the circumcising **of the child**[3], his name was called JESUS, which was so named of the angel before he was conceived in the womb.

22 And when the days of

her[4] purification according to the law of Moses were accomplished, they brought him to Jerusalem, to present *him* to the Lord;

23 (As it is written in the law of the Lord, Every male that openeth the womb shall be called holy to the Lord;)

24 And to offer a sacrifice according to that which is said in the law of the Lord, A pair of turtledoves, or two young pigeons.

25 And, behold, there was a man in Jerusalem, whose name *was* Simeon; and the same man *was* just and devout, waiting for the consolation of Israel: and the Holy **Ghost**[5] was upon him.

26 And it was revealed unto him by the Holy Ghost, that he should not see death, before he had seen the Lord's Christ.

27 And he came by the Spirit into the temple: and when the parents brought in the child Jesus, to do for him after the custom of the law,

---

[1] WH changed they made known **abroad** (**die**gnOrisan) to *they made known* (*egnOrisan*). Both Aor Act Ind. [prefix dropped]

[2] WH changed turned **upon** (epestreṣan) to *turned **under*** (*ʰupestreṣan*). Both Aor Act Ind. [prefix changed]

[3] WH changed of **the child** (**to paid**ion) to *of him* (*auton*).

[4] WH changed her (aut**As**) to *their* {i.e. boys} (*autOn*). Gen **Sing Fem** to Gen *Plur Masc*. [number & gender]

[5] WH changed the word order from GHOST Holy was to *Holy was* GHOST.

28 Then took he him up in his arms, and blessed God, and said,

29 Lord, now lettest thou thy servant depart in peace, according to thy word:

30 For mine eyes have seen thy salvation,

31 Which thou hast prepared before the face of all people;

32 A light to lighten the Gentiles, and the glory of thy people Israel.

33 And **Joseph**[1] and his mother marvelled at those things which were spoken of him.

34 And Simeon blessed them, and said unto Mary his mother, Behold, this *child* is set for the fall and rising again of many in Israel; and for a sign which shall be spoken against;

35 (Yea, a sword shall pierce through thy own soul also,) that the thoughts of many hearts may be revealed.

36 And there was one Anna, a prophetess, the daughter of Phanuel, of the tribe of Aser: she was of a great age, and had lived with an husband seven years from her virginity;

37 And she *was* a widow **of about**[2] fourscore and four years, which departed not from the temple, but served *God* with fastings and prayers night and day.

38 And ~~she~~[3] coming in that instant gave thanks likewise unto the **Lord**[4], and spake of him to all them that looked for redemption ~~in~~[5] Jerusalem.

39 And when they had performed **all things**[6] according to the law of the Lord, they returned into Galilee, to their own city Nazareth.

40 And the child grew, and waxed strong ~~in spirit~~[7], filled with wisdom: and the grace of God was upon him.

41 Now his parents went to Jerusalem every year at the feast of the passover.

---

[2] WH changed **of about** (^{h}Os) to *until* (^{h}eOs).

[3] WH omitted she (autA).

[4] WH changed **Lord** (**kuriO**) to *God (~~the~~eO)*.

[5] WH omitted in (en) and forced the case of Jerusalem to supply the prepositon.

[6] WH changed all things (^{h}**a-panta**) to *all things* (*panta*). [prefix dropped]

[7] WH omitted in spirit (pneumati).

---

[1] WH changed **Joseph** (**iO-sAf**) to *the father of him* (^{h}*o patAr autou*).

42 And when he was twelve years old, they **went up**[1] **to Jerusalem**[2] after the custom of the feast.

43 And when they had fulfilled the days, as they returned, the child Jesus tarried behind in Jerusalem; and **Joseph and his mother**[3] **knew**[4] not *of it*.

44 But they, supposing him to have been in the company, went a day's journey; and they sought him among *their* kinsfolk and **[among]**[5] acquaintance.

45 And when they found **him**[6] not, they turned back again to Jerusalem, **seeking**[7]

him.

46 And it came to pass, that after three days they found him in the temple, sitting in the midst of the doctors, both hearing them, and asking them questions.

47 And all that heard him were astonished at his understanding and answers.

48 And when they saw him, they were amazed: and his mother said unto him, Son, why hast thou thus dealt with us? behold, thy father and I have sought thee sorrowing.

49 And he said unto them, How is it that ye sought me? wist ye not that I must be about my Father's business?

50 And they understood not the saying which he spake unto them.

51 And he went down with them, and came to Nazareth, and was subject unto them: but his mother kept all **these**[8] sayings in her heart.

52 And Jesus increased in wisdom and stature, and in favour with God and man.

---

[1] WH changed **having gone up** (*anabantOn*) to *going up* (*anabainontOn*). **Aor** Act Part to *Pres* Act Part. [tense]

[2] WH omitted to Jerusalem (eis ierosoluma).

[3] WH changed **Joseph and the mother of him** (*iOsAf kai* ᶣ**a mAtAr outou**) to *the parents* (ᶣ*oi goneis*).

[4] WH changed {**he**} knew (*egnO*) to {**they**} *knew* (*egnOssan*). Both Aor Act Ind. 3rd **Sing** to 3rd *Plur*.

[5] WH omitted the untranslated among (en).

[6] WH omitted him (auton).

[7] WH changed seeking (zAtountes) to *seeking out*

(*anazAtountes*). [prefix added]

[8] WH omitted these (tauta) from the phrase the sayings these.

CHAPTER 3

1 Now in the fifteenth year of the reign of Tiberius Caesar, Pontius Pilate being governor of Judaea, and Herod being tetrarch of Galilee, and his brother Philip tetrarch of Ituraea and of the region of Trachonitis, and Lysanias the tetrarch of Abilene,

2 Annas and Caiaphas **being**[1] **the high priests**[2], the word of God came unto John the son of Zacharias in the wilderness.

3 And he came into all the country about Jordan, preaching the baptism of repentance for the remission of sins;

4 As it is written in the book of the words of Esaias the prophet, ~~saying~~[3], The voice of one crying in the wilderness, Prepare ye the way of the Lord, make his paths straight.

5 Every valley shall be filled, and every mountain and hill shall be brought low; and the crooked shall be made **straight**[4], and the rough ways *shall be* made smooth;

6 And all flesh shall see the salvation of God.

7 Then said he to the multitude that came forth to be baptized of him, O generation of vipers, who hath warned you to flee from the wrath to come?

8 Bring forth therefore fruits worthy of repentance, and begin not to say within yourselves, We have Abraham to *our* father: for I say unto you, That God is able of these stones to raise up children unto Abraham.

9 And now also the axe is laid unto the root of the trees: every tree therefore which bringeth not forth good fruit is hewn down, and cast into the fire.

10 And the people asked him, saying, What **shall we do**[5] then?

11 He answereth and

---

[1] WH changed <u>upon</u> (ep') to *upon* (ep**i**). [spell]

[2] WH changed <u>highpriests</u> (arciereO**n**) to *highpriest* (arciereO**s**). Gen **Plur** Masc to Gen *Sing* Masc. [number]

[3] WH omitted <u>saying</u> (<u>legontos</u>).

[4] WH changed <u>straight</u> (<u>eu~~t~~heian</u>) to *straight*. (*eu~~t~~heias*). Acc Fem **Sing** to Acc Fem *Plur*. [number]

[5] WH changed **shall** we do (<u>poiAsomen</u>) to *were we doing* (*poiAsOmen*). **Fut** Act Ind to *Impf* Act Ind. [tense]

saith[1] unto them, He that hath two coats, let him impart to him that hath none; and he that hath meat, let him do likewise.

12 Then came also publicans to be baptized, and said unto him, Master, what **shall we do**[2]?

13 And he said unto them, Exact no more than that which is appointed you.

14 And the soldiers likewise demanded of him, saying, **And what**[3] **shall we do**[4]? And he said unto them, Do violence to no man, neither accuse *any* falsely; and be content with your wages.

15 And as the people were in expectation, and all men mused in their hearts of John, whether he were the Christ, or not;

16 John answered, saying unto *them* all, I indeed baptize you with water; but one mightier than I cometh, the latchet of whose shoes I am not worthy to unloose: he shall baptize you with the Holy Ghost and with fire:

17 Whose fan *is* in his hand, **and he will throughly purge**[5] his floor, and **will gather**[6] the wheat into his garner; but the chaff he will burn with fire unquenchable.

18 And many other things in his exhortation preached he unto the people.

19 But Herod the tetrarch, being reproved by him for Herodias his brother ~~Philip~~'s[7] wife, and for all the evils which Herod had done,

20 Added ~~yet~~[8] this above

---

[1] WH changed <u>says</u> (<u>legei</u>) to *was* sa*ying* (*elegen*). **Pres** Act **Part** to *Impf* Act *Ind*.

[2] WH changed **shall** we do (<u>poiAsomen</u>) to *were we do-ing* (*poiAsOmen*). **Fut** Act Ind to *Impf* Act Ind.

[3] WH changed the word order from <u>AND OURSELVES</u> <u>what</u> **shall** <u>we do</u> to *what were we doing AND OURSELVES*.

[4] WH changed **shall** we do (<u>poiAsomen</u>) to *were we do-ing* (*poiAsOmen*). **Fut** Act Ind to *Impf* Act Ind. [tense]

[5] WH changed **and he will** throughly purge (**kai** diaka~~th~~ariei) to *to throughly purge* (*diaka~~th~~arai*). **Fut** Act **Ind** to *Aor* Act *Inf*. [tense & mood]

[6] WH changed **will** gather (<u>sunaxei</u>) to *to gather* (*sunagagein*). **Fut** Act **Ind** to *Aor* Act *Inf*. [tense & mood]

[7] WH omitted <u>of Philip</u> (<u>filippou</u>) from <u>the wife of Philip</u>.

[8] WH omitted <u>yet</u> (<u>kai</u>).

all, that he shut up John in [~~the~~][1] prison.

21 Now when all the people were baptized, it came to pass, that Jesus also being baptized, and praying, the heaven was opened,

22 And the Holy Ghost descended in a bodily shape **like**[2] a dove upon him, and a voice came from heaven, which said, Thou art my beloved Son; in thee I am well pleased.

23 And Jesus himself **began to be**[3] about thirty years of age, being (as was supposed) **the son**[4] of Joseph, which was *the son* of Heli,

24 Which was *the son* of Matthat, which was *the son* of Levi, which was *the son* of Melchi, which was *the son* of

Janna[5], which was *the son* of Joseph,

25 Which was *the son* of Mattathias, which was *the son* of Amos, which was *the son* of Naum, which was *the son* of Esli, which was *the son* of Nagge,

26 Which was *the son* of Maath, which was *the son* of Mattathias, which was *the son* of **Semei**[6], which was *the son* of **Joseph**[7], which was *the son* of **Juda**[8],

27 Which was *the son* of **Joanna**[9], which was *the son* of Rhesa, which was *the son* of Zorobabel, which was *the son* of Salathiel, which was *the son* of Neri,

28 Which was *the son* of Melchi, which was *the son* of Addi, which was *the son* of Cosam, which was *the son* of **Elmodam**[10], which was *the*

---

[1] WH omitted the untranslated the (kai).

[2] WH changed like if (^hOsei) to like (^hOs).

[3] WH changed the word order from about years of age thirty BEGAN TO BE to *BEGAN TO BE about years of age thirty*.

[4] WH changed the word order from being (as was supposed {THE} SON to *being {THE} SON (as was supposed)*.

---

[5] WH changed Janna (ianna) to *Jannai* (*iannai*).

[6] WH changed Semei (semei) to *Semeein* (*semeein*).

[7] WH changed Joseph (iOsAf) to *Josech* (*iOsAc*).

[8] WH changed Juda (iouda) to *Joda* (*iOda*).

[9] WH changed Joanna (iOanna) to *Joanan* (*iOanan*).

[10] WH changed Elmodam (elmOdam) to *Elmadam* (*elmadam*).

son of Er,

29 Which was *the son* of **Jose**[1], which was *the son* of Eliezer, which was *the son* of Jorim, which was *the son* of Matthat, which was *the son* of Levi,

30 Which was *the son* of Simeon, which was *the son* of Juda, which was *the son* of Joseph, which was *the son* of **Jonan**[2], which was *the son* of Eliakim,

31 Which was *the son* of Melea, which was *the son* of **Menan**[3], which was *the son* of Mattatha, which was *the son* of Nathan, which was *the son* of David,

32 Which was *the son* of Jesse, which was *the son* of Obed, which was *the son* of Booz, which was *the son* of **Salmon**[4], which was *the son* of Naasson,

33 Which was *the son* of **Aminadab**[5], which was *the*

son of **Aram**[6], which was *the son* of Esrom, which was *the son* of Phares, which was *the son* of Juda,

34 Which was *the son* of Jacob, which was *the son* of Isaac, which was *the son* of Abraham, which was *the son* of Thara, which was *the son* of Nachor,

35 Which was *the son* of Saruch, which was *the son* of Ragau, which was *the son* of Phalec, which was *the son* of **Heber**[7], which was *the son* of Sala,

36 Which was *the son* of Cainan, which was *the son* of Arphaxad, which was *the son* of Sem, which was *the son* of Noe, which was *the son* of Lamech,

37 Which was *the son* of Mathusala, which was *the son* of Enoch, which was *the son* of Jared, which was *the son* of Maleleel, which was *the son* of Cainan,

38 Which was *the son* of Enos, which was *the son* of Seth, which was *the son* of

---

[1] WH changed <u>Jose</u> (<u>iOsA</u>) to *Josu* (*iOsou*).
[2] WH changed <u>Jonan</u> (<u>iOnan</u>) to *Jonam* (*iOnam*).
[3] WH changed <u>Menan</u> (<u>menam</u>) to *Menna* (*menna*).
[4] In their margin, WH changed <u>Salmon</u> (<u>salmOn</u>) to *Sala* (*sala*).
[5] In their margin, WH added *Admein* either after or instead

of <u>Aminadab</u>.
[6] WH changed <u>Aram</u> (<u>aram</u>) to *Arnei* (*arnei*) in their text, but retained <u>Aram</u> (<u>aram</u>) in their margin.
[7] WH changed <u>Heber</u> (<u>ʰeber</u>) to *Eber* (*eber*).

Adam, which was *the son* of God.

CHAPTER 4

1 And Jesus being full of the Holy Ghost returned from Jordan, and was led by the Spirit **into**[1] **the wilderness**[2],

2 Being forty days tempted of the devil. And in those days he did eat nothing: and when they were ended, he ~~afterward~~[3] hungered.

3 **And** the devil **said**[4] unto him, If thou be the Son of God, command this stone that it be made bread.

4 And Jesus answered him, ~~saying~~[5], It is written, That man shall not live by bread alone, ~~but by every word of God~~[6].

5 And ~~the devil~~[7], taking him up ~~into an high mountain~~[8], shewed unto him all the kingdoms of the world in a moment of time.

6 And the devil said unto him, All this power will I give thee, and the glory of them: for that is delivered unto me; and to whomsoever I will I give it.

7 If thou therefore wilt worship **me**[9], **all**[10] shall be thine.

8 And Jesus answered and said unto him, ~~Get thee behind me, Satan~~: ~~for~~[11] it is written, **Thou shalt worship**[12] the Lord thy God, and him only shalt thou serve.

---

[1] WH changed into (eis) to *in* (*en*).

[2] WH changed the wilderness (tAn erAmon) to *the wilderness* (*tA erAmO*). **Acc** to **Dat**. [case]

[3] WH omitted afterward (hus-teron).

[4] WH changed **and** (kai) to *but* (*de*) and put the verb said (eipen) first after it dropped the final letter (n).

[5] WH omitted saying (legOn).

[6] WH omitted but by every word of God (all' epi panti hrAmati theou).

[7] WH omitted the devil (ho diabolos).

[8] WH omitted into an high mountain (eis oros husAlon).

[9] WH changed me (mou) to *me* (*emou*). [**Regular** form to **Intensive** form]

[10] WH changed all {**things**} (panta) to all {**this**} (*pasa*). Nom **Pl Neut** to Nom *Sing Fem*. [number & gender]

[11] WH omitted get thee behind me Satan for (hupage hopisO mou satana gar).

[12] WH changed the word order from THOU SHALT WORSHIP Lord the God of thee to *Lord the God of thee THOU SHALT WORSHIP*.

9 **And he brought**[1] him to Jerusalem, and set him on a pinnacle of the temple, and said unto him, If thou be ~~the~~[2] Son of God, cast thyself down from hence:

10 For it is written, He shall give his angels charge over thee, to keep thee:

11 And in *their* hands they shall bear thee up, lest at any time thou dash thy foot against a stone.

12 And Jesus answering said unto him, It is said, Thou shalt not tempt the Lord thy God.

13 And when the devil had ended all the temptation, he departed from him for a season.

14 And Jesus returned in the power of the Spirit into Galilee: and there went out a fame of him through all the region round about.

15 And he taught in their synagogues, being glorified of all.

16 And he came to Nazareth, where he had been brought up: and, as his custom was, he went into the synagogue on the sabbath day, and stood up for to read.

17 And there was delivered unto him the book of the prophet **Esaias**[3]. And **when he had opened**[4] the book, he found the place where it was written,

18 The Spirit of the Lord *is* upon me, because he hath anointed me **to preach the gospel**[5] to the poor; he hath sent me ~~to heal the brokenhearted~~[6], to preach deliverance to the captives, and recovering of sight to the blind, to set at liberty them that are bruised,

19 To preach the acceptable year of the Lord.

20 And he closed the

---

[1] WH changed **and** (**kai**) to *but* (*de*) and placed the verb first.

[2] WH omitted the (^h̲o̲).

[3] WH changed the word order from of ISAIAH the prophet to *of the prophet ISAIAH*.

[4] WH changed when he had **unrolled** (an**aptu**xas) to *when he had **opened*** (an**oi**xas). Aor Act Part of an**aptussO** to Aor Act Part of *anoigO*. [syn]

[5] WH changed to be preaching the gospel (euaggelizesthai) to *to preach the gospel* (*euaggelisasthai*). **Pres** Mid Inf to *Aor* Mid Inf. [tense]

[6] WH omitted to heal the broken hearted (iasasthai tous suntetrimmenous tAn kardian).

book, and he gave *it* again to the minister, and sat down. And **the eyes**[1] of all them that were in the synagogue were fastened on him.

21 And he began to say unto them, This day is this scripture fulfilled in your ears.

22 And all bare him witness, and wondered at the gracious words which proceeded out of his mouth. And they said, Is not this Joseph's son?

23 And he said unto them, Ye will surely say unto me this proverb, Physician, heal thyself: whatsoever we have heard done **in**[2] Capernaum, do also here in thy country.

24 And he said, Verily I say unto you, No prophet is accepted in his own country.

25 But I tell you of a truth, many widows were in Israel in the days of Elias, when the heaven was shut up three years and six months, when great famine was throughout all the land;

26 But unto none of them was Elias sent, save unto Sarepta, *a city* **of Sidon**[3], unto a woman *that was* a widow.

27 And many lepers were **in Israel**[4] in the time of Eliseus the prophet; and none of them was cleansed, saving Naaman the Syrian.

28 And all they in the synagogue, when they heard these things, were filled with wrath,

29 And rose up, and thrust him out of the city, and led him unto ~~the~~[5] brow of the hill whereon their city was built, **that**[6] they might cast him down headlong.

30 But he passing through the midst of them went his way,

31 And came down to Capernaum, a city of Galilee, and taught them on the sabbath days.

---

[1] WH changed the word order from in the synagogue THE EYES to *THE EYES in the synagugue*.

[2] WH changed **in** {the} (**en** tA) to *into* {the} (**eis** *tAs*).

[3] WH changed of Sidon (sidOnos) to *Sidonian* (*sidOnia*). [**noun** to *adjective*]

[4] WH changed the word order from in the time of Eliseus the prophet IN {THE} ISRAEL to *IN* {*THE*} *ISRAEL in the time of Eliseus the prophet*.

[5] WH omitted the (tAs).

[6] WH changed that (**eis to**) to *so that* (*ʰOste*).

32 And they were aston-ished at his doctrine: for his word was with power.

33 And in the synagogue there was a man, which had a spirit of an unclean devil, and cried out with a loud voice,

34 ~~Saying~~[1], Let *us* alone; what have we to do with thee, *thou* Jesus of Nazareth? art thou come to destroy us? I know thee who thou art; the Holy One of God.

35 And Jesus rebuked him, saying, Hold thy peace, and come out **of**[2] him. And when the devil had thrown him in the midst, he came out of him, and hurt him not.

36 And they were all amazed, and spake among themselves, saying, What a word *is* this! for with author-ity and power he com-mandeth the unclean spirits, and they come out.

37 And the fame of him went out into every place of the country round about.

38 And he arose **out of**[3] the synagogue, and entered into Simon's house. And [the][4] Simon's wife's mother was taken with a great fever; and they besought him for her.

39 And he stood over her, and rebuked the fever; and it left her: and immediately she arose and ministered unto them.

40 Now when the sun was setting, all they that had any sick with divers diseases brought them unto him; and he laid his hands on every one of them, and healed them.

41 And devils also came out of many, crying out, and saying, Thou art ~~Christ~~[5] the Son of God. And he rebuking *them* suffered them not to speak: for they knew that he was Christ.

42 And when it was day, he departed and went into a desert place: and the people **sought**[6] him, and came unto him, and stayed him, that he should not depart from them.

43 And he said unto them,

---

[1] WH omitted saying (legOn).
[2] WH changed {out} **of** (**ex**) to *from* (**ap'**).
[3] WH changed **out of** (**ek**) to *from* (**apo**).

[4] WH omitted the (ʰA) in the mother-in-law of the Simon (ʰA pent̶hera tou SimOnos).
[5] WH omitted the Christ (ʰo cristos).
[6] WH changed sought (exA-toun) to *sought for* (epexA-toun). Both are Impf Act Ind. [prefix added]

I must preach the kingdom of God to other cities also: **for**[1] therefore **am I sent**[2].

44 And he preached **in the synagogues**[3] of **Galilee**[4].

CHAPTER 5

1 And it came to pass, that, as the people pressed upon him **[the]**[5] to hear the word of God, he stood by the lake of Gennesaret,

2 And saw two ships standing by the lake: but the fishermen were gone out of them, and **were washing**[6]

their nets.

3 And he entered into one of the ships, which was Simon's, and prayed him that he would thrust out a little from the land. **And he sat down**[7], and taught the people out of the ship.

4 Now when he had left speaking, he said unto Simon, Launch out into the deep, and let down your nets for a draught.

5 And Simon answering said ~~unto him~~[8], Master, we have toiled all ~~the~~[9] night, and have taken nothing: nevertheless at thy word I will let down **the net**[10].

6 And when they had this done, they inclosed a great multitude of fishes: and their net brake.

7 And they beckoned unto *their* partners, ~~which~~

---

[1] WH changed **for** (**eis**) to *upon* (**epi**). They changed **into** this [for therefore] (**eis touto**) to **upon** *this* (**epi touto**).

[2] WH changed I **have been** sent (apestal**mai**) to *I was sent* (*apesta**lan***). **Pf** Pass Ind to *Aor* Pass Ind. [tense]

[3] WH changed in the synagogues (**en** tais sunagOgais) to *into the synagogues* (**eis** tas sunagOgas). [prep & case]

[4] In their margin, WH changed **Galilee** (**galil**aias) to *Judea* (*ioudaias*).

[5] WH changed the untranslated **the** (**tou**) to *and* (**kai**).

[6] WH changed wash**ed off** (**ape**plunan) to *were washing*

(eplunon). **Aor** Act Ind of **apo**plunO to *Impf* Act Ind of *plunO*. [tense & prefix dropped]

[7] WH changed **and** (**kai**) to *but* (*de*) and placed it after he sat down (kathisas).

[8] WH omitted unto him (autO).

[9] WH omitted the (tAs).

[10] WH changed the net (**to** dikton) to *the nets* (*ta dikta*). [number]

were[1] in the other ship, that they should come and help them. And they came, and filled both the ships, so that they began to sink.

8   When Simon Peter saw *it*, he fell down at Jesus' knees, saying, Depart from me; for I am a sinful man, O Lord.

9   For he was astonished, and all that were with him, at the draught of the fishes **which**[2] they had taken:

10   And so *was* also James, and John, the sons of Zebedee, which were partners with Simon. And Jesus said unto Simon, Fear not; from henceforth thou shalt catch men.

11   And when they had brought their ships to land, they forsook all, and followed him.

12   And it came to pass, when he was in a certain city, behold a man full of leprosy: **who seeing**[3] Jesus fell on *his*

face, and besought him, saying, Lord, if thou wilt, thou canst make me clean.

13   And he put forth *his* hand, and touched him, **saying**[4], I will: be thou clean. And immediately the leprosy departed from him.

14   And he charged him to tell no man: but go, and shew thyself to the priest, and offer for thy cleansing, according as Moses commanded, for a testimony unto them.

15   But so much the more went there a fame abroad of him: and great multitudes came together to hear, and to be healed **by him**[5] of their infirmities.

16   And he withdrew himself into the wilderness, and prayed.

17   And it came to pass on a certain day, as he was teaching, that there were Pharisees and doctors of the law sitting by, which were

---

[1] WH omitted which were (tois--the {ones}).
[2] WH changed which {one} (^hA) to which {ones} (^hOn). **Dat Sing Fem** to *Gen Plur Masc*. [case, number, & gender]
[3] WH changed **who** seeing (**kai** idOn--and having seen) to *but seeing* (idOn de-- hav-

ing seen but).
[4] WH changed **having said** (**eipOn**) to *saying* (*legOn*). **Aor** Act Part to *Pres* Act Part. [tense]
[5] WH omitted by him (^hup' autou).

come out of every town of Galilee, and Judaea, and Jerusalem: and the power of the Lord was *present* to heal **them**[1].

18 And, behold, men brought in a bed a man which was taken with a palsy: and they sought *means* to bring him in, and to lay *him* before him.

19 And when they could not find ~~by~~[2] what *way* they might bring him in because of the multitude, they went upon the housetop, and let him down through the tiling with *his* couch into the midst before Jesus.

20 And when he saw their faith, he said ~~unto him~~[3], Man, thy sins are forgiven thee.

21 And the scribes and th e Pharisees began to reason, saying, Who is this which speaketh blasphemies? Who can forgive sins, but God alone?

22 But when Jesus perceived their thoughts, he answering said unto them, What reason ye in your hearts?

23 Whether is easier, to say, Thy sins be forgiven thee; or to say, Rise up and walk?

24 But that ye may know that the Son of man hath power upon earth to forgive sins, (he said unto the sick of the palsy,) I say unto thee, Arise, and take up thy couch, and go into thine house.

25 And immediately he rose up before them, and took up that whereon he lay, and departed to his own house, glorifying God.

26 And they were all amazed, and they glorified God, and were filled with fear, saying, We have seen strange things to day.

27 And after these things he went forth, and saw a publican, named Levi, sitting at the receipt of custom: and he said unto him, Follow me.

28 And he left **all**[4], rose up, and **followed**[5] him.

29 And Levi made him a

---

[1] WH changed **them** (aut**ous**) to *him* (*auton*). **Plur** to *Sing*. [number] They retained them (autous) in their margin, however.
[2] WH omitted by (dia).
[3] WH omitted unto him (autO).

[4] WH changed all (**h**apanta) to *all* (*panta*).
[5] WH changed followed (Akolou**th**Asen) to *was following* (*Akolou**th**ei*). **Aor** Act Ind to *Impf* Act Ind. [tense]

great feast in his own house: and there was a great company of publicans and of others that sat down with them.

30 But their scribes **and Pharisees**[1] murmured against his disciples, saying, Why do ye eat and drink with [∧the][2] publicans and sinners?

31 And Jesus answering said unto them, They that are whole need not a physician; but they that are sick.

32 I came not to call the righteous, but sinners to repentance.

33 And they said unto him, ~~Why~~[3] do the disciples of John fast often, and make prayers, and likewise *the disciples* of the Pharisees; but thine eat and drink?

34 And [∧Jesus][4] he said unto them, Can ye make the children of the bridechamber fast, while the bridegroom is with them?

35 But the days will come, when the bridegroom shall be taken away from them, and then shall they fast in those days.

36 And he spake also a parable unto them; No man [∧**having torn**][5] putteth a piece [∧**from**][6] of a new garment upon an old; if otherwise, then both the new **maketh a rent**[7], and ∧**the**[8] piece that was *taken* out of the new **agreeth**[9] not with the old.

37 And no man putteth new wine into old bottles; else the new wine will burst the bottles, and be spilled, and the bottles shall perish.

38 But new wine must be put into new bottles; ~~and both are preserved~~[10].

---

[1] WH changed the word order from the scribes of them AND THE PHARISEES to *THE PHARISEES AND the scribes of them.*

[2] WH added *the (tOn).*

[3] WH omitted why (diati).

[4] WH added *Jesus (iAsous).* [They changed and the {one} said to *and the Jesus said.*]

[5] WH added *having torn (scisas).*

[6] WH added *from (apo).* They changed a piece {of} (noun in **genitive** case) to *a piece from (apo).*

[7] WH changed tears (scizei) to *will tear (scisei).* **Pres** Act Ind to *Fut* Act Ind. [tense]

[8] WH added *the (ton)* as the KJV supplied.

[9] WH changed agrees (sumfOnei) to *will agree (sumfOnAsei).* **Pres** Act Ind to *Fut* Act Ind. [tense]

[10] WH omitted and both are preserved (kai amfoteroi suntArountai).

39 No man also having drunk old *wine* ~~straightway~~[1] desireth new: for he saith, The old is **better**[2].

CHAPTER 6

1   And it came to pass on the ~~second~~ sabbath ~~after the first~~[3], that he went through ~~the~~ corn fields; and his disciples plucked the ears of corn, and did eat, rubbing *them* in *their* hands.

2   And certain of the Pharisees said ~~unto them~~[4], Why do ye that which is not lawful to do ~~on~~[5] the sabbath days?

3   And Jesus answering them said, Have ye not read so much as this, what David did, **when**[6] himself was an

hungred, and they which were with him;

4   How he went into the house of God, and **did take**[7] ~~and~~[8] eat the shewbread, and gave also to them that were with him; which it is not lawful to eat but for the priests alone?

5   And he said unto them, That the Son of man is Lord ~~also~~[9] of the sabbath.

6   And it came to pass ~~also~~[10] on another sabbath, that he entered into the synagogue and taught: and **there**[11] was a man whose right hand was withered.

7   And the scribes and Pharisees **watched**[12] him, whether he would heal on the sabbath day; that they might

---

to *when* (^hote).

[7] WH changed **did** take (**elabe**) to *having taken* (la-b**On**). Aor Act **Ind** to Aor Act *Part*. [mood]

[8] WH omitted and (kai).

[9] WH omitted also (kai).

[10] WH omitted also (kai).

[11] WH changed the word order from and was THERE a man to *and was a man THERE*.

[12] WH changed were watching (paretAroun) to were watching {*for themselves*} (paretArounto). Impf **Act** Ind to Impf *Mid* Ind [voice]

[1] WH omitted straightway (eutheOs).

[2] WH changed **better** (crAsteros) to *good* (crAstos) in their text, but retained better in their margin.

[3] WH omitted "second-first" (deutero-prOtO) in their text, but retained the term in their margin.

[4] WH omitted unto them (autois).

[5] WH omitted on (en), leaving the dative case to supply the preposition.

[6] WH changed when (^opote)

find **an accusation against**[1] him.

8 But he knew their thoughts, **and**[2] said to the man which had the withered hand, Rise up, and stand forth in the midst. **And**[3] ~~**he**~~[4] arose and stood forth.

9 **Then**[5] said Jesus unto them, **I will ask**[6] you **one thing**[7]; Is it lawful **on the sabbath days**[8] to do good, or to do evil? to save life, or to destroy *it*?

10 And looking round about upon them all, **he said unto the man**[9], Stretch forth thy hand. And he did ~~**so**~~[10]: and his hand was restored ~~**whole as the other**~~[11].

11 And they were filled with madness; and communed one with another what they might do to Jesus.

12 And it came to pass in those days, that **[^himself]**[12] **he went out**[13] into a mountain to pray, and continued all night in prayer to God.

13 And when it was day, he called *unto him* his disciples: and of them he chose twelve, whom also he named apostles;

14 Simon, (whom he also named Peter,) and Andrew his brother, **[^and]**[14] James

---

[1] WH changed an accusation against (katAgorian) to ***to be making** an accusation against* (*katAgorein*). **Noun** Acc Sing Fem to ***Verb*** Pres Act Inf.

[2] WH changed **and** (**kai**) to ***but*** (*de*) and placed it after said.

[3] WH changed and (**de**) to *and* (***kai***).

[4] WH omitted he (^h^o—the {one}).

[5] WH changed **then** (**oun**) to ***but*** (*de*).

[6] WH changed I **will** ask (eperOtAsO) to *I **am asking*** (*eperOtO*). **Fut** Act Ind to ***Pres*** Act Ind. [tense]

[7] WH changed **some thing** (**ti**) to ***if*** (*ei*).*

[8] WH changed on the sabbath days (**tois** sabbasin) to *on the sabbath day* (*tO sabbatO*). Dat **Plur** to Dat ***Sing***. [number]

[9] WH changed he said unto **the man** (eipe **tO anthrOpO**) to *he said unto **him*** (*eipen **autO***).

[10] WH omitted so (^h^utO).

[11] WH omitted whole as the other (^h^ugiAs ^h^Os ^h^A allA).

[12] WH added *himself* (*auton*).

[13] WH changed **he went** out (exAlthen) to ***to go** out* (*exelthein*). Aor Act **Ind** to Aor Act ***Inf***. [mood]

[14] WH added *and* (*kai*).

and John, [∧and]¹ Philip and Bartholomew,

15 [∧and]² Matthew and Thomas, James ~~the son of~~ [the]³ Alphaeus, and Simon called Zelotes,

16 And Judas *the brother* of James, and Judas Iscariot, which ~~also~~⁴ was the traitor.

17 And he came down with them, and stood in the plain, and the [∧great]⁵ company of his disciples, and a great multitude of people out of all Judaea and Jerusalem, and from the sea coast of Tyre and Sidon, which came to hear him, and to be healed of their diseases;

18 And they **that were vexed**⁶ **with**⁷ unclean spirits: ~~and~~⁸ they were healed.

19 And the whole multitude sought to touch him: for there went virtue out of him,

and healed *them* all.

20 And he lifted up his eyes on his disciples, and said, Blessed *be ye* poor: for yours is the kingdom of God.

21 Blessed *are ye* that hunger now: for ye shall be filled. Blessed *are ye* that weep now: for ye shall laugh.

22 Blessed are ye, when men shall hate you, and when they shall separate you *from their company*, and shall reproach *you*, and cast out your name as evil, for the Son of man's sake.

23 **Rejoice**⁹ ye in that day, and leap for joy: for, behold, your reward *is* great in heaven: for in **the like manner**¹⁰ did their fathers unto the prophets.

24 But woe unto you that are rich! for ye have received your consolation.

25 Woe unto you that are full [∧now]¹¹! for ye shall hunger. Woe ~~unto you~~¹² that laugh now! for ye shall

---

¹ WH added *and* (kai).
² WH added *and* (kai).
³ WH omitted the [son] of the (ton tou).
⁴ WH omitted also (kai).
⁵ WH added *great* (polus).
⁶ WH changed that were vexed (ocloumenoi) to *that were vexed* (**enocloumenoi**). Both Pres Pass Part. [prefix added]
⁷ WH changed **with** (ʰupo) to *from* (apo).
⁸ WH omitted and (kai).

⁹ WH changed **be** rejoic**ing** (cairete) to *rejoice* (*cairate*). **Pres Act** Imp to *Aor Pass* Imp. [tense & voice]
¹⁰ WH changed **these** {things} (tauta) to *the same* {things} (*ta auta*).
¹¹ WH added *now* (nun).
¹² WH omitted unto you (ʰumin).

mourn and weep.

26 Woe ~~unto you~~,[1] when all men shall speak well of you! for **so**[2] did their fathers to the false prophets.

27 But I say unto you which hear, Love your enemies, do good to them which hate you,

28 Bless them that curse you, ~~and~~[3] pray for them which despitefully use you.

29 And unto him that smiteth thee on the *one* cheek offer also the other; and him that taketh away thy cloke forbid not *to take thy* coat also.

30 [and][4] Give to every man ~~that~~[5] asketh of thee; and of him that taketh away thy goods ask *them* not again.

31 And as ye would that men should do to you, do ye also to them likewise.

32 For if ye love them which love you, what thank

have ye? for sinners also love those that love them.

33 And if ye do good to them which do good to you, what thank have ye? for sinners also do even the same.

34 And if ye lend *to them* of whom ye hope **to receive**[6], what thank have ye? ~~for~~ [the][7] sinners also lend to sinners, to receive as much again.

35 But love ye your enemies, and do good, and lend, hoping for **nothing**[8] again; and your reward shall be great, and ye shall be the children of the Highest: for he is kind unto the unthankful and *to* the evil.

36 Be ye ~~therefore~~[9] merciful, as your Father ~~also~~[10] is merciful.

37 [∧and][11] Judge not, and ye shall not be judged:

---

[6] WH changed <u>to receive</u> {**from**} (**apo**labein) to *to receive* (*labein*). Both Aor Act Inf. [prefix dropped]

[7] WH omitted <u>for</u> (<u>gar</u>) and the untranslated <u>the</u> (^hoi).

[8] In their margin, WH changed **nothing** (mAden) to *nothing* (*mAdena*).

[9] WH omitted <u>therefore</u> (<u>oun</u>).

[10] WH omitted <u>also</u> (<u>kai</u>).

[11] WH added *and* (*kai*).

---

[1] WH omitted <u>unto you</u> (^humin).

[2] WH changed <u>according to</u> **these** {things} (<u>kata tauta</u>) to *according to the same* {things} (kata *ta auta*).

[3] WH omitted <u>and</u> (<u>kai</u>).

[4] WH omitted the untranslated <u>and</u> (<u>de</u>).

[5] WH omitted <u>that</u> (<u>tO</u>--the {one}).

[ᴧand]¹ condemn not, and ye shall not be condemned: forgive, and ye shall be forgiven:

38 Give, and it shall be given unto you; good measure, pressed down, **and**² shaken together, **and**³ running over, shall men give into your bosom. For with ~~the same~~⁴ measure **that**⁵ ye mete withal it shall be measured to you again.

39 And he spake [ᴧalso]⁶ a parable unto them, Can the blind lead the blind? **shall they** not both **fall**⁷ into the ditch?

40 The disciple is not above **his**⁸ master: but every one that is perfect shall be as his master.

41 And why beholdest thou the mote that is in thy brother's eye, but perceivest not the beam that is in thine own eye?

42 Either how canst thou say to thy brother, Brother, let me pull out the mote that is in thine eye, when thou thyself beholdest not the beam that is in thine own eye? Thou hypocrite, cast out first the beam out of thine own eye, and then shalt thou see clearly to pull out the mote that is in thy brother's eye.

43 For a good tree bringeth not forth corrupt fruit; neither [ᴧagain]⁹ doth a corrupt tree bring forth good fruit.

44 For every tree is known by his own fruit. For of thorns men do not gather figs, nor of a bramble bush gather they grapes.

45 A good man out of the good treasure of his heart bringeth forth that which is good; and an evil **man**¹⁰ out of the evil ~~treasure of his heart~~¹¹ bringeth forth that

---

¹ WH added *and* (*kai*).
² WH omitted <u>and</u> (<u>kai</u>).
³ WH omitted <u>and</u> (<u>kai</u>).
⁴ WH omitted <u>the same</u> (<u>tO autO</u>).
⁵ WH changed the word order from <u>for</u> <u>with</u> **the same** <u>measure</u> THAT to *for with THAT measure*.
⁶ WH added *also* (*kai*).
⁷ WH changed <u>shall they fall</u> (<u>pesountai</u>) to *shall they fall in* (*empesountai*). Both Fut M/P Ind. [prefix added]
⁸ WH omitted <u>of him</u> (<u>autou</u>) from <u>the</u> <u>master of him</u>.

⁹ WH added *again* (*palin*).
¹⁰ WH omitted <u>man</u> (<u>anthrOpos</u>) and forced <u>evil</u> to supply the implied *one*.
¹¹ WH omitted <u>treasure</u> of his heart (<u>thAsaurou tAs kardias autou</u>).

which is evil: for of ~~the~~[1] abundance of ~~the~~[2] heart his mouth speaketh.

46 And why call ye me, Lord, Lord, and do not the things which I say?

47 Whosoever cometh to me, and heareth my sayings, and doeth them, I will shew you to whom he is like:

48 He is like a man which built an house, and digged deep, and laid the foundation on a rock: and when the flood arose, the stream beat vehemently upon that house, and could not shake it: **for it was founded upon a rock**[3].

49 But he that heareth, and doeth not, is like a man that without a foundation built an house upon the earth; against which the stream did beat vehemently, and **immediately**[4] **it fell**[5]; and the ruin

of that house was great.

CHAPTER 7

1 **Now when**[6] he had ended all his sayings in the audience of the people, he entered into Capernaum.

2 And a certain centurion's servant, who was dear unto him, was sick, and ready to die.

3 And when he heard of Jesus, he sent unto him the elders of the Jews, beseeching him that he would come and heal his servant.

4 And when they came to Jesus, they besought him instantly, saying, That he was worthy for whom **he should do**[7] this:

5 For he loveth our nation, and he hath built us a synagogue.

6 Then Jesus went with

---

[1] WH omitted the (tou).
[2] WH omitted the (tAs).
[3] WH changed **for** it was **founded upon a rock** (te**th**emeliOto **gar epi tAn petran**) to *because it was well built* (*dia to kalOs oikodomAs**th**ai autAn*). They retained the KJV reading in their margin, however.
[4] WH changed **immediately** (eu**th**eOs) to *suddenly* (*eu**th**us*).

---

[5] WH changed it fell (epese) to *it fell **together*** (*sunepese*). Both Aor Act Ind. [prefix added]
[6] WH changed now when (epei de) to *now when* (*ep-eidA*).
[7] WH changed he will do (parexei) to he will do {**for himself**} (*parexA*). Fut **Act** Ind to 2Fut *MidDep* Ind. [voice]

them. And when he was now not far from the house, the centurion sent friends to him, saying unto him, Lord, trouble not thyself: for I am not worthy that thou shouldest enter under my roof:

7 Wherefore neither thought I myself worthy to come unto thee: but say in a word, and my servant shall be healed.

8 For I also am a man set under authority, having under me soldiers, and I say unto one, Go, and he goeth; and to another, Come, and he cometh; and to my servant, Do this, and he doeth *it*.

9 When Jesus heard these things, he marvelled at him, and turned him about, and said unto the people that followed him, I say unto you, I have not found so great faith, no, not in Israel.

10 And they that were sent, returning **to the house**[1], found the servant whole ~~that had been sick~~[2].

11 And it came to pass **the**[3] day after, that **he went**[4] into a city called Nain; and ~~many of~~[5] his disciples went with him, and much people.

12 Now when he came nigh to the gate of the city, behold, there was a dead man carried out, the only son of his mother, and she was a widow: and much people of the city was with her.

13 And when the Lord saw her, he had compassion on her, and said unto her, Weep not.

14 And he came and touched the bier: and they that bare *him* stood still. And he said, Young man, I say unto thee, Arise.

15 And he that was dead sat up, and began to speak. And he delivered him to his mother.

16 And there came a fear on all: and they glorified

---

[1] WH changed the word order from and returning they that were sent TO THE HOUSE found to *and returning TO THE HOUSE* **they that were sent** *found*.
[2] WH omitted that had been sick, the single word (asthenounta).
[3] WH changed the (tA) to *the* (*tO*) in their text, but retained the (tA) in their margin. Fem to Masc. [gender]
[4] WH changed he **was going** (eporeueto) to *he went* (eporeue*thA*). **Impf** M/P Ind to *Aor* Pass Ind. [tense]
[5] WH omitted many of ([h]ika-noi).

God, saying, That a great prophet **is risen up**[1] among us; and, That God hath visited his people.

17 And this rumour of him went forth throughout all Judaea, and **throughout**[2] all the region round about.

18 And the disciples of John shewed him of all these things.

19 And John calling *unto him* two of his disciples sent *them* to **Jesus**[3], saying, Art thou he that should come? or look we for another?

20 When the men were come unto him, they said, John Baptist hath sent us unto thee, saying, Art thou he that should come? or look we for another?

21 **And**[4] in **that same**[5] hour he cured many of *their* infirmities and plagues, and of evil spirits; and unto many

that were blind he gave **[the]**[6] sight.

22 Then **Jesus**[7] answering said unto them, Go your way, and tell John what things ye have seen and heard; how **that**[8] the blind see, the lame walk, the lepers are cleansed, **[ʌand]**[9] the deaf hear, the dead are raised, to the poor the gospel is preached.

23 And blessed is *he*, whosoever shall not be offended in me.

24 And when the messengers of John were departed, he began to speak unto the people concerning John, What **went ye out**[10] into the wilderness for to see? A reed shaken with the wind?

25 But what **went ye out**[11]

---

[1] WH changed **has** risen **up** (**eg**Ager**tai**) to *was risen* (*Ager**thA***). **Pf** Pass Ind to *Aor* Pass Ind. [tense & prefix dropped]

[2] WH omitted throughout (en).

[3] WH changed {the} **Jesus** (ton iAsoun) to *the **Lord*** (*ton kurion*).

[4] WH omitted and (de).

[5] WH change {that} **same** (**autA**) to *that* (*ekeinA*).

[6] WH omitted the untranslated the (to) from graciously-granted the to see (ecarisato to blepein).

[7] WH omitted the Jesus ([h]o iAsous) and forced the verb to supply the subject *he*.

[8] WH omitted that ([h]oti).

[9] WH added *and* (kai).

[10] WH changed **have** ye **gone** out (exe**I**Alut**h**ate) to *went ye out* (*exAl**th**ate*). **Pf** Act Ind to *Aor* Act Ind. [tense]

[11] WH changed **have** ye **gone** out (exe**I**Alut**h**ate) to *went ye out* (*exAl**th**ate*). **Pf** Act Ind to *Aor* Act Ind. [tense]

for to see? A man clothed in soft raiment? Behold, they which are gorgeously apparelled, and live delicately, are in kings' courts.

26 But what **went ye out**[1] for to see? A prophet? yea, I say unto you, and much more than a prophet.

27 This is *he*, of whom it is written, Behold, I send my messenger before thy face, which shall prepare thy way before thee.

28 ~~For~~[2] I say unto you, Among those that are born of women there is not a greater ~~prophet~~[3] than John ~~the Baptist~~[4]: but he that is least in the kingdom of God is greater than he.

29 And all the people that heard *him*, and the publicans, justified God, being baptized with the baptism of John.

30 But the Pharisees and lawyers rejected the counsel of God against themselves, being not baptized of him.

31 ~~And the Lord said~~[5], Whereunto then shall I liken the men of this generation? and to what are they like?

32 They are like unto children sitting in the marketplace, and calling one to another, **and**[6] **saying**[7], We have piped unto you, and ye have not danced; we have mourned ~~to you~~[8], and ye have not wept.

33 For John the Baptist came **neither**[9] eating bread nor drinking wine; and ye say, He hath a devil.

34 The Son of man is come eating and drinking; and ye say, Behold a gluttonous man, and a winebibber, a friend of publicans and sinners!

35 But wisdom is justified of all her children.

36 And one of the Pharisees desired him that he

---

[1] WH changed **have ye gone** out (*exelAluthate*) to *went ye out* (*exAlthate*). **Pf** Act Ind to *Aor* Act Ind. [tense]

[2] WH omitted <u>for</u> (gar).

[3] WH omitted prophet (profAtAs).

[4] WH omitted the Baptist (to baptistou).

[5] WH omitted <u>and the Lord said</u> (eipe de [h]o kurios).

[6] WH changed **and** (**kai**) to *which* {*things*} (*[h]a*).

[7] WH changed saying (le-**gousin**) to *he says* (*legei*). Pres Act **Part** 3rd **Plur** to Pres Act *Ind* 3rd *Sing*. [mood & number]

[8] WH omitted <u>to you</u> ([h]umin).

[9] WH changed **neither** (mAte) to *not* (mA).

would eat with him. And he went into the Pharisee's house, and **sat down to meat**[1].

37 And, behold, a woman in the city, **which was**[2] a sinner, when she knew that *Jesus* **sat at meat**[3] in the Pharisee's house, brought an alabaster box of ointment,

38 And stood at his feet **behind**[4] *him* weeping, and began to wash his feet with tears, and **did wipe**[5] *them* with the hairs of her head, and kissed his feet, and anointed *them* with the oint-

ment.

39 Now when the Pharisee which had bidden him saw *it*, he spake within himself, saying, This man, if he were a **[the]**[6] prophet, would have known who and what manner of woman *this* *is* that toucheth him: for she is a sinner.

40 And Jesus answering said unto him, Simon, I have somewhat to say unto thee. And he saith, Master, say on.

41 There was a certain creditor which had two debtors: the one owed five hundred pence, and the other fifty.

42 ~~And~~[7] when they had nothing to pay, he frankly forgave them both. ~~Tell me~~[8] therefore, which of them will love him most?

43 **[but]**[9] Simon answered and said, I suppose that *he*, to whom he forgave most. And he said unto him, Thou hast rightly judged.

44 And he turned to the woman, and said unto Simon,

---

[1] WH changed was sat {**up**} (**an**eklit*h*A) to *was sat* {*down*} (*kateklit*h*A*). Both Aor Pass Ind. [prefix changed]

[2] WH changed the word order from in the city WHICH WAS to *WHICH WAS in the city*.

[3] WH changed is sitting {**up**} (**ana**keitai) to *is sitting* {*down*} (*katakeitai*). Both Pres M/P Ind. [prefix changed]

[4] WH changed the word order from at his feet BEHIND to *BEHIND at his feet*.

[5] WH changed **was** wip**ing** (exemasse) to *wiped* (*exemaxe*). **Impf** Act Ind to *Aor* Act Ind. [tense]

[6] In their margin, WH added *the* (*ʰo*).

[7] WH omitted and (de).

[8] WH omitted tell {me} (eipe).

[9] WH omitted the untranslated but (de).

Seest thou this woman? I entered into thine house, thou gavest me no water for my feet: but she hath washed my feet with tears, and wiped *them* with the hairs of her **head**[1].

45 Thou gavest me no kiss: but this woman since the time I came in hath not ceased to kiss my feet.

46 My head with oil thou didst not anoint: but this woman hath anointed my feet with ointment.

47 Wherefore I say unto thee, Her sins, which are many, are forgiven; for she loved much: but to whom little is forgiven, *the same* loveth little.

48 And he said unto her, Thy sins are forgiven.

49 And they that sat at meat with him began to say within themselves, Who is this that forgiveth sins also?

50 And he said to the woman, Thy faith hath saved thee; go in peace.

CHAPTER 8

1　And it came to pass afterward, that he went throughout every city and village, preaching and shewing the glad tidings of the kingdom of God: and the twelve *were* with him,

2　And certain women, which had been healed of evil spirits and infirmities, Mary called Magdalene, out of whom went seven devils,

3　And Joanna the wife of Chuza Herod's steward, and Susanna, and many others, which ministered **unto him**[2] **of**[3] their substance.

4　And when much people were gathered together, and were come to him out of every city, he spake by a parable:

5　A sower went out to sow his seed: and as he sowed, some fell by the way side; and it was trodden down, and the fowls of the air devoured it.

6　And some **fell**[4] upon a rock; and as soon as it was

---

[1] WH omitted of the head (tAs kefalAs) from the hairs of the head of her.

[2] WH changed unto **him** (aut**O**) to unto *them* (*autois*). Dat **Sing** to Dat *Plur*. [number]

[3] WH changed of (**apo**) to *out* of (*ek*).

[4] WH changed fell (*epesen*) to *fell* ***down*** (*katepesen*). Both Aor Act Ind. [prefix added]

sprung up, it withered away, because it lacked moisture.

7   And some fell among thorns; and the thorns sprang up with it, and choked it.

8   And other fell **on**[1] good ground, and sprang up, and bare fruit an hundredfold. And when he had said these things, he cried, He that hath ears to hear, let him hear.

9   And his disciples asked him, ~~saying~~[2], What might this parable be?

10   And he said, Unto you it is given to know the mysteries of the kingdom of God: but to others in parables; that seeing they might not see, and hearing they might not understand.

11   Now the parable is this: The seed is the word of God.

12   Those by the way side are they that **hear**[3]; then cometh the devil, and taketh away the word out of their hearts, lest they should believe and be saved.

13   They on the rock *are they*, which, when they hear, receive the word with joy; and these have no root, which for a while believe, and in time of temptation fall away.

14   And that which fell among thorns are they, which, when they have heard, go forth, and are choked with cares and riches and pleasures of *this* life, and bring no fruit to perfection.

15   But that on the good ground are they, which in an honest and good heart, having heard the word, keep *it*, and bring forth fruit with patience.

16   No man, when he hath lighted a candle, covereth it with a vessel, or putteth *it* under a bed; but **setteth**[4] *it* on a candlestick, that they which enter in may see the light.

17   For nothing is secret, that shall not be made manifest; neither *any thing* hid, that **shall** not [∧**not**][5] **be known**[6] and come abroad.

---

[1] WH changed **on** (**epi**) to *into* (*eis*).

[2] WH omitted saying (legontes).

[3] WH changed hearing (akouontes) to *having heard* (*akousontes*). **Pres** Act Part to *Aor* Act Part. [tense]

[4] WH changed sets {**upon**}(**epi**tithAsin) to *sets* (*ti*thAsin). Both Pres Act Ind. [prefix dropped]

[5] WH added *not* (*mA*) to strengthen the negative.

[6] WH changed **shall be** known (gnOsthAsetai) to *might* be known (*gnOsthA*). **Fut** Pass **Ind** to *Aor* Pass *Sub*. [tense & mood]

18 Take heed therefore how ye hear: for whosoever hath, to him shall be given; and whosoever hath not, from him shall be taken even that which he seemeth to have.

19 Then came to him *his* mother and his brethren, and could not come at him for the press.

20 **And** **it was told**[1] him *by certain* ~~which said~~[2], Thy mother and thy brethren stand without, desiring to see thee.

21 And he answered and said unto them, My mother and my brethren are these which hear the word of God, and do ~~it~~[3].

22 **Now** **it came to pass**[4] a on certain day, that he went into a ship with his disciples: and he said unto them, Let us go over unto the other side of the lake. And they launched forth.

23 But as they sailed he fell asleep: and there came down a storm of wind on the lake; and they were filled *with water*, and were in jeopardy.

24 And they came to him, and awoke him, saying, Master, master, we perish. Then **he arose**[5], and rebuked the wind and the raging of the water: and they ceased, and there was a calm.

25 And he said unto them, Where ~~is~~[6] your faith? And they being afraid wondered, saying one to another, What manner of man is this! for he commandeth even the winds and water, and they obey him.

26 And they arrived at the country of the **Gadarenes**[7], which is over against Galilee.

27 And when he went forth to land, there met ~~him~~[8] out of the city a certain man,

---

[1] WH changed **and** (**kai**) to *but* (*de*) and put it was told (apAggelA) first.

[2] WH omitted the participle saying (legontOn).

[3] WH omitted it (auton).

[4] WH changed **and** (**kai**) to *but* (*de*) and put it came to pass (egeneto) first.

[5] WH changed he arose (eger~~th~~eis) to *he arose **up*** (dieger~~th~~eis). Both Aor Act Part. [prefix added]

[6] WH omitted is (estin).

[7] WH changed Gadarenes (gadarAnOn) to Garasenes (garasAnOn). In their margin, they have *Gergesenes* (gergesAnOn) or Gadarenes (gadarAnOn).

[8] WH omitted him (autO).

~~which~~[1] __had__[2] devils [~~out of~~][3] __long time__[4], __and__ __ware__[5] no __clothes__[6], neither abode in *any* house, but in the tombs.

28 When he saw Jesus, he cried out, ~~and~~[7] fell down before him, and with a loud voice said, What have I to do with thee, Jesus, *thou* Son of God most high? I beseech thee, torment me not.

29 (For __he had commanded__[8] the unclean spirit to come out of the man. For oftentimes it had caught him: and __he was kept bound__[9] with chains and in fetters; and he brake the bands, and was driven of the __devil__[10] into the wilderness.)

30 And Jesus asked him, ~~saying~~[11], What is thy name? And he said, Legion: because many devils were entered into him.

31 And they besought him that he would not command them to go out into the deep.

32 And there was there an herd of many swine __feeding__[12] on the mountain: and they besought him that he would

---

[1] WH omitted <u>which</u> (<u>**ʰos**</u>).

[2] WH changed __were__ having (<u>eice</u>) to *having* (<u>ecoOn</u>). **Impf** Act **Ind** to *Pres* Act *Part.* [tense & mood]

[3] WH omitted the untranslated <u>out of</u> (<u>ek</u>).

[4] WH changed {of} <u>long times</u> (<u>cronOn ʰikanOn</u>) to {**for**} *long time* (<u>cronO ʰikanO</u>). **Gen Plur** to *Dat Sing.* [case & number]

[5] changed __was wearing__ (<u>enedidusketo</u>) to *wore* (<u>enedusato</u>) **Impf** Mid Ind to *Aor* Mid Ind

[6] WH changed the word order from __out of__ <u>times</u> <u>long</u> <small>AND CLOTHING</small> <u>not</u> **was wearing** to *AND* {*for*} *time long not* **wore** *CLOTHING*.

[7] WH omitted <u>and</u> (<u>kai</u>).

[8] WH changed he **was** commanding (parAggeile) to *he commanded* (parAggelle).

Impf Act Ind to *Aor* Act Ind. [tense]

[9] WH changed <u>he was being bound</u> (<u>edesmeito</u>) to *he was being bound* (<u>edesmeueto</u>). Both Impf Pass Ind of <u>desmeuO</u>. [spell]

[10] WH changed <u>devil</u> (<u>daimonos</u>) to *devil* (<u>daimoniou</u>). Gen Sing **Masc** to Gen Sing *Neut.* [gender]

[11] WH omitted <u>saying</u> (<u>legOn</u>).

[12] WH changed <u>being fed</u> (<u>boskomenOn</u>) to *being fed* (<u>boskomenA</u>). Both Pres Pass Part. **Gen Plur Masc** to *Nom Sing Fem.* [case, number, & gender]

suffer them to enter into them. And he suffered them.

33 Then went the devils out of the man, and entered into the swine: and the herd ran violently down a steep place into the lake, and were choked.

34 When they that fed *them* saw what **was done**[1], they fled, and **went**[2] and told *it* in the city and in the country.

35 Then they went out to see what was done; and came to Jesus, and found the man, out of whom the devils **were departed**[3], sitting at the feet of Jesus, clothed, and in his right mind: and they were afraid.

36 They **also**[4] which saw *it* told them by what means he that was possessed of the devils was healed.

37 Then the whole multitude of the country of the **Gadarenes**[5] round about **besought**[6] him to depart from them; for they were taken with great fear: and he went up into **the**[7] ship, and returned back again.

38 Now the man out of whom the devils were departed besought him that he might be with him: but **Jesus**[8] sent him away, saying,

39 Return to thine own house, and shew how great things God hath done unto thee. And he went his way, and published throughout the whole city how great things Jesus had done unto him.

40 **And** ~~it came to pass~~[9],

---

[1] WH changed having **been** done (gegen**Amenon**) to *having done* (*gegonos*). Pf **Pass** Part to Pf *Act* Part. [voice]

[2] WH omitted having gone (apel~~th~~ontes).

[3] WH changed **had** departed (exel~~A~~lu~~th~~ei) to *departed* (*exAl~~then~~*). **PastPf** Act Ind to **Aor** Act Ind. [tense]

[4] WH omitted also (kai).

[5] WH changed Gadarenes (**gadar**AnOn) to *Gerasenes* (*gerasAnOn*). In their margin, they have *Gergesenes* (*gergesAnOn*) or Gadarenes (gadarAnOn).

[6] WH changed {**they**} besought (ArOtAsan) to {**it**} *besought* (*ArOtAsen*). Both Aor Act Ind. **Plur** to *Sing*. [number]

[7] WH omitted the (to).

[8] WH omitted the Jesus ([h]o iAsous) and forced the verb to supply the subject *he*.

[9] WH omitted it came to pass, the single word egeneto and forced and (de) back to its usual second-place position.

that, **when** Jesus **was re-turned**[1], the people *gladly* received him: for they were all waiting for him.

41 And, behold, there came a man named Jairus, and he was a ruler of the synagogue: and he fell down at Jesus' feet, and besought him that he would come into his house:

42 For he had one only daughter, about twelve years of age, and she lay a dying. But as he went the people thronged him.

43 And a woman having an issue of blood twelve years, which **had spent all her living**[2] **upon**[3] **physicians**[4], neither could be healed **of**[5] any,

44 Came behind *him*, and touched the border of his garment: and immediately her issue of blood stanched.

45 And Jesus said, Who touched me? When all denied, Peter **and they that were with him**[6] said, Master, the multitude throng thee and press *thee*, **and sayest thou, Who touched me**[7]?

46 And Jesus said, Somebody hath touched me: for I perceive that virtue **is gone out**[8] of me.

47 And when the woman saw that she was not hid, she came trembling, and falling down before him, she declared **unto him**[9] before all the people for what cause she had touched him, and how she was healed immediately.

48 And he said unto her, Daughter, **be of good comfort**[10]: thy faith hath made

---

[1] WH changed to return (*hu-postresai*) to *to be returning* (*hupostrefein*). **Aor** Act Inf to *Pres* Act Inf. [tense]

[2] In their margin, WH omitted had spent all her living (*prosanalOsasa holon ton bion*).

[3] WH omitted upon (*eis*) and forced physicians to supply the implied preposition.

[4] WH changed physicians (*iatrous*) to *physicians* (*iatrois*). **Acc** Masc Plur to *Dat* Masc Plur. [case]

[5] WH changed by (*hup'*) to *from* (*ap'*).

[6] In their margin, WH omitted and the {ones} with him (*kai hoi met' autou*).

[7] WH omitted and sayest thou who touched me (*kai legeis tis ho hasamenos mou*).

[8] WH changed **went** out (*exelthousan*) to *has gone out* (*exelAluthuian*). **Aor** Act Part to *Pf* Act Part. [tense]

[9] WH omitted {unto} him (*autO*).

[10] WH omitted be of good comfort (*tharsei*).

thee whole; go in peace.

49 While he yet spake, there cometh one from the ruler of the synagogue's *house*, saying ~~to him~~[1], Thy daughter is dead; trouble not the Master.

50 But when Jesus heard *it*, he answered him, ~~saying~~[2], Fear not: believe only, and she shall be made whole.

51 And **when he came**[3] into the house, he suffered **no man**[4] to go in, save Peter, and **James,** and **John**[5], and the father and the mother of the maiden.

52 And all wept, and bewailed her: but he said, Weep **not**[6]; she is not dead, but sleepeth.

53 And they laughed him to scorn, knowing that she was dead.

54 And he ~~put them all out, and~~[7] took her by the hand, and called, saying, Maid, arise.

55 And her spirit came again, and she arose straightway: and he commanded to give her meat.

56 And her parents were astonished: but he charged them that they should tell no man what was done.

CHAPTER 9

1 Then he called ~~his~~ twelve ~~disciples~~[8] together, and gave them power and authority over all devils, and to cure diseases.

2 And he sent them to preach the kingdom of God, and to heal ~~the sick~~[9].

3 And he said unto them, Take nothing for *your* journey,

---

[1] WH omitted {unto} him (autO).

[2] WH omitted saying (legOn).

[3] WH changed when he entered {into}(eiselthOn) to *when he entered* (elthOn). [prefix dropped]

[4] WH changed **no man** (**oudena**) to *anyone with him* (**tina sun autO**). The WH change resulted in *he did not permit anyone to enter with him.*

[5] WH changed the word order from JAMES and JOHN to *JOHN and JAMES.*

[6] WH changed not (ouk) to *for* not (ou gar).

[7] WH omitted put out outside them all and (ekbalOn exO pantas kai).

[8] WH omitted disciples of him (mathAtas autou) from the twelve disciples of him.

[9] WH omitted the sick (tous asthenountas).

neither **staves**[1], nor scrip, neither bread, neither money; neither have two coats **apiece**[2].

4 And whatsoever house ye enter into, there abide, and thence depart.

5 And whosoever **will** not **receive**[3] you, when ye go out of that city, shake off the **very**[4] dust from your feet for a testimony against them.

6 And they departed, and went through the towns, preaching the gospel, and healing every where.

7 Now Herod the tetrarch heard of all that was done **by him**[5]: and he was perplexed, because that it was said of some, that John **was risen**[6] from the dead;

8 And of some, that Elias had appeared; and of others, that **one**[7] of the old prophets was risen again.

9 **And**[8] Herod **said**, John have I beheaded: but who is this, of whom I **[myself]**[9] hear such things? And he desired to see him.

10 And the apostles, when they were returned, told him all that they had done. And he took them, and went aside privately into **a desert place**[10] **belonging to the city**[11] **called**[12] Bethsaida.

11 And the people, when they knew *it*, followed him:

Ind to *Aor* Pass Ind. [tense]

[7] WH changed one (**h**eis) to *a certain one* (*tis*).

[8] WH changed **and** (**kai**) to *but* (*de*) and put said (eipen) first in the verse.

[9] WH omitted the untranslated intensive pronoun myself (egO).

[10] WH omitted a desert place (topon erAmon).

[11] WH changed **belonging to the** city (poleOs) to *city* (*polin*). **Gen** Sing Fem to *Dat* Sing Fem. [case].

[12] WH changed being called (kaloumenAs) to *being called* (kaloumenAn) Both Pres Pass Part. **Gen** Sing Fem to *Dat* Sing Fem. [case]

---

[1] WH changed staffs (**h**rabdous) to *staff* (**h**rabdon). Acc **Plur** Fem to Acc *Sing* Fem. [number]

[2] WH omitted apiece (ana).

[3] WH changed **might** receive (dexOntai) to *receiving* (decOntai). **Aor** Mid-D **Sub** to *Pres* M/P-D *Part*. [tense & mood]

[4] WH omitted very (kai).

[5] WH omitted by him (**h**up' autou).

[6] WH changed **has been** raised (egAgerti) to *was raised* (Ager**th**A). **Pf** Pass

and he **received**[1] them, and spake unto them of the kingdom of God, and healed them that had need of healing.

12 And when the day began to wear away, then came the twelve, and said unto him, Send the multitude away, that **they may go**[2] into the towns and [~~the~~][3] country round about, and lodge, and get victuals: for we are here in a desert place.

13 But he said unto them, Give ye them to eat. And they said, We have no more but five loaves and two fishes; except we should go and buy meat for all this people.

14 For they were about five thousand men. And he said to his disciples, Make them sit down by fifties [∧**as it were**][4] in a company.

15 And they did so, and **made** them all **sit down**[5].

16 Then he took the five loaves and the two fishes, and looking up to heaven, he blessed them, and brake, and gave to the disciples to set before the multitude.

17 And they did eat, and were all filled: and there was taken up of fragments that remained to them twelve baskets.

18 And it came to pass, as he was alone praying, his disciples were with him: and he asked them, saying, Whom say the people that I am?

19 They answering said, John the Baptist; but some *say*, Elias; and others *say*, that one of the old prophets is risen again.

20 He said unto them, But whom say ye that I am? Peter answering said, The Christ of God.

21 And he straitly charged them, and commanded *them* **to tell**[6] no man that thing;

22 Saying, The Son of

---

[1] WH changed <u>received</u> (<u>dexamenos</u>) to *received from* (*apodexamenos*). Both Aor Mid-D Part. [prefix added]

[2] WH changed <u>having gone</u> (**apelth**<u>ontes</u>) to *having gone* (*poreu**th**entes*). Aor **Act** Part of **aperc**omai to Aor *Pass-D* Part of *poreuomai*. [voice & syn]

[3] WH omitted the untranslated <u>the</u> (<u>tous</u>).

[4] WH added <u>as it were</u> (<u>[h]osei</u>).

[5] WH changed <u>made sit down</u> (**an**eklinan) to *made sit down* (*kateklinan*). Both Aor Act Ind. [prefix changed & syn]

[6] WH changed <u>to tell</u> (**eip**ein) to *to be telling* (*legein*). **Aor** Act Inf to *Pres* Act Inf. [tense]

man must suffer many things, and be rejected of the elders and chief priests and scribes, and be slain, and be raised the third day.

23　And he said to *them* all, If any *man* **will <u>come</u>**[1] after me, **<u>let him deny</u>**[2] himself, and take up his cross daily, and follow me.

24　For whosoever will save his life shall lose it: but whosoever will lose his life for my sake, the same shall save it.

25　For what is a man advantaged, if he gain the whole world, and lose himself, or be cast away?

26　For whosoever shall be ashamed of me and of my words, of him shall the Son of man be ashamed, when he shall come in his own glory, and *in his* Father's, and of the holy angels.

27　But I tell you of a

truth, there be some standing here, which shall not taste of death, till they see the kingdom of God.

28　And it came to pass about an eight days after these sayings, he took Peter and John and James, and went up into a mountain to pray.

29　And as he prayed, the fashion of his countenance was altered, and his raiment *was* white *and* glistering.

30　And, behold, there talked with him two men, which were Moses and Elias:

31　Who appeared in glory, and spake of his decease which he should accomplish at Jerusalem.

32　But Peter and they that were with him were heavy with sleep: and when they were awake, they saw his glory, and the two men that stood with him.

33　And it came to pass, as they departed from him, Peter said unto Jesus, Master, it is good for us to be here: and let us make three tabernacles; one for thee, and one for Moses, and one for Elias: not knowing what he said.

34　While he thus spake, there came a cloud, and overshadowed them: and they

---

[1] WH changed <u>wills</u> to <u>come</u> (t̶helei **elthein**) to *wills to be* com<u>*ing*</u> (t̶helei **erces̶thai**). <u>**Aor**</u> Act Inf to ***Pres*** M/P-D Inf. [tense & voice]

[2] WH changed <u>let him deny</u> (**ap**arnAsast̶hO) to *let him deny* (*arnAsast̶hO*). Both Aor Mid-D Imp. [prefix dropped & syn]

feared as **they entered**[1] into the cloud.

35 And there came a voice out of the cloud, saying, This is my **beloved**[2] Son: hear him.

36 And when the voice was past, Jesus was found alone. And they kept *it* close, and told no man in those days any of those things which they had seen.

37 And it came to pass, that on the next day, when they were come down from the hill, much people met him.

38 And, behold, a man of the company **cried out**[3], saying, Master, I beseech thee, **look**[4] upon my son: for he is mine only child.

39 And, lo, a spirit taketh him, and he suddenly crieth out; and it teareth him that he foameth again, and bruising him hardly departeth from him.

40 And I besought thy disciples to **cast** him **out**[5]; and they could not.

41 And Jesus answering said, O faithless and perverse generation, how long shall I be with you, and suffer you? Bring thy son hither.

42 And as he was yet a coming, the devil threw him down, and tare *him*. And Jesus rebuked the unclean spirit, and healed the child, and delivered him again to his father.

43 And they were all amazed at the mighty power of God. But while they wondered every one at all things which ~~Jesus~~[6] **did**[7], he said

---

[1] WH changed **those** {ones} entered (**ekeinous** eiselthein) to *they entered* (*eiselthein autous*). [synonym]

[2] WH changed **beloved** (**aga-pAt**os) to *having been chosen out* (*eklelegmenos*). Nom Sing Masc **Noun** to Pf Pass Part Nom Sing Masc *Verbal*. [noun to verbal]. WH retained beloved in their margin, however.

[3] WH changed cried **out** (**ane**bonse) to *cried* (*ebonse*). [prefix dropped & syn]

[4] WH changed look (epible**s on**) to *to look* (*epiblesai*). Aor Act **Imp** to Aor Act **Inf**.

[mood]

[5] WH changed **may be casting** out (ekballOsin) to *might cast out* (*ekbalOsin*). **Pres** Act Sub to *Aor* Act Sub. [tense]

[6] WH omitted the Jesus (ho iAsous).

[7] WH changed **did** (epoi-Asen) to *was doing* (*epoiei*). **Aor** Act Ind to *Impf* Act Ind. [tense]

unto his disciples,

44 Let these sayings sink down into your ears: for the Son of man shall be delivered into the hands of men.

45 But they understood not this saying, and it was hid from them, that they perceived it not: and they feared to ask him of that saying.

46 Then there arose a reasoning among them, which of them should be greatest.

47 And Jesus, perceiving the thought of their heart, took **a child**[1], and set him by him,

48 And said unto them, Whosoever shall receive this child in my name receiveth me: and whosoever shall receive me receiveth him that sent me: for he that is least among you all, the same **shall be**[2] great.

49 And John answered and said, Master, we saw one casting out [~~the~~][3] devils **in**[4]

thy name; and **we forbad**[5] him, because he followeth not with us.

50 **And**[6] Jesus **said** unto him, Forbid *him* not: for he that is not against **us**[7] is for **us**[8].

51 And it came to pass, when the time was come that he should be received up, he stedfastly set his face to go to Jerusalem,

52 And sent messengers before his face: and they went, and entered into a village of the Samaritans, to make ready for him.

53 And they did not receive him, because his face was as though he would go to Jerusalem.

54 And when his disciples James and John saw *this*, they said, Lord, wilt thou that we command fire to come down

---

[1] WH changed a child (paidio**u**) to *a child* (*paidion*). **Gen** to *Acc.* [case]

[2] WH changed **shall be** (estai) to *is* (*esti*). **Fut** Ind to *Pres* Ind. [tense]

[3] WH omitted the untranslated the (ta).

[4] WH changed **upon** (ep**i**) to *in* (*en*).

[5] WH changed we forbade (ekOlusamen) to *we were forbidding* (*ekOluomen*). **Aor** Act Ind to *Impf* Act Ind. [tense]

[6] WH changed **and** (**kai**) to *but* (*de*) and placed said (eipe) at the beginning of the verse.

[7] WH changed **us** (^{h}AmOn) to *you* (^{h}umOn).

[8] WH changed **us** (^{h}AmOn) to *you* (^{h}umOn).

from heaven, and consume them, ~~even as Elias did~~[1]?

55 But he turned, and rebuked them, ~~and said, Ye know not what manner of spirit ye are of~~.

56 ~~For the Son of man is not come to destroy men's lives, but to save *them*~~[2]. And they went to another village.

57 ~~And~~[3] it came to pass[4], that, as they went in the way, a certain *man* said unto him, ~~Lord~~[5], I will follow thee whithersoever thou goest.

58 And Jesus said unto him, Foxes have holes, and birds of the air *have* nests; but the Son of man hath not where to lay *his* head.

59 And he said unto another, Follow me. But he said, Lord, suffer me first to go and bury my father.

60 ~~Jesus~~[6] said unto him, Let the dead bury their dead: but go thou and preach the kingdom of God.

61 And another also said, Lord, I will follow thee; but let me first go bid them farewell, which are at home at my house.

62 And Jesus said unto him, No man, having put his hand to the plough, and looking back, is fit for the kingdom of God.

CHAPTER 10

1 After these things the Lord appointed other seventy ~~[two by two]~~[7] ~~also~~[8], and sent them two and two before his face into every city and place, whither he himself would come.

---

[1] WH omitted <u>even as Elias did</u> (^h<u>Os kai Alias epoiAse</u>) in their text, but retained it in their margin.

[2] WH omitted <u>and said ye know not what manner of spirit ye are of for the son of man is not come to destroy men's lives but to save</u> [them] (<u>kai eipen ouk oidate oiou pneumatos este</u> ^h<u>umeis</u> ^h<u>o gar</u> ^h<u>uios tou anthOpou ouk Althe</u> ^h<u>ucas anthrOpOn apolesai alla sOsai</u>). WH omitted these words in their text, but retained them in their margin.

[3] WH changed <u>and</u> (**de**) to <u>and</u> (**kai**).

[4] WH omitted <u>and it came to pass</u> (<u>egeneto</u>).

[5] WH omitted <u>Lord</u> (<u>kurie</u>).

[6] WH omitted <u>the Jesus</u> (^h<u>o iAsous</u>) and forced the verb to supply the subject *he*.

[7] In their margin, WH added *two by two* (*duo*).

[8] WH omitted <u>also</u> (<u>kai</u>).

2   **Therefore**[1]   said   he unto them, The harvest truly *is* great, but the labourers *are* few: pray ye therefore the Lord of the harvest, that he would   send   forth   labourers into his harvest.

3   Go your ways: behold, I send you forth as lambs among wolves.

4   Carry   neither   purse, nor scrip, **nor**[2] shoes: and salute no man by the way.

5   And   into   whatsoever **house**[3] **ye enter**[4], first say, Peace *be* to this house.

6   And if [indeed][5] **the**[6] son of peace be there, your peace shall rest upon it: if not, it shall turn to you again.

7   And in the same house remain, eating and drinking such things as they give: for

the labourer is worthy of his hire. Go not from house to house.

8   And into [also][7] whatsoever city ye enter, and they receive you, eat such things as are set before you:

9   And heal the sick that are   therein,   and   say   unto them, The kingdom of God is come nigh unto you.

10 But   into   whatsoever city **ye enter**[8], and they receive you not, go your ways out into the streets of the same, and say,

11 Even the very dust of your   city   [ʌon   **the   feet**][9], which cleaveth on us, we do wipe off against you: notwithstanding be ye sure of this, that the kingdom of God is come nigh unto you[10].

12 **But**[11]   I say unto you, that it shall be more tolerable in that day for Sodom, than for that city.

---

[1] WH changed **therefore** (**oun**) to *then* (*de*).

[2] WH changed **but** not (**mAde**) to *not* (*mA*).

[3] WH changed the word order from HOUSE ye enter to *ye enter HOUSE.*

[4] WH changed ye **may be** entering (eisercAsthe) to *ye might enter* (eiselthAte). **Pres** M/P-D Sub to *Aor* Act Sub. [tense]

[5] WH omitted the untranslated indeed (men).

[6] WH omitted the (ho).

[7] WH omitted the untranslated also (de).

[8] WH changed ye **may** enter (eisercAsthe) to *ye might enter* (eiselthAte). **Pres** M/P-D Sub to *Aor* Act Sub. [tense]

[9] WH added *on the feet* (eis tous podas).

[10] WH omitted unto you (ef humas).

[11] WH omitted but (de).

13 Woe unto thee, Chorazin! woe unto thee, Bethsaida! for if the mighty works **had been done**[1] in Tyre and Sidon, which have been done in you, they had a great while ago repented, **sitting**[2] in sackcloth and ashes.

14 But it shall be more tolerable for Tyre and Sidon at the judgment, than for you.

15 And thou, Capernaum, **which**[3] **art exalted**[4] to heaven, shalt be thrust down to hell.

16 He that heareth you heareth me; and he that despiseth you despiseth me; and he that despiseth me despiseth him that sent me.

17 And the seventy returned **[two by two]**[5] again

with joy, saying, Lord, even the devils are subject unto us through thy name.

18 And he said unto them, I beheld Satan as lightning fall from heaven.

19 Behold, **I give**[6] unto you power to tread on serpents and scorpions, and over all the power of the enemy: and nothing shall by any means hurt you.

20 Notwithstanding in this rejoice not, that the spirits are subject unto you; but **rather**[7] rejoice, because your names **are written**[8] in heaven.

21 In that hour ~~Jesus~~[9] rejoiced in spirit [∧**the holy**][10],

---

[1] WH changed became (egen**onto**) to *were become* (egenA*th*Asan). Aor **Mid** Ind to Aor *Pass*-D Ind. [voice]

[2] WH changed sitting (ka*th*Amenai) to sitting (ka*th*Amenoi). Both Pres M/P-D Part. Nom Plur **Fem** to Nom Plur *Masc*. [gender]

[3] WH changed **which** (ʰA) to *not* (*mA*).

[4] WH changed **having been** exalted (ʰu*s*O*th*eisa) to *will be exalted* (ʰu*s*O*th*AsA). **Aor** Pass **Part** to *Fut* Pass **Ind**. [tense & mood]

[5] In their margin, WH add

two by two (*duo*).

[6] WH changed I **am** giving (did**Omi**) to *I have given* (dedOka). **Pres** Act Ind to *Pf* Act Ind. [tense]

[7] WH omitted rather (mallon).

[8] WH changed **were** written (egrafA) to *have been written in* (eggegraptai). **Aor** Pass Ind of grafO to *Pf* Pass Ind of *eggrafO*. [tense & prefix added]

[9] WH omitted Jesus (ʰo iAsous) and forced the verb to supply the subject he.

[10] WH added *the holy* (tO ʰaggiO). The result was *the spirit the holy* or *the Holy Spirit*.

and said, I thank thee, O Father, Lord of heaven and earth, that thou hast hid these things from the wise and prudent, and hast revealed them unto babes: even so, Father; for so it seemed good in thy sight.

22 All things are delivered to me of my Father: and no man knoweth who the Son is, but the Father; and who the Father is, but the Son, and *he* to whom the Son will reveal *him*.

23 And he turned him unto *his* disciples, and said privately, Blessed *are* the eyes which see the things that ye see:

24 For I tell you, that many prophets and kings have desired to see those things which ye see, and have not seen *them*; and to hear those things which ye hear, and have not heard *them*.

25 And, behold, a certain lawyer stood up, and tempted him, [~~and~~][1] saying, Master, what shall I do to inherit eternal life?

26 He said unto him, What is written in the law? how readest thou?

27 And he answering said, Thou shalt love the Lord thy God with all thy heart, and **with all thy soul**[2], and **with all thy strength**[3], and **with all thy mind**[4]; and thy neighbour as thyself.

28 And he said unto him, Thou hast answered right: this do, and thou shalt live.

29 But he, willing **to justify**[5] himself, said unto Jesus, And who is my neighbour?

30 ~~**And**~~[6] Jesus answering said, A certain *man* went down from Jerusalem to Jericho, and fell among thieves, which stripped him of his raiment, and wounded *him*, and departed, leaving *him* half dead [~~**being**~~][7].

31 And by chance there

---

[1] WH omitted the untranslated and (kai).

[2] WH changed **out of** all thy soul (**ex** [h]olAs tAs [s]ucAs sou) to *in all thy soul* (*en* [h]olA tA [s]ucA sou) [prep & case]

[3] WH changed **out of** all thy strength (**ex** [h]olAs tAs iscuos sou) to *in all thy strength* (*en* [h]olA tA iscui sou). [case]

[4] WH changed **out of** all thy mind (**ex** [h]olAs tAs dianoias sou) to *in all thy mind* (*en* [h]olA tA dianoia sou). [case]

[5] WH changed to **be justifying** (dikaioun) to *to justify* (*dikaiOsai*). **Pres** Act Inf to *Aor* Act Inf. [tense]

[6] WH omitted and (de).

[7] WH omitted the untranslated being (tugcanonta).

came down a certain priest that way: and when he saw him, he passed by on the other side.

32 And likewise a Levite, ~~when he was~~[1] at the place, came and looked *on him*, and passed by on the other side.

33 But a certain Samaritan, as he journeyed, came where he was: and when he saw **him**[2], he had compassion *on him*,

34 And went to *him*, and bound up his wounds, pouring in oil and wine, and set him on his own beast, and brought him to an inn, and took care of him.

35 And on the morrow ~~when he departed~~[3], he took out two pence, and gave *them* to the host, and said ~~unto him~~[4], Take care of him; and whatsoever thou spendest more, when I come again, I will repay thee.

36 Which ~~now~~[5] of these three, thinkest thou, was neighbour unto him that fell among the thieves?

37 And he said, He that shewed mercy on him. **Then**[6] said Jesus unto him, Go, and do thou likewise.

38 **Now** ~~it came to pass~~[7], **as**[8] they went, that he **[also]**[9] entered into a certain village: and a certain woman named Martha received him into her house.

39 And she had a sister called Mary, which also **sat at**[10] **Jesus'**[11] feet, and heard his word.

40 But Martha was cumbered about much serving, and came to him, and said, Lord, dost thou not care that my sister **hath left**[12] me to

---

[6] WH changed <u>then</u> (**oun**) to then (*de*).

[7] WH omitted <u>it came to pass</u> (<u>egeneto</u>).

[8] WH reversed the word order of <u>now</u> (<u>de</u>) and <u>as</u> (<u>en</u>).

[9] WH omitted the untranslated <u>also</u> (<u>kai</u>).

[10] WH changed <u>sat **at**</u> (<u>paraka~~this~~asa **para**</u>) to *was sat towards* (*paraka~~thes~~~~the~~isa pros*). Aor **Act** Part to Aor *Pass* Part. [voice]

[11] WH changed **Jesus'** (<u>tou iAsou</u>) to *Lord's* (*tou kuriou*).

[12] WH changed <u>left</u> (<u>katelipe</u>) to *was leaving* (*kateleipe*). **Aor** Act Ind to *Impf* Act Ind. [tense]

---

[1] WH omitted <u>when he was</u> (<u>genomenos</u>).

[2] WH omitted <u>him</u> (<u>auton</u>).

[3] WH omitted <u>when he departed</u> (<u>ekel~~th~~On</u>).

[4] WH omitted <u>unto him</u> (<u>autO</u>).

[5] WH omitted <u>now</u> (<u>oun</u>).

serve alone? bid her therefore that she help me.

41 And **Jesus**[1] answered and said unto her, Martha, Martha, **thou art careful and**[2] **troubled**[3] **about many things**:

42 **But one thing is needful**[4]: [5]**and**[6] Mary hath chosen that good part, which shall not be taken away from her.

CHAPTER 11

1 And it came to pass, that, as he was praying in a certain place, when he ceased, one of his disciples said unto him, Lord, teach us to pray, as John also taught his disciples.

2 And he said unto them, When ye pray, say, ~~Our~~ Father ~~which art in heaven~~[7], hallowed be thy name. Thy kingdom come. ~~Thy will be done, as in heaven, so in earth~~[8].

3 Give us day by day our daily bread.

4 And forgive us our sins; for we also forgive every one that is indebted to us. And lead us not into temptation; ~~but deliver us from evil~~[9].

5 And he said unto them,

---

[1] WH changed the **Jesus** ([h]o iAsous) to *the Lord* ([h]o *kurious*).

[2] In their margin, WH omitted thou are careful and (merimnas kai).

[3] WH changed being troubled (**tur**bazA) to *being troubled* (**th**orubazA). Both Pres Pass Ind. [spell]

[4] In another marginal note, WH changed but one **thing** is needful ([h]**enos** de esti creia) to *but of few one is needful* ([h]**oligOn** de esti creia [h]**A** [h]enos).

[5] In their margin, WH omitted about many things but one thing is needful and (peri polla [h]enos de esti creia de).

[6] WH changed **and** (**de**) to *for* (**gar**).

[7] WH omitted our the in the heavens ([h]AmOn [h]o en tois ouranois) in their text, but retained these words in their margin.

[8] WH omitted thy will be done as in heaven so in earth (genAthAtO to thelAma sou [h]Os en ouranO kai epi tAs gAs) in their text, but retained these words in their margin.

[9] WH omitted but deliver us from evil (alla [h]rusai [h]Amas apo tou ponArou), but retained these words in their margin.

Which of you shall have a friend, and shall go unto him at midnight, and say unto him, Friend, lend me three loaves;

6 For a friend of mine in his journey is come to me, and I have nothing to set before him?

7 And he from within shall answer and say, Trouble me not: the door is now shut, and my children are with me in bed; I cannot rise and give thee.

8 I say unto you, Though he will not rise and give him, because he is his friend, yet because of his importunity he will rise and give him as many as he needeth.

9 And I say unto you, Ask, and it shall be given you; seek, and ye shall find; knock, and it shall be opened unto you.

10 For every one that asketh receiveth; and he that seeketh findeth; and to him that knocketh it shall be opened.

11 If a son shall ask **bread** of any [ʌ**out of**][1] of you that is a father, **will he give him a stone**? **or** [2]**if** *he ask* a fish,

will he for a fish give him a serpent?

12 Or **if**[4] **he shall ask**[5] an egg, will he offer him a scorpion?

13 If ye then, being evil, know how to give good gifts unto your children: how much more shall *your* heavenly Father give the Holy Spirit to them that ask him?

14 And he was casting out a devil, **and it was**[6] dumb. And it came to pass, when the devil was gone out, the dumb spake; and the people wondered.

15 But some of them said, He casteth out devils through Beelzebub ʌ**the**[7] chief of the devils.

16 And others, tempting *him*, sought of him a sign **from heaven**.[8]

---

ted <u>bread</u> <u>will he give him</u> a stone <u>or</u> <u>if</u> (arton mA lithon epidOsei autO ei kai).

[4] WH omitted <u>if</u> (ean).

[5] WH changed <u>he **might** ask</u> (aitAsA) to *he will ask* (aitAsei). **Aor** Act **Sub** to *Fut* Act *Ind*. [tense & mood]

[6] WH omitted <u>and it was</u> (kai auto An).

[7] WH added *the* (to) as the KJV supplied.

[8] WH changed the word order from <u>of him sought FROM HEAVEN</u> to *FROM HEAVEN sought of him.*

---

[1] WH added *out of* (ex).

[2] WH changed <u>or if</u> (<u>ei</u> kai) to *or and* (ʰA kai).

[3] In their margin, WH omit-

17 But he, knowing their thoughts, said unto them, Every kingdom divided against itself is brought to desolation; and a house *divided* against a house falleth.

18 If Satan also be divided against himself, how shall his kingdom stand? because ye say that I cast out devils through Beelzebub.

19 And if I by Beelzebub cast out devils, by whom do your sons cast *them* out? therefore shall they be your judges.

20 But if I [ʌ**myself**]¹ with the finger of God cast out devils, no doubt the kingdom of God is come upon you.

21 When a strong man armed keepeth his palace, his goods are in peace:

22 But when [**the**]² a stronger than he shall come upon him, and overcome him, he taketh from him all his armour wherein he trusted, and divideth his spoils.

23 He that is not with me is against me: and he that gathereth not with me scattereth.

24 When the unclean spirit is gone out of a man, he walketh through dry places, seeking rest; and finding none, he saith, I will return unto my house whence I came out.

25 And when he cometh, he findeth *it* swept and garnished.

26 Then goeth he, and taketh *to him* seven other spirits more wicked than himself; and they enter in, and dwell there: and the last *state* of that man is worse than the first.

27 And it came to pass, as he spake these things, a certain woman of the company lifted up her **voice**³, and said unto him, Blessed *is* the womb that bare thee, and the paps which thou hast sucked.

28 But he said, **Yea rather**⁴, blessed *are* they that hear the word of God, and keep **it**⁵.

29 And when the people were gathered thick together, he began to say, This is an

---

¹ WH added the intensive *myself* (*egO*).
² WH omitted the untranslated the (ʰ**o**).

³ WH changed the word order from woman VOICE to *VOICE woman*.
⁴ WH changed **yea** rather (meno**unge**) to *rather* (*menoun*). **Stronger** form to *Weaker* form.
⁵ WH omitted it (auton).

evil generation: **they seek**[1] a sign; and there shall no sign be given it, but the sign of Jonas ~~the prophet~~[2].

30 For as Jonas was a sign unto the Ninevites, so shall also the Son of man be to this generation.

31 The queen of the south shall rise up in the judgment with the men of this generation, and condemn them: for she came from the utmost parts of the earth to hear the wisdom of Solomon; and, behold, a greater than Solomon *is* here.

32 The men of Nineve shall rise up in the judgment with this generation, and shall condemn it: for they repented at the preaching of Jonas; and, behold, a greater than Jonas *is* here.

33 ~~[and]~~[3] No man, when he hath lighted a candle, putteth *it* in **a secret place**[4], nei-

ther under a bushel, but on a candlestick, that they which come in may see the **light**[5].

34 The light of the body is the eye [∧**of thou**][6] : ~~therefore~~[7] when thine eye is single, thy whole body also is full of light; but when *thine eye* is evil, thy body also *is* full of darkness.

35 Take heed therefore that the light which is in thee be not darkness.

36 If thy whole body therefore *be* full of light, having no part dark, the whole shall be full of light, as when the bright shining of a candle doth give thee light.

37 And as he spake, ~~a certain~~[8] Pharisee **besought**[9] him to dine with him: and he went in, and sat down to meat.

38 And when the Pharisee saw *it*, he marvelled that he

Neut to Acc Sing *Fem*. **Adj** to *Noun*. [gender]

[1] WH changed they seek {**for**} (**epiz**Atei) to *they seek* (*zAtei*). [prefix dropped & syn]

[2] WH omitted the prophet (tou profAtou).

[3] WH omitted the untranslated and (de).

[4] WH changed a secret {**place**} (krupton) to *a secret place* (*kruoptAn*). Acc Sing

[5] WH changed light-**glow** (**feggos**) to light-**beam** (*fOs*). [syn]

[6] WH added *of thou* (*sou*).

[7] WH omitted therefore (oun).

[8] WH omitted a certain (tis).

[9] WH changed **was** ask**ing** (**ArOta**) to *asks* (*erOta*). **Impf** Act Ind to **Pres** Act Ind [tense]

had not first washed before dinner.

39 And the Lord said unto him, Now do ye Pharisees make clean the outside of the cup and the platter; but your inward part is full of ravening and wickedness.

40 *Ye* fools, did not he that made that which is without make that which is within also?

41 But rather give alms of such things as ye have; and, behold, all things are clean unto you.

42 But woe unto you, Pharisees! for ye tithe mint and rue and all manner of herbs, and pass over judgment and the love of God: [∧but]¹ these ought ye to have done, and not to leave the other undone.

43 Woe unto you, Pharisees! for ye love the uppermost seats in the synagogues, and greetings in the markets.

44 Woe unto you, ~~scribes and Pharisees, hypocrites!~~ ² for ye are as graves which appear not, and the men that walk over *them* are not aware

of them.

45 Then answered one of the lawyers, and said unto him, Master, thus saying thou reproachest us also.

46 And he said, Woe unto you also, *ye* lawyers! for ye lade men with burdens grievous to be borne, and ye yourselves touch not the burdens with one of your fingers.

47 Woe unto you! for ye build the sepulchres of the prophets, and your fathers killed them.

48 Truly **ye bear witness**³ that ye allow the deeds of your fathers: for they indeed killed them, and ye build **their sepulchres**⁴.

49 Therefore also said the wisdom of God, I will send them prophets and apostles, and *some* of them they shall slay and **persecute**⁵:

50 That the blood of all the prophets, which was shed

---

¹ WH added *but* (*de*).

² WH omitted scribes and Pharisees hypocrites (grammateis kai farisaioi ʰupokritai).

³ WH changed ye **bear** witness (martureite) to *ye are* witness (*martures este*). **Verb** to *Noun + Verb*.

⁴ WH omitted their sepulchres (outOn ta mnAmeia).

⁵ WH changed they shall persecute {out} (ekdiOxousin) to *they shall persecute* (*diOxousin*). [prefix dropped & syn]

from the foundation of the world, may be required of this generation;

51 From the blood of Abel unto the blood of Zacharias, which perished between the altar and the temple: verily I say unto you, It shall be required of this generation.

52 Woe unto you, lawyers! for ye have taken away the key of knowledge: ye entered not in yourselves, and them that were entering in ye hindered.

53 **And as he said these things unto them**[1], the scribes and the Pharisees began to urge *him* vehemently, and to provoke him to speak of many things:

54 Laying wait for him, ~~and seeking~~[2] to catch something out of his mouth, ~~that they might accuse him~~[3].

CHAPTER 12

1 In the mean time, when there were gathered together an innumerable multitude of people, insomuch that they trode one upon another, he began to say unto his disciples first of all, Beware ye of the leaven of the Pharisees, which is hypocrisy.

2 For there is nothing covered, that shall not be revealed; neither hid, that shall not be known.

3 Therefore whatsoever ye have spoken in darkness shall be heard in the light; and that which ye have spoken in the ear in closets shall be proclaimed upon the housetops.

4 And I say unto you my friends, Be not afraid of them that kill the body, and after that have no more that they can do.

5 But I will forewarn you whom ye shall fear: Fear him, which after he hath killed hath power to cast into hell; yea, I say unto you, Fear him.

6 Are not five sparrows sold for two farthings, and not one of them is forgotten before God?

7 But even the very hairs of your head are all numbered.

---

[1] WH changed <u>and</u> as he said these <u>things</u> <u>unto</u> <u>them</u> (**le-gontos de autou tauta pros** <u>autous</u>) to *and afterwards when he had gone* (**kakeithen exelthontos** *autou*).

[2] WH omitted <u>and</u> seeking (<u>kai</u> <u>zAtountes</u>).

[3] WH omitted <u>that</u> <u>they</u> <u>might</u> <u>accuse</u> <u>him</u> ([h]<u>ina</u> katAgorA-sOsin autou).

Fear not **therefore**[1]: ye are of more value than many sparrows.

8   Also I say unto you, Whosoever shall confess me before men, him shall the Son of man also confess before the angels of God:

9   But he that denieth me before men shall be denied before the angels of God.

10   And whosoever shall speak a word against the Son of man, it shall be forgiven him: but unto him that blasphemeth against the Holy Ghost it shall not be forgiven.

11   And when **they bring**[2] you unto the synagogues, and *unto* magistrates, and powers, **take ye** no **thought**[3] how or what thing ye shall answer, or what ye shall say:

12   For the Holy Ghost shall teach you in the same

hour what ye ought to say.

13   And one of the company said **unto him**[4], Master, speak to my brother, that he divide the inheritance with me.

14   And he said unto him, Man, who made me **a judge**[5] or a divider over you?

15   And he said unto them, Take heed, and beware of **[the]**[6] covetousness: for a man's life consisteth not in the abundance of the things which he possesseth.

16   And he spake a parable unto them, saying, The ground of a certain rich man brought forth plentifully:

17   And he thought within himself, saying, What shall I do, because I have no room where to bestow my fruits?

18   And he said, This will I do: I will pull down my barns, and build greater; and there will I bestow all **my**[7]

---

[1] WH omitted <u>therefore</u> (<u>oun</u>).

[2] WH changed <u>they may bring</u> {**toward**} (**pros-**<u>fer</u>**Osin**) to *they may bring* {**into**} (*eiferOsin*). Both Pres Act Sub. [prefix changed & syn]

[3] WH changed **be** tak**ing** <u>thought</u> (<u>merimnate</u>) to *ye might take thought* (*merimnAsAte*). **Pres** Act **Imp** to *Aor* Act **Sub**. [tense & mood]

[4] WH changed the word order from <u>UNTO HIM</u> <u>out</u> of <u>the</u> <u>company</u> to *out of the company UNTO HIM*.

[5] WH changed <u>a judge</u> (**di-**<u>kast</u>**An**) to *a judge* (*kritAn*). [syn]

[6] WH changed the untranslated <u>**the**</u> (**tAn**) to *all* (*pas*).

[7] WH omitted <u>of me</u> (<u>mou</u>) from <u>the</u> <u>fruits</u> <u>of me</u> (<u>ta</u> <u>genAmata</u> <u>mou</u>).

fruits[1] and my goods.

19 And I will say to my soul, Soul, thou hast much goods laid up for many years; take thine ease, eat, drink, *and* be merry.

20 But God said unto him, *Thou* fool, this night thy soul shall be required of thee: then whose shall those things be, which thou hast provided?

21 So *is* he that layeth up treasure for himself, and is not rich toward God.

22 And he said unto his disciples, Therefore I say **unto you**[2], Take no thought for ~~your~~[3] life, what ye shall eat; neither for the body [∧of thee][4], what ye shall put on.

23 [∧for][5] The life is more than meat, and the body *is more* than raiment.

24 Consider the ravens: for they neither sow nor reap; which neither have storehouse nor barn; and God feedeth them: how much more are ye better than the fowls?

25 And which of you with taking thought can add to his stature ~~one~~[6] cubit?

26 If ye then be **not**[7] able to do that thing which is least, why take ye thought for the rest?

27 Consider the lilies how they grow: they toil not, they spin not; and yet I say unto you, that Solomon in all his glory was not arrayed like one of these.

28 If then God so clothe the grass, which is to day **in the**[8] **field**[9], and to morrow is cast into the oven; how much more *will he clothe* you, O ye of little faith?

29 And seek not ye what ye shall eat, **or**[10] what ye shall drink, neither be ye of doubtful mind.

---

[1] WH changed the **fruits** (**ta genAmata**) to *the wheat* (*ton siton*).

[2] WH changed the word order from UNTO YOU I say to *I say UNTO YOU.*

[3] WH omitted of you ([h]umOn) from the life of you (tA sucA [h]umOn).

[4] WH added *of thee* (*[h]umOn*).

[5] WH added *for* (*gar*).

[6] WH omitted one ([h]ena).

[7] WH changed not (oute) to *not* (*oude*).

[8] WH omitted the (tO) before field.

[9] WH changed the word order from the grass IN **the** FIELD today which is to *IN FIELD the grass today which is.*

[10] WH changed **or** (**A**) to *and* (*kai*).

221

30 For all these things do the nations of the world seek after: and your Father knoweth that ye have need of these things.

31 But rather seek ye the kingdom of **God**[1]; and ~~all~~[2] these things shall be added unto you.

32 Fear not, little flock; for it is your Father's good pleasure to give you the kingdom.

33 Sell that ye have, and give alms; provide yourselves bags which wax not old, a treasure in the heavens that faileth not, where no thief approacheth, neither moth corrupteth.

34 For where your treasure is, there will your heart be also.

35 Let your loins be girded about, and *your* lights burning;

36 And ye yourselves like unto men that wait for their lord, when **he will return**[3] from the wedding; that when

he cometh and knocketh, they may open unto him immediately.

37 Blessed *are* those servants, whom the lord when he cometh shall find watching: verily I say unto you, that he shall gird himself, and make them to sit down to meat, and will come forth and serve them.

38 **And if**[4] ~~he shall come~~[5] in the second ~~watch~~[6], **or**[7] come in the third watch, and find *them* so, blessed are those ~~servants~~[8].

39 And this know, that if the goodman of the house had known what hour the thief would come, he would have watched, and not [ever][9] have suffered his house to be broken through.

40 Be ye **therefore**[10] ready also: for the Son of man

---

[1] WH changed <u>the **God**</u> (<u>tou</u> <u>~~the~~ou</u>) to *him* (*autou*) in their text, but retained <u>God</u> in their margin.

[2] WH omitted <u>all</u> (<u>panta</u>).

[3] WH changed <u>he **will** return</u> (<u>analusei</u>) to *he might return* (*analusA*). **Fut** Act **Ind** to *Aor* Act *Sub*. [tense & mood]

---

[4] WH changed <u>and if</u> (<u>kai</u> <u>ean</u>) to *and if* (*kan*).

[5] WH omitted <u>he shall come</u> (<u>el~~th~~A</u>).

[6] WH omitted <u>watch</u> (<u>fu-lakA</u>).

[7] WH changed <u>**or**</u> (<u>kai</u>) to *and if* (*kan*).

[8] WH omitted <u>the servants</u> from <u>the servants those</u>.

[9] WH omitted the untranslated <u>ever</u> (<u>an</u>).

[10] WH omitted <u>therefore</u> (<u>oun</u>).

cometh at an hour when ye think not.

41 Then Peter said ~~unto him~~[1], Lord, speakest thou this parable unto us, or even to all?

42 **And**[2] the Lord **said**, Who then is that faithful **and**[3] wise steward, whom *his* lord shall make ruler over his household, to give *them their* portion of meat in due season?

43 Blessed *is* that servant, whom his lord when he cometh shall find so doing.

44 Of a truth I say unto you, that he will make him ruler over all that he hath.

45 But and if that servant say in his heart, My lord delayeth his coming; and shall begin to beat the menservants and maidens, and to eat and drink, and to be drunken;

46 The lord of that servant will come in a day when he looketh not for *him*, and at an hour when he is not aware, and will cut him in sunder, and will appoint him his por-

tion with the unbelievers.

47 And that servant, which knew his **lord's**[4] will, and prepared not *himself*, **neither**[5] did according to his will, shall be beaten with many *stripes*.

48 But he that knew not, and did commit things worthy of stripes, shall be beaten with few *stripes*. For unto whomsoever much is given, of him shall be much required: and to whom men have committed much, of him they will ask the more.

49 I am come to send fire **on**[6] the earth; and what will I, if it be already kindled?

50 But I have a baptism to be baptized with; and how am I straitened till **[that]**[7] it be accomplished!

51 Suppose ye that I am come to give peace on earth? I tell you, Nay; but rather division:

52 For from henceforth

---

[1] WH omitted <u>unto him</u> (<u>autO</u>).
[2] WH changed **and** (**kai**) to *but* (*de*) and put <u>said</u> at the beginning of the verse.
[3] WH changed **and** (**kai**) to *the* (*ʰo*).

[4] WH changed <u>of himself</u> (*ʰ*eautou) to *of him* (*autou*) in the will of the lord of himself.
[5] WH changed **neither** (**mAde**) to *or* (*A*).
[6] WH changed **into** (**eis**) to *upon* (*epi*).
[7] WH changed the untranslated **that** (<u>ou</u>) to *while* (*ʰotou*).

there shall be five in one **house**[1] divided, three against two, and two against three.

53 The father **shall be divided**[2] against the son, and the son against the father; the mother against the **daughter**[3], and the daughter against _∧the[4] **mother**[5]; the mother in law against her daughter in law, and the daughter in law against **her**[6] mother in law.

54 And he said also to the people, When ye see [~~the~~][7] a

cloud rise **out of**[8] the west, straightway ye say [_∧**that**][9], There cometh a shower; and so it is.

55 And when *ye see* the south wind blow, ye say, There will be heat; and it cometh to pass.

56 *Ye* hypocrites, ye can discern the face of the **sky** and of the **earth**[10]; but how is it that **ye do not**[11] [_∧**know**][12] **discern**[13] this time?

57 Yea, and why even of yourselves judge ye not what is right?

58 When thou goest with thine adversary to the magistrate, *as thou art* in the way, give diligence that thou mayest be delivered from him; lest he hale thee to the judge,

---

[1] WH changed the word order from HOUSE one to *one HOUSE*.

[2] WH changed {**he**} shall be divided (diameristhAsetai) to {**they**} *shall be divided* (*diameristhAsontai*). Both Fut Pass Ind. 3rd **Sing** to 3rd *Plur*. [number]

[3] WH changed daughter (thugatri) to *daughter* (*thugatera*). **Dat** S Fem to *Acc* S Fem. [case]

[4] WH added *the* (*tAn*) as supplied by the KJV.

[5] WH changed mother (mAtri) to *mother* (*mAtera*). **Dat** Sing Fem to *Acc* Sing Fem. [case]

[6] WH omitted of her (autAs) from the mother-in-law of her.

[7] WH omitted the untranslated the (tAn).

---

[8] WH changed **from** (**apo**) to *upon* (*epi*).

[9] WH added *that* (^h*oti*).

[10] WH changed the word order from of the HEAVEN and the EARTH to *of the EARTH and the HEAVEN*.

[11] WH changed not (ou) to *not* (*ouk*). [spell]

[12] WH added *know* (*oidate*).

[13] WH changed **you**^p **are** discerning (dokimazete) to *to be discerning* (*dokimazein*). Pres Act **Ind** to Pres Act *Inf*. [mood]

and the judge **deliver**[1] thee to the officer, and the officer **cast**[2] thee into prison.

59 I tell thee, thou shalt not depart thence, till thou hast paid the very last mite.

CHAPTER 13

1 There were present at that season some that told him of the Galilaeans, whose blood Pilate had mingled with their sacrifices.

2 And ~~Jesus~~[3] answering said unto them, Suppose ye that these Galilaeans were sinners above all the Galilaeans, because they suffered **such things**[4]?

3 I tell you, Nay: but, except ye repent, ye shall all **likewise**[5] perish.

4 Or those eighteen, upon whom the tower in Siloam fell, and slew them, think ye that **they**[6] were sinners above all [ᴧthe][7] men that dwelt ~~in~~[8] Jerusalem?

5 I tell you, Nay: but, except ye repent, ye shall all **likewise**[9] perish.

6 He spake also this parable; A certain *man* had a fig tree **planted**[10] in his vineyard; and he came and sought **fruit**[11] thereon, and found none.

7 Then said he unto the dresser of his vineyard, Behold, these three years [ᴧ**from which**][12] I come seeking fruit on this fig tree, and find none: cut it down;

---

[1] WH changed **might** deliver (paradO) to *will deliver* (*paradOsei*). **Aor** Act **Sub** to *Fut* Act *Ind*. [tense & mood]

[2] WH changed **might** cast (ballA) to *will cast* (*ballei*). **Aor** Act **Sub** to *Fut* Act *Ind*. [tense & mood]

[3] WH omitted the Jesus (ʰo iAsous).

[4] WH changed **such** things (toiauta) to *these* {things} (*tauta*).

[5] WH changed likewise (ʰ**OsautOs**) to *likewise* (ʰo-

moiOs). [syn]

[6] WH changed these (outoi) to *they* (*autoi*).

[7] WH added *the* (*tous*).

[8] WH omitted in (en).

[9] WH changed likewise (ʰo-moiOs) to *likewise* (ʰ**OsautOs**). [syn]

[10] WH changed the word order from in his vineyard PLANTED to *PLANTED in his vineyard*.

[11] WH changed the word order from FRUIT sought to *sought FRUIT*.

[12] WH added *from which* (*ap' ou*).

why cumbereth it the ground?

8   And he answering said unto him, Lord, let it alone this year also, till I shall dig about it, and dung *it*:

9   And if it bear fruit, *well*: and if not, *then* **after that**[1] thou shalt cut it down.

10   And he was teaching in one of the synagogues on the sabbath.

11   And, behold, ~~there was~~[2] a woman which had a spirit of infirmity eighteen years, and was bowed together, and could in no wise lift up *herself.*

12   And when Jesus saw her, he called *her to him*, and said unto her, Woman, thou art loosed from thine infirmity.

13   And he laid *his* hands on her: and immediately she was made straight, and glorified God.

14   And the ruler of the synagogue answered with indignation, because that Jesus had healed on the sabbath day, and said unto the people, There are six days in which

men ought to work: in **them**[3] therefore come and be healed, and not on the sabbath day.

15   The Lord **then**[4] answered him, and said, *Thou* **hypocrite**[5], doth not each one of you on the sabbath loose his ox or *his* ass from the stall, and lead *him* away to watering?

16   And ought not this woman, being a daughter of Abraham, whom Satan hath bound, lo, these eighteen years, be loosed from this bond on the sabbath day?

17   And when he had said these things, all his adversaries were ashamed: and all the people rejoiced for all the glorious things that were done by him.

18   **Then said**[6] he, Unto what is the kingdom of God like? and whereunto shall I resemble it?

---

[1] WH changed the word order from and if not [then] AFTER THAT to [*then*] AFTER THAT *and if not.*

[2] WH omitted there was (An).

[3] WH changed these (**t**autais) to *them* (*autais*). [syn]

[4] WH changed then (**oun**) to *then* (*de*).

[5] WH changed hypocrite ('u-pokrita) to *hypocrites* ('*upo-critai*). Voc **Sing** Masc to Voc ***Plur*** Masc. [number]

[6] WH changed then (*de*) to *then* (*oun*) and then put said first in the verse.

19 It is like a grain of mustard seed, which a man took, and cast into his garden; and it grew, and waxed a **great**[1] tree; and the fowls of the air lodged in the branches of it.

20 And again he said, Whereunto shall I liken the kingdom of God?

21 It is like leaven, which a woman took and **hid**[2] in three measures of meal, till the whole was leavened.

22 And he went through the cities and villages, teaching, and journeying toward Jerusalem.

23 Then said one unto him, Lord, are there few that be saved? And he said unto them,

24 Strive to enter in at the strait **gate**[3]: for many, I say unto you, will seek to enter in, and shall not be able.

25 When once the master of the house is risen up, and hath shut to the door, and ye begin to stand without, and to knock at the door, saying, Lord, ~~Lord~~[4], open unto us;

and he shall answer and say unto you, I know you not whence ye are:

26 Then shall ye begin to say, We have eaten and drunk in thy presence, and thou hast taught in our streets.

27 But he shall say, I tell you, I know ~~you~~[5] not whence ye are; depart from me, all *ye* [~~the~~][6] workers of [~~the~~][7] iniquity.

28 There shall be weeping and gnashing of teeth, when ye shall see Abraham, and Isaac, and Jacob, and all the prophets, in the kingdom of God, and you *yourselves* thrust out.

29 And they shall come from the east, and *from* the west, and from the north, and *from* the south, and shall sit down in the kingdom of God.

30 And, behold, there are last which shall be first, and there are first which shall be last.

31 The same **day**[8] there came certain of the Pharisees, saying unto him, Get thee

---

[1] WH omitted <u>great</u> (<u>mega</u>).
[2] WH changed <u>hid</u> {**in**}(**en**ekru̞̱<u>s</u>en) to *hid* (*ekru̞̱sen*). [prefix dropped]
[3] WH changed **gate** (**pulA**s) to *door* (*ẗhuras*). [syn]
[4] WH omitted <u>Lord</u> (<u>kurie</u>).

[5] WH omitted <u>you</u> (^h<u>umas</u>).
[6] WH omitted the untranslated <u>the</u> (<u>oi</u>).
[7] WH omitted the untranslated <u>the</u> (<u>tAs</u>).
[8] WH changed **day** (^h**Ame**ra) to *hour* (^h*Ora*).

out, and depart hence: for Herod will kill thee.

32 And he said unto them, Go ye, and tell that fox, Behold, I cast out devils, and **I do**[1] cures to day and to morrow, and the third *day* I shall be perfected.

33 Nevertheless I must walk to day, and to morrow, and the *day* following: for it cannot be that a prophet perish out of Jerusalem.

34 O Jerusalem, Jerusalem, which killest the prophets, and stonest them that are sent unto thee; how often would I have gathered thy children together, as a hen doth *gather* her brood under *her* wings, and ye would not!

35 Behold, your house is left unto you ~~desolate~~[2]: **and verily**[3] **I say**[4] unto you, [~~that~~][5] Ye shall not see me, until *the time* ~~come when~~[6] ye

shall say, Blessed *is* he that cometh in the name of the Lord.

CHAPTER 14

1 And it came to pass, as he went into the house of one of the chief Pharisees to eat bread on the sabbath day, that they watched him.

2 And, behold, there was a certain man before him which had the dropsy.

3 And Jesus answering spake unto the lawyers and Pharisees, saying, [~~If~~][7] Is it lawful **to heal**[8] [∧**or not**][9] on the sabbath day?

4 And they held their peace. And he took *him*, and healed him, and let him go;

5 And ~~answered~~[10] them, saying, Which of you **shall have an ass**[11] or an ox

---

[1] WH changed I do (**epitelO**) to *I do* (**apotelO**). [prefix changed & syn]

[2] WH omitted desolate (erAmos).

[3] WH omitted verily (amAn).

[4] After WH omitted desolate and verily, they forced I say (legO) to precede and (de).

[5] WH omitted the untranslated that ([h]oti).

[6] WH omitted [the time]

come when (an [h]AxA [h]ote).

[7] WH omitted the untranslated if (ei).

[8] WH changed to be heal~~ing~~ (~~th~~erapeuein) to *to heal* (~~th~~erapeusai). **Pres** Act Inf to *Aor* Act Inf. [tense]

[9] WH added or not ([h]A ou).

[10] WH omitted answered (apokri~~th~~eis).

[11] In their margin, WH changed **an ass** (**on**os) to *a son* (*[h]uios*).

fallen[1] into a pit, and will not straightway pull him out on the sabbath day?

6 And they could not answer ~~him~~[2] again to these things.

7 And he put forth a parable to those which were bidden, when he marked how they chose out the chief rooms; saying unto them,

8 When thou art bidden of any *man* to a wedding, sit not down in the highest room; lest a more honourable man than thou be bidden of him;

9 And he that bade thee and him come and **say**[3] to thee, Give this man place; and thou begin with shame to take the lowest room.

10 But when thou art bidden, go and sit down in the lowest room; that when he that bade thee cometh, he may say unto thee, Friend, go up higher: then shalt thou have worship in the presence of [∧all][4] them that sit at meat with thee.

11 For whosoever exalteth himself shall be abased; and he that humbleth himself shall be exalted.

12 Then said he also to him that bade him, When thou makest a dinner or a supper, call not thy friends, nor thy brethren, neither thy kinsmen, nor *thy* rich neighbours; lest they also bid thee again, and a recompence be made **thee**[5].

13 But when thou makest a feast, call the poor, the maimed, the lame, the blind:

14 And thou shalt be blessed; for they cannot recompense thee: for thou shalt be recompensed at the resurrection of the just.

15 And when one of them that sat at meat with him heard these things, he said unto him, Blessed *is* he **that**[6] shall eat bread in the kingdom of God.

16 Then said he unto him, A certain man **made**[7] a great

---

[1] WH changed will fall **into** (**empe**seitai) to *will fall* (*pe-seitai*). [prefix dropped]

[2] WH omitted him (autO).

[3] WH changed **might** say (eipA) to ***will** say* (*eipei*). **Aor** Act **Sub** to *Fut* Act *Ind*. [tense & mood]

[4] WH added *all* (*pantOn*).

[5] WH changed the order from THEE a recompense to *a recompense THEE*.

[6] WH changed who (hos) to *whoever* (hostis).

[7] WH changed made (epoi-Ase) to ***was** making* (*epoiei*). **Aor** Act Ind to *Impf* Act Ind. [tense]

supper, and bade many:

17 And sent his servant at supper time to say to them that were bidden, Come; for ~~all things~~[1] are now ready.

18 And they **all**[2] with one *consent* began to make excuse. The first said unto him, I have bought a piece of ground, and I must needs **go**[3] ~~and~~[4] see it: I pray thee have me excused.

19 And another said, I have bought five yoke of oxen, and I go to prove them: I pray thee have me excused.

20 And another said, I have married a wife, and therefore I cannot come.

21 So ~~that~~[5] servant came, and shewed his lord these things. Then the master of the house being angry said to his servant, Go out quickly into the streets and lanes of the city, and bring in hither the poor, and the maimed, and the **halt**, and the **blind**[6].

22 And the servant said, Lord, it is done **as**[7] thou hast commanded, and yet there is room.

23 And the lord said unto the servant, Go out into the highways and hedges, and compel *them* to come in, that my house may be filled.

24 For I say unto you, That none of those men which were bidden shall taste of my supper.

25 And there went great multitudes with him: and he turned, and said unto them,

26 If any *man* come to me, and hate not his father, and mother, and wife, and children, and brethren, and sisters, **yea**[8], and his own life also, he cannot be my disciple.

27 ~~And~~[9] whosoever doth not bear **his**[10] cross, and come after me, cannot be my

---

[1] WH omitted <u>all</u> {things} (<u>panta</u>).

[2] WH changed the word order from <u>to make excuse</u> <u>ALL</u> to *ALL to make excuse*.

[3] WH changed **to go** (exel~~the~~in) to **having gone** (*exel~~th~~On*). Aor Act **Inf** to Aor Act *Part*. [mood]

[4] WH omitted <u>and</u> (<u>kai</u>).

[5] WH omitted <u>that</u> (<u>ekeinos</u>) from <u>the servant that</u> {one} (^h<u>o</u> <u>doulos</u> <u>ekeinos</u>).

[6] WH changed the word order from <u>LAME</u> <u>and</u> <u>BLIND</u> to *BLIND and LAME*.

[7] WH changed **as** (^h**Os**) to *the* (^h**o**).

[8] WH changed **yea** (<u>de</u>) to *both* (*te*).

[9] WH omitted <u>and</u> (<u>kai</u>).

[10] WH changed <u>of him</u> (<u>autou</u>) in <u>the cross of him</u> to *of himself* (*eautou*).

disciple.

28 For which of you, intending to build a tower, sitteth not down first, and counteth the cost, whether he have [~~the {means}~~][1] *suffi-cient* **to**[2] finish *it*?

29 Lest haply, after he hath laid the foundation, and is not able to finish *it*, all that behold *it* begin to mock him,

30 Saying, This man began to build, and was not able to finish.

31 Or what king, going to make war against another king, sitteth not down first, and **consulteth**[3] whether he be able with ten thousand **to meet**[4] him that cometh against him with twenty thousand?

32 Or else, while the other is yet a great way off, he sen-

deth an ambassage, and desireth conditions of peace.

33 So likewise, whosoever he be of you that forsaketh not all that he hath, he cannot be my disciple.

34 Salt   *is*   good [∧**therefore**][5]: but if [∧**also**][6] the salt have lost his savour, wherewith shall it be seasoned?

35 It is neither fit for the land, nor yet for the dunghill; *but* men cast it out. He that hath ears to hear, let him hear.

CHAPTER 15

1 Then drew near unto him all the publicans and sinners for to hear him.

2 And   [∧**both**][7]   the Pharisees and scribes murmured, saying, This man receiveth sinners, and eateth with them.

3 And he spake this parable unto them, saying,

4 What man of you, having an hundred sheep, if he lose **one**[8] of them, doth not leave the ninety and nine in

---

[1] WH omitted the untranslated the {means} (<u>ta</u>).

[2] WH changed <u>to</u> (**pros**) to *into* (**eis**). The result changed the {means} <u>to-wards</u> <u>completion</u> to *unto completion*.

[3] WH changed <u>consults</u> (<u>bouleuetai</u>) to **will** *consult* (*bouleusetai*). **Pres** M/P Ind to *Fut* Mid Ind. [tense]

[4] WH changed <u>to meet</u> (**ap-antAsai**) to *to meet* (*ʰ**upantA-**sai*). Both Aor Act Inf. [prefix changed & syn]

[5] WH added *therefore* (*oun*).

[6] WH added *also* (*kai*).

[7] WH added *both* (*te*).

[8] WH changed the word order from <u>ONE</u> <u>of</u> <u>them</u> to *of them ONE*.

the wilderness, and go after that which is lost, until he find it?

5 And when he hath found *it*, he layeth *it* on **his**[1] shoulders, rejoicing.

6 And when he cometh home, he calleth together *his* friends and neighbours, saying unto them, Rejoice with me; for I have found my sheep which was lost.

7 I say unto you, that likewise joy shall be in heaven over one sinner that repenteth, more than over ninety and nine just persons, which need no repentance.

8 Either what woman having ten pieces of silver, if she lose one piece, doth not light a candle, and sweep the house, and seek diligently till she find *it*?

9 And when she hath found *it*, **she calleth**[2] *her* friends and *her* **[the]**[3] neighbours together, saying,

Rejoice with me; for I have found the piece which I had lost.

10 Likewise, I say unto you, there is **joy**[4] in the presence of the angels of God over one sinner that repenteth.

11 And he said, A certain man had two sons:

12 And the younger of them said to *his* father, Father, give me the portion of goods that falleth *to me*. **And**[5] he divided unto them *his* living.

13 And not many days after the younger son gathered all together, and took his journey into a far country, and there wasted his substance with riotous living.

14 And when he had spent all, there arose a mighty famine in that land; and he began to be in want.

15 And he went and joined himself to a citizen of that country; and he sent him into his fields to feed swine.

16 And he would fain

---

[1] WH changed of himself (ʰeautou) to *of him* (*autou*) in the shoulders of himself.

[2] WH changed she calls {for herself} (sugkaleitai) to *she calls* (*sugkalei*). Pres **Mid** Ind to Pres *Act* Ind. [voice]

[3] WH omitted the untranslated the (tas).

[4] WH changed the word order from JOY there is to *there is JOY*.

[5] WH changed and (**kai**) to *and the* {one} (ʰo de).

have filled[1] ~~his belly~~[2] **with**[3] the husks that the swine did eat: and no man gave unto him.

17 And when he came to himself, **he said**[4], How many hired servants of my father's **have** bread **enough and to spare**[5], and I perish with hunger [∧**here**][6]!

18 I will arise and go to my father, and will say unto him, Father, I have sinned against heaven, and before thee,

19 ~~And~~[7] am no more worthy to be called thy son: make me as one of thy hired servants.

20 And he arose, and came to his father. But when he was yet a great way off, his father saw him, and had compassion, and ran, and fell on his neck, and kissed him.

21 And the son said unto him, Father, I have sinned against heaven, and in thy sight, ~~and~~ [8] am no more worthy to be called thy son. [**Make me as one of thy hired servants.**][9]

22 But the father said to his servants [∧**in haste**][10], Bring forth the best [~~the~~][11] robe, and put *it* on him; and put a ring on his hand, and shoes on *his* feet:

23 And **bring hither**[12] the fatted calf, and kill *it*; and let us eat, and be merry:

24 For this my son was

---

[1] WH changed to fill (**gemisai**) to *to be filled* (*cortas~~th~~Anai*). Aor **Act** Inf to Aor *Pass* Inf. [voice & syn]

[2] WH omitted his belly (tAn koilian autou)

[3] WH changed **from** (**apo**) to *out of* (*ek*).

[4] WH changed he said (eipe) to *was saying* (efA). **Aor** Act Ind of **legO** to *Impf* Ind of *fAmi*. [tense & synonym]

[5] WH changed have in abundance (perisseuo**usin**) to *have in abundance* {**for themselves**} (*perisseuontai*). Pres *Act* Ind to Pres **Mid** Ind. [voice]

[6] WH added here (*hOde*).

[7] WH omitted and (kai).

[8] WH omitted and (kai).

[9] In their margin, WH added make me as one of thy hired servants (poiAson me [h]Os [h]ena tOn misthiOn sou).

[10] WH added in haste (tacu).

[11] WH omitted the untranslated the (tAn).

[12] WH changed **having brought** hither (**enegkantes**) to *be bringing* hither (*ferete*). **Aor** Act **Part** to *Pres* Act *Imp*. [tense & voice]

dead, and is alive again; [**and**]¹ he was **lost**², and is found. And they began to be merry.

25 Now his elder son was in the field: and as he came and drew nigh to the house, he heard musick and dancing.

26 And he called one of the servants, and asked what [∧ever]³ these things meant.

27 And he said unto him, Thy brother is come; and thy father hath killed the fatted calf, because he hath received him safe and sound.

28 And he was angry, and would not go in: **therefore**⁴ came his father out, and intreated him.

29 And he answering said to *his* father [∧of him]⁵, Lo, these many years do I serve thee, neither transgressed I at any time thy commandment: and yet thou never gavest me a kid, that I might make merry with my friends:

30 But as soon as this thy son was come, which hath devoured thy living with [∧the]⁶ harlots, thou hast killed for him the **fatted** [the]⁷ **calf**⁸.

31 And he said unto him, Son, thou art ever with me, and all that I have is thine.

32 It was meet that we should make merry, and be glad: for this thy brother was dead, and **is alive again**⁹; and ~~was~~¹⁰ lost, and is found.

CHAPTER 16

1 And he said also unto ~~his~~¹¹ disciples, There was a certain rich man, which had a steward; and the same was accused unto him that he had wasted his goods.

2 And he called him, and said unto him, How is it that I hear this of thee? give an account of thy stewardship; for

---

¹ WH omitted the untranslated <u>and</u> (<u>kai</u>).
² WH changed the word order from <u>LOST</u> <u>he was</u> to *he was LOST*.
³ WH added *ever* (*an*).
⁴ WH changed **therefore** (**oun**) to **then** (**de**).
⁵ WH added *of him* (*autou*).

⁶ WH added *the* (*tOn*).
⁷ WH omitted the untranslated <u>the</u> (<u>ton</u>).
⁸ WH changed the word order from CALF <u>the</u> <u>fatted</u> to *fatted CALF*
⁹ WH changed is alive **again** (**anezAse**) to *is alive* (*ezAse*). [prefix dropped & syn]
¹⁰ WH omitted <u>was</u> (<u>An</u>).
¹¹ WH omitted <u>of him</u> (<u>autou</u>) from <u>the</u> <u>disciples</u> <u>of him</u>.

thou **mayest be**[1] no longer steward.

3 Then the steward said within himself, What shall I do? for my lord taketh away from me the stewardship: I cannot dig; to beg I am ashamed.

4 I am resolved what to do, that, when I am put ˄out of[2] the stewardship, they may receive me into **their**[3] houses.

5 So he called every one of his lord's debtors _unto him_, and said unto the first, How much owest thou unto my lord?

6 **And**[4] he said, An hundred measures of oil. And he said unto him, Take **thy bill**[5],

and sit down quickly, and write fifty.

7 Then said he to another, And how much owest thou? And he said, An hundred measures of wheat. **And**[6] he said unto him, Take **thy bill**[7], and write fourscore.

8 And the lord commended the unjust steward, because he had done wisely: for the children of this world are in their [˄**the]**[8] generation wiser than the children of light.

9 And I say unto you, Make to yourselves friends of the mammon of unrighteousness; that, when **ye fail**[9], they may receive you into everlasting habitations.

10 He that is faithful in that which is least is faithful

---

[1] WH changed **will** be (dunAsA) to _are being_ (dunA). **Fut** Mid Ind to _Pres_ M/P Ind. [tense]

[2] WH added _out of_ (ek) as the KJV supplied from the genitive case.

[3] WH changed of them (autOn) to _of themselves_ ("eautOn) in the houses **of them**.

[4] WH changed **and** (**kai**) to _but the_ {one} ("o de).

[5] WH changed the bill (**to** gramma) to _the bills_ (_ta grammata_) in the bill of him. Acc **Sing** Neut to Acc _Plur_

Neut. [number]

[6] WH omitted and (kai).

[7] WH changed the bill (**to** gramma) to _the bills_ (_ta grammata_) in the bill of him. Acc **Sing** Neut to Acc _Plur_ Neut. [number]

[8] WH added _the_ (_tAn_) to of themselves in the generation of themselves.

[9] WH changed **ye** might fail (eklipAte) to _it might fail_ (_eklipA_). Aor Act Sub **2**[nd] **Plur** to Aor Act Sub _3_[rd] **Sing**. [person & number]

also in much: and he that is unjust in the least is unjust also in much.

11 If therefore ye have not been faithful in the unrighteous mammon, who will commit to your trust the true *riches*?

12 And if ye have not been faithful in that which is another man's, who shall **give**[1] you that which is **your own**[2]?

13 No servant can serve two masters: for either he will hate the one, and love the other; or else he will hold to the one, and despise the other. Ye cannot serve God and mammon.

14 And the Pharisees ~~also~~[3], who were covetous, heard all these things: and they derided him.

15 And he said unto them, ye are they which justify yourselves before men; but God knoweth your hearts: for that which is highly esteemed among men ~~is~~[4] abomination in the sight of God.

16 The law and the proph-

ets *were* **until**[5] John: since that time the kingdom of God is preached, and every man presseth into it.

17 And it is easier for heaven and earth to pass, than one tittle of the law to fail.

18 ~~Whosoever~~[6] putteth away his wife, and marrieth another, committeth adultery: and whosoever marrieth her that is put away from *her* husband committeth adultery.

19 ~~There was~~[7] a certain rich man, which was clothed in purple and fine linen, and fared sumptuously every day:

20 And there was a certain beggar named Lazarus, which was laid at his gate, full of sores,

21 And desiring to be fed with the ~~crumbs which~~[8] fell from the rich man's table: moreover the dogs came and **licked**[9] his sores.

---

[1] WH changed the word order from {to} you GIVE to *GIVE* {to} *you.*

[2] In their margin, WH changed **your** own (*[h]umeteron*) to *thy own* (*[h]Ameteron*). [number]

[3] WH omitted also (kai).

[4] WH omitted is (estin).

[5] WH changed until (*[h]eOs*) to *until* (*mecri*). [syn]

[6] WH omitted all (pas) from all the (pas *[h]o*).

[7] WH omitted there was (An).

[8] WH omitted crumbs which (*[s]iciOn tOn*).

[9] WH changed was licking {from} (apeleicon) to *was licking* {upon} (*epeleicon*). Both Impf Act Ind 3rd Plur. [prefix changed & syn]

22 And it came to pass, that the beggar died, and was carried by the angels into Abraham's bosom: the rich man also died, and was buried;

23 And in hell he lift up his eyes, being in torments, and seeth Abraham afar off, and Lazarus in his bosom.

24 And he cried and said, Father Abraham, have mercy on me, and send Lazarus, that he may dip the tip of his finger in water, and cool my tongue; for I am tormented in this flame.

25 But Abraham said, Son, remember that thou [**thyself**]¹ in thy lifetime receivedst thy good things, and likewise Lazarus evil things: but now he [this {one} here]² is comforted, and thou art tormented.

26 And **beside**³ all this, between us and you there is a great gulf fixed: so that they which would pass **from hence**⁴ to you cannot; neither can they pass to us, **that**⁵ *would come* from thence.

27 Then he said, I pray thee therefore, father, that thou wouldest send him to my father's house:

28 For I have five brethren; that he may testify unto them, lest they also come into this place of torment.

29 [∧**but**]⁶ Abraham saith **unto him**⁷, They have Moses and the prophets; let them hear them.

30 And he said, Nay, father Abraham: but if one went unto them from the dead, they will repent.

31 And he said unto him, If they hear not Moses and the prophets, neither will they be persuaded, though one rose from the dead.

CHAPTER 17

1   Then said he unto the disciples [∧of him]⁸, It is impossible

---

¹ WH omitted the intensive thyself (su).
² WH changed the untranslated **this {one}** here (ʰode) to *here* (ʰOde). **Demonstrative pronoun** to *Adverb*.
³ WH changed **upon** (e̲p̲i) to *in* (e̲n).

⁴ WH changed from here (e̲n̲t̲e̲u̲t̲h̲e̲n) to *from here* (e̲n̲t̲h̲e̲n). [syn]
⁵ WH omitted that (ʰo̲i--the {ones that}).
⁶ WH added *but* (de).
⁷ WH omitted unto him (a̲u̲t̲O).
⁸ WH added *of him* (autou).

but that **offences**[1] will come: **but** **woe**[2] *unto him*, through whom they come!

2 It were better for him that **a millstone**[3] were hanged about his neck, and he cast into the sea, than that he should offend **one**[4] of these little ones.

3 Take heed to yourselves: [but][5] If thy brother trespass **against thee**[6], rebuke him; and if he repent, forgive him.

4 And if he trespass against thee seven times in a day, and seven times ~~in a~~ ~~day~~[7] turn again **to**[8] thee, saying, I repent; thou shalt forgive him.

5 And the apostles said unto the Lord, Increase our faith.

6 And the Lord said, If **ye had**[9] faith as a grain of mustard seed, ye might say unto this sycamine tree, Be thou plucked up by the root, and be thou planted in the sea; and it should obey you.

7 But which of you, having a servant plowing or feeding cattle, will say ⋏**unto him**[10] by and by, when he is come from the field, Go and **sit down to meat**[11]?

8 And will not rather say unto him, Make ready wherewith I may sup, and gird thyself, and serve me, till

---

[1] WH changed the word order from <u>not</u> <u>to come</u> THE OFFENSES to *THE OFFENCES not to come.*

[2] WH changed <u>but</u> (**de**) to *but* (***plAn***) and put (*but*) *plAn* after <u>woe</u> (<u>ouai</u>).

[3] WH changed <u>millstone</u> (**mul**os **on**ikos--millstone turned by an ass) to *millstone* (*li**th**os **mul**ikos*--stone belonging to a mill).

[4] WH changed the word order from ONE of the <u>little</u> <u>ones</u> <u>these</u> to *of the little ones these ONE.*

[5] WH omitted the untranslated <u>but</u> (<u>de</u>).

[6] WH omitted <u>against</u> <u>thee</u> (<u>eis</u> <u>se</u>).

[7] WH omitted <u>in a</u> <u>day</u> (<u>t</u>As ʰ<u>Ameras</u>).

[8] WH changed **upon** (**epi**) to *toward* (*pros*).

[9] WH changed <u>ye</u> **were** having (<u>eicete</u>) to *ye* ***are*** *having* (*ecete*). **Impf** Act Ind ***Pres*** Act Ind. [tense]

[10] WH added *unto him* (*auto*) as the KJV supplied.

[11] WH changed <u>sit</u> <u>down</u> <u>to</u> <u>meat</u> {**for yourself**} (*anapesai*) to *sit down to meat* (*anapese*). Aor **Mid** Imp to Aor ***Act*** Imp. [voice]

I have eaten and drunken; and afterward thou shalt eat and drink?

9 Doth he thank **that**[1] servant because he did the things that were commanded **him**? ~~I trow not~~[2].

10 So likewise ye, when ye shall have done all those things which are commanded you, say, **[~~that~~]**[3] We are unprofitable servants: we have done that which was our duty to do.

11 And it came to pass, as ~~**he**~~[4] went to Jerusalem, that he passed through **the midst**[5] of Samaria and Galilee.

12 And as he entered into a certain village, there met him ten men that were lepers, which stood afar off:

13 And they lifted up *their* voices, and said, Jesus, Master, have mercy on us.

14 And when he saw *them*, he said unto them, Go shew yourselves unto the priests. And it came to pass, that, as they went, they were cleansed.

15 And one of them, when he saw that he was healed, turned back, and with a loud voice glorified God,

16 And fell down on *his* face at his feet, giving him thanks: and he was a Samaritan.

17 And Jesus answering said, Were there not ten cleansed? but where *are* the nine?

18 There are not found that returned to give glory to God, save this stranger.

19 And he said unto him, Arise, go thy way: thy faith hath made thee whole.

20 And when he was demanded of the Pharisees, when the kingdom of God should come, he answered them and said, The kingdom of God cometh not with observation:

21 Neither shall they say, Lo here! or, ~~**lo**~~[6] there! for, behold, the kingdom of God is within you.

22 And he said unto the disciples, The days will come, when ye shall desire to see one of the days of the Son of man, and ye shall not see *it*.

---

[1] WH omitted <u>that</u> (ekeinO) from <u>the servant that</u> {one}.
[2] WH omitted <u>him</u> <u>I think</u> <u>not</u> (<u>autO</u> <u>ou</u> <u>dokO</u>).
[3] WH omitted the untranslated <u>that</u> (^h<u>oti</u>).
[4] WH omitted <u>he</u> (<u>auton</u>).
[5] WH changed <u>the midst</u> (<u>meso**u**</u>) to *the midst* (<u>meso**n**</u>). **Gen** Sing Neut to *Acc* Sing Neut. [case]

---

[6] WH omitted <u>lo</u> (<u>idou</u>).

23 And they shall say to you, See **here**; ~~or~~[1], see **there**[2]: go not after *them*, nor follow *them*.

24 For as the lightning, ~~that~~[3] lighteneth out of the one *part* **under**[4] [∧**the**][5] heaven, shineth unto the other *part* under heaven; so shall ~~also~~[6] the Son of man be in his day[7].

25 But first must he suffer many things, and be rejected of this generation.

26 And as it was in the days of Noe, so shall it be also in the days of the Son of man.

27 They did eat, they drank, they married wives, **they were given in marriage**[8], until the day that Noe

entered into the ark, and the flood came, and destroyed them all.

28 Likewise **also as**[9] it was in the days of Lot; they did eat, they drank, they bought, they sold, they planted, they builded;

29 But the same day that Lot went out of Sodom it rained fire and brimstone from heaven, and destroyed *them* all.

30 **Even thus**[10] shall it be in the day when the Son of man is revealed.

31 In that day, he which shall be upon the housetop, and his stuff in the house, let him not come down to take it away: and he that is in the field, let him likewise not return back.

32 Remember Lot's wife.

33 Whosoever shall seek **to save**[11] his life shall lose it;

---

[1] WH omitted or (A).

[2] WH changed the word order from HERE **or** see THERE to *THERE see HERE*

[3] WH omitted that ([h]A).

[4] WH changed under (hup') to *under* (hupo). [spell]

[5] WH added the (ton).

[6] WH omitted also (kai).

[7] In their margin, WH omitted in his day (en tA [h]Amera auton).

[8] WH changed they were given {**away**} in marriage (**exegamizonto**) to *they were given in marriage* (egamizonto). Both Impf Act Ind. [prefix dropped & syn]

[9] WH changed **also** as (kai [h]Os) to *even as* (ka[th]Os).

[10] WH changed **these** {things} (tauta) to *the same* {things} (*ta auta*) in the paraphrase even thus (kata tauta--according to these {things}).

[11] WH changed to **save** (sOsai) to *to preserve* {*for himself*} (peripoiAsas[th]ai). Aor **Act** Inf of **sOzO** to Aor *Mid* Inf of *peripoieomai*.

and[1] **whosoever**[2] shall lose his life shall preserve ~~it~~[3].

34 I tell you, in that night there shall be two *men* in one bed; the one shall be taken, and the other shall be left.

35 **Two**[4] *women* shall be grinding together; the one shall be taken, **and the**[5] other left.

36 ~~Two *men* shall be in the field; the one shall be taken, and the other left.~~ [6]

37 And they answered and said unto him, Where, Lord? And he said unto them,

Wheresoever the body *is*, thither **will** [ᴧalso][7] **the eagles**[8] **be gathered together**[9].

CHAPTER 18

1 And he spake a parable [~~also~~][10] unto them *to this end*, that ᴧ**men**[11] ought always to pray, and not **to faint**[12];

2 Saying, There was in a city a judge, which feared not God, neither regarded man:

3 And there was a widow in that city; and she came unto him, saying, Avenge me of mine adversary.

---

[1] WH changed <u>and</u> (**kai**) to *and* (**de**).

[2] WH changed <u>ever</u> (**ean**) to *ever* (**an**) in <u>whosoever</u> (ʰos ean) and placed <u>whoso</u> (ʰos) first.

[3] WH omitted <u>it</u> (<u>autAn</u>).

[4] WH changed the word order from <small>TWO</small> <u>shall be</u> to <u>shall be</u> <small>TWO</small>.

[5] WH changed **and** (**kai**) to *but* (**de**) and placed <u>the</u> (ʰA) first.

[6] WH omitted <u>two</u> [men] <u>shall be in the field the one shall be taken and the other left</u> (<u>duo esontai en tO agrO</u> ʰo ais <u>paralafthasetai kai</u> ʰo ʰeteros <u>afethAsetai</u>). WH omitted all Luke 17:36 words in their text; but retained them in their margin.

[7] WH added *also* (*kai*).

[8] WH changed the word order from <u>will be gathered together</u> <small>THE EAGLES</small> to ***also*** *THE EAGLES will be gathered together*.

[9] WH changed <u>will be gathered together</u> (<u>sunacthAsountai</u>) to *will be gathered together* {***beside***} (*episunacthAsontai*) [syn, prefix added].

[10] WH omitted the untranslated <u>also</u> (<u>kai</u>).

[11] WH added *they* (*autous*) where the KJV supplied *men*.

[12] WH changed <u>to be fainting</u> (<u>ekkakein</u>) to *to be fainting* (*egkakein*). Both Pres Act Inf of *ekkakeO*. [spell]

4   And **he would**[1] not for a while: but afterward he said within himself, Though I fear not God, **nor**[2] regard **man;**[3]

5   Yet because this widow troubleth me, I will avenge her, lest by her continual coming she weary me.

6   And the Lord said, Hear what the unjust judge saith.

7   And **shall** not God **avenge**[4] his own elect, which cry day and night ~~unto~~[5] **him**[6], **though he bear long**[7] with

them?

8   I tell you that he will avenge them speedily. Nevertheless when the Son of man cometh, shall he find faith on the earth?

9   And he spake this parable unto certain which trusted in themselves that they were righteous, and despised others:

10   Two men went up into the temple to pray; the one a Pharisee, and the other a publican.

11   The Pharisee stood and prayed **thus**[8] with himself, God, I thank thee, that I am not as other men *are*, extortioners, unjust, adulterers, or even as this publican.

12   I fast twice in the week, I give tithes of all that I possess.

13   **And the**[9] publican, standing afar off, would not **lift up**[10] so much as *his* eyes

---

[1] WH changed he **willed** (A~~th~~el**A**sen) to *he was willing* (*A~~th~~elen*). **Aor** Act Ind to *Impf* Act Ind. [tense]

[2] WH changed **and not** (**kai ouk**) to *not even* (*oude*).

[3] WH changed the word order from and MAN not to *not even MAN*.

[4] WH changed **shall** carry out (poiAsei) to *might carry out* (*poiAsA*) in shall carry out the vengeance (poiAsei tAn edikAsin) **Fut** Act **Ind** to *Aor* Act *Sub*. [tense & mood].

[5] WH omitted unto (pros).

[6] WH changed him (aut**on**) to him (aut**O**). *Acc* Sing Masc to *Dat* Sing Masc. [case]

[7] WH changed bear**ing** long (makro~~th~~um**On**) to *he bears long* (*makro~~th~~umei*). Pres

Act **Part** to Pres Act *Ind*. [mood]

[8] WH changed the word order from with himself THUS to *THUS with himself*.

[9] WH changed **and** (**kai**) to *but* (*de*) and put the (h**o**) first in the verse.

[10] WH changed the word order from unto heaven lift up to *LIFT UP unto heaven*.

unto heaven, but smote ~~upon~~[1] his breast, saying, God be merciful to me a sinner.

14 I tell you, this man went down to his house justified *rather* than the other: for every one that exalteth himself shall be abased; and he that humbleth himself shall be exalted.

15 And they brought unto him also infants, that he would touch them: but when *his* disciples saw *it*, **they rebuked**[2] them.

16 But Jesus **called**[3] them *unto him*, and **said**[4], Suffer little children to come unto me, and forbid them not: for of such is the kingdom of God.

17 Verily I say unto you, whosoever shall not receive the kingdom of God as a little child shall in no wise enter therein.

18 And a certain ruler asked him, saying, Good Master, what shall I do to inherit eternal life?

19 And Jesus said unto him, Why callest thou me good? none *is* good, save one, *that is*, God.

20 Thou knowest the commandments, Do not commit adultery, Do not kill, Do not steal, Do not bear false witness, Honour thy father and ~~thy~~[5] mother.

21 And he said, All these have I kept from my youth up.

22 Now when Jesus heard ~~these things~~[6], he said unto him, Yet lackest thou one thing: sell all that thou hast, and distribute unto the poor, and thou shalt have treasure in [∧the][7] **heaven**[8]: and come, follow me.

23 And when he heard

---

[1] WH omitted upon (eis).
[2] WH changed they rebuked (epetim**A**san) to *they were rebuking* (epetim**O**n). **Aor** Act Ind to *Impf* Act Ind. [tense]
[3] WH changed **having** called (proskalesa**menos**) to *he called* (*prosekalesato*). Aor Mid **Part** to Aor Mid *Ind* [mood]
[4] WH changed said (**eipen**) to *saying* (*legOn*). **Aor** Act **Ind** to *Pres* Act *Part*. [tense & mood]

[5] WH omitted of thee (sou) from the mother of thee.
[6] WH omitted these things (touta).
[7] WH added *the* (*tois*).
[8] WH changed heaven (ouran**O**) to *heavens* (*ouranois*). [number]

this, **he was**[1] very sorrowful: for he was very rich.

24 And when Jesus saw that he was very sorrow-ful[2], he said, How hardly shall they that have riches enter into the kingdom of God!

25 For it is easier for a camel to go through **a needle's eye**[3], than for a rich man to enter into the kingdom of God.

26 And they that heard *it* said, Who then can be saved?

27 And he said, The things which are impossible with men are possible with God.

28 Then Peter said, Lo, **we have left**[4] **all**[5], **and**[6] fol-lowed thee.

29 And he said unto them, Verily I say unto you, There is no man that hath left house, or **parents**, or brethren, or **wife**[7], or children, for the kingdom of God's sake,

30 Who shall not receive manifold more in this present time, and in the world to come life everlasting.

31 Then he took *unto him* the twelve, and said unto them, Behold, we go up to Jerusalem, and all things that are written by the prophets concerning the Son of man shall be accomplished.

32 For he shall be delivered unto the Gentiles, and shall be mocked, and spitefully entreated, and spitted on:

33 And they shall scourge *him*, and put him to death: and the third day he shall rise again.

34 And they understood none of these things: and this saying was hid from them, neither knew they the things

---

[1] WH changed he became {**for himself**} (egeneto) to *he was become* (egenА*th*А). Aor **Mid** Ind to Aor *Pass-D* Ind. [voice]

[2] WH omitted that he was very sorrowful (perilupon genomenon).

[3] WH changed a needle's eye (t**rumalias** **ʰraṣidos**) to *a needle's eye* (tr*Amatos belonАs*). Gen Sing **Fem** to Gen Sing *Neut*. [gender & syn]

[4] WH changed **we** left **all** (af**Akamen**) to *having left* (*afentes*). Aor Act **Ind** to Aor Act *Part*. [mood]

[5] WH changed **all** (**panta**) to *the* {things} *of our own* (*ta idia*). [**Adj** to *Article + Adj*]

[6] WH omitted and (kai).

[7] WH changed the word order from PARENTS or brethren or WIFE to *WIFE or brethren or PARENTS*.

which were spoken.

35 And it came to pass, that as he was come nigh unto Jericho, a certain blind man sat by the way side begging:

36 And hearing the multitude pass by, he asked what it meant.

37 And they told him, that Jesus of Nazareth passeth by.

38 And he cried, saying, Jesus, *thou* Son of David, have mercy on me.

39 And they which went before rebuked him, that **he should hold his peace**[1]: but he cried so much the more, *Thou* Son of David, have mercy on me.

40 And Jesus stood, and commanded him to be brought unto him: and when he was come near, he asked him,

41 ~~Saying~~[2], What wilt thou that I shall do unto thee? And he said, Lord, that I may receive my sight.

42 And Jesus said unto him, Receive thy sight: thy

faith hath saved thee.

43 And immediately he received his sight, and followed him, glorifying God: and all the people, when they saw *it*, gave praise unto God.

CHAPTER 19

1 And *Jesus* entered and passed through Jericho.

2 And, behold, *there was* a man named Zacchaeus, which was the chief among the publicans, and **[this {one}]**[3] ~~he was~~[4] rich.

3 And he sought to see Jesus who he was; and could not for the press, because he was little of stature.

4 And he ran **[ᴧ into the]**[5] before, and climbed up into a sycomore tree to see him: for he was to pass **[~~through~~]**[6] that *way*.

5 And when Jesus came to the place, he looked up, and ~~saw him, and~~[7] said unto him, Zacchaeus, make haste,

---

[1] WH changed he might hold his peace (siOpAsA) to *he might hold his peace* (*sigAsA*). Aor Act Sub of siOpO to Aor Act Sub of *siagO*. [syn]

[2] WH omitted saying (legOn).

[3] WH changed the untranslated **this** {one} (ᴴoutos) to *himself* or *the same* (*autos*).

[4] WH omitted he was (An)

[5] WH added *into the* (*eis to*).

[6] WH omitted the untranslated through (di').

[7] WH omitted saw him and (eiden auton kai).

and come down; for to day I must abide at thy house.

6 And he made haste, and came down, and received him joyfully.

7 And when they saw *it*, they **all**[1] murmured, saying, That he was gone to be guest with a man that is a sinner.

8 And Zacchaeus stood, and said unto the Lord; Behold, Lord, the half of my goods I give to the poor; and if I have taken any thing from any man by false accusation, I restore *him* fourfold.

9 And Jesus said unto him, This day is salvation come to this house, forsomuch as he also is a son of Abraham.

10 For the Son of man is come to seek and to save that which was lost.

11 And as they heard these things, he added and spake a parable, because he was nigh to Jerusalem, and because they thought that the kingdom of God should immediately appear.

12 He said therefore, A certain nobleman went into a far country to receive for himself a kingdom, and to return.

13 And he called his ten servants, and delivered them ten pounds, and said unto them, Occupy till I come.

14 But his citizens hated him, and sent a message after him, saying, We will not have this *man* to reign over us.

15 And it came to pass, that when he was returned, having received the kingdom, then he commanded these servants to be called unto him, to whom **he had given**[2] the money, that he might know how much **every man**[3] **had gained by trading**[4].

16 Then came the first, saying, **Lord**[5], thy pound hath gained ten pounds.

17 And he said unto him, Well, thou good servant: because thou hast been faithful in a very little, have thou authority over ten cities.

---

[2] WH changed <u>he gave</u> (edOke) to *he **had given** (dedOkei)*. **Aor** Act Ind to ***PastPf*** Act Ind. [tense]

[3] WH omitted <u>every man</u> (<u>tis</u>).

[4] WH changed **he** <u>had gained by trading</u> (<u>diepragmateusato</u>) to ***they** had gained by trading (diepragmateusanto)*. Aor Mid-D Ind 3rd **Sing** to Aor Mid-D Ind 3rd ***Plur***. [number]

[5] WH changed the word order from <u>LORD</u> thy <u>pound</u> to *thy pound LORD*.

---

[1] WH changed <u>all</u> (**ʰapantes**) to *all (pantes)*. [syn]

18 And the second came, saying, Lord, thy pound hath gained five pounds.

19 And he said likewise to him, Be thou also over five cities.

20 And [∧the]¹ another came, saying, Lord, behold, *here is* thy pound, which I have kept laid up in a napkin:

21 For I feared thee, because thou art an austere man: thou takest up that thou layedst not down, and reapest that thou didst not sow.

22 **And**² he saith unto him, Out of thine own mouth will I judge thee, *thou* wicked servant. Thou knewest that I was an austere man, taking up that I laid not down, and reaping that I did not sow:

23 Wherefore then gavest not thou my money into **the**³ bank, that at my coming I might have required mine own with usury?

24 And he said unto them that stood by, Take from him the pound, and give *it* to him that hath ten pounds.

25 (And they said unto him, Lord, he hath ten pounds.)

26 **For**⁴ I say unto you, That unto every one which hath shall be given; and from him that hath not, even that he hath shall be taken away from him.

27 But **those**⁵ mine enemies, which would not that I should reign over them, bring hither, and slay ∧*them*⁶ before me.

28 And when he had thus spoken, he went before, ascending up to Jerusalem.

29 And it came to pass, when he was come nigh to Bethphage and Bethany, at the mount called *the mount* of Olives, he sent two of **his**⁷ disciples,

30 Saying, Go ye into the village over against *you*; in the which at your entering ye shall find a colt tied, whereon yet never man sat: loose him, and bring *him hither*.

31 And if any man ask you, Why do ye loose *him*? thus shall ye say **unto him**⁸,

---

¹ WH added *the* (ʰ*o*).
² WH omitted <u>and</u> (<u>de</u>).
³ WH omitted <u>the</u> (<u>tAn</u>).

⁴ WH omitted <u>for</u> (<u>gar</u>).
⁵ WH changed <u>those</u> (**ekeinous**) to *these* (**toutous**).
⁶ WH added *them* (*autous*) where the KJV supplied it.
⁷ WH omitted <u>of him</u> (<u>autou</u>) from <u>the disciples of him</u>.
⁸ WH omitted <u>unto him</u> (<u>autO</u>).

Because the Lord hath need of him.

32 And they that were sent went their way, and found even as he had said unto them.

33 And as they were loosing the colt, the owners thereof said unto them, Why loose ye the colt?

34 And they said, The Lord hath need of him.

35 And they brought him to Jesus: and they cast **their**¹ garments upon the colt, and they set Jesus thereon.

36 And as he went, they spread their clothes in the way.

37 And when he was come nigh, even now at the descent of the mount of Olives, the whole multitude of the disciples began to rejoice and praise God with a loud voice for all the mighty works that they had seen;

38 Saying, Blessed *be* the King that cometh in the name of the Lord: peace in heaven, and glory in the highest.

39 And some of the Pharisees from among the multitude said unto him, Master, rebuke thy disciples.

40 And he answered and said ~~unto them~~,² I tell you that, if these **should hold their peace**³, the stones **would immediately cry out**⁴.

41 And when he was come near, he beheld the city, and wept over it,

42 Saying, If thou hadst known, ~~even thou~~, ~~at least~~⁵ in this **thy**⁶ day [∧even thou]⁷, the things *which belong* unto ~~thy~~⁸ peace! but now they are hid from thine eyes.

43 For the days shall come

---

¹ WH changed of them**selves** (**ʰ**eautOn) to *of them (autOn)* in the garments of themselves.

² WH omitted unto them (autois).

³ WH changed **might** hold their peace (siOpAsOsin) to *will hold their peace (siOpAsousin)*. **Aor** Act **Sub** to *Fut* Act *Ind.* [tense & mood]

⁴ WH changed **will** {immediately} cry out (**kekraxontai**) to *will {immediately} cry out (kraxousi)*. 2Fut **Mid-D** Ind to Fut *Act* Ind. [voice]

⁵ WH omitted even thou at least (kai su kai ge).

⁶ WH omitted of thee (sou) from in the day of thee.

⁷ WH added *even thou (kai su)*.

⁸ WH omitted of thou (sou) from the peace of thou.

upon thee, that thine enemies shall cast a trench about thee, and compass thee round, and keep thee in on every side,

44 And shall lay thee even with the ground, and thy children within thee; and they shall not leave **in thee**[1] one stone upon another; because thou knewest not the time of thy visitation.

45 And he went into the temple, and began to cast out them that sold ~~therein, and them that bought~~[2];

46 Saying unto them, It is written, [∧**and**][3] My house [4]**is**[5] the house of prayer: but ye have made it a den of thieves.

47 And he taught daily in the temple. But the chief priests and the scribes and the chief of the people sought to destroy him,

48 And could not find what they might do: for all the people were very attentive to hear him.

CHAPTER 20

1 And it came to pass, *that* on one of ~~those~~[6] days, as he taught the people in the temple, and preached the gospel, the chief priests and the scribes came upon *him* with the elders,

2 And spake unto him, **saying**[7], Tell us, by what authority doest thou these things? or who is he that gave thee this authority?

3 And he answered and said unto them, I will also ask you ~~one~~[8] thing; and answer me:

4 The baptism of John, was it from heaven, or of men?

5 And they reasoned with

---

[1] WH changed the word order from IN THEE stone upon stone to *stone upon stone IN THEE*.

[2] WH omitted in it and them that bought (en autO kai agorazontas).

[3] WH added *and* (*kai*).

[4] WH changed the word order from my house house of prayer IS to *and WILL BE my house house of prayer*.

[5] WH changed is (*estin*) to *will be* (*estai*) **Pres** Ind to *Fut* Ind. [tense]

[6] WH omitted those (ekeinOn) from one of the days those.

[7] WH changed the word order from unto him SAYING to *SAYING unto him*.

[8] WH omitted one ([h]ena) and left *I will ask you a word* (logon)

themselves, saying, If we shall say, From heaven; he will say, Why **then**[1] believed ye him not?

6　But and if we say, Of men; **all**[2] **the people**[3] will stone us: for they be persuaded that John was a prophet.

7　And they answered, that they could not tell whence *it was*.

8　And Jesus said unto them, Neither tell I you by what authority I do these things.

9　Then began he to speak to the people this parable; A ~~certain~~[4] man planted a vineyard, and let it forth to husbandmen, and went into a far country for a long time.

10　And ~~at~~[5] the season he sent a servant to the husbandmen, that **they should give**[6] him of the fruit of the

vineyard: but the husbandmen beat him, and sent *him* away empty.

11　And again he sent another servant: and they beat him also, and entreated *him* shamefully, and sent *him* away empty.

12　And again he sent a third: and they wounded him also, and cast *him* out.

13　Then said the lord of the vineyard, What shall I do? I will send my beloved son: it may be they will reverence *him* ~~when they see~~[7] him.

14　But when the husbandmen saw him, they reasoned among **themselves**[8], saying, This is the heir: ~~come~~[9], let us kill him, that the inheritance may be ours.

15　So they cast him out of the vineyard, and killed *him*. What therefore shall the lord of the vineyard do unto them?

16　He shall come and destroy these husbandmen, and

---

[1] WH omitted <u>then</u> (<u>oun</u>).
[2] WH changed <u>all</u> (<u>pas</u>) to *all* (*ʰapas*). [syn]
[3] WH changed the word order from <u>all</u> THE PEOPLE to *THE PEOPLE all*.
[4] WH omitted <u>certain</u> (<u>tis</u>).
[5] WH omitted <u>at</u> (<u>en</u>) and let the dative case supply the prepositon.
[6] WH changed <u>they **might** give</u> (<u>dOsin</u>) to *they **will** give*

(*dOsousin*). **Aor** Act **Sub** to *Fut* Act *Ind*. [tense & mood]
[7] WH omitted <u>having seen</u> (<u>idontes</u>).
[8] WH changed **themselves** (**ʰeaut**<u>ous</u>) to *one another* (*allAlous*).
[9] WH omitted the interjection <u>come</u> (<u>deute</u>).

shall give the vineyard to others. And when they heard *it*, they said, God forbid.

17 And he beheld them, and said, What is this then that is written, The stone which the builders rejected, the same is become the head of the corner?

18 Whosoever shall fall upon that stone shall be broken; but on whomsoever it shall fall, it will grind him to powder.

19 And the **chief priests** and the **scribes**[1] the same hour sought to lay hands on him; and they feared the people: for they perceived that he had spoken this parable against them.

20 And they watched *him*, and sent forth spies, which should feign themselves just men, that they might take hold of his words, **that so**[2] they might deliver him unto the power and authority of the governor.

21 And they asked him, saying, Master, we know that thou sayest and teachest rightly, neither acceptest thou the person *of any*, but teachest the way of God truly:

22 Is it lawful **for us**[3] to give tribute unto Caesar, or no?

23 But he perceived their craftiness, and said unto them, ~~Why tempt ye me?~~ [4]

24 **Shew**[5] me a penny. Whose image and superscription hath it? **They answered and**[6] said, Caesar's.

25 And he said unto them, **Render**[7] therefore unto Caesar the things which be Caesar's, and unto God the things which be God's.

26 And they could not

---

[1] WH changed the word order from CHIEF PRIESTS and the SCRIBES to *SCRIBES and the CHIEF PRIESTS*.

[2] WH changed **into the** {end}) (**eis to**) to *so that* (*ʰOste*).

[3] WH changed for us (ʰAmin) to *for us* (ʰAmas). **Dat** Plur to *Acc* Plur. [case]

[4] WH omitted why tempt ye me (ti me peirazete).

[5] WH changed show {**upon**} (**epi**deixate) to *show* (*deixate*). Both Aor Act Imp. [prefix dropped & syn]

[6] WH changed **they answered** {and} (**apokri**𝚝**entes**) to *the* {ones} (ʰoi).

[7] WH changed the word order from RENDER therefore to *therefore RENDER*.

take hold of **his**[1] words before the people: and they marvelled at his answer, and held their peace.

27 Then came to *him* certain of the Sadducees, which **deny**[2] that there is any resurrection; and they asked him,

28 Saying, Master, Moses wrote unto us, If any man's brother die, having a wife, and **he die**[3] without children, that his brother should take his wife, and raise up seed unto his brother.

29 There were therefore seven brethren: and the first took a wife, and died without children.

30 And the second ~~took her to wife, and he died childless~~[4].

31 And the third took her;

and in like manner the seven also: ~~and~~[5] they left no children, and died.

32 Last ~~of all~~[6] the woman died also.

33 Therefore in the resurrection whose wife of them **is she**[7]? for seven had her to wife.

34 And Jesus ~~answering~~[8] said unto them, The children of this world marry, and **are given in marriage**[9]:

35 But they which shall be accounted worthy to obtain that world, and the resurrection from the dead, neither marry, nor **are given in marriage**[10]:

---

[1] WH changed of **him** (**ou**tou) to *of the* (*tou*).

[2] WH changed saying **against** (**anti**legontes) to *saying* (*legontes*). Both Pres Act Part. [antonym, prefix dropped]

[3] WH changed he **might die** (**apo**thanA) to *he may be* (*A*). **Aor** Act Sub of **apothnAskO** to *Pres* Sub of *eimi*.

[4] WH omitted took the woman and this one died childless (elaben tAn gunaika kai [h]outos apethanen ateknos).

[5] WH omitted and (kai).

[6] WH omitted of all (pantOn).

[7] WH changed **becomes** she (**gine**tai) to *is she* (*estai*).

[8] WH omitted having answered (apokritheis).

[9] WH changed are being given {**away**} in marriage (**ek**gamiskontai) to *are being given in marriage* (*gamiskontai*). Both Pres Pass Ind. [prefix dropped & syn]

[10] WH changed are given {**away**} in marriage (**ek**gamiskontai) to *are given in marriage* (*gamizontai*). Both Pres Pass Ind. [prefix dropped & spell]

36 **Neither**[1] can they die any more: for they are equal unto the angels; and are the children of God, being the children of the resurrection.

37 Now that the dead are raised, even Moses shewed at the bush, when he calleth the Lord the God of Abraham, and ~~the~~[2] God of Isaac, and ~~the~~[3] God of Jacob.

38 For he is not a God of the dead, but of the living: for all live unto him.

39 Then certain of the scribes answering said, Master, thou hast well said.

40 **And**[4] after that they durst not ask him any *question at all.*

41 And he said unto them, How say they that Christ is David's son?

42 **And** David **himself**[5] saith in the book of Psalms, The LORD said unto my Lord, Sit thou on my right hand,

43 Till I make thine ene-mies thy footstool.

44 David therefore calleth him Lord, how is he then his son?

45 Then in the audience of all the people he said unto his disciples,

46 Beware of the scribes, which desire to walk in long robes, and love greetings in the markets, and the highest seats in the synagogues, and the chief rooms at feasts;

47 Which devour widows' houses, and for a shew make long prayers: the same shall receive greater damnation.

CHAPTER 21

1 And he looked up, and saw the rich men casting **their gifts**[6] into the treasury.

2 And he saw ~~also~~[7] a certain poor widow casting in thither two mites.

3 And he said, Of a truth I say unto you, that this poor widow hath cast in more than they all:

4 For **all**[8] these have of

---

[1] WH changed <u>neither</u> (<u>oute</u>) to *neither* (*oude*).
[2] WH omitted <u>the</u> (<u>ton</u>).
[3] WH omitted <u>the</u> (<u>ton</u>).
[4] WH changed **and** (**de**) to *for* (*gar*).
[5] WH changed **and** (**kai**) to *for* (*gar*) and put <u>himself</u> (<u>autos</u>) first in the verse.

[6] WH changed the word order from <u>their gifts into the treasury</u> to *into the treasury their gifts*.
[7] WH omitted <u>also</u> (<u>kai</u>).
[8] WH changed <u>all</u> (<u>ᵸapantes</u>) to *all* (*pantes*).

their abundance cast in unto the offerings ~~of God~~[1]: but she of her penury hath cast in **all**[2] the living that she had.

5 And as some spake of the temple, how it was adorned with goodly stones and gifts, he said,

6 *As for* these things which ye behold, the days will come, in the which there shall not be left one stone upon another [∧**here**][3], that shall not be thrown down.

7 And they asked him, saying, Master, but when shall these things be? and what sign *will there be* when these things shall come to pass?

8 And he said, Take heed that ye be not deceived: for many shall come in my name, saying, I am *Christ*; and the time draweth near: go ye not ~~**therefore**~~[4] after them.

9 But when ye shall hear of wars and commotions, be not terrified: for these things must first come to pass; but the end *is* not by and by.

10 Then said he unto them, Nation shall rise against nation, and kingdom against kingdom:

11 And great earthquakes shall be in divers places, **and**[5] famines, and pestilences; and fearful sights and great signs shall there be from heaven.

12 But before **all**[6] these, they shall lay their hands on you, and persecute *you*, delivering *you* up to ∧**the**[7] synagogues, and into prisons, **being brought**[8] before kings and rulers for my name's sake.

13 ~~**And**~~[9] it shall turn to you for a testimony.

14 **Settle**[10] *it* therefore **in**[11]

---

[1] WH omitted of the God (tou ~~theou~~)

[2] WH changed all (**ʰapantes**) to *all* (*pantes*).

[3] WH added *here* (ʰ*Ode*).

[4] WH omitted therefore (oun).

[5] WH changed the word order from in divers places AND to *AND in divers places*.

[6] WH changed all (**ʰapantOn**) to *all* (*pantOn*).

[7] WH added *the* (*tas*) where the KJV supplied it.

[8] WH changed being brought (*agomenous*) to *being brought* {**away**} (*apagomenous*). Both Pres Pass Part. [prefix added]

[9] WH omitted and (de).

[10] WH changed settle {**for yourselves**} (~~thesthe~~) to *settle* (*thete*). Aor *Mid* Imp to Aor *Act* Imp. [voice]

[11] WH changed **into** (eis) to *in* (*en*). [prep]

your hearts[1], not to meditate before what ye shall answer:

15 For I will give you a mouth and wisdom, which all your adversaries shall not be able to gainsay nor **resist**[2].

16 And ye shall be betrayed both by parents, and brethren, and kinsfolks, and friends; and *some* of you shall they cause to be put to death.

17 And ye shall be hated of all *men* for my name's sake.

18 But there shall not an hair of your head perish.

19 In your patience **possess ye**[3] your souls.

20 And when ye shall see Jerusalem compassed with armies, then know that the desolation thereof is nigh.

21 Then let them which are in Judaea flee to the mountains; and let them which are in the midst of it depart out; and let not them that are in the countries enter thereinto.

22 For these be the days of vengeance, that all things which are written **may be fulfilled**[4].

23 ~~But~~[5] woe unto them that are with child, and to them that give suck, in those days! for there shall be great distress in the land, and wrath ~~upon~~[6] this people.

24 And they shall fall by the edge of the sword, and shall be led away captive into all nations: and Jerusalem shall be trodden down of the Gentiles, until the times of the Gentiles be fulfilled.

25 And **there shall be**[7] signs in the sun, and in the moon, and in the stars; and upon the earth distress of nations, with perplexity; the sea

---

[1] WH changed <u>the</u> <u>hearts</u> <u>of</u> <u>you</u> (<u>tas</u> <u>kardias</u> <u>ʰumOn</u>) to *the hearts of you* (*tais kardiais ʰumOn*). [case]

[2] WH changed the word order from <u>to gainsay</u> <u>nor</u> <u>RESIST</u> to *to RESIST nor gainsay*.

[3] WH changed <u>possess ye</u> (<u>ktAsasthe</u>) to <u>ye</u> **will** <u>possess</u> (*ktAsesthe*). **Aor** Mid-D **Imp** to *Fut* Mid-D *Ind*. [tense & mood]

[4] WH changed <u>to be fulfilled</u> (<u>plArOthAnai</u>) to *to be fulfilled* (*plAsthAnai*). Aor Pass Inf of <u>plAroO</u> to Aor Pass Inf of *plAthO*. [syn]

[5] WH omitted <u>but</u> (<u>de</u>).

[6] WH omitted <u>upon</u> (<u>en</u>) and let the dative case supply the preposition.

[7] WH changed **it shall be** (<u>estai</u>) to **they** *shall be* (*esontai*). Fut Ind 3rd **Sing** to Fut Ind 3rd *Plur*. [number]

and the waves **roaring**[1];

26 Men's hearts failing them for fear, and for looking after those things which are coming on the earth: for the powers of heaven shall be shaken.

27 And then shall they see the Son of man coming in a cloud with power and great glory.

28 And when these things begin to come to pass, then look up, and lift up your heads; for your redemption draweth nigh.

29 And he spake to them a parable; Behold the fig tree, and all the trees;

30 When they now shoot forth, ye see and know of your own selves that summer is now nigh at hand.

31 So likewise ye, when ye see these things come to pass, know ye that the kingdom of God is nigh at hand.

32 Verily I say unto you, This generation shall not pass away, till all be fulfilled.

33 Heaven and earth shall pass away: but my words **shall** not **pass away**[2].

34 And take heed to yourselves, lest at any time your hearts **be overcharged**[3] with surfeiting, and drunkenness, and cares of this life, and *so* that day come upon you unawares.

35 For as a snare shall it come on all them that dwell on the face of the whole earth.

36 Watch ye **therefore**[4], and pray always, that **ye may be accounted worthy**[5] to escape all these things that shall come to pass, and to stand before the Son of man.

37 And in the day time he was teaching in the temple; and at night he went out, and

---

pass away (*pareleusontai*). **Aor** Act **Sub** to *Fut* Mid-D *Ind*. [tense & mood]

[3] WH changed <u>might be over-</u>**charged** (<u>barunthOsin</u>) to *might be overburdened* (*barAthOsin*). Aor Pass Sub of <u>barunO</u> to Aor Pass Sub of *bareO*. [syn]

[4] WH changed **therefore** (<u>oun</u>) to *then* (*de*).

[5] WH changed <u>ye</u> **might be accounted worthy** (<u>kataxiOthAte</u>) to ye *may overcome* (*katiscusAte*). **Aor Pass** Sub of <u>kataxioO</u> to *Pres Act* Sub of *katiscuO*. [tense, voice, & syn]

---

[1] WH changed <u>roar**ing**</u> (<u>Acous**As**</u>) to *a roar* (*Acous*). Pres Act Part to Noun.

[2] WH changed **might** <u>pass</u> <u>away</u> (<u>parel**th**Osi</u>) to *will*

abode in the mount that is called *the mount* of Olives.

38 And all the people came early in the morning to him in the temple, for to hear him.

CHAPTER 22

1 Now the feast of unleavened bread drew nigh, which is called the Passover.

2 And the chief priests and scribes sought how they might kill him; for they feared the people.

3 Then entered Satan into Judas **surnamed**[1] Iscariot, being of the number of the twelve.

4 And he went his way, and communed with the chief priests and [the][2] captains, how he might betray him unto them.

5 And they were glad, and covenanted to give him money.

6 And he promised, and sought opportunity to betray him unto them in the absence of the multitude.

7 Then came the day of unleavened bread, when the passover must be killed.

8 And he sent Peter and John, saying, Go and prepare us the passover, that we may eat.

9 And they said unto him, Where wilt thou that we prepare?

10 And he said unto them, Behold, when ye are entered into the city, there shall a man meet you, bearing a pitcher of water; follow him into the house **where**[3] he entereth in.

11 And ye shall say unto the goodman of the house, The Master saith unto thee, Where is the guestchamber, where I shall eat the passover with my disciples?

12 And he shall shew you a large upper room furnished: there make ready.

13 And they went, and found as **he had said**[4] unto them: and they made ready the passover.

14 And when the hour was come, he sat down, and the

---

[1] WH changed **sur**named (**epi**kaloumenon) to *named* (*kaloumenon*). Both Pres Pass Part. [prefix dropped]
[2] WH omitted the untranslated the (tois).

[3] WH changed **where** (**ou**) to *into which* (**eis An**).
[4] WH changed he has said (eirAken) to *he had said* (*eirAkei*). **Pf** Act Ind to *PastPf* Act Ind. [tense]

twelve[1] apostles with him.

15 And he said unto them, With desire I have desired to eat this passover with you before I suffer:

16 For I say unto you, I will not ~~any more~~[2] eat **there**[3] ~~of~~[4], until it be fulfilled in the kingdom of God.

17 And he took the cup, and gave thanks, and said, Take this, and divide *it* ᴧ**among**[5] yourselves:

18 For I say unto you, I will not drink [ᴧ**from the present**][6] of the fruit of the vine, until the kingdom of God shall come.

19 And he took bread, and gave thanks, and brake *it*, and gave unto them, saying, This is my body **which is given for you: this do in remem-brance of me**[7].

20 **Likewise**[8] **also the cup after supper, saying, This cup *is* the new testament in my blood, which is shed for you.**[9]

21 But, behold, the hand of him that betrayeth me *is* with me on the table.

22 **And**[10] **truly**[11] the Son of man **goeth**[12], as it was determined: but woe unto that man by whom he is betrayed!

23 And they began to enquire among themselves, which of them it was that should do this thing.

24 And there was also a strife among them, which of them should be accounted the

---

[1] WH omitted twelve (dO-deka).

[2] WH omitted no longer (ouketi).

[3] WH omitted out of (ex) from out of it [thereof].

[4] WH changed it (auto**u**) to *it* (*auto*) in out of it [thereof]. [case]

[5] WH added *among* (*eis*--into) where the KJV supplied it.

[6] WH added from the present (apo tou nun).

[7] In their margin, WH omitted the last half of Luke 22:19.

[8] In their text, WH changed the word order from LIKEWISE also the cup to *also the cup LIKEWISE*.

[9] In their margin, WH omitted all of Luke 22:20.

[10] WH changed **and** (**kai**) to *because* (*[h]oti*).

[11] WH changed the word order from **and** the TRULY son to *because the son TRULY*.

[12] WH changed the word order from GOETH as it was determined to *as it was determined GOETH*.

greatest.

25 And he said unto them, The kings of the Gentiles exercise lordship over them; and they that exercise authority upon them are called benefactors.

26 But ye *shall* not *be* so: but he that is greatest among you, **let him be**[1] as the younger; and he that is chief, as he that doth serve.

27 For whether *is* greater, he that sitteth at meat, or he that serveth? *is* not he that sitteth at meat? but **I am**[2] among you as he that serveth.

28 Ye are they which have continued with me in my temptations.

29 And I appoint unto you a kingdom, as my Father hath appointed unto me;

30 That ye may eat and drink at my table in my kingdom, and **sit**[3] on thrones judging the twelve tribes of Israel.

31 ~~**And the Lord said**~~[4], Simon, Simon, behold, Satan hath desired *to have* you, that he may sift *you* as wheat:

32 But I have prayed for thee, that thy faith **fail**[5] not: and when thou art converted, strengthen thy brethren.

33 And he said unto him, Lord, I am ready to go with thee, both into prison, and to death.

34 And he said, I tell thee, Peter, the cock shall not [~~not~~][6] crow this day, **before that**[7] **thou shalt** thrice [~~not~~][8] deny that thou knowest **me**[9].

D *Ind* of *kathAmai*. [syn; tense & mood]
[4] WH omitted <u>and the Lord said</u> (eipe de <u>ʰo kurios</u>).
[5] WH changed **may** fail (ekleipA) to **might** *fail* (*eklipA*). **Pres** Act Sub to *Aor* Act Sub. [tense]
[6] WH omitted an untranslated second <u>not</u> (mA)
[7] WH changed **before that** (**prin A**) to *until* (*ʰeOs*).
[8] WH omitted the untranslated <u>not</u> (mA).
[9] WH changed the word order from <u>thou shalt</u> <u>not</u> deny that thou knowest ME *to* ME *thou shalt deny that thy knowest*.

---

[1] WH changed <u>let him be</u> (<u>genesthO</u>) to *be letting him be* (*ginesthO*). **Aor** Mid-D Imp to *Pres* M/P-D Imp. [tense]
[2] WH changed the word order from <u>I am</u> <u>among</u> <u>you</u> to *among you I am*.
[3] WH changed **might** sit (kathisAsthe) to *may sit* (*kathisesthe*). **Aor** Mid-D **Sub** of <u>kathizO</u> to *Pres* M/P-

35 And he said unto them, When I sent you without purse, and scrip, and shoes, lacked ye any thing? And they said, Nothing.

36 **Then** **said** **he**[1] unto them, But now, he that hath a purse, let him take *it*, and likewise *his* scrip: and he that hath no sword, let him sell his garment, and buy one.

37 For I say unto you, that this that is written must ~~yet~~[2] be accomplished in me, And he was reckoned among the transgressors: for **the things**[3] concerning me have an end.

38 And they said, Lord, behold, here *are* two swords. And he said unto them, It is enough.

39 And he came out, and went, as he was wont, to the mount of Olives; and ~~his~~[4] disciples also followed him.

40 And when he was at the place, he said unto them, Pray that ye enter not into temptation.

41 And he was withdrawn from them about a stone's cast, and kneeled down, and prayed,

42 Saying, Father, if thou be willing, remove **this**[5] cup from me: nevertheless not my will, but thine, **be done**[6].

43 **And** **there** **appeared** **an** **angel** **unto** **him** **from** **heaven,** **strengthening** **him.**

44 **And** **being** **in** **an** **ag-** **ony** **he** **prayed** **more** **ear-** **nestly:** **and** **his** **sweat** **was** **as** **it** **were** **great** **drops** **of** **blood** **falling** **down** **to** **the** **ground.**[7]

45 And when he rose up from prayer, and was come to ~~his~~[8] disciples, he found them sleeping for sorrow,

46 And said unto them, Why sleep ye? rise and pray, lest ye enter into temptation.

47 ~~And~~[9] while he yet

---

[1] WH changed **then** (**oun**) to *but the* {one} (*^{h}o de*); and put this change before he said (eipen).

[2] WH omitted yet (eti).

[3] WH changed the things (**ta**) to *the thing* (*to*). [number]

[4] WH omitted of him (autou) from the disciples of him.

[5] WH changed the word order from the cup THIS to *THIS the cup.*

[6] WH changed be done (genes*th*O) to *be* ***being*** *done* (gines*th*O). **Aor** Mid-D Imp to ***Pres*** M/P-D Imp. [tense]

[7] In their margin, WH omitted verses 43 & 44.

[8] WH omitted of him (autou) from the disciples of him.

[9] WH omitted and (de).

spake, behold a multitude, and he that was called Judas, one of the twelve, went before them, and drew near unto Jesus to kiss him.

48 But Jesus said unto him, Judas, betrayest thou the Son of man with a kiss?

49 When they which were about him saw what would follow, they said unto him, Lord, shall we smite with the sword?

50 And one of them smote the servant of the high priest, and cut off his right ear.

51 And Jesus answered and said, Suffer ye thus far. And he touched ~~his~~[1] ear, and healed him.

52 Then Jesus said unto the chief priests, and captains of the temple, and the elders, which were come to him, Be ye come out, as against a thief, with swords and staves?

53 When I was daily with you in the temple, ye stretched forth no hands against me: but this is your hour, and the power of darkness.

54 Then took they him, and led *him*, and brought

~~him~~[2] into the high priest's house. And Peter followed afar off.

55 And **when they had kindled**[3] a fire in the midst of the hall, and **[they]**[4] were set down together, Peter sat down among them.

56 But a certain maid beheld him as he sat by the fire, and earnestly looked upon him, and said, This man was also with him.

57 And he denied **him**[5], saying, **Woman**[6], I know him not.

58 And after a little while another saw him, and said, Thou art also of them. And Peter **said**[7], Man, I am not.

59 And about the space of

---

[1] WH omitted of him (autou) from the ear of him.

[2] WH omitted him (auton).

[3] WH changed when they had kindled (^{h}aςantOn) to *when they had kindled* {**around**} (*periaςantOn*). Both Aor Act Part. [prefix added]

[4] WH omitted the untranslated they (autOn).

[5] WH omitted him (auton).

[6] WH changed the word order from WOMAN not I know him to *not I know him* WOMAN.

[7] WH changed said (**eipen**) to *was saying* (*efA*). **Aor** Act Ind of **epO** to *Impf* Ind of *fAmi*. [synonym & tense]

one hour after another confidently affirmed, saying, Of a truth this *fellow* also was with him: for he is a Galilaean.

60 And Peter said, Man, I know not what thou sayest. And immediately, while he yet spake, ~~the~~[1] cock crew.

61 And the Lord turned, and looked upon Peter. And Peter remembered the **word**[2] of the Lord, how he had said unto him, Before the cock crow [∧**this day**][3], thou shalt deny me thrice.

62 And ~~Peter~~[4] went out, and wept bitterly.

63 And the men that held **Jesus**[5] mocked him, and smote *him*.

64 And when they had blindfolded him, they ~~struck him on the face, and~~[6] asked him, saying, Prophesy, who is it that smote thee?

65 And many other things blasphemously spake they against him.

66 And as soon as it was day, the elders of the people and the chief priests and the scribes came together, and **led**[7] him into **their**[8] council, saying,

67 Art thou the Christ? tell us. And he said unto them, If I tell you, ye will not believe:

68 And if I ~~also~~[9] ask *you*, ye will not answer me, ~~nor let *me* go~~[10].

69 [∧**but**][11] Hereafter shall the Son of man sit on the right hand of the power of God.

70 Then said they all, Art thou then the Son of God? And he said unto them, Ye say that I am.

71 And they said, What need we any further witness? for we ourselves have heard

---

[1] WH omitted the (ʰo).
[2] WH changed word (**logou**) to *word* (ʰ*rAmatos*). Both Gen Sing Masc. [syn]
[3] WH added *this day* (*sAmeron*).
[4] WH omitted the Peter (ʰo petros).
[5] WH changed the Jesus (ʰo iAsous) to *him* (*auton*).
[6] WH omitted struck him on the face and (etupton autou to prosOpon kai).

[7] WH changed led {up} (anAgagon) to *led* {away} (*apAgagon*). Both Aor Act Ind. [prefix changed]
[8] WH changed of them**selves** (ʰeautOn) to *of them* (*autOn*).
[9] WH omitted also (kai).
[10] WH omitted nor let [me] go (moi ʰA apolusAte).
[11] WH added *but* (*de*).

of his own mouth.

CHAPTER 23

1   And the whole multitude of them arose, and **led**[1] him unto Pilate.

2   And they began to accuse him, saying, We found this *fellow* perverting the nation [ʌ**of us**][2], and forbidding to give tribute to Caesar, [ʌ**and**][3] saying that he himself is Christ a King.

3   And Pilate **asked**[4] him, saying, Art thou the King of the Jews? And he answered him and said, Thou sayest *it*.

4   Then said Pilate to the chief priests and *to* the people, I find no fault in this man.

5   And they were the more fierce, saying, He stirreth up the people, teaching throughout all Jewry,

[ʌ**even**][5]   beginning from Galilee to this place.

6   When Pilate heard ~~of Galilee~~[6], he asked whether the man were a Galilaean.

7   And as soon as he knew that he belonged unto Herod's jurisdiction, he sent him to Herod, who himself also was at Jerusalem at that time.

8   And when Herod saw Jesus, he was exceeding glad: for **he was desirous**[7] to see him **of a long**[8] ʌ*season*[9], because he had heard ~~many things~~[10] of him; and he hoped to have seen some miracle done by him.

9   Then he questioned with him in many words; but he answered him nothing.

---

[1] WH changed {**it**} <u>led</u> (<u>Agagen</u>) to {**they**} led (*Agagon*). Aor Act Ind 3rd **Sing** to Aor Act Ind 3rd *Plur.* [number]

[2] WH added *of us* (ʰ*Amon*).

[3] WH added *and* (*kai*).

[4] WH changed <u>asked</u> {**of**} (**ep**A*r*O*t*Asen) to *asked* (*A*r*O*t*Asen*). Both Aor Act Ind. [prefix dropped]

---

[5] WH added *even* (*kai*).

[6] WH omitted <u>of Galilee</u> (<u>galilaian</u>).

[7] WH changed the word order from <u>WILLING</u> <u>out of</u> <u>a</u> <u>long</u> <u>to see</u> <u>him</u> to *out of a long season* WILLING *to see him.*

[8] WH changed <u>a long</u> (ʰ<u>ikanou</u>) to *a long* (ʰ*ikanOn*). **Gen** to *Dat.* [case].

[9] WH added *season* (*cronoOn*) as the KJV supplied.

[10] WH omitted <u>many</u> [things] (<u>polla</u>).

10 And the chief priests and scribes stood and vehemently accused him.

11 And Herod with his men of war set him at nought, and mocked *him*, and arrayed ~~him~~¹ in a gorgeous robe, and sent him again to Pilate.

12 And the same day [~~both~~]² **Pilate** and **Herod**³ were made friends together: for before they were at enmity between themselves.

13 And Pilate, when he had called together the chief priests and the rulers and the people,

14 Said unto them, Ye have brought this man unto me, as one that perverteth the people: and, behold, I, having examined *him* before you, have found no fault in this man touching those things whereof ye accuse him:

15 No, nor yet Herod: for **I sent**⁴ **you**⁵ to **him**⁶; and, lo,

nothing worthy of death is done unto him.

16 I will therefore chastise him, and release *him*.

17 ~~(For of necessity he must release one unto them at the feast.)~~ ⁷

18 And they cried out all at once, saying, Away with this *man*, and release unto us Barabbas:

19 (Who for a certain sedition made in the city, and for murder, **was cast**⁸ **into**⁹ [∧**the**]¹⁰ **prison**¹¹.)

20 Pilate therefore, willing

---

¹ WH omitted <u>him</u> (*auton*).
² WH omitted the untranslated <u>both</u> (*te*).
³ WH changed the word order from <u>PILATE</u> <u>and</u> <u>HEROD</u> to *HEROD and PILATE.*
⁴ WH changed **I** sent (*anepemsa*) to *he sent* (*anepemse*). Aor Act Ind **1ʳˢᵗ** Sing to Aor Act Ind *3ʳᵈ* Sing. [person]

⁵ WH changed <u>**you**</u> (ʰ<u>umas</u>) to *us* (ʰ<u>Amas</u>).
⁶ WH changed the word order from <u>**you**</u> <u>to</u> <u>HIM</u> to *HIM to us.*
⁷ WH omitted <u>for</u> of necessity he must release <u>one</u> <u>unto</u> them at the <u>feast</u> (*anagkAn de eicen* ʰ*apoluein autois kata* ʰ*eortan* ʰ*ena*) from their text. In their margin, WH retained Luke 23:17.
⁸ WH changed **has been** cast (*beblAmenos*) to *was cast* (*blAtheis*) **Pf** Pass Part to *Aor* Pass Part. [tense]
⁹ WH changed <u>into</u> (<u>eis</u>) to *in* (*en*).
¹⁰ WH added *the* (*tAn*).
¹¹ WH changed <u>prision</u> (<u>fulakAn</u>) to *prision* (*fulakA*) [case].

to release Jesus, spake again
ʌto them[1].

21 But they cried, saying,
Crucify *him*, crucify him.

22 And he said unto them
the third time, Why, what evil
hath he done? I have found
no cause of death in him: I
will therefore chastise him,
and let *him* go.

23 And they were instant
with loud voices, requiring
that he might be crucified.
And the voices of them ~~and
of the chief priests~~[2] prevailed.

24 **And**[3] Pilate gave sentence that it should be as they
required.

25 And he released ~~unto
them~~[4] him that for sedition
and murder was cast into
[**the**][5] prison, whom they had
desired; but he delivered Jesus to their will.

26 And as they led him
away, they laid hold upon
one **Simon**, **a Cyrenian**[6],
~~[the {one}]~~[7] **coming**[8] out of
the country, and on him they
laid the cross, that he might
bear *it* after Jesus.

27 And there followed him
a great company of people,
and of women, which ~~also~~[9]
bewailed and lamented him.

28 But Jesus turning unto
them said, Daughters of Jerusalem, weep not for me, but
weep for yourselves, and for
your children.

29 For, behold, the days
are coming, in the which they
shall say, Blessed *are* the barren, and ʌ**the**[10] wombs that
never bare, and the paps
which never **gave suck**[11].

---

[1] WH added *to them* (*autois*)
as the KJV supplied.
[2] WH omitted <u>and of the
chief priests</u> (<u>kai tOn arci-
ereOn</u>).
[3] WH changed **but the** (**ʰo
de**) to *and* (*kai*).
[4] WH omitted <u>unto them</u>
(<u>autois</u>).
[5] WH omitted the untranslated <u>the</u> (<u>tAn</u>).

---

[6] WH changed <u>Simon</u> one **of
Cyrene** (<u>simOnos tinos
kurAnaiou</u>) to *Simon one a
Cyrenian* (*simOna tina
kurAnaion*). [case]
[7] WH omitted the untranslated <u>the {one}</u> (<u>tou</u>).
[8] WH changed <u>coming</u> (<u>er-
comenou</u>) to *coming* (*er-
comenon*). [case]
[9] WH omitted <u>also</u> (<u>kai</u>).
[10] WH added *the* (*ai*) as the
KJV supplied.
[11] WH changed <u>gave suck</u>
(<u>ethAlasan</u>) to *gave suck*
(*ethreşan*). Aor Act Ind of
<u>thAlazO</u> to Aor Act Ind of
trefO. [syn]

30 Then shall they begin to say to the mountains, Fall on us; and to the hills, Cover us.

31 For if they do these things in a green tree, what shall be done in the dry?

32 And there were also two other, malefactors, led with him to be put to death.

33 And when **they were come**[1] to the place, which is called Calvary, there they crucified him, and the malefactors, one on the right hand, and the other on the left.

34 **Then said Jesus, Father, forgive them; for they know not what they do.**[2] And they parted his raiment, and cast lots.

35 And the people stood beholding. And the rulers also ~~with them~~[3] derided *him*, saying, He saved others; let him save himself, if he be Christ, **the chosen**[4] of God.

36 And the soldiers also mocked him, coming to him, **and**[5] offering him vinegar,

37 And saying, If thou be the king of the Jews, save thyself.

38 And a superscription also ~~was written~~[6] over him ~~in letters of Greek, and Latin, and Hebrew~~[7], **THIS**[8] ~~IS~~[9] THE KING OF THE JEWS.

39 And one of the malefactors which were hanged railed on him, saying, **If**[10] thou be Christ, save thyself and us.

40 But the other answering **rebuked**[11] **him**,

CHOSEN to *of the God* THE *CHOSEN*.

[5] WH omitted <u>and</u> (<u>kai</u>).

[6] WH omitted <u>was written</u> (<u>gegrammenA</u>).

[7] WH omitted <u>in letters of Greek</u> <u>and</u> <u>Latin</u> <u>and</u> <u>Hebrew</u> (<u>grammasin</u> [h]<u>AllAnikois kai</u> [h]<u>rOmaikois kai</u> [h]<u>Abraikois</u>).

[8] WH changed the word order from <u>THIS</u> **is** <u>the</u> <u>king</u> of <u>the</u> <u>jews</u> to *the king of the jews THIS*.

[9] WH omitted <u>is</u> (<u>estin</u>).

[10] WH changed if (**ei**) to *by no means* (*ouci*).

[11] WH changed **was** rebuking (**epetima**) to *rebuking* (*epetimOn*). **Impf** Act <u>Ind</u> to ***Pres*** Act ***Part***. [tense mood]

---

[1] WH changed <u>they were come</u> {**from**} (**apAlthon**) to *they were come* (*AlThon*). Both Aor Act Ind. [prefix dropped]

[2] In their margin, WH omitted the first two-thirds of Luke 23:34.

[3] WH omitted <u>with</u> <u>them</u> (<u>sun autois</u>).

[4] WH changed the word order from <u>THE</u> of the <u>God</u>

saying[1], Dost not thou fear God, seeing thou art in the same condemnation?

41 And we indeed justly; for we receive the due reward of our deeds: but this man hath done nothing amiss.

42 And he said unto [the][2] Jesus, ~~Lord~~[3], remember me when thou comest **into**[4] **thy kingdom**[5].

43 And ~~Jesus~~[6] said unto him, Verily I say unto thee, To day shalt thou be with me in paradise.

44 **And it was**[7] [^**now**][8] about the sixth hour, and there was a darkness over all the earth until the ninth hour.

45 ~~And~~[9] [10]**the sun**[11] **was darkened**[12], **and**[13] the veil of the temple **was rent**[14] in the midst.

46 And when Jesus had cried with a loud voice, he said, Father, into thy hands **I commend**[15] my spirit: **and**[16] having said **thus**[17], he gave up the ghost.

---

[1] WH changed saying (**legOn**) to *was saying* (*efA*). **Pres** Act **Part** of legO to *Impf Ind* of *fAmi*. [tense, mood, & syn]

[2] WH omitted the untranslated the (tO).

[3] WH omitted Lord (kurie).

[4] WH changed in (**en**) to *into* (*eis*).

[5] and changed the kingdom of thee (tA basileia sou) to *the kingdom of thee* (*tAn basileian sou*) **Dat** to *Acc*. [case].

[6] WH omitted the Jesus (^ho iAsous).

[7] WH changed and (*de*) to *and* (*kai*) and put *and* (*kai*) first in the verse.

[8] WH added *now* (*AdA*).

[9] WH omitted and (kai).

[10] WH changed the word order from **and was darkened** THE SUN to *THE SUN failing*.

[11] WH changed the sun (^hAlios) to *the sun* (^hAliou) **Nom** to *Gen*. [case];

[12] WH changed **was darkened** (eskotisthA) to *failing* or *eclipsing* (*ekleipontos*). **Aor** **Pass** **Ind** of skotizO to *Pres Act Part* of ekleipO. [tense, voice, & mood].

[13] WH changed and (kai) to *but* (*de*); and put *but* (*de*) second in the verse.

[14] WH changed the word order from WAS RENT **but** to *and WAS RENT*.

[15] WH changed I **will** commend (parathAsomai) to *I am commending* (*paratithemai*). **Fut** Mid Ind to *Pres* Mid Ind. [tense]

[16] WH changed **and** (kai) to *then* (*de*).

[17] WH changed thus (tauta) to *this* (*tauto*). [number]

47 Now when the centurion saw what was done, **he glorified**[1] God, saying, Certainly this was a righteous man.

48 And all the people that came together to that sight, **beholding**[2] the things which were done, smote **their**[3] breasts, and returned.

49 And all **his**[4] acquaintance, and the women that **followed**[5] him from Galilee, stood [∧**from**][6] afar off, beholding these things.

50 And, behold, *there was* a man named Joseph, a counsellor; *and he was* a good man, and a just:

51 (The same had not consented to the counsel and deed of them;) he was of Arimathaea, a city of the Jews: [~~and~~][7] who ~~also himself~~[8] waited for the kingdom of God.

52 This *man* went unto Pilate, and begged the body of Jesus.

53 And he took ~~it~~[9] down, and wrapped it in linen, and laid **it**[10] in a sepulchre that was hewn in stone, wherein **never man before**[11] was laid.

54 And that day was **the preparation**[12], and the sabbath drew on.

55 And the women **also**[13],

---

[1] WH changed he glorif**ied** (edoxase) to *he was glorifying* (edoxaze). **Aor** Act Ind to *Impf* Act Ind. [tense]

[2] WH changed behold**ing** (~~the~~Orou**ntes**) to *having beheld* (~~the~~OrAs**antes**). **Pres** Act Part to *Aor* Act Part. [tense]

[3] WH omitted of themselves ([h]eautOn) from the breasts of themselves.

[4] WH changed **of** him (aut**ou**) to *to* him (aut**O**). [case]

[5] WH changed **having** fol**lowed** (sunakolou~~th~~**As**asai) to *following* (sunakolou~~th~~**ousai**). **Aor** Act Part to *Pres* Act Part. [tense]

[6] WH added *from* (apo).

[7] WH omitted the untranslated and (kai).

[8] WH omitted also himself (kai autos).

[9] WH omitted it (auto).

[10] WH changed it (aut**o**) to *it* (aut**on**). **Neut** to *Masc*. [gender]

[11] WH changed not yet **anyone** (oudepO oudeis) to *not yet no one* (oudeis [h]oupO).

[12] WH changed the preparation (paraskeuA) to *the preparation* (paraskeuAs). **Nom** Sing Fem to *Gen* Sing Fem. [case]

[13] WH changed **also** (kai) to *the* (ai) and placed the *the* (ai) where the KJV supplied the.

which came ~~with him~~[1] from Galilee, followed after, and beheld the sepulchre, and how his body was laid.

56 And they returned, and prepared spices and ointments; and rested the sabbath day according to the commandment.

CHAPTER 24

1 Now upon the first *day* of the week, very early in the morning, they came unto the sepulchre, bringing the spices which they had prepared, ~~and certain *others* with them~~[2].

2 And they found the stone rolled away from the sepulchre.

3 **And they entered in**[3], and found not the body **of the Lord Jesus**[4].

4 And it came to pass, as

they were much perplexed[5] thereabout, behold, two men stood by them in shining garments:

5 And as they were afraid, and bowed down **_their faces_**[6] to the earth, they said unto them, Why seek ye the living among the dead?

6 **He is not here, but is risen**[7]: remember how he spake unto you when he was yet in Galilee,

7 Saying, The Son of man **must**[8] be delivered into the hands of sinful men, and be crucified, and the third day rise again.

8 And they remembered his words,

9 And returned **from the**

---

[1] WH omitted with him (autO).

[2] WH omitted and certain [others] with them (kai tines sun autais).

[3] WH changed and (**kai**) to *and* (*de*) and put they entered in at the beginning of the verse.

[4] In their margin, WH omitted of the Lord Jesus (tou kuriou iAsou).

[5] WH changed to be **much** perplexed (**dia**poreisthai) to *to be perplexed* (*aporeisthai*). Both Pres Pass Inf. [prefix dropped]

[6] WH changed the face (**to** prosOpon) to *the faces* (*ta prosOpa*). Acc **Sing** Neut to Acc *Plur* Neut. [number]

[7] In their margin, WH omitted he is not here but is risen (ouk estin [h]Ode all' AgerthA).

[8] WH changed the word order from THAT MUST the son of man to *the son of man THAT MUST.*

sepulchre[1], and told all these things unto the eleven, and to all the rest.

10 It was Mary Magdalene, and Joanna, and Mary *the mother* of [∧the][2] James, and other *women that were* with them, which told these things unto the apostles.

11 And **their**[3] words seemed to them as idle tales, and they believed them not.

12 Then arose Peter, and ran unto the sepulchre; and stooping down, he beheld the linen clothes ~~laid~~[4] by themselves, and departed, wondering in himself at that which was come to pass.[5]

13 And, behold, two of them **went**[6] that same day to a village called Emmaus, which was from Jerusalem *about* threescore furlongs.

14 And they talked together of all these things which had happened.

15 And it came to pass, that, while they communed *together* and reasoned, Jesus himself drew near, and went with them.

16 But their eyes were holden that they should not know him.

17 And he said unto them, What manner of communications *are* these that ye have one to another, as ye walk, and **are**[7] sad?

18 And ~~the~~[8] one of them, **whose name was**[9] Cleopas, answering said unto him, Art thou only a stranger ~~in~~[10] Jerusalem, and hast not known the things which are come to pass there in these days? And he said unto them, What things? And they said unto him, Concerning Jesus

---

[1] In their margin, WH omitted (apo tou mnAmeiou).
[2] WH added *the* (*h*A).
[3] WH changed of them (autOn) to *these* (tautA) in the words of them.
[4] In their text, WH omitted laid (keimena).
[5] In their margin, WH omitted all of Luke 24:12.
[6] WH changed the word order from WENT that same day to *that same day WENT.*

[7] WH changed **are being** (este) to *was stood* (esta*th*Asan). **Pres** Ind of eimi to *Aor* Pass Ind of *h*istAmi.
[8] WH omitted the untranslated the (*h*o).
[9] WH changed **whose** name was (*h*O onoma) to *named* (onomati).
[10] WH omitted in (en).

of **Nazareth**[1], which was a prophet mighty in deed and word before God and all the people:

20 And how the chief priests and our rulers delivered him to be condemned to death, and have crucified him.

21 But [∧also][2] we trusted that it had been he which should have redeemed Israel: and beside all this, ~~to day~~[3] is the third day since these things were done.

22 Yea, and certain women also of our company made us astonished, which were **early**[4] at the sepulchre;

23 And when they found not his body, they came, saying, that they had also seen a vision of angels, which said that he was alive.

24 And certain of them which were with us went to the sepulchre, and found *it* ~~even~~[5] so as the women had said: but him they saw not.

25 Then he said unto them, O fools, and slow of heart to believe all that the prophets have spoken:

26 Ought not Christ to have suffered these things, and to enter into his glory?

27 And beginning at Moses and all the prophets, **he expounded**[6] unto them in all the scriptures the things concerning himself.

28 And they drew nigh unto the village, whither they went: and he made as though he would have gone further.

29 But they constrained him, saying, Abide with us: for it is toward evening, and the day is far spent. And he went in to tarry with them.

30 And it came to pass, as he sat at meat with them, he took bread, and blessed *it*, and brake, and gave to them.

31 And their eyes were opened, and they knew him; and he vanished out of their sight.

32 And they said one to another, Did not our heart burn within us, while he talked with us by the way,

---

[1] WH changed Nazareth (na-zOraiou) to Nazareth (*nazarAnou*).

[2] WH added *also* (kai).

[3] WH omitted to day (sAmeron).

[4] WH changed early (or~~th~~riai) to early (or~~th~~rinai).

[5] WH omitted even (kai).

[6] WH changed he **was** expounding (diArmAneuen) to *he expounded* (*diermAneusen*). **Impf** Act Ind to *Aor* Act Ind. [tense]

and[1] while he opened to us the scriptures?

33 And they rose up the same hour, and returned to Jerusalem, and found the eleven **gathered together**[2], and them that were with them,

34 Saying, The Lord is risen **indeed**[3], and hath appeared to Simon.

35 And they told what things *were done* in the way, and how he was known of them in breaking of bread.

36 And as they thus spake, ~~Jesus~~[4] himself stood in the midst of them, **and saith unto them, Peace** *be* **unto you**[5].

37 But they were terrified and affrighted, and supposed that they had seen a spirit.

38 And he said unto them, Why are ye troubled? and why do thoughts arise in **your hearts**[6]?

39 Behold my hands and my feet, that it is I **myself**[7]: handle me, and see; for a spirit hath not flesh and bones, as ye see me have.

40 **And when he had thus spoken, he shewed**[8] **them** *his* **hands and** *his* **feet.**[9]

41 And while they yet believed not for joy, and wondered, he said unto them, Have ye here any meat?

42 And they gave him a piece of a broiled fish, ~~and of an honeycomb~~[10].

43 And he took *it*, and did

---

[1] WH omitted and (kai).

[2] WH changed gathered together (sunAthroismenous) to *gathered* (A*throismenous*). Both Pf Pass Part. [prefix dropped]

[3] WH changed the word order from is risen the Lord INDEED to *INDEED is risen the Lord.*

[4] WH omitted the Jesus (ho iAsous).

[5] In their margin, WH omitted and saith unto them peace [be] unto you (kai legei autois eirAnA humin).

[6] WH changed the hearts of you (**tais** kardiais) to *the heart of you* (*tA kardia*). Dat **Plur** Fem to Dat *Sing* Fem. [number]

[7] WH changed the word order from he MYSELF I am to *MYSELF I am he.*

[8] In their text, WH changed he showed {**upon**} (**epe**deixen) to *showed* (*edeixen*). Both Aor Act Ind. [prefex dropped]

[9] In their margin, WH omitted all of Luke 24:40.

[10] WH omitted and of an honeycomb (kai apo melissiou kAriou).

eat before them.

44 And he said **unto them**[1], These *are* the words [∧**of me**][2] which I spake unto you, while I was yet with you, that all things must be fulfilled, which were written in the law of Moses, and *in* the prophets, and *in* the psalms, concerning me.

45 Then opened he their understanding, that they might understand the scriptures,

46 And said unto them, Thus it is written, ~~and thus it behoved~~[3] Christ to suffer, and to rise from the dead the third day:

47 And that repentance **and**[4] remission of sins should be preached in his name among all nations, **beginning**[5] at Jerusalem.

---

[1] WH changed unto them (auto**is**) to *unto them* (**pros** auto**us**).
[2] WH added *of me* (**mou**).
[3] WH omitted and thus it behoved (kai [h]out**Os** edei).
[4] In their margin, WH changed **and** (**kai**) to *unto* (**eis**).
[5] WH changed having begun ([h]apxameno**n**) to *having begun* ([h]apxameno**i**). Aor Mid Part Nom **Sing Neut** to Aor Mid Part Nom ***Plur Masc***.

48 And ye are witnesses of these things.

49 And, behold, **I send**[6] the promise of my Father upon you: but tarry ye in the city ~~of Jerusalem~~[7], until ye be endued with **power**[8] from on high.

50 And he led them ~~out~~[9] as far as **to**[10] Bethany, and he lifted up his hands, and blessed them.

51 And it came to pass, while he blessed them, he was parted from them, **and carried up into heaven**[11].

52 And they **worshipped him, and**[12] returned to Jerusalem with great joy:

53 And were continually in

[number & gender]
[6] WH changed I send (apostell**O**) to *I send out* (**ekapostellO**). Both Pres Act Ind. [synonym, prefix added]
[7] WH omitted of Jerusalem ([h]ierousal**Am**).
[8] WH changed the word order from POWER from on high to *from on high POWER*.
[9] WH omitted out (ex**O**).
[10] WH changed **into** (**eis**) to *toward* (**pros**).
[11] In their margin, WH omitted (kai anefereto eis ton ouranon).
[12] In their margin, WH omitted (proskunAsantes auton).

the temple, ~~praising and~~[1]
blessing God. ~~Amen~~.[2]

---

[1] WH omitted <u>praising</u> <u>and</u>
(<u>ainountes</u> <u>kai</u>).
[2] WH omitted <u>Amen</u>
(<u>AmAn</u>).

JOHN

CHAPTER 1

1 In the beginning was the Word, and the Word was with God, and the Word was God.

2 The same was in the beginning with God.

3 All things were made by him; and without him was not any thing made that was made.

4 In him was life; and the life was the light of men.

5 And the light shineth in darkness; and the darkness comprehended it not.

6 There was a man sent from God, whose name *was* John.

7 The same came for a witness, to bear witness of the Light, that all *men* through him might believe.

8 He was not that Light, but *was sent* to bear witness of that Light.

9 *That* was the true Light, which lighteth every man that cometh into the world.

10 He was in the world, and the world was made by him, and the world knew him not.

11 He came unto his own,

and his own received him not.

12 But as many as received him, to them gave he power to become the sons of God, *even* to them that believe on his name:

13 Which were born, not of blood, nor of the will of the flesh, nor of the will of man, but of God.

14 And the Word was made flesh, and dwelt among us, (and we beheld his glory, the glory as of the only begotten of the Father,) full of grace and truth.

15 John bare witness of him, and cried, saying, This was he **of whom I spake**[1], He that cometh after me is preferred before me: for he was before me.

16 **And**[2] of his fulness have all we received, and grace for grace.

17 For the law was given by Moses, *but* grace and truth came by Jesus Christ.

18 No man hath seen God

---

[1] In their margin, WH changed **of whom** I spoke ([h]**on** eipon) to *himself having spoken* ([h]*o eipOn*). **Acc** Sing Masc to *Nom* Sing Masc and Aor Act **Ind** to Aor Act *Part*. [case & mood]

[2] WH changed **and** (**kai**) to *because* ([h]*oti*).

at any time; **the**[1] only begotten **Son**[2], which is in the bosom of the Father, he hath declared *him*.

19 And this is the record of John, when the Jews sent [∧**to him**][3] priests and Levites from Jerusalem to ask him, Who art thou?

20 And he confessed, and denied not; but confessed, I am not the Christ.

21 And they asked him, What then? Art thou Elias? And he saith, I am not. Art thou that prophet? And he answered, No.

22 Then said they unto him, Who art thou? that we may give an answer to them that sent us. What sayest thou of thyself?

23 He said, I *am* the voice of one crying in the wilderness, Make straight the way of the Lord, as said the prophet Esaias.

24 And ~~they~~[4] which were sent were of the Pharisees.

25 And they asked him, and said unto him, Why baptizest thou then, if thou be not that Christ, **nor**[5] Elias, **neither**[6] that prophet?

26 John answered them, saying, I baptize with water: **but**[7] there standeth one among you, whom ye know not;

27 ~~He it is~~[8], who coming after me ~~is preferred before me~~[9], whose shoe's latchet I am not worthy to unloose.

28 These things were done in **Bethabara**[10] beyond Jordan, where John was baptizing.

29 The next day **John**[11] seeth Jesus coming unto him,

---

[5] WH changed <u>nor</u> (<u>oute</u>) to *nor* (*oude*).
[6] WH changed <u>neither</u> (<u>oute</u>) to *neither* (*oude*).
[7] WH omitted <u>but</u> (<u>de</u>).
[8] WH omitted <u>he</u> <u>it is</u> (<u>autos estin</u>).
[9] WH omitted <u>who</u> before <u>me</u> has become (^h<u>os</u> emprosthen mou gegonen).
[10] WH changed <u>Bethabara</u> (b<u>A</u>thabara) to *Bethany* (b<u>A</u>thania). In their margin, WH suggested <u>Bethabara</u> (b<u>A</u>thabara) or *Betharaba* (b<u>A</u>tharaba)
[11] WH omitted <u>the</u> John (^h<u>o</u> iOnnAs).

---

[1] In their margin, WH omitted <u>the</u> (^h<u>o</u>).
[2] In their margin, WH changed <u>son</u> (^h<u>uios</u>) to *God* (*theos*).
[3] WH added *to him* (*pros auton*).
[4] WH omitted <u>the</u> (ones) (^h<u>oi</u>).

and saith, Behold the Lamb of God, which taketh away the sin of the world.

30 This is he **of**[1] whom I said, After me cometh a man which is preferred before me: for he was before me.

31 And I knew him not: but that he should be made manifest to Israel, therefore am I come baptizing with [**the**][2] water.

32 And John bare record, saying, I saw the Spirit descending from heaven **like**[3] a dove, and it abode upon him.

33 And I knew him not: but he that sent me to baptize with water, the same said unto me, Upon whom thou shalt see the Spirit descending, and remaining on him, the same is he which baptizeth with the Holy Ghost.

34 And I saw, and bare record that this is the Son of God.

35 Again the next day after John stood, and two of his disciples;

36 And looking upon Jesus as he walked, he saith, Behold the Lamb of God!

37 And the two disciples heard **him**[4] speak, and they followed Jesus.

38 Then Jesus turned, and saw them following, and saith unto them, What seek ye? They said unto him, Rabbi, (which is to say, **being interpreted**[5], Master,) where dwellest thou?

39 He saith unto them, Come and **see**[6]. They came [∧**therefore**][7] and saw where he dwelt, and abode with him that day: **for**[8] it was about the tenth hour.

40 One of the two which heard John *speak*, and followed him, was Andrew, Simon Peter's brother.

---

[1] WH changed **about** (**peri**) to *on behalf of* (*ʰuper*).
[2] WH omitted the untranslated the (tO).
[3] WH changed as if (ʰOsei) to *as* (*ʰOs*).

[4] WH changed the word order from heard {of} HIM the two disciples to *heard the two disciples* {of} HIM
[5] WH changed being interpreted (ʰermAneuomenon) to *being interpreted* {with} (*meʰthermAneuomenon*). Both Pres Pass Part. [prefix added]
[6] WH changed see {ye} (**idete**) to *ye will see* (*oʂ esʰthe*). **Aor Act Imp** of **eidO** to *Fut Mid-D Ind* of *ʰoraO*. [syn, tense, voice, & mood]
[7] WH added *therefore* (*oun*).
[8] WH omitted for (de).

41 He **first**[1] findeth his own brother Simon, and saith unto him, We have found ~~the~~[2] Messias, which is, being interpreted, the Christ.

42 ~~And~~[3] he brought him to Jesus. ~~And~~[4] when Jesus beheld him, he said, Thou art Simon the son of **Jona**[5]: thou shalt be called Cephas, which is by interpretation, A stone.

43 The day following ~~Jesus~~[6] would go forth into Galilee, and findeth Philip, and [∧**the Jesus**][7] saith unto him, Follow me.

44 Now Philip was of Bethsaida, the city of Andrew and Peter.

45 Philip findeth Nathanael, and saith unto him, We have found him, of whom Moses in the law, and the prophets, did write, Jesus of Nazareth, **the**[8] son of Joseph.

46 And Nathanael said unto him, Can there any good thing come out of Nazareth? Philip saith unto him, Come and see.

47 Jesus saw Nathanael coming to him, and saith of him, Behold an Israelite indeed, in whom is no guile!

48 Nathanael saith unto him, Whence knowest thou me? Jesus answered and said unto him, Before that Philip called thee, when thou wast under the fig tree, I saw thee.

49 Nathanael answered [∧**him**][9] ~~and saith unto him~~[10], Rabbi, thou art the Son of God; thou art **the**[11] **King**[12] of Israel.

50 Jesus answered and said unto him, Because I said unto thee, [∧**that**][13] I saw thee under the fig tree, believest thou? thou shalt see greater things than these.

51 And he saith unto him, Verily, verily, I say unto you,

---

[1] WH changed <u>first</u> (<u>protos</u>) to *first* (*proton*). **Nom** to *Acc.* [case]

[2] WH omitted <u>the</u> (^h<u>o</u>).

[3] WH omitted <u>and</u> (<u>kai</u>).

[4] WH omitted <u>and</u> (<u>de</u>).

[5] WH changed <u>Jona</u> (<u>iOna</u>) to *John* (*iOanou*).

[6] WH omitted <u>the</u> <u>Jesus</u> (^h<u>o</u> <u>iAsous</u>) and forced the verb to supply the subject *he*.

[7] WH added *the Jesus* (^h*o iAsous*).

[8] WH omitted <u>the</u> (<u>ton</u>).

[9] WH added *him* (*autO*).

[10] WH omitted <u>and</u> <u>saith</u> <u>unto</u> <u>him</u> (<u>kai</u> <u>legei</u> <u>autO</u>).

[11] WH omitted <u>the</u> (^h<u>o</u>).

[12] WH changed the word order from <u>are</u> **the** KING to *KING are*.

[13] WH added *that* (^h*oti*).

~~Hereafter~~[1] ye shall see heaven open, and the angels of God ascending and descending upon the Son of man.

CHAPTER 2

1　And the third day there was a marriage in Cana of Galilee; and the mother of Jesus was there:

2　And both Jesus was called, and his disciples, to the marriage.

3　And when they wanted wine, the mother of Jesus saith unto him, They have no wine.

4　[∧and][2] Jesus saith unto her, Woman, what have I to do with thee? mine hour is not yet come.

5　His mother saith unto the servants, Whatsoever he saith unto you, do *it*.

6　And there ~~were set~~[3] there six **waterpots**[4] of stone, after the manner of the purifying of the Jews

[∧standing][5], containing two or three firkins apiece.

7　Jesus saith unto them, Fill the waterpots with water. And they filled them up to the brim.

8　And he saith unto them, Draw out now, and bear unto the governor of the feast. **And**[6] they bare *it*.

9　When the ruler of the feast had tasted the water that was made wine, and knew not whence it was: (but the servants which drew the water knew;) the governor of the feast called the bridegroom,

10　And saith unto him, Every man at the beginning doth set forth good wine; and when men have well drunk, ~~then~~[7] that which is worse: *but* thou hast kept the good wine until now.

11　This [~~the~~][8] beginning of miracles did Jesus in Cana of Galilee, and manifested forth his glory; and his disciples believed on him.

12　After this he went

---

[1] WH omitted hereafter (ap' arti).
[2] WH added *and* (*kai*).
[3] WH omitted were set (keimenai).
[4] WH changed the word order from WATERPOTS of stone to *of stone* WATERPOTS.

---

[5] WH added *standing* (*keimenai*).
[6] WH changed **and** (*kai*) to *then the* {ones} (*oi de*).
[7] WH omitted then (tote).
[8] WH omitted the untranslated the (tAn).

down to Capernaum, he, and his mother, and ~~his~~[1] brethren, and his disciples: and they continued there not many days.

13 And the Jews' passover was at hand, and Jesus went up to Jerusalem,

14 And found in the temple those that sold oxen and sheep and doves, and the changers of money sitting:

15 And when he had made a scourge of small cords, he drove them all out of the temple, and the sheep, and the oxen; and poured out **the** changers' **money**[2], and overthrew the tables;

16 And said unto them that sold doves, Take these things hence; make not my Father's house an house of merchandise.

17 ~~And~~[3] his disciples remembered that it was written, The zeal of thine house **hath eaten** me **up**[4].

18 Then answered the Jews and said unto him, What sign shewest thou unto us, seeing that thou doest these things?

19 Jesus answered and said unto them, Destroy this temple, and in three days I will raise it up.

20 Then said the Jews, Forty and six years was this temple in building, and wilt thou rear it up in three days?

21 But he spake of the temple of his body.

22 When therefore he was risen from the dead, his disciples remembered that he had said this ~~unto them~~[5]; and they believed the scripture, and the word which Jesus had said.

23 Now when he was in Jerusalem at the passover, in the feast *day*, many believed in his name, when they saw the miracles which he did.

24 But Jesus did not commit **himself**[6] unto them, because he knew all *men*,

25 And needed not that any should testify of man: for

---

[1] WH omitted <u>of him</u> (<u>autou</u>) from <u>the</u> <u>brethren of him</u>.

[2] WH changed <u>the</u> <u>coin</u> (<u>to kerma</u>) to *the coins* (*ta kermata*). Acc **Sing** Neut to Acc **Plur** Neut. [number]

[3] WH omitted <u>and</u> (<u>de</u>).

[4] WH changed <u>ate up</u> (<u>katefage</u>) to *will eat up* (*katafagetai*). **Aor** **Act** Ind to

Fut Mid-D Ind. [tense & voice]

[5] WH omitted <u>unto them</u> (<u>autois</u>).

[6] WH changed <u>himself</u> (^h<u>eauton</u>) to *him* (*auton*).

he knew what was in man.

CHAPTER 3

1　There was a man of the Pharisees, named Nicodemus, a ruler of the Jews:

2　The same came to **Je-sus**[1] by night, and said unto him, Rabbi, we know that thou art a teacher come from God: for no man can do these miracles that thou doest, except God be with him.

3　Jesus answered and said unto him, Verily, verily, I say unto thee, Except a man be born again, he cannot see the kingdom of God.

4　Nicodemus saith unto him, How can a man be born when he is old? can he enter the second time into his mother's womb, and be born?

5　Jesus answered, Verily, verily, I say unto thee, Except a man be born of water and *of* the Spirit, he cannot enter into the kingdom of God.

6　That which is born of the flesh is flesh; and that which is born of the Spirit is spirit.

7　Marvel not that I said unto thee, ye must be born again.

8　The wind bloweth where it listeth, and thou hearest the sound thereof, but canst not tell whence it cometh, and whither it goeth: so is every one that is born of the Spirit.

9　Nicodemus answered and said unto him, How can these things be?

10　Jesus answered and said unto him, Art thou a master of Israel, and knowest not these things?

11　Verily, verily, I say unto thee, We speak that we do know, and testify that we have seen; and ye receive not our witness.

12　If I have told you earthly things, and ye believe not, how shall ye believe, if I tell you *of* heavenly things?

13　And no man hath ascended up to heaven, but he that came down from heaven, *even* the Son of man <u>which is in heaven</u>[2].

14　And as Moses lifted up the serpent in the wilderness, even so must the Son of man be lifted up:

15　That whosoever believeth **in** <u>**him**</u>[3] ~~should not perish,~~

---

[1] WH changed <u>the</u> **Jesus** (**ton iAsoun**) to *him* (*auton*).

[2] In their margin, WH omitted <u>which</u> is <u>in</u> heaven ([h]<u>o On</u> en tO ouranO).

[3] WH changed <u>into</u> him (**eis** <u>auton</u>) to *in him* (*en autO*).

but[1] have eternal life.

16 For God so loved the world, that he gave his only begotten Son, that whosoever believeth in him should not perish, but have everlasting life.

17 For God sent not **his**[2] Son into the world to condemn the world; but that the world through him might be saved.

18 He that believeth on him is not condemned: **but**[3] he that believeth not is condemned already, because he hath not believed in the name of the only begotten Son of God.

19 And this is the condemnation, that light is come into the world, and men loved darkness rather than light, because their deeds were evil.

20 For every one that doeth evil hateth the light, neither cometh to the light, lest his deeds should be reproved.

21 But he that doeth truth cometh to the light, that his deeds may be made manifest, that they are wrought in God.

22 After these things came Jesus and his disciples into the land of Judaea; and there he tarried with them, and baptized.

23 And John also was baptizing in Aenon near to Salim, because there was much water there: and they came, and were baptized.

24 For John was not yet cast into prison.

25 Then there arose a question between *some* of John's disciples and **the Jews**[4] about purifying.

26 And they came unto John, and said unto him, Rabbi, he that was with thee beyond Jordan, to whom thou barest witness, behold, the same baptizeth, and all *men* come to him.

27 John answered and said, A man can receive nothing, except it be given him from heaven.

28 Ye yourselves bear me witness, that I said, I am not the Christ, but that I am sent before him.

29 He that hath the bride is the bridegroom: but the

---

[1] WH omitted <u>not</u> <u>should perish</u> <u>but</u> (mA apolAtai all').
[2] WH omitted <u>of him</u> (autou) from <u>the son</u> of him.
[3] WH omitted <u>but</u> (de).

[4] WH changed **the Jews** (<u>ioudaiOn</u>) to *a Jew* (<u>ioudaiou</u>). Gen **Plur** Masc to Gen *Sing* Masc. [number]

friend of the bridegroom, which standeth and heareth him, rejoiceth greatly because of the bridegroom's voice: this my joy therefore is fulfilled.

30 He must increase, but I *must* decrease.

31 He that cometh from above is above all: he that is of the earth is earthly, and speaketh of the earth: he that cometh from heaven is above all[1].

32 ~~And~~[2] what he hath seen and heard, that he testifieth; and no man receiveth his testimony.

33 He that hath received his testimony hath set to his seal that God is true.

34 For he whom God hath sent speaketh the words of God: for ~~God~~[3] giveth not the Spirit by measure *unto him*.

35 The Father loveth the Son, and hath given all things into his hand.

36 He that believeth on the Son hath everlasting life: and he that believeth not the Son shall not see life; but the wrath of God abideth on him.

---

[1] In their margin, WH omitted (epanO pantOn esti).

[2] WH omitted *and* (kai).

[3] WH omitted *the God* ([h]o ~~theos~~) and forced the verb to supply the subject *he*.

CHAPTER 4

1 When therefore the Lord knew how the Pharisees had heard that Jesus made and baptized more disciples than John,

2 (Though Jesus himself baptized not, but his disciples,)

3 He left Judaea, and departed again into Galilee.

4 And he must needs go through Samaria.

5 Then cometh he to a city of Samaria, which is called Sychar, near to the parcel of ground that Jacob gave to his son Joseph.

6 Now Jacob's well was there. Jesus therefore, being wearied with *his* journey, sat thus on the well: *and* it was **about the**[4] sixth hour.

7 There cometh a woman of Samaria to draw water: Jesus saith unto her, Give me to drink.

8 (For his disciples were gone away unto the city to buy meat.)

9 Then saith the woman of Samaria unto him, How is it that thou, being a Jew, askest drink of me, which am a woman of Samaria? **for the**

---

[4] WH changed *as if* ([h]Osei) to *as* ([h]Os).

283

Jews have no dealings with the Samaritans[1].

10 Jesus answered and said unto her, If thou knewest the gift of God, and who it is that saith to thee, Give me to drink; thou wouldest have asked of him, and he would have given thee living water.

11 The woman saith unto him, Sir, thou hast nothing to draw with, and the well is deep: from whence then hast thou that living water?

12 Art thou greater than our father Jacob, which gave us the well, and drank thereof himself, and his children, and his cattle?

13 Jesus answered and said unto her, Whosoever drinketh of this water shall thirst again:

14 But whosoever drinketh of the water that I shall give him **shall** never **thirst**[2]; but the water that I [ʌ**myself**][3] shall give him shall be in him a well of water springing up into ev-

erlasting life.

15 The woman saith unto him, Sir, give me this water, that I thirst not, neither **come**[4] hither to draw.

16 Jesus saith unto her, Go, call thy husband, and come hither.

17 The woman answered and said [ʌ**unto him**[5]], I have no husband. Jesus said unto her, Thou hast well said, I have no husband:

18 For thou hast had five husbands; and he whom thou now hast is not thy husband: in that saidst thou truly.

19 The woman saith unto him, Sir, I perceive that thou art a prophet.

20 Our fathers worshipped in this mountain; and ye say, that in Jerusalem is the place where men ought to worship.

21 Jesus saith unto her, **Woman**[6], **believe**[7] me, the

---

[1] In their margin, WH omitted <u>for the Jews have no dealings with the Samaritans</u> (<u>ou gar sugchrOntai ioudaioi zamareitais</u>).
[2] WH changed **might** thirst (di$AsA) to *will thirst* (*di$Asei*). **Aor** Act **Sub** to *Fut* Act *Ind*. [tense & mood]
[3] WH added *myself* (*egO*).

[4] WH changed <u>may come</u> (<u>er-cOmai</u>) to *may come* {**through**} (d<u>i</u>ercOmai). Both Pres M/P Sub. [prefix added]
[5] WH added *unto him* (*autO*).
[6] WH changed the word order from <u>WOMAN</u> believe me to *believe me WOMAN*.
[7] WH changed <u>believe</u> (pisteus**on**) to **be** *believing* (*pisteue*) **Aor** Act Imp to *Pres* Act Imp. [tense];

284

hour cometh, when ye shall neither in this mountain, nor yet at Jerusalem, worship the Father.

22 Ye worship ye know not what: we know what we worship: for salvation is of the Jews.

23 But the hour cometh, and now is, when the true worshippers shall worship the Father in spirit and in truth: for the Father seeketh such to worship him.

24 God *is* a Spirit: and they that worship him must worship *him* in spirit and in truth.

25 The woman saith unto him, I know that Messias cometh, which is called Christ: when he is come, he will tell us all things.

26 Jesus saith unto her, I that speak unto thee am *he*.

27 And upon this came his disciples, and **marvelled**[1] that he talked with the woman: yet no man said, What seekest thou? or, Why talkest thou with her?

28 The woman then left her waterpot, and went her way into the city, and saith to the men,

29 Come, see a man, which told me all things **that ever**[2] I did: is not this the Christ?

30 ~~Then~~[3] they went out of the city, and came unto him.

31 **[but]**[4] In the mean while his disciples prayed him, saying, Master, eat.

32 But he said unto them, I have meat to eat that ye know not of.

33 Therefore said the disciples one to another, hath any man brought him *ought* to eat?

34 Jesus saith unto them, My meat is **to do**[5] the will of him that sent me, and to finish his work.

35 Say not ye, There are yet **four months**[6], and *then*

---

[1] WH changed marvell**ed** (e~~th~~aumas**an**) to *were marvelling* (e*th*aumaz**an**). **Aor** Act Ind to *Impf* Act Ind. [tense]

[2] WH changed that **ever** (^h**osa**) to that (*a*).

[3] WH omitted then (oun).

[4] WH omitted the untranslated but (de).

[5] WH changed that I **may be** do**ing** (^hina poiO) to *that I might* do (^hina poiAsO). **Pres** Act Sub to *Aor* Act Sub. [tense]

[6] WH changed four months (tetramAno**n**) to (*tetramAnos*). Nom Sing **Neut** to Nom Sing *Masc*. [gender]

cometh harvest? behold, I say unto you, Lift up your eyes, and look on the fields; for they are white already to harvest.

36 ~~And~~[1] he that reapeth receiveth wages, and gathereth fruit unto life eternal: that ~~both~~[2] he that soweth and he that reapeth may rejoice together.

37 And herein is that saying true, One soweth, and another reapeth.

38 I sent you to reap that whereon ye bestowed no labour: other men laboured, and ye are entered into their labours.

39 And many of the Samaritans of that city believed on him for the saying of the woman, which testified, He told me all **that ~~ever~~**[3] ~~that~~ when the Samaritans were come unto him, they besought him that he would tarry with them: and he abode there two days.

41 And many more believed because of his own word;

42 And said unto the woman, Now we believe, not because of thy saying: for we have heard *him* ourselves, and know that this is indeed ~~the Christ~~[4], the Saviour of the world.

43 Now after two days he departed thence, ~~and went~~[5] into Galilee.

44 For Jesus himself testified, that a prophet hath no honour in his own country.

45 Then when he was come into Galilee, the Galilaeans received him, having seen all **the things**[6] that he did at Jerusalem at the feast: for they also went unto the feast.

46 So ~~Jesus~~[7] came again into Cana of Galilee, where he made the water wine. And there was a certain nobleman, whose son was sick at Capernaum.

47 When he heard that Jesus was come out of Judaea into Galilee, he went unto him, and besought **him**[8] that he would come down, and

---

[1] WH omitted and (kai).
[2] WH omitted both (kai).
[3] WH changed that **ever** (^{h}osa) to *that* (^{h}a).

[4] WH omitted the Christ (^{h}o cristos).
[5] WH omitted and went (kai apAlthen).
[6] WH changed **the things** (^{h}a) to *how much* (^{h}osa).
[7] WH omitted the Jesus (^{h}o iAsous).
[8] WH omitted him (auton).

heal his son: for he was at the point of death.

48 Then said Jesus unto him, Except ye see signs and wonders, ye will not believe.

49 The nobleman saith unto him, Sir, come down ere my child die.

50 Jesus saith unto him, Go thy way; thy son liveth. ~~And~~[1] the man believed the word that Jesus had spoken unto him, and he went his way.

51 And as he was now going down, his servants **met**[2] him, ~~and told~~[3] *him*, saying, **Thy**[4] son liveth.

52 Then enquired he of them the hour when he began to amend. **And**[5] **they said**[6] unto him, Yesterday at the seventh hour the fever left him.

53 So the father knew that *it was* ~~**at**~~[7] the same hour, in the which Jesus said unto him, **[~~that~~]**[8] Thy son liveth: and himself believed, and his whole house.

54 This *is* again the second miracle *that* Jesus did, when he was come out of Judaea into Galilee.

CHAPTER 5

1 After this there was **[^the]**[9] a feast of the Jews; and Jesus went up to Jerusalem.

2 Now there is at Jerusalem by the sheep *market* a pool, which is called in the Hebrew tongue **Bethesda**[10], having five porches.

3 In these lay a **great**[11] multitude of impotent folk, of

---

[1] WH omitted <u>and</u> (<u>kai</u>).

[2] WH changed <u>met</u> {**from**} (<u>apAntAsan</u>) to *met* {**by**} (*^h*<u>upAntAsan</u>). Both Aor Act Ind. [prefix changed]

[3] WH omitted <u>and told</u> (<u>kai apAggeilan</u>).

[4] WH changed <u>of **thou**</u> (<u>sou</u>) to *of **him*** (*autou*) in <u>the son of thou</u>.

[5] WH changed **<u>and</u>** (**<u>kai</u>**) to *therefore* (*oun*).

[6] WH changed the word order from **<u>and</u>** THEY SAID to *THEY SAID* ***therefore***.

[7] WH omitted <u>at</u> (<u>en</u>) and forced the dative case to supply the implied preposition.

[8] WH omitted the untranslated <u>that</u> (*^h*<u>oti</u>).

[9] WH added *the* (*^hA*) making it *the* <u>feast</u> instead of <u>a</u> <u>feast</u>.

[10] In their margin, WH changed <u>Bethesda</u> (<u>bAthesda</u>) to *Bethsaida* (*bA*<del>*th*</del>*saida*) or *Bethzatha* (*bA*<del>*th*</del>*zatha*).

[11] WH omitted <u>great</u> (<u>polu</u>).

blind, halt, withered, ~~waiting for the moving of the water~~.

4 ~~For an angel~~ [ʌof lord][1] ~~went down at a certain season into the pool, and troubled the water: whosoever then first after the troubling of the water stepped in was made whole of whatsoever disease he had.~~ [2]

5 And a certain man was there, which had an infirmity [ʌof him][3] thirty and eight years.

---

[1] WH added *of lord* (*kuriou*).
[2] WH omitted <u>waiting for the moving of the water for an angel went down at a certain season into the pool and troubled the water whosoever then first after the troubling of the water stepped in was made whole of whatsoever disease he had</u> (ekdecomenOn tAn tou ^hudatos kinAsin aggelos gar kata kairon katebainen en tA kolumbAthra kai etarasse to ^hudOr ^ho oun prOtos embas meta tAn taracAn tou ^hudatos ^hugias egineto ^hO dApote kateiceto nosAmati). WH omitted these words [the last third of John 5:3 and all of verse 4] in their text, but retained them in their margin.
[3] WH added *of him* (*autou*).

6 When Jesus saw him lie, and knew that he had been now a long time *in that case*, he saith unto him, Wilt thou be made whole?

7 The impotent man answered him, Sir, I have no man, when the water is troubled, **to put**[4] me into the pool: but while I am coming, another steppeth down before me.

8 Jesus saith unto him, Rise, take up thy bed, and walk.

9 And immediately the man was made whole, and took up his bed, and walked: and on the same day was the sabbath.

10 The Jews therefore said unto him that was cured, It is the sabbath day: [ʌand][5] it is not lawful for thee to carry *thy* bed.

11 [ʌwho then][6] He answered them, He that made me whole, the same said unto me, Take up thy bed, and walk.

---

[4] WH changed <u>he **may** put</u> (ball**A**) to *he **might** put* (bal**An**). **Pres** Act Sub to *Aor* Act Sub. [tense]
[5] WH added *and* (*kai*).
[6] WH added *who then* (^hos de), replacing the verb-supplied <u>he</u> with *who then*.

12 ~~Then~~[1] asked they him, What man is that which said unto thee, Take up ~~thy bed~~[2], and walk?

13 And he that was healed wist not who it was: for Jesus had conveyed himself away, a multitude being in *that* place.

14 Afterward Jesus findeth him in the temple, and said unto him, Behold, thou art made whole: sin no more, lest a worse **thing**[3] come unto thee.

15 The man departed, and told the Jews that it was Jesus, which had made him whole.

16 And therefore did the Jews persecute **Jesus**[4], ~~and sought to slay him~~[5], because he had done these things on the sabbath day.

17 But Jesus answered them, My Father worketh

hitherto, and I work.

18 Therefore the Jews sought the more to kill him, because he not only had broken the sabbath, but said also that God was his Father, making himself equal with God.

19 Then answered Jesus and said unto them, Verily, verily, I say unto you, The Son can do nothing of himself, but what he seeth the Father do: for what things soever he doeth, these also doeth the Son likewise.

20 For the Father loveth the Son, and sheweth him all things that himself doeth: and he will shew him greater works than these, that ye may marvel.

21 For as the Father raiseth up the dead, and quickeneth *them*; even so the Son quickeneth whom he will.

22 For the Father judgeth no man, but hath committed all judgment unto the Son:

23 That all *men* should honour the Son, even as they honour the Father. He that honoureth not the Son honoureth not the Father which hath sent him.

24 Verily, verily, I say unto you, He that heareth my word, and believeth on him that sent me, hath everlasting

---

[1] WH omitted then (oun).

[2] WH omitted the bed of thou [you^s] (ton krabbaton sou).

[3] WH changed the word order from THING unto thee to *unto thee THING*.

[4] WH changed the word order from did persecute THE JESUS the Jews to *did persecute the Jews THE JESUS*.

[5] WH omitted and sought to slay him (kai exAtoun auton apokteinai).

life, and shall not come into condemnation; but is passed from death unto life.

25 Verily, verily, I say unto you, The hour is coming, and now is, when the dead shall hear the voice of the Son of God: and they that hear shall live.

26 For as the Father hath life in himself; so **hath he given**[1] to the Son to have life in himself;

27 And hath given him authority to execute judgment **also**[2], because he is the Son of man.

28 Marvel not at this: for the hour is coming, in the which all that are in the graves shall hear his voice,

29 And shall come forth; they that have done good, unto the resurrection of life; and they that have done evil, unto the resurrection of damnation.

30 I can of mine own self do nothing: as I hear, I judge: and my judgment is just; because I seek not mine own will, but the will of the **Fa-**

ther[3] which hath sent me.

31 If I bear witness of myself, my witness is not true.

32 There is another that beareth witness of me; and I know that the witness which he witnesseth of me is true.

33 Ye sent unto John, and he bare witness unto the truth.

34 But I receive not testimony from man: but these things I say, that ye might be saved.

35 He was a burning and a shining light: and ye were willing for a season to rejoice in his light.

36 But I have greater witness than *that* of John: for the works which the Father **hath given**[4] me to finish, the same works that I **[I {myself}]**[5] do, bear witness of me, that the Father hath sent me.

37 And the Father **himself**,[6] which hath sent me,

---

[3] WH omitted <u>Father</u> (<u>pa-tros</u>), forcing the <u>the</u> to supply the implied *one*.
[4] WH changed <u>gave</u> (<u>edOke</u>) to *has given* (*dedOke*). **Aor** Act Ind to *Pf* Act Ind. [tense]
[5] WH omitted the intensive <u>I</u> {myself} (<u>egO</u>).
[6] WH changed **himself** (**aut**os) to *that* {one} (*ekei-nos*).

---

[1] WH changed the word order from <u>HATH HE GIVEN</u> also to the <u>Son</u> to *also to the Son* HATH HE GIVEN.
[2] WH omitted <u>also</u> (<u>kai</u>).

hath borne witness of me. Ye have neither heard his voice **at any time**[1], nor seen his shape.

38 And ye have not his word **abiding**[2] in you: for whom he hath sent, him ye believe not.

39 Search the scriptures; for in them ye think ye have eternal life: and they are they which testify of me.

40 And ye will not come to me, that ye might have life.

41 I receive not honour from men.

42 But I know you, that ye have not the love of God in you.

43 I am come in my Father's name, and ye receive me not: if another shall come in his own name, him ye will receive.

44 How can ye believe, which receive honour one of another, and seek not the honour that *cometh* from **God**[3] only?

45 Do not think that I will accuse you to the Father: there is *one* that accuseth you, *even* Moses, in whom ye trust.

46 For had ye believed Moses, ye would have believed me: for he wrote of me.

47 But if ye believe not his writings, how shall ye believe my words?

CHAPTER 6

1 After these things Jesus went over the sea of Galilee, which is *the sea* of Tiberias.

2 **And** a great multitude **followed**[4] him, because they **saw**[5] ~~his~~[6] miracles which he did on them that were diseased.

3 And Jesus went up into a mountain, and there he sat with his disciples.

---

[1] WH changed the word order from ye have heard AT ANY TIME to *AT ANY TIME ye have heard.*

[2] WH changed the word order from ABIDING in you to *in you ABIDING.*

[3] In their margin, WH omitted God (~~theou~~) and forced

the change from the only **God** to *the only* {**one**}.

[4] WH changed **and** (**kai**) to *but* (*de*); and placed followed at the beginning of the verse.

[5] WH changed were seeing (**^heOrOn**) to *were seeing* (*e~~th~~Oroun*). Impf Act Ind of **^horaO** to Impf Act Ind of *~~the~~OreO.* [syn]

[6] WH omitted of him (autou) from the miracles of him.

4 And the passover, a feast of the Jews, was nigh.

5 When Jesus then lifted up *his* eyes, and saw a great company come unto him, he saith unto Philip, Whence **shall we buy**[1] bread, that these may eat?

6 And this he said to prove him: for he himself knew what he would do.

7 Philip answered him, Two hundred pennyworth of bread is not sufficient for them, that every one ~~of them~~[2] may take a little.

8 One of his disciples, Andrew, Simon Peter's brother, saith unto him,

9 There is [~~one~~][3] a lad here, which hath five barley loaves, and two small fishes: but what are they among so many?

10 And Jesus said, Make the men sit down. Now there was much grass in the place. So the men sat down, in number **about**[4] five thousand.

11 ~~And~~[5] Jesus took the loaves; and when he had given thanks, he distributed ~~to the disciples, and the disciples~~[6] to them that were set down; and likewise of the fishes as much as they would.

12 When they were filled, he said unto his disciples, Gather up the fragments that remain, that nothing be lost.

13 Therefore they gathered *them* together, and filled twelve baskets with the fragments of the five barley loaves, which remained over and above unto them that had eaten.

14 Then those men, when they had seen <u>the miracle that ~~Jesus~~</u>[7] <u>did</u>,[8] said, This is of a truth that prophet that should come into the world.

---

[1] WH changed **shall** <u>we buy</u> (<u>agoraso</u>men) to *might* we *buy* (agoras*Omen*). **Fut** Act **Ind** to *Aor* Act *Sub*. [tense & mood]

[2] WH omitted <u>of them</u> (<u>aut</u>On).

[3] WH omitted the untranslated <u>one</u> ([h]<u>en</u>), changing from <u>one</u> <u>lad</u> to *a lad*.

[4] WH changed <u>as **if**</u> ([h]<u>Osei</u>) to *as* ([h]*Os*).

[5] WH omitted <u>and</u> (<u>de</u>).

[6] WH omitted <u>to the</u> <u>disciples</u> <u>and</u> <u>the disciples</u> (<u>tois</u> <u>mathAtais, oi de math</u>[h]<u>Atai</u>).

[7] WH omitted <u>the Jesus</u> ([h]<u>o iAsous</u>).

[8] In their margin, WH changed <u>the miracle</u> <u>that</u> **Jesus** <u>did</u> ([h]<u>o</u> <u>epoiAse</u> **sAmeion** [h]<u>o iAsous</u>) to *the miracles that he did* ([h]*a epoiAse sAmeia*). [number]

292

15 When Jesus therefore perceived that they would come and take him by force, to make him a king, he departed again into a mountain himself alone.

16 And when even was *now* come, his disciples went down unto the sea,

17 And entered into [~~the~~][1] a ship, and went over the sea toward Capernaum. And it was now dark, and Jesus was **not**[2] come to them.

18 And the sea arose by reason of a great wind that blew.

19 So when they had rowed about five and twenty or thirty furlongs, they see Jesus walking on the sea, and drawing nigh unto the ship: and they were afraid.

20 But he saith unto them, It is I; be not afraid.

21 Then they willingly received him into the ship: and immediately the ship was at the land whither they went.

22 The day following, when the people which stood on the other side of the sea **saw**[3] that there was none

other boat there, save ~~that~~ one ~~whereinto his disciples were entered~~[4], and that Jesus went not with his disciples into the **boat**[5], but *that* his disciples were gone away alone;

23 (Howbeit [~~then~~][6] there came other boats from Tiberias nigh unto the place where they did eat bread, after that the Lord had given thanks:)

24 When the people therefore saw that Jesus was not there, neither his disciples, they ~~also~~[7] took **shipping**[8], and came to Capernaum, seeking for Jesus.

25 And when they had

(id**O**n) to *saw* (*eidon*). Aor Act **Part** to Aor Act *Ind*. [mood]
[4] WH omitted that whereinto his disciples were entered (ekeino eis ʰo enebAsan ʰo mathAtai autou).
[5] WH changed **boat** (ploi**ari**on--**small** ship) to **ship** (*ploion*--ship). [syn]
[6] WH omitted the untranslated then (de), changing but **then** (alla **de**) to *but* (*alla*).
[7] WH omitted also (kai).
[8] WH changed shipping (eis ta ploia--into the ships) to *shipping* (*eis ta ploiaria*--into the **small** ships).

---

[1] WH omitted the untranslated the (to).
[2] WH changed not (ouk) to *not yet* (*oupO*).
[3] WH changed **having seen**

293

found him on the other side of the sea, they said unto him, Rabbi, when camest thou hither?

26 Jesus answered them and said, Verily, verily, I say unto you, ye seek me, not because ye saw the miracles, but because ye did eat of the loaves, and were filled.

27 Labour not for the meat which perisheth, but for that meat which endureth unto everlasting life, which the Son of man shall give unto you: for him hath God the Father sealed.

28 Then said they unto him, What shall we do, that we might work the works of God?

29 Jesus answered and said unto them, This is the work of God, that **ye be-lieve**[1] on him whom he hath sent.

30 They said therefore unto him, What sign shewest thou then, that we may see, and believe thee? what dost thou work?

31 Our fathers did eat manna in the desert; as it is written, He gave them bread from heaven to eat.

32 Then Jesus said unto them, Verily, verily, I say unto you, Moses **gave**[2] you not that bread from heaven; but my Father giveth you the true bread from heaven.

33 For the bread of God is he which cometh down from heaven, and giveth life unto the world.

34 Then said they unto him, Lord, evermore give us this bread.

35 ~~**And**~~[3] Jesus said unto them, I am the bread of life: he that cometh to me shall never hunger; and he that believeth on me **shall** never **thirst**[4].

36 But I said unto you, That ye also have seen me, and believe not.

37 All that the Father giveth me shall come to me; and him that cometh to me I will in no wise cast out.

---

[1] WH changed ye **might** be-lieve (*pisteusAte*) to *ye may be believing* (*pisteuAte*). **Aor** Act Sub to *Pres* Act Sub. [tense]

[2] WH changed **has given** (**dedOken**) to *gave* (*edOken*). **Pf** Act Ind to *Aor* Act Ind. [tense]

[3] WH omitted and (de).

[4] WH changed **might** thirst (di§ AsA) to *will thirst* (di§Asei). **Aor** Act **Sub** to *Fut* Act *Ind*. [tense & mood]

38 For I came down **from**[1] heaven, not to do mine own will, but the will of him that sent me.

39 And this is the ~~Father's~~[2] will which hath sent me, that of all which he hath given me I should lose nothing, but should raise it up again ~~at~~[3] the last day.

40 **And**[4] this is the will of **him that sent me**[5], that every one which seeth the Son, and believeth on him, may have everlasting life: and I will raise him up at the last day.

41 The Jews then murmured at him, because he said, I am the bread which came down from heaven.

42 And they said, Is not this Jesus, the son of Joseph, whose father and mother we know? how is it **then**[6] that he

saith [~~this {thing}~~][7], I came down from heaven?

43 Jesus **therefore**[8] answered and said unto them, Murmur not among yourselves.

44 No man can come to me, except the Father which hath sent me draw him: and I will raise him up ∧**at**[9] the last day.

45 It is written in the prophets, And they shall be all taught of God. Every man **therefore**[10] that hath heard, and hath learned of the Father, cometh unto me.

46 Not that any man hath seen the Father, save he which is of God, he hath seen the Father.

47 Verily, verily, I say unto you, He that believeth ~~on me~~[11] hath everlasting life.

48 I am that bread of life.

49 Your fathers did eat

---

[1] WH changed **out of** (**ek**) to _from_ (**apo**).

[2] WH omitted Father (patros) from the will of the having sent me Father. They let the implied _one_ take its place.

[3] WH omitted at (en).

[4] WH changed **de** (**and**) to _for_ (**gar**).

[5] WH changed **him that sent me** (**tou pemṣantos me**) to _my father_ (_tou patros mou_).

[6] WH changed **then** (**oun**) to _now_ (**nun**)

[7] WH omitted the untranslated this {thing} (_ʰoutos_).

[8] WH omitted therefore (oun).

[9] WH added _at_ (_en_) where the KJV supplied it.

[10] WH omitted therefore (oun).

[11] WH omitted on me (eis eme).

manna[1] in the wilderness, and are dead.

50 This is the bread which cometh down from heaven, that a man may eat thereof, and not die.

51 I am the living bread which came down from heaven: if any man eat of this bread, he shall live for ever: and the bread that I will give is my flesh, ~~which I will give~~[2] for the life of the world.

52 The Jews therefore strove among themselves, saying, How can this man give us *his* flesh to eat?

53 Then Jesus said unto them, Verily, verily, I say unto you, Except ye eat the flesh of the Son of man, and drink his blood, ye have no life in you.

54 Whoso eateth my flesh, and drinketh my blood, hath eternal life; and I will raise him up at the last day.

55 For my flesh is meat **indeed**[3], and my blood is drink **indeed**[4].

56 He that eateth my flesh, and drinketh my blood, dwelleth in me, and I in him.

57 As the living Father hath sent me, and I live by the Father: so he that eateth me, even he shall live by me.

58 This is that bread which came down from heaven: not as ~~your~~[5] fathers did eat **manna**[6], and are dead: he that eateth of this bread shall live for ever.

59 These things said he in the synagogue, as he taught in Capernaum.

60 Many therefore of his disciples, when they had heard *this*, said, This is an hard saying; who can hear it?

61 When Jesus knew in himself that his disciples murmured at it, he said unto them, doth this offend you?

62 *What* and if ye shall see the Son of man ascend up where he was before?

63 It is the spirit that quickeneth; the flesh profiteth

---

[1] WH changed the word order from <u>the</u> manna <u>in</u> THE WILDERNESS to *in THE WILDERNESS the manna.*

[2] WH omitted <u>which</u> I {myself} <u>will give</u> ([h]An egO dOsO).

[3] WH changed <u>truly</u> (alA͞thOs) to *true* (*alA͞thAs*).

Adv to *Adj.*

[4] WH changed <u>truly</u> (alA͞thOs) to *true* (alA͞thAs).

[5] WH omitted <u>of you</u> ([h]umOn) from <u>the</u> fathers <u>of</u> you.

[6] WH omitted <u>the</u> manna (to manna).

nothing: the words that I **speak**[1] unto you, *they* are spirit, and *they* are life.

64 But there are some of you that believe not. For Jesus knew from the beginning who they were that believed not, and who should betray him.

65 And he said, Therefore said I unto you, that no man can come unto me, except it were given unto him of **my**[2] Father.

66 From that *time* many of his disciples went back, and walked no more with him.

67 Then said Jesus unto the twelve, Will ye also go away?

68 **Then**[3] Simon Peter answered him, Lord, to whom shall we go? thou hast the words of eternal life.

69 And we believe and are sure that thou art **that Christ, the Son**[4] of ~~the liv-~~

~~ing~~[5] God.

70 Jesus answered them, Have not I chosen you twelve, and one of you is a devil?

71 He spake of Judas **Iscariot**[6] *the son* of Simon: for he it was that should betray him, ~~being~~[7] one of the twelve.

CHAPTER 7

1 After these things **Jesus walked**[8] in Galilee: for he would not walk in Jewry, because the Jews sought to kill him.

2 Now the Jews' feast of tabernacles was at hand.

3 His brethren therefore said unto him, Depart hence, and go into Judaea, that thy disciples also may see the works that thou doest.

4 For *there is* no man

---

[1] WH changed **am speaking** (lal**O**) to *have spoken* (*lelalAka*). **Pres** Act Ind to *Pf* Act Ind. [tense]

[2] WH omitted of me (mou) from the father of me.

[3] WH omitted then (oun).

[4] WH changed **that Christ the Son** (ʰo **cristos** ʰo ʰuios) to *the holy* {one} (ʰo ʰagios).

[5] WH omitted the living (tou zOntos).

[6] WH changed Iscariot (iskariOtAn) to *Iscariot* (*iskariOtou*). **Acc** Sing Masc to *Gen* Sing Masc. [case]

[7] WH omitted being (On).

[8] WH changed the word order from WALKED THE JESUS after these {things} to *after these* {things} WALKED THE JESUS.

that doeth any thing in secret, and he **himself**[1] seeketh to be known openly. If thou do these things, shew thyself to the world.

5 For neither did his brethren believe in him.

6 Then Jesus said unto them, My time is not yet come: but your time is alway ready.

7 The world cannot hate you; but me it hateth, because I testify of it, that the works thereof are evil.

8 Go ye up unto ~~this~~[2] feast: I go **not** up **yet**[3] unto this feast; for my time is not yet full come.

9 When he had said these words unto them, he abode *still* in Galilee.

10 But when his brethren were gone up, then went he also up **unto the feast**[4], not

openly, but as it were in secret.

11 Then the Jews sought him at the feast, and said, Where is he?

12 And there was **much**[5] murmuring among the people concerning him: for some said, He is a good man: others said, Nay; but he deceiveth the people.

13 Howbeit no man spake openly of him for fear of the Jews.

14 Now about the midst of the feast Jesus went up into the temple, and taught.

15 **And** the Jews **marvelled**[6], saying, How knoweth this man letters, having never learned?

16 Jesus answered them, and said, My doctrine is not mine, but his that sent me.

17 If any man will do his will, he shall know of the doctrine, whether it be of God, or *whether* I speak of myself.

18 He that speaketh of himself seeketh his own

---

[1] In their margin, WH changed himself (auto**s**) to *himself (auto)*. [case]

[2] WH omitted this (taut**An**) from the feast this (t**An** [h]eort**An** taut**An**).

[3] WH changed not **yet** (oup**O**) to *not (ou**k**)*.

[4] WH changed the word order from then also he himself went up UNTO THE FEAST to *UNTO THE FEAST then also he himself went up.*

[5] WH changed the word order from MUCH concerning him there was to *concerning him there was MUCH.*

[6] WH changed **and** (kai) to *therefore (oun)*; and placed marvelled first in the verse.

glory: but he that seeketh his glory that sent him, the same is true, and no unrighteousness is in him.

19 **Did** not Moses **give**[1] you the law, and *yet* none of you keepeth the law? Why go ye about to kill me?

20 The people answered ~~and said~~[2], Thou hast a devil: who goeth about to kill thee?

21 Jesus answered and said unto them, I have done one work, and ye all marvel.

22 Moses therefore gave unto you circumcision; (not because it is of Moses, but of the fathers;) and ye on the sabbath day circumcise a man.

23 If a man on the sabbath day receive circumcision, that the law of Moses should not be broken; are ye angry at me, because I have made a man every whit whole on the sabbath day?

24 Judge not according to the appearance, but judge righteous judgment.

25 Then said some of them of Jerusalem, Is not this he, whom they seek to kill?

26 But, lo, he speaketh boldly, and they say nothing unto him. Do the rulers know indeed that this is ~~the very~~[3] Christ?

27 Howbeit we know this man whence he is: but when Christ cometh, no man knoweth whence he is.

28 Then cried Jesus in the temple as he taught, saying, Ye both know me, and ye know whence I am: and I am not come of myself, but he that sent me is true, whom ye know not.

29 ~~But~~[4] I know him: for I am from him, and he hath sent me.

30 Then they sought to take him: but no man laid hands on him, because his hour was not yet come.

31 **And many**[5] of the people believed on him, and said, **[that]**[6] When Christ cometh, **[perchance]**[7] will he do more

---

[3] WH omitted <u>the very</u> (<u>alAthOs</u>).

[4] WH omitted <u>but</u> (<u>de</u>).

[5] WH changed the word order from <u>AND MANY</u> <u>of the people</u> to *of the people AND MANY*.

[6] WH omitted the untranslated <u>that</u> (^h<u>oti</u>).

[7] WH changed the untranslated **perchance** (<u>mAti</u>) to *not* (*mA*).

---

[1] WH changed **has** <u>given</u> (<u>dedOken</u>) to *gave* (*edOken*). **Pf** Act Ind to *Aor* Act Ind. [tense]

[2] WH omitted <u>and said</u> (<u>kai eipe</u>).

miracles ~~than these~~[1] which this *man* hath done?

32 The Pharisees heard that the people murmured such things concerning him; and the **Pharisees** and the **chief priests**[2] sent officers to take him.

33 Then said Jesus ~~unto them~~[3], Yet a little while am I with you, and *then* I go unto him that sent me.

34 Ye shall seek me, and shall not find ∧*me*[4]: and where I am, *thither* ye cannot come.

35 Then said the Jews among themselves, Whither will he go, that we shall not find him? will he go unto the dispersed among the Gentiles, and teach the Gentiles?

36 What *manner of* saying is this that he said, Ye shall seek me, and shall not find ∧*me*[5]: and where I am,

thither ye cannot come?

37 In the last day, that great *day* of the feast, Jesus stood and cried, saying, If any man thirst, let him come unto me, and drink.

38 He that believeth on me, as the scripture hath said, out of his belly shall flow rivers of living water.

39 (But this spake he of the Spirit, which they that **believe**[6] on him should receive: for the ~~Holy~~[7] Ghost was not yet *given*[8]; because that Jesus was **not yet**[9] glorified.)

40 ~~Many~~[10] of the people **therefore**[11], when they heard

---

[6] WH changed believ**ing** (pisteuontes) to *having believed* (pisteusontes). **Pres** Act Part to *Aor* Act Part. [tense]

[7] WH omitted holy ([h]agion) in their text, but retained it in their margin.

[8] In their margin, WH added *given* (dedomenon) where the KJV supplied it.

[9] WH changed not yet (oudepO) to *not yet* (eupO). [syn]

[10] WH omitted many (polloi).

[11] WH changed the word order from **many** THEREFORE of the people to *of the people THEREFORE*.

---

[1] WH omitted than these (toutOn).

[2] WH changed the word order from PHARISEES and the CHIEF PRIESTS to *CHIEF PRISTS and the PHARISEES*.

[3] WH omitted unto them (autois).

[4] WH added me (me) where the KJV supplied it.

[5] WH added me (me) where the KJV supplied it.

this saying[1] [∧**these**][2], said, Of a truth this is the Prophet.

41 Others said, This is the Christ. But **some**[3] said, Shall Christ come out of Galilee?

42 Hath not the scripture said, That Christ **cometh**[4] of the seed of David, and out of the town of Bethlehem, where David was?

43 So **there was**[5] a division among the people because of him.

44 And some of them would have taken him; but no man laid hands on him.

45 Then came the officers to the chief priests and Pharisees; and they said unto them, Why have ye not brought him?

46 The officers answered, Never man [**thus**] **spake**[6] ~~like~~ ~~this man~~[7].

47 Then answered them the Pharisees, Are ye also deceived?

48 Have any of the rulers or of the Pharisees believed on him?

49 But this people who knoweth not the law are **cursed**[8].

50 Nicodemus saith unto them, (he that came to Jesus [∧**before**][9] ~~by night~~[10], being one of them,)

51 Doth our law judge *any* man, **before**[11] it hear **him**[12], and know what he doeth?

52 They answered and

---

[1] WH changed the word (<u>ton logon</u>) to {**of**} *the words these* (*tOn logOn toutOn.* **Acc Sing** Masc to *Gen Plur* Masc. [case & number]

[2] WH added *these* (*toutOn*);

[3] WH changed <u>some</u> (**alloi**) to *the {ones}* (*oi*).

[4] WH changed the word order from <u>Christ</u> COMETH to *COMETH Christ.*

[5] WH changed the word order from <u>among the people</u> THERE WAS to *THERE WAS among the people.*

[6] WH changed the word order from <u>thus</u> SPOKE to *SPOKE thus.* [The KJV left thus ([h]outOs) untranslated.]

[7] WH omitted <u>like</u> <u>this</u> <u>the man</u> ([h]Os outos [h]o anthrOpos).

[8] WH changed <u>cursed</u> (epi-kataratoi) to *cursed* (*eparatoi*). [synonym]

[9] WH added *before* (*proteron*) after <u>him</u> (auton) [This <u>auton</u> was rendered <u>Jesus</u> in the KJV].

[10] WH omitted <u>by night</u> (nuktos).

[11] WH changed **before** (proteron) to *first* (*prOton*).

[12] WH changed the word order from FROM HIM **before** to *first FROM HIM.*

said unto him, Art thou also of Galilee? Search, and look: for out of Galilee **ariseth**[1] no **prophet**[2].

[3][53. And every man **went**[4] unto his own house.

CHAPTER 8

1   Jesus went unto the mount of Olives.
2   And early in the morning he came again into the temple, and all the people came unto him; and he sat down, and taught them.
3   And the scribes and Pharisees brought **unto him**[5]

a woman taken **in**[6] adultery; and when they had set her in the midst,
4   They say unto him, Master, this woman **was taken**[7] in adultery, in the very act.
5   Now Moses in the law commanded us, that such **should be stoned**[8]: but what sayest thou [∧**about her**][9]?
6   This they said, tempting him, that they might have to accuse him. But Jesus stooped down, and with *his* finger **wrote**[10] on the ground, *as though he heard them not.*[11]
7   So when they continued

---

[1] WH changed **has been** raised (eg**Ager**tai) to *is being raised* (*egeiretai*). **Pf** Pass Ind to *Pres* Pass Ind. [tense]
[2] WH changed the word order from PROPHET out of Galilee to *out of Galilee* PROPHET.
[3] In their text, WH put John 7:53-John 8:11 in brackets. In their margin, WH virtually rejected this passage.
[4] WH changed {**he**} went (eporeuth**A**) to {*they*} *went* (eporeuth**Asan**). Aor Pass-D Ind 3rd **Sing** to Aor Pass-D Ind 3rd *Plur.* [number]
[5] WH omitted to him (pros auton).

[6] WH changed **in** (en) to *upon* (*epi*).
[7] WH changed **was** taken (kateilAf**th**A) to *has been taken* (*kateilAptai*). **Aor** Pass Ind to *Pf* Pass Ind. [tense]
[8] WH changed to **be stoned** (lit**h**oboleisthai) *to stone* (*li**th**azein*). Pres **Pass** Inf of lit**h**oboleO to Pres *Act* Inf of *li**th**azO.* [syn & voice]
[9] WH added about her (peri autAs).
[10] WH changed wrote (egrafen) to *wrote {down}* (*kategrafen*). [prefix added]
[11] WH omitted pretending not {to hear} (mA prospoioumenos).

asking him, he lifted up himself, and said unto them, He that is without sin among you, let him first cast **[the]**[1] a stone at her.

8   And again he stooped down, and **[∧{with} the fingers]**[2] wrote on the ground.

9   And they which heard it, ~~being convicted by *their own* conscience~~[3], went out one by one, beginning at the eldest, *even* unto the last: and Jesus was left alone, and the woman **standing**[4] in the midst.

10   When Jesus had lifted up himself, ~~and saw none but the woman~~[5], he said unto her, Woman, where are ~~those thine accusers~~[6]? hath no man condemned thee?

11   She said, No man, Lord. And Jesus [7]said **unto her**[8], Neither do I condemn thee: go, **and** sin no more.][9]

12   Then spake Jesus again unto them, saying, I am the light of the world: he that followeth me **shall** not **walk**[10] in darkness, but shall have the light of life.

13   The Pharisees therefore said unto him, Thou bearest record of thyself; thy record is not true.

14   Jesus answered and said unto them, Though I bear record of myself, *yet* my record is true: for I know whence I came, and whither I go; but ye cannot tell whence I come, **and**[11] whither I go.

---

[1] WH omitted the untranslated the (ton).

[2] WH added {with} *the fingers* (*to daktulO*).

[3] WH omitted being convicted by [their own] conscience (kai ʰupo tAs suneidAseOs elegcomenoi).

[4] WH changed **stand**ing (ʰestOsa) to *being* (*ousa*).

[5] WH omitted and saw none but the woman (kai mAdena theasamenos palAn tAs gunaikos).

[6] WH omitted those thine accusers (ekeinoi ʰoi katAgoroi sou).

[7] WH changed **and** (**kai**) to *from the now* (**apo tou nun**).

[8] WH omitted unto her (autA).

[9] In their text, WH put John 7:53-John 8:11 in brackets. In their margin, WH virtually reject this passage.

[10] WH changed **shall** walk (peripatAsei) to *might walk* (*peripatAsA*). **Fut** Act **Ind** to *Aor* Act *Sub*. [tense & mood]

[11] WH changed **and** (**kai**) to *or* (ʰA).

15 Ye judge after the flesh; I judge no man.

16 And yet if I judge, my judgment is true: for I am not alone, but I and the Father that sent me.

17 It is also written in your law, that the testimony of two men is true.

18 I am one that bear witness of myself, and the Father that sent me beareth witness of me.

19 Then said they unto him, Where is thy Father? Jesus answered, Ye neither know me, nor my Father: if ye had known me, ye should have known my Father also.

20 These words spake ~~Jesus~~[1] in the treasury, as he taught in the temple: and no man laid hands on him; for his hour was not yet come.

21 Then said ~~Jesus~~[2] again unto them, I go my way, and ye shall seek me, and shall die in your sins: whither I go, ye cannot come.

22 Then said the Jews, Will he kill himself? because he saith, Whither I go, ye cannot come.

23 And **he said**[3] unto them, Ye are from beneath; I am from above: ye are of this world; I am not of this world.

24 I said therefore unto you, that ye shall die in your sins: for if ye believe not that I am *he*, ye shall die in your sins.

25 Then said they unto him, Who art thou? **And**[4] Jesus saith unto them, Even *the same* **that**[5] I said unto you from the beginning.

26 I have many things to say and to judge of you: but he that sent me is true; and **I speak**[6] to the world those things which I have heard of him.

27 They understood not that he spake to them of the Father.

28 Then said Jesus ~~unto~~

---

[1] WH omitted <u>the Jesus</u> (^ho iAsous) and forced the verb to supply the subject *he*.
[2] WH omitted <u>the Jesus</u> (^ho iAsous) and forced the verb to supply the subject *he*.
[3] WH changed <u>he said</u> (<u>eipen</u>) to he *was* sa*ying* (*elegen*). **Aor** Act Ind to *Impf* Act Ind of. [tense]
[4] WH omitted <u>and</u> (<u>kai</u>).
[5] In their margin, WH changed <u>some</u> {thing} (<u>ti</u>) to *that* (^h*oti*)
[6] WH changed <u>I speak</u> (<u>legO</u>) to *I speak* (*lalO*). Pres Act Ind of **legO** to Pres Act Ind of *laleO*. [syn]

~~them~~[1], When ye have lifted up the Son of man, then shall ye know that I am *he,* and *that* I do nothing of myself; but as ~~my~~[2] Father hath taught me, I speak these things.

29 And he that sent me is with me: ~~the Father~~[3] hath not left me alone; for I do always those things that please him.

30 As he spake these words, many believed on him.

31 Then said Jesus to those Jews which believed on him, If ye continue in my word, *then* are ye my disciples indeed;

32 And ye shall know the truth, and the truth shall make you free.

33 They answered **him**[4], We be Abraham's seed, and were never in bondage to any man: how sayest thou, Ye shall be made free?

34 Jesus answered them, Verily, verily, I say unto you, Whosoever committeth sin is the servant of sin.

35 And the servant abideth not in the house for ever: *but* the Son abideth ever.

36 If the Son therefore shall make you free, ye shall be free indeed.

37 I know that ye are Abraham's seed; but ye seek to kill me, because my word hath no place in you.

38 I speak **that which**[5] I have seen with ~~my~~[6] Father: and ye do **that which**[7] **ye have seen**[8] with ~~your~~[9] **father**[10].

39 They answered and

---

[5] WH changed <u>that</u> {thing} <u>which</u> (^{h}**o**) to *those* {things} *which* (^{h}*a*). Acc **Sing** Neut to Acc ***Plur*** Neut. [number]

[6] WH omitted <u>of me</u> (<u>mou</u>) from <u>the</u> <u>father</u> <u>of me</u>.

[7] WH changed <u>that</u> {thing} <u>which</u> (^{h}**o**) to *those* {things} *which* (^{h}*a*). Acc **Sing** Neut to Acc ***Plur*** Neut. [number]

[8] WH changed ye **have seen** (^{h}**eOrak**<u>ate</u>) to *ye heard* (*Ak-ousate*). **Pf** Act Ind of **euriskO** to *Aor* Act Ind of *akouO*. [verb & tense]

[9] WH omitted <u>of you</u> (^{h}<u>u-mOn</u>) from <u>the</u> <u>father</u> <u>of you</u>.

[10] WH changed <u>the</u> <u>father</u> (t**O** patri) to *the father* (*tou pa-tros*). **Dat** Masc Sing to ***Gen*** Masc Sing [case]

---

[1] WH omitted <u>unto them</u> (<u>autois</u>).

[2] WH omitted <u>of me</u> (<u>mou</u>) from <u>the</u> <u>father</u> <u>of me</u>.

[3] WH omitted <u>the</u> <u>Father</u> (^{h}<u>o patAr</u>) and forced the verb to supply the subject *he*.

[4] WH changed <u>him</u> (<u>autO</u>) to *to him* (***pros auton***).

said unto him, Abraham is our father. Jesus saith unto them, If **ye were**[1] Abraham's children, **ye would do**[2] [**ever**][3] the works of Abraham.

40 But now ye seek to kill me, a man that hath told you the truth, which I have heard of God: this did not Abraham.

41 Ye do the deeds of your father. ~~Then~~[4] said they to him, **We be** not **born**[5] of fornication; we have one Father, *even* God.

42 Jesus said unto them, If God were your Father, ye would love me: for I proceeded forth and came from God; neither came I of myself, but he sent me.

43 Why do ye not understand my speech? *even* because ye cannot hear my word.

44 Ye are of *your* [∧**the**][6] father the devil, and the lusts of your father ye will do. He was a murderer from the beginning, and abode **not**[7] in the truth, because there is no truth in him. When he speaketh a lie, he speaketh of his own: for he is a liar, and the father of it.

45 And because I tell *you* the truth, ye believe me not.

46 Which of you convinceth me of sin? ~~And~~[8] if I say the truth, why do ye not believe me?

47 He that is of God heareth God's words: ye therefore hear *them* not, because ye are not of God.

48 ~~Then~~[9] answered the Jews, and said unto him, Say we not well that thou art a Samaritan, and hast a devil?

49 Jesus answered, I have not a devil; but I honour my Father, and ye do dishonour

---

[1] WH changed ye **were** (**A**te) to *ye are* (*este*). **Impf** Ind to *Pres* Ind. [tense]

[2] In their margin, WH changed **ye were** doing (**epoieite**) to *be ye doing* (*poieite*). **Impf** Act **Ind** to *Pres* Act *Imp*. [tense & mood]

[3] WH omitted the untranslated ever (an).

[4] WH omitted then (oun).

[5] WH changed we **have been** born (**gegennAmetha**) to *we were born* (*egennAthAmen*). **Pf** Pass Ind to *Aor* Pass Ind. [tense]

[6] WH added *the* (*tou*).

[7] WH changed not (ouc) to not (ouk) in their text, but not in their margin. [spell]

[8] WH omitted and (de).

[9] WH omitted then (oun).

me.

50 And I seek not mine own glory: there is one that seeketh and judgeth.

51 Verily, verily, I say unto you, If a man keep my saying, he shall never see death.

52 ~~Then~~[1] said the Jews unto him, Now we know that thou hast a devil. Abraham is dead, and the prophets; and thou sayest, If a man keep my saying, he **shall** never **taste**[2] of death.

53 Art thou greater than our father Abraham, which is dead? and the prophets are dead: whom makest ~~thou~~[3] thyself?

54 Jesus answered, If I honour myself, my honour is nothing: it is my Father that honoureth me; of whom ye say, that he is your God:

55 Yet ye have not known him; but I know him: and if I should say, I know him not, I shall be a liar like unto you: but I know him, and keep his

saying.

56 Your father Abraham rejoiced to see my day: and he saw *it*, and was glad.

57 Then said the Jews unto him, Thou art not yet fifty years old, and hast thou seen Abraham?

58 Jesus said unto them, Verily, verily, I say unto you, Before Abraham was, I am.

59 Then took they up stones to cast at him: but Jesus hid himself, and went out of the temple, ~~going through the midst of them, and so passed by~~[4].

CHAPTER 9

1 And as *Jesus* passed by, he saw a man which was blind from *his* birth.

2 And his disciples asked him, saying, Master, who did sin, this man, or his parents, that he was born blind?

3 Jesus answered, Neither hath this man sinned, nor

---

[1] WH omitted then (oun).
[2] WH changed **shall** taste (geusetai) to *might* taste (*geusAtai*). **Fut** Mid-D **Ind** to *Aor* Mid-D *Sub*. [tense & mood]
[3] WH omitted thou [you^s] (su).

[4] WH omitted going through the midst of them and so passed by (dielthOn dia mesou autOn kai parAgen ^houtOs) from their text, but retained these words in their margin. Their margin prefixes *kai* to dielthOn and adds *eporeueto* after autOn.

his parents: but that the works of God should be made manifest in him.

4　**I**[1] must work the works of him that sent me, while it is day: the night cometh, when no man can work.

5　As long as I am in the world, I am the light of the world.

6　When he had thus spoken, he spat on the ground, and made clay of the spittle, and he anointed [∧**him**][2] the eyes ~~of the blind man~~[3] with the clay,

7　And said unto him, Go, wash in the pool of Siloam, (which is by interpretation, Sent.) He went his way therefore, and washed, and came seeing.

8　The neighbours therefore, and they which before had seen him that he was **blind**[4], said, Is not this he that sat and begged?

9　Some said, This is he: others *said*, He is like him: **_but_**[5] he said, I am *he*.

10　Therefore said they unto him, How [∧**then**][6] were thine eyes opened?

11　He answered ~~and said~~[7], [∧**the**][8] A man that is called Jesus made clay, and anointed mine eyes, and said unto me, [∧**that**][9] Go to ~~the pool~~[10] **of** [**the**][11] Siloam, and wash: **_and_**[12] I went and washed, and I received sight.

12　[∧**and**][13] ~~Then~~[14] said they unto him, Where is he? He said, I know not.

13　They brought to the Pharisees him that aforetime was blind.

14　And it was the sabbath

_h_oti) to *said, No, but* (*elegon ouci, alla'*).

[6] WH added *then* (*oun*).

[7] WH omitted <u>and said</u> (<u>kai eipen</u>).

[8] WH added the definite article *the* (*h_o*).

[9] WH added *that* (*h_oti*).

[10] WH omitted <u>the pool</u> (<u>tAn kolumbAthran</u>).

[11] WH changed <u>of the</u> (<u>tou</u>) to <u>the</u> (*ton*). **Gen** to *Acc*. [case] They changed from <u>Go to **the pool of the** Siloam</u> to *Go to **the** Siloam*.

[12] WH changed **_and_** (**_de_**) to *then* (*oun*).

[13] WH added *and* (*kai*).

[14] WH omitted <u>then</u> (<u>oun</u>).

---

[1] WH changed **I** (<u>eme</u>) to *we* (*h_Amas*).

[2] WH added *him* (*autou*).

[3] WH omitted <u>of the</u> blind {man} (<u>tou tuflou</u>).

[4] WH changed **blind** (**tuflos**) to *a beggar* (*prosaitAs*).

[5] WH changed **but that** (**de**

day **when**[1] Jesus made the clay, and opened his eyes.

15 Then again the Pharisees also asked him how he had received his sight. He said unto them, He put clay upon **mine**[2] eyes, and I washed, and do see.

16 Therefore said some of the Pharisees, **This man**[3] is not of [~~the~~][4] God, because he keepeth not the sabbath day. [∧**but**][5] Others said, How can a man that is a sinner do such miracles? And there was a division among them.

17 They say [∧**therefore**][6] unto the blind man again, What sayest **thou**[7] of him, that he hath opened thine eyes? He said, He is a prophet.

18 But the Jews did not believe concerning him, that he had been blind, and received his sight, until they called the parents of him that had received his sight.

19 And they asked them, saying, Is this your son, who ye say was born blind? how then doth he now see?

20 His parents answered ~~**them**~~[8] and said, We know that this is our son, and that he was born blind:

21 But by what means he now seeth, we know not; or who hath opened his eyes, we know not: he [~~**himself**~~][9] is of age; **ask him**[10]: he shall speak for **himself**[11].

22 These *words* spake his parents, because they feared the Jews: for the Jews had agreed already, that if any man did confess that he was Christ, he should be put out of the synagogue.

23 Therefore said his parents, He is of age; ask him.

---

[1] WH changed **when** (ʰote) to *in the day* (*en* ʰ*A* ʰ*Amera*).

[2] WH changed the word order from upon the eyes OF ME to *OF ME upon the eyes.*

[3] WH changed the word order from THIS THE MAN not is from **the** God to *not is THIS from God THE MAN.*

[4] WH omitted the untranslated the (tou).

[5] WH added *but* (*de*).

[6] WH added *therefore* (oun).

[7] WH changed the word order from THOU what to *what THOU.*

[8] WH omitted them (autois).

[9] WH omitted the untranslated himself (autos).

[10] WH changed the word order from **himself** of age he is, HIM ASK to *HIM ASK, of age he is.*

[11] WH changed himself (autou) to *himself* (ʰ*eautou*).

24 Then **again**[1] called they the man that was blind, and said unto him, Give God the praise: we know that this man is a sinner.

25 He answered ~~and said~~[2], Whether he be a sinner *or no*, I know not: one thing I know, that, whereas I was blind, now I see.

26 **Then**[3] said they to him ~~again~~[4], What did he to thee? how opened he thine eyes?

27 He answered them, I have told you already, and ye did not hear: wherefore would ye hear *it* again? will ye also be his disciples?

28 [∧**and**][5] ~~Then~~[6] they reviled him, and said, Thou art his disciple; but we are Moses' disciples.

29 We know that God spake unto Moses: *as for* this *fellow*, we know not from whence he is.

30 The man answered and said unto them, Why herein is

[∧**the**][7] a marvellous thing, that ye know not from whence he is, and *yet* he hath opened mine eyes.

31 ~~Now~~[8] we know that God heareth not sinners: but if any man be a worshipper of God, and doeth his will, him he heareth.

32 Since the world began was it not heard that any man opened the eyes of one that was born blind.

33 If this man were not of God, he could do nothing.

34 They answered and said unto him, Thou wast altogether born in sins, and dost thou teach us? And they cast him out.

35 Jesus heard that they had cast him out; and when he had found him, he said ~~unto him~~[9], Dost thou believe on the Son of **God**[10]?

36 He answered and said, [∧**and**][11] Who is he, Lord, that I might believe on him?

---

[1] WH changed the word order from AGAIN the man to *the man* AGAIN.

[2] WH omitted and said (kai eipen).

[3] WH changed then (**de**) to *then* (**oun**).

[4] WH omitted again (pailin).

[5] WH added *and* (kai).

[6] WH omitted then (oun).

---

[7] WH added *the* (*to*) before wonderful.

[8] WH omitted now (de).

[9] WH omitted unto him (autO).

[10] In their margin, WH changed **God** (~~theos~~) to *man* (*an**thr**Opos*).

[11] WH added *and* (kai).

37 ~~And~~[1] Jesus said unto him, Thou hast both seen him, and it is he that talketh with thee.

38 And he said, Lord, I believe. And he worshipped him.

39 And Jesus said, For judgment I am come into this world, that they which see not might see; and that they which see might be made blind.

40 ~~And~~[2] *some* of the Pharisees which **were**[3] with him heard these words, and said unto him, Are we blind also?

41 Jesus said unto them, If ye were blind, ye should have no sin: but now ye say, We see; ~~therefore~~[4] your sin remaineth.

CHAPTER 10

1 Verily, verily, I say unto you, He that entereth not by the door into the sheepfold, but climbeth up some other way, the same is a thief and a robber.

2 But he that entereth in by the door is the shepherd of the sheep.

3 To him the porter openeth; and the sheep hear his voice: and **he calleth**[5] his own sheep by name, and leadeth them out.

4 ~~And~~[6] when he putteth forth his own **sheep**[7], he goeth before them, and the sheep follow him: for they know his voice.

5 And a stranger **will they** not **follow**[8], but will flee from him: for they know not the voice of strangers.

6 This parable spake Jesus unto them: but they understood not what things they were which he spake unto them.

7 Then said Jesus unto them again, Verily, verily, I

---

[1] WH omitted and (de).
[2] WH omitted and (kai).
[3] WH changed the word order from WERE with him to *with him* WERE
[4] WH omitted therefore (oun).

[5] WH changed he calls (**kalei**) to *he calls* (*fOnei*). Both Pres Act Ind. [syn]
[6] WH omitted and (kai).
[7] WH changed **sheep** (**probata**) to *all* (*panta*).
[8] WH changed they **might** follow (akolouthAsOsin) to *they* **will** *follow* (*akolouthAsousin*). **Aor** Act **Sub** to *Fut* Act **Ind**. [tense & mood]

say unto you, [**that**][1] I am the door of the sheep.

8   All that ever **came**[2] before me are thieves and robbers: but the sheep did not hear them.

9   I am the door: by me if any man enter in, he shall be saved, and shall go in and out, and find pasture.

10 The thief cometh not, but for to steal, and to kill, and to destroy: I am come that they might have life, and that they might have *it* more abundantly.

11 I am the good shepherd: the good shepherd giveth his life for the sheep.

12 **But**[3] he that is an hireling, and not the shepherd, whose own the sheep are not, seeth the wolf coming, and leaveth the sheep, and fleeth: and the wolf catcheth them, and scattereth **the sheep**[4].

13 **The hireling fleeth**[5],

because he is an hireling, and careth not for the sheep.

14 I am the good shepherd, and know my *sheep*, and **am known**[6] **of mine**[7].

15 As the Father knoweth me, even so know I the Father: and I lay down my life for the sheep.

16 And other sheep I have, which are not of this fold: them also I **must**[8] bring, and they shall hear my voice; and **there shall be**[9] one fold, *and* one shepherd.

17 Therefore doth my **Father**[10] love me, because I lay down my life, that I might

---

[1] WH omitted the untranslated <u>that</u> (<u>h</u>oti).

[2] WH changed the word order from <u>before me</u> CAME to *CAME before me.*

[3] WH omitted <u>but</u> (<u>de</u>).

[4] WH omitted <u>the sheep</u> (<u>ta probata</u>).

[5] WH omitted <u>but the hireling fleeth</u> (<u>h</u>o <u>de misthOtos feugei</u>).

[6] WH changed **I am being known** (<u>ginOskomai</u>) to *they are knowing* (*ginOskousi*). Pres **Pass** Ind 1st **Sing** to Pres *Act* Ind 3rd **Plur**. [voice, number, & person]

[7] WH changed **by** <u>the of my own</u> {things} (<u>h</u>**upo** <u>tOn emOn</u>) to *me the my own* {things} (*me ta ema*).

[8] WH changed the word order from <u>I</u> MUST to *MUST I.*

[9] WH changed **it shall be** (<u>genAsetai</u>) to *they shall be* (*genAsontai*). Fut Mid-D Ind 3 **Sing** to Fut Mid-D Ind 3 *Plur*. [number]

[10] WH changed the word order from <u>the</u> FATHER <u>of me</u> to *of me the FATHER.*

take it again.

18 No man **taketh**[1] it from me, but I lay it down of myself. I have power to lay it down, and I have power to take it again. This commandment have I received of my Father.

19 There was a division ~~therefore~~[2] again among the Jews for these sayings.

20 And many of them said, He hath a devil, and is mad; why hear ye him?

21 Others said, These are not the words of him that hath a devil. Can a devil open the eyes of the blind?

22 **And**[3] it was at Jerusalem the feast of the dedication, ~~and~~[4] it was winter.

23 And Jesus walked in the temple in Solomon's porch.

24 Then came the Jews round about him, and said unto him, How long dost thou make us to doubt? If thou be the Christ, tell us plainly.

25 Jesus answered them, I told you, and ye believed not: the works that I do in my Father's name, they bear witness of me.

26 But ye believe not, **because** ye are **not**[5] of my sheep, ~~as I said unto you~~[6].

27 My sheep hear my voice, and I know them, and they follow me:

28 And I give unto them eternal life; and they shall never perish, neither shall any *man* pluck them out of my hand.

29 My Father, **which**[7] gave *them* me, **is greater than**[8] **all**[9]; and no *man* is able

---

[1] In their margin, WH changed takes (**airei**) to *took* (*Aren*). **Pres** Act Ind to *Aor* Act Ind. [tense]

[2] WH omitted therefore (oun).

[3] In their margin, WH changed **and** (de) to *then* (*tote*).

[4] WH omitted and (kai).

[5] WH changed **because** not (**ou gar**) to *that not* (*[h]oti oun*).

[6] WH omitted as I said unto you (kathOs eipon [h]umin).

[7] In their margin, WH changed **which** ([h]os) to *the* ([h]o).

[8] In their margin, WH changed greater than (me-zOn) to *greater than* (*mezon*) [spell]

[9] In their margin, WH changed the word order from greater than ALL is to *ALL greater than is.*

to pluck _them_ out of **my**[1] Father's hand.

30 I and _my_ Father are one.

31 ~~Then~~[2] the Jews took up stones again to stone him.

32 Jesus answered them, Many good works have I shewed you from my Father; for which of those works do ye stone me?

33 The Jews answered him, ~~saying~~[3], For a good work we stone thee not; but for blasphemy; and because that thou, being a man, makest thyself God.

34 Jesus answered them, Is it not written in your law, [∧**that**][4] I said, Ye are gods?

35 If he called them gods, unto whom the word of God came, and the scripture cannot be broken;

36 Say ye of him, whom the Father hath sanctified, and sent into the world, Thou blasphemest; because I said, I am the Son of God?

37 If I do not the works of my Father, believe me not.

38 But if I do, though ye

believe not me, **believe**[5] the works: that ye may know, and **believe**[6], that the Father _is_ in me, and I in **him**[7].

39 ~~Therefore~~[8] they sought again to take him: but he escaped out of their hand,

40 And went away again beyond Jordan into the place where John at first baptized; and there he abode.

41 And many resorted unto him, and said, John did no miracle: but all things that John spake of this man were true.

42 And **many believed on him there**[9].

CHAPTER 11

1   Now a certain _man_ was

---

[1] WH omitted <u>of me</u> (<u>mou</u>) from <u>the</u> <u>father</u> of me.

[2] WH omitted <u>then</u> (<u>oun</u>).

[3] WH omitted <u>saying</u> (<u>legontes</u>).

[4] WH added _that_ (<u>[h]oti</u>).

[5] WH changed <u>believe</u> (<u>pisteusate</u>) to _be believing_ (_pisteuete_). **Aor** Act Imp to _Pres_ Act Imp [tense]

[6] WH changed **might believe** (**pisteus**<u>Ate</u>) to _may know_ (_gin_**Osk**_Ate_). **Aor** Act Sub of pisteuO to _Pres_ Act Sub of ginOskO. [tense & verb]

[7] WH changed **him** (**aut**<u>O</u>) to _the father_ (_to patri_).

[8] WH omitted <u>therefore</u> (<u>oun</u>).

[9] WH changed the word order from BELIEVED MANY THERE <u>ON</u> <u>HIM</u> to _MANY BELIEVED ON THERE HIM._

sick, *named* Lazarus, of Bethany, the town of Mary and her sister Martha.

2　(It was *that* Mary which anointed the Lord with ointment, and wiped his feet with her hair, whose brother Lazarus was sick.)

3　Therefore his sisters sent unto him, saying, Lord, behold, he whom thou lovest is sick.

4　When Jesus heard *that*, he said, This sickness is not unto death, but for the glory of God, that the Son of God might be glorified thereby.

5　Now Jesus loved Martha, and her sister, and Lazarus.

6　When he had heard therefore that he was sick, he abode two days still in the same place where he was.

7　Then after that saith he to *his* disciples, Let us go into Judaea again.

8　*His* disciples say unto him, Master, the Jews of late sought to stone thee; and goest thou thither again?

9　Jesus answered, Are there not twelve hours in the day? If any man walk in the day, he stumbleth not, because he seeth the light of this world.

10　But if a man walk in the night, he stumbleth, because there is no light in him.

11　These things said he: and after that he saith unto them, Our friend Lazarus sleepeth; but I go, that I may awake him out of sleep.

12　Then said [ʌ**to him**]¹ **his**² disciples, Lord, if he sleep, he shall do well.

13　Howbeit Jesus spake of his death: but they thought that he had spoken of taking of rest in sleep.

14　Then said Jesus unto them plainly, Lazarus is dead.

15　And I am glad for your sakes that I was not there, to the intent ye may believe; nevertheless let us go unto him.

16　Then said Thomas, which is called Didymus, unto his fellowdisciples, Let us also go, that we may die with him.

17　Then when Jesus came, he found that he had *lain* in the grave four days already.

18　Now Bethany was nigh unto Jerusalem, about fifteen furlongs off:

19　**And** **many**³ of the Jews came to [**the** {ones}

---

¹ WH added *to him* (*autO*).
² WH omitted *of him* (*autou*) from the disciples of him.
³ WH changed **and** (**kai**) to *but* (*de*) and put many first.

around]¹ Martha and Mary, to comfort them concerning ~~their~~² brother.

20 Then Martha, as soon as she heard that Jesus was coming, went and met him: but Mary sat *still* in the house.

21 Then said Martha unto Jesus, Lord, if thou hadst been here, **my brother**³ **had** not **died**⁴.

22 ~~But~~⁵ I know, that even now, whatsoever thou wilt ask of God, God will give *it* thee.

23 Jesus saith unto her, Thy brother shall rise again.

24 Martha saith unto him, I know that he shall rise again in the resurrection at the last day.

25 Jesus said unto her, I am the resurrection, and the life: he that believeth in me, though he were dead, yet shall he live:

26 And whosoever liveth and believeth in me shall never die. Believest thou this?

27 She saith unto him, Yea, Lord: I believe that thou art the Christ, the Son of God, which should come into the world.

28 And when she had so said [**these** {things}]⁶, she went her way, and called Mary her sister secretly, saying, The Master is come, and calleth for thee.

29 [∧**but**]⁷ As soon as she heard *that*, **she arose**⁸ quickly, and **came**⁹ unto him.

30 Now Jesus was not yet come into the town, but was

---

¹ WH changed the untranslated the {ones} **around** (**tas peri**) to *the* (*tAn*).

² WH omited of them (autOn) from the brother of them.

³ WH changed the word order from THE BROTHER OF ME not ever **had** died to *not ever died THE BROTHER OF ME.*

⁴ WH changed **had** died (etethnAkei) to *died* (*apethanen*). **PastPf** Act Ind to *Aor* Act Ind. [tense]

⁵ WH omitted but (alla).

⁶ WH changed the untranslated these {things} (tauta) to *this* {thing} (*touta*). Acc **Plur** Nom to Acc *Sing* Nom. [number]

⁷ WH added *but* (de).

⁸ WH changed she **is being** raised (egeiretai) to *she was raised* (*AgerthA*). **Pres** Pass Ind to *Aor* Pass Ind. [tense]

⁹ WH changed comes (ercetai) to *were coming* (*Arceto*). **Pres** M/P Ind to *Impf* M/P Ind. [tense]

[ʌstill][1] in that place where Martha met him.

31 The Jews then which were with her in the house, and comforted her, when they saw Mary, that she rose up hastily and went out, followed her, saying, She goeth unto the grave to weep there.

32 Then when Mary was come where Jesus was, and saw him, she fell down at his feet, **saying**[2] unto him, Lord, if thou hadst been here, my brother had not died.

33 When Jesus therefore saw her weeping, and the Jews also weeping which came with her, he groaned in the spirit, and was troubled,

34 And said, Where have ye laid him? They said unto him, Lord, come and see.

35 Jesus wept.

36 Then said the Jews, Behold how he loved him!

37 And some of them said, Could not this man, which opened the eyes of the blind, have caused that even this man should not have died?

38 Jesus therefore again groaning in himself cometh to the grave. It was a cave, and a stone lay upon it.

39 Jesus said, Take ye away the stone. Martha, the sister of him **that was dead**[3], saith unto him, Lord, by this time he stinketh: for he hath been *dead* four days.

40 Jesus saith unto her, Said I not unto thee, that, if thou wouldest believe, thou shouldest see the glory of God?

41 Then they took away the stone *from the place* ~~where the dead was laid~~[4]. And Jesus lifted up *his* eyes, and said, Father, I thank thee that thou hast heard me.

42 And I knew that thou hearest me always: but because of the people which stand by I said *it*, that they may believe that thou hast sent me.

43 And when he thus had spoken, he cried with a loud voice, Lazarus, come forth.

---

[1] WH added *still* (*eti*).
[2] WH changed **saying** (**legontes**) to *having supposed* (*doxantes*). **Pres** Act Part of legO to *Aor* Act Part of *dokeO*. [tense & verb]

[3] WH changed that was dead (tethnAkotos) to *that was dead* (*teteleutAkotos*). Pf Act Part of thAxO to Pf Act Part of *teleutaO*. [syn]
[4] WH omitted where the dead was laid (ou An [h]o tethnAkOs keimenos).

44 ~~And~~[1] he that was dead came forth, bound hand and foot with graveclothes: and his face was bound about with a napkin. Jesus saith unto them, Loose him, and let ʌ**him**[2] go.

45 Then many of the Jews which came to Mary, and had seen the things which Jesus did, believed on him.

46 But some of them went their ways to the Pharisees, and told them **what things**[3] ~~Jesus~~[4] had done.

47 Then gathered the chief priests and the Pharisees a council, and said, What do we? for this man doeth many miracles.

48 If we let him thus alone, all *men* will believe on him: and the Romans shall come and take away both our place and nation.

49 And one of them, *named* Caiaphas, being the high priest that same year, said unto them, Ye know nothing at all,

50 Nor **consider**[5] that it is expedient **for us**[6], that one man should die for the people, and that the whole nation perish not.

51 And this spake he not of himself: but being high priest that year, he prophesied that Jesus should die for that nation;

52 And not for that nation only, but that also he should gather together in one the children of God that were scattered abroad.

53 Then from that day forth **they took counsel together**[7] for to put him to death.

54 Jesus therefore walked no more openly among the Jews; but went thence unto a country near to the wilderness,

---

[1] WH omitted and (kai).

[2] WH added *him* (*auton*) where the KJV supplied it.

[3] In their text, WH changed what {thing} (ʰ**a**) to *what* {*things*} (ʰ**o**). *Acc Neut Plur* to **Nom Masc Sing**. [case, gender, number] They did not make this change in their margin.

[4] WH omitted the Jesus (ʰo iAsous) and forced the verb to supply the subject *he*.

[5] WH changed consider (**dia**logizes~~th~~e) to *consider* (*logizes*~~th~~*e*). [prefix dropped]

[6] WH changed for us (ʰAmin) to *for you* (ʰ*umin*). [person]

[7] WH changed they took counsel **together** (**sune**bouleusanto) to *they took counsel* (*ebouleusanto*). [prefix dropped]

into a city called Ephraim, and there **continued**[1] with **his**[2] disciples.

55 And the Jews' passover was nigh at hand: and many went out of the country up to Jerusalem before the passover, to purify themselves.

56 Then sought they for Jesus, and spake among themselves, as they stood in the temple, What think ye, that he will not come to the feast?

57 Now **both**[3] the chief priests and the Pharisees had given **a commandment**[4], that, if any man knew where he were, he should shew *it*, that they might take him.

CHAPTER 12

1   Then Jesus six days before the passover came to

---

[1] WH changed **were staying** (**dietribe**) to *remained* (*emeine*). **Impf** Act Ind of diatribO [rub through] to *Aor* Act Ind of *menO*. [syn & tense]

[2] WH omitted of him (autou) from the disciples of him.

[3] WH omitted both (kai).

[4] WH changed a commandment (entolAn) to *commandments* (*entolas*). Acc **Sing** Fem to Acc *Plur* Fem. [number]

Bethany, where Lazarus was ~~which had been dead~~[5], whom [ᴧ**Jesus**][6] he raised from the dead.

2   There they made him a supper; and Martha served: but Lazarus was one [ᴧ**out of**][7] of them **that sat at the table with**[8] him.

3   Then took Mary a pound of ointment of spikenard, very costly, and anointed the feet of Jesus, and wiped his feet with her hair: and the house was filled with the odour of the ointment.

4   **Then**[9] saith one **of**[10] his

---

[5] WH omitted who had been dead (ᵸo tethnAkOs).

[6] WH added *Jesus* (*iAsous*) and replaced the he supplied by the verb.

[7] WH added *out of* (*ek*) and replaced the of supplied by the genitive case.

[8] WH removed the prefix with (sun) from that sat at the table with (**sun**anakeimenOn) and made it a separate preposition after the verb (*anakeimenOn sun*). [prefix moved]

[9] WH changed then (**oun**) to *then* (*de*).

[10] WH omitted of (ek) and left the genitive case to supply the *of*.

disciples, Judas [ʌ**the**]¹ Iscariot, ~~**Simon's son**~~,² which should betray him,

5   Why was not this ointment sold for three hundred pence, and given to the poor?

6   This he said, not that he cared for the poor; but because he was a thief, **and**³ **had**⁴ the bag, and bare what was put therein.

7   Then said Jesus, Let her alone: [ʌ**in order that**]⁵ against the day of my burying **hath she kept**⁶ this.

8   For the poor always ye have with you; but me ye have not always.

9   Much [ʌ**the**]⁷ people of the Jews therefore knew that he was there: and they came not for Jesus' sake only, but that they might see Lazarus also, whom he had raised from the dead.

10   But the chief priests consulted that they might put Lazarus also to death;

11   Because that by reason of him many of the Jews went away, and believed on Jesus.

12   On the next day much [**the**]⁸ people that were come to the feast, when they heard that Jesus was coming to Jerusalem,

13   Took branches of palm trees, and went forth to meet him, and **cried**⁹, Hosanna: Blessed *is* [ʌ**even**]¹⁰ the King of Israel that cometh in the name of the Lord.

14   And Jesus, when he had found a young ass, sat thereon; as it is written,

15   Fear not, daughter of Sion: behold, thy King cometh, sitting on an ass's colt.

---

¹ WH added *the* (ʰ*o*) before Iscariot.
² WH omitted of Simon (simOnos).
³ WH omitted and (kai).
⁴ WH changed **was** having (eice) to *having* (ecOn). **Impf** Act **Ind** to *Pres* Act *Part*. [tense & mood]
⁵ WH added *in order that* (ʰ*ina*) before against (eis).
⁶ WH changed she **has** kept (**tetArAken**) to *she **might** keep* (**tArAsA**). **Pf** Act **Ind** to *Aor* Act *Sub*. [tense & mood]
⁷ WH added *the* (ʰ*o*) before people (oclos).

⁸ In their margin, WH added *the* (ʰ*o*) before people (oclos).
⁹ WH changed were crying (ekrazon) to *were crying* (*ekraugazon*). Impf Act Ind of krazO to Impf Act Ind of *kraugazO*. [syn]
¹⁰ WH added *even* (kai).

16 [**but**]¹ These things understood not his disciples at the first: but when Jesus was glorified, then remembered they that these things were written of him, and *that* they had done these things unto him.

17 The people therefore that was with him when he called Lazarus out of his grave, and raised him from the dead, bare record.

18 For this cause the people also met him, for that **they heard**² that he had done this miracle.

19 The Pharisees therefore said among themselves, Perceive ye how ye prevail nothing? behold, the world is gone after him.

20 And there were certain Greeks among them that came up to worship at the feast:

21 The same came therefore to Philip, which was of Bethsaida of Galilee, and desired him, saying, Sir, we would see Jesus.

22 Philip cometh and telleth Andrew: **and again**³ Andrew and Philip [∧**and**]⁴ tell Jesus.

23 And Jesus **answered**⁵ them, saying, The hour is come, that the Son of man should be glorified.

24 Verily, verily, I say unto you, Except a corn of wheat fall into the ground and die, it abideth alone: but if it die, it bringeth forth much fruit.

25 He that loveth his life **shall lose**⁶ it; and he that hateth his life in this world shall keep it unto life eternal.

26 If any man serve me, let him follow me; and where I am, there shall also my servant be: [**and**]⁷ if any man serve me, him will *my* Father

---

¹ WH omitted the untranslated <u>but</u> (<u>de</u>).

² WH changed **it** <u>heard</u> (<u>Akouse</u>) to *they heard* (*Akousan*). Aor Act Ind 3 **Sing** to Aor Act Ind 3 *Plur.* [number]

³ WH changed **and again** (**kai palin**) to *he comes* (*ercetai*). Pres M-P Ind 3 sing.

⁴ WH added *and* (*kai*).

⁵ WH changed <u>answered</u> (<u>apekrinato</u>) to *answers* (*apokrinetai*). **Aor** M/P-D Ind to *Pres* M/P-D Ind. [tense]

⁶ WH changed **shall** lose (<u>apolesei</u>) to *loses* (*apolluei*). **Fut** Act Ind to *Pres* Act Ind. [tense]

⁷ WH omitted the untranslated <u>and</u> (<u>kai</u>).

honour.

27 Now is my soul troubled; and what shall I say? Father, save me from this hour: but for this cause came I unto this hour.

28 Father, glorify thy name. Then came there a voice from heaven, *saying*, I have both glorified *it*, and will glorify *it* again.

29 The people therefore, that stood by, and heard *it*, said that it thundered: others said, An angel spake to him.

30 Jesus answered and said, This voice came not because of me, but for your sakes.

31 Now is the judgment of this world: now shall the prince of this world be cast out.

32 And I, if I be lifted up from the earth, will draw all *men* unto me.

33 This he said, signifying what death he should die.

34 The people [ʌ**therefore**]¹ answered him, We have heard out of the law that Christ abideth for ever: and how sayest thou, The Son of man must be lifted up? who is this Son of man?

35 Then Jesus said unto them, Yet a little while is the light **with you**². Walk **while**³ ye have the light, lest darkness come upon you: for he that walketh in darkness knoweth not whither he goeth.

36 **while**⁴ ye have light, believe in the light, that ye may be the children of light. These things spake Jesus, and departed, and did hide himself from them.

37 But though he had done so many miracles before them, yet they believed not on him:

38 That the saying of Esaias the prophet might be fulfilled, which he spake, Lord, who hath believed our report? and to whom hath the arm of the Lord been revealed?

39 Therefore they could not believe, because that Esaias said again,

40 He hath blinded their eyes, and **hardened**⁵ their

---

² WH changed **with** you (**meth'** ʰ**umOn**) to *in you* (*en* ʰ*umin*). **Gen** to *Dat*. [prep & case]

³ WH changed **while** (ʰ**eOs**) to **as** (ʰ*Os*).

⁴ WH changed **while** (ʰ**eOs**) to **as** (ʰ*Os*).

⁵ WH changed **has** hardened (**pepOrOken**) to *hardened* (*epOrOsen*). **Pf** Act Ind to *Aor* Act Ind. [tense]

---

¹ WH added *therefore* (*oun*).

heart; that they should not see with *their* eyes, nor understand with *their* heart, and **be converted**[1], and **I should heal**[2] them.

41 These things said Esaias, **when**[3] he saw his glory, and spake of him.

42 Nevertheless among the chief rulers also many believed on him; but because of the Pharisees they did not confess *him*, lest they should be put out of the synagogue:

43 For they loved the praise of men more than the praise of God.

44 Jesus cried and said, He that believeth on me, believeth not on me, but on him that sent me.

45 And he that seeth me seeth him that sent me.

46 I am come a light into the world, that whosoever believeth on me should not abide in darkness.

47 And if any man hear my words, and **believe**[4] not, I judge him not: for I came not to judge the world, but to save the world.

48 He that rejecteth me, and receiveth not my words, hath one that judgeth him: the word that I have spoken, the same shall judge him in the last day.

49 For I have not spoken of myself; but the Father which sent me, he **gave**[5] me a commandment, what I should say, and what I should speak.

50 And I know that his commandment is life everlasting: whatsoever I **speak**[6] therefore, even as the Father said unto me, so I speak.

CHAPTER 13

1 Now before the feast of the passover, when Jesus knew that his hour **was come**[7] that he should depart

---

[1] WH changed be turned **upon** (**epi**straf**Osi**) to *be turned* (*strafOsi*). [prefix dropped]

[2] WH changed I **might** heal (ias**O**mai) to *I will heal* (*iasomai*). **Aor** Mid-D **Sub** to *Fut* Mid-D *Ind*. [tense & mood]

[3] WH changed **when** (ʰote) to *because* (ʰoti).

[4] WH changed **believe** (pisteusA) to *keep* (fulaxA). Both Aor Act Sub. [verb]

[5] WH changed gave (edOke) to *has given* (dedOke). **Aor** Act Ind to *Pf* Act Ind. [tense]

[6] WH changed the word order from SPEAK I-myself to *I-myself SPEAK*.

[7] WH changed **has come** (**el**Aluthen) to *came* (*Althen*). **Pf** Act Ind to *Aor* Act Ind. [tense]

out of this world unto the Father, having loved his own which were in the world, he loved them unto the end.

2　And supper **being ended**[1], the devil having now put into the heart of **Judas**[2] **Iscariot**[3], Simon's *son*, to **betray**[4] **him**;[5]

3　**Jesus**[6] knowing that the Father **had given**[7] all things into his hands, and that he was come from God, and went to God;

---

[1] WH changed **having end**ed (**genomenou**) to *ending* (*ginomenou*). **Aor** Mid-D Part to *Pres* M/P-D Part. [tense]

[2] WH changed Juda (*iouda*) to *Judas* (*ioudas*) [spell].

[3] WH changed {of} Iscariot (iskariO**tou**) to *Iscariot* (*iscariOt***As***). **Gen** to *Nom*. [case]

[4] WH changed he might betray (parad**O**) to *he might betray* (*parado**i***). Both [h]ina + Aor Act Sub 3 Sing. [spell]

[5] WH changed the word order from in order that HIM he might betray to *in order that he might betray HIM*.

[6] WH omitted the Jesus ([h]o iAsous) and forced the verb to supply the subject *he*.

[7] WH changed **has** given (de-dOken) to *gave* (*edOken*). **Pf** Act Ind to *Aor* Act Ind. [tense]

4　He riseth from supper, and laid aside his garments; and took a towel, and girded himself.

5　After that he poureth water into a bason, and began to wash the disciples' feet, and to wipe *them* with the towel wherewith he was girded.

6　Then cometh he to Simon Peter: and **Peter**[8] saith unto him, Lord, dost thou wash my feet?

7　Jesus answered and said unto him, What I do thou knowest not now; but thou shalt know hereafter.

8　Peter saith unto him, Thou shalt never wash my feet. Jesus answered him, If I wash thee not, thou hast no part with me.

9　Simon Peter saith unto him, Lord, not my feet only, but also *my* hands and *my* head.

10　Jesus saith to him, He that is washed needeth not **save**[9] to wash *his* **feet**[10], but is

---

[8] WH omitted that {one} [i.e. Peter] (ekeinos) and forced the verb to supply the subject *he*.

[9] WH changed **either** (**A**--either, or, than) to *if not* (*ei mA*--i.e. except)

[10] In their margin, WH omitted the feet (tous podas).

clean every whit: and ye are clean, but not all.

11 For he knew who should betray him; therefore said he, [∧that]¹ Ye are not all clean.

12 So after he had washed their feet, and had taken his garments, ∧and² **was set down**³ again, he said unto them, Know ye what I have done to you?

13 Ye call me Master and Lord: and ye say well; for *so* I am.

14 If I then, *your* Lord and Master, have washed your feet; ye also ought to wash one another's feet.

15 For **I have given**⁴ you an example, that ye should do as I have done to you.

16 Verily, verily, I say unto you, The servant is not greater than his lord; neither he that is sent greater than he that sent him.

17 If ye know these things, happy are ye if ye do them.

18 I speak not of you all: I know whom I have chosen: but that the scripture may be fulfilled, He that eateth bread with **me**⁵ hath lifted up his heel against me.

19 Now I tell you before it come, that, when it is come to pass, **ye may believe**⁶ that I am *he*.

20 Verily, verily, I say unto you, He that receiveth whomsoever I send receiveth me; and he that receiveth me receiveth him that sent me.

21 When Jesus had thus said, he was troubled in spirit, and testified, and said, Verily, verily, I say unto you, that one of you shall betray me.

22 ~~Then~~⁷ the disciples looked one on another, doubting of whom he spake.

23 ~~Now~~⁸ there was leaning

---

¹ WH added *that* (*ʰoti*).
² WH added *and* (*kai*) where the KJV supplied it.
³ WH changed **having** reclined (**anapesOn**) to *reclined* (*anapese*). Aor Act **Part** to Aor Act ***Ind.*** [mood]
⁴ WH changed I **gave** (**edOke**) to I **have given** (*dedOka*). **Aor** Act Ind to ***Pf*** Act Ind. [tense]

⁵ In their text, WH changed me (**emou**) to me (*mou*), but not in their margin. Prolonged form to shortened form.
⁶ WH changed the word order from when it is come to pass YE MAY BELIEVE to *YE MAY BELIEVE when it is come to pass.*
⁷ WH omitted then (oun).
⁸ WH omitted now (de).

on Jesus' bosom one [**out of**]¹ of his disciples, whom Jesus loved.

24 Simon Peter therefore beckoned to him, **that he should ask who it should be**² of whom he spake.

25 He **then**³ **lying**⁴ [**in this manner**]⁵ on Jesus' breast saith unto him, Lord, who is it?

26 Jesus [**therefore**]⁶ answered, He it is, to whom [**also**]⁷ **I shall give**⁸ [**him**]⁹¹⁰ a sop, **when I have dipped**¹⁰

---

¹ WH added *out of* (*ek*) in place of the *of* supplied by the genitive case.
² WH changed **that he should ask** who it **should be** (**puthestai** tis **an** ei*A*) to and *says to him Tell* who it *is* (*kai legei autO eipe tis esti*).
³ WH omitted then (*de*).
⁴ WH changed lying {**upon**} (**epipesOn**) to lying {**down**} (*anapesOn*). [prefix changed]
⁵ WH added *in this manner* (*ʰoutOs*).
⁶ WH added *therefore* (*oun*).
⁷ WH added *also* (*kai*).
⁸ WH changed I shall give (**epid**OsO) to *I shall give* (*dOsO*). [prefix dropped]
⁹ WH added *him* (*autO*).
¹⁰ WH changed **having dipped** (ba*s*as) to *I will dip* (*baṣO*). **Aor** Act **Part** to *Fut* Act *Ind*. [tense & mood]

---

it. **And when he had dipped**¹¹ the sop, [**he took and**]¹² he gave *it* to Judas **Iscariot**¹³, *the son* of Simon.

27 And after the sop Satan entered into him. Then said Jesus unto him, That thou doest, do quickly.

28 Now no man at the table knew for what intent he spake this unto him.

29 For some *of them* thought, because Judas had the bag, that Jesus had said unto him, Buy *those things* that we have need of against the feast; or, that he should give something to the poor.

30 He then having received the sop **went immediately**¹⁴ **out**¹⁵: and it was

---

¹¹ WH changed **and** when he had dipped (**kai emba**ṣas) to *when he had dipped therefore* (*baṣas oun*).
¹² WH added he took and (lambanei kai--lit. he takes and).
¹³ WH changed Iscariot (iskariOt*A*) to *of Iscariot* (*iscariOtou*). **Dat** to *Gen*. [case]
¹⁴ WH changed immediately (eutheOs) to *immediately* (*eutheus*). [spell]
¹⁵ WH changed the word order from WENT immediately OUT to *WENT OUT immediately*.

night.

31 Therefore, when he was gone out, Jesus said, Now is the Son of man glorified, and God is glorified in him.

32 ~~If God be glorified in him~~[1], God shall also glorify him in **himself**[2], and shall straightway glorify him.

33 Little children, yet a little while I am with you. Ye shall seek me: and as I said unto the Jews, Whither I **go**[3], ye cannot come; so now I say to you.

34 A new commandment I give unto you, That ye love one another; as I have loved you, that ye also love one another.

35 By this shall all *men* know that ye are my disciples, if ye have love one to another.

36 Simon Peter said unto him, Lord, whither goest thou? [~~the~~][4] Jesus answered

him[5], Whither I go, thou canst not follow me now; but thou shalt follow ~~me~~[6] **afterwards**[7].

37 Peter said unto him, Lord, why cannot I follow thee now? I will lay down my life for thy sake.

38 [~~the~~][8] Jesus **answered** ~~him~~[10], Wilt thou lay down thy life for my sake? Verily, verily, I say unto thee, The cock **shall** not **crow**[11], till **thou has denied**[12] me thrice.

---

[5] WH omitted <u>him</u> (<u>autO</u>).

[6] WH omitted <u>me</u> (<u>moi</u>).

[7] WH changed the word order from <u>but</u> AFTERWARDS <u>thou shalt follow</u> **me** to *but thou shalt follow* AFTERWARDS.

[8] WH omitted the untranslated <u>the</u> (^h<u>o</u>).

[9] WH changed <u>answered</u> (<u>apekrith</u>**A**) to *answers* (*apokrinetai*). **Aor** Mid-D Ind to ***Pres*** M/P-D Ind. [tense]

[10] WH omitted <u>him</u> (<u>autO</u>).

[11] WH changed **shall** <u>crow</u> (<u>fOnAsei</u>) to ***might*** *crow* (*fOnAsA*). **Fut** Act **Ind** to ***Aor*** Act ***Sub***. [tense & mood]

[12] WH changed <u>thou hast denied</u> (**apa**rnAsA) to *thou hast denied* (*arnAsA*). [prefix dropped]

---

[1] WH omitted <u>if the God be glorified in him</u> (ei ^h<u>o</u> <u>theos</u> <u>edoxasth</u>**A** <u>en</u> <u>autO</u>).

[2] WH changed <u>himself</u> (^h<u>eautO</u>) to *himsef* (*autO*).

[3] WH changed the word order from <u>GO</u> <u>I-myself</u> to *I-myself GO*.

[4] WH omitted the untranslated <u>the</u> (^h<u>o</u>).

CHAPTER 14

1　Let not your heart be troubled: ye believe in God, believe also in me.

2　In my Father's house are many mansions: if *it were* not *so*, I would have told you. I go to prepare a place for you.

3　And if I go and prepare a place for you, I will come again, and receive you unto myself; that where I am, *there* ye may be also.

4　And whither I go ye know, ~~and~~[1] the way ~~ye know~~[2].

5　Thomas saith unto him, Lord, we know not whither thou goest; ~~and~~[3] how can **we know**[4] **the way**[5]?

6　Jesus saith unto him, I am the way, the truth, and the life: no man cometh unto the Father, but by me.

7　If ye had known me, **ye should have known**[6] [7] **[ever]**[8] my Father also: ~~and~~[9] from henceforth ye know him, and have seen him.

8　Philip saith unto him, Lord, shew us the Father, and it sufficeth us.

9　Jesus saith unto him, Have I been so long time with you, and yet hast thou not known me, Philip? he that hath seen me hath seen the Father; ~~and~~[10] how sayest thou *then*, Shew us the Father?

10　Believest thou not that I am in the Father, and the Father in me? the words that I **speak**[11] unto you I speak not of myself: but the Father ~~that~~[12] dwelleth in me, **he**

---

[1] WH omitted <u>and</u> (<u>kai</u>).

[2] WH omitted <u>ye know</u> (<u>oi-date</u>).

[3] WH omitted <u>and</u> (<u>kai</u>).

[4] WH changed **to** have know**n** (**eidenai**) to *we have know* (*oidamen*). Pf Act **Inf** to Pf Act ***Ind***. [mood]

[5] WH changed the word order from THE WAY we know to *we know THE WAY*.

[6] WH changed <u>ye **had** known</u> (**egnOk**eite an) to *ye **have** known* (*an Adeite*). **PastPf** Act Ind of <u>ginOskO</u> to *Pf* Act Ind of *eidO*. [tense & syn]

[7] WH added *ever* (*an*).

[8] WH changed the word order from <u>ye **had** known</u> EVER (<u>an</u>) to *EVER* (<u>an</u>) *ye **have** known*.

[9] WH omitted <u>and</u> (<u>kai</u>).

[10] WH omitted <u>and</u> (<u>kai</u>).

[11] WH changed <u>speak</u> (<u>lalO</u>) to *speak* (*legO*). Both Pres Act Ind. [syn]

[12] WH omitted <u>the</u> {one} (<u>h͑o</u>) before <u>dwelling</u> (<u>menOn</u>).

[himself][1] **doeth the works**[2].

11 Believe me that I *am* in the Father, and the Father in me: or else believe me for the very works' sake.

12 Verily, verily, I say unto you, He that believeth on me, the works that I do shall he do also; and greater *works* than these shall he do; because I go unto **my**[3] Father.

13 And whatsoever ye shall ask in my name, that will I do, that the Father may be glorified in the Son.

14 If ye shall ask [∧**me**][4] any thing in my name, **I**[5] will do *it*.

15 If ye love me, **keep**[6] my

---

[1] WH changed the untranslated <u>himself</u> (<u>autos</u>) to *of him* (*autou*). **Nom** to **Gen**. [case]

[2] They then changed the word order from **himself** HE <u>DOETH</u> <u>THE</u> <u>WORKS</u> to *HE DOETH THE WORKS* **of him**.

[3] WH omitted <u>of me</u> (<u>mou</u>) from <u>the father of me</u>.

[4] In their text, WH added *me* (*me*), but not in their margin.

[5] WH changed **I-myself** (**egO**) to *this* {one} (*touto*).

[6] WH changed <u>keep</u> (<u>tArAsate</u>) to *ye will keep* (*tArAsete*). **Aor** Act **Imp** to *Fut* Act **Ind**. [tense & mood]

---

commandments.

16 And I will pray the Father, and he shall give you another Comforter, that **he may abide**[7] with you for ever;

17 *Even* the Spirit of truth; whom the world cannot receive, because it seeth him not, neither knoweth him: **but**[8] ye know him; for he dwelleth with you, and shall be in you.

18 I will not leave you comfortless: I will come to you.

19 Yet a little while, and the world seeth me no more; but ye see me: because I live, ye shall live also.

20 At that day ye shall know that I *am* in my Father, and ye in me, and I in you.

21 He that hath my commandments, and keepeth them, he it is that loveth me: and he that loveth me shall be loved of my Father, and I will love him, and will manifest myself to him.

22 Judas saith unto him, not Iscariot, Lord, how is it that thou wilt manifest thyself

---

[7] WH changed <u>he may</u> **abide** (**menA**) to *he may be* (*A*). Pres Act Sub of <u>menO</u> to Pres NV Sub of *eimi*. [syn]

[8] WH omitted <u>but</u> (<u>de</u>).

unto us, and not unto the world?

23 Jesus answered and said unto him, If a man love me, he will keep my words: and my Father will love him, and we will come unto him, and **make**[1] our abode with him.

24 He that loveth me not keepeth not my sayings: and the word which ye hear is not mine, but the Father's which sent me.

25 These things have I spoken unto you, being *yet* present with you.

26 But the Comforter, *which is* the Holy Ghost, whom the Father will send in my name, he shall teach you all things, and bring all things to your remembrance, whatsoever I have said unto you.

27 Peace I leave with you, my peace I give unto you: not as the world giveth, give I unto you. Let not your heart be troubled, neither let it be afraid.

28 Ye have heard how I said unto you, I go away, and come *again* unto you. If ye loved me, ye would rejoice, because ~~I said~~[2], I go unto the Father: for ~~my~~[3] Father is greater than I.

29 And now I have told you before it come to pass, that, when it is come to pass, ye might believe.

30 Hereafter I will not talk much with you: for the prince of ~~this~~[4] world cometh, and hath nothing in me.

31 But that the world may know that I love the Father; and as the Father gave me commandment, even so I do. Arise, let us go hence.

CHAPTER 15

1 I am the true vine, and my Father is the husbandman.

2 Every branch in me that beareth not fruit he taketh away: and every *branch* that beareth fruit, he purgeth it, that it may bring forth more fruit.

3 Now ye are clean through the word which I have spoken unto you.

4 Abide in me, and I in you. As the branch cannot

---

[1] WH changed <u>we will make</u> (poiAsome**n**) to *we will make* [**for ourselves**] (*poi-Asome**tha***). Fut **Act** Ind to Fut *Mid-D* Ind. [voice]

[2] WH omitted <u>I said</u> (eipon).
[3] WH omitted <u>of me</u> (mou) from <u>the</u> <u>father</u> of me.
[4] WH omitted <u>this</u> (toutou) from <u>of the world</u> <u>this</u>.

bear fruit of itself, except it abide in the vine; no more can ye, except ye abide in me.

5   I am the vine, ye *are* the branches: He that abideth in me, and I in him, the same bringeth forth much fruit: for without me ye can do nothing.

6   If a man abide not in me, he is cast forth as a branch, and is withered; and men gather them, and cast *them* into ∧**the**[1] fire, and they are burned.

7   If ye abide in me, and my words abide in you, <u>**ye shall ask**</u>[2] what ye will, and it shall be done unto you.

8   Herein is my Father glorified, that ye bear much fruit; so <u>**shall ye be**</u>[3] my disciples.

9   As the Father hath loved me, so have I loved you: continue ye in my love.

10 If ye keep my commandments, ye shall abide in my love; even as I have kept my Father's commandments, and abide in his love.

11 These things have I spoken unto you, that my joy <u>**might remain**</u>[4] in you, and *that* your joy might be full.

12 This is my commandment, That ye love one another, as I have loved you.

13 Greater love hath no man than this, that a man lay down his life for his friends.

14 Ye are my friends, if ye do <u>**whatsoever**</u>[5] I command you.

15 Henceforth I call <u>**you**</u>[6] not servants; for the servant knoweth not what his lord doeth: but I have called you friends; for all things that I have heard of my Father I have made known unto you.

16 Ye have not chosen me, but I have chosen you, and ordained you, that ye should go and bring forth fruit, and *that* your fruit

---

[1] WH added *the* (*to*) where the KJV supplied it.

[2] WH changed <u>**ye shall** ask</u> (ait~~A~~sest~~he~~) to *ask* **ye** (*ait~~A~~sas~~the~~*). **Fut** Mid **Ind** to *Aor* Mid *Imp*. [tense & mood]

[3] In their margin, WH changed <u>shall ye be</u> (gen~~A~~sest~~he~~) to *shall ye be* (*gen~~A~~s~~the~~*). Both Fut Mid-D Ind. [<u>rare</u> sp to *common* sp]

---

[4] WH changed <u>**might remain**</u> (<u>**mein**</u>A) to *may be* (*A*). <u>**Aor**</u> Act Sub of <u>menO</u> to *Pres* NV Sub of *eimi*. [tense & syn]

[5] WH changed <u>whats**oever**</u> (^h<u>**osa**</u>) to *what* (^h*a*).

[6] WH changed the word order from <u>YOU</u> I call to *I call YOU*.

should remain: that whatsoever ye shall ask of the Father in my name, he may give it you.

17 These things I command you, that ye love one another.

18 If the world hate you, ye know that it hated me before *it hated* you.

19 If ye were of the world, the world would love his own: but because ye are not of the world, but I have chosen you out of the world, therefore the world hateth you.

20 Remember the word that I said unto you, The servant is not greater than his lord. If they have persecuted me, they will also persecute you; if they have kept my saying, they will keep yours also.

21 But all these things will they do ∧**unto**[1] **you**[2] for my name's sake, because they know not him that sent me.

22 If I had not come and spoken unto them, they had not had sin: but now they have no cloke for their sin.

23 He that hateth me hateth my Father also.

24 If I had not done among them the works which none other man **did**[3], they had not had sin: but now have they both seen and hated both me and my Father.

25 But *this cometh to pass*, that the word might be fulfilled that is written in their law, They hated me without a cause.

26 But when the Comforter is come, whom I will send unto you from the Father, *even* the Spirit of truth, which proceedeth from the Father, he shall testify of me:

27 And ye also shall bear witness, because ye have been with me from the beginning.

CHAPTER 16

1 These things have I spoken unto you, that ye should not be offended.

2 They shall put you out of the synagogues: yea, the time cometh, that whosoever killeth you will think that he

---

[1] WH added *unto* (*eis*) as the KJV supplied from the dative case.

[2] WH changed {unto} you (ʰ**umin**) to *unto you* (*eis* ʰ**u-mas**). [case & prep added]

---

[3] WH changed **has done** (**pe-poiAken**) to *did* (*epoiAsen*). **Pf** Act Ind to *Aor* Act Ind. [tense]

doeth God service.

3   And these things will they do ~~unto you~~[1], because they have not known the Father, nor me.

4   But these things have I told you, that when the time [∧**of them**][2] shall come, ye may remember that I told you of them. And these things I said not unto you at the beginning, because I was with you.

5   But now I go my way to him that sent me; and none of you asketh me, Whither goest thou?

6   But because I have said these things unto you, sorrow hath filled your heart.

7   Nevertheless I tell you the truth; It is expedient for you that I go away: for if I go not away, the Comforter will not come unto you; but if I depart, I will send him unto you.

8   And when he is come, he will reprove the world of sin, and of righteousness, and of judgment:

9   Of sin, because they believe not on me;

10 Of righteousness, be-cause I go to ~~my~~[3] Father, and ye see me no more;

11 Of judgment, because the prince of this world is judged.

12 I have yet many things to say unto you, but ye cannot bear them now.

13 Howbeit when he, the Spirit of truth, is come, he will guide you into all truth: for he shall not speak of himself; but ~~whatso~~ever[4] **he shall hear**[5], *that* shall he speak: and he will shew you things to come.

14 He shall glorify me: for he shall receive of mine, and shall shew *it* unto you.

15 All things that the Father hath are mine: therefore said I, that **he shall take**[6] of mine, and shall shew *it* unto you.

16 A little while, and ye

---

[3] WH omitted <u>of me</u> (<u>mou</u>) from <u>the father</u> of me.
[4] WH omitted <u>ever</u> (<u>an</u>) from **whatso**<u>ever</u> (**<u>osa</u>** <u>an</u>).
[5] WH changed <u>he **might** hear</u> (<u>akousA</u>) to *he will hear* (*ak-ousei*). <u>**Aor**</u> Act <u>**Sub**</u> to *Fut* Act *Ind*. [tense & mood]
[6] WH changed <u>he **shall** take</u> (<u>lABetai</u>) to *he takes* (*lam-banei*). **Fut** Mid-D Ind to *Pres* Act Ind. [tense]

---

[1] WH omitted <u>unto you</u>[p] (<u>[h]umin</u>).
[2] WH added *of them* (*autOn*).

shall **not**[1] see me: and again, a little while, and ye shall see me, ~~because I go to the Father~~[2].

17 Then said *some* of his disciples among themselves, What is this that he saith unto us, A little while, and ye shall not see me: and again, a little while, and ye shall see me: and, Because [~~myself~~][3] I go to the Father?

18 They said therefore, What is **this**[4] that he saith, A little while? we cannot tell what he saith.

19 ~~Now~~ [**the**][5] Jesus knew that they were desirous to ask him, and said unto them, Do ye enquire among yourselves of that I said, A little while, and ye shall not see me: and again, a little while, and ye shall see me?

20 Verily, verily, I say unto you, That ye shall weep and lament, ~~but~~[6] the world shall rejoice: and ye shall be sorrowful, but your sorrow shall be turned into joy.

21 A woman when she is in travail hath sorrow, because her hour is come: but as soon as she is delivered of the child, she remembereth no more the anguish, for joy that a man is born into the world.

22 And ye **now** therefore [**indeed**] have **sorrow**:[7] but I will see you again, and your heart shall rejoice, and your joy no man taketh from you.

23 And in that day ye shall ask me nothing. Verily, verily, I say unto you, [**that**][8] **Whatsoever**[9] ye shall ask the Father **in my name**[10], he will give *it* you.

24 Hitherto have ye asked nothing in my name: ask, and

---

[1] WH changed **not** (<u>ou</u>) to *no longer* (*ou**keti***).

[2] WH omitted <u>because</u> <u>myself</u> <u>I go</u> <u>to the Father</u> (^hoti <u>egO</u> ^hupagO <u>pros</u> <u>ton</u> <u>patera</u>).

[3] WH omitted the untranslated <u>myself</u> (<u>egO</u>).

[4] WH changed the word order from <u>THIS</u> <u>what</u> <u>is</u> to *what is THIS*.

[5] WH omitted <u>now</u> & the untranslated <u>the</u> (<u>oun</u> ^h<u>o</u>).

[6] WH omitted <u>but</u> (<u>de</u>).

[7] WH changed the word order from <u>sorrow</u> <u>indeed</u> <u>now</u> to *now indeed sorrow*.

[8] WH omitted the untranslated <u>that</u> (^h<u>oti</u>).

[9] WH changed <u>whatso</u> (^h**osa**) to *what* (*ti*) and put <u>ever</u> (<u>an</u>) last.

[10] WH changed the word order from <u>IN</u> <u>THE</u> <u>NAME</u> <u>OF ME</u> <u>he will give</u> <u>you</u> to *he will give you IN THE NAME OF ME.*

ye shall receive, that your joy may be full.

25 These things have I spoken unto you in proverbs: but the time cometh, when I shall no more speak unto you in proverbs, but **I shall shew** you **plainly**[1] of the Father.

26 At that day ye shall ask in my name: and I say not unto you, that I will pray the Father for you:

27 For the Father himself loveth you, because ye have loved me, and have believed that I came out from **God**[2].

28 I came forth **from**[3] the Father, and am come into the world: again, I leave the world, and go to the Father.

29 His disciples said ~~unto him~~[4], Lo, now speakest thou plainly, and speakest no proverb.

30 Now are we sure that thou knowest all things, and needest not that any man should ask thee: by this we believe that thou camest forth from God.

31 Jesus answered them, Do ye now believe?

32 Behold, the hour cometh, yea, is ~~now~~[5] come, that ye shall be scattered, every man to his own, and shall leave me alone: and yet I am not alone, because the Father is with me.

33 These things I have spoken unto you, that in me ye might have peace. In the world **ye shall have**[6] tribulation: but be of good cheer; I have overcome the world.

CHAPTER 17

1 These words spake Jesus, and **lifted up**[7] his eyes to heaven, ~~and~~[8] said, Father, the hour is come; glorify ~~thy~~[9]

---

[1] WH changed I shall show plainly (**anaggelO**) to *I shall show plainly* (*apaggelO*). Both Fut Act Ind. [prefix changed]

[2] WH changed {the} **God** (tou ~~theou~~) to {the} *father* (*tou patros*).

[3] WH changed **from** (**para**) to *out of* (*ek*).

[4] WH omitted unto him (autO).

[5] WH omitted now (nun).

[6] WH changed ye **shall** have (exete) to *ye are having* (*ecete*). **Fut** Act Ind to *Pres* Act Ind. [tense]

[7] WH changed lifted up (epAre) to *having lifted up* (*eparas*). Aor Act **Ind** to Aor Act *Part*. [mood]

[8] WH omitted and (kai).

[9] WH omitted of thee [you^s] (sou) from the son of thee.

Son, that thy Son ~~also~~[1] may glorify thee:

2　As thou hast given him power over all flesh, that he should give eternal life to as many as thou hast given him.

3　And this is life eternal, that they might know thee the only true God, and Jesus Christ, whom thou hast sent.

4　I have glorified thee on the earth: **I have finished**[2] the work which thou gavest me to do.

5　And now, O Father, glorify thou me with thine own self with the glory which I had with thee before the world was.

6　I have manifested thy name unto the men which **thou gavest**[3] me out of the world: thine they were, and **thou gavest**[4] them me; and they have kept thy word.

7　Now they have known that all things whatsoever thou hast given me are of thee.

8　For I have given unto them the words which **thou gavest**[5] me; and they have received *them*, and have known surely that I came out from thee, and they have believed that thou didst send me.

9　I pray for them: I pray not for the world, but for them which thou hast given me; for they are thine.

10　And all mine are thine, and thine are mine; and I am glorified in them.

11　And now I am no more in the world, but these are in the world, and I come to thee. Holy Father, keep through thine own name those **whom**[6] thou hast given me, that they may be one, as we *are*.

12　While I was with them ~~in the world~~[7], I kept them in

---

[1] WH omitted <u>also</u> (<u>kai</u>).

[2] WH changed **I finished** (*eteleiOsa*) to *having finished* (*teleiOsas*). Aor Act **Ind** to Aor Act *Part*. [mood]

[3] WH changed <u>you</u>ˢ **have given** (<u>dedOkas</u>) to *you*ˢ *gave* (*edOkas*). **Pf** Act Ind to *Aor* Act Ind. [tense]

[4] WH changed <u>you</u>ˢ **have given** (<u>dedOkas</u>) to *you*ˢ *gave* (*edOkas*). **Pf** Act Ind to *Aor* Act Ind. [tense]

[5] WH changed <u>you</u>ˢ **have given** (<u>dedOkas</u>) to *you*ˢ *gave* (*edOkas*). **Pf** Act Ind to *Aor* Act Ind. [tense]

[6] WH changed **whom** (**ous**) to *which* (*O*). **Acc Masc Plur** to *Dat Neut Sing*. [case, gender, & number]

[7] WH omitted <u>in the world</u> (<u>en</u> <u>tO</u> <u>kosmO</u>).

thy name: those **that**[1] thou gavest me [∧**also**][2] I have kept, and none of them is lost, but the son of perdition; that the scripture might be fulfilled.

13 And now come I to thee; and these things I speak in the world, that they might have my joy fulfilled in **themselves**[3].

14 I have given them thy word; and the world hath hated them, because they are not of the world, even as I am not of the world.

15 I pray not that thou shouldest take them out of the world, but that thou shouldest keep them from the evil.

16 They are not of the world, even as I am not of the world.

17 Sanctify them through ~~thy~~[4] truth: thy word is truth.

18 As thou hast sent me into the world, even so have I also sent them into the world.

19 And for their sakes I sanctify myself, that they also **might be**[5] sanctified through the truth.

20 Neither pray I for these alone, but for them also which **shall believe**[6] on me through their word;

21 That they all may be one; as thou, Father, *art* in me, and I in thee, that they also may be ~~one~~[7] in us: that the world may believe that thou hast sent me.

22 And the glory which thou gavest me I have given them; that they may be one, even as we ~~are~~[8] one:

23 I in them, and thou in me, that they may be made perfect in one; ~~and~~[9] that the world may know that thou hast sent me, and hast loved them, as thou hast loved me.

24 Father, I will that they also, **whom**[10] thou hast given me, be with me where I am;

---

[1] WH changed that (ous) to *that* (*O*). **Acc Masc Plur** to *Dat Neut Sing*. [case, gender, & number]

[2] WH added also (kai).

[3] WH changed themselves (autois) to *themselves* (*eautois*).

[4] WH omitted of thee [you^s] (sou) from *the truth of thee*.

[5] WH changed the word order from also they MIGHT BE to *MIGHT BE also they*.

[6] WH changed **shall** believe (pisteusontOn) to *is believing* (*pisteuontOn*). **Fut** Act Part to *Pres* Act Part. [tense]

[7] WH omitted one (^{h}en).

[8] WH omitted are (esmen).

[9] WH omitted and (kai).

[10] WH changed **whom** (**ous**) to *which* (^{h}*o*)

that they may behold my glory, which **thou hast given**[1] me: for thou lovedst me before the foundation of the world.

25 O righteous Father, the world hath not known thee: but I have known thee, and these have known that thou hast sent me.

26 And I have declared unto them thy name, and will declare *it*: that the love wherewith thou hast loved me may be in them, and I in them.

CHAPTER 18

1 When Jesus had spoken these words, he went forth with his disciples over the brook Cedron, where was a garden, into the which he entered, and his disciples.

2 And Judas also, which betrayed him, knew the place: for Jesus ofttimes resorted thither with his disciples.

3 Judas then, having received a band *of men* and officers from the chief priests and [∧**the**][2] Pharisees,

cometh thither with lanterns and torches and weapons.

4 Jesus therefore, knowing all things that should come upon him, **went forth**[3], ∧**and**[4] **said**[5] unto them, Whom seek ye?

5 They answered him, Jesus of Nazareth. Jesus saith unto them, I am *he*. And Judas also, which betrayed him, stood with them.

6 As soon then as he had said unto them, [**that**][6] I am *he*, they went backward, and fell to the ground.

7 Then asked he them again, Whom seek ye? And they said, Jesus of Nazareth.

8 Jesus answered, I have told you that I am *he*: if therefore ye seek me, let these go their way:

9 That the saying might be fulfilled, which he spake, Of them which thou gavest me have I lost none.

---

[1] WH changed you[s] gave (*edOkas*) to *you[s] have given* (*dedOkas*). **Aor** Act Ind to *Pf* Act Ind. [tense]

[2] WH added *the* (*tOn*).

[3] WH changed **having gone forth** (*exelthOn*) to *went forth* (*exelthe*). Aor Act **Part** to Aor Act *Ind*. [mood]

[4] WH added and (*kai*) where the KJV supplied it.

[5] WH changed said (**eipen**) to *says* (*legai*). **Aor** Act Ind to *Pres* Act Ind. [tense]

[6] WH omitted the untranslated that ([h]*oti*).

10 Then Simon Peter having a sword drew it, and smote the high priest's servant, and cut off his right **ear**[1]. The servant's name was Malchus.

11 Then said Jesus unto Peter, Put up ~~thy~~[2] sword into the sheath: the cup which my Father hath given me, shall I not drink it?

12 Then the band and the captain and officers of the Jews took Jesus, and bound him,

13 And **led** ~~him~~[3] **away**[4] to Annas first; for he was father in law to Caiaphas, which was the high priest that same year.

14 Now Caiaphas was he, which gave counsel to the Jews, that it was expedient that one man **should die**[5] for

the people.

15 And Simon Peter followed Jesus, and *so did* another disciple: that disciple was known unto the high priest, and went in with Jesus into the palace of the high priest.

16 But Peter stood at the door without. Then went out that other disciple, which was known unto the high priest, and spake unto her that kept the door, and brought in Peter.

17 Then saith the damsel that kept the door unto Peter, Art not thou also *one* of this man's disciples? He saith, I am not.

18 And the servants and officers stood there, who had made a fire of coals; for it was cold: and they warmed themselves: **and**[6] Peter stood **with them**,[7] and warmed himself.

19 The high priest then asked Jesus of his disciples, and of his doctrine.

20 Jesus answered him, **I**

---

[1] WH changed <u>ear</u> (<u>Otion</u>) to *ear* (*Otarion*). [**normal** form to **diminutive** form]

[2] WH omitted <u>of thee</u> [you^s] (<u>sou</u>) from <u>the sword of thee</u>.

[3] WH omitted <u>him</u> (<u>auton</u>).

[4] WH <u>led **away** (**ap**Agagon)</u> to *led* (*Agagon*). [prefix dropped]

[5] WH changed <u>to die</u> {**for himself**} (<u>apo**les**thai</u>) to *to die* (*apo**tha**nein*). Aor **Mid** Inf <u>ap**pollumi**</u> to Aor *Act* Inf of *apo**thn**AskO*. [voice &

syn]

[6] WH changed <u>and</u> (**de**) to *and* (**kai**).

[7] WH changed the word order from <u>and</u> WITH THEM <u>the Peter</u> to *and the Peter* WITH THEM.

spake[1] openly to the world; I ever taught in the synagogue, and in the temple, whither **the**[2] Jews **always**[3] resort; and in secret have I said nothing.

21 Why **askest thou**[4] me? **ask**[5] them which heard me, what I have said unto them: behold, they know what I said.

22 And when he had thus spoken, one of the officers which stood by struck Jesus with the palm of his hand, saying, Answerest thou the high priest so?

23 Jesus answered him, If I have spoken evil, bear witness of the evil: but if well, why smitest thou me?

24 Now Annas had sent him bound unto Caiaphas the high priest.

25 And Simon Peter stood and warmed himself. They said therefore unto him, Art not thou also *one* of his disciples? He denied *it*, and said, I am not.

26 One of the servants of the high priest, being *his* kinsman whose ear Peter cut off, saith, Did not I see thee in the garden with him?

27 Peter then denied again: and immediately the cock crew.

28 Then led they Jesus from Caiaphas unto the hall of judgment: and it was early; and they themselves went not into the judgment hall, lest they should be defiled; **but**[6] **that**[7] they might eat the passover.

29 Pilate then went out [∧**outside**][8] unto them, and **said**[9], What accusation bring ye against this man?

30 They answered and said unto him, If he were not a malefactor, we would not have delivered him up unto

---

[1] WH changed I spoke (ela-lAsa) to *I have spoken (lela-lAka)*. **Aor** Act Ind to *Pf* Act Ind. [tense]

[2] WH omitted the (tA).

[3] WH changed always (pantote) to *all (pantes)*.

[4] WH changed askest thou {**upon**} (**eper**Otas) to *askest thou (erOtas)*. Both Pres Act Ind [prefix dropped]

[5] WH changed ask (**eper**O-tAson) {**upon**} to *ask (erO-tAson)*. Both Aor Act Imp. [prefix dropped]

[6] WH changed but (all') to *but (alla)*. **Contraction** to *Full* spell. [spell]

[7] WH omitted that (hina).

[8] WH added *outside (exO)*.

[9] WH changed said (eipe) to *says (fAsi)*. **Aor** Act Ind to *Pres* NV Ind. [tense & syn]

thee.

31 Then said Pilate unto them, Take ye him, and judge him according to your law. The Jews ~~therefore~~[1] said unto him, It is not lawful for us to put any man to death:

32 That the saying of Jesus might be fulfilled, which he spake, signifying what death he should die.

33 Then Pilate entered into the judgment hall **again**[2], and called Jesus, and said unto him, Art thou the King of the Jews?

34 [~~the~~][3] Jesus answered ~~him~~[4], Sayest thou this thing of thyself, or did others tell it thee of me?

35 Pilate answered, Am I a Jew? Thine own nation and the chief priests have delivered thee unto me: what hast thou done?

36 Jesus answered, My kingdom is not of this world: if my kingdom were of this world, then would my servants fight, that I should not be delivered to the Jews: but now is my kingdom not from hence.

37 Pilate therefore said unto him, Art thou a king then? Jesus answered, Thou sayest that I am a king. To this end was I born, and for this cause came I into the world, that I should bear witness unto the truth. Every one that is of the truth heareth my voice.

38 Pilate saith unto him, What is truth? And when he had said this, he went out again unto the Jews, and saith unto them, I find in him no fault *at all*.

39 But ye have a custom, that I should release unto you one at the passover: will ye therefore that I release unto you the King of the Jews?

40 Then cried they ~~all~~[5] again, saying, Not this man, but Barabbas. Now Barabbas was a robber.

CHAPTER 19

1 Then Pilate therefore took Jesus, and scourged *him*.

2 And the soldiers platted a crown of thorns, and put *it*

---

[1] WH omitted therefore (oun).

[2] WH changed the word order from into the judgment hall AGAIN to *AGAIN into the judgment hall*.

[3] WH omitted the untranslated the (^{h}o).

[4] WH omitted him (autO).

[5] WH omitted all (pantes).

on his head, and they put on him a purple robe [ʌ**and went to him**]¹,

3   And said, Hail, King of the Jews! and they smote him with their hands.

4   [ʌ**then**]² Pilate ~~therefore³~~ went forth again, and saith unto them, Behold, I bring him forth to you, that ye may know that I find no fault in him.

5   Then came Jesus forth, wearing the crown of thorns, and the purple robe. And *Pilate* saith unto them, Behold the man!

6   When the chief priests therefore and officers saw him, they cried out, saying, Crucify *him*, crucify *him*. Pilate saith unto them, Take ye him, and crucify *him*: for I find no fault in him.

7   The Jews answered him, We have a law, and by ~~our⁴~~ law he ought to die, because he made himself the Son of God.

8   When Pilate therefore heard that saying, he was the more afraid;

9   And went again into the judgment hall, and saith unto Jesus, Whence art thou? But Jesus gave him no answer.

10   Then saith Pilate unto him, Speakest thou not unto me? knowest thou not that I have power **to crucify** thee, and have power **to release**⁵ thee?

11   Jesus answered, Thou couldest have no power *at all* against me, except it were given thee from above: therefore he that **delivered**⁶ me unto thee hath the greater sin.

12   And from thenceforth Pilate sought to release him: but the Jews cried out, saying, If thou let this man go, thou art not Caesar's friend: whosoever maketh **himself**⁷ a

---

¹ WH added *and went to him* (*kai Akrconto pros auton*-- literally "and were going to him").
² WH added *then* (*kai*).
³ WH omitted therefore (oun).
⁴ WH omitted of us (ʰAmOn) from the law of us.

⁵ WH changed the word order from TO CRUCIFY thee and power I have TO RELEASE thee to *TO RELEASE thee and power I have TO CRUCIFY thee.*
⁶ WH changed delivering (paradidous) to *having delivered* (paradous). **Pres** Act Part to *Aor* Act Part. [tense]
⁷ WH changed himself (auton) to himself (*eauton*).

king speaketh against Caesar.

13 When Pilate therefore heard **that saying**[1], he brought Jesus forth, and sat down in ~~the~~[2] judgment seat in a place that is called the Pavement, but in the Hebrew, Gabbatha.

14 And it was the preparation of the passover, **and about**[3] the sixth hour: and he saith unto the Jews, Behold your King!

15 **But they cried out**[4], Away with *him*, away with *him*, crucify him. Pilate saith unto them, Shall I crucify your King? The chief priests answered, We have no king but Caesar.

16 Then delivered he him therefore unto them to be crucified. **And**[5] they took Je-sus, ~~**and led *him* away**~~[6].

17 And he bearing **his cross**[7] went forth into a place called *the place* of a skull, **which**[8] is called in the Hebrew Golgotha:

18 Where they crucified him, and two other with him, on either side one, and Jesus in the midst.

19 And Pilate wrote a title, and put *it* on the cross. And the writing was, JESUS OF NAZARETH THE KING OF THE JEWS.

20 This title then read many of the Jews: for the place where Jesus was crucified was nigh to **the city**[9]: and it was written in Hebrew, *and* Greek, *and* **Latin**[10].

21 Then said the chief priests of the Jews to Pilate, Write not, The King of the

---

[1] WH changed that saying (touton ton logon) to *that saying* (toutOn tOn logOn). [case]

[2] WH omitted the (tou).

[3] WH changed **and about** (de ^hOsei) to *it was like* (*An ^hOs*).

[4] WH changed **but they** (de oi) to *therefore these* (*oun ekeinoi*). They also put the verb first.

[5] WH changed **and** (de) to *therefore* (*oun*).

[6] WH omitted and led away (kai apAgagon).

[7] WH changed of him (autou) in the cross of him to *of himself* (*eautou*) and put it before the cross.

[8] WH changed which (^hos) to *the* {one} (^ho).

[9] WH changed the word order from THE CITY the place to *the place THE CITY.*

[10] WH changed the word order from Greek LATIN to *LATIN Greek.*

Jews; but that he said, I am King of the Jews.

22 Pilate answered, What I have written I have written.

23 Then the soldiers, when they had crucified Jesus, took his garments, and made four parts, to every soldier a part; and also *his* coat: now the coat was without seam, woven from the top throughout.

24 They said therefore among themselves, Let us not rend it, but cast lots for it, whose it shall be: that the scripture might be fulfilled, which saith, They parted my raiment among them, and for my vesture they did cast lots. These things therefore the soldiers did.

25 Now there stood by the cross of Jesus his mother, and his mother's sister, Mary the *wife* of Cleophas, and Mary Magdalene.

26 When Jesus therefore saw his mother, and the disciple standing by, whom he loved, he saith unto ~~his~~[1] mother, Woman, behold thy son!

27 Then saith he to the disciple, Behold thy mother! And from that hour that dis-

ciple took her unto his own *home*.

28 After this, Jesus knowing that all things were now accomplished, that the scripture might be fulfilled, saith, I thirst.

29 ~~Now~~[2] there was set a vessel full of vinegar: **and**[3] **they filled**[4] **a spunge**[5] with [ᴧ**the**][6] vinegar, ~~and~~[7] put *it* upon hyssop, and put *it* to his mouth.

30 When Jesus therefore had received the vinegar, he said, It is finished: and he bowed his head, and gave up the ghost.

31 The Jews therefore, because it was the preparation, that the bodies should not remain upon the cross on the sabbath day, (for that sabbath day was an high day,) besought Pilate that their legs might be broken, and *that*

---

[1] WH omitted <u>of him</u> (<u>autou</u>) from <u>the mother of him</u>.

[2] WH omitted <u>now</u> (<u>oun</u>).

[3] WH changed **and** (**de**) to *therefore* (*oun*).

[4] WH changed **they filled** (^h**oi plAsantes**) to *full* (*meston*).

[5] WH changed the word order from **and they filled** A SPONGE with vinegar **and** to A *SPONGE* ***therefore full*** with *the* vinegar.

[6] WH added *the* (*tou*);

[7] WH omitted <u>and</u> (<u>kai</u>).

they might be taken away.

32 Then came the soldiers, and brake the legs of the first, and of the other which was crucified with him.

33 But when they came to Jesus, and saw that he was dead already, they brake not his legs:

34 But one of the soldiers with a spear pierced his side, and **forthwith**[1] came there out blood and water.

35 And he that saw *it* bare record, and his record is true: and he knoweth that he saith true, that [**ʌalso**][2] ye might believe.

36 For these things were done, that the scripture should be fulfilled, A bone of him shall not be broken.

37 And again another scripture saith, They shall look on him whom they pierced.

38 And after this Joseph of Arimathaea, being a disciple of Jesus, but secretly for fear of the Jews, besought Pilate that he might take away the body of Jesus: and Pilate gave *him* leave. He came

therefore, and took the body **of Jesus**[3].

39 And there came also Nicodemus, which at the first came to **Jesus**[4] by night, and brought a mixture of myrrh and aloes, **about**[5] an hundred pound *weight*.

40 Then took they the body of Jesus, and wound it in linen clothes with the spices, as the manner of the Jews is to bury.

41 Now in the place where he was crucified there was a garden; and in the garden a new sepulchre, wherein was never man yet laid.

42 There laid they Jesus therefore because of the Jews' preparation *day*; for the sepulchre was nigh at hand.

CHAPTER 20

1 The first *day* of the week cometh Mary Magdalene early, when it was yet dark, unto the sepulchre, and seeth the stone taken away from the sepulchre.

---

[1] WH changed the word order from FORTHWITH came there out to *came there out* FORTHWITH.

[2] WH added *also* (*kai*).

[3] WH changed of {**the**} **Jesus** (**tou iAsou**) to *of him* (*autou*).

[4] WH changed {**the**} **Jesus** to *him* (*auton*).

[5] WH changed *about* ([h]**Osei**) to *like* ([h]*Os*).

2   Then she runneth, and cometh to Simon Peter, and to the other disciple, whom Jesus loved, and saith unto them, They have taken away the Lord out of the sepulchre, and we know not where they have laid him.

3   Peter therefore went forth, and that other disciple, and came to the sepulchre.

4   So they ran both together: and the other disciple did outrun Peter, and came first to the sepulchre.

5   And he stooping down, *and looking in*, saw the linen clothes lying; yet went he not in.

6   Then cometh [∧**also**]¹ Simon Peter following him, and went into the sepulchre, and seeth the linen clothes lie,

7   And the napkin, that was about his head, not lying with the linen clothes, but wrapped together in a place by itself.

8   Then went in also that other disciple, which came first to the sepulchre, and he saw, and believed.

9   For as yet they knew not the scripture, that he must rise again from the dead.

10   Then the disciples went away again unto their own home.

11   But Mary stood without at **the sepulchre**² **weeping**³: and as she wept, she stooped down, *and looked* into the sepulchre,

12   And seeth two angels in white sitting, the one at the head, and the other at the feet, where the body of Jesus had lain.

13   And they say unto her, Woman, why weepest thou? She saith unto them, Because they have taken away my Lord, and I know not where they have laid him.

14   ~~**And**~~⁴ when she had thus said, she turned herself back, and saw Jesus standing, and knew not that it was Jesus.

15   Jesus saith unto her, Woman, why weepest thou? whom seekest thou? She, supposing him to be the gardener, saith unto him, Sir, if thou have borne him hence, tell me where thou hast laid

---

¹ WH added *also* (*kai*).

² WH changed <u>the</u> <u>sepulchre</u> (<u>**to** mnAmeion</u>) to *the sepulchre* (*tO mnAmeiO*). **Acc** to ***Dat***. [case]

³ WH changed the word order from <u>WEEPING</u> <u>without</u> to *without WEEPING*.

⁴ WH omitted <u>and</u> (<u>kai</u>).

him, and I will take him away.

16 Jesus saith unto her, Mary. She turned herself, and saith unto him [∧**in He-brew**][1], Rabboni; which is to say, Master.

17 Jesus saith unto her, Touch me not; for I am not yet ascended to ~~my~~[2] Father: but go to my brethren, and say unto them, I ascend unto my Father, and your Father; and *to* my God, and your God.

18 Mary Magdalene came and **told**[3] the disciples that **she had seen**[4] the Lord, and *that* he had spoken these things unto her.

19 Then the same day at evening, being the first *day* of **the**[5] week, when the doors were shut where the disciples were ~~**assembled**~~[6] for fear of the Jews, came Jesus and stood in the midst, and saith unto them, Peace *be* unto you.

20 And when he had so said, he shewed **unto them**[7] *his* hands and ~~**his**~~[8] side. Then were the disciples glad, when they saw the Lord.

21 Then said Jesus to them again, Peace *be* unto you: as *my* Father hath sent me, even so send I you.

22 And when he had said this, he breathed on *them*, and saith unto them, Receive ye the Holy Ghost:

23 Whose soever sins ye remit, they are remitted unto them; *and* whose soever *sins* ye retain, they are retained.

24 But Thomas, one of the twelve, called Didymus, was not with them when Jesus came.

25 The other disciples therefore said unto him, We have seen the Lord. But he

---

[1] WH added *in Hebrew* (*[h]Abraisti*).

[2] WH omitted <u>of me</u> (<u>mou</u>) from <u>the father</u> <u>of me</u>.

[3] WH changed <u>told</u> {**from**} (**ap**<u>agellousa</u>) to *told* (*aggel-lousa*). [prefix dropped]

[4] WH changed **she** <u>has seen</u> (*[h]eOrak**e***) to *I have seen* (*[h]eOrak**a***). Pf Act Ind **3** Sing to Pf Act Ind **1** Sing. [number]

[5] WH omitted <u>the</u> (<u>tOn</u>).

---

[6] WH omitted <u>assembled</u> (<u>su-nAgmenoi</u>).

[7] WH changed the word or-der from UNTO THEM <u>the hands</u> <u>and</u> <u>the side</u> **of him** to *the hands and the side* UNTO THEM.

[8] WH omitted <u>of him</u> (<u>autou</u>) from <u>the</u> <u>side</u> <u>of him</u>.

said unto them, Except I shall see in his hands the print of the nails, and put my finger into the print of the nails, and thrust my hand into his side, I will not believe.

26 And after eight days again his **disciples** were within, and **Thomas** with them: *then* came Jesus, the doors being shut, and stood in the midst, and said, Peace *be* unto you.

27 Then saith he to Thomas, Reach hither thy finger, and behold my hands; and reach hither thy hand, and thrust *it* into my side: and be not faithless, but believing.

28 ~~And~~[1] Thomas answered and said unto him, My Lord and my God.

29 Jesus saith unto him, ~~Thomas~~[2], because thou hast seen me, thou hast believed: blessed *are* they that have not seen, and *yet* have believed.

30 And many other signs truly did Jesus in the presence of ~~his~~[3] disciples, which are not written in this book:

31 But these are written, that ye might believe that Jesus is the Christ, the Son of God; and that believing ye might have life through his name.

CHAPTER 21

1 After these things Jesus shewed himself again to the disciples at the sea of Tiberias; and on this wise shewed he *himself.*

2 There were together Simon Peter, and Thomas called Didymus, and Nathanael of Cana in Galilee, and the *sons* of Zebedee, and two other of his disciples.

3 Simon Peter saith unto them, I go a fishing. They say unto him, We also go with thee. They went forth, and **entered**[4] into a ship ~~immediately~~[5]; and that night they caught nothing.

4 But **when** the morning was now **come**[6], Jesus stood on the shore: but the disciples

---

[1] WH omitted <u>and</u> (<u>kai</u>).
[2] WH omitted <u>Thomas</u> (<u>th</u>Oma).
[3] WH omitted <u>of him</u> (<u>autou</u>) from <u>the</u> <u>disciples</u> <u>of him</u>.

[4] WH changed <u>entered</u> (<u>ane</u>bAsan) to *entered* (*ene*basan). Aor Act Ind of <u>ana</u>bainO to Aor Act Ind of *em*bainO. [prefix changed]
[5] WH omitted <u>immediately</u> (<u>eut</u>hus).
[6] WH changed <u>having come</u> (<u>genomen</u>As) to *having come* (*ginomen*As). Both Aor Mid-D Part. **Common** to *Rare*. [spell]

knew not that it was Jesus.

5   Then Jesus saith unto them, Children, have ye any meat? They answered him, No.

6   And he said unto them, Cast the net on the right side of the ship, and ye shall find. They cast therefore, and now **they were** not **able**[1] to draw it for the multitude of fishes.

7   Therefore that disciple whom Jesus loved saith unto Peter, It is the Lord. Now when Simon Peter heard that it was the Lord, he girt *his* fisher's coat *unto him,* (for he was naked,) and did cast himself into the sea.

8   And the other disciples came in a little ship; (for they were not far from land, but as it were two hundred cubits,) dragging the net with fishes.

9   As soon then as they were come to land, they saw a fire of coals there, and fish laid thereon, and bread.

10   Jesus saith unto them, Bring of the fish which ye have now caught.

11   [∧**therefore**][2]   Simon Peter went up, and drew the net **to land**[3] full of great fishes, an hundred and fifty and three: and for all there were so many, yet was not the net broken.

12   Jesus saith unto them, Come *and* dine. And none of the disciples durst ask him, Who art thou? knowing that it was the Lord.

13   [**the**][4]   Jesus   **then**[5] cometh, and taketh bread, and giveth them, and fish likewise.

14   This is now the third time that Jesus shewed himself to **his**[6] disciples, after that he was risen from the dead.

15   So   when   they   had dined, Jesus saith to Simon Peter, Simon, *son* **of Jonas**[7], lovest thou me more than these? He saith unto him, Yea, Lord; thou knowest that I love thee. He saith unto

---

[1] WH changed they were able (iscusan) to they were **being** *able* (iscuon). **Aor** Act Ind to *Impf* Act Ind. [tense]

[2] WH added *therefore* (oun).

[3] WH changed **upon** the land (**epi** tAs gAs) to *into the land* (*eis tAn gAn*). [prep & case]

[4] WH omitted the untranslated the ([h]o).

[5] WH omitted then (oun).

[6] WH omitted of him (autou) from the disciples of him.

[7] WH changed {of} Jonas (iOna) to *of Jonas* (*iOnou*). [case]

him, Feed my lambs.

16 He saith to him again the second time, Simon, *son* **of Jonas**[1], lovest thou me? He saith unto him, Yea, Lord; thou knowest that I love thee. He saith unto him, Feed my sheep.

17 He saith unto him the third time, Simon, *son* **of Jonas**[2], lovest thou me? Peter was grieved because he said unto him the third time, lovest thou me? And he said unto him, Lord, thou [**thyself**][3] knowest all things; thou knowest that I love thee. Jesus saith unto him, Feed my **sheep**[4].

18 Verily, verily, I say unto thee, When thou wast young, thou girdedst thyself, and walkedst whither thou wouldest: but when thou shalt be old, thou shalt stretch forth thy hands, and another shall gird thee, and carry *thee* whither thou wouldest not.

19 This spake he, signifying by what death he should glorify God. And when he had spoken this, he saith unto him, Follow me.

20 ~~**Then**~~[5] Peter, turning about, seeth the disciple whom Jesus loved following; which also leaned on his breast at supper, and said, Lord, which is he that betrayeth thee?

21 Peter seeing him saith to Jesus, Lord, and what *shall* this man *do*?

22 Jesus saith unto him, If I will that he tarry till I come, what *is that* to thee? follow thou me.

23 Then went this saying abroad among the brethren, that that disciple should not die: yet Jesus said not unto him, He shall not die; but, If I will that he tarry till I come, what *is that* to thee?

24 This is the disciple which testifieth of these things, and wrote these things: and we know that his testimony is true.

25 And there are also

---

[1] WH changed {of} Jonas (*iOna*) to *of Jonas* (*iOnou*). [case]

[2] WH changed {of} Jonas (*iOna*) to *of Jonas* (*iOnou*). [case]

[3] WH changed the word order from THYSELF all {things} to *all* {things} THYSELF

[4] WH changed sheep (probata) to *sheep* (*probatia*). [from common to rare form]

[5] WH omitted then (de).

many other things **which**[1] Jesus did, the which, if they
should be written every one, I
suppose that even the world
itself **could** not **contain**[2] the
books that should be written.
~~**Amen**~~[3].

---

[1] WH changed the <u>which</u>
(^h<u>**osa**</u>--**as great as**) to *which*
(^h*a*).
[2] WH changed **could** contain
(<u>cOrAsai</u>) to *will contain*
(*cOrAsein*). **2 Aor** Act Inf to
Fut Act Inf. [tense]
[3] WH omitted <u>Amen</u> (<u>amAn</u>).

ACTS

CHAPTER 1

1 The former treatise have I made, O Theophilus, of all that Jesus began both to do and teach,

2 Until the day in which he was taken up, after that he through the Holy Ghost had given commandments unto the apostles whom he had chosen:

3 To whom also he shewed himself alive after his passion by many infallible proofs, being seen of them forty days, and speaking of the things pertaining to the kingdom of God:

4 And, being assembled together with them[1], commanded them that they should not depart from Jerusalem, but wait for the promise of the Father, which, *saith he*, ye have heard of me.

5 For John truly baptized with water; but ye shall be baptized with the Holy Ghost not many days hence.

6 When they therefore were come together, they asked of him, saying, Lord, wilt thou at this time restore

again the kingdom to Israel?

7 And he said unto them, It is not for you to know the times or the seasons, which the Father hath put in his own power.

8 But ye shall receive power, after that the Holy Ghost is come upon you: and ye shall be witnesses **unto me**[2] both in Jerusalem, and in all Judaea, and in Samaria, and unto the uttermost part of the earth.

9 And when he had spoken these things, while they beheld, he was taken up; and a cloud received him out of their sight.

10 And while they looked stedfastly toward heaven as he went up, behold, two men stood by them in **white apparel**[3];

11 Which also said, Ye men of Galilee, why stand ye **gazing up**[4] into heaven? this

---

[1] WH omitted with them (met' autOn).

[2] WH changed **unto** me (moi) to *of me* (*mou*). **Dat** Sing to *Gen* Sing. [case]

[3] WH changed white apparel (esthAti leukA) to *white apparels* (*esthAsesi leukais*). Dat Fem **Sing** to Dat Fem *Plur*. [number]

[4] WH changed gazing **up** (**em**blepontes) to *gazing* (*blepontes*). [prefix dropped]

same Jesus, which is taken up from you into heaven, shall so come in like manner as ye have seen him go into heaven.

12 Then returned they unto Jerusalem from the mount called Olivet, which is from Jerusalem a sabbath day's journey.

13 And when they were come in, **they went up**[1] into an upper room, where abode both Peter, and **James**, and **John**[2], and Andrew, Philip, and Thomas, Bartholomew, and Matthew, James *the son* of Alphaeus, and Simon Zelotes, and Judas *the brother* of James.

14 These all continued with one accord in prayer ~~and sup-plication~~[3], with the women, and Mary the mother of Jesus, and with his brethren.

15 And in those days Peter stood up in the midst of the **disciples**[4], and said, (the number of names together were about an hundred and twenty,)

16 Men *and* brethren, ~~this~~[5] scripture must needs have been fulfilled, which the Holy Ghost by the mouth of David spake before concerning Judas, which was guide to them that took Jesus.

17 For he was numbered **with**[6] us, and had obtained part of this ministry.

18 Now this man pur-chased a field with ~~the~~[7] re-ward of iniquity; and falling headlong, he burst asunder in the midst, and all his bowels gushed out.

19 And it was known unto all the dwellers at Jerusalem; insomuch as that field is called in their ~~proper~~[8] tongue, Aceldama, that is to say, The field of blood.

20 For it is written in the book of Psalms, Let his habi-tation be desolate, and let no man dwell therein: and his bishoprick **let** another **take**[9].

---

[1] WH changed the word or-der from THEY WENT UP into the upper room *to into the upper room THEY WENT UP.*
[2] WH changed the word or-der from JAMES and JOHN to *JOHN and JAMES.*
[3] WH omitted and {the} sup-plication (kai tA deAsei).
[4] WH changed **disciples** (**math**AtOn) to *brethren* (*adelfOn*).

[5] WH omitted this (tautAn).
[6] WH changed **with** (**sun**) to *in* (*en*).
[7] WH omitted the (tou). [8] WH omitted proper (idia).
[9] WH changed **should** take (laboi) to *let take* (*labetO*). Aor Act **Opt** to Aor Act *Imp*. [mood]

21 Wherefore of these men which have companied with us all the time [**in**]¹ that the Lord Jesus went in and out among us,

22 Beginning from the baptism of John, unto that same day that he was taken up from us, must one be ordained **to be**² a witness with us of his resurrection.

23 And they appointed two, Joseph called **Barsabas**³, who was surnamed Justus, and Matthias.

24 And they prayed, and said, Thou, Lord, which knowest the hearts of all *men*, shew **whether** of these two **thou hast chosen**⁴,

25 That he may take **part**⁵

of this ministry and apostleship, **from**⁶ which Judas by transgression fell, that he might go to his own place.

26 And they gave forth **their**⁷ lots; and the lot fell upon Matthias; and he was numbered with the eleven apostles.

CHAPTER 2

1 And when the day of Pentecost was fully come, they were **all**⁸ **with one accord**⁹ in one place.

2 And suddenly there came a sound from heaven as of a rushing mighty wind, and it filled all the house where they were sitting.

---

¹ WH omitted the untranslated in (**en**) before that (ʰ<u>O</u>).
² WH changed the word order from <u>TO BE</u> with <u>us</u> to *with us TO BE.*
³ WH changed <u>Barsabas</u> (*bar-saban*) to *Barsabbas* (*bar-sabban*). [spell]
⁴ WH changed the word order from <u>out of</u> <u>these</u> <u>the</u> <u>two</u> <u>WHICH</u> <u>ONE</u> <u>HAST THOU</u> <u>CHOSEN</u> to *WHICH HAST THOU CHOSEN out of these the two ONE.*
⁵ WH changed **part** (**klAr**on)

to *place* (*top*on).
⁶ WH changed **out** from (**ex**) to *away from* (*ap'*).
⁷ WH changed <u>lots</u> **of** them (<u>klArous</u> aut<u>On</u>) to *lots to them* (*klArous autois*). **Gen** to *Dat*. [case]
⁸ WH changed <u>all</u> (ʰ<u>apantes</u>) to *all* (*pantes*) [prefix dropped]
⁹ WH changed **with one accord** (ʰomo**th**umadon) to *together* (ʰ*omou*) [root dropped]

3 And there appeared unto them cloven tongues like as of fire, **and**[1] it sat upon each of them.

4 And they were **all**[2] filled with the Holy Ghost, and began to speak with other tongues, as the Spirit gave **them**[3] utterance.

5 And there were dwelling at Jerusalem Jews, devout men, out of every nation under heaven.

6 Now when this was noised abroad, the multitude came together, and were confounded, because that every man heard them speak in his own language.

7 And they were all amazed and marvelled, saying ~~one to another~~[4], Behold, are not **all**[5] these which speak Galilaeans?

8 And how hear we every man in our own tongue,

wherein we were born?

9 Parthians, and Medes, and Elamites, and the dwellers in Mesopotamia, and in Judaea, and Cappadocia, in Pontus, and Asia,

10 Phrygia, and Pamphylia, in Egypt, and in the parts of Libya about Cyrene, and strangers of Rome, Jews and proselytes,

11 Cretes and Arabians, we do hear them speak in our tongues the wonderful works of God.

12 And they were all amazed, and **were in doubt**[6], saying one to another, What [**ever**][7] **meaneth**[8] this?

13 Others **mocking**[9] said, These men are full of new wine.

14 But Peter, standing up with the eleven, lifted up his

---

[1] WH changed and (**te**) to and (**kai**). [syn]

[2] WH changed all (ʰ**apantes**) to all (*pantes*). [prefix dropped]

[3] WH changed the word order from THEM utterance to *utterance THEM.*

[4] WH omitted one to another (pros allAlous).

[5] WH changed all (pantes) to all (ʰ*apantes*). [prefix added]

[6] WH changed were in doubt (diAporoun) to *were in doubt* (*diAporounto*). Impf **Act** Ind to Impf *Mid* Ind. [voice]

[7] WH omitted the untranslated ever (an).

[8] WH changed **should** mean (theloi) to *means (thele).* Pres Act **Opt** to Pres Act *Ind.* [mood]

[9] WH changed mocking (cleuazontes) to *mocking* {*thoroughly*} (*dia*cleuazontes). [prefix added]

voice, and said unto them, ye men of Judaea, and **all**[1] *ye* that dwell at Jerusalem, be this known unto you, and hearken to my words:

15 For these are not drunken, as ye suppose, seeing it is *but* the third hour of the day.

16 But this is that which was spoken by the prophet Joel;

17 And it shall come to pass in the last days, saith God, I will pour out of my Spirit upon all flesh: and your sons and your daughters shall prophesy, and your young men shall see visions, and your old men shall dream **dreams**[2]:

18 And on my servants and on my handmaidens I will pour out in those days of my Spirit; and they shall prophesy:

19 And I will shew wonders in heaven above, and signs in the earth beneath; blood, and fire, and vapour of smoke:

20 The sun shall be turned into darkness, and the moon into blood, before [~~even~~][3] that great and notable [~~the~~][4] day of the Lord come:

21 And it shall come to pass, *that* whosoever shall call on the name of the Lord shall be saved.

22 Ye men of Israel, hear these words; Jesus of Nazareth, a man **approved**[5] of God among you by miracles and wonders and signs, which God did by him in the midst of you, as ye yourselves **also**[6] know:

23 Him, being delivered by the determinate counsel and foreknowledge of God, ~~ye have taken~~[7], and by wicked **hands**[8] have crucified and slain:

24 Whom God hath raised up, having loosed the pains of

---

[3] WH omitted the untranslated even (^hA).
[4] WH omitted the untranslated the (tAn).
[5] WH changed the word order from by the God APPROVED to *APPROVED by the God.*
[6] WH omitted also (kai).
[7] WH omitted ye have taken (labontes).
[8] WH changed hands (cei-rOn) to *hand (ceiros).* **Plur** to **Sing.** [number]

---

[1] WH changed all (^hapantes) to *all (pantes).* [prefix dropped]
[2] WH changed dreams (enup-nia) to *dreams (enupniois).* **Acc** to **Dat.** [case]

death: because it was not possible that he should be holden of it.

25 For David speaketh concerning him, I foresaw the Lord always before my face, for he is on my right hand, that I should not be moved:

26 Therefore did my heart rejoice, and my tongue was glad; moreover also my flesh shall rest in hope:

27 Because thou wilt not leave my soul in hell, neither wilt thou suffer thine Holy One to see corruption.

28 Thou hast made known to me the ways of life; thou shalt make me full of joy with thy countenance.

29 Men *and* brethren, let me freely speak unto you of the patriarch David, that he is both dead and buried, and his sepulchre is with us unto this day.

30 Therefore being a prophet, and knowing that God had sworn with an oath to him, that of the fruit of his loins, ~~according to the flesh, he would raise up Christ~~[1] to sit on **his throne**[2];

31 He seeing this before spake of the resurrection of Christ, that ~~his soul~~[3] **was not**[4] **left**[5] in hell, **neither**[6] his flesh did see corruption.

32 This Jesus hath God raised up, whereof we all are witnesses.

33 Therefore being by the right hand of God exalted, and having received of the Father the promise of the Holy Ghost, he hath shed forth this, which ye ~~now~~[7] see and hear.

34 For David is not ascended into the heavens: but he saith himself, The LORD said unto my Lord, Sit thou on my right hand,

35 Until I make thy foes thy footstool.

36 Therefore let all the house of Israel know assuredly, that God hath made

---

(*ton* ~~thronon~~). **Gen** to *Acc.* [case]

[3] WH omitted the soul of him (^hA sucA autou).

[4] WH changed not (ou) to *not even* (*oute*).

[5] WH changed was left (kateleifthA) to *was left* {**out**} (*egkateleifthA*). [prefix added]

[6] WH changed neither (oude) to *neither* (*oute*).

[7] WH omitted now (nun).

---

[1] WH omitted the according to flesh to raise up the Christ (to kata sarka anastAsein ton criston).

[2] WH changed the thrown (tou ~~thronou~~) to *the thrown*

[**him**]¹ that same Jesus, whom ye have crucified, both Lord and Christ.

37 Now when they heard *this*, they were pricked **in their heart**², and said unto Peter and to the rest of the apostles, Men *and* brethren, what **shall we do**³?

38 Then Peter ~~said~~⁴ unto them, Repent, and be baptized every one of you **in**⁵ the name of Jesus Christ for the remission of [ʌ**the**]⁶ sins [ʌ**of you**]⁷, and ye shall receive the gift of the Holy Ghost.

39 For the promise is unto you, and to your children, and to all that are afar off,

even as many as the Lord our God shall call.

40 And with many other words **did he testify**⁸ and exhort [ʌ**them**]⁹, saying, Save yourselves from this untoward generation.

41 Then they that ~~gladly~~¹⁰ received his word were baptized: and [ʌ**in**]¹¹ the same day there were added *unto them* about three thousand souls.

42 And they continued stedfastly in the apostles' doctrine and fellowship, ~~and~~¹² in breaking of bread, and in prayers.

43 And fear **came upon**¹³ every soul: and many wonders and signs were done by the apostles.

---

¹ WH changed the word order from <u>and</u> <u>Christ</u> <u>HIM</u> to *HIM and Christ*.

² WH changed {in} <u>the</u> <u>heart</u> (<u>tA kardia</u>) to {in} *the heart* (*tAn kardian*). **Dat** to *Acc*. [case]

³ WH changed **shall** we do (<u>poiAsomen</u>) to *might we do* (*poiAsOmen*). **Fut** Act **Ind** to *Aor* Act *Sub*. [tense & mood]

⁴ WH omitted <u>said</u> (<u>efA</u>).

⁵ WH changed **upon** (<u>epi</u>) to *in* (*en*).

⁶ WH added *the* (*tOn*) before <u>sins</u>.

⁷ WH added *of you*ᵖ (*ʰumOn*) after <u>sins</u>.

⁸ WH changed <u>he</u> **was** <u>testifying</u> (<u>diemartureo</u>) to *he testified* (*diemarturato*). **Impf** M/P-D Ind to *Aor* Mid Ind. [tense]

⁹ WH added *them* (*autous*) after <u>exhort</u>.

¹⁰ WH omitted <u>gladly</u> (<u>asmenOs</u>).

¹¹ WH added *in* (*en*) before <u>the</u> <u>same</u> <u>day</u>.

¹² WH omitted <u>and</u> (<u>kai</u>).

¹³ WH changed **came** <u>upon</u> (<u>egeneto</u>) to *was coming upon* (*egineto*). **Aor** M-D Ind to *Impf* Mid Ind. [tense]

44 And all that believed were together, and had all things common;

45 And sold their possessions and goods, and parted them to all *men*, as every man had need.

46 And they, continuing daily with one accord in the temple, and breaking bread from house to house, did eat their meat with gladness and singleness of heart,

47 Praising God, and having favour with all the people. And the Lord added **to the church**[1] daily such as should be saved.

CHAPTER 3

1 **[upon the same]**[2] **Now**[3] Peter and John went up together into the temple at the hour of prayer, *being* the ninth *hour*.

2 And a certain man lame from his mother's womb was carried, whom they laid daily at the gate of the temple

which is called Beautiful, to ask alms of them that entered into the temple;

3 Who seeing Peter and John about to go into the temple asked [ʌ**to receive**][4] an alms.

4 And Peter, fastening his eyes upon him with John, said, Look on us.

5 And he gave heed unto them, expecting to receive something of them.

6 Then Peter said, Silver and gold have I none; but such as I have give I thee: In the name of Jesus Christ of Nazareth ~~rise up and~~[5] walk.

7 And he took him by the right hand, and lifted ʌ*him*[6] up: and immediately his feet and ankle bones received strength.

8 And he leaping up stood, and walked, and entered with them into the temple, walking, and leaping, and praising God.

9 And all the people saw him walking and praising God:

---

[1] WH changed {**to**} the **church** (t**A ekklAsia**) to *upon the same* (*epi to auto*).
[2] WH omitted upon the same (epi to auto).
[3] WH changed the word order from NOW Peter to *Peter NOW*.

[4] WH added *to receive* (*labein*).
[5] WH omitted rise up and (egeirai kai).
[6] WH added *him* (*auton*) as the KJV supplied it.

10 **And**[1] they knew that it was he which sat for alms at the Beautiful gate of the temple: and they were filled with wonder and amazement at that which had happened unto him.

11 And ~~as the~~[2] ~~lame man~~[3] ~~which was healed~~[4] held Peter and John, all the people ran together unto them in the porch that is called Solomon's, greatly wondering.

12 And when Peter saw *it*, he answered unto the people, Ye men of Israel, why marvel ye at this? or why look ye so earnestly on us, as though by our own power or holiness we had made this man to walk?

13 The God of Abraham, and of Isaac, and of Jacob, the God of our fathers, hath glorified his Son Jesus; whom ye [ʌ**indeed**][5] delivered up, and denied ~~him~~[6] in the presence of Pilate, when he was determined to let *him* go.

14 But ye denied the Holy One and the Just, and desired a murderer to be granted unto you;

15 And killed the Prince of life, whom God hath raised from the dead; whereof we are witnesses.

16 And his name through faith in his name hath made this man strong, whom ye see and know: yea, the faith which is by him hath given him this perfect soundness in the presence of you all.

17 And now, brethren, I wot that through ignorance ye did *it*, as *did* also your rulers.

18 But those things, which God before had shewed by the mouth of all **his**[7] prophets, that Christ should suffer, he hath so fulfilled.

19 Repent ye therefore, and be converted, that your sins may be blotted out, when the times of refreshing shall come from the presence of the Lord;

20 And he shall send **Jesus**[8] Christ, **which before**

---

[1] WH changed <u>and</u> (<u>te</u>) to *and* (*de*).
[2] WH omitted <u>as the</u> (<u>tou</u>)
[3] WH changed **lame man** (**cOl**ou) to *he* (*autou*).
[4] WH omitted <u>which was healed</u> (^hiathentos).
[5] WH added *indeed* (*men*) after the intensive <u>ye</u>.
[6] WH omitted <u>him</u> (auton).

---

[7] WH changed the word order from <u>the prophets</u> OF HIM <u>to suffer the Christ</u> to *the prophets to suffer the Christ OF HIM*.
[8] WH changed the word order from JESUS Christ to *Christ JESUS*.

was preached[1] unto you:

21 Whom the heaven must receive until the times of restitution of all things, which God hath spoken by the mouth **of all**[2] his holy prophets **since the world began**[3].

22 ~~For~~ Moses truly said ~~unto the fathers~~[4], A prophet shall the Lord ~~your~~[5] God raise up unto you of your brethren, like unto me; him shall ye hear in all things whatsoever he shall say unto you.

23 And it shall come to pass, *that* every soul, which will not hear that prophet, shall be destroyed from among the people.

24 Yea, and all the prophets from Samuel and those that follow after, as many as have spoken, have likewise **foretold**[6] of these days.

25 Ye are ∧**the**[7] children of the prophets, and of the covenant which God made with **our**[8] fathers, saying unto Abraham, And ∧**in**[9] thy seed shall all the kindreds of the earth be blessed.

26 Unto you first God, having raised up his Son ~~Jesus~~[10], sent him to bless you, in turning away every one of you from his iniquities.

CHAPTER 4

1 And as they spake unto the people, the **priests**[11], and

---

[1] WH changed which before was **preached** (prokekA-**rug**menon) to *which before was **appointed*** (*prokeceiris-menon*). Pf Pass Part of prokArussO to Pf Pass Part of *proceirizomai.*

[2] WH changed of **all** (**pan**tOn) to *of the* (*tOn*).

[3] WH changed the word order from holy of him prophets FROM ETERNITY to *holy FROM ETERNITY of him prophets.*

[4] WH omitted for unto the fathers (gar pros tous pateras).

[5] WH omitted of you ([h]umOn) from Lord the God of you.

[6] WH changed **foretold** (**pro**katAggeilan) to *told* (katAggeilan). [prefix dropped]

[7] WH added the ([h]oi) as the KJV supplied it.

[8] WH changed the fathers of us (tous pateras [h]AmOn) to *the fathers of you* (*tous pateras [h]umOn*). [person]

[9] WH added in (en) where the KJV supplied it based on the dative case.

[10] WH omitted Jesus (iAsoun).

[11] In their margin, WH changed priests ([h]iereis) to *high priests* (*arciereis*). [prefix added]

361

the captain of the temple, and the Sadducees, came upon them,

2 Being grieved that they taught the people, and preached through Jesus the resurrection from the dead.

3 And they laid hands on them, and put *them* in hold unto the next day: for it was now eventide.

4 Howbeit many of them which heard the word believed; and ~~the~~[1] number of the men was about five thousand.

5 And it came to pass on the morrow, that their rulers, and [ʌthe][2] elders, and [ʌthe][3] scribes,

6 And **Annas the high priest, and Caiaphas, and John, and Alexander**[4], and

---

[1] WH omitted the (ʰo).
[2] WH added *the* (*tous*) before elders.
[3] WH added *the* (*tous*) before scribes.
[4] WH changed Annas the high priest and Caiaphas, and John and Alexander (anna**n** ton arciere**a** kai kaiafan kai iOannAn kai alexandro**n**) to *Annas the high preist and Caiaphas and John and Alexander* (annas ʰo arciereus kai kaiafas kai iOannAs kai alexandros). [case]

as many as were of the kindred of the high priest, were gathered together **at**[5] Jerusalem.

7 And when they had set them in the midst, they asked, By what power, or by what name, have ye done this?

8 Then Peter, filled with the Holy Ghost, said unto them, ye rulers of the people, and elders ~~of Israel~~[6],

9 If we this day be examined of the good deed done to the impotent man, by what means he is made whole;

10 Be it known unto you all, and to all the people of Israel, that by the name of Jesus Christ of Nazareth, whom ye crucified, whom God raised from the dead, *even* by him doth this man stand here before you whole.

11 This is the stone which was set at nought of you builders, which is become the head of the corner.

12 Neither is there salvation in any other: for there is **none**[7] other name under heaven given among men,

---

[5] WH changed into (eis) to *in* (en).
[6] WH omitted of the Israel (tou israAl).
[7] WH changed none (oute) to *none* (oude).

whereby we must be saved.

13 Now when they saw the boldness of Peter and John, and perceived that they were unlearned and ignorant men, they marvelled; and they took knowledge of them, that they had been with Jesus.

14 **And**[1] beholding the man which was healed standing with them, they could say nothing against it.

15 But when they had commanded them to go aside out of the council, they conferred among themselves,

16 Saying, What **shall we do**[2] to these men? for that indeed a notable miracle hath been done by them *is* manifest to all them that dwell in Jerusalem; and we cannot **deny**[3] *it*.

17 But that it spread no further among the people, let us **straitly**[4] threaten them,

that they speak henceforth to no man in this name.

18 And they called them, and commanded **them**[5] not to speak at all nor teach in the name of Jesus.

19 But Peter and John answered and said unto them, Whether it be right in the sight of God to hearken unto you more than unto God, judge ye.

20 For we cannot but speak the things which we have seen and heard.

21 So when they had further threatened them, they let them go, finding nothing how they might punish them, because of the people: for all *men* glorified God for that which was done.

22 For the man was above forty years old, on whom this miracle of healing was shewed.

23 And being let go, they went to their own company, and reported all that the chief priests and elders had said unto them.

24 And when they heard that, they lifted up their voice to God with one accord, and said, Lord, thou *art* **God**[6], which hast made heaven, and

---

[1] WH changed and (**de**) to *and* (*te*).

[2] WH changed **shall** we do (poiAsomen) to *might we do* (*poiAsOmen*). **Fut** Act **Ind** to *Aor* Act *Sub*. [tense & mood]

[3] WH changed to deny (ar-nAsasthai) to *to be denying* (*arneisthai*). **Aor** Mid-D Inf to *Pres* Mid Inf. [tense]

[4] WH omitted straightly (apeilA—by threatening).

[5] WH omitted them (autois).

[6] WH omitted the God (^{h}o theos).

earth, and the sea, and all that in them is:

25 Who by the mouth of ~~thy~~[1] servant David hast said, Why did the heathen rage, and the people imagine vain things?

26 The kings of the earth stood up, and the rulers were gathered together against the Lord, and against his Christ.

27 For of a truth [∧in the city this {one}][2] against thy holy child Jesus, whom thou hast anointed, both Herod, and Pontius Pilate, with the Gentiles, and the people of Israel, were gathered together,

28 For to do whatsoever thy hand and thy counsel determined before to be done.

29 And now, Lord, behold their threatenings: and grant unto thy servants, that with all boldness they may speak thy word,

30 By stretching forth thine hand to heal; and that signs and wonders may be done by the name of thy holy child Jesus.

31 And when they had prayed, the place was shaken where they were assembled together; and they were all filled with ∧**the**[3] Holy **Ghost**[4], and they spake the word of God with boldness.

32 And the multitude of them that believed were of [**the**][5] one heart and of [**the**][6] one soul: neither said any *of them* that ought of the things which he possessed was his own; but they had all things common.

33 And with great power gave the apostles witness of the resurrection of the Lord Jesus [∧**Christ**][7]: and great grace was upon them all.

34 Neither was there any among them that lacked: for as many as **were**[8] possessors of lands or houses sold them, and brought the prices of the

---

[1] WH omitted <u>of thee</u> [you[s]] (<u>tou</u>) from <u>the</u> <u>servant</u> <u>of</u> <u>thee</u>.

[2] WH added *in the city this {one}* (*en tA polei tautA*).

[3] WH added *the* (*tou*) where the KJV supplied it.

[4] WH changed the word order from GHOST <u>holy</u> to ***the*** *holy* GHOST.

[5] WH omitted the untranslated <u>the</u> ([h]<u>A</u>).

[6] WH omitted the untranslated <u>the</u> ([h]<u>A</u>).

[7] WH added *Christ* (*cristou*).

[8] WH changed <u>were</u> ([h]**upArcen**) to *were* (*An*). Impf Act Ind of [h]<u>uparcO</u> to Impf Act Ind of *eimi*.

things that were sold,

35 And laid *them* down at the apostles' feet: and distribution was made unto every man according as he had need.

36 And **<u>Joses</u>**[1], who **<u>by</u>**[2] the apostles was surnamed Barnabas, (which is, being interpreted, The son of consolation,) a Levite, *and* of the country of Cyprus,

37 Having land, sold *it*, and brought the money, and laid *it* at the apostles' feet.

CHAPTER 5

1 But a certain man named Ananias, with Sapphira **<s>his</s>**[3] wife, sold a possession,

2 And kept back *part* of the price, his wife also being privy *to it*, and brought a certain part, and laid *it* at the apostles' feet.

3 But Peter said, Ananias, why hath Satan filled thine heart to lie to the Holy Ghost, and to keep back *part* of the price of the land?

4 Whiles it remained, was it not thine own? and after it was sold, was it not in thine own power? why hast thou conceived this thing in thine heart? thou hast not lied unto men, but unto God.

5 And Ananias hearing these words fell down, and gave up the ghost: and great fear came on all them that heard **<s>these things</s>**[4].

6 And the young men arose, wound him up, and carried *him* out, and buried *him*.

7 And it was about the space of three hours after, when his wife, not knowing what was done, came in.

8 And Peter answered ʌunto[5] **<u>her</u>**[6], Tell me whether ye sold the land for so much? And she said, Yea, for so much.

9 Then Peter **<s>said</s>**[7] unto her, How is it that ye have agreed together to tempt the

---

[1] WH changed <u>Joses</u> (<u>iOsAs</u>) to *Joseph* (*iOsAf*).

[2] WH changed **<u>by</u>** (**^h<u>upo</u>**) to *from* (*apo*).

[3] WH omitted of him (<u>autou</u>) from <u>the wife of him</u>.

[4] WH omitted <u>these things</u> (<u>tauta</u>).

[5] WH added *unto* (*pros*) where the KJV supplied it based on the dative case of <u>her</u>.

[6] WH changed her (<u>autA</u>) to *her* (*autAn*). The final <u>n</u> here is a matter of taste.

[7] WH omitted <u>said</u> (<u>eipe</u>).

Spirit of the Lord? behold, the feet of them which have buried thy husband *are* at the door, and shall carry thee out.

10 Then fell she down straightway **at**[1] his feet, and yielded up the ghost: and the young men came in, and found her dead, and, carrying *her* forth, buried *her* by her husband.

11 And great fear came upon all the church, and upon as many as heard these things.

12 And by the hands of the apostles were many signs and wonders wrought among the people; (and they were all with one accord in Solomon's porch.

13 And of the rest durst no man join himself to them: but the people magnified them.

14 And believers were the more added to the Lord, multitudes both of men and women.)

15 Insomuch that they brought forth the sick **into**[2] the streets, and laid *them* on **beds**[3] and couches, that at the least the shadow of Peter passing by might overshadow some of them.

16 There came also a multitude *out* of the cities round about **unto**[4] Jerusalem, bringing sick folks, and them which were vexed with unclean spirits: and they were healed every one.

17 Then the high priest rose up, and all they that were with him, (which is the sect of the Sadducees,) and were filled with indignation,

18 And laid **their**[5] hands on the apostles, and put them in the common prison.

19 But the angel of the Lord by **[the]**[6] night opened the prison doors, and brought them forth, and said,

20 Go, stand and speak in the temple to the people all the words of this life.

21 And when they heard *that*, they entered into the temple early in the morning, and taught. But the high priest came, and they that were with him, and called the council together, and all the

---

[1] WH changed at (**para**) to *at* (*pros*).
[2] WH changed into (*kata*) to *also into* (*kai eis*).
[3] WH changed beds (*klinOn*) to *small beds* (*klinariOn*).
[4] WH omitted unto (*eis*).
[5] WH omitted of them (*autOn*) from the hands of them.
[6] WH omitted the untranslated the (*tAs*).

senate of the children of Israel, and sent to the prison to have them brought.

22 But when the **officers**[1] came, and found them not in the prison, they returned, and told,

23 Saying, The prison ~~truly~~[2] found we shut with all safety, and the keepers standing ~~without~~[3] **before**[4] the doors: but when we had opened, we found no man within.

24 Now when the ~~high priest and the~~[5] captain of the temple and the chief priests heard these things, they doubted of them whereunto this would grow.

25 Then came one and told them, ~~saying~~[6], Behold, the men whom ye put in prison are standing in the temple, and teaching the people.

26 Then went the captain with the officers, and brought them without violence: for they feared the people, ~~lest~~[7] they should have been stoned.

27 And when they had brought them, they set *them* before the council: and the high priest asked them,

28 Saying, Did ~~not~~[8] we straitly command you that ye should not teach in this name? and, behold, ye have filled Jerusalem with your doctrine, and intend to bring this man's blood upon us.

29 Then Peter and the *other* apostles answered and said, We ought to obey God rather than men.

30 The God of our fathers raised up Jesus, whom ye slew and hanged on a tree.

31 Him hath God exalted with his right hand *to be* a Prince and a Saviour, [∧**the**][9] for to give repentance to Israel, and forgiveness of sins.

32 And we are ~~his~~[10] witnesses of these things; and *so is* ~~also~~[11] the Holy Ghost,

---

[1] WH changed the word order from the OFFICERS having come to *having come the OFFICERS*.

[2] WH omitted truly (men).

[3] WH omitted without (exO).

[4] WH changed **before** (**pro**) to *upon* (*epi*).

[5] WH omited high priest and the (ʰiereus kai ʰo).

[6] WH omitted saying (legOn).

[7] WH omitted lest (ʰina).

[8] WH omitted not (ou).

[9] WH added *the* (*tou*).

[10] WH omitted his (autou) in their text. In their margin, however, WH changed his (autou) to *in him* (*en autO*).

[11] WH omitted also (de).

~~whom~~[1] God hath given to them that obey him.

33 When they heard *that*, they were cut *to the heart*, and **took counsel**[2] to slay them.

34 Then stood there up one in the council, a Pharisee, named Gamaliel, a doctor of the law, had in reputation among all the people, and commanded to put the **apostles**[3] forth [~~for~~][4] a little space;

35 And said unto them, Ye men of Israel, take heed to yourselves what ye intend to do as touching these men.

36 For before these days rose up Theudas, boasting himself to be somebody; to whom a number **of men**[5], **about**[6] four hundred, **joined**

themselves[7]: who was slain; and all, as many as obeyed him, were scattered, and brought to nought.

37 After this man rose up Judas of Galilee in the days of the taxing, and drew away ~~much~~[8] people after him: he also perished; and all, *even* as many as obeyed him, were dispersed.

38 And now I say unto you, Refrain from these men, and **let** them **alone**[9]: for if this counsel or this work be of men, it will come to nought:

39 But if it be of God, **ye can**not[10] overthrow **it**[11]; lest

---

[1] WH omitted whom (^ho).

[2] WH changed took counsel (ebouleuonto) to *took counsel (eboulonto)*. Impf **M/P-D** Ind to Impf **Mid** Ind. [voice]

[3] WH changed **apostles** (apostolous) to *men (anthrOpous)*.

[4] WH omitted the untranslated for (ti).

[5] WH changed the word order from joined themselves four hundred OF MEN about to *joined themselves OF MEN four hundred about.*

[6] WH changed as if (^hOsei) to *as (^hOs).*

[7] WH changed joined themselves (prosekollAthA) to *joined themselves (proseklithA)*. Aor Pass Ind of proskollaomai to Aor Pass Ind of *prosklinomai*. [syn]

[8] WH omitted much (^hikanon).

[9] WH changed **let** alone (easate) to *leave alone (afete)*. Aor Act Imp of **eaO** to Aor Act Imp of *afiAmi*. [syn]

[10] WH changed ye **are** able (dunasthe) to *ye will be able (dunAsesthe)*. **Pres** M/P Ind to *Fut* Mid Ind. [tense]

[11] WH changed it (auto) to *them (autous)*. Acc Neut **Sing** to Acc Neut *Plur*. [number]

haply ye be found even to fight against God.

40 And to him they agreed: and when they had called the apostles, and beaten *them*, they commanded that they should not speak in the name of Jesus, and let **them**[1] go.

41 And they departed from the presence of the council, rejoicing that **they were counted worthy**[2] to suffer shame for **his**[3] name.

42 And daily in the temple, and in every house, they ceased not to teach and preach **Jesus**[4] Christ.

CHAPTER 6

1 And in those days, when the number of the disciples was multiplied, there arose a murmuring of the Grecians against the He-

---

[1] WH omitted <u>them</u> (<u>autous</u>).

[2] WH changed the word order from <u>for</u> the <u>name</u> **of him** THEY WERE COUNTED WORTHY to *THEY WERE COUNTED WORTHY for the name*.

[3] WH omitted <u>of him</u> (<u>outou</u>) from <u>the</u> <u>name</u> <u>of him</u>.

[4] WH changed the word order from <u>JESUS</u> the <u>Christ</u> to *the Christ JESUS*.

brews, because their widows were neglected in the daily ministration.

2 Then the twelve called the multitude of the disciples *unto them*, and said, It is not reason that we should leave the word of God, and serve tables.

3 Wherefore, brethren, look ye out among you seven men of honest report, full of the **Holy**[5] Ghost and wisdom, whom we may appoint over this business.

4 But we will give ourselves continually to prayer, and to the ministry of the word.

5 And the saying pleased the whole multitude: and they chose Stephen, a man full of faith and of the Holy Ghost, and Philip, and Prochorus, and Nicanor, and Timon, and Parmenas, and Nicolas a proselyte of Antioch:

6 Whom they set before the apostles: and when they had prayed, they laid *their* hands on them.

7 And the word of God increased; and the number of the disciples multiplied in Jerusalem greatly; and a great company of the priests were obedient to the faith.

---

[5] WH omitted <u>Holy</u> (^h<u>agiou</u>).

8 And Stephen, full **of faith**[1] and power, did great wonders and miracles among the people.

9 Then there arose certain of the synagogue, which is called *the synagogue* of the libertines, and Cyrenians, and Alexandrians, and of them of Cilicia and of Asia, disputing with Stephen.

10 And they were not able to resist the wisdom and the spirit by which he spake.

11 Then they suborned men, which said, We have heard him speak blasphemous words against Moses, and *against* God.

12 And they stirred up the people, and the elders, and the scribes, and came upon *him*, and caught him, and brought *him* to the council,

13 And set up false witnesses, which said, This man ceaseth not to speak ~~blasphemous~~[2] words against this holy place, and the law:

14 For we have heard him say, that this Jesus of Nazareth shall destroy this place, and shall change the customs which Moses delivered us.

15 And **all**[3] that sat in the council, looking stedfastly on him, saw his face as it had been the face of an angel.

CHAPTER 7

1 Then said the high priest, Are **[therefore]**[4] these things so?

2 And he said, Men, brethren, and fathers, hearken; The God of glory appeared unto our father Abraham, when he was in Mesopotamia, before he dwelt in Charran,

3 And said unto him, Get thee out of thy country, and from thy kindred, and come into ˄the[5] land which I shall shew thee.

4 Then came he out of the land of the Chaldaeans, and dwelt in Charran: and from thence, when his father was dead, he removed him into this land, wherein ye now dwell.

5 And he gave him none inheritance in it, no, not *so*

---

[1] WH changed of **faith** (**pisteOs**) to *of love* (*caritas*).

[2] WH omitted blasphemous (blasfAma).

[3] WH changed all (ᵃapantes) to *all* (*pantes*). [prefix dropped]

[4] WH omitted the untranslated therefore (ara).

[5] WH added *the* (*tAn*) as the KJV supplied it.

much as to set his foot on: yet he promised that he would give it to him for a possession, and to his seed after him, when *as yet* he had no child.

6 And God spake on this wise, That his seed should sojourn in a strange land; and that they should bring them into bondage, and entreat *them* evil four hundred years.

7 And the nation to whom **they shall be in bondage**[1] will I judge, said God: and after that shall they come forth, and serve me in this place.

8 And he gave him the covenant of circumcision: and so *Abraham* begat Isaac, and circumcised him the eighth day; and Isaac *begat* Jacob; and Jacob *begat* the twelve patriarchs.

9 And the patriarchs, moved with envy, sold Joseph into Egypt: but God was with him,

10 And delivered him out of all his afflictions, and gave him favour and wisdom in the sight of Pharaoh king of Egypt; and he made him governor over Egypt and all his house.

11 Now there came a dearth over all the ~~land~~[2] **of Egypt**[3] and Chanaan, and great affliction: and our fathers found no sustenance.

12 But when Jacob heard that there was **corn**[4] **in Egypt**[5], he sent out our fathers first.

13 And at the second *time* Joseph was made known to his brethren; and Joseph's kindred was made known unto Pharaoh.

14 Then sent Joseph, and called his father **Jacob**[6] to *him*, and all ~~his~~[7] kindred, threescore and fifteen souls.

---

[1] WH changed they **might** serve as slaves (douleus**O**si) to *they **shall** serve as slaves* (*douleusousi*). **Aor** Act **Sub** to *Fut* Act *Ind*. [tense & mood]*

[2] WH omitted land (gAn).

[3] WH changed **of** Egypt (ai-gupto**u**) to *Egypt* (*aigupton*). [case]

[4] WH changed grain (sita) to *grain* (*sitia*). Acc **Masc** Plur to Acc **Neut** Plur. [gender]

[5] WH changed in Egypt (**en** aigupt**O**) to *into Egypt* (*eis aigupton*). [prep & case]

[6] WH changed the word order from the father of him JACOB to *JACOB the father of him*.

[7] WH omitted of him (autou) in the father of him.

15 So Jacob went down into Egypt, and died, he, and our fathers,

16 And were carried over into Sychem, and laid in the sepulchre that Abraham bought for a sum of money of the sons of **Emmor**[1] *the*[2] *father* of Sychem.

17 But when the time of the promise drew nigh, which God **had sworn**[3] to Abraham, the people grew and multiplied in Egypt,

18 Till another king [∧**from Egypt**][4] arose, which knew not Joseph.

19 The same dealt subtilly with our kindred, and evil entreated our fathers, so that they cast out their young children, to the end they might not live.

20 In which time Moses was born, and was exceeding fair, and nourished up in **his**[5]

father's house three months:

21 And **when he was cast out**[6], Pharaoh's daughter took him up, and nourished him for her own son.

22 And Moses was learned in all the wisdom of the Egyptians, and was mighty in words and **in**[7] deeds [∧**of him**][8].

23 And when he was full forty years old, it came into his heart to visit his brethren the children of Israel.

24 And seeing one *of them* suffer wrong, he defended *him*, and avenged him that was oppressed, and smote the Egyptian:

25 For he supposed **his**[9] brethren would have understood how that God by his hand would deliver **them**[10]:

---

in the house of the father of him.

[6] WH changed having been cast out (ektethenta auton) to *having been cast out* (ektethentos autou). Aor Pass Part **Acc** to Aor Pass Part *Gen*. [case]

[7] WH omitted *in* (en).

[8] WH added *of him* (autou).

[9] WH omitted of him (autou) from his brethren.

[10] WH changed the word order from give TO THEM deliverance to *give deliverance TO THEM*.

---

[1] WH changed Emmor (emor) to *Emmor* (*emmOr*). [spell]

[2] WH changed **the** (**tou**) to *in* (*en*). Article to Prep.

[3] WH changed **swore** (Omosen) to *promised* (*"OmologAsen*). Aor Act Ind of omnuO to Aor Act Ind of *"omologeO*. [syn v]

[4] WH added *from Egypt* (*ep' aigupton*).

[5] WH omitted of him (autou)

but they understood not.

26 **And**[1] the next day he shewed himself unto them as they strove, and **would have set**[2] them at one again, saying, Sirs, ye [~~yourselves~~][3] are brethren; why do ye wrong one to another?

27 But he that did his neighbour wrong thrust him away, saying, Who made thee a ruler and a judge over **us**[4]?

28 Wilt thou kill me, as thou diddest the Egyptian yesterday?

29 Then fled Moses at this saying, and was a stranger in the land of Madian, where he begat two sons.

30 And when forty years were expired, there appeared to him in the wilderness of mount Sina an angel ~~of the Lord~~[5] in a flame of fire in a bush.

31 When Moses saw *it*, he wondered at the sight: and as he drew near to behold *it*, the voice of the Lord came ~~unto him~~[6],

32 *Saying*, I *am* the God of thy fathers, the God of Abraham, and ~~the God~~[7] of Isaac, and the God of Jacob. Then Moses trembled, and durst not behold.

33 Then said the Lord to him, Put off thy shoes from thy feet: for the place **where**[8] thou standest is holy ground.

34 I have seen, I have seen the affliction of my people which is in Egypt, and I have heard their groaning, and am come down to deliver them. And now come, **I will send**[9] thee into Egypt.

35 This Moses whom they refused, saying, Who made thee a ruler and a judge? the

---

[1] WH changed <u>and</u> (**de**) to *and* (*te*).

[2] WH changed <u>set</u> (<u>sunA-lasen</u>) to *was setting* (*sunAl-lassen*). **Aor** Act Ind of <u>sunAlasen</u> to *Impf* Act Ind of *sunAllassen*. [tense & {mis}spell]

[3] WH omitted the untranslated <u>yourselves</u>[p] (^h<u>umeis</u>).

[4] WH changed <u>us</u> (^h<u>Amas</u>) to *us* (^h*AmOn*). **Acc** Plur to *Gen* Plur. [case]

[5] WH omitted <u>of Lord</u> (ku-riou).

[6] WH omitted <u>unto him</u> (<u>pros auton</u>).

[7] WH omitted <u>the God</u> (^h<u>o</u> ~~theos~~).

[8] WH changed **in** <u>which</u> (<u>en</u> ^h<u>O</u>) to **upon** which (*ef'* ^h*O*). [prep changed]

[9] WH changed I **will** send (<u>apostelO</u>) to *I **might** send* (*aposteilO*). **Fut** Act **Ind** to *Aor* Act *Sub*. [tense & mood]

same **did** God **send**[1] *to be*
[ʌalso][2] a ruler and a deliverer **by**[3] the hand of the angel
which appeared to him in the
bush.

36 He brought them out,
after that he had shewed
wonders and signs in ʌthe[4]
~~land~~[5] **of Egypt**[6], and in the
Red sea, and in the wilder-
ness forty years.

37 This is that Moses,
which said unto the children
of Israel, A prophet shall ~~the~~
~~Lord~~[7] ~~your~~[8] God raise up
unto you of your brethren,
like unto me; ~~him shall ye~~
~~hear~~[9].

38 This is he, that was in
the church in the wilderness

---

[1] WH changed **did send**
(apest**eilen**) to *has sent*
(*apestalke*). **Aor** Act Ind to
Pf Act Ind. [tense]
[2] WH added *also* (*kai*).
[3] WH changed **by** (**en**) to
with (*sun*).
[4] WH added *the* (*tA*) as the
KJV supplied it.
[5] WH omitted land (gA).
[6] WH changed **of Egypt** (aiguptou) to *Egypt* (*aiguptO*).
Gen to *Dat*. [case]
[7] WH omitted Lord (kurios).
[8] WH omitted of you from
the Lord your God.
[9] WH omitted him shall ye
hear (autou akousest~~he~~).

with the angel which spake to
him in the mount Sina, and
with our fathers: who received the lively oracles to
give unto us:

39 To whom our fathers
would not obey, but thrust
him from them, and ʌin[10]
their hearts turned back again
into Egypt,

40 Saying unto Aaron,
Make us gods to go before
us: for *as for* this Moses,
which brought us out of the
land of Egypt, we wot not
what **is become**[11] of him.

41 And they made a calf in
those days, and offered sacrifice unto the idol, and rejoiced in the works of their
own hands.

42 Then God turned, and
gave them up to worship the
host of heaven; as it is written
in the book of the prophets,
O ye house of Israel, have ye
offered to me slain beasts and
sacrifices *by the space of*
forty years in the wilderness?

43 Yea, ye took up the
tabernacle of Moloch, and the

---

[10] WH added *in* (*en*) as the
KJV supplied it.
[11] WH changed **has become**
(**gegonen**) to *became*
(*egeneto*). **Pf Act** Ind to *Aor*
Mid Ind. [tense & voice]

374

star of ~~your~~[1] god **Remphan**[2], figures which ye made to worship them: and I will carry you away beyond Babylon.

44 Our fathers had the tabernacle of witness in the wilderness, as he had appointed, speaking unto Moses, that he should make it according to the fashion that he had seen.

45 Which also our fathers that came after brought in with Jesus into the possession of the Gentiles, whom God drave out before the face of our fathers, unto the days of David;

46 Who found favour before God, and desired to find a tabernacle for the God of Jacob.

47 But Solomon built him an house.

48 Howbeit the most High dwelleth not in **temples**[3] made with hands; as saith the prophet,

49 Heaven *is* my throne, and earth *is* my footstool: what house will ye build me?

saith the Lord: or what *is* the place of my rest?

50 Hath not my hand made all these things?

51 Ye stiffnecked and uncircumcised **in** [~~the~~][4] **heart**[5] and ears, ye do always resist the Holy Ghost: as your fathers *did,* so *do* ye.

52 Which of the prophets have not your fathers persecuted? and they have slain them which shewed before of the coming of the Just One; of whom ye **have been**[6] now the betrayers and murderers:

53 Who have received the law by the disposition of angels, and have not kept *it.*

54 When they heard these things, they were cut to the heart, and they gnashed on him with *their* teeth.

55 But he, being full of the Holy Ghost, looked up stedfastly into heaven, and saw the glory of God, and Jesus standing on the right hand of God,

---

[1] WH omitted of you from the god of you.
[2] WH changed Remphan (remfan) to *Rephan* (*refan*). [spell]
[3] WH omitted temple (naois).

[4] WH omitted the untranslated the (tA).
[5] WH changed {in} heart (kardia) to {in} *hearts* (kardia**s**).
[6] WH changed **have been** (gegenAsthe) to *were* (egenesthe). **Pf Pass** Ind to *Aor Mid* Ind. [tense & voice]

56 And said, Behold, I see the heavens **opened**[1], and the Son of man standing on the right hand of God.

57 Then they cried out with a loud voice, and stopped their ears, and ran upon him with one accord,

58 And cast *him* out of the city, and stoned *him*: and the witnesses laid down their clothes at a young man's feet, whose name was Saul.

59 And they stoned Stephen, calling upon *God*, and saying, Lord Jesus, receive my spirit.

60 And he kneeled down, and cried with a loud voice, Lord, lay not this sin to their charge. And when he had said this, he fell asleep.

CHAPTER 8

1 And Saul was consenting unto his death. And at that time there was a great persecution against the church which was at Jerusalem; **and**[2] they were all scattered abroad throughout the regions of Judaea and Samaria, except the apostles.

2 And devout men carried Stephen *to his burial*, and **made**[3] great lamentation over him.

3 As for Saul, he made havock of the church, entering into every house, and haling men and women committed *them* to prison.

4 Therefore they that were scattered abroad went every where preaching the word.

5 Then Philip went down to ᴧ**the**[4] city of Samaria, and preached Christ unto them.

6 **And**[5] the people with one accord gave heed unto those things which Philip spake, hearing and seeing the miracles which he did.

7 For unclean spirits, crying with loud voice, **came out**[6]

---

[1] WH changed having been opened **up** (**aneO**gmenous) to *having been opened* ***through*** (*di***Anoi**gmenous*). Pf Pass Part of anoigO to Pf Pass Part of *dianoigO*. [prefix changed]

[2] WH changed and (**te**) to *and* (*de*).

[3] WH changed made (epoi-Asanto) to *made* {**for himself**} (*epoiAsan*). Aor **Mid** Ind to Aor *Act* Ind. [voice]

[4] WH added *the* (*tAn*) as the KJV supplied it.

[5] WH changed and (*te*) to *and* (*de*).

[6] WH changed the word order from with loud voice CAME OUT to *CAME OUT with loud voice*.

of many[1] that were possessed *with them*: and many taken with palsies, and that were lame, were healed.

8　**And**[2] there was **great**[3] **joy**[4] in that city.

9　But there was a certain man, called Simon, which beforetime in the same city used sorcery, and bewitched the people of Samaria, giving out that himself was some great one:

10　To whom they all gave heed, from the least to the greatest, saying, This man is [ᴧ**calling**][5] the great power of God.

11　And to him they had regard, because that of long time he had bewitched them with sorceries.

12　But when they believed Philip preaching ~~the things~~[6]

concerning the kingdom of God, and the name of Jesus Christ, they were baptized, both men and women.

13　Then Simon himself believed also: and when he was baptized, he continued with Philip, and wondered, beholding the **miracles** and **signs**[7] **which were done**[8].

14　Now when the apostles which were at Jerusalem heard that Samaria had received the word of God, they sent unto them Peter and John:

15　Who, when they were come down, prayed for them, that they might receive the Holy Ghost:

16　(For **as yet**[9] he was fallen upon none of them: only they were baptized in the name of the Lord Jesus.)

17　Then laid they *their*

---

[1] WH changed **of** many (pol-lOn) to *many* (*polloi*). **Gen** Masc Plur to *Nom* Masc Plur. [case]

[2] WH changed and (**kai**) to *but* (*de*).

[3] WH changed **great** (**mega**lA) to *much* (*poll*A).

[4] WH changed the word order from **AND** there was JOY **great** to *there was BUT much JOY*.

[5] WH added *calling* (*ka-loumenA*).

[6] WH omitted the things (ta).

---

[7] WH changed the word order from MIRACLES and SIGNS being done to *SIGNS and MIRACLES being done.*

[8] WH changed which were done (ginomena) to *which were done* (*ginomenas*). Pres M/P Part Acc **Neut** Plur to Pres Mid Part Acc *Fem* Plur. signs is neuter and miracles is *feminine.* [gender]

[9] WH changed as yet ([h]oupO) to *as yet* ([h]oudepO).

hands on them, and they received the Holy Ghost.

18 And **when** Simon **saw**[1] that through laying on of the apostles' hands **the Holy**[2] Ghost was given, he offered them money,

19 Saying, Give me also this power, that on whomsoever I lay hands, he may receive the Holy Ghost.

20 But Peter said unto him, Thy money perish with thee, because thou hast thought that the gift of God may be purchased with money.

21 Thou hast neither part nor lot in this matter: for thy heart is not right **in the sight**[3] of God.

22 Repent therefore of this thy wickedness, and pray **God**[4], if perhaps the thought of thine heart may be for-

given thee.

23 For I perceive that thou art in the gall of bitterness, and *in* the bond of iniquity.

24 Then answered Simon, and said, Pray ye to the Lord for me, that none of these things which ye have spoken come upon me.

25 And they, when they had testified and preached the word of the Lord, **returned**[5] to Jerusalem, and **preached the gospel**[6] in many villages of the Samaritans.

26 And the angel of the Lord spake unto Philip, saying, Arise, and go toward the south unto the way that goeth down from Jerusalem unto Gaza, which is desert.

27 And he arose and went: and, behold, a man of Ethiopia, an eunuch of great authority under Candace **[the]**[7] queen of the Ethiopians, who had the charge of all her

---

[1] WH changed having **observed** (theasamenos) to *having seen* (*idOn*). Aor **Mid-D** Part of theaomai to Aor *Act* Part of *[h]oraO*. [syn]

[2] In their margin, WH omitted the Holy (to [h]agion).

[3] WH changed in the sight (en**Opion**) to *in the sight* (*enanti*). [syn]

[4] WH changed the God (tou theou) to *the Lord* (*tou kuriou*).

[5] WH changed returned ([h]upestre$an) to *were returning* (*[h]upestrefon*). **Aor** Act Ind to *Impf* Act Ind. [tense]

[6] WH changed preached the gospel (auAggelisanto) to *was preaching the gospel* (*euAggelizonto*). **Aor** Mid Ind to *Impf* Mid Ind. [tense]

[7] WH omitted the untranslated the (tAs).

treasure, and had come to Jerusalem for to worship,

28 Was returning, and sitting in his chariot read Esaias the prophet.

29 Then the Spirit said unto Philip, Go near, and join thyself to this chariot.

30 And Philip ran thither to *him*, and heard him read the prophet **Esaias**[1], and said, Understandest thou what thou readest?

31 And he said, How can I, except some man **should guide**[2] me? And he desired Philip that he would come up and sit with him.

32 The place of the scripture which he read was this, He was led as a sheep to the slaughter; and like a lamb dumb before his shearer, so opened he not his mouth:

33 In ~~his~~[3] humiliation his judgment was taken away: ~~and~~[4] who shall declare his generation? for his life is taken from the earth.

34 And the eunuch answered Philip, and said, I pray thee, of whom speaketh the prophet this? of himself, or of some other man?

35 Then Philip opened his mouth, and began at the same scripture, and preached unto him Jesus.

36 And as they went on *their* way, they came unto a certain water: and the eunuch said, See, *here is* water; what doth hinder me to be baptized?

37 ~~And Philip said, If thou believest with all thine heart, thou mayest. And he answered and said, I believe that Jesus Christ is the Son of God.~~[5]

38 And he commanded the chariot to stand still: and they went down both into the water, both Philip and the

---

[1] WH changed the word order from the prophet ISAIAH to *ISAIAH the prophet*.

[2] WH changed **might** guide (ʰodAgAsA) to *will guide* (ʰodAgAsei). **Aor** Act **Sub** to *Fut* Act *Ind.* [tense & mood]

[3] WH omitted of him (autou) from the humiliation of him.

[4] WH omitted and (de).

[5] WH omitted and the Phillip said if thou believest with all thine heart thou mayest and he answered and said I believe that Jesus Christ is the Son of the God (eipe de ʰo filippos ei pisteueis ex ʰolAs tAs kardias exestin apokritheis de eipe pisteuO ton ʰuion tou theou einai ton iasoun criston). WH omitted all of Acts 8:37.

eunuch; and he baptized him.

39 And when they were come up out of the water, the Spirit of the Lord caught away Philip, that the eunuch saw him no more: and he went on his way rejoicing.

40 But Philip was found at Azotus: and passing through he preached in all the cities, till he came to Caesarea.

CHAPTER 9

1 And Saul, yet breathing out threatenings and slaughter against the disciples of the Lord, went unto the high priest,

2 And desired of him letters to Damascus to the synagogues, that if he found any of this way, whether they were men or women, he might bring them bound unto Jerusalem.

3 And as he journeyed, he came near Damascus: **and**[1] **suddenly**[2] there shined round about him a light **from**[3] heaven:

4 And he fell to the earth, and heard a voice saying unto him, Saul, Saul, why persecutest thou me?

5 And he said, Who art thou, Lord? And the ~~Lord said~~[4], I am Jesus whom thou persecutest: *~~it is hard for thee to kick against the pricks~~*[5].

6 ~~And he trembling and astonished said, Lord, what wilt thou have me to do? And the Lord *said* unto him,~~[6] [∧**but**][7] Arise, and go into the city, and it shall be told thee [∧**the**][8] what thou must do.

7 And the men which

---

[4] WH omitted <u>Lord</u> <u>said</u> (<u>kurios</u> <u>eipen</u>).

[5] In their text, WH omitted <u>hard</u> <u>for thee</u> <u>to kick</u> <u>against</u> <u>pricks</u> (<u>sklAron</u> <u>soi</u> <u>pros</u> <u>kentra</u> <u>laktizein</u>). They retained these words in their margin, however.

[6] WH omitted <u>and he trembling</u> <u>and</u> <u>astonished</u> <u>said</u> <u>Lord</u> <u>what</u> <u>wilt thou have</u> <u>me</u> <u>to do?</u> <u>and</u> <u>the Lord</u> <u>said</u> <u>unto</u> <u>him</u> (<u>tremOn</u> <u>te</u> <u>kai</u> ~~thambOn~~ <u>eipe</u> <u>kurie</u> <u>ti</u> <u>me</u> ~~theleis~~ <u>poiAsai;</u> <u>kai</u> [h]<u>o</u> <u>kurios</u> <u>pros</u> <u>auton</u>).

[7] WH added <u>but</u> (<u>alla</u>).

[8] WH added *the* ([h]*o*) before <u>what</u> (<u>ti</u>).

---

[1] WH changed <u>and</u> (**kai**) to *and* (*te*).

[2] WH changed the word order from **and** SUDDENLY to *SUDDENLY **and**.*

[3] WH changed **from** (**apo**) to *out of* (*ek*).

journeyed with him stood speechless, hearing a voice, but seeing **no man**[1].

8 And Saul arose from the earth; and when his eyes were opened, he saw no man: but they led him by the hand, and brought *him* into Damascus.

9 And he was three days without sight, and neither did eat nor drink.

10 And there was a certain disciple at Damascus, named Ananias; and to him said **the Lord**[2] in a vision, Ananias. And he said, Behold, I *am here*, Lord.

11 And the Lord *said* unto him, Arise, and go into the street which is called Straight, and enquire in the house of Judas for *one* called Saul, of Tarsus: for, behold, he prayeth,

12 And hath seen ~~in a vision~~[3] a man **named**[4] Ananias

coming in, and putting ∧*his*[5] **hand**[6] on him, that he might receive his sight.

13 Then Ananias answered, Lord, **I have heard**[7] by many of this man, how much evil he hath done to thy saints at Jerusalem:

14 And here he hath authority from the chief priests to bind all that call on thy name.

15 But the Lord said unto him, Go thy way: for he **is**[8] a chosen vessel unto me, to bear my name before ∧**the**[9] Gentiles, [∧**also**][10] and kings, and the children of Israel:

16 For I will shew him how great things he must suffer for my name's sake.

---

[1] WH changed no **man** (oudena) to *no thing* (ouden). Acc **Masc** Sing to Acc *Neut* Sing. [gender]

[2] WH changed the word order from THE LORD in a vision to *in a vision THE LORD*.

[3] WH omitted in a vision (en ʰoramati).

[4] WH changed the word order from NAMED Ananias to *Ananias NAMED*.

[5] WH added *the* (tas) where the KJV supplied his.

[6] WH changed hand (ceira) to *hands* (ceiras). They changed from putting **a hand** to *putting **the hands***. [number]

[7] WH changed I **have** heard (**akAkoa**) to *I heard* (*Akousa*). **Pf** Act Ind to *Aor* Act Ind. [tense]

[8] WH changed the word order from unto me IS he to *IS unto me he*

[9] WH added *the* (tOn) as the KJV supplied it.

[10] WH added *also* (te) after Gentiles (ethnOn).

17 And Ananias went his way, and entered into the house; and putting his hands on him said, Brother Saul, the Lord, *even* Jesus, that appeared unto thee in the way as thou camest, hath sent me, that thou mightest receive thy sight, and be filled with the Holy Ghost.

18 And immediately there fell from his eyes as it had been scales: and he received sight ~~forthwith~~[1], and arose, and was baptized.

19 And when he had received meat, he was strengthened. Then was ~~Saul~~[2] certain days with the disciples which were at Damascus.

20 And straightway he preached **Christ**[3] in the synagogues, that he is the Son of God.

21 But all that heard *him* were amazed, and said; Is not this he that destroyed them which called on this name in Jerusalem, and came hither for that intent, that he might bring them bound unto the chief priests?

22 But Saul increased the more in strength, and confounded ~~the~~[4] Jews which dwelt at Damascus, proving that this is very Christ.

23 And after that many days were fulfilled, the Jews took counsel to kill him:

24 But their laying await was known of Saul. And **they watched**[5] [∧also][6] the gates day and night to kill him.

25 Then **the disciples**[7] took **him**[8] by night, and **let ∧*him***[9] **down**[10] by the wall in a basket.

26 And when ~~Saul~~[11] was

---

[4] WH omitted the (*tous*).

[5] WH changed they were watching (*paretAroun*) to *they were watching* {**for themselves**} (*paratArounto*). Impf **Act** Ind to Impf *Mid* Ind. [voice]

[6] WH added *also* (*kai*) after (te).

[7] WH changed the word order from him THE DISCIPLES to *THE DISCIPLES **of him***.

[8] WH changed him (*auto**n***) to *of him* (*auto**u***). [case]

[9] WH added *him* (*auton*) as the KJV supplied.

[10] WH changed the word order from LET {**him**} DOWN by the wall to *by the wall LET **him** DOWN*.

[11] WH omitted the Saul (^{h}o saulos).

---

[1] WH omitted forthwith (*paracrAma*).

[2] WH omitted the Saul (^{h}o saulos).

[3] WH changed **Christ** (**criston**) to *Jesus* (*iAsoun*).

come to Jerusalem, **he as-sayed**[1] to join himself to the disciples: but they were all afraid of him, and believed not that he was a disciple.

27 But Barnabas took him, and brought *him* to the apostles, and declared unto them how he had seen the Lord in the way, and that he had spoken to him, and how he had preached boldly at Damascus in the name of Jesus.

28 And he was with them coming in and going out **at**[2] Jerusalem.

29 **And**[3] he spake boldly in the name of the Lord ~~Jesus~~[4], and disputed against the Grecians: but they went about to slay him.

30 *Which* when the brethren knew, they brought him down to Caesarea, and sent him forth to Tarsus.

31 Then   **had**[5]   **the**

churches[6] rest throughout all Judaea and Galilee and Samaria, **and were edified**[7]; and **walking**[8] in the fear of the Lord, and in the comfort of the Holy Ghost, **were multiplied**[9].

32 And it came to pass, as Peter passed throughout all *quarters,* he came down also to the saints which dwelt at Lydda.

33 And there he found a certain man named Aeneas, which had kept his **bed**[10]

---

[1] WH changed he assayed (epeira**o**) to *he assayed* (*epeiraze*). Impf **M/P-D** Ind of peira**aomai** to Impf *Act* Ind of *peirazO*. [voice & syn]

[2] WH changed in (**en**) to *into* (*eis*).

[3] WH omitted and (kai).

[4] WH omitted Jesus (iAsou).

[5] WH changed **they** had (ei-con) to *she had* (*eicen*). 3rd **Plur** to 3rd *Sing*. [number]

[6] WH changed the churches (**ai** ekklAsiai) to *the church* (*"A ekklAsia*). [number]

[7] WH changed and **they were** being edified (oikodo-moumenai) to *and it was being edified* (*oikodo-moumenA*). Both Pres Pass Part. Nom Fem **Plur** to Nom Fem *Sing*. [number]

[8] WH changed walking (poreuomenai) to *walking* (*poreuomenA*). Pres M/P-D Part to Pres Mid Part. Nom Fem **Plur** to Nom Fem *Sing*. [number]

[9] WH changed **they were** multiplied (eplAthunonto) to *it was multiplied* (*eplAthuneto*). Both Impf Pass Ind. 3rd **Plur** to 3rd *Sing*. [number]

[10] WH changed bed (krabbat**O**) to *bed* (*krabbatou*). **Dat** Masc Sing to *Gen* Masc Sing. [case]

eight years, and was sick of the palsy.

34 And Peter said unto him, Aeneas, Jesus **[the]**[1] Christ maketh thee whole: arise, and make thy bed. And he arose immediately.

35 And all that dwelt at Lydda and Saron saw him, and turned to the Lord.

36 Now there was at Joppa a certain disciple named Tabitha, which by interpretation is called Dorcas: this woman was full of good works and almsdeeds which she did.

37 And it came to pass in those days, that she was sick, and died: whom when they had washed, they laid *her* in an upper chamber.

38 And forasmuch as Lydda was nigh to Joppa, and the disciples had heard that Peter was there, they sent unto him two men, desiring *him* that he would not **delay**[2] to come to **them**[3].

39 Then Peter arose and went with them. When he was come, they brought him into the upper chamber: and all the widows stood by him weeping, and shewing the coats and garments which Dorcas made, while she was with them.

40 But Peter **[ʌalso]**[4] put them all forth, and kneeled down, and prayed; and turning *him* to the body said, Tabitha, arise. And she opened her eyes: and when she saw Peter, she sat up.

41 And he gave her *his* hand, and lifted her up, and when he had called the saints and widows, presented her alive.

42 And it was known throughout all Joppa; and many believed in the Lord.

43 And it came to pass, that he tarried many days in Joppa with one Simon a tanner.

CHAPTER 10

1 ~~There was~~[5] a certain man in Caesarea called Cornelius, a centurion of the band called the Italian *band*,

2 *A* devout *man*, and one

---

[1] WH omitted the untranslated the (*ʰo*).
[2] WH changed **to delay** (*oknAsai*) to *you*[s] *might delay* (*oknAsAs*). Aor Act **Inf** to Aor Act *Sub* 2nd Sing. [mood & number]
[3] WH changed **them** (*autOn*) to *us* (*ʰAmOn*). [person]

[4] WH added *also* (*kai*).
[5] WH omitted <u>there was</u> (*An*).

that feared God with all his house, which **[also]**[1] gave much alms to the people, and prayed to God alway.

3   He saw in a vision evidently about **[˄around]**[2] the ninth hour of the day an angel of God coming in to him, and saying unto him, Cornelius.

4   And when he looked on him, he was afraid, and said, What is it, Lord? And he said unto him, Thy prayers and thine alms are come up for a memorial **before**[3] God.

5   And now send **men**[4] to Joppa, and call for ˄*one*[5] Simon, whose surname is Peter:

6   He lodgeth with one Simon a tanner, whose house is by the sea side: ~~he shall tell thee what thou oughtest to do~~.[6]

7   And when the angel which spake **unto Cornelius**[7] was departed, he called two of **his**[8] household servants, and a devout soldier of them that waited on him continually;

8   And when he had declared all *these* things unto them, he sent them to Joppa.

9   On the morrow, as they went on their journey, and drew nigh unto the city, Peter went up upon the housetop to pray about the sixth hour:

10 And he became very hungry, and would have eaten: but while **they**[9] made ready, he **fell**[10] into a trance,

11 And saw heaven opened, and a certain vessel descending ~~unto him~~[11], as it

---

[1] WH omitted the untranslated also (*te*).

[2] WH added *around* (*peri*).

[3] WH changed before (*enO-pion*) to *before* (*em-prosthen*). [syn]

[4] WH changed the word order from into Joppa MEN to MEN into Joppa.

[5] WH added *one* (*tina*) as the KJV supplied it.

[6] WH omitted he shall tell thee what thou outest to do (*outos lalAsei soi ti se dei poiein*).

[7] WH changed {unto} the **Cornelius** (**tO kornAliO**) to {unto} *him* (*autO*).

[8] WH omitted of him (*autou*) from two of the household servants of him.

[9] WH changed those (*ekeinOn*) to *they* (*autOn*).

[10] WH changed **fell** (*epepesen*) to *was* (*egeneto*). Aor **Act** Ind of **epipiptO** to Aor *Mid* Ind of **ginomai**. [voice & verb]

[11] WH omitted unto him (*ep' auton*).

had been a great sheet ~~knit~~[1] at the four corners, ~~and~~[2] let down to the earth:

12 Wherein were all manner of fourfooted beasts ~~of the earth, and wild beasts~~,[3] and **[the]**[4] creeping things [∧**of the earth]**[5], and **[the]**[6] fowls of the air.

13 And there came a voice to him, Rise, Peter; kill, and eat.

14 But Peter said, Not so, Lord; for I have never eaten any thing that is common **or**[7] unclean.

15 And the voice *spake* unto him again the second time, What God hath cleansed, *that* call not thou common.

16 This was done thrice: and the vessel was received up **again**[8] into heaven.

17 Now while Peter doubted in himself what this vision which he had seen should mean, **[and]**[9] behold, the men which were sent **from**[10] Cornelius had made enquiry for Simon's house, and stood before the gate,

18 And called, and asked whether Simon, which was surnamed Peter, were lodged there.

19 While Peter **thought**[11] on the vision, the Spirit said unto him, Behold, three men seek thee.

20 Arise therefore, and get thee down, and go with them, doubting nothing: **for**[12] I have sent them.

21 Then Peter went down to the men ~~which were sent unto him from Cornelius~~[13];

---

[1] WH omitted <u>knit</u> (<u>dedemenon</u>).

[2] WH omitted <u>and</u> (<u>kai</u>).

[3] WH omitted <u>of the</u> <u>earth</u> <u>and the</u> <u>wild beasts</u> (<u>tAs gAs kai ta thAria</u>).

[4] WH omitted the untranslated <u>the</u> (<u>ta</u>).

[5] WH added {of} *the earth* (<u>*tAs gAs*</u>).

[6] WH omitted the untranslated <u>the</u> (<u>ta</u>).

[7] WH changed <u>or</u> (**A**) to *and* (*kai*).

[8] WH changed **again** (**palin**) to *immediately* (*euthus*).

[9] WH omitted the untranslated <u>and</u> (<u>kai</u>).

[10] WH changed **from** (<u>apo</u>) to *by* (*ʰupo*).

[11] WH changed <u>thought</u> (<u>enthumoumenou</u>) to *thought* {*through*} (*dienthumoumenou*). [prefix added]

[12] WH changed <u>for</u> (<u>dioti</u>) to *for* (*ʰoti*). [prefix dropped]

[13] WH omitted <u>which</u> <u>were</u> <u>sent</u> <u>unto</u> <u>him</u> <u>from</u> <u>Cornelius</u> (<u>tous apestalmenous apo tou kornAliou pros auton</u>).

and said, Behold, I am he whom ye seek: what *is* the cause wherefore ye are come?

22 And they said, Cornelius the centurion, a just man, and one that feareth God, and of good report among all the nation of the Jews, was warned from God by an holy angel to send for thee into his house, and to hear words of thee.

23 Then called he them in, and lodged *them.* And on the morrow **Peter**[1] went away with them, and certain brethren from Joppa accompanied him.

24 **And the**[2] morrow after **they entered**[3] into Caesarea. And Cornelius waited for them, and had called together his kinsmen and near friends.

25 And as Peter was [∧the][4] coming in, Cornelius met him, and fell down at his feet, and worshipped *him.*

26 But Peter took him up, saying, Stand up; I myself also am a man.

27 And as he talked with him, he went in, and found many that were come together.

28 And he said unto them, Ye know how that it is an unlawful thing for a man that is a Jew to keep company, or come unto one of another nation; but God hath shewed me that I should not call any man common or unclean.

29 Therefore came I *unto you* without gainsaying, as soon as I was sent for: I ask therefore for what intent ye have sent for me?

30 And Cornelius said, Four days ago I was ~~fasting~~ until this hour; ~~and~~[5] at the ninth ~~hour~~[6] I prayed in my house, and, behold, a man stood before me in bright clothing,

---

[1] WH changed **Peter** (^h**o pet-ros**) to *having risen (anastas)*. They changed **Peter** went away to *having risen he went away.* They supplied the subject *he* from the verb went away.

[2] WH changed and (**kai**) to *but* (**de**) and, as a result, put the (t**A**) first in the verse.

[3] In their margin, WH changed **they** entered (ei-sAl~~th~~on) to *he entered* (*eisA ~~th~~en*). Both Aor Act Ind 3rd. **Plur** to *Sing.* [number]

[4] WH added *the (tou)* before the infinitive translated coming in.

[5] WH omitted fasting and (nAsteuOn kai).

[6] WH omitted hour (^hOran).

31 And said, Cornelius, thy prayer is heard, and thine alms are had in remembrance in the sight of God.

32 Send therefore to Joppa, and call hither Simon, whose surname is Peter; he is lodged in the house of *one* Simon a tanner by the sea side: ~~who, when he cometh, shall speak unto thee~~[1].

33 Immediately therefore I sent to thee; and thou hast well done that thou art come. Now therefore are we all here present before God, to hear all things that are commanded thee of **God**[2].

34 Then Peter opened *his* mouth, and said, Of a truth I perceive that God is no respecter of persons:

35 But in every nation he that feareth him, and worketh righteousness, is accepted with him.

36 The word <u>which</u>[3] *God* sent unto the children of Israel, preaching peace by Jesus Christ: (he is Lord of all:)

37 That word, *I say*, ye know, which was published throughout all Judaea, and <u>began</u>[4] from Galilee, after the baptism which John preached;

38 How God anointed Jesus of Nazareth with the Holy Ghost and with power: who went about doing good, and healing all that were oppressed of the devil; for God was with him.

39 And we ~~are~~[5] witnesses of all things which he did both in the land of the Jews, and in Jerusalem; whom [∧**also**][6] they slew and hanged on a tree:

40 Him God raised up the third day, and shewed him openly;

41 Not to all the people, but unto witnesses chosen before of God, *even* to us, who did eat and drink with him after he rose from the dead.

42 And he commanded us to preach unto the people,

---

[1] WH omitted <u>who</u> <u>when</u> <u>he</u> <u>cometh</u> <u>shall</u> <u>speak</u> <u>unto</u> <u>thee</u> (<u>ʰos</u> <u>paragenomenos</u> <u>lalAsei</u> <u>soi</u>).
[2] WH changed <u>of</u> {<u>the</u>} **<u>God</u>** (<u>apo</u> <u>tou</u> **theou**) to *of the Lord* (*apo tou kuriou*).
[3] In their margin, WH omitted <u>which</u> (<u>ʰon</u>).

[4] WH changed {**it**} <u>began</u> (<u>arxamenon</u>) to {**he**} *began* (*arxamenos*). Aor Mid Part **Acc Neut** Sing to Aor Mid Part ***Nom Masc*** Sing. [case & gender]
[5] WH omitted <u>are</u> (<u>esmen</u>).
[6] WH added *also* (*kai*).

and to testify that it is **he**[1] which was ordained of God *to be* the Judge of quick and dead.

43 To him give all the prophets witness, that through his name whosoever believeth in him shall receive remission of sins.

44 While Peter yet spake these words, the Holy Ghost fell on all them which heard the word.

45 And they of the circumcision which believed were astonished, as many as came with Peter, because that on the Gentiles also was poured out the gift of the Holy Ghost.

46 For they heard them speak with tongues, and magnify God. Then answered Peter,

47 Can any man forbid water, that these should not be baptized, which have received the Holy Ghost **as well**[2] as we?

48 **And**[3] he commanded

them **to be baptized**[4] in the name of **the Lord**[5]. Then prayed they him to tarry certain days.

CHAPTER 11

1 And the apostles and brethren that were in Judaea heard that the Gentiles had also received the word of God.

2 **And when**[6] Peter was come up to Jerusalem, they that were of the circumcision contended with him,

3 Saying, Thou wentest in to men uncircumcised, and didst eat with them.

4 But Peter rehearsed *the matter* from the beginning, and expounded *it* by order unto them, saying,

5 I was in the city of Joppa praying: and in a trance I saw a vision, A certain vessel descend, as it had

---

[1] WH changed he {**himself**} (**autos**) to *he {this one}* (**^houtos**).

[2] WH changed **just** as (**kathOs**) to *as* (**^hOs**). [prefix dropped]

[3] WH changed and (**te**) to *and* (*de*).

---

[4] WH changed the word order from TO BE BAPTIZED in the name of **the Lord** to *in the name of Jesus Christ TO BE BAPTIZED*.

[5] WH change **the Lord** (**tou kuriou**) to *Jesus Christ* (*iAsou cristou*).

[6] WH changed **and** (**kai**) to *but* (*de*). As a result the word when (**^hote**) was put first in the verse.

been a great sheet, let down from heaven by four corners; and it came even to me:

6   Upon the which when I had fastened mine eyes, I considered, and saw four-footed beasts of the earth, and wild beasts, and creeping things, and fowls of the air.

7   And I heard [∧also]¹ a voice saying unto me, Arise, Peter; slay and eat.

8   But I said, Not so, Lord: for ~~nothing~~² common or unclean hath at any time entered into my mouth.

9   But the voice answered ~~me~~³ again from heaven, What God hath cleansed, *that* call not thou common.

10   And this was done three times: and all were drawn up again into heaven.

11   And, behold, immediately there were three men already come unto the house where **I was**⁴, sent from Caesarea unto me.

12   And the Spirit bade me go with them, nothing **doubt-**

ing⁵. Moreover these six brethren accompanied me, and we entered into the man's house:

13   And he shewed us how he had seen an angel in his house, which stood and said ~~unto him~~⁶, Send ~~men~~⁷ to Joppa, and call for Simon, whose surname is Peter;

14   Who shall tell thee words, whereby thou and all thy house shall be saved.

15   And as I began to speak, the Holy Ghost fell on them, as on us at the beginning.

16   Then remembered I the word of the Lord, how that he said, John indeed baptized with water; but ye shall be baptized with the Holy Ghost.

17   Forasmuch then as God gave them the like gift as *he did* unto us, who believed on the Lord Jesus Christ; **[then]**⁸ what was I, that I could withstand God?

---

¹ WH added <u>also</u> (<u>kai</u>).
² WH omitted <u>nothing</u> (<u>pas</u>-- lit. all).
³ WH omitted <u>me</u> (<u>moi</u>).
⁴ WH changed **I was** (AmAn) to *we were* (*Amen*). Impf NV Ind 1ˢᵗ **Sing** to Impf *Act* Ind 1ˢᵗ *Plur.* [number]

⁵ WH changed <u>doubting</u> (<u>diakrinomenon</u>) to *having doubted* (*diakrinanta*). **Pres Mid** Part to *Aor Act* Part. [tense & voice]
⁶ WH omitted <u>unto him</u> (<u>autO</u>).
⁷ WH omitted <u>men</u> (<u>andras</u>).
⁸ WH omitted the untranslated <u>then</u> (<u>de</u>).

18 When they heard these things, they held their peace, and **glorified**[1] God, saying, **Then**[2] **hath** God also to the Gentiles **granted**[3] repentance unto life.

19 Now they which were scattered abroad upon the persecution that arose about Stephen travelled as far as Phenice, and Cyprus, and Antioch, preaching the word to none but unto the Jews only.

20 And some of them were men of Cyprus and Cyrene, which, **when they were come**[4] to Antioch, spake [ʌ**also**][5] unto the **Grecians**[6], preaching the Lord

Jesus.

21 And the hand of the Lord was with them: and a great number [ʌ**the**][7] believed, and turned unto the Lord.

22 Then tidings of these things came unto the ears of the church which ʌ**was**[8] in Jerusalem: and they sent forth Barnabas, ~~that he should go~~[9] as far as Antioch.

23 Who, when he came, and had seen the grace [ʌ**the**][10] of God, was glad, and exhorted them all, that

---

[1] WH changed **were glorifying** (edoxaz*on*) to *glorified* (edoxas*an*). **Impf** Act Ind to *Aor* Act Ind. [tense]

[2] WH changed then (ara**ge**) to *then* (ara). [emphatic root dropped]

[3] WH changed the word order from repentance HATH GRANTED unto life to *repentance unto life HATH GRANTED.*

[4] WH changed when they were come {**into**} (eiselt̶hontes) to *when they were come* (elt̶hontes). [prefix dropped]

[5] WH added *also* (kai).

[6] WH changed Grecians ([h]ell̶Anist*as*) to *Greeks* ([h]ell̶Anas) in their text. Acc Masc Plur of [h]ell̶Anist*As*--Hellenist (one who uses the Greek language and customs) to Acc Masc Plur of [h]ell̶An--Greek. They retained Grecians ([h]ell̶Anist*as*) in their margin, however.

[7] WH added a singular *the* ([h]o) before the Aor Sing Part believed.

[8] WH added *was* (ous*As*--being) just as the KJV supplied it. (They changed from which [**no verb**] in Jerusalem to *which being in Jerusalem.*)

[9] WH omitted that he should go (dielt̶hein).

[10] WH added *the* (tAn) before of the God (tou t̶heou).

with purpose of heart they would cleave **unto**[1] the Lord.

24 For he was a good man, and full of the Holy Ghost and of faith: and much people was added unto the Lord.

25 Then departed ~~Barnabas~~[2] to Tarsus, for to seek Saul:

26 And when he had found **him**[3], he brought **him**[4] unto Antioch. And it came to pass, that a whole year **they**[5] assembled themselves with the church, and taught much people. And the disciples were called Christians first in Antioch.

27 And in these days came prophets from Jerusalem unto Antioch.

28 And there stood up one of them named Agabus, and signified by the Spirit that there should be great dearth throughout all the world:

which **[also]**[6] came to pass in the days of Claudius ~~Caesar~~[7].

29 Then the disciples, every man according to his ability, determined to send relief unto the brethren which dwelt in Judaea:

30 Which also they did, and sent it to the elders by the hands of Barnabas and Saul.

CHAPTER 12

1 Now about that time Herod the king stretched forth *his* hands to vex certain of the church.

2 And he killed James the brother of John with the sword.

3 **And because he saw**[8] it pleased the Jews, he proceeded further to take Peter also. (Then were the days of unleavened bread.)

4 And when he had apprehended him, he put *him* in prison, and delivered *him* to four quaternions of soldiers

---

[1] In their margin, WH added *in* (*en*) where the KJV supplied *unto* (from the dative case).
[2] WH omitted the Barnabas (ʰo barnabas).
[3] WH omitted him (auton).
[4] WH omitted him (auton).
[5] WH changed they (auto**us**) to *they* (*autois*). **Acc** Masc Plur to **Dat** Masc Plur. [case]

[6] WH omitted the untranslated also (kai).
[7] WH omitted Caesar (kaisaros).
[8] WH changed and (**kai**) to *and* (*de*). As a result they put because he saw (idOn) first in the verse.

to keep him; intending after Easter to bring him forth to the people.

5 Peter therefore was kept in prison: but prayer was made **without ceasing**[1] of the church unto God **for**[2] him.

6 And when Herod would have brought him forth, the same night Peter was sleeping between two soldiers, bound with two chains: and the keepers before the door kept the prison.

7 And, behold, the angel of the Lord came upon *him*, and a light shined in the prison: and he smote Peter on the side, and raised him up, saying, Arise up quickly. And his chains fell off from *his* hands.

8 And the angel said unto him, **Gird thyself**[3], and bind on thy sandals. And so he did. And he saith unto him,

---

[1] WH changed <u>constant</u> (ek-<u>tenAs</u>) to *constantly* (*ek-tenOs*). **<u>Nom</u>** Fem Sing **<u>Adjective</u>** to *Dat* Fem Sing *Adverb.* [case & part of speech]
[2] WH changed **on behalf of** (^h**<u>uper</u>**) to *concerning* (*peri*).
[3] WH changed <u>gird thyself</u> {**around**} (**<u>periz</u>Osai**) to *gird thyself* (*zOsai*). [prefix dropped]

Cast thy garment about thee, and follow me.

9 And he went out, and followed **him**[4]; and wist not that it was true which was done by the angel; but thought he saw a vision.

10 When they were past the first and the second ward, they came unto the iron gate that leadeth unto the city; which opened to them of his own accord: and they went out, and passed on through one street; and forthwith the angel departed from him.

11 And when Peter was come to himself, he said, Now I know of a surety, that the Lord hath sent his angel, and hath delivered me out of the hand of Herod, and *from* all the expectation of the people of the Jews.

12 And when he had considered *the thing*, he came to the house of Mary the mother of John, whose surname was Mark; where many were gathered together praying.

13 And as **Peter**[5] knocked at the door of the gate, a damsel came to hearken, named Rhoda.

14 And when she knew

---

[4] WH omitted <u>him</u> (autO).
[5] WH changed **the Peter** (**<u>tou</u> petr<u>ou</u>**) to *he* (*autou*).

Peter's voice, she opened not the gate for gladness, but ran in, and told how Peter stood before the gate.

15 And they said unto her, Thou art mad. But she constantly affirmed that it was even so. Then said they, It is his angel.

16 But Peter continued knocking: and when they had opened *the door*, and saw him, they were astonished.

17 But he, beckoning unto them with the hand to hold-their peace, declared unto them how the Lord had brought him out of the prison. **And**[1] he said, Go shew these things unto James, and to the brethren. And he departed, and went into another place.

18 Now as soon as it was day, there was no small stir among the soldiers, what was become of Peter.

19 And when ~~Herod~~[2] had sought for him, and found him not, he examined the keepers, and commanded that *they* should be put to death. And he went down from Judaea to Caesarea, and *there* abode.

20 And Herod was highly displeased with them of Tyre and Sidon: but they came with one accord to him, and, having made Blastus the king's chamberlain their friend, desired peace; because their country was nourished by the king's *country*.

21 And upon a set day Herod, arrayed in royal apparel, **[even]**[3] sat upon his throne, and made an oration unto them.

22 And the people gave a shout, *saying, It is* the voice of a god, and not of a man.

23 And immediately the angel of the Lord smote him, because he gave not God the glory: and he was eaten of worms, and gave up the ghost.

24 But the word of God grew and multiplied.

25 And Barnabas and Saul returned **from**[4] Jerusalem, when they had fulfilled *their* ministry, and took with them **[also]**[5] John, whose surname was Mark.

---

[1] WH changed <u>and</u> (**de**) to *and* (**te**).
[2] WH omitted <u>the Herod</u> (<u>^ho ^hArOdAs</u>).

[3] WH omitted the untranslated <u>even</u> (<u>kai</u>).
[4] In their margin, WH changed **out from** (<u>ex</u>) to *into* (*eis*).
[5] WH omitted the untranslated <u>also</u> (<u>kai</u>).

CHAPTER 13

1 Now there were in the church that was at Antioch ~~certain~~[1] prophets and teachers; as Barnabas, and Simeon that was called Niger, and Lucius of Cyrene, and Manaen, which had been brought up with Herod the tetrarch, and Saul.

2 As they ministered to the Lord, and fasted, the Holy Ghost said, Separate me [~~also~~][2] Barnabas and Saul for the work whereunto I have called them.

3 And when they had fasted and prayed, and laid *their* hands on them, they sent *them* away.

4 So **they**[3], being sent forth by the Holy Ghost, departed unto Seleucia; and from thence they sailed to Cyprus.

5 And when they were at Salamis, they preached the word of God in the synagogues of the Jews: and they had also John to *their* minister.

6 And when they had gone through [∧all][4] the isle unto Paphos, they found [∧man][5] a certain sorcerer, a false prophet, a Jew, whose name *was* Barjesus:

7 Which was with the deputy of the country, Sergius Paulus, a prudent man; who called for Barnabas and Saul, and desired to hear the word of God.

8 But Elymas the sorcerer (for so is his name by interpretation) withstood them, seeking to turn away the deputy from the faith.

9 Then Saul, (who also *is called* Paul,) filled with the Holy Ghost, [~~also~~][6] set his eyes on him,

10 And said, O full of all subtilty and all mischief, *thou* child of the devil, *thou* enemy of all righteousness, wilt thou not cease to pervert the right ways of the Lord?

11 And now, behold, the hand of the Lord *is* upon thee, and thou shalt be blind, not seeing the sun for a season. And immediately **there fell**[7] on him a mist and a darkness; and he went about

---

[1] WH omitted <u>certain</u> (<u>tines</u>).
[2] WH omitted the untranslated <u>also</u> (<u>te</u>).
[3] WH changed <u>these</u> (^h<u>outoi</u>) to *they* (*autoi*).
[4] WH added *all* (^h*olAn*).

[5] WH added *man* (*andra*).
[6] WH omitted the untranslated <u>also</u> (<u>kai</u>).
[7] WH changed <u>there fell</u> {**upon**} (<u>epepesen</u>) to *there fell* (*epesen*). [prefix dropped]

seeking some to lead him by the hand.

12 Then the deputy, when he saw what was done, believed, being astonished at the doctrine of the Lord.

13 Now when Paul and his company loosed from Paphos, they came to Perga in Pamphylia: and John departing from them returned to Jerusalem.

14 But when they departed from Perga, they came to Antioch **in Pisidia**[1], and **went**[2] into the synagogue on the sabbath day, and sat down.

15 And after the reading of the law and the prophets the rulers of the synagogue sent unto them, saying, *Ye* men *and* brethren, if [ʌ**anyone**][3] ye have any word of exhortation for the people, say on.

16 Then Paul stood up, and beckoning with *his* hand said, Men of Israel, and ye that fear God, give audience.

17 The God of this people of Israel chose our fathers, and exalted the people when they dwelt as strangers in the land **of Egypt**[4], and with an high arm brought he them out of it.

18 And about the time of forty years **suffered he**[5] their manners in the wilderness.

19 And when he had destroyed seven nations in the land of Chanaan, **he divided** their land ~~to them~~[6] **by lot**[7].

20 **And after that**[8] he

---

[1] WH changed **in** the Pisidia (t**As** pisidi**as**) to *the Pisidia* (t**An** pisidi**an**). **Gen** (Antioch {**of**} the Pisidia) to *Acc* (Antioch the Pisidia). [case]

[2] WH changed **went** {**into**} (**eiselth**ontes) to *went* (**el th**ontes). [prefix dropped]

[3] WH added *anyone* (*tis*). They changed if **he** has to *if anyone has*.

[4] WH changed of Egypt (aigupt**O**) to *of Egypt* (*aiguptou*). **Dative** (in land **to** Egypt) to *Genitive* (in land *of* Egypt). [case]

[5] In their margin, WH changed suffered he ([h]etropoforAsen) to *suffered he* ([h]etrofoforAsen). [spell]

[6] WH omitted to them (autois).

[7] WH changed he divided by **lot** (katekl**A**rodot**A**sen) to *he divided by law* (*katekl**A**ronom**A**se*). Aor Ind of katak-l**A**rodoteO to Aor Ind of *kataklAronomeO*.

[8] WH changed the word order from AND AFTER THAT about years four hundred and fifty to *about years four hundred and fifty AND AFTER THAT.*

gave ~~unto them~~[1] judges about the space of four hundred and fifty years, until Samuel ~~the~~[2] prophet.

21 And afterward they desired a king: and God gave unto them Saul the son of Cis, a man of the tribe of Benjamin, by the space of forty years.

22 And when he had removed him, he raised up **unto them**[3] David to be their king; to whom also he gave testimony, and said, I have found David the *son* of Jesse, a man after mine own heart, which shall fulfil all my will.

23 Of this man's seed hath God according to *his* promise **raised**[4] unto Israel a Saviour, Jesus:

24 When John had first preached before his coming the baptism of repentance to all the people of Israel.

25 And as John fulfilled his course, he said, **Whom**[5] think ye that **I**[6] am? I am not *he*. But, behold, there cometh one after me, whose shoes of *his* feet I am not worthy to loose.

26 Men *and* brethren, children of the stock of Abraham, and whosoever among you feareth God, **to you**[7] **is** the word of this salvation **sent**[8].

27 For they that dwell at Jerusalem, and their rulers, because they knew him not, nor yet the voices of the prophets which are read every sabbath day, they have fulfilled *them* in condemning *him*.

28 And though they found no cause of death *in him*, yet desired they Pilate that he should be slain.

29 And when they had fulfilled **all**[9] that was written of

---

[1] WH omitted the unto them (autois) supplied by the KJV in italics.`

[2] WH omitted the (tou).

[3] WH changed the word order from UNTO THEM the David to *the David UNTO THEM*.

[4] WH changed **raised** (Ageire) to *led* (*Agage*). Aor Act Ind of **egeirO** to Aor Act Ind of *agO*.

[5] WH changed whom (tina) to *what* (*ti*). Acc **Masc** Sing to Acc *Neut* Sing. [gender]

[6] WH changed I (me) to *I* (*eme*). [spell]

[7] WH changed to **you** (ʰumin) *to us* (ʰAmin).

[8] WH changed is sent (apestalA) to *is sent* {**out**} (*exapestalA*). [prefix added]

[9] WH changed all (ʰapanta) to *all* (*panta*). [prefix dropped]

him, they took *him* down from the tree, and laid *him* in a sepulchre.

30 But God raised him from the dead:

31 And he was seen many days of them which came up with him from Galilee to Jerusalem, who [∧now][1] are his witnesses unto the people.

32 And we declare unto you glad tidings, how that the promise which was made unto the fathers,

33 God hath fulfilled the same **unto us**[2] ~~their~~[3] children, in that he hath raised up Jesus again; as it is also written in the second psalm, Thou art my Son, this day have I begotten thee.

34 And as concerning that he raised him up from the dead, *now* no more to return to corruption, he said on this wise, I will give you the sure mercies of David.

35 **Wherefore**[4] he saith also in another *psalm*, Thou

shalt not suffer thine Holy One to see corruption.

36 For David, after he had served his own generation by the will of God, fell on sleep, and was laid unto his fathers, and saw corruption:

37 But he, whom God raised again, saw no corruption.

38 Be it known unto you therefore, men *and* brethren, that through this man is preached unto you the forgiveness of sins:

39 And by him all that believe are justified from all things, from which ye could not be justified by the law of Moses.

40 Beware therefore, lest that come ~~upon you~~[5], which is spoken of in the prophets;

41 Behold, ye despisers, and wonder, and perish: for I **work**[6] a work in your days, a work which ye shall in no wise believe, though a man declare it unto you.

42 And when **the Jews**[7]

---

[1] WH added *now* (*nun*).

[2] WH changed **unto** us (ʰAm<u>in</u>) to *of us* (ʰ*AmOn*). **Dat** Plur to *Gen* Plur. [case]

[3] WH omitted <u>of them</u> (<u>autOn</u>) from <u>the children of them</u>.

[4] WH changed <u>wherefore</u> (<u>dio</u>) to *wherefore* (*dioti*).

[5] WH omitted <u>upon you</u> (<u>ep'</u> ʰ<u>umas</u>).

[6] WH changed the word order from <u>I-myself</u> WORK to *WORK I-myself.*

[7] WH changed **the Jews** (**tOn Ioudai**<u>On</u>) to *they* (***autOn***).

were gone ~~out of the syna-gogue~~[1], ~~the Gentiles~~[2] besought that these words might be preached to them the next sabbath.

43 Now when the congregation was broken up, many of the Jews and religious proselytes followed Paul and Barnabas: who, speaking to them, persuaded them **to continue**[3] in the grace of God.

44 And the next sabbath day came almost the whole city together to hear the word of God[4].

45 But when the Jews saw the multitudes, they were filled with envy, and spake against those things which **were spoken**[5] by Paul, ~~con-~~

~~tradicting and~~[6] blaspheming.

46 **Then**[7] Paul and Barnabas waxed bold, and said, It was necessary that the word of God should first have been spoken to you: ~~but~~[8] seeing ye put it from you, and judge yourselves unworthy of everlasting life, lo, we turn to the Gentiles.

47 For so hath the Lord commanded us, *saying*, I have set thee to be a light of the Gentiles, that thou shouldest be for salvation unto the ends of the earth.

48 And when the Gentiles heard this, they were glad, and glorified the word of the **Lord**[9]: and as many as were ordained to eternal life believed.

49 And the word of the Lord was published throughout all the region.

50 But the Jews stirred up

---

[1] WH omitted <u>out of the</u> <u>synagogue</u> (<u>ek</u> <u>tAs</u> suna-gOgAs).
[2] WH omitted <u>the</u> <u>Gentiles</u> (ta ethnA) and let the verb supply the subject *they*.
[3] WH changed <u>to continue</u> (**epi**menein) to *to continue* (*prosmenein*). [prefix changed]
[4] In their margin, WH changed of the **God** (tou theou) to *of the Lord* (*tou kuriou*).
[5] WH changed <u>were being</u> <u>spoken</u> (**lego**menois) to *were*

being spoken (*laloumenois*). Pres Pass Part of **legO** to Pres Pass Part of *laleO*. [syn]
[6] WH omitted <u>contradicting</u> <u>and</u> (<u>antilegontes</u> <u>kai</u>).
[7] WH changed <u>then</u> (<u>de</u>) to *then* (*te*).
[8] WH omitted <u>but</u> (<u>de</u>).
[9] WH changed **Lord** (**ku-ri**ou) to *God (theou)*. They retained **Lord** (**kuri**ou) in their margin.

the devout and honourable women, **and**[1] the chief men of the city, and raised persecution against Paul and Barnabas, and expelled them out of their coasts.

51 But they shook off the dust of **their**[2] feet against them, and came unto Iconium.

52 And the disciples were filled with joy, and with the Holy Ghost.

CHAPTER 14

1   And it came to pass in Iconium, that they went both together into the synagogue of the Jews, and so spake, that a great multitude both of the Jews and also of the Greeks believed.

2   But the **unbelieving**[3] Jews stirred up the Gentiles, and made their minds evil affected against the brethren.

3   Long time therefore abode they speaking boldly in the Lord, which gave testimony unto the word of his grace, **and**[4] granted signs and wonders to be done by their hands.

4   But the multitude of the city was divided: and part held with the Jews, and part with the apostles.

5   And when there was an assault made both of the Gentiles, and also of the Jews with their rulers, to use *them* despitefully, and to stone them,

6   They were ware of *it*, and fled unto Lystra and Derbe, cities of Lycaonia, and unto the region that lieth round about:

7   And   there   they preached the gospel.

8   And there sat a certain man at Lystra, impotent in his feet, **being**[5] a cripple from his mother's womb, who never **had walked**[6]:

9   The same heard Paul speak: who stedfastly beholding him, and perceiving that he had faith to be healed,

---

[1] WH omitted <u>and</u> (<u>kai</u>).
[2] WH omitted <u>of them</u> (<u>autOn</u>) from <u>of the</u> <u>feet</u> of <u>them</u>.
[3] WH changed <u>unbeliev**ing**</u> (<u>apei**thou**ntes</u>) to *having unbelieved* (*apei**thAsantes***).
Pres Act Part to *Aor* Act Part. [tense]

[4] WH omitted <u>and</u> (<u>kai</u>).
[5] WH omitted <u>being</u> (<u>ʰupar-cOn</u>).
[6] WH changed **had** <u>walked</u> (<u>perie**pep**atAkei</u>) to *walked* (*periepatAsen*). **PastPf** Act Ind to *Aor* Act Ind. [tense]

10　Said with a loud [the]¹ voice, Stand upright on thy feet. And **he leaped**² and walked.

11　**And**³ when the people saw what Paul had done, they lifted up their voices, saying in the speech of Lycaonia, The gods are come down to us in the likeness of men.

12　And they [then]⁴ called Barnabas, Jupiter; and Paul, Mercurius, because he was the chief speaker.

13　**Then**⁵ the priest of Jupiter, which was before their⁶ city, brought oxen and garlands unto the gates, and would have done sacrifice with the people.

14　*Which* when the apostles, Barnabas and Paul, heard *of*, they rent their clothes, and **ran in**⁷ among the people, crying out,

15　And saying, Sirs, why do ye these things? We also are men of like passions with you, and preach unto you that ye should turn from these vanities unto the⁸ living [the]⁹ God, which made heaven, and earth, and the sea, and all things that are therein:

16　Who in times past suffered all nations to walk in their own ways.

17　Nevertheless [though]¹⁰ he left not himself without witness, **in that he did good**¹¹, and gave **us**¹² rain from heaven, and fruitful

---

¹ WH omitted the untranslated the (tA).
² WH changed he **was leaping** (ʰAlleto) to (ʰAlato) *he leaped*. **Impf** M/P-D Ind to *Aor* Mid Ind. [tense]
³ WH changed and (**de**) to *and* (*te*).
⁴ WH omitted the untranslated then (men).
⁵ WH changed then (**de**) to *then* (*te*).
⁶ WH omitted of them (autOn) from the city of them.

⁷ WH changed ran **in** (**eis**epAdAsan) to *ran out* (*ex*epAdAsan). [prefix changed]
⁸ WH omitted the (ton).
⁹ WH omitted the untranslated the (ton).
¹⁰ WH omitted the untranslated though (ge).
¹¹ WH changed in that he **did good** (agathopoiOn) to *in that he worked good* (*agathourgOn*). Pres Act Part of agathopoieO to Pres Act Part of *agathoergeO*. [syn]
¹² WH changed **us** (ʰAmin) to *you* (ʰumin). [person]

401

seasons, filling **our**[1] hearts with food and gladness.

18 And with these sayings scarce restrained they the people, that they had not done sacrifice unto them.

19 And there came thither *certain* Jews from Antioch and Iconium, who persuaded the people, and, having stoned Paul, drew *him* out of the city, **supposing**[2] he had been dead.

20 Howbeit, as the disciples stood round about him, he rose up, and came into the city: and the next day he departed with Barnabas to Derbe.

21 And when they had preached the gospel to that city, and had taught many, they returned again to Lystra, and *to* Iconium, and [∧**into**][3] Antioch,

22 Confirming the souls of the disciples, *and* exhorting them to continue in the faith, and that we must through much tribulation enter into the kingdom of God.

23 And when they had ordained them elders in every church, and had prayed with fasting, they commended them to the Lord, on whom they believed.

24 And after they had passed throughout Pisidia, they came to Pamphylia.

25 And when they had preached the word in Perga, they went down into Attalia:

26 And thence sailed to Antioch, from whence they had been recommended to the grace of God for the work which they fulfilled.

27 And when they were come, and had gathered the church together, **they rehearsed**[4] all that God had done with them, and how he had opened the door of faith unto the Gentiles.

28 And **there**[5] they abode long time with the disciples.

CHAPTER 15

1 And certain men which

---

[1] WH changed <u>of **us**</u> (<u>[h]**AmOn**</u>) to *of you* (*[h]**umOn***) in <u>the</u> <u>hearts</u> <u>of us</u>. [person]
[2] WH changed **having** <u>sup-posed</u> (<u>nomisantes</u>) to *sup-posing* (*nomizontes*). **Aor** Act Part to *Pres* Act Part. [tense]
[3] WH added *into* (*eis*).

[4] WH changed <u>they rehears**ed**</u> (<u>anAggeilan</u>) to *they **were** rehears**ing*** (*anAggellen*). **Aor** Act Ind to *Impf* Act Ind. [tense]
[5] WH omitted <u>there</u> (<u>ekei</u>).

came down from Judaea taught the brethren, *and said,* Except **ye be circumcised**[1] after the manner of Moses, ye cannot be saved.

2   When **therefore**[2] Paul and Barnabas had no small dissension and **disputation**[3] with them, they determined that Paul and Barnabas, and certain other of them, should go up to Jerusalem unto the apostles and elders about this question.

3   And being brought on their way by the church, they passed through [∧**both**][4] Phenice and Samaria, declaring the conversion of the Gentiles: and they caused great joy unto all the brethren.

4   And when they were come to Jerusalem, **they were received**[5] of the church,

and *of* the apostles and elders, and they declared all things that God had done with them.

5   But there rose up certain of the sect of the Pharisees which believed, saying, That it was needful to circumcise them, and to command *them* to keep the law of Moses.

6   And the apostles and elders came together for to consider of this matter.

7   And when there had been much **disputing**[6], Peter rose up, and said unto them, Men *and* brethren, ye know how that a good while ago **God**[7] made choice among us, that the Gentiles by my mouth should hear the word of the gospel, and believe.

8   And   God,   which knoweth   the   hearts,   bare

---

[1] WH changed ye **may** be circumcised (peritemnAsthe) to *ye* ***might*** *be circumcised* (peritmA thAte). **Pres** Pass Sub to *Aor* Pass Sub. [tense]
[2] WH change **therefore** (**oun**) to *then* (*de*).
[3] WH changed **heated** dispute (**suz**AtAseOs) to *dispute* (zAtAseOs). [prefix dropped]
[4] WH added *both* (*te*).
[5] WH changed they were re-

ceived {**from**} (apedecthAsan) to *they were received* {**beside**} (*paredecthAsan*). [prefix changed]
[6] WH changed **heated** dispute (**suz**AtAseOs) to *dispute* (zAtAseOs). [prefix dropped]
[7] WH changed the word order from THE GOD among us made choice to *among us made choice* THE GOD.

them witness, giving **them**[1] the Holy Ghost, even as *he did* unto us;

9 And put no difference between us and them, purifying their hearts by faith.

10 Now therefore why tempt ye God, to put a yoke upon the neck of the disciples, which neither our fathers nor we were able to bear?

11 But we believe that through the grace of the Lord Jesus ~~Christ~~[2] we shall be saved, even as they.

12 Then all the multitude kept silence, and gave audience to Barnabas and Paul, declaring what miracles and wonders God had wrought among the Gentiles by them.

13 And after they had held their peace, James answered, saying, Men *and* brethren, hearken unto me:

14 Simeon hath declared how God at the first did visit the Gentiles, to take out of them a people ~~for~~[3] his name.

15 And to this agree the words of the prophets; as it is written,

16 After this I will return, and will build again the tabernacle of David, which is fallen down; and I will build again the **ruins**[4] thereof, and I will set it up:

17 That the residue of men might seek after the Lord, and all the Gentiles, upon whom my name is called, saith the Lord, who doeth **all**[5] these things.

18 Known ~~unto God are all his works~~[6] from the beginning of the world.

19 Wherefore my sentence is, that we trouble not them, which from among the Gentiles are turned to God:

20 But that we write unto them, that they abstain from pollutions of idols, and *from* fornication, and *from* things strangled, and *from* blood.

21 For Moses of old time hath in every city them that preach him, being read in the synagogues every sabbath day.

---

[1] WH omitted them (autois).
[2] WH omitted Christ (cristou).
[3] WH omitted for (epi) and forced the dative case to supply the preposition *for*.

[4] WH changed ruins (kateskammena) to *ruins* (katestrammena). Both Pf Pass Part. [spell]
[5] WH omitted all (panta).
[6] WH omitted unto God are all his works (esti tO theO panta ta egra autou).

22 Then pleased it the apostles and elders, with the whole church, to send chosen men of their own company to Antioch with Paul and Barnabas; *namely*, Judas **surnamed Barsabas**[1], and Silas, chief men among the brethren:

23 And they wrote *letters* by them ~~after this manner~~[2]; The apostles ~~and~~ [the][3] elders and brethren *send* greeting unto the brethren which are of the Gentiles in Antioch and Syria and Cilicia:

24 Forasmuch as we have heard, that certain **which went out**[4] from us have troubled you with words, subverting your souls, ~~saying, Ye must be circumcised, and keep the law~~[5]: to whom we gave no *such* commandment:

25 It seemed good unto us, being assembled with one accord, to send chosen men unto you with our beloved Barnabas and Paul,

26 Men that have hazarded their lives for the name of our Lord Jesus Christ.

27 We have sent therefore Judas and Silas, who shall also tell *you* the same things by mouth.

28 For it seemed good to the Holy Ghost, and to us, to lay upon you no greater burden than these necessary things;

29 That ye abstain from meats offered to idols, and from blood, and **from things strangled**[6], and from fornication: from which if ye keep yourselves, ye shall do well. Fare ye well.

30 So when they were dismissed, **they came**[7] to Antioch: and when they had gathered the multitude together, they delivered the

---

[1] WH changed **sur**named Barsabas (**epi**kaloumenon barsaban) to *named Barsabbas* (*kaloumenon barsabban*). [prefix dropped & spell]

[2] WH omitted after this manner (tade).

[3] WH omitted and (kai) and the untranslated the (ʰoi).

[4] In their margin, WH omitted which went out (exelthontes).

[5] WH omitted saying be circumcised and keep the law (legontes peritemnesthai kai tArein ton nomon).

[6] WH changed {from} strangled {thing} (pniktou) to ({from} *strangled* {thing*s*}) (*pniktOn*). Gen Neut *Sing* to Gen Neut *Plur*. [number]

[7] WH changed they came (Althon) to *they came down* (*kataAlthon*). [prefix added]

epistle:

31 *Which* when they had read, they rejoiced for the consolation.

32 **And**[1] Judas and Silas, being prophets also themselves, exhorted the brethren with many words, and confirmed *them*.

33 And after they had tarried *there* a space, they were let go in peace from the brethren unto the **apostles**[2].

34 ~~Notwithstanding it pleased Silas to abide there still.~~[3]

35 Paul also and Barnabas continued in Antioch, teaching and preaching the word of the Lord, with many others also.

36 And some days after Paul said unto Barnabas, Let us go again and visit ~~our~~[4]

brethren in every city where we have preached the word of the Lord, *and see* how they do.

37 And Barnabas **determined**[5] to take with them **[the]**[6] **[ᴧalso]**[7] John, whose surname was Mark.

38 But Paul thought not good **to take**[8] him with them, who departed from them from Pamphylia, and went not with them to the work.

39 **And**[9] the contention was so sharp between them, that they departed asunder one from the other: and so Barnabas took Mark, and sailed unto Cyprus;

40 And Paul chose Silas, and departed, being recommended by the brethren unto

---

[1] WH changed <u>and</u> (<u>de</u>) to *and* (*te*).

[2] WH changed **apostles** (<u>apostolous</u>) to *having sent them* {*ones*} (*aposteilantas autous*). [noun to participle phrase]

[3] WH omitted <u>Notwithstanding it pleased Silas to abide there still</u> (<u>edoxe de tO sila epimeinai autou</u>) in their text. They retained this verse, however, in their margin.

[4] WH omitted <u>of us</u> (^hAmOn) from <u>the brethren of us</u>.

[5] WH changed <u>determined</u> (<u>ebouleusato</u>) to *was determining* (*ebouleto*). **Aor** Mid-D Ind of <u>bouleuomai</u> to *Impf* Mid Ind of *boulomai*. [tense & syn]

[6] WH omitted the untranslated <u>the</u> (<u>ton</u>).

[7] WH added *also* (*kai*).

[8] WH changed <u>to take</u> (<u>sumparalabein</u>) to *to be taking* (*sumparalambanein*). **Aor** Act Inf to *Pres* Act Inf. [tense]

[9] WH changed <u>and</u> (**oun--therefore**) to *and* (*de*--**but**).

the grace of **God**[1].

41 And he went through Syria and Cilicia, confirming the churches.

CHAPTER 16

1 Then came he [∧**also**][2] to Derbe and [∧**into**][3] Lystra: and, behold, a certain disciple was there, named Timotheus, the son of a ~~certain~~[4] woman, which was a Jewess, and believed; but his father *was* a Greek:

2 Which was well reported of by the brethren that were at Lystra and Iconium.

3 Him would Paul have to go forth with him; and took and circumcised him because of the Jews which were in those quarters: for they knew all that his **father**[5] was **a Greek**[6].

4 And as they went through the cities, they delivered them the decrees for to keep, that were ordained of the apostles and [~~the~~][7] elders which were at Jerusalem.

5 And so were the churches established in the faith, and increased in number daily.

6 Now **when they had gone throughout**[8] Phrygia and the region of [~~the~~][9] Galatia, and were forbidden of the Holy Ghost to preach the word in Asia,

7 [∧**but**][10] After they were come to Mysia, they assayed **to go**[11] **into**[12] Bithynia:

GREEK {was} *the father of him.*

[7] WH omitted the untranslated the (tOn).

[8] WH changed **having gone through** (dielthontes) to *they went through* (diAlthon). Aor Act **Part** to Aor Act **Ind**. [mood]

[9] WH omitted the untranslated the (tAn).

[10] WH added *but* (de).

[11] WH changed to **be going** (poreuesthai) to *to go* (poreuthAnai). **Pres** M/P Inf to *Aor* Pass Inf. [tense]

[12] WH changed into (kata) to *into* (eis).

---

[1] WH changed of the **God** (tou theou) to *of the Lord* (*tou kuriou*).

[2] WH added *also* (*kai*).

[3] WH added *into* (*eis*).

[4] WH omitted certain (tinos).

[5] WH changed the father (**ton patera**) to *the father* ([h]**o patAr**). **Acc** Masc Sing to *Nom* Masc Sing. [case]

[6] WH changed the word order from the father of him that {was} A GREEK to *that A*

but the Spirit [ʌ**of Jesus**][1] suffered them not.

8   And they passing by Mysia came down to Troas.

9   And a vision appeared to Paul in ~~the~~[2] night; There stood a man **of Macedonia**[3], ʌ**and**[4] prayed him, saying, Come over into Macedonia, and help us.

10   And after he had seen the vision, immediately we endeavoured to go into Macedonia, assuredly gathering that the **Lord**[5] had called us for to preach the gospel unto them.

11   Therefore loosing from Troas, we came with a straight course to Samothracia, **and**[6] the next *day* to **Neapolis**[7];

12   ~~And~~[8] **from thence**[9] to Philippi, which is the chief city of that part of [~~the~~][10] Macedonia, *and* a colony: and we were in that city abiding certain days.

13   And on the sabbath we went out of the **city**[11] by a river side, where **prayer**[12] **was wont**[13] to be made; and we sat down, and spake unto the women which resorted *thither*.

14   And a certain woman named Lydia, a seller of purple, of the city of Thyatira, which worshipped God, heard *us*: whose heart the Lord opened, that she attended unto the things which

---

[1] WH added *of Jesus* (*iAsou*).
[2] WH omitted the (*tAs*).
[3] WH changed the word order from <u>man</u> <u>someone</u> <u>was</u> <u>MACEDONIAN</u> <u>standing</u> to *man MACEDONIAN someone was standing.*
[4] WH added *and* (*kai*) as the KJV supplied it.
[5] WH changed **Lord** (**kuri**os) to *God* (*theos*).
[6] WH changed <u>and</u> (<u>te</u>) to *and* (*de*).
[7] WH changed <u>Neapolis</u> (<u>neapolin</u>) to *Nea Polis* (*nean polin*).

[8] WH omitted <u>and</u> (<u>te</u>).
[9] WH changed <u>from thence</u> (**ekei**then) to ***and from thence*** (*kakeithen*).
[10] WH omitted the untranslated <u>the</u> (<u>tAs</u>).
[11] WH changed **city** (**pole**Os) to *gate* (*pulAs*).
[12] WH changed <u>prayer</u> (<u>proseucA</u>) to *prayer* (*proseucAn*). **Nom** to *Acc*. [case]
[13] WH changed **was being supposed** (<u>enomizeto</u>) to *we were supposing* (*enomizomen*). Impf **Pass** Ind **3ʳᵈ Sing** to Impf *Act* Ind *1ʳˢᵗ Plur*. [voice person number]

were spoken of Paul.

15 And when she was baptized, and her household, she besought *us*, saying, If ye have judged me to be faithful to the Lord, come into my house, and abide *there*. And she constrained us.

16 And it came to pass, as we went to [ʌ**the**]¹ prayer, a certain damsel possessed with a spirit **of divination**² **met**³ us, which brought her masters much gain by soothsaying:

17 The same **followed**⁴ Paul and us, and cried, saying, These men are the servants of the most high God, which shew unto **us**⁵ the way of salvation.

---

¹ WH added *the* (*tAn*).
² WH changed spirit **of** divination (pu**th**Onos) to *divination* spirit (*pu**th**Ona*). **Gen** Masc Sing to *Acc* Masc Sing. [case]
³ WH changed to meet (**apan-tAsai**) to *to meet* (*ʰupantA-sai*). Both Aor Act Inf. [prefix changed]
⁴ WH changed **having** followed (katakolou**th**A**sa**sa) to *following* (*katakolou**th**ousa*). **Aor** Act Part to *Pres* Act Part. [tense]
⁵ WH changed **us** (ʰAmin) to *you* (*ʰumin*). [person]

18 And this did she many days. But Paul, being grieved, turned and said to the spirit, I command thee in the name of Jesus Christ to come out of her. And he came out the same hour.

19 And when her masters saw that the hope of their gains was gone, they caught Paul and Silas, and drew *them* into the marketplace unto the rulers,

20 And brought them to the magistrates, saying, These men, being Jews, do exceedingly trouble our city,

21 And teach customs, which are not lawful for us to receive, neither to observe, being Romans.

22 And the multitude rose up together against them: and the magistrates rent off their clothes, and commanded to beat *them*.

23 And when they had laid many stripes upon them, they cast *them* into prison, charging the jailor to keep them safely:

24 Who, **having received**⁶ such a charge, thrust them into the inner prison, and

---

⁶ WH changed having received (**eilAfOs**) to *having received* (*labOn*). **Pf** Act Part to *Aor* Act Part. [tense]

made their feet fast in the stocks.

25 And at midnight Paul and Silas prayed, and sang praises unto God: and the prisoners heard them.

26 And suddenly there was a great earthquake, so that the foundations of the prison were shaken: **and**[1] immediately all the doors were opened, and every one's bands were loosed.

27 And the keeper of the prison awaking out of his sleep, and seeing the prison doors open, he drew out ∧**his**[2] sword, and would have killed himself, supposing that the prisoners had been fled.

28 But Paul cried with a loud voice, saying, Do thyself no harm: for we are all here.

29 Then he called for a light, and sprang in, and came trembling, and fell down before Paul and Silas,

30 And brought them out, and said, Sirs, what must I do to be saved?

31 And they said, Believe on the Lord Jesus ~~Christ~~[3],

and thou shalt be saved, and thy house.

32 And they spake unto him the word of the **Lord**[4], and to all that were in his house.

33 And he took them the same hour of the night, and washed *their* stripes; and was baptized, he and all his, straightway.

34 And when he had brought them into **his**[5] house, he set meat before them, and rejoiced, believing in God with all his house.

35 And when it was day, the magistrates sent the serjeants, saying, Let those men go.

36 And the keeper of the prison told ~~this~~[6] saying to Paul, The magistrates have sent to let you go: now therefore depart, and go in peace.

37 But Paul said unto them, They have beaten us openly uncondemned, being Romans, and have cast *us* into prison; and now do they thrust us out

---

[1] WH changed <u>and</u> (<u>te</u>) to *and* (*de*).

[2] WH added *the* (*tAn*) where the KJV supplied <u>his</u>.

[3] WH omitted <u>Christ</u> (<u>criston</u>).

[4] In their margin, WH changed **<u>Lord</u>** (**<u>kuri</u>**ou) to *God* (*~~th~~eou*).

[5] WH omitted <u>of him</u> (<u>autou</u>) from <u>the house of him</u>.

[6] WH omitted <u>these</u> (<u>toutous</u>) from <u>the words these</u>.

privily? nay verily; but let them come themselves and fetch us out.

38 And the serjeants **told**[1] these words unto the magistrates: **and**[2] they feared, when they heard that they were Romans.

39 And they came and besought them, and brought *them* out, and desired *them* **to depart out**[3] [**from**][4] of the city.

40 And they went out of the prison, and entered **into**[5] *the house of* Lydia: and when they had seen the brethren, **they comforted**[6] ~~them~~[7], and departed.

---

[1] WH changed <u>told</u> (<u>anAg-geilan</u>) to *told* (*apAggeilan*). [prefix changed]

[2] WH changed <u>and</u> (**kai**) to *and* (*de*). As a result, the conjunction <u>de</u> dropped behind <u>they feared</u>.

[3] WH changed <u>to depart **out**</u> (<u>exelthein</u>) to *to depart from* (*apelthein*). [prefix changed]

[4] WH added *from* (*apo*).

[5] WH changed **into** (**eis**) to *toward* (*pros*).

[6] WH changed the word order from <u>the</u> <u>brethren</u> THEY COMFORTED **them** to *THEY COMFORTED the brethren.*

[7] WH omitted <u>them</u> (<u>autous</u>).

CHAPTER 17

1 Now when they had passed through Amphipolis and Apollonia, they came to Thessalonica, where was [**the**][8] a synagogue of the Jews:

2 And Paul, as his manner was, went in unto them, and three sabbath days **reasoned**[9] with them out of the scriptures,

3 Opening and alleging, that Christ must needs have suffered, and risen again from the dead; and that this [**the**][10] Jesus, whom I preach unto you, is Christ.

4 And some of them believed, and consorted with Paul and Silas; and of the devout Greeks a great multitude, and of the chief women not a few.

5 But the Jews ~~which believed not~~[11], moved with envy, took unto them certain

---

[8] WH omitted the untranslated <u>the</u> (<u>hA</u>).

[9] WH changed **was reasoning** (<u>dielegeto</u>) to *reasoned* (*dielexato*). **Impf** M/P Ind to *Aor* Mid Ind. [tense]

[10] WH added *the* (*ho*).

[11] WH omitted <u>which believed not</u> (<u>apeithountes</u>).

lewd fellows of the baser sort, and gathered a company, and set all the city on an uproar, **and**¹ assaulted the house of Jason, and sought to **bring** them **out**² to the people.

6 And when they found them not, they drew Jason and certain brethren unto the rulers of the city, crying, These that have turned the world upside down are come hither also;

7 Whom Jason hath received: and these all do contrary to the decrees of Caesar, saying that there is another king, *one* Jesus.

8 And they troubled the people and the rulers of the city, when they heard these things.

9 And when they had taken security of Jason, and of the other, they let them go.

10 And the brethren immediately sent away Paul and Silas by [~~the~~]³ night unto Berea: who coming *thither* went into the synagogue of the Jews.

11 These were more noble than those in Thessalonica, in that they received the word with all readiness of mind, and searched the scriptures daily, whether those things were so.

12 Therefore many of them believed; also of honourable women which were Greeks, and of men, not a few.

13 But when the Jews of Thessalonica had knowledge that the word of God was preached of Paul at Berea, they came thither also, and stirred up [∧**and agitated**]⁴ the people.

14 And then immediately the brethren sent away Paul to go **as it were**⁵ to the sea: **but**⁶ Silas and Timotheus **abode**⁷ there still.

15 And they that conducted

---

¹ WH changed *and* (**te**) to *and* (**kai**). This forced the conjunction to move in front of <u>assaulted</u>.
² WH changed <u>bring</u> {out} (<u>agagein</u>) to *bring **out*** (***proagagein***). [prefix added]
³ WH omitted the untranslated <u>the</u> (<u>tAs</u>).

⁴ WH added <u>and</u> <u>agitated</u> (<u>kai tarassontes</u>).
⁵ WH changed <u>as **it were**</u> (ʰOs) to *as **far as*** (ʰeOs).
⁶ WH changed <u>but</u> (**de**) to <u>but</u> (*te*).
⁷ WH changed **were** remain-**ing** (ʰupemenon) to *remained* (ʰupemeinan). **Impf** Act Ind to *Aor* Act Ind. [tense]

Paul brought **him**¹ unto Athens: and receiving a commandment unto Silas and Timotheus for to come to him with all speed, they departed.

16 Now while Paul waited for them at Athens, his spirit was stirred in him, **when he saw**² the city wholly given to idolatry.

17 Therefore disputed he in the synagogue with the Jews, and with the devout persons, and in the market daily with them that met with him.

18 Then certain philosophers [∧**also**]³ of the Epicureans, and of **the**⁴ Stoicks, encountered him. And some said, What will this babbler say? other some, He seemeth to be a setter forth of strange gods: because he preached **unto them**⁵ Jesus, and the resurrection.

19 And they took him, and brought him unto Areopagus,

saying, May we know what this new doctrine, whereof thou speakest, *is*?

20 For thou bringest certain strange things to our ears: **we would**⁶ know therefore **what**⁷ these things mean.

21 (For all the Athenians and strangers which were there spent their time in nothing else, but either to tell [∧**something**]⁸, **or**⁹ to hear some new thing.)

22 Then Paul stood in the midst of Mars' hill, and said, *Ye* men of Athens, I perceive that in all things ye are too superstitious.

23 For as I passed by, and beheld your devotions, I found an altar with this inscription, TO THE UNKNOWN GOD. **Whom**¹⁰

---

¹ WH omitted <u>him</u> (*auton*).
² WH changed <u>seeing</u> (*theOrounti*) to *seeing* (*theOrountos*). Pres Act Part **Dat** Masc Sing to Pres Act Part *Gen* Masc Sing. [case]
³ WH added *also* (*kai*).
⁴ WH omitted <u>the</u> (*tOn*).
⁵ WH omitted <u>unto them</u> (*autois*).

⁶ WH changed <u>we should</u> (*theloi*) to *we would* (*thelei*). Pres Act **Opt** to Pres Act *Ind*. [mood]
⁷ WH changed <u>what</u> (ti **an**) to *what* (*tina*).
⁸ WH added *something* (*ti*) after <u>to hear</u>. The result is *to tell something or to hear something new*.
⁹ WH changed <u>or</u> (**kai**) to *or* (*ʰA*).
¹⁰ WH changed <u>whom</u> (*ʰon*) to *what* (*ʰo*). Acc **Masc** Sing to Acc *Neut* Sing. [gender]

therefore ye ignorantly worship, **him**[1] declare I unto you.

24 God that made the world and all things therein, seeing that he is Lord of heaven and earth, dwelleth not in temples made with hands;

25 Neither is worshipped with **men's**[2] hands, as though he needed any thing, seeing he giveth to all life, and breath, and all things;

26 And hath made of one ~~blood~~[3] all nations of men for to dwell on **all** ~~the~~[4] **face**[5] of the earth, and **hath determined**[6] the times before appointed, and the bounds of their habitation;

27 That they should seek the **Lord**[7], if haply they might feel after him, and find him, **though**[8] he be not far from every one of us:

28 For in him we live, and move, and have our being; as certain also of your own poets have said, For we are also his offspring.

29 Forasmuch then as we are the offspring of God, we ought not to think that the Godhead is like unto gold, or silver, or stone, graven by art and man's device.

30 And the times of this ignorance God winked at; but now **commandeth**[9] **all**[10] men

---

[1] WH changed **him** (touton) to *this* (touto). Acc **Masc** Sing to Acc *Neut* Sing. [gender]

[2] WH changed of men (anthrOpOn) to *of men* (anthrOpinOn). Gen **Masc** Plur of anthrOpos to Gen *Fem* Plur of anthrOpinos. [gender & syn]

[3] WH omitted blood ([h]aimatos).

[4] WH omitted the (to).

[5] WH changed every face (pan prosOpon) to *every face* (pantos prosOpou). **Acc** Neut Sing to **Gen** Neut Sing. [case]

[6] WH changed hath determined {**beforehand**} (protetagmenous) to *hath determined* {**toward**} (prostetagmenous). Pf Pass Part of protassO to Pf Pass Part of prostassO. [prefix changed]

[7] WH changed **Lord** (kurion) to *God* ([th]eon).

[8] WH changed **though** (kaitoige) to *and indeed* (kai ge)

[9] In their margin, WH changed commandeth {**beside**} (**par**aggellei) to *commandeth* {**from**} (apagellei). [prefix changed]

[10] WH changed all (pasi) to *all* (pantas). **Dat** Masc Plur to *Acc* Masc Plur. [case]

every where to repent:

31 **Because**[1] he hath appointed a day, in the which he will judge the world in righteousness by *that* man whom he hath ordained; *whereof* he hath given assurance unto all *men*, in that he hath raised him from the dead.

32 And when they heard of the resurrection of the dead, some mocked: and others said, We will hear thee **again**[2] of this *matter*.

33 ~~So~~[3] Paul departed from among them.

34 Howbeit certain men clave unto him, and believed: among the which *was* Dionysius the Areopagite, and a woman named Damaris, and others with them.

CHAPTER 18

1 [~~but~~][4] After these things ~~Paul~~[5] departed from Athens, and came to Corinth;

2 And found a certain Jew named Aquila, born in Pontus, lately come from Italy, with his wife Priscilla; (because that Claudius had commanded all Jews to depart **from**[6] Rome:) and came unto them.

3 And because he was of the same craft, he abode with them, and **wrought**[7]: for **by their occupation**[8] they were tentmakers.

4 And he reasoned in the synagogue every sabbath, and persuaded the Jews and the Greeks.

5 And when Silas and Timotheus were come from Macedonia, Paul was pressed in the **spirit**[9], and testified to the Jews *that* Jesus [∧to be][10]

---

[1] WH changed <u>because</u> (**dioti**) to *because* (**ka*th*oti**). [prefix changed]

[2] WH changed the word order from <u>AGAIN</u> <u>of this</u> also to *of this also AGAIN*.

[3] WH omitted <u>so</u> (**kai**).

[4] WH omitted the untranslated but (**de**).

[5] WH omitted <u>the Paul</u> (<u>h</u><u>o</u> <u>Paulos</u>).

[6] WH changed **out of** (**ek**) to **from** (*apo*).

[7] WH changed **he was** working (**eirgazeto**) to *they were working* (*Argazonto*). Both Impf M/P-D Ind. 3rd **Sing** to 3rd **Plur**. [number]

[8] WH changed {by} <u>the occupation</u> (**tAn tecnAn**) to {*by*} *the occupation* (*tA tecnA*). **Acc** Fem Sing to *Dat* Fem Sing. [case]

[9] WH changed **spirit** (**pneumati**) to *word* (*logO*).

[10] WH added *to be* (*einai*) where the KJV supplied <u>was</u>.

was Christ.

6 And when they opposed themselves, and blasphemed, he shook *his* raiment, and said unto them, Your blood *be* upon your own heads; I *am* clean: from henceforth I will go unto the Gentiles.

7 And he departed thence, and entered into a certain *man's* house, named [∧Titus][1] Justus, *one* that worshipped God, whose house joined hard to the synagogue.

8 And Crispus, the chief ruler of the synagogue, believed on the Lord with all his house; and many of the Corinthians hearing believed, and were baptized.

9 Then spake the Lord to Paul in the night **by a vision**[2], Be not afraid, but speak, and hold not thy peace:

10 For I am with thee, and no man shall set on thee to hurt thee: for I have much people in this city.

11 **And**[3] he continued

there a year and six months, teaching the word of God among them.

12 And when Gallio was the deputy of Achaia, the Jews made insurrection with one accord against Paul, and brought him to the judgment seat,

13 Saying, **This**[4] *fellow* persuadeth men to worship God contrary to the law.

14 And when Paul was now about to open *his* mouth, Gallio said unto the Jews, If **[therefore]**[5] it were a matter of wrong or wicked lewdness, O *ye* Jews, reason would that I should bear with you:

15 But if it be **a question**[6] of words and names, and *of* your law, look ye *to it*; **for**[7] I will be no judge of such *matters*.

16 And he drave them from the judgment seat.

---

[4] WH changed the word order from THIS persuadeth to *persuadeth THIS.*
[5] WH omitted the untranslated therefore (oun).
[6] WH changed **a question** (zAtAma) to *questions* (zAtAmata). Nom Neut **Sing** to Nom Neut *Plur.* [number]
[7] WH omitted for (gar).

---

[1] WH added *Titus* (*titou*) before Justus.
[2] WH changed the word order from BY VISION in night to *in night BY VISION.*
[3] WH changed and (te) to *and* (*de*). [syn]

416

17 Then all ~~the Greeks~~[1] took Sosthenes, the chief ruler of the synagogue, and beat *him* before the judgment seat. And Gallio cared for none of those things.

18 And Paul *after this* tarried *there* yet a good while, and then took his leave of the brethren, and sailed thence into Syria, and with him Priscilla and Aquila; having shorn *his* head in Cenchrea: for he had a vow.

19 And **he came**[2] to Ephesus, and left them there: but he himself entered into the synagogue, and reasoned with the Jews.

20 When they desired *him* to tarry longer time ~~with them~~[3], he consented not;

21 **But**[4] **bade** ~~them~~[5] **farewell**[6], [ʌand][7] saying, ~~I must~~ ~~must by all means keep this~~ ~~feast that cometh in Jerusa-~~ ~~lem~~[8]: ~~but~~[9] I will return again unto you, if God will. ~~And~~[10] he sailed from Ephesus.

22 And when he had landed at Caesarea, and gone up, and saluted the church, he went down to Antioch.

23 And after he had spent some time *there*, he departed, and went over *all* the country of Galatia and Phrygia in order, **strengthening**[11] all the disciples.

24 And a certain Jew named Apollos, born at Alexandria, an eloquent man, *and* mighty in the scriptures, came to Ephesus.

25 This man was instructed in the way of the

---

[1] WH omitted the Greeks (ʰoi ʰellAnes).
[2] WH changed **he** came (katAntAse) to *they came* (katAntAsan). 3rd **Sing** to 3rd **Plur**. [number]
[3] WH omitted with them (par' autois).
[4] WH changed but (all') to but (alla). [spell]
[5] WH omitted **them** (**autois**).
[6] WH changed **bade** farewell (apetaxato) to *having bid farewell* (apotaxamenos).

Aor M-D **Ind** to Aor Mid *Part*. [mood]
[7] WH added *and* (kai).
[8] WH omitted I must by all means keep this feast that cometh in Jerusalem (dei me pantOs tAn ʰertAn tAn ercomenAn poiAsai eis ʰierosoluma).
[9] WH omitted but (de).
[10] WH omitted and (kai).
[11] WH changed strengthening (**epi**sArizOn) to *strengthening* (stArizOn). [prefix dropped]

417

Lord[1]; and being fervent in the spirit, he spake and taught diligently the things of the Lord, knowing only the baptism of John.

26 And he began to speak boldly in the synagogue: whom when **Aquila** and **Priscilla**[2] had heard, they took him unto *them*, and expounded unto him the way of God more perfectly.

27 And when he was disposed to pass into Achaia, the brethren wrote, exhorting the disciples to receive him: who, when he was come, helped them much which had believed through grace:

28 For he mightily convinced the Jews, *and that* publickly, shewing by the scriptures that Jesus was Christ.

CHAPTER 19

1 And it came to pass, that, while Apollos was at Corinth, Paul having passed through the upper coasts came to Ephesus: and **find-**ing[3] certain disciples,

2 He said [∧**also**][4] unto them, Have ye received the Holy Ghost since ye believed? And they ~~said~~[5] unto him, We have not so much as heard whether there be any Holy Ghost.

3 And he said ~~unto them~~[6], Unto what then were ye baptized? And they said, Unto John's baptism.

4 Then said Paul, John ~~verily~~[7] baptized with the baptism of repentance, saying unto the people, that they should believe on him which should come after him, that is, on ~~Christ~~[8] Jesus.

5 When they heard *this*, they were baptized in the name of the Lord Jesus.

6 And when Paul had laid *his* [**the**][9] hands upon them,

---

[3] WH changed **having found** (^h^eurOn) to *to find* (^h^eurein). Aor Act **Part** to Aor Act *Inf*. [mood]

[4] WH added *also* (te).

[5] WH omitted said (eipon).

[6] WH omitted unto them (pros autous).

[7] WH omitted verily (men).

[8] WH omitted Christ (criston) from the Christ Jesus (ton criston iAsoun).

[9] WH omitted the untranslated the (tas).

---

[1] WH changed **Lord** (kuriou) to *Jesus* (iAsou).

[2] WH changed the word order from AQUILA and PRISCILLA to PRISCILLA and AQUILA.

the Holy Ghost came on them; and they spake with tongues, and prophesied.

7   And all the men were about twelve.

8   And he went into the synagogue, and spake boldly for the space of three months, disputing and persuading the things concerning the kingdom of God.

9   But when divers were hardened, and believed not, but spake evil of that way before the multitude, he departed from them, and separated the disciples, disputing daily in the school of ~~one~~[1] Tyrannus.

10   And this continued by the space of two years; so that all they which dwelt in Asia heard the word of the Lord ~~Jesus~~[2], both Jews and Greeks.

11   And God wrought special miracles by the hands of Paul:

12   So that from his body **were brought**[3] unto the sick handkerchiefs or aprons, and

the diseases departed from them, and the evil spirits **went out**[4] ~~of them~~[5].

13   Then certain [∧**also**][6] [~~from~~][7] of the vagabond Jews, exorcists, took upon them to call over them which had evil spirits the name of the Lord Jesus, saying, **We adjure**[8] you by Jesus whom Paul preacheth.

14   And there were seven **sons**[9] of **one**[10] Sceva, a Jew,

---

[1] WH omited one (tinos).

[2] WH omitted Jesus (iAsou).

[3] WH changed were brought {**upon**} (epiferestha) to *were brought* {**from**} (*apoferesthai*). [prefix changed]

[4] WH changed to be going out (**exerc**esthai) to *to be going out* (*ekporeuesthai*). Pres M/P Inf of **exerc**omai to Pres Mid Inf of *ekporeuomai*. [syn]

[5] WH omitted of them (ap' autOn).

[6] WH added *also* (*kai*).

[7] WH omitted from (apo) and forced the Genitive case to supply the of.

[8] WH changed **we** adjure (orki**zomen**) to *I adjure* (*orkizO*). 1ˢᵗ **Plur** to 1ˢᵗ *Sing*.[number]

[9] WH changed seven **the** (ʰepta ʰoi) to *seven sons* (ʰepta ʰuioi) as the KJV did.

[10] WH changed certain **sons** (tines ʰuioi) to *a certain Sceva* (*tinos sceua*) as the KJV did by placing one in italics. **Plur** to *Sing*. [number]

and chief of the priests, which did so.

15 And the evil spirit answered and said [ʌto them]¹, Jesus I know, and Paul I know; but who are ye?

16 And the man in whom the evil spirit was **leaped**² on them, ~~and~~³ overcame **them**⁴, and prevailed against them, so that they fled out of that house naked and wounded.

17 And this was known to all the Jews and Greeks also dwelling at Ephesus; and fear fell on them all, and the name of the Lord Jesus was magnified.

18 And many that believed came, and confessed, and shewed their deeds.

19 Many of them also which used curious arts brought their books together, and burned them before all *men*: and they counted the price of them, and found *it* fifty thousand *pieces* of silver.

20 So mightily grew **the word**⁵ of God and prevailed.

21 After these things were ended, Paul purposed in the spirit, when he had passed through Macedonia and Achaia, to go to Jerusalem, saying, After I have been there, I must also see Rome.

22 So he sent into Macedonia two of them that ministered unto him, Timotheus and Erastus; but he himself stayed in Asia for a season.

23 And the same time there arose no small stir about that way.

24 For a certain *man* named Demetrius, a silversmith, which made silver shrines for Diana, brought no small gain unto the craftsmen;

25 Whom he called together with the workmen of like occupation, and said,

---

¹ WH added *to them* (*autois*).
² WH changed leap**ing** (*efallomenos*) to *having* leaped (*efalomenos*). **Pres** M/P-D Part to *Aor* Mid Part. [tense]
³ WH omitted and (kai).
⁴ WH changed them (au̅On) to *all* (*amfoterOn*).

⁵ WH changed the word order from THE WORD of the Lord to *of the Lord THE WORD*. [For some reason the KJV treated tou kuriou (the Lord) as if it had been *theou* (*God*). Scriveners, Stephens, BIZ, WH, NA27 all agree that the Greek words are {of} the Lord (tou kuriou) NOT {of} *God* (*theou*). The Latin Vulgate has *God* (*dei*).]

Sirs, ye know that by this craft we have **our**[1] wealth.

26 Moreover ye see and hear, that not alone at Ephesus, but almost throughout all Asia, this Paul hath persuaded and turned away much people, saying that they be no gods, which are made with hands:

27 So that not only this our craft is in danger to be set at nought; but also that the temple of the great goddess Diana should be despised, and her **magnificence**[2] should be destroyed, whom all Asia and the world worshippeth.

28 And when they heard *these sayings*, they were full of wrath, and cried out, saying, Great *is* Diana of the Ephesians.

29 And the **whole**[3] city was filled with confusion: and

having caught Gaius and Aristarchus, men of Macedonia, Paul's companions in travel, they rushed with one accord into the theatre.

30 And when Paul would have entered in unto the people, the disciples suffered him not.

31 And certain of the chief of Asia, which were his friends, sent unto him, desiring *him* that he would not adventure himself into the theatre.

32 Some therefore cried one thing, and some another: for the assembly was confused; and the more part knew not wherefore they were come together.

33 And **they drew**[4] Alexander out of the multitude, the Jews **putting** him **forward**[5]. And Alexander beckoned with the hand, and would have made his defence unto the people.

34 But when they knew that he was a Jew, all with

---

[1] WH changed {**of**} us (ʰAmOn) to {*to*} *us* (ʰAmin) **Gen** Plur to *Dat* Plur. [case]

[2] WH changed the magnificence of her (tAn megaleiotAta autAs) to *of the magnificence of her* (*tAs megaleiotAtos autAs*). **Acc** Fem Sing to *Gen* Fem Sing. [case]

[3] WH changed **whole** (ʰolA) to *of the* (*tAs*).

[4] WH changed they drew {**out**} (**pro**ebibasan) to *they drew* {*together*} (*sunebibasan*). [prefix changed]

[5] WH changed putting forward (proballontOn) to *putting forward* (*probalontOn*). Both Pres Act Part. [spell]

one voice about the space of two hours cried out, Great *is* Diana of the Ephesians.

35 And when the town-clerk had appeased the people, he said, *Ye* men of Ephesus, what **man**[1] is there that knoweth not how that the city of the Ephesians is a worshipper of the great ~~goddess~~[2] Diana, and of the *image* which fell down from Jupiter?

36 Seeing then that these things cannot be spoken against, ye ought to be quiet, and to do nothing rashly.

37 For ye have brought hither these men, which are neither robbers of churches, nor yet blasphemers of **your goddess**[3].

38 Wherefore if Demetrius, and the craftsmen which are with him, have a matter against any man, the law is open, and there are deputies: let them implead one another.

39 But if ye enquire any thing concerning other matters, it shall be determined in a lawful assembly.

40 For we are in danger to be called in question for this day's uproar, there being no cause whereby [∧**not**][4] we may give an account [∧**concerning**][5] of this concourse.

41 And when he had thus spoken, he dismissed the assembly.

CHAPTER 20

1 And after the uproar was ceased, Paul **called unto**[6] *him* the disciples, and [∧**having encouraged**][7] embraced *them*, and departed

---

[1] WH changed <u>what</u> **man** (tis anthrOpos) to *who of men* (tis anthrOpON). **Nom** Masc **Sing** to *Gen* Masc *Plur*. [case & number]

[2] WH omitted <u>goddess</u> (theas).

[3] WH changed <u>your</u> **goddess** (tAn thean ʰumOn) to *our god* (tAn theon ʰAmOn). **Accusative Fem** Sing to *Genitive Masc* Sing. [gender & case]

[4] WH added a *not* (ou) after <u>whereby</u> (peri ou).

[5] WH added *concerning* (peri) after <u>account</u> (logon). This addition replaced the <u>of</u> supplied by the Genitive case.

[6] WH changed **called unto** (**proskales**amenos) to *sent with* (metapemšamenos). Both Aor Mid Part Nom Masc Sing. [root & prefix changed]

[7] WH added *having encouraged* (parakalesas).

for to go[1] into Macedonia.

2   And when he had gone over those parts, and had given them much exhortation, he came into Greece,

3   And *there* abode three months. And when the Jews laid wait for him, as he was about to sail into Syria, **he purposed**[2] to return through Macedonia.

4   And there accompanied him **into Asia**[3] Sopater [∧**of Pyrrhus**][4] of Berea; and of the Thessalonians, Aristarchus and Secundus; and Gaius of Derbe, and Timotheus; and of Asia, Tychicus and Trophimus.

5   [∧**but**][5] These **going**

before[6] tarried for us at Troas.

6   And we sailed away from Philippi after the days of unleavened bread, and came unto them to Troas in five days; where we abode seven days.

7   And upon the first *day* of the week, when **the disciples**[7] came together to break bread, Paul preached unto them, ready to depart on the morrow; and continued his speech until midnight.

8   And there were many lights in the upper chamber, where **they were**[8] gathered together.

9   And there **sat**[9] in a

---

[1] WH changed to go (poreu~~th~~**An**ai) to *to be going* (*poreues~~th~~ai*). **Aor Pass-D** Inf to *Pres Mid-D* Inf. [tense & voice]
[2] WH changed he purposed (egeneto gnOm**A**) to *he purposed* (*egeneto gnOmA**s***). **Nom** Fem Sing (i.e. his mind was) to **Gen** Fem Sing (i.e. he was of a mind). [case]
[3] In their margin, WH omitted into Asia (acri tAs Asias).
[4] WH added *of Pyrrhus* (*purros*) after Sopater.
[5] WH added *but* (*de*) after these (^houtoi) in the Greek text, but since *de* is translated

before the word it follows it was put at the beginning here.
[6] In their margin, WH changed going **before** (proel~~th~~ontes) to *going toward* (*prosel~~th~~ontes*). [prefix changed]
[7] WH changed **the disciples** (**tOn** ma~~th~~**AtOn** tou) to *we* (^**AmOn**).
[8] WH changed **they** were (**As**an) to *we were* (*Amen*). **3ʳᵈ** Plur to *1ˢᵗ* Plur. [person]
[9] WH changed sitting (ka~~th~~**Amenos**) to *sitting* (*ka~~th~~ezomenos*). Both Pres Part. [verb root]

window a certain young man named Eutychus, being fallen into a deep sleep: and as Paul was long preaching, he sunk down with sleep, and fell down from the third loft, and was taken up dead.

10 And Paul went down, and fell on him, and embracing *him* said, Trouble not yourselves; for his life is in him.

11 When he therefore was come up again, and had broken [ʌthe]¹ bread, and eaten, and talked a long while, even till break of day, so he departed.

12 And they brought the young man alive, and were not a little comforted.

13 And we went before to ship, and sailed **unto**² Assos, there intending to take in Paul: for so had he appointed, minding himself to go afoot.

14 And when **he met**³ with us at Assos, we took him in, and came to Mitylene.

15 And we sailed thence, and came the next *day* over against Chios; and the next *day* we arrived at Samos, **and tarried at Trogyllium**⁴; ʌ**and**⁵ the next *day* we came to Miletus.

16 For Paul **had determined**⁶ to sail by Ephesus, because he would not spend the time in Asia: for he hasted, if **it were**⁷ possible for him, to be at Jerusalem the day of Pentecost.

17 And from Miletus he sent to Ephesus, and called the elders of the church.

18 And when they were come to him, he said unto them, Ye know, from the first day that I came into Asia, after what manner I have been with you at all seasons,

19 Serving the Lord with all humility of mind, and with

---

⁴ WH omitted <u>and</u> <u>tarried</u> <u>at</u> <u>Trogyllium</u> (<u>kai</u> <u>minantes</u> <u>en</u> <u>TrOgulliO</u>) in their text, but retained it in their margin.
⁵ WH added *and* (*de*) as the KJV supplied it.
⁶ WH changed <u>determined</u> (<u>ekrine</u>) to **had** *determined* (*kekrikei*). **Aor** Act Ind to *PastPf* Act Ind. [verb tense]
⁷ WH changed <u>it</u> **were** (**An**) to *it* **should be** (*ein*). **Impf Ind** to *Pres* Act *Opt*. [tense & mood]

---

¹ WH added *the* (*ton*).
² WH change **unto** (**eis**) to *upon* (*epi*).
³ WH changed <u>he met</u> (<u>sunebalen</u>) to *he met* (*suneballen*). [spell]

~~**many**~~[1] tears, and temptations, which befell me by the lying in wait of the Jews:

20 *And* how I kept back nothing that was profitable *unto you*, but have shewed you, and have taught you publickly, and from house to house,

21 Testifying both to the Jews, and also to the Greeks, repentance toward God, and [~~**the**~~][2] faith toward our Lord Jesus <u>**Christ**</u>[3].

22 And now, behold, I go bound in the spirit unto Jerusalem, not knowing the things that shall befall me there:

23 Save that the Holy Ghost witnesseth [∧**of me**][4] in every city, saying that bonds and afflictions abide me.

24 But none **of these things**[5] move me, ~~**neither count I**~~[6] **my**[7] life dear unto myself, so that I might finish my course ~~**with joy**~~[8], and the ministry, which I have received of the Lord Jesus, to testify the gospel of the grace of God.

25 And now, behold, I know that ye all, among whom I have gone preaching the kingdom ~~**of God**~~[9], shall see my face no more.

26 **<u>Wherefore</u>**[10] I take you to record this day, that **<u>I</u>**[11] *am* pure from the blood of all *men.*

27 For I have not shunned to declare unto you all the counsel of God.

28 Take heed ~~**therefore**~~[12] unto yourselves, and to all the flock, over the which the Holy Ghost hath made you overseers, to feed the church of <u>**God**</u>[13], which he hath

---

[1] WH omitted <u>many</u> (<u>pollOn</u>).

[2] WH omitted the untranslated <u>the</u> (<u>tAn</u>).

[3] In their margin, WH omitted <u>Christ</u> (<u>criston</u>).

[4] WH added *of me* (*mou*).

[5] WH changed <u>word</u> (<u>logo**n**</u>) to {**of**} *word* (*logou*). **Acc** M Sing to *Gen* M Sing. [case]

[6] WH omitted <u>neither count I</u> (<u>oude ecO</u>).

[7] WH omitted <u>my</u> (<u>mou</u>—of me).

[8] WH omitted <u>with joy</u> (<u>meta caras</u>).

[9] WH omitted <u>of the God</u> (<u>tou ~~theou~~</u>).

[10] WH changed **<u>wherefore</u>** (<u>dio</u>) to *therefore* (*dioti*).

[11] WH changed <u>I</u> (<u>eg**O**</u>) to *I am* (*eimi*).

[12] WH omitted <u>therefore</u> (<u>oun</u>).

[13] In their margin, WH changed **<u>God</u>** (<u>~~th~~eou</u>) to *Lord* (*kuriou*).

purchased with his own **blood**[1].

29 ~~For~~[2] I know **this**[3], that after my departing shall grievous wolves enter in among you, not sparing the flock.

30 Also of your own selves shall men arise, speaking perverse things, to draw away disciples after them.

31 Therefore watch, and remember, that by the space of three years I ceased not to warn every one night and day with tears.

32 And now, ~~brethren~~[4], I commend you to **God**[5], and to the word of his grace, which is able **to build** you **up**[6], and to give ~~you~~[7] [∧the][8] an inheritance among all them

which are sanctified.

33 I have coveted no man's silver, or gold, or apparel.

34 ~~Yea~~[9], ye yourselves know, that these hands have ministered unto my necessities, and to them that were with me.

35 I have shewed you all things, how that so labouring ye ought to support the weak, and to remember the words of the Lord Jesus, how he said, It is more blessed to give **than**[10] to receive.

36 And when he had thus spoken, he kneeled down, and prayed with them all.

37 And they all wept sore, and fell on Paul's neck, and kissed him,

38 Sorrowing most of all for the words which he spake, that they should see his face no more. And they accompanied him unto the ship.

CHAPTER 21

1 And it came to pass, that after we were gotten from them, and had launched,

---

[1] WH changed the word order from his own BLOOD to *BLOOD his own.*

[2] WH omitted for (gar).

[3] WH omitted this (touto).

[4] WH omitted brethren (adelfoi).

[5] In their margin, WH changed **God** (~~the~~O) to *Lord* (*kuriO*).

[6] WH changed to build up {**upon**} (**epoikodomAsai**) to *to build up (oikodomAsai).* [prefix dropped]

[7] WH omitted you ([h]umin).

[8] WH added *the (tAn)* and replaced the supplied an.

[9] WH omitted yea (de).

[10] WH changed the word order from to give THAN to *THAN to give.*

we came with a straight course unto **Coos**[1], and the *day* following unto Rhodes, and from thence unto Patara:

2   And finding a ship sailing over unto Phenicia, we went aboard, and set forth.

3   Now when we had discovered Cyprus, we left it on the left hand, and sailed into Syria, and **landed**[2] at Tyre: for there the ship was to unlade her burden.

4   **And**[3] finding disciples, we tarried there seven days: who said to Paul through the Spirit, that he should not **go up**[4] to Jerusalem.

5   And when we had accomplished those days, we departed and went our way; and they all brought us on our way, with wives and children, till *we were* out of the city: and we kneeled down on the shore, and **prayed**[5].

6   ~~And~~[6] **when we had taken our leave**[7] one of another, **[ʌand]**[8] **we took**[9] ship; and they returned home again.

7   And when we had finished *our* course from Tyre, we came to Ptolemais, and saluted the brethren, and abode with them one day.

8   And the next *day* we ~~that were of Paul's company~~[10] departed, and came unto Caesarea: and we entered into the house of Philip the evangelist, **[the {one}]**[11]

---

[1] WH changed from Coos (k**O**n) to *Cos* (k**O**). Both Acc Fem Sing. [spell]

[2] WH changed it was landed (katAc~~th~~Amen) to *we landed* (katAl~~th~~omen). Aor **Pass** Ind. 1[rst] **Sing** to *Aor Act Inc 1[rst] Plur*. [voice & number]

[3] WH changed **and** (**kai**) to *but* (*de*).

[4] WH changed go **up** (ana-bainein) to *go on* (*epi-bainein*). [prefix changed]

[5] WH changed **we prayed** (pros**A**uxame**th**a) to *having prayed* (*proseuxame**noi***). Aor Mid-D **Ind** to Aor Mid *Part*. [mood]

[6] WH omitted *and* (kai).

[7] WH changed **having taken our leave** (aspasame**noi**) to *we took our leave **from*** (*apaspasame**th**a*). Aor Mid-D **Part** to Aor Mid *Ind*. [mood & prefix added]

[8] WH added *and* (kai).

[9] WH changed we went **on** (epeb**A**men) to *we went in* (*eneb**A**men*). [prefix changed]

[10] WH omitted the {ones} concerning the Paul (oi peri ton paulon).

[11] WH omitted the untranslated the {one} (tou).

which was *one* of the seven; and abode with him.

9 And the same man had four daughters, **virgins**[1], which did prophesy.

10 And as we [we {our-selves}][2] tarried *there* many days, there came down from Judaea a certain prophet, named Agabus.

11 And when he was come unto us, he took Paul's girdle, and bound [both][3] **his own**[4] hands and **feet**[5], and said, Thus saith the Holy Ghost, So shall the Jews at Jerusalem bind the man that owneth this girdle, and shall deliver *him* into the hands of the Gentiles.

12 And when we heard these things, both we, and they of that place, besought him not to go up to Jerusalem.

13 **Then**[6] Paul answered, What mean ye to weep and to break mine heart? for I am ready not to be bound only, but also to die at Jerusalem for the name of the Lord Jesus.

14 And when he would not be persuaded, we ceased, saying, The will of the Lord be done.

15 And after those days **we took up our carriages**[7], and went up to Jerusalem.

16 There went with us also *certain* of the disciples of Caesarea, and brought with them one Mnason of Cyprus, an old disciple, with whom we should lodge.

17 And when we were come to Jerusalem, the brethren **received**[8] us gladly.

18 And the *day* following

---

[1] WH changed the word order from VIRGINS four to *four VIRGINS*.
[2] WH omitted the untranslated intensive we {our-selves} ([h]AmOn).
[3] WH omitted the untranslated both (te).
[4] WH changed of him (autou) to *of himself* ([h]eautou). [prefix added]
[5] WH changed the word order from the hands and the FEET to *the FEET and the hands*.

[6] WH changed then (**de**) to *then* (**tote**).
[7] WH changed having packed up **and left** (**apo**skeuasamenoi) to *having packed up* (*episkeuasamenoi*). Both Aor Mid-D Part. [prefix changed]
[8] WH changed received (edexanto) to *received favorably* (apedexanto). [prefix added]

Paul went in with us unto James; and all the elders were present.

19 And when he had saluted them, he declared particularly what things God had wrought among the Gentiles by his ministry.

20 And when they heard *it*, they glorified the **Lord**[1], and said unto him, Thou seest, brother, how many thousands **of Jews**[2] there are which believe; and they are all zealous of the law:

21 And they are informed of thee, that thou teachest all the Jews which are among the Gentiles to forsake Moses, saying that they ought not to circumcise *their* children, neither to walk after the customs.

22 What is it therefore? ~~the multitude must needs come together~~[3]: ~~for~~[4] they will hear that thou art come.

23 Do therefore this that we say to thee: We have four men which have a vow on them;

24 Them take, and purify thyself with them, and be at charges with them, that **they may shave**[5] *their* heads: and all **may know**[6] that those things, whereof they were informed concerning thee, are nothing; but *that* thou thyself also walkest orderly, and keepest the law.

25 As touching the Gentiles which believe, we **have written**[7] *and* concluded ~~that they observe no such thing, save only~~[8] that they keep

---

[1] WH changed **Lord** (**ku-rion**) to *God* (~~the~~*O*).

[2] WH changed **of** Jews (iou-dai**On**) to **among the Jews** (*in tois ioudaiois*).

[3] WH omitted it is necessary for multitude to come together (dei plAthos su-nel~~th~~ein).

[4] WH omitted for (gar).

[5] WH changed they **might** shave (xurAs**O**ntai) to *they will shave* (*xurAsontai*). **Aor** Mid **Sub** D to *Fut* Mid *Ind*. [tense & mood]

[6] WH changed **might** know (gn**Osi**) to *will know* (*gnOs-ontai*). **Aor Act Sub** to *Fut Mid Ind*. [tense, voice, & mood]

[7] In their margin, WH changed have sent **word to** (epesteilamen) to *have sent with authority from* (*apesteilamen*). [prefix changed]

[8] WH omitted nothing of such a kind they observe except (mAden toiouton tArein autous ei mA).

themselves from *things* offered to idols, and from **[the]**[1] blood, and from strangled, and from fornication.

26 Then Paul took the men, and the next day purifying himself with them entered into the temple, to signify the accomplishment of the days of purification, until that an offering should be offered for every one of them.

27 And when the seven days were almost ended, the Jews which were of Asia, when they saw him in the temple, stirred up all the people, and laid hands on him,

28 Crying out, Men of Israel, help: This is the man, that teacheth all *men* every where against the people, and the law, and this place: and further brought Greeks also into the temple, and hath polluted this holy place.

29 (For they had seen before with him in the city Trophimus an Ephesian, whom they supposed that Paul had brought into the temple.)

30 And all the city was moved, and the people ran together: and they took Paul, and drew him out of the temple: and forthwith the doors were shut.

31 **And**[2] as they went about to kill him, tidings came unto the chief captain of the band, that all Jerusalem **was in an uproar**[3].

32 Who immediately took soldiers and centurions, and ran down unto them: and when they saw the chief captain and the soldiers, they left beating of Paul.

33 Then the chief captain came near, and took him, and commanded *him* to be bound with two chains; and demanded who **[ever]**[4] he was, and what he had done.

34 And some **cried**[5] one thing, some another, among the multitude: and when he could not know the certainty for the tumult, he commanded him to be carried into the castle.

---

[2] WH changed **and** (**de**) to *both* (*te*).

[3] WH changed **had been** in an uproar (**sugkecutai**) to *is being* in an uproar (*sugcunetai*). *Pf* Pass Ind to *Pres* Pass Ind. [tense]

[4] WH omitted the untranslated ever (an)

[5] WH changed cried (eboOn) to *cried* (*epefOnoun*). Impf Act Ind of **boaO** to Impf Act Ind of *epifOneO*. [syn]

---

[1] WH omitted the untranslated the (to).

35 And when he came upon the stairs, so it was, that he was borne of the soldiers for the violence of the people.

36 For the multitude of the people followed after, crying, Away with him.

37 And as Paul was to be led into the castle, he said unto the chief captain, May I speak unto thee? Who said, Canst thou speak Greek?

38 Art not thou that Egyptian, which before these days madest an uproar, and leddest out into the wilderness four thousand men that were murderers?

39 But Paul said, I am a man *which am* a Jew of Tarsus, *a city* in Cilicia, a citizen of no mean city: and, I beseech thee, suffer me to speak unto the people.

40 And when he had given him licence, Paul stood on the stairs, and beckoned with the hand unto the people. And when there was made a great silence, he spake unto *them* in the Hebrew tongue, saying,

CHAPTER 22

1 Men, brethren, and fathers, hear ye my defence *which I make* now unto you.

2 (And when they heard that he spake in the Hebrew tongue to them, they kept the more silence: and he saith,)

3 I am ~~verily~~[1] a man *which am* a Jew, born in Tarsus, *a city* in Cilicia, yet brought up in this city at the feet of Gamaliel, *and* taught according to the perfect manner of the law of the fathers, and was zealous toward God, as ye all are this day.

4 And I persecuted this way unto the death, binding and delivering into prisons both men and women.

5 As also the high priest doth bear me witness, and all the estate of the elders: from whom also I received letters unto the brethren, and went to Damascus, to bring them which were there bound unto Jerusalem, for to be punished.

6 And it came to pass, that, as I made my journey, and was come nigh unto Damascus about noon, suddenly there shone from heaven a great light round about me.

7 And I fell unto the ground, and heard a voice saying unto me, Saul, Saul, why persecutest thou me?

8 And I answered, Who art thou, Lord? And he said unto me, I am Jesus of Nazareth, whom thou persecutest.

---

[1] WH omitted verily (men).

431

9 And they that were with me saw indeed the light, ~~and were afraid~~[1]; but they heard not the voice of him that spake to me.

10 And I said, What shall I do, Lord? And the Lord said unto me, Arise, and go into Damascus; and there it shall be told thee of all things which are appointed for thee to do.

11 And when I could not see for the glory of that light, being led by the hand of them that were with me, I came into Damascus.

12 And one Ananias, a **devout**[2] man according to the law, having a good report of all the Jews which dwelt *there*,

13 Came unto me, and stood, and said unto me, Brother Saul, receive thy sight. And the same hour I looked up upon him.

14 And he said, The God of our fathers hath chosen thee, that thou shouldest know his will, and see that Just One, and shouldest hear the voice of his mouth.

15 For thou shalt be his witness unto all men of what thou hast seen and heard.

16 And now why tarriest thou? arise, and be baptized, and wash away thy sins, calling on the name **of the Lord**[3].

17 And it came to pass, that, when I was come again to Jerusalem, even while I prayed in the temple, I was in a trance;

18 And saw him saying unto me, Make haste, and get thee quickly out of Jerusalem: for they will not receive ~~thy~~[4] testimony concerning me.

19 And I said, Lord, they know that I imprisoned and beat in every synagogue them that believed on thee:

20 And when the blood of thy martyr Stephen was shed, I also was standing by, and consenting ~~unto his death~~[5], and kept the raiment of them that slew him.

21 And he said unto me,

---

[1] WH omitted <u>and were afraid</u> (<u>kai</u> <u>emfoboi egenonto</u>).
[2] WH changed <u>devout</u> (<u>euse-bAs</u>) to *devout* (*eulabAs*). [adj]

[3] WH change of **the Lord** (**tou kuri**ou) to *of him* (*autou*).
[4] WH omitted <u>the</u> (<u>tAn</u>) from <u>of thee</u> <u>the testimony</u>.
[5] WH omitted <u>unto the death of him</u> (<u>tA anairesei autou</u>).

Depart: for I will send thee far hence unto the Gentiles.

22 And they gave him audience unto this word, and *then* lifted up their voices, and said, Away with such a *fellow* from the earth: for it is not fit that he should live.

23 And as they cried out, and cast off *their* clothes, and threw dust into the air,

24 The chief captain commanded him to be brought into the castle, and bade that he should be examined by scourging; that he might know wherefore they cried so against him.

25 And as they bound him with thongs, Paul said unto the centurion that stood by, Is it lawful for you to scourge a man that is a Roman, and uncondemned?

26 When the centurion heard *that*, he went and **told**[1] the chief captain, saying, **Take heed**[2] what thou doest: for this man is a Roman.

27 Then the chief captain came, and said unto him, Tell me, **[if]**[3] art thou a Roman?

He said, Yea.

28 **And**[4] the chief captain answered, With a great sum obtained I this freedom. And Paul said, But I was *free* born.

29 Then straightway they departed from him which should have examined him: and the chief captain also was afraid, after he knew that he was a Roman, and because he had bound him.

30 On the morrow, because he would have known the certainty wherefore he was accused **of**[5] the Jews, he loosed him **from *his* bands**[6], and commanded the chief priests and **all**[7] **their**[8] council **to appear**[9], and brought Paul down, and set him before them.

---

[1] WH changed the word order from TOLD the chief captain to *the chief captain TOLD*.

[2] WH omitted take heed (^hora)

[3] WH omitted the untrans-lated if (ei).

[4] WH changed **and** (te) to *but* (de).

[5] WH changed of (**para**) to *by* (^hupo).

[6] WH omitted from the bands (apo tOn desmOn).

[7] WH changed all (^holon) to *all* (**pan**). [syn]

[8] WH omitted of them (autOn).

[9] WH changed to appear (elthein) to *to appear together* (**sun**elthein). [prefix added]

CHAPTER 23

1 And Paul, earnestly beholding the council, said, Men *and* brethren, I have lived in all good conscience before God until this day.

2 And the high priest Ananias commanded them that stood by him to smite him on the mouth.

3 Then said Paul unto him, God shall smite thee, *thou* whited wall: for sittest thou to judge me after the law, and commandest me to be smitten contrary to the law?

4 And they that stood by said, Revilest thou God's high priest?

5 Then said Paul, I wist not, brethren, that he was the high priest: for it is written, Thou shalt not speak evil of the ruler of thy people.

6 But when Paul perceived that the one part were Sadducees, and the other Pharisees, **he cried out**[1] in the council, Men *and* brethren, I am a Pharisee, the son **of a Pharisee**[2]: of the hope

and resurrection of the dead I am called in question.

7 And **when he had** so **said**[3], there arose a dissension between the Pharisees and **the**[4] Sadducees: and the multitude was divided.

8 For the Sadducees say that there is no resurrection, **neither**[5] angel, nor spirit: but the Pharisees confess both.

9 And there arose a great cry: and [∧**some**][6] **the scribes**[7] *that were* of the Pharisees' part arose, and strove, saying, We find no evil in this man: but if a spirit or an angel hath spoken to him, ~~let us not fight against God~~[8].

(*farisaiOn*). [number]
[3] WH changed <u>having said</u> (**lalAsantos**) to *having said* (**eipontos**). Both Aor Act Part Gen Masc Sing. <u>laleO</u> to *legO*. [syn]
[4] WH omitted <u>the</u> (<u>tOn</u>).
[5] WH changed <u>not</u> **but** (<u>mAde</u>) to *not* **and** (*mAte*). [syn conj]
[6] WH added *some* (*tines*) before <u>the</u> <u>scribes</u>.
[7] WH changed <u>the</u> <u>scribes</u> (<u>^hoi</u> <u>grammateis</u>) to *of the scribes* (*tOn grammateOn*). **Nom** to **Gen**. [case]
[8] WH omitted <u>let us</u> <u>not</u> <u>fight</u> against God (<u>ma</u> ~~th~~<u>eomacOmen</u>).

---

[1] WH changed <u>he cried out</u> (<u>ekraxen</u>) to *he was crying out* (*ekrazen*). **Aor** to *Impf*. [tense]
[2] WH changed <u>of</u> **a** Pharisee (<u>farisaiou</u>) to *of Pharisees*

10 And **when there arose**[1] a great dissension, the chief captain, **fearing**[2] lest Paul should have been pulled in pieces of them, commanded the soldiers to go down, and to take him by force from among them, and to bring *him* into the castle.

11 And the night following the Lord stood by him, and said, Be of good cheer, ~~Paul~~[3]: for as thou hast testified of me in Jerusalem, so must thou bear witness also at Rome.

12 And when it was day, ~~certain~~[4] **of the Jews**[5] banded **together**[6], and bound themselves under a curse, saying that they would neither eat nor drink till they had killed Paul.

13 And they were more than forty which **had made**[7] this conspiracy.

14 And they came to the chief priests and elders, and said, We have bound ourselves under a great curse, that we will eat nothing until we have slain Paul.

15 Now therefore ye with the council signify to the chief captain that he bring **him**[8] down **unto**[9] you ~~to morrow~~[10], as though ye would enquire something more perfectly concerning him: and we, or ever he come near, are ready to kill him.

16 And when Paul's sister's son heard of their lying in wait, he went and entered into the castle, and told Paul.

17 Then Paul called one of

---

[1] WH changed **having** arisen (genomenAs) to *arising* (*ginomenAs*). **Aor** Part to *Pres* Part. [tense]

[2] WH changed having feared (eulabAtheis) to *having feared* (*fobAtheis*). Both Aor Pass Part. [syn]

[3] WH omitted Paul (paule).

[4] WH omitted some (tines).

[5] WH changed of the Jews (**tOn** ioudaiOn) to *the Jews* (*^{h}oi ioudaioi*). **Gen** to *Nom*. [case]

[6] WH changed the word order from having made **some** of the Jews A PLOT to *having made A PLOT the Jews*.

[7] WH changed **had** made (**pepoiAkotes**) to *made* (*poiAsamenoi*). **Pf Act** Part to *Aor Mid* Part. [tense & voice]

[8] WH changed the word order from HIM he bring down to *he bring down HIM*.

[9] WH changed **unto** (**pros**) to *into* (*eis*).

[10] WH omitted tomorrow (aurion).

the centurions unto *him*, and said, Bring this young man unto the chief captain: for he hath a certain thing to tell him.

18 So he took him, and brought *him* to the chief captain, and said, Paul the prisoner called me unto *him*, and prayed me to bring this young man unto thee, who hath something to say unto thee.

19 Then the chief captain took him by the hand, and went *with him* aside privately, and asked *him*, What is that thou hast to tell me?

20 And he said, The Jews have agreed to desire thee that thou wouldest bring down Paul to morrow into the council, as **though they would**[1] enquire somewhat of him more perfectly.

21 But do not thou yield unto them: for there lie in wait for him of them more than forty men, which have bound themselves with an oath, that they will neither eat nor drink till they have killed him: and now are they ready, looking for a promise from

thee.

22 So the chief captain *then* let the young man depart, and charged *him, See thou* tell no man that thou hast shewed these things to me.

23 And he called unto *him* two centurions, saying, Make ready two hundred soldiers to go to Caesarea, and horsemen threescore and ten, and spearmen two hundred, at the third hour of the night;

24 And provide *them* beasts, that they may set Paul on, and bring *him* safe unto Felix the governor.

25 And he wrote a letter **after**[2] this manner:

26 Claudius Lysias unto the most excellent governor Felix *sendeth* greeting.

27 This man was taken of the Jews, and should have been killed of them: then came I with an army, and rescued **him**[3], having understood that he was a Roman.

28 **And**[4] when I would

---

[1] WH changed though **they** would (mell**ontes**) to *though it would* (mell**On**). Both Pres Act Part. Nom Masc **Plur** to Nom Masc *Sing*. [number]

[2] WH changed having **about** (**peri**ecousan) to *having* (ecousan). Both Pres Act Part. [prefix dropped]
[3] WH omitted him (auton).
[4] WH changed and (**de**) to *and* (te).

~~have known~~[1] the cause wherefore they accused him, ~~I brought him forth into their council~~[2]:

29 Whom I perceived to be accused of questions of their law, but to have nothing laid to his charge worthy of death or of bonds.

30 And when it was told me how that ~~the Jews~~[3] ~~laid~~[4] wait for the man, I sent straightway to thee, and gave commandment to his accusers also to say **[that]**[5] before thee what *they had* against him. ~~Farewell~~[6].

31 Then the soldiers, as it was commanded them, took Paul, and brought *him* by

[the][7] night to Antipatris.

32 On the morrow they left the horsemen **to go**[8] with him, and returned to the castle:

33 Who, when they came to Caesarea, and delivered the epistle to the governor, presented Paul also before him.

34 And when ~~the governor~~[9] had read *the letter*, he asked of what province he was. And when he understood that *he was* of Cilicia;

35 I will hear thee, said he, when thine accusers are also come. ~~And~~[10] **he commanded**[11] **him**[12] to be kept in Herod's judgment hall.

---

[1] WH changed to know (gnOnai) to *to know exactly* (*epignOnai*). Both Aor Act Inf. [prefix added]

[2] WH omitted I brought him forth into their council (katAgagon auton eis to sunedrion autOn).

[3] WH omitted by the Jews (ʰupo tOn ioudaiOn).

[4] WH omitted laid (mellein— to be intending).

[5] WH omitted the untranslated that (ta).

[6] WH omitted farewell (errOso), although they retained it in their margin.

[7] WH omitted the untranslated the (tAs).

[8] WH changed to go (poreuesthai) to *to go away* (*apercesthai*). [syn]

[9] WH omitted the governor (ʰo ʰAgemOn) and forced the verb to supply the subject *he*.

[10] WH omitted and (te).

[11] WH changed **he commanded** (ekeleuse) to *having commanded* (*keleusas*). Aor Act **Ind** to Aor Act *Part*. [mood]

[12] WH moved him (auton) from after he commanded (ekeleuse) to after *to be kept* (*fulassesthai*).

CHAPTER 24

1　And after five days Ananias the high priest descended with **the**[1] **elders**[2], and *with* a certain orator *named* Tertullus, who informed the governor against Paul.

2　And when he was called forth, Tertullus began to accuse *him*, saying, Seeing that by thee we enjoy great quietness, and that **very worthy deeds**[3] are done unto this nation by thy providence,

3　We accept *it* always, and in all places, most noble Felix, with all thankfulness.

4　Notwithstanding, that I be not further tedious unto thee, I pray thee that thou wouldest hear us of thy clemency a few words.

5　For we have found this man *a* pesti-lent *fellow*, and a mover of **sedition**[4] among all the Jews throughout the world, and a ringleader of the sect of the Nazarenes:

6　Who also hath gone about to profane the temple: whom we took, ~~and would have judged according to our law~~.

7　~~But the chief captain Lysias came *upon us*, and with great violence took *him* away out of our hands,~~

8　~~Commanding his accusers to come unto thee:~~[5]

---

[1] WH changed **the** (**tOn**) to *several* (*tinOn*).

[2] WH changed the word order from the ELDERS to ELDERS *several*.

[3] WH changed very worthy deeds (**katorthOmatOn**— **success, prosperity**) to *very worthy deeds* (*diorthOmatOn*— **improvements, reforms**). [prefix changed]

[4] WH changed sedition (stasin) to *seditions* (*staseis*). **Sing** to *Plur*. [number]

[5] WH omitted and would have judged according to our law but the chief captain Lysias came [upon us] and with great violence took [him] away out of our hands commanding his accusers to come unto thee (kai kata ton [h]Ameteron nomon AthelAsamen krinein parelthOn de lusias [h]o ciliarcos meta pollAs bias ek tOn ceirOn [h]AmOn apAgage keleusas tous katAborous autou ercestai epi se) They retained these words, however, in their original margin. [Modern printings of WH and the computerized version omit these words in their text itself without brackets.]

by examining of whom thyself mayest take knowledge of all these things, whereof we accuse him.

9 And the Jews also **assented**[1], saying that these things were so.

10 **Then**[2] Paul, after that the governor had beckoned unto him to speak, answered, Forasmuch as I know that thou hast been of many years a judge unto this nation, I do the more cheerfully answer for myself:

11 Because that thou mayest understand, that there are ~~yet but~~[3] twelve days since I went up **to**[4] Jerusalem for to worship.

12 And they neither found me in the temple disputing with any man, neither **raising up**[5] the people, neither in the synagogues, nor in the city:

13 **Neither**[6] can [ₐto thee][7] they prove the things whereof they now accuse me.

14 But this I confess unto thee, that after the way which they call heresy, so worship I the God of my fathers, believing all things which are written in the law and [ₐthe {things} in][8] in the prophets:

15 And have hope toward God, which they themselves also allow, that there shall be a resurrection ~~of the dead~~[9], both of the just and unjust.

16 **And**[10] herein do I exercise myself, to have always a conscience void of offence toward God, and *toward* men.

17 Now after many years **I came**[11] to bring alms to my

---

[1] WH changed **assented** (sune~~th~~ento) to *joined in the attack* (sunepe~~th~~ento). [prefix added]

[2] WH changed **then** (**de**) to *then* (*te*). [syn]

[3] WH omitted yet but (**A**).

[4] WH changed in (**en**) to *into* (*eis*).

[5] WH changed raising up **with** (episustasin) *to raising* up (*epistasin*). [prefix dropped]

[6] WH changed neither (oute—not **and**) to *neither* (*oude*—not **but**).

[7] WH added *to thee* (*soi*) resulting in *neither are they able to prove **to thee***.

[8] WH added *the {things} in* (*tois en*), letting *in* take the place of the in supplied by the dative case.

[9] WH omitted of the dead (nekrOn).

[10] WH changed and (**de**) to *and* (**kai**).

[11] WH changed the word order from I CAME alms to bring to the nation of me to *alms to bring to the nation of me I CAME.*

nation, and offerings.

18 **Whereupon**[1] [ʌ**rather**][2] certain Jews from Asia found me purified in the temple, neither with multitude, nor with tumult.

19 Who ought to have been here before thee, and object, if they had ought against me.

20 Or else let these same *here* say, ~~if~~[3] they have found any evil doing ~~in me~~[4], while I stood before the council,

21 Except it be for this one voice, that I cried **standing**[5] among them, Touching the resurrection of the dead I am called in question **by**[6] you

this day.

22 **And** ~~when~~ **Felix**[7] ~~heard these things~~[8], having more perfect knowledge of *that* way, he deferred them, and said, When Lysias the chief captain shall come down, I will know the uttermost of your matter.

23 ~~And~~[9] he commanded a centurion to keep **Paul**[10], and to let *him* have liberty, and that he should forbid none of his acquaintance to minister ~~or come~~[11] unto him.

24 And after certain days, when Felix came with ~~his~~[12] [ʌ**own**][13] wife Drusilla, which was a Jewess, he sent for

---

[1] WH changed in which {**neut** things} (en ois) to *in which* {**fem** things} (en ais). Dat **Neut** Plur to Dat *Fem* Plur. [gender]

[2] WH added *rather* (de) after certain (tines) in the Greek text. The word would come before certain in the English text.

[3] WH omitted if (ei).

[4] WH omitted in me (en emoi).

[5] WH changed the word order from STANDING among them to *among them STANDING*.

[6] WH changed by (ʰ**uf**) to *by* (*ef*).

[7] WH changed the word order from **having heard** THEN **these** {**things**} THE FELIX deferred them to *deferred* THEN *them THE FELIX*.

[8] WH omitted having heard these things (akousas tauta).

[9] WH omitted and (te).

[10] WH changed **the Paul** (ton paulon) to *him* (*auton*).

[11] WH omitted or come (A prosercest̶hai).

[12] WH omitted of him (autou).

[13] WH added *own* (idia). In other words, they changed the wife **of him** (tA gunaiki **autou**) to *the own wife* (*tA idia gunaiki*).

Paul, and heard him concerning the faith in Christ [ʌ**Jesus**][1].

25 And as he reasoned of righteousness, temperance, and judgment [~~shall be~~][2] to come, Felix trembled, and answered, Go thy way for this time; when I have a convenient season, I will call for thee.

26 [~~and~~][3] He hoped also that money should have been given him of Paul, ~~that he might loose him~~[4]: wherefore he sent for him the oftener, and communed with him.

27 But after two years Porcius Festus came into Felix' room: and Felix, willing to shew the Jews **a pleasure**[5], left Paul bound.

CHAPTER 25

1 Now when Festus was come into the province, after three days he ascended from Caesarea to Jerusalem.

2 **Then**[6] **the high priest**[7] and the chief of the Jews informed him against Paul, and besought him,

3 And desired favour against him, that he would send for him to Jerusalem, laying wait in the way to kill him.

4 But Festus answered, that Paul should be kept **at Caesarea**[8], and that he himself would depart shortly *thither*.

5 Let them therefore, said he, which among you **are able**[9], go down with *me*, and accuse this man, if there be any **wickedness**[10] in him.

---

[1] WH added *Jesus* (*iAsoun*).
[2] WH omitted the untranslated shall be (*eses̶thai*) in the judgment the coming shall be.
[3] WH omitted the untranslated and (*de*).
[4] WH omitted that he might loose him (ʰopOs lusA auton).
[5] WH changed graces (caritas) to *grace* (*carita*). **Plur** to *Sing*. [number]

[6] WH changed **then** (**de**) to *and* (*te*).
[7] WH changed the high priest (ʰo arciereus) to *the high priests* (ʰoi arciereis). **Sing** to *Plur*. [number]
[8] WH changed in Caesarea (en kaisareia) to *into Caesarea* (*eis kaisareian*). [prep & case]
[9] WH changed the word order from ARE BEING ABLE among you he said to *among you he said* ARE BEING ABLE.
[10] WH changed the word order from WICKEDNESS in the man to *in the man* WICKEDNESS.

6 And when he had tarried among them [ᴧnot]¹ more than [ᴧeight]² ten days, he went down unto Caesarea; and the next day sitting on the judgment seat commanded Paul to be brought.

7 And when he was come, the Jews which came down from Jerusalem stood round about [ᴧhim]³, and **laid** many and grievous **complaints**⁴ **against**⁵ ~~Paul~~⁶, which they could not prove.

8 While [ᴧPaul]⁷ he answered ~~for himself~~⁸, Neither against the law of the Jews, neither against the temple, nor yet against Caesar, have I offended any thing at all.

9 But Festus, willing to

---

¹ WH added *not* (*ou*).
² WH added *eight* (*octO*).
³ WH added *him* (*auton*).
⁴ WH changed complaints (aitiamata) to *complaints* (*aitiOmata*).
⁵ WH changed laid AGAINST (ferontes KATA) to *AGAINST laid* (*KATAferontes*). [2 words to 1 word]
⁶ WH omitted the Paul (tou paulou).
⁷ WH added *Paul* (*tou paulou*), replacing the subject (he) supplied by the verb.
⁸ WH omitted for himself (autou).

do the Jews a pleasure, answered Paul, and said, Wilt thou go up to Jerusalem, and there be judged of these things before me?

10 Then said Paul, I stand at Caesar's judgment seat, where I ought to be judged: to the Jews have I done no wrong, as thou very well knowest.

11 **For**⁹ if I be an offender, or have committed any thing worthy of death, I refuse not to die: but if there be none of these things whereof these accuse me, no man may deliver me unto them. I appeal unto Caesar.

12 Then Festus, when he had conferred with the council, answered, Hast thou appealed unto Caesar? unto Caesar shalt thou go.

13 And after certain days king Agrippa and Bernice came unto Caesarea to **salute**¹⁰ Festus.

14 And when they had been there many days, Festus declared Paul's cause unto the

---

⁹ WH changed **for** (**gar**) to *therefore* (*oun*).
¹⁰ WH changed **will be** greeting (aspasomenoi) to *having* greet**ed** (*aspasamenoi*). **Fut** Mid Part to *Aor* Mid Part. [tense]

king, saying, There is a certain man left in bonds by Felix:

15 About whom, when I was at Jerusalem, the chief priests and the elders of the Jews informed *me*, desiring *to have* **judgment**[1] against him.

16 To whom I answered, It is not the manner of the Romans to deliver any man ~~to die~~[2], before that he which is accused have the accusers face to face, and have licence to answer for himself concerning the crime laid against him.

17 Therefore, when they were come hither, without any delay on the morrow I sat on the judgment seat, and commanded the man to be brought forth.

18 Against whom when the accusers stood up, **they brought**[3] none accusation of

such things as I **supposed**[4]: [∧**of evil {things}}**][5]

19 But had certain questions against him of their own superstition, and of one Jesus, which was dead, whom Paul affirmed to be alive.

20 And because I doubted [~~into~~][6] of **such**[7] manner of questions, I asked *him* whether he would go to Jerusalem, and there be judged of these matters.

21 But when Paul had appealed to be reserved unto the hearing of Augustus, I commanded him to be kept till **I might send**[8] him to Caesar.

22 Then Agrippa ~~said~~[9]

---

[1] WH changed **judgment** (di-kAn) to *condemnation* (*katadikAn*). [prefix added]
[2] WH omitted to die (eis apOleian).
[3] WH changed **you were bringing upon** (epeferon) to *they were bringing* (*eferon*). Both Impf Act Ind. **2**[nd] person Pl to *3*[rd] person Pl. [person]

[4] WH changed the word order from SUPPOSED I {myself} to *I* {myself} *SUPPOSED*.
[5] WH added of evil {things} (ponArOn).
[6] WH omitted into (eis) from into the about this question.
[7] WH changed this {kind} of question to (toutou zAtAsin) to *these* {kinds} *of questions* (*toutOn zAtAsin*). Gen **Masc Sing** to Gen *Neut Plur*. [gender & number]
[8] WH changed I might send (pemşO) to *I might send up* (*anapemşO*). Both Aor Act Sub. [prefix added]
[9] WH omitted said (efA).

unto Festus, I would also hear the man myself. [~~but the~~][1] To morrow, said he, thou shalt hear him.

23 And on the morrow, when Agrippa was come, and Bernice, with great pomp, and was entered into the place of hearing, with ~~the~~[2] chief captains, and principal men [~~being~~][3] of the city, at Festus' commandment Paul was brought forth.

24 And Festus said, King Agrippa, and all men which are here present with us, ye see this man, about whom **all**[4] the multitude of the Jews have dealt with me, both at Jerusalem, and *also* here, **crying**[5] that he ought not to live any longer.

25 But when I **found**[6] that he had committed nothing

worthy of death, **~~and~~**[7] that he himself hath appealed to Augustus, I have determined to send **~~him~~**[8].

26 Of whom I have no certain thing to write unto my lord. Wherefore I have brought him forth before you, and specially before thee, O king Agrippa, that, after examination had, I might have somewhat **to write**[9].

27 For it seemeth to me unreasonable to send a prisoner, and not withal to signify the crimes *laid* against him.

CHAPTER 26

1 Then Agrippa said unto Paul, Thou art permitted to speak for thyself. Then Paul stretched forth the hand, **and answered for himself**[10]:

---

[1] WH omitted the untranslated <u>but</u> <u>the</u> (^h<u>o</u> <u>de</u>).

[2] WH omitted <u>the</u> (<u>tois</u>).

[3] WH omitted the untranslated <u>being</u> (<u>ousi</u>).

[4] WH changed <u>all</u> (<u>pan</u>) to *all* (^h<u>apan</u>).

[5] WH changed <u>crying</u> {**out**} (**epi**bo**Ontes**) to *crying* (*boOntes*). [prefix dropped]

[6] WH changed **having** <u>found</u> (<u>kata</u>labo**menos**) to *I found* (*katelabomAn*). Aor Mid **Part** to Aor Mid *Ind*. [mood]

[7] WH omitted <u>and</u> (<u>kai</u>).

[8] WH omitted <u>him</u> (<u>auton</u>).

[9] WH changed **to** <u>write</u> (gras**ai**) to *I might* write (gra**s**O). Aor Act **Inf** to Aor Act *Sub*. [mood]

[10] WH changed the word order from <u>then</u> <u>the</u> <u>Paul</u> was speaking in his own defence having stretched <u>forth</u> <u>the</u> <u>hand</u> to *then the Paul having stretched forth the hand* was speaking in his own defence.

2   I think myself happy, king Agrippa, because **I shall answer for myself**[1] this day before thee touching all the things whereof I am accused of the Jews:

3   Especially ~~because I know~~[2] thee to be expert in all customs and questions which are among the Jews: wherefore I beseech ~~thee~~[3] to hear me patiently.

4   My manner of life from my youth, which was at the first among mine own nation [˄**also**][4] at Jerusalem, know all ~~the~~[5] Jews;

5   Which knew me from the beginning, if they would testify, that after the most straitest sect of our religion I lived a Pharisee.

6   And now I stand and am judged for the hope of the promise made of God **unto**[6]

our fathers [˄**of us**][7]:

7   Unto which *promise* our twelve tribes, instantly serving *God* day and night, hope to come. For which hope's sake, ~~king Agrippa~~[8], I am accused of ~~the~~[9] Jews [˄**O King**][10].

8   Why should it be thought a thing incredible with you, that God should raise the dead?

9   I verily thought with myself, that I ought to do many things contrary to the name of Jesus of Nazareth.

10   Which thing I also did in Jerusalem: and many [˄**also**][11] of the saints did I shut up ~~in~~[12] in prison, having received authority from the chief priests; and when they were put to death, I gave my voice against *them*.

11   And I punished them oft in every synagogue, and compelled *them* to blaspheme; and being exceedingly mad against *them*, I persecuted them unto

---

[1] WH changed the word order from I SHALL ANSWER FOR MYSELF upon of you day to upon of you I SHALL day ANSWER FOR MYSELF.

[2] WH omitted because I know (eidOs). [The KJV put the words in italics.]

[3] WH omitted thee (sou).

[4] WH added also (te) after in (en) in the Greek text.

[5] WH omitted the (ʰoi).

[6] WH changed unto (**pros**) to

into (**eis**).

[7] WH added *of us* (ʰAmOn).

[8] WH omitted King Agrippa (basileu agrippa).

[9] WH omitted the (tOn).

[10] WH added O King (basileu).

[11] WH added also (te).

[12] WH omitted in (en).

strange cities.

12 Whereupon **[also]**[1] as I went to Damascus with authority and commission **from**[2] the chief priests,

13 At midday, O king, I saw in the way a light from heaven, above the brightness of the sun, shining round about me and them which journeyed with me.

14 **And**[3] when we were all fallen to the earth, I heard a voice **speaking**[4] unto me, **and saying**[5] in the Hebrew tongue, Saul, Saul, why persecutest thou me? *it is* hard for thee to kick against the pricks.

15 And I said, Who art thou, Lord? And **[∧Lord]**[6] he said, I am Jesus whom thou persecutest.

16 But rise, and stand upon thy feet: for I have appeared unto thee for this purpose, to make thee a minister and a witness both of these things which thou hast seen **[∧me]**[7], and of those things in the which I will appear unto thee;

17 Delivering thee from the people, and **[∧out of]**[8] *from* the Gentiles, unto whom **now**[9] I **[∧myself]**[10] send **thee**[11],

18 To open their eyes, **and**[12] to turn *them* from darkness to light, and *from* the power of Satan unto God, that they may receive forgiveness of sins, and inheritance among them which are sanctified by faith that is in me.

19 Whereupon, O king Agrippa, I was not disobedient unto the heavenly vision:

---

[1] WH omitted the untranslated <u>also</u> (<u>kai</u>).

[2] WH omitted <u>from</u> (<u>para</u>) and forced the genitive case to supply the preposition.

[3] WH changed <u>and</u> (<u>de</u>) to *and* (**te**).

[4] WH changed **speak**ing (**lal**ousan) to *saying* (*legousan*). Both Pres Act Part. [syn]

[5] WH omitted <u>and</u> <u>saying</u> (<u>kai</u> <u>legousan</u>).

[6] WH added *Lord* (*kurios*), making the verse say, "And the *Lord* said."

[7] WH added *me* (*me*) in their text (but not in their margin).

[8] WH added *out of* (*ek*).

[9] WH omitted <u>now</u> (<u>nun</u>).

[10] WH added the intensive pronoun *myself* (*egO*).

[11] WH changed the word order from <u>THEE</u> <u>I send</u> to *I send* <u>THEE</u>.

[12] WH changed **and** (**kai**) to *the* (*tou*).

20 But shewed first unto them of Damascus, [ʌ**both**]¹ and at Jerusalem, and ~~throughout~~² all the coasts of Judaea, and *then* to the Gentiles, that they should repent and turn to God, and do works meet for repentance.

21 For these causes **the**³ Jews caught me in the temple, and went about to kill *me*.

22 Having therefore obtained help **of**⁴ God, I continue unto this day, **witnessing**⁵ both to small and great, saying none other things than those which the prophets and Moses did say should come:

23 That Christ should suffer, *and* that he should be the first that should rise from the dead, and should shew light unto [ʌ**both**]⁶ the people, and to the Gentiles.

24 And as he thus spake for himself, Festus **said**⁷ with a loud voice, Paul, thou art beside thyself; much learning doth make thee mad.

25 But [ʌ**Paul**]⁸ he said, I am not mad, most noble Festus; but speak forth the words of truth and soberness.

26 For the king knoweth of these things, before whom also I speak freely: for I am persuaded that none of these things are hidden from him; for this thing was not done in a corner.

27 King Agrippa, believest thou the prophets? I know that thou believest.

28 Then Agrippa **said**⁹ unto Paul, Almost thou persuadest me **to be**¹⁰ a Christian.

29 And Paul **said**¹¹, I would to God, that not only thou, but also all that hear me this day, were both almost,

---

¹ WH added *both* (*te*), making their text read *both also at Jerusalem.*

² WH omitted throughout (eis).

³ WH omitted the (ʰoi).

⁴ WH change **of** (**para**) to *from* (*apo*).

⁵ WH changed witnessing (marturo**u**menos) to *witnessing* (*marturomenos*). mar- ture**O** to *marturomai.* [syn]

⁶ WH added *both* (*te*) after the (t**O**) in their text.

---

⁷ WH changed **was saying** (ef**A**) to *says* (*f**A**si*). **Impf** NV Ind to **Pres** NV Ind. [tense]

⁸ WH added *Paul* (*paulos*).

⁹ WH omitted said (af**A**).

¹⁰ WH changed to be (**genest**hai) to *to make* (*poi- Asai*). Both Aor Act Inf.

¹¹ WH omitted said (eipen).

and **altogether**[1] such as I am, except these bonds.

30 ~~And when he had thus spoken~~[2], the king [∧**both**][3] rose up, and the governor, and Bernice, and they that sat with them:

31 And when they were gone aside, they talked between themselves, saying, This man doeth nothing worthy of death or of bonds.

32 Then said Agrippa unto Festus, This man might have been set at liberty, if he had not appealed unto Caesar.

CHAPTER 27

1 And when it was determined that we should sail into Italy, they delivered Paul and certain other prisoners unto *one* named Julius, a centurion of Augustus' band.

2 And entering into a ship of Adramyttium, we launched, **meaning**[4] to sail [∧**into**][5] by the coasts of Asia; *one* Aristarchus, a Macedonian of Thessalonica, being with us.

3 And the next *day* we touched at Sidon. And Julius courteously entreated Paul, and gave *him* liberty to go unto his friends to refresh himself.

4 And when we had launched from thence, we sailed under Cyprus, because the winds were contrary.

5 And when we had sailed over the sea of Cilicia and Pamphylia, we came to Myra, *a city* of Lycia.

6 And there the centurion found a ship of Alexandria sailing into Italy; and he put us therein.

7 And when we had sailed slowly many days, and scarce were come over against Cnidus, the wind not suffering us, we sailed under Crete, over against Salmone;

---

[1] WH changed <u>altogether</u> (**poll**O—**many**) to *altogether* (*megalO*—**great**).
[2] WH omitted <u>and</u> <u>these</u> {things} <u>having spoken of him</u> (<u>kai</u> <u>tauta</u> <u>eipontos autou</u>).
[3] WH added *both* (<u>te</u>) after <u>rose up</u> (<u>anestA</u>) in their Greek text.

[4] WH changed <u>meaning</u> (<u>mellontes</u>) to *meaning* (*mellonti*). Nom **Masc Plur** (i.e. **we men** meaning) to Dat *Neut Sing* (i.e. *the ship* meaning). [gender & number]
[5] WH added *into* (*eis*) making their text read <u>into</u> <u>the according to the Asia place</u>.

8 And, hardly passing it, came unto a place which is called The fair havens; nigh whereunto was the city *of* Lasea.

9 Now when much time was spent, and when sailing was now dangerous, because the fast was now already past, Paul admonished *them*,

10 And said unto them, Sirs, I perceive that this voyage will be with hurt and much damage, not only of the **lading**[1] and ship, but also of our lives.

11 Nevertheless the centurion **believed**[2] the master and the owner of the ship, more than those things which were spoken by Paul.

12 And because the haven was not commodious to winter in, the more part advised to depart **thence also**[3], if by any means they might attain to Phenice, *and there* to winter; *which is* an haven of Crete, and lieth toward the south west and north west.

13 And when the south wind blew softly, supposing that they had obtained *their* purpose, loosing *thence*, they sailed close by Crete.

14 But not long after there arose against it a tempestuous wind, called **Euroclydon**[4].

15 And when the ship was caught, and could not bear up into the wind, we let *her* drive.

16 And running under a certain island which is called **Clauda**[5], we had **much**[6] work to come by the boat:

17 Which when they had taken up, they used helps, undergirding the ship; and, fearing lest they should fall into the quicksands, strake

---

[1] WH changed <u>lading</u> (<u>por-tou</u>) to *lading* (*portiou*). **Masc** to *Neut*. [gender]

[2] WH changed the word order from <u>BELIEVED</u> more to *more BELIEVED*.

[3] WH changed **also** from there (**kakei**t̶h̶en) to *from there* (*ekei*t̶h̶en). [prefix changed]

[4] WH changed <u>Euroc**lyd**on</u> (<u>euro**klud**On</u>) to *Eurokulon* (*eurakulOn*). **Southe**ast wind to *North*east wind.

[5] WH changed <u>Clauda</u> (<u>klau-d**An**</u>) to *Cauda* (*kaud**a***) in their text. Acc **Fem** to Acc **Neut**. They had <u>Clauda</u> (claud**a**) in their margin. [gender & spell]

[6] WH changed the word order from <u>MUCH</u> we used strength to we used strength <u>MUCH</u>.

sail, and so were driven.

18 And we being exceedingly tossed with a tempest, the next *day* they lightened the ship;

19 And the third *day* **we cast out**[1] with our own hands the tackling of the ship.

20 And when neither sun nor stars in many days appeared, and no small tempest lay on *us*, all hope that we should be saved was then taken away.

21 **But**[2] after long abstinence Paul stood forth in the midst of them, and said, Sirs, ye should have hearkened unto me, and not have loosed from Crete, and to have gained this harm and loss.

22 And now I exhort you to be of good cheer: for there shall be no loss of *any man's* life among you, but of the ship.

23 For there stood by me this night the **angel**[3] of God,

whose I am, and whom I serve,

24 Saying, Fear not, Paul; thou must be brought before Caesar: and, lo, God hath given thee all them that sail with thee.

25 Wherefore, sirs, be of good cheer: for I believe God, that it shall be even as it was told me.

26 Howbeit we must be cast upon a certain island.

27 But when the fourteenth night was come, as we were driven up and down in Adria, about midnight the shipmen deemed that they drew near to some country;

28 And sounded, and found *it* twenty fathoms: and when they had gone a little further, they sounded again, and found *it* fifteen fathoms.

29 Then fearing **lest**[4] we should have fallen **upon**[5] rocks, they cast four anchors out of the stern, and wished for the day.

30 And as the shipmen were about to flee out of the

---

[1] WH changed **we** cast out (erri*samen*) to *they cast out* (erri*san*). **1**[st] Plur to *3*[rd] Plur. [number]

[2] WH changed **but** (**de**) to *and so* (*te*).

[3] WH changed the word order from ANGEL of the God of whom I am for whom also I serve to *of the God of*

whom I am for whom also I serve ANGEL.

[4] WH change lest (mApOs) to *lest* (*mA pOs*). **one**-word to *two* words [spell]

[5] WH changed **upon** (**eis**) to *according to* (*kata*).

ship, when they had let down the boat into the sea, under colour as though they would have cast anchors out of the foreship,

31 Paul said to the centurion and to the soldiers, Except these abide in the ship, ye cannot be saved.

32 Then the soldiers cut off the ropes of the boat, and let her fall off.

33 And while the day was coming on, Paul besought *them* all to take meat, saying, This day is the fourteenth day that ye have tarried and continued fasting, having taken nothing.

34 Wherefore I pray you **to take**[1] *some* meat: for this is for your health: for there **shall** not an hair **fall**[2] **from**[3] the head of any of you.

35 And when he had thus spoken, he took bread, and gave thanks to God in presence of them all: and when he had broken *it*, he began to eat.

36 Then were they all of good cheer, and they also took *some* meat.

37 And we were in all in the ship **two hundred**[4] threescore and sixteen souls.

38 And when they had eaten enough, they lightened the ship, and cast out the wheat into the sea.

39 And when it was day, they knew not the land: but they discovered a certain creek with a shore, into the which **they were minded**[5], if it were possible, to **thrust in**[6] the ship.

40 And when they had taken up the anchors, they committed *themselves* unto the sea, and loosed the rudder bands, and hoised up the mainsail to the wind, and made toward shore.

41 And falling into a place

---

[1] WH changed to take {**before**} (**pros**labein) to *to take* {**with**} (*metalabein*). [prefix changed]

[2] WH changed shall **fall** (**pe**seitai) to *shall **be destroyed*** (*apoleitai*).

[3] WH changed from (**ek**— **out of**) to *from* (*apo*—**from**).

[4] In their margin, WH changed **two hundred** (**dia-kosiai**) to *about* (*Os*).

[5] WH changed they planned (ebouleusanto) to *they **were** planning* (*ebouleuonto*). **Aor** Mid Ind to *Impf* Mid Ind. [tense]

[6] In their margin, WH changed thrust in (**ex**Osai) to *thrust in* (*eks*Osai). **One** letter to *two* letters. [spell]

where two seas met, **they ran** the ship **aground**[1]; and the forepart stuck fast, and remained unmoveable, but the hinder part was broken with the violence ~~of the waves~~[2].

42 And the soldiers' counsel was to kill the prisoners, lest any of them should swim out, and escape.

43 But the centurion, willing to save Paul, kept them from *their* purpose; and commanded that they which could swim should cast *themselves* first *into the sea*, and get to land:

44 And the rest, some on boards, and some on *broken pieces* of the ship. And so it came to pass, that they escaped all safe to land.

CHAPTER 28

1 And when they were escaped, then **they knew**[3]

that the island was called **Melita**[4].

2 **And**[5] the barbarous people shewed us no little kindness: for they kindled a fire, and received us every one, because of the present rain, and because of the cold.

3 And when Paul had gathered a bundle of sticks [∧**some**][6], and laid *them* on the fire, there came a viper **out of**[7] the heat, and fastened on his hand.

4 And when the barbarians saw the *venomous* beast hang on his hand, they said among themselves, No doubt this man is a murderer, whom, though he hath escaped the sea, yet vengeance suffereth not to live.

5 And he shook off the beast into the fire, and felt no harm.

6 Howbeit they looked when he should have swollen, or fallen down dead suddenly:

---

[1] WH changed they ran aground (epOkeilan) to *they ran aground* (epekeilan). Both Aor Act Ind 3rd Plur. epokellO to *epikellO*. [spell]
[2] WH omitted of the waves (tOn kumatOn).
[3] WH changed **they** knew (epegnOsan) to *we knew* (epegnOmen). Both Aor Act

Ind. **3rd** Plur to *1rst* Plur. [person]
[4] In their margin, WH changed Melita (melitA) to *Melitan* (*melitAnA*). [spell]
[5] WH changed and (**de**) to *and* (*te*).
[6] WH added *some* (*ti*).
[7] WH changed **out of** (ek) to *from* (*apo*).

but after they had looked a great while, and saw no harm come to him, **they changed their minds**[1], and said that he was a god.

7　In the same quarters were possessions of the chief man of the island, whose name was Publius; who received us, and lodged us three days courteously.

8　And it came to pass, that the father of Publius lay sick of a fever and of a bloody flux: to whom Paul entered in, and prayed, and laid his hands on him, and healed him.

9　**So**[2] when this was done, others also, which had diseases **in the island**[3], came, and were healed:

10　Who also honoured us with many honours; and when we departed, they laded *us* with such things as **were necessary**[4].

11　And after three months we departed in a ship of Alexandria, which had wintered in the isle, whose sign was Castor and Pollux.

12　And landing at Syracuse, we tarried *there* three days.

13　And from thence **we fetched a compass**[5], and came to Rhegium: and after one day the south wind blew, and we came the next day to Puteoli:

14　Where we found brethren, and were desired to tarry **with**[6] them seven days: and so we went toward Rome.

15　And from thence, when the brethren heard of us, **they came**[7] to meet us as far as Appii forum, and The three taverns: whom when Paul

---

[1] WH changed chang**ing** their minds (metaball**o**menoi) to *having* changed their minds (metaba**lo**menoi). **Pres** Mid Part to *Aor* Mid Part. [tense]

[2] WH changed **so** (**oun**) to *but* (*de*).

[3] WH changed the word order from having diseases IN THE ISLAND to *IN THE ISLAND having diseases.*

[4] WH changed the need (t**An** creian) to *the needs* (*tas creias*). **Sing** to *Plur*. [number]

[5] In their margin, WH changed we **sailed around** (perie**lth**ontes) to *we cut anchor* (*perielontes*).

[6] WH changed **upon** (**ep'**) to *with* (*par'*).

[7] WH changed they came {**out**} (**ex**Al**th**on) to *they came* (*Al**th**on*). [prefix dropped]

saw, he thanked God, and took courage.

16 And when **we came**[1] to Rome, ~~the centurion delivered the prisoners to the captain of the guard~~: ~~but~~[2] **Paul**[3] was suffered to dwell by himself with a soldier that kept him.

17 And it came to pass, that after three days **Paul**[4] called the chief of the Jews together: and when they were come together, he said unto them, Men *and* brethren, though I **[myself]**[5] have committed nothing against the people, or customs of our

fathers, yet was I delivered prisoner from Jerusalem into the hands of the Romans.

18 Who, when they had examined me, would have let *me* go, because there was no cause of death in me.

19 But when the Jews spake against *it*, I was constrained to appeal unto Caesar; not that I had ought to accuse my nation of.

20 For this cause therefore have I called for you, to see *you*, and to speak with *you*: because that for the hope of Israel I am bound with this chain.

21 And they said unto him, We neither received letters out of Judaea concerning thee, neither any of the brethren that came shewed or spake any harm of thee.

22 But we desire to hear of thee what thou thinkest: for as concerning this sect, **we**[6] know that every where it is spoken against.

23 And when they had appointed him a day, there came many to him into *his* lodging; to whom he expounded and testified the kingdom of God, persuading

---

[1] WH changed <u>we came</u> (Al~~th~~homen) to *we came* {**into**} (*eisAl~~th~~homen*). [prefix added]

[2] WH omitted <u>the centurion delivered the prisoners to the captain of the guard but</u> (^{h}o ^{h}ekatonrcos paredOke <u>tous desmious</u> <u>tO stratopedarcA de</u>).

[3] WH changed the word order from THE PAUL <u>was suffered</u> to *was suffered THE PAUL.*

[4] WH changed <u>Paul</u> (<u>ton paulon</u>) to **him** (*auton*).

[5] WH changed the word order from <u>men brethren</u> MYSELF to *MYSELF men brethren.*

[6] WH changed the word order from <u>known are WE</u> to *known WE are.*

them [~~the {things}~~]¹ concerning Jesus, both out of the
law of Moses, and *out of* the
prophets, from morning till
evening.

24 And some believed the
things which were spoken,
and some believed not.

25 And when they agreed
not among themselves, they
departed, after that Paul had
spoken one word, Well spake
the Holy Ghost by Esaias the
prophet unto **our**² fathers,

26 Saying, Go unto this
people, and say, Hearing ye
shall hear, and shall not understand; and seeing ye shall
see, and not perceive:

27 For the heart of this
people is waxed gross, and
their ears are dull of hearing,
and their eyes have they
closed; lest they should see
with *their* eyes, and hear with
their ears, and understand
with *their* heart, and should
be converted, and **I should
heal**³ them.

28 Be it known therefore
unto you, that the salvation
of God is sent [ᴧ**this**]⁴ unto
the Gentiles, and *that* they
will hear it.

29 ~~And when he had
said these words, the Jews
departed, and had great
reasoning among them-
selves.~~⁵

30 And ~~Paul~~⁶ **dwelt**⁷ two
whole years in his own hired
house, and received all that
came in unto him,

31 Preaching the kingdom
of God, and teaching those
things which concern the
Lord Jesus Christ, with all
confidence, no man forbidding him.

---

¹ WH omitted the untrans-
lated the {things}.

² WH changed of us (ʰ**AmOn**)
in the fathers of us to *of you*
(ʰ*umOn*). [person]

³ WH changed I might heal
(ʰ**iasOmai**) to *I will heal* (ʰ*i-
asomai*). **Aor** Mid Sub to
Fut Mid-D Ind. [tense]

⁴ WH added *this* (*touto*).

⁵ WH omitted and when he
had said these words the
Jews departed and had great
reasoning among themselves
(kai tauta autou eipontos ʰa-
pAlthon ʰoi ioudaioi pollAn
econtes en ʰeautois suzAtA-
sin).

⁶ WH omitted the Paul (ʰo
paulos), letting the verb supply he as the subject.

⁷ WH changed dwelt
(emeine) to *dwelt* {*in*} (*ene-
meine*). [prefix added]

ROMANS

CHAPTER 1

1   Paul, a servant of Jesus Christ, called *to be* an apostle, separated unto the gospel of God,

2   (Which he had promised afore by his prophets in the holy scriptures,)

3   Concerning his Son Jesus Christ our Lord, which was made of the seed of David according to the flesh;

4   And declared *to be* the Son of God with power, according to the spirit of holiness, by the resurrection from the dead:

5   By whom we have received grace and apostleship, for obedience to the faith among all nations, for his name:

6   Among whom are ye also the called of Jesus Christ:

7   To all that be in Rome, beloved of God, called *to be* saints: Grace to you and peace from God our Father, and the Lord Jesus Christ.

8   First, I thank my God through Jesus Christ **for**[1] you all, that your faith is spoken of throughout the whole world.

9   For God is my witness, whom I serve with my spirit in the gospel of his Son, that without ceasing I make mention of you always in my prayers;

10   Making request, if by any means now at length I might have a prosperous journey by the will of God to come unto you.

11   For I long to see you, that I may impart unto you some spiritual gift, to the end ye may be established;

12   That is, that I may be comforted together with you by the mutual faith both of you and me.

13   Now I would not have you ignorant, brethren, that oftentimes I purposed to come unto you, (but was let hitherto,) that I might have some **fruit**[2] among you also, even as among other Gentiles.

14   I am debtor both to the Greeks, and to the barbarians; both to the wise, and to the unwise.

15   So, as much as in me is, I am ready to preach the gospel to you that are at Rome

---

[1] WH changed **for** (**ʰuper**) to *about* (*peri*).

[2] WH changed the word order from FRUIT some to *some FRUIT*.

also.

16 For I am not ashamed of the gospel ~~of Christ~~[1]: for it is the power of God unto salvation to every one that believeth; to the Jew first, and also to the Greek.

17 For therein is the righteousness of God revealed from faith to faith: as it is written, The just shall live by faith.

18 For the wrath of God is revealed from heaven against all ungodliness and unrighteousness of men, who hold the truth in unrighteousness;

19 Because that which may be known of God is manifest in them; for **God**[2] hath shewed *it* unto them.

20 For the invisible things of him from the creation of the world are clearly seen, being understood by the things that are made, *even* his eternal power and Godhead; so that they are without excuse:

21 Because that, when they knew God, they glorified *him* not as God, neither were thankful; but became vain in their imaginations, and their foolish heart was darkened.

22 Professing themselves to be wise, they became fools,

23 And changed the glory of the uncorruptible God into an image made like to corruptible man, and to birds, and fourfooted beasts, and creeping things.

24 Wherefore God **also**[3] gave them up to uncleanness through the lusts of their own hearts, to dishonour their own bodies between **themselves**[4]:

25 Who changed the truth of God into a lie, and worshipped and served the creature more than the Creator, who is blessed for ever. Amen.

26 For this cause God gave them up unto vile affections: for even their women did change the natural use into that which is against nature:

27 And likewise also the men, leaving the natural use of the woman, burned in their lust one toward another; men

---

[1] WH omitted of the Christ (tou cristou).

[2] WH changed the word order from for GOD to *GOD for*.

[3] WH omitted also (kai).

[4] WH changed themselves (ʰeautois) to *them* (*autois*). **Reflexive** to *Personal* Pronoun.

with men working that which is unseemly, and receiving in themselves that recompence of their error which was meet.

28 And even as they did not like to retain God in *their* knowledge, God gave them over to a reprobate mind, to do those things which are not convenient;

29 Being filled with all unrighteousness, fornication, ~~wickedness~~[1], covetousness, maliciousness; full of envy, murder, debate, deceit, malignity; whisperers,

30 Backbiters, haters of God, despiteful, proud, boasters, inventors of evil things, disobedient to parents,

31 Without understanding, covenantbreakers, without natural affection, ~~implacable~~[2], unmerciful:

32 Who knowing the judgment of God, that they which commit such things are worthy of death, not only do the same, but have pleasure in them that do them.

CHAPTER 2

1 Therefore thou art inexcusable, O man, whosoever thou art that judgest: for wherein thou judgest another, thou condemnest thyself; for thou that judgest doest the same things.

2 **But**[3] we are sure that the judgment of God is according to truth against them which commit such things.

3 And thinkest thou this, O man, that judgest them which do such things, and doest the same, that thou shalt escape the judgment of God?

4 Or despisest thou the riches of his goodness and forbearance and longsuffering; not knowing that the goodness of God leadeth thee to repentance?

5 But after thy hardness and impenitent heart treasurest up unto thyself wrath against the day of wrath and revelation of the righteous judgment of God;

6 Who will render to every man according to his deeds:

7 To them who by patient continuance in well doing seek for glory and honour

---

[1] WH omitted <u>wickedness</u> (<u>porneia</u>).

[2] WH omitted <u>implacable</u> (<u>aspondous</u>).

[3] In their margin, WH changed **but** (**de**) to *for* (**gar**).

and immortality, eternal life:

8 But unto them that are contentious, and do not obey [~~on the one hand~~][1] the truth, but obey unrighteousness, indignation and **wrath**[2],

9 Tribulation and anguish, upon every soul of man that doeth evil, of the Jew first, and also of the Gentile;

10 But glory, honour, and peace, to every man that worketh good, to the Jew first, and also to the Gentile:

11 For there is no respect of persons with God.

12 For as many as have sinned without law shall also perish without law: and as many as have sinned in the law shall be judged by the law;

13 (For not the hearers of **the**[3] law *are* just before God, but the doers of **the**[4] law shall be justified.

14 For when the Gentiles, which have not the law, **do**[5]

by nature the things contained in the law, these, having not the law, are a law unto themselves:

15 Which shew the work of the law written in their hearts, their conscience also bearing witness, and *their* thoughts the mean while accusing or else excusing one another;)

16 In the day when God shall judge the secrets of men by Jesus Christ according to my gospel.

17 **Behold**[6], thou art called a Jew, and restest in **the**[7] law, and makest thy boast of God,

18 And knowest *his* will, and approvest the things that are more excellent, being instructed out of the law;

19 And art confident that thou thyself art a guide of the blind, a light of them which are in darkness,

20 An instructor of the foolish, a teacher of babes, which hast the form of knowledge and of the truth in

---

[1] WH omitted the untranslated <u>on the one hand</u> (<u>men</u>).

[2] WH changed the word order from <u>indignation</u> <u>and</u> <u>WRATH</u> to *WRATH and indignation.*

[3] WH omitted <u>the</u> (<u>tou</u>).

[4] WH omitted <u>the</u> (<u>tou</u>).

[5] WH changed **he** <u>may do</u>

(<u>poiA</u>) to *they may do* (*poiOsin*). Both Pres Act Sub. 3rd **<u>Sing</u>** to 3rd *Plur*. [number]

[6] WH changed **behold** (<u>ide</u>) to *if but* (*ei de*).

[7] WH omitted <u>the</u> (<u>tO</u>).

the law.

21 Thou therefore which teachest another, teachest thou not thyself? thou that preachest a man should not steal, dost thou steal?

22 Thou that sayest a man should not commit adultery, dost thou commit adultery? thou that abhorrest idols, dost thou commit sacrilege?

23 Thou that makest thy boast of the law, through breaking the law dishonourest thou God?

24 For the name of God is blasphemed among the Gentiles through you, as it is written.

25 For circumcision verily profiteth, if thou keep the law: but if thou be a breaker of the law, thy circumcision is made uncircumcision.

26 Therefore if the uncircumcision keep the righteousness of the law, shall not his uncircumcision be counted for circumcision?

27 And shall not uncircumcision which is by nature, if it fulfil the law, judge thee, who by the letter and circumcision dost transgress the law?

28 For he is not a Jew, which is one outwardly; neither *is* *that* circumcision, which is outward in the flesh:

29 But he *is* a Jew, which is one inwardly; and circumcision *is* *that* of the heart, in the spirit, *and* not in the letter; whose praise *is* not of men, but of God.

CHAPTER 3

1 What advantage then hath the Jew? or what profit *is there* of circumcision?

2 Much every way: chiefly, ~~because~~[1] that unto them were committed the oracles of God.

3 For what if some did not believe? shall their unbelief make the faith of God without effect?

4 God forbid: yea, let God be true, but every man a liar; as it is written, That thou mightest be justified in thy sayings, and mightest overcome when thou art judged.

5 But if our unrighteousness commend the righteousness of God, what shall we say? *Is* God unrighteous who taketh vengeance? (I speak as a man)

6 God forbid: for then how shall God judge the world?

---

[1] WH omitted <u>for</u> (<u>gar</u>) from <u>for</u> **on the other hand** (<u>men gar</u>).

7 **For**[1] if the truth of God hath more abounded through my lie unto his glory; why yet am I also judged as a sinner?

8 And not *rather*, (as we be slanderously reported, and as some affirm that we say,) Let us do evil, that good may come? whose damnation is just.

9 What then? are we better *than they*? No, in no wise: for we have before proved both Jews and Gentiles, that they are all under sin;

10 As it is written, There is none righteous, no, not one:

11 There is none that understandeth, there is none that seeketh after God.

12 They are all gone out of the way, they are together become unprofitable; there is none that doeth good, no, not one.

13 Their throat *is* an open sepulchre; with their tongues they have used deceit; the poison of asps *is* under their lips:

14 Whose mouth *is* full of cursing and bitterness:

15 Their feet *are* swift to shed blood:

16 Destruction and misery *are* in their ways:

17 And the way of peace have they not known:

18 There is no fear of God before their eyes.

19 Now we know that what things soever the law saith, it saith to them who are under the law: that every mouth may be stopped, and all the world may become guilty before God.

20 Therefore by the deeds of the law there shall no flesh be justified in his sight: for by the law *is* the knowledge of sin.

21 But now the righteousness of God without the law is manifested, being witnessed by the law and the prophets;

22 Even the righteousness of God *which is* by faith of Jesus Christ unto all ~~and upon all~~[2] them that believe: for there is no difference:

23 For all have sinned, and come short of the glory of God;

24 Being justified freely by his grace through the

---

[1] WH changed **for** (**gar**) to *but* (*de*), although they retained <u>for</u> (<u>gar</u>) in their margin.

[2] WH omitted <u>and</u> <u>upon</u> <u>all</u> (<u>kai</u> <u>epi</u> <u>pantas</u>) from their text but retained it in their margin.

redemption that is in Christ Jesus:

25 Whom God hath set forth *to be* a propitiation through faith in his blood, to declare his righteousness for the remission of sins that are past, through the forbearance of God;

26 To [ₐthe]¹ declare, *I say*, at this time his righteousness: that he might be just, and the justifier of him which believeth in Jesus.

27 Where *is* boasting then? It is excluded. By what law? of works? Nay: but by the law of faith.

28 **Therefore**² we conclude that a man is justified **by faith**³ without the deeds of the law.

29 *Is he* the God of the Jews only? *is he* not ~~also~~⁴ of the Gentiles? Yes, of the Gentiles also:

30 **Seeing**⁵ *it is* one God,

which shall justify the circumcision by faith, and uncircumcision through faith.

31 Do we then make void the law through faith? God forbid: yea, we establish the law.

CHAPTER 4

1 What shall we say then that **Abraham our father**⁶, as pertaining to the flesh, **hath found**⁷?

2 For if Abraham were justified by works, he hath *whereof* to glory; but not before God.

3 For what saith the scripture? Abraham believed God, and it was counted unto him for righteousness.

4 Now to him that worketh is the reward not reckoned of grace, but of [the]⁸ debt.

5 But to him that

---

¹ WH added *the* (*tAn*).
² In their margin, WH changed **therefore** (**oun**) to *for* (*gar*).
³ WH changed the word order from BY FAITH is justified to *is justified BY FAITH*.
⁴ WH omitted <u>also</u> (<u>de</u>).
⁵ WH changed <u>since</u> **indeed** (<u>epeiper</u>) to *since* (*eiper*). [prefix dropped]

⁶ In their margin, WH omitted <u>Abraham</u> <u>the</u> <u>father</u> <u>of us</u> <u>has found</u> (<u>abraam</u> <u>ton</u> <u>patera</u> ʰ<u>AmOn</u> <u>eurAkenai</u>).
⁷ WH changed the word order from <u>Abraham</u> <u>the</u> <u>father</u> <u>of us</u> HAS FOUND to *HAS FOUND Abraham the father of us*.
⁸ WH omitted the untranslated <u>the</u> (<u>to</u>).

worketh not, but believeth on him that justifieth the ungodly, his faith is counted for righteousness.

6   Even as David also describeth the blessedness of the man, unto whom God imputeth righteousness without works,

7   *Saying*, Blessed *are* they whose iniquities are forgiven, and whose sins are covered.

8   Blessed *is* the man to whom the Lord will not impute sin.

9   *Cometh* this blessedness then upon the circumcision *only*, or upon the uncircumcision also? for we say **that**[1] faith was reckoned to Abraham for righteousness.

10   How was it then reckoned? when he was in circumcision, or in uncircumcision? Not in circumcision, but in uncircumcision.

11   And he received the sign of circumcision, a seal of the righteousness of the faith which *he had yet* being uncircumcised: that he might be the father of all them that believe, though they be not circumcised; that righteousness might be imputed unto them **also**[2]:

12   And the father of circumcision to them who are not of the circumcision only, but who also walk in the steps of that faith of our father Abraham, which *he had* being *yet* **[the]**[3] uncircumcised.

13   For the promise, that he should be the heir of **the**[4] world, *was* not to Abraham, or to his seed, through the law, but through the righteousness of faith.

14   For if they which are of the law *be* heirs, faith is made void, and the promise made of none effect:

15   Because the law worketh wrath: **for**[5] where no law is, *there is* no transgression.

16   Therefore *it is* of faith, that *it might be* by grace; to the end the promise might be sure to all the seed; not to that only which is of the law, but to that also which is of the faith of Abraham; who is the father of us all,

17   (As it is written, I have made thee a father of many nations,) before him whom he believed, *even* God, who

---

[1] WH omitted <u>that</u> (^hoti).
[2] WH omitted <u>also</u> (<u>kai</u>).

[3] WH omitted the untranslated <u>the</u> (<u>tA</u>).
[4] WH omitted <u>the</u> (<u>tou</u>).
[5] WH changed **for** (**gar**) to **but** (**de**).

quickeneth the dead, and calleth those things which be not as though they were.

18 Who against hope believed in hope, that he might become the father of many nations, according to that which was spoken, So shall thy seed be.

19 And being not weak in faith, he considered **not**[1] his own body **now**[2] dead, when he was about an hundred years old, neither yet the deadness of Sara's womb:

20 He staggered not at the promise of God through unbelief; but was strong in faith, giving glory to God;

21 And being fully persuaded that, what he had promised, he was able also to perform.

22 And therefore it was imputed to him for righteousness.

23 Now it was not written for his sake alone, that it was imputed to him;

24 But for us also, to whom it shall be imputed, if we believe on him that raised up Jesus our Lord from the dead;

25 Who was delivered for our offences, and was raised

again for our justification.

CHAPTER 5

1 Therefore being justified by faith, **we have**[3] peace with God through our Lord Jesus Christ:

2 By whom also we have access by **faith**[4] into this grace wherein we stand, and rejoice in hope of the glory of God.

3 And not only *so*, but we glory in tribulations also: knowing that tribulation worketh patience;

4 And patience, experience; and experience, hope:

5 And hope maketh not ashamed; because the love of God is shed abroad in our hearts by the Holy Ghost which is given unto us.

6 For when we were yet without strength, [ʌyet][5] in due time Christ died for the ungodly.

7 For scarcely for a righteous man will one die:

---

[1] WH omitted not (ou).
[2] In their margin, WH omitted now (AdA).

[3] WH changed we **are** having (ecomen) to we **may have** (ecOmen). Pres Act **Ind** to Pres Act **Sub**. They retained (ecomen) in their margin, however. [mood]
[4] In their margin, WH omitted the faith (tA pistei).
[5] WH added yet (eti).

yet peradventure for a good man some would even dare to die.

8 But God commendeth his love toward us, in that, while we were yet sinners, Christ died for us.

9 Much more then, being now justified by his blood, we shall be saved from wrath through him.

10 For if, when we were enemies, we were reconciled to God by the death of his Son, much more, being reconciled, we shall be saved by his life.

11 And not only *so*, but we also joy in God through our Lord Jesus Christ, by whom we have now received the atonement.

12 Wherefore, as by one man sin entered into the world, and death by sin; and so death passed upon all men, for that all have sinned:

13 (For until the law sin was in the world: but sin is not imputed when there is no law.

14 Nevertheless death reigned from Adam to Moses, even over them that had not sinned after the similitude of Adam's transgression, who is the figure of him that was to come.

15 But not as the offence, so also *is* the free gift. For if

through the offence of one many be dead, much more the grace of God, and the gift by grace, *which is* by one man, Jesus Christ, hath abounded unto many.

16 And not as *it was* by one that sinned, *so is* the gift: for the judgment *was* by one to condemnation, but the free gift *is* of many offences unto justification.

17 For if by one man's offence death reigned by one; much more they which receive abundance of grace and **of the gift**[1] of righteousness shall reign in life by one, Jesus Christ.)

18 Therefore as by the offence of one *judgment came* upon all men to condemnation; even so by the righteousness of one *the free gift came* upon all men unto justification of life.

19 For as by one man's disobedience many were made sinners, so by the obedience of one shall many be made righteous.

20 Moreover the law entered, that the offence might abound. But where sin abounded, grace did much more abound:

---

[1] In their margin, WH omitted <u>of the gift</u> (<u>tAs</u> <u>dOreas</u>).

21 That as sin hath reigned unto death, even so might grace reign through righteousness unto eternal life by Jesus Christ our Lord.

CHAPTER 6

1 What shall we say then? **Shall we continue**[1] in sin, that grace may abound?

2 God forbid. How shall we, that are dead to sin, live any longer therein?

3 Know ye not, that so many of us as were baptized into Jesus Christ were baptized into his death?

4 Therefore we are buried with him by baptism into death: that like as Christ was raised up from the dead by the glory of the Father, even so we also should walk in newness of life.

5 For if we have been planted together in the likeness of his death, we shall be also *in the likeness* of *his* resurrection:

6 Knowing this, that our old man is crucified with *him*, that the body of sin might be destroyed, that henceforth we should not serve sin.

7 For he that is dead is freed from sin.

8 Now if we be dead with Christ, we believe that we shall also live with him:

9 Knowing that Christ being raised from the dead dieth no more; death hath no more dominion over him.

10 For in that he died, he died unto sin once: but in that he liveth, he liveth unto God.

11 Likewise reckon ye also yourselves to be dead indeed unto sin, but alive unto God through Jesus Christ ~~our Lord~~[2].

12 Let not sin therefore reign in your mortal body, that ye should obey ~~it in~~[3] the lusts thereof.

13 Neither yield ye your members *as* instruments of unrighteousness unto sin: but yield yourselves unto God, **as**[4] those that are alive from the dead, and your members *as* instruments of righteousness unto God.

14 For sin shall not have dominion over you: for ye are

---

[1] WH changed **shall** we continue (epimeno**u**men) to *may we continue* (epimen**O**men). **Fut** Act **Ind** to *Pres* Act *Sub*. [tense & mood]

[2] WH omitted the Lord of us (tO kuriO ^hAmOn).

[3] WH omitted it in (autA en).

[4] WH changed as (^hOs) to *as if* (^hOsei).

not under the law, but under grace.

15 What then? **shall we sin**[1], because we are not under the law, but under grace? God forbid.

16 Know ye not, that to whom ye yield yourselves servants to obey, his servants ye are to whom ye obey; whether of sin unto death, or of obedience unto righteousness?

17 But God be thanked, that ye were the servants of sin, but ye have obeyed from the heart that form of doctrine which was delivered you.

18 Being then made free from sin, ye became the servants of righteousness.

19 I speak after the manner of men because of the infirmity of your flesh: for as ye have yielded your members servants to uncleanness and to iniquity unto iniquity; even so now yield your members servants to righteousness unto holiness.

20 For when ye were the servants of sin, ye were free from righteousness.

21 What fruit had ye then in those things whereof ye are now ashamed? for the end of those things *is* death.

22 But now being made free from sin, and become servants to God, ye have your fruit unto holiness, and the end everlasting life.

23 For the wages of sin *is* death; but the gift of God *is* eternal life through Jesus Christ our Lord.

CHAPTER 7

1 Know ye not, brethren, (for I speak to them that know the law,) how that the law hath dominion over a man as long as he liveth?

2 For the woman which hath an husband is bound by the law to *her* husband so long as he liveth; but if the husband be dead, she is loosed from the law of *her* husband.

3 So then if, while *her* husband liveth, she be married to another man, she shall be called an adulteress: but if her husband be dead, she is free from that law; so that she is no adulteress, though she be married to another man.

4 Wherefore, my brethren, ye also are become dead to the law by the body of

---

[1] WH changed **shall** we sin (ᵸamartAsomen) to *might we sin* (ᵸamartAsOmen). **Fut** Act **Ind** to *Aor* Act ***Sub***. [tense & mood]

Christ; that ye should be married to another, *even* to him who is raised from the dead, that we should bring forth fruit unto God.

5   For when we were in the flesh, the motions of sins, which were by the law, did work in our members to bring forth fruit unto death.

6   But now we are delivered from the law, **that being dead**[1] wherein we were held; that we should serve in newness of spirit, and not *in* the oldness of the letter.

7   What shall we say then? *Is* the law sin? God forbid. Nay, I had not known sin, but by the law: for I had not known lust, except the law had said, Thou shalt not covet.

8   But sin, taking occasion by the commandment, wrought in me all manner of concupiscence. For without the law sin *was* dead.

9   For I was alive without the law once: but when the commandment came, sin revived, and I died.

10   And the command-

ment, which *was ordained* to life, I found *to be* unto death.

11   For sin, taking occasion by the commandment, deceived me, and by it slew *me*.

12   Wherefore the law *is* holy, and the commandment holy, and just, and good.

13   **Was** then that which is good **made**[2] death unto me? God forbid. But sin, that it might appear sin, working death in me by that which is good; that sin by the commandment might become exceeding sinful.

14   For we know that the law is spiritual: but I am **carnal**[3], sold under sin.

15   For that which I do I allow not: for what I would, that do I not; but what I hate, that do I.

16   If then I do that which I would not, I consent unto the law that *it is* good.

17   Now then it is no more I that do it, but sin that dwelleth in me.

18   For I know that in me

---

[1] WH changed **that** being dead (apoŧhanontos) to **those** being dead (apopŧhanontes). Both Aor Act Part. **Gen** Masc **Sing** to *Nom* Masc *Plur*. [case & number]

[2] WH changed **has** become (**gegone**) to *became* (*egeneto*). **Pf** Act Ind to *Aor* Mid Ind. [tense]

[3] WH changed fleshly-- **belonging** to the flesh) (sarkikos) to *fleshly-- consisting* of the flesh (*sarkinos*). [syn]

(that is, in my flesh,) dwelleth no good thing: for to will is present with me; but *how* to perform that which is good ~~I~~ **find**[1] **not**[2].

19 For the good that I would I do not: but the evil which I would not, that I do.

20 Now if I do that I [~~my-self~~][3] would not, it is no more I that do it, but sin that dwelleth in me.

21 I find then a law, that, when I would do good, evil is present with me.

22 For I delight in the law of God after the inward man:

23 But I see another law in my members, warring against the law of my mind, and bringing me into captivity [ʌ**in**][4] to the law of sin which is in my members.

24 O wretched man that I

---

[1] WH omitted <u>I find</u> (<u>euriskO</u>).
[2] WH changed the spelling of <u>not</u> (<u>ou</u>) to *not* (*ouc*). [spell]
[3] WH omitted the untranslated intensive <u>myself</u> (<u>egO</u>).
[4] WH added <u>in</u> (*en*) right after <u>bringing into captivity me</u> (<u>aicmalOizonta me</u>) and replaced the preposition supplied by the dative case of <u>the law</u>. WH added <u>in</u> (*en*) in their text but not in their margin.

am! who shall deliver me from the body of this death?

25 **I thank**[5] God through Jesus Christ our Lord. So then with the mind I myself serve the law of God; but with the flesh the law of sin.

CHAPTER 8

1 *There is* therefore now no condemnation to them which are in Christ Jesus, ~~who walk not after the flesh, but after the Spirit~~[6].

2 For the law of the Spirit of life in Christ Jesus hath made me free from the law of sin and death.

3 For what the law could not do, in that it was weak through the flesh, God sending his own Son in the likeness of sinful flesh, and for sin, condemned sin in the flesh:

4 That the righteousness of the law might be fulfilled in us, who walk not after the flesh, but after the Spirit.

5 For they that are after

---

[5] In their margin, WH changed **I thank** (**eucaristO**) to **but grace** (*caris de*).
[6] WH omitted <u>who walk not after the flesh but after the spirit</u> (<u>mA kata sarka peripatousin alla kata pneuma</u>).

the flesh do mind the things of the flesh; but they that are after the Spirit the things of the Spirit.

6 For to be carnally minded *is* death; but to be spiritually minded *is* life and peace.

7 Because the carnal mind *is* enmity against God: for it is not subject to the law of God, neither indeed can be.

8 So then they that are in the flesh cannot please God.

9 But ye are not in the flesh, but in the Spirit, if so be that the Spirit of God dwell in you. Now if any man have not the Spirit of Christ, he is none of his.

10 And if Christ *be* in you, the body *is* dead because of sin; but the Spirit *is* life because of righteousness.

11 But if the Spirit of him that raised up Jesus from the dead dwell in you, he that raised up **[the]**[1] Christ **[ʌJesus]**[2] from the dead shall also quicken your mortal bodies by **his Spirit that dwelleth in you**[3].

12 Therefore, brethren, we are debtors, not to the flesh, to live after the flesh.

13 For if ye live after the flesh, ye shall die: but if ye through the Spirit do mortify the deeds of the body, ye shall live.

14 For as many as are led by the Spirit of God, they are the sons of God.

15 For ye have not received the spirit of bondage again to fear; but ye have received the Spirit of adoption, whereby we cry, Abba, Father.

16 The Spirit itself beareth witness with our spirit, that we are the children of God:

17 And if children, then heirs; heirs of God, and joint-heirs with Christ; if so be that we suffer with *him*, that we may be also glorified together.

18 For I reckon that the sufferings of this present time *are* not worthy *to be compared* with the glory which shall be revealed in us.

19 For the earnest expectation of the creature waiteth

---

[1] WH omitted the untranslated the (ton).

[2] WH added *Jesus* (*iasousn*).

[3] In their margin, WH changed the dwelling in you spirit (tou enoikountos autou pneumatos) to *the dwelling in you spirit* (*to enoikoun autou pneuma*). Gen to Acc. [case]

for the manifestation of the sons of God.

20 For the creature was made subject to vanity, not willingly, but by reason of him who hath subjected *the same* in hope,

21 Because the creature itself also shall be delivered from the bondage of corruption into the glorious liberty of the children of God.

22 For we know that the whole creation groaneth and travaileth in pain together until now.

23 And not only *they*, but ourselves also, which have the firstfruits of the Spirit, even **we**[1] ourselves groan within ourselves, waiting for the adoption, *to wit*, the redemption of our body.

24 For we are saved by hope: but hope that is seen is not hope: for what a man seeth, ~~why~~ doth he ~~yet~~[2] hope for[3]?

25 But if we hope for that

we see not, *then* do we with patience wait for *it*.

26 Likewise the Spirit also helpeth **our infirmities**[4]: for we know not what we should pray for as we ought: but the Spirit itself maketh intercession ~~for us~~[5] with groanings which cannot be uttered.

27 And he that searcheth the hearts knoweth what *is* the mind of the Spirit, because he maketh intercession for the saints according to *the will of* God.

28 And we know that all things work together **[the God]**[6] for good to them that love God, to them who are the called according to *his* purpose.

29 For whom he did foreknow, he also did predestinate *to be* conformed to the image of his Son, that he might be the firstborn among many brethren.

---

[1] WH changed the word order from even WE to *WE even.*

[2] WH omitted why yet (ti kai) in their text but not their margin.

[3] In their margin, WH changed doth he **hope for** (**elpiz**ei) to *doth he* **endure** (**[h]upomen**ei).

[4] WH changed the infirmities of us (t**ais** as**th**eneia**is** [h]AmOn) to *the* **infirmity** *of us* (t**A** as**th**eneia [h]AmOn). **Plur** to **Sing.** [number]

[5] WH omitted for us ([h]uper [h]AmOn).

[6] In their margin, WH added *the God* ([h]o **th**eos), making the clause read **God** *works together all things for good.*

30 Moreover whom he did predestinate, them he also called: and whom he called, them he also justified: and whom he justified, them he also glorified.

31 What shall we then say to these things? If God *be* for us, who *can be* against us?

32 He that spared not his own Son, but delivered him up for us all, how shall he not with him also freely give us all things?

33 Who shall lay any thing to the charge of God's elect? *It is* God that justifieth.

34 Who *is* he that condemneth? *It is* Christ [ʌ**Jesus**][1] that died, yea [~~also~~][2] rather, that is risen again [ʌ**out of dead {ones}**][3], who is ~~even~~[4] at the right hand of God, who also maketh intercession for us.

35 Who shall separate us from the love of **Christ**[5]? *shall* tribulation, or distress, or persecution, or famine, or nakedness, or peril, or sword?

36 As it is written, For thy sake we are killed all the day long; we are accounted as sheep for the slaughter.

37 Nay, in all these things we are more than conquerors through him that loved us.

38 For I am persuaded, that neither death, nor life, nor angels, nor principalities, **nor powers**[6], nor things present, nor things to come,

39 Nor height, nor depth, nor any other creature, shall be able to separate us from the love of God, which is in Christ Jesus our Lord.

CHAPTER 9

1 I say the truth in Christ, I lie not, my conscience also bearing me witness in the Holy Ghost,

2 That I have great heaviness and continual sorrow in my heart.

3 For I could wish that myself **were accursed**[7] from

---

[1] WH added *Jesus* (*iAsous*).
[2] WH omitted the untranslated _also_ (kai).
[3] WH added _out of dead_ {ones} (ek nekrOn).
[4] WH omitted _even_ (kai).
[5] In their margin, WH changed **Christ** (**crist**ou) to **God** (~~th~~eou).

[6] WH changed the word order by moving NOR POWERS (oute dunameis) so that it followed _nor things to come_ instead of _nor principalities_.
[7] WH changed the word order from myself I ACCURSED TO BE to *ACCURSED TO BE myself I*.

Christ for my brethren, my kinsmen according to the flesh:

4 Who are Israelites; to whom *pertaineth* the adoption, and the glory, and the covenants, and the giving of the law, and the service *of God*, and the promises;

5 Whose *are* the fathers, and of whom as concerning the flesh Christ *came*, who is over all, God blessed for ever. Amen.

6 Not as though the word of God hath taken none effect. For they *are* not all Israel, which are of Israel:

7 Neither, because they are the seed of Abraham, *are they* all children: but, In Isaac shall thy seed be called.

8 That is, They which are the children of the flesh, these *are* not the children of God: but the children of the promise are counted for the seed.

9 For this *is* the word of promise, At this time will I come, and Sara shall have a son.

10 And not only *this*; but when Rebecca also had conceived by one, *even* by our father Isaac;

11 (For *the children* being not yet born, neither having

done any good or **evil**[1], that the **purpose**[2] of God according to election might stand, not of works, but of him that calleth;)

12 It was said unto her, The elder shall serve the younger.

13 As it is written, Jacob have I loved, but Esau have I hated.

14 What shall we say then? *Is there* unrighteousness with God? God forbid.

15 For he saith to Moses, I will have mercy on whom I will have mercy, and I will have compassion on whom I will have compassion.

16 So then *it is* not of him that willeth, nor of him that runneth, but of God that sheweth mercy.

17 For the scripture saith unto Pharaoh, Even for this same purpose have I raised thee up, that I might shew my power in thee, and that my name might be declared throughout all the earth.

18 Therefore hath he mercy on whom he will *have mercy*, and whom he will he

---

[1] WH changed evil (**kak**on) to *evil* (***paulon***). [syn]
[2] WH changed the word order from <u>of the</u> <u>God</u> PURPOSE to *PURPOSE of the God*

hardeneth.

19 Thou wilt say **then**[1] unto me, Why doth he yet find fault? For who hath resisted his will?

20 **Nay but**[2], O man, who art thou that repliest against God? Shall the thing formed say to him that formed *it*, Why hast thou made me thus?

21 Hath not the potter power over the clay, of the same lump to make one vessel unto honour, and another unto dishonour?

22 *What* if God, willing to shew *his* wrath, and to make his power known, endured with much longsuffering the vessels of wrath fitted to destruction:

23 **And**[3] that he might make known the riches of his glory on the vessels of mercy, which he had afore prepared unto glory,

24 Even us, whom he hath called, not of the Jews only, but also of the Gentiles?

25 As he saith also in Osee, I will call them my people, which were not my people; and her beloved, which was not beloved.

26 And it shall come to pass, *that* in the place where it was said unto them, Ye *are* not my people; there shall they be called the children of the living God.

27 Esaias also crieth concerning Israel, Though the number of the children of Israel be as the sand of the sea, a **remnant**[4] shall be saved:

28 For he will finish the work, and cut *it* short ~~in righteousness: because a short work~~[5] will the Lord make upon the earth.

29 And as Esaias said before, Except the Lord of Sabaoth had left us a seed, we had been as Sodoma, and been made like unto Gomorrha.

30 What shall we say then? That the Gentiles, which followed not after

---

[1] WH changed the word order from THEN unto me to *unto me THEN*.
[2] WH changed the word order from NAY BUT O man to *O man NAY BUT*.
[3] In their margin, WH omitted and (kai). [4] WH changed remnant (**kata**leimma) to *remnant (ʰupoleimma)*. [prefix changed]

[5] WH omitted in righteousness because a short work (en dikaiosunA ʰoti logon suntetmAmenon).

righteousness, have attained to righteousness, even the righteousness which is of faith.

31 But Israel, which followed after the law of righteousness, hath not attained to the law ~~of righteousness~~[1].

32 Wherefore? Because *they sought it* not by faith, but as it were by the works ~~of the law~~[2]. ~~For~~[3] they stumbled at that stumblingstone;

33 As it is written, Behold, I lay in Sion a stumblingstone and rock of offence: and ~~whosoever~~[4] believeth on him shall not be ashamed.

CHAPTER 10

1 Brethren, my heart's desire and prayer **[the]**[5] to God for **Israel**[6] ~~is~~[7], that they might be saved.

2 For I bear them record that they have a zeal of God, but not according to knowledge.

3 For they being ignorant of God's righteousness, and going about to establish their own ~~righteousness~~[8], have not submitted themselves unto the righteousness of God.

4 For Christ *is* the end of the law for righteousness to every one that believeth.

5 For Moses describeth [∧**that**][9] the righteousness which is of ~~the~~[10] law, ~~That~~[11] the man which doeth ~~those things~~[12] shall live by **them**[13].

6 But the righteousness which is of faith speaketh on this wise, Say not in thine heart, Who shall ascend into heaven? (that is, to bring Christ down *from above*:)

7 Or, Who shall descend

---

[1] WH omitted <u>of righteousness</u> (<u>dikaiosunAs</u>).

[2] WH omitted <u>of the law</u> (<u>nomou</u>).

[3] WH omitted <u>for</u> (<u>gar</u>).

[4] WH omitted <u>all</u> (<u>pas</u>) from <u>all</u> <u>the</u> {ones} <u>believing</u> <u>upon</u> <u>him</u>.

[5] WH omitted the untranslated <u>the</u> (^hA).

[6] WH changed **Israel** (**is-raAl**) to *them* (*autOn*).

[7] WH omitted <u>is</u> (<u>estin</u>).

[8] WH omitted <u>righteousness</u> (<u>dikaiosunAn</u>).

[9] WH added *that* (^hoti).

[10] WH omitted <u>the</u> (<u>tou</u>).

[11] WH omitted <u>that</u> (^hoti).

[12] WH omitted <u>these things</u> (<u>ta</u>).

[13] WH changed **them** (**autois**) to *her* (*autA*). Dat **Neut Plur** (**these** {things}) to Dat *Fem Sing* (her). [gender & number]

into the deep? (that is, to bring up Christ again from the dead.)

8   But what saith it? The word is nigh thee, *even* in thy mouth, and in thy heart: that is, the word of faith, which we preach;

9   That if thou shalt confess **[the word]**[1] with thy mouth the Lord Jesus **[that]**[2], and shalt believe in thine heart that God hath raised him from the dead, thou shalt be saved.

10   For with the heart man believeth unto righteousness; and with the mouth confession is made unto salvation.

11   For the scripture saith, Whosoever believeth on him shall not be ashamed.

12   For there is no difference between the Jew and the Greek: for the same Lord over all is rich unto all that call upon him.

13   For whosoever shall call upon the name of the Lord shall be saved.

14   How then **shall they call**[3] on him in whom they

have not believed? and how **shall they believe**[4] in him of whom they have not heard? and how **shall they hear**[5] without a preacher?

15   And how **shall they preach**[6], except they be sent? as it is written, How beautiful are the feet ~~of them that preach the gospel of peace~~[7], and bring glad tidings of **[the]**[8] good things!

16   But they have not all

---

[1] In their margin, WH added *the word* (*to* [h]*rAma*).

[2] In their margin, WH added *that* ([h]*oti*).

[3] WH changed **shall we call** (*epikalesontai*) to *might we call* (*epikalesOntai*). **Fut** Mid

Ind to *Aor* Mid **Sub**. [tense & mood]

[4] WH changed **shall** they believe (*pisteusousin*) to *might they believe* (*episteusOsin*). **Fut** Act **Ind** to *Aor* Act **Sub**. [tense & mood]

[5] WH changed **shall** they hear (*akousousi*) to *might they hear* (*akousOsi*). **Fut** Act **Ind** to *Aor* Act **Sub**. [tense & mood]

[6] WH changed **shall** they preach (*kAruxousin*) to *might they preach* (*kAruxOsin*). **Fut** Act **Ind** to *Aor* Act **Sub**. [tense & mood]

[7] WH omitted of them that preach the gospel of peace (*tOn euaggelizomenOn eiranAn*). [They also retranslated and (*tOn*) as *of them that*.]

[8] WH omitted the untranslated *the* (*ta*).

obeyed the gospel. For Esaias saith, Lord, who hath believed our report?

17 So then faith *cometh* by hearing, and hearing by the word **of God**[1].

18 But I say, Have they not heard? Yes verily, their sound went into all the earth, and their words unto the ends of the world.

19 But I say, Did not **Israel**[2] know? First Moses saith, I will provoke you to jealousy by *them that are* no people, *and* by a foolish nation I will anger you.

20 But Esaias is very bold, and saith, I was found of them that sought me not; I was made manifest unto them that asked not after me.

21 But to Israel he saith, All day long I have stretched forth my hands unto a disobedient and gainsaying people.

CHAPTER 11

1 I say then, hath God cast away his people? God forbid. For I also am an Isra-elite, of the seed of Abraham, *of* the tribe of Benjamin.

2 God hath not cast away his people which he foreknew. Wot ye not what the scripture saith of Elias? how he maketh intercession to God against Israel, ~~saying~~[3],

3 Lord, they have killed thy prophets, ~~and~~[4] digged down thine altars; and I am left alone, and they seek my life.

4 But what saith the answer of God unto him? I have reserved to myself seven thousand men, who have not bowed the knee to *the image of* Baal.

5 Even so then at this present time also there is a remnant according to the election of grace.

6 And if by grace, then *is it* no more of works: otherwise grace is no more grace. ~~But if *it be* of works, then is it no more grace: otherwise work is no more work~~[5].

7 What then? Israel hath

---

[1] WH changed of **God** (~~th~~eou) to *of Christ* (*cristou*).
[2] WH changed the word order from <u>not</u> <u>did</u> <u>know</u> ISRAEL to *ISRAEL not did know*.

[3] WH omitted <u>saying</u> (<u>legOn</u>).
[4] WH omitted <u>and</u> (<u>kai</u>).
[5] WH omitted <u>but</u> <u>if</u> [it be] <u>of</u> <u>works</u> <u>then</u> <u>it</u> <u>is</u> <u>not</u> <u>more</u> <u>grace</u> <u>otherwise</u> <u>work</u> <u>is</u> <u>no</u> <u>more</u> <u>work</u> (<u>ei</u> <u>de</u> <u>ex</u> <u>ergOn</u> <u>ouketi</u> <u>esti</u> <u>caris</u> <u>epei</u> <u>to</u> <u>ergon</u> <u>ouketi</u> <u>estin</u> <u>ergon</u>).

not obtained **that**[1] which he seeketh for; but the election hath obtained it, and the rest were blinded

8 (According as it is written, God hath given them the spirit of slumber, eyes that they should not see, and ears that they should not hear;) unto this day.

9 And David saith, Let their table be made a snare, and a trap, and a stumblingblock, and a recompence unto them:

10 Let their eyes be darkened, that they may not see, and bow down their back alway.

11 I say then, Have they stumbled that they should fall? God forbid: but *rather* through their fall salvation *is come* unto the Gentiles, for to provoke them to jealousy.

12 Now if the fall of them *be* the riches of the world, and the diminishing of them the riches of the Gentiles; how much more their fulness?

13 **For**[2] I speak to you Gentiles, inasmuch as [˄**therefore**][3] I am the apostle of the Gentiles, I magnify mine office:

14 If by any means I may provoke to emulation *them which are* my flesh, and might save some of them.

15 For if the casting away of them *be* the reconciling of the world, what *shall* the receiving *of them be*, but life from the dead?

16 For if the firstfruit *be* holy, the lump *is* also *holy*: and if the root *be* holy, so *are* the branches.

17 And if some of the branches be broken off, and thou, being a wild olive tree, wert graffed in among them, and with them partakest of the root ~~and~~[4] fatness of the olive tree;

18 Boast not against the branches. But if thou boast, thou bearest not the root, but the root thee.

19 Thou wilt say then, ~~The~~[5] branches were broken off, that I might be graffed in.

20 Well; because of unbelief they were broken off, and

---

[1] WH changed **of** that (tou-tou) to *that* (*touto*). **Gen** Neut Sing (**of** that) to *Acc* Neut Sing (*that*). [case]
[2] WH changed **for** (**gar**) to *but* (*de*).

[3] WH added *therefore* (*oun*).
[4] WH omitted and (kai) from their text, but kept it in their margin.
[5] WH omitted the (ʰoi).

thou standest by faith. Be not highminded, but fear:

21 For if God spared not the natural branches, *take heed* ~~lest~~ **he** ~~also~~[1] **spare**[2] not thee.

22 Behold therefore the goodness and severity of God: on them which fell, <u>**severity**</u>[3]; but toward thee, <u>**goodness**</u>[4] [∧**of God**][5], if thou continue in *his* goodness: otherwise thou also shalt be cut off.

23 And they also, if they abide not still in unbelief, shall be graffed in: for God is able to graff them in again.

24 For if thou wert cut out of the olive tree which is wild by nature, and wert graffed contrary to nature into a

good olive tree: how much more shall these, which be the natural *branches*, be graffed into their own olive tree?

25 For I would not, brethren, that ye should be ignorant of this mystery, lest ye should be wise in your own conceits; that blindness in part is happened to Israel, until the fulness of the Gentiles be come in.

26 And so all Israel shall be saved: as it is written, There shall come out of Sion the Deliverer, ~~and~~[6] shall turn away ungodliness from Jacob:

27 For this *is* my covenant unto them, when I shall take away their sins.

28 As concerning the gospel, *they are* enemies for your sakes: but as touching the election, *they are* beloved for the fathers' sakes.

29 For the gifts and calling of God *are* without repentance.

30 For as ye [~~also~~][7] in times past have not believed God, yet have now obtained mercy through their unbelief:

31 Even so have these also

---

[1] WH omitted <u>least also</u> (mApOs).
[2] WH changed <u>he **might** spare</u> (*feisAtai*) to *he will spare* (*feisetai*). **Aor** Mid **Sub** to *Fut* Mid *Ind*. [tense & mood]
[3] WH changed <u>severity</u> (<u>apotomia**n**</u>) to *severity* (*apotomia*). **Fem** Sing to *Nom* Fem Sing. [gender]
[4] WH changed <u>kindness</u> (<u>crAstotA**ta**</u>) to *kindness* (*crAstotA**s***). **Acc** Fem Sing to *Nom* Fem Sing. [gender]
[5] WH added *of God* (~~t~~*heou*).

[6] WH omitted <u>and</u> (kai).
[7] WH omitted the untranslated <u>also</u> (kai).

now not believed, that through your mercy they [∧**now**]¹ also may obtain mercy.

32 For God hath concluded them all in unbelief, that he might have mercy upon all.

33 O the depth of the riches both of the wisdom and knowledge of God! how unsearchable *are* his judgments, and his ways past finding out!

34 For who hath known the mind of the Lord? or who hath been his counsellor?

35 Or who hath first given to him, and it shall be recompensed unto him again?

36 For of him, and through him, and to him, *are* all things: to whom *be* glory for ever. Amen.

CHAPTER 12

1 I beseech you therefore, brethren, by the mercies of God, that ye present your bodies a living sacrifice, holy, acceptable unto God, *which is* your reasonable service.

2 And be not conformed to this world: but be ye transformed by the renewing of **your**² mind, that ye may prove what *is* that good, and acceptable, and perfect, will of God.

3 For I say, through the grace given unto me, to every man that is among you, not to think *of himself* more highly than he ought to think; but to think soberly, according as God hath dealt to every man the measure of faith.

4 For as we have many **members**³ in one body, and all members have not the same office:

5 So we, *being* many, are one body in Christ, and [**the**]⁴ every one members one of another.

6 Having then gifts differing according to the grace that is given to us, whether prophecy, *let us prophesy* according to the proportion of faith;

7 Or ministry, *let us wait*

---

¹ WH added *now* (*nun*) after the intensive they.

² WH omitted of you (ʰu-mOn) from the phrase the mind of you.

³ WH changed the word order from MEMBERS many to *many* MEMBERS.

⁴ WH changed the untranslated the (ʰo) to *the* (*to*). Nom **Masc** Sing to Nom *Neut* Sing. [gender]

on *our* ministering: or he that teacheth, on teaching;

8 Or he that exhorteth, on exhortation: he that giveth, *let him do it* with simplicity; he that ruleth, with diligence; he that sheweth mercy, with cheerfulness.

9 *Let* love be without dissimulation. Abhor that which is evil; cleave to that which is good.

10 *Be* kindly affectioned one to another with brotherly love; in honour preferring one another;

11 Not slothful in business; fervent in spirit; serving **the Lord**[1];

12 Rejoicing in hope; patient in tribulation; continuing instant in prayer;

13 Distributing to the necessity of saints; given to hospitality.

14 Bless them which persecute you: bless, and curse not.

15 Rejoice with them that do rejoice, **and**[2] weep with them that weep.

16 *Be* of the same mind one toward another. Mind not high things, but condescend to men of low estate. Be not wise in your own conceits.

17 Recompense to no man evil for evil. Provide things honest in the sight of all men.

18 If it be possible, as much as lieth in you, live peaceably with all men.

19 Dearly beloved, avenge not yourselves, but *rather* give place unto wrath: for it is written, Vengeance *is* mine; I will repay, saith the Lord.

20 **Therefore**[3] **if**[4] thine enemy hunger, feed him; if he thirst, give him drink: for in so doing thou shalt heap coals of fire on his head.

21 Be not overcome of evil, but overcome evil with good.

CHAPTER 13

1 Let every soul be subject unto the higher powers. For there is no power but **of**[5]

---

[1] In their margin, WH changed **the Lord** (**tO kuriO**) to *in time* (*kairO*). Both Dat Masc Sing.
[2] WH omitted and (kai).
[3] WH changed **therefore** (**oun**) to *but* (*alla*).
[4] WH changed the word order and made IF (ean) the second word rather than the first word in the verse.
[5] WH changed **of** (apo) to *by* (**upo**).

God: the ~~powers~~[1] that be are ordained of **[the]**[2] God.

2 Whosoever therefore resisteth the power, resisteth the ordinance of God: and they that resist shall receive to themselves damnation.

3 For rulers are not a terror **to good works**[3], but **to the evil**[4]. Wilt thou then not be afraid of the power? do that which is good, and thou shalt have praise of the same:

4 For he is the minister of God to thee for good. But if thou do that which is evil, be afraid; for he beareth not the sword in vain: for he is the minister of God, a revenger to *execute* wrath upon him that doeth evil.

5 Wherefore *ye* must needs be subject, not only for wrath, but also for con-science sake.

6 For for this cause pay ye tribute also: for they are God's ministers, attending continually upon this very thing.

7 Render **therefore**[5] to all their dues: tribute to whom tribute *is due*; custom to whom custom; fear to whom fear; honour to whom honour.

8 Owe no man any thing, but to love one another: for he that loveth another hath fulfilled the law.

9 For this, Thou shalt not commit adultery, Thou shalt not kill, Thou shalt not steal, ~~Thou shalt not bear false witness~~[6], Thou shalt not covet; and if *there be* any other commandment, it is briefly comprehended in this saying, namely, Thou shalt love thy neighbour as thyself.

10 Love worketh no ill to his neighbour: therefore love *is* the fulfilling of the law.

11 And that, knowing the time, that **now**[7] it is

---

[1] WH omitted powers (exousiai) and changed the translation of the (ta) to *the {ones}*.

[2] WH omitted the untranslated the (tou).

[3] WH changed to the good works (tOn agathOn ergOn) to *to the good work (tO agathO ergO)*. **Plur** to *Sing*. [number]

[4] WH change to the evil {ones} (tOn kakOn) to *to the evil {one} (tO kakO)*. **Plur** to *Sing*. [number]

[5] WH omitted therefore (oun).

[6] WH omitted thou shalt not bear false witness (ou seudomarturaseis).

[7] WH changed the word order from time of us NOW to *time NOW of you*.

high[1] time to awake out of sleep: for now *is* our salvation nearer than when we believed.

12 The night is far spent, the day is at hand: let us therefore cast off the works of darkness, **and**[2] let us put on the armour of light.

13 Let us walk honestly, as in the day; not in rioting and drunkenness, not in chambering and wantonness, not in strife and envying.

14 But put ye on the Lord Jesus Christ, and make not provision for the flesh, to *fulfil* the lusts *thereof.*

CHAPTER 14

1 Him that is weak in the faith receive ye, *but* not to doubtful disputations.

2 For one believeth that he may eat all things: another, who is weak, eateth herbs.

3 Let not him that eateth despise him that eateth not; **and**[3] let not him which eateth

not judge him that eateth: for God hath received him.

4 Who art thou that judgest another man's servant? to his own master he standeth or falleth. Yea, he shall be holden up: for **God**[4] **is able**[5] to make him stand.

5 One man esteemeth one day above another: another esteemeth every day *alike.* Let every man be fully persuaded in his own mind.

6 He that regardeth the day, regardeth *it* unto the Lord; ~~and he that regardeth not the day, to the Lord he doth not regard *it*.~~[6] [ʌand][7] He that eateth, eateth to the Lord, for he giveth God thanks; and he that eateth not, to the Lord he eateth not, and giveth God thanks.

---

[1] WH changed of **us** (ʰΑmas) to *of you* (ʰumas). [person]
[2] WH changed **and** (**kai**) to *but* (*de*) and changed the word order so that *de* was the second Greek word after darkness.
[3] WH changed **and** (**kai**) to

but (*de*).
[4] WH changed the **God** (ʰo ~~theos~~) to *the Lord* (ʰo *kurios*).
[5] WH changed is able (duna-tos **estin**) to *is able* (*dunatei*). Adj-Verb to Verb. They changed for ABLE is the **God** to *for is ABLE the Lord*.
[6] WH omitted and he that regardeth not the day, to the Lord he doth not regard [it] (kai ʰo mA fronOn tAn ʰam-eran kuriO ou fronei).
[7] WH added **and** (kai).

7 For none of us liveth to himself, and no man dieth to himself.

8 For whether we live, we live unto the Lord; and whether we die, we die unto the Lord: whether we live therefore, or die, we are the Lord's.

9 For to this end Christ ~~both~~[1] died, and ~~rose, and~~[2] **revived**[3], that he might be Lord both of the dead and living.

10 But why dost thou judge thy brother? or why dost thou set at nought thy brother? for we shall all stand before the judgment seat of Christ.

11 For it is written, *As* I live, saith the Lord, every knee shall bow to me, and every tongue shall confess to **God**[4].

12 So then every one of us shall give account of himself to God.

13 Let us not therefore judge one another any more: but judge this rather, that no man put a stumblingblock or an occasion to fall in *his* brother's way.

14 I know, and am persuaded by the Lord Jesus, that *there is* nothing unclean of itself: but to him that esteemeth any thing to be unclean, to him *it is* unclean.

15 **But**[5] if thy brother be grieved with *thy* meat, now walkest thou not charitably. Destroy not him with thy meat, for whom Christ died.

16 Let not then your good be evil spoken of:

17 For the kingdom of God is not meat and drink; but righteousness, and peace, and joy in the Holy Ghost.

18 For he that in **these things**[6] serveth Christ *is* acceptable to God, and approved of men.

19 **Let us** therefore **follow after**[7] the things which make

---

[1] WH omitted <u>and</u> (<u>kai</u>).

[2] WH omitted <u>rose and</u> (<u>anestA</u> <u>kai</u>).

[3] WH changed <u>lived **again**</u> (**an**<u>ezAsen</u>) to *lived* (*ezAsen*). Both Aor Act Ind. [prefix dropped]

[4] WH changed **Christ** (**cris-tou**) to *God* (*~~th~~eou*).

[5] WH changed **but** (**de**) to *for* (*gar*).

[6] WH changed <u>these</u> {things} (<u>tout**ois**</u>) to *this* {*thing*} (*tout**O***). **Plur** to *Sing*. [number]

[7] In their margin, WH changed <u>let us follow after</u> (<u>diOkOmen</u>) to *let us follow after* (*diOkomen*). [spell]

for peace, and things wherewith one may edify another.

20 For meat destroy not the work of God. All things indeed *are* pure; but *it is* evil for that man who eateth with offence.

21 *It is* good neither to eat flesh, nor to drink wine, nor *any thing* whereby thy brother stumbleth, ~~or is offended, or is made weak~~[1].

22 Hast thou faith? [^which][2] have *it* to thyself before God. Happy *is* he that condemneth not himself in that thing which he alloweth.

23 And he that doubteth is damned if he eat, because *he eateth* not of faith: for whatsoever *is* not of faith is sin.

[xx Now to him that is of power to stablish you according to my gospel, and the preaching of Jesus Christ, according to the revelation of the mystery, which was kept secret since the world began,

xx But now is made manifest, and by the scriptures of the prophets, according to the commandment of the everlasting God, made known to all nations for the obedience of faith:

xx To God only wise, *be* glory through Jesus Christ [to whom] for ever. Amen.][3].

CHAPTER 15

1 We then that are strong ought to bear the infirmities of the weak, and not to please ourselves.

2 [~~for~~][4] Let every one of us please *his* neighbour for *his* good to edification.

3 For even Christ pleased not himself; but, as it is written, The reproaches of them that reproached thee fell on me.

4 For whatsoever things were written aforetime **were written**[5] for our learning,

---

[1] WH omitted or is offended or is made weak (A skandalizetai A asthenei) but retained these words in their margin.

[2] WH added *which* (An).

[3] In their margin, WH inserted Romans 16:25-27 here. Their margin omitted Romans 16:25-27 at the end of the book.

[4] WH omitted the untranslated for (gar).

[5] WH changed were written {**before**} (**pro**egrafA) to *were written* (egrafA). [prefix dropped]

that we through patience and [ʌ**through**]¹ comfort of the scriptures might have hope.

5 Now the God of patience and consolation grant you to be likeminded one toward another according to Christ Jesus:

6 That ye may with one mind *and* one mouth glorify God, even the Father of our Lord Jesus Christ.

7 Wherefore receive ye one another, as Christ also received **us**² to the glory of God.

8 **Now**³ I say that ~~Jesus~~⁴ Christ was a minister of the circumcision for the truth of God, to confirm the promises *made* unto the fathers:

9 And that the Gentiles might glorify God for *his* mercy; as it is written, For this cause I will confess to thee among the Gentiles, and sing unto thy name.

10 And again he saith, Rejoice, ye Gentiles, with his people.

11 And again, Praise **the Lord**⁵, all ye Gentiles; and **laud**⁶ him, all ye people.

12 And again, Esaias saith, There shall be a root of Jesse, and he that shall rise to reign over the Gentiles; in him shall the Gentiles trust.

13 Now the God of hope fill you with all joy and peace in believing, that ye may abound in hope, through the power of the Holy Ghost.

14 And I myself also am persuaded of you, my brethren, that ye also are full of goodness, filled with all knowledge, able also to admonish one another.

15 Nevertheless, ~~brethren~~⁷, I have written the more boldly unto you in some sort, as putting you in mind, because of the grace that is given to me **of**⁸ God,

---

¹ WH added *through* (*dia*).
² WH changed **us** (ᵸ**Amas**) to *you* (ʰ*umas*) in their text but not their margin. [person]
³ WH changed **now** (**de**) to *for* (*gar*).
⁴ WH omitted **Jesus** (iAsoun).

⁵ WH changed the word order from THE LORD all the gentiles to *all the gentiles THE LORD.*
⁶ WH changed **You**ᵖ Praise! (epainesate) *Let them Praise!* (epainesat**Otan**). Both Aor Act Imp. **2ⁿᵈ** Plur to *3ʳᵈ* Plur. [number]
⁷ WH omitted brothers (adle-foi).
⁸ WH changed **by** (ʰ**u**po) to *from* (*apo*).

16 That I should be the minister of **Jesus**[1] Christ to the Gentiles, ministering the gospel of God, that the offering up of the Gentiles might be acceptable, being sanctified by the Holy Ghost.

17 I have therefore [∧**the**][2] whereof I may glory through Jesus Christ in those things which pertain to God.

18 For I will not dare **to speak**[3] of any of those things which Christ hath not wrought by me, to make the Gentiles obedient, by word and deed,

19 Through mighty signs and wonders, by the power of the Spirit **of God**[4]; so that from Jerusalem, and round about unto Illyricum, I have fully preached the gospel of Christ.

20 Yea, so have I strived to preach the gospel, not where Christ was named, lest I should build upon another man's foundation:

21 But as it is written, To whom he was not spoken of, **they shall see**[5]: and they that have not heard shall understand.

22 For which cause also I have been much hindered from coming to you.

23 But now having no more place in these parts, and having a great desire these many years to come unto you;

24 **Whensoever**[6] I take my journey into Spain, ~~I will come to you~~[7]: for I trust to see you in my journey, and to be brought on my way thitherward by you, if first I be somewhat filled with your *company*.

25 But now I go unto Jerusalem to minister unto the saints.

26 For it hath pleased

---

[1] WH changed the word order from J_ESUS_ Christ to *Christ J_ESUS_.*

[2] WH added *the* (*tAn*).

[3] WH changed the word order from T_O SPEAK_ of any to *of any T_O SPEAK_.*

[4] WH changed of **God** (~~th~~eou) to *of holy* (*ʰagiou*) in their text. They retained ~~th~~eou in their margin or omitted both words.

[5] WH changed the word order from to whom he was not spoken of T_HEY SHALL SEE_ to T_HEY SHALL SEE_ to whom he was not spoken of.

[6] WH changed the *if* (**ean**) in whensoever (ʰOs ean—as if) to *if* (*an*). [syn]

[7] WH omitted I will come to you (eleusomai pros ʰumas).

them of Macedonia and Achaia to make a certain contribution for the poor saints which are at Jerusalem.

27 It hath pleased them verily; and their debtors they are. For if the Gentiles have been made partakers of their spiritual things, their duty **is**[1] also to minister unto them in carnal things.

28 When therefore I have performed this, and have sealed to them this fruit, I will come by you into Spain.

29 And I am sure that, when I come unto you, I shall come in the fulness of the blessing of ~~the gospel of~~[2] Christ.

30 Now I beseech you, brethren, for the Lord Jesus Christ's sake, and for the love of the Spirit, that ye strive together with me in *your* prayers to God for me;

31 That I may be delivered from them that do not believe in Judaea; and ~~that~~[3] my service which *I have* for Jerusalem **may be**[4] accepted of the saints;

32 That **I may come**[5] unto you with joy by the will of God, ~~and~~[6] may with you be refreshed.

33 Now the God of peace *be* with you all. Amen.

CHAPTER 16

1 I commend unto you Phebe our sister, which is a servant of the church which is at Cenchrea:

2 That ye receive her in the Lord, as becometh saints, and that ye assist her in whatsoever business she hath need of you: for she hath been a succourer of many, and **of myself**[7] also.

3 Greet **Priscilla**[8] and Aquila my helpers in Christ Jesus:

---

[1] WH changed the word order from <u>duty</u> <u>of them</u> IS to *duty* IS *of them*.

[2] WH omitted <u>the</u> <u>gospel</u> <u>of</u> the (tou euaggeliou tou).

[3] WH omitted <u>that</u> (^{h}ina).

[4] WH changed the word or-

der from <u>accepted</u> MAY BE of the <u>saints</u> to *accepted of the saints* MAY BE.

[5] WH changed **I might** <u>come</u> (e~~l~~thO) to *having come* (el~~th~~On). Aor Act **Sub** to Aor Act *Part*. [mood]

[6] WH omitted <u>and</u> (kai).

[7] WH changed the word order from <u>also</u> OF MYSELF to *OF MYSELF also*.

[8] WH changed <u>Priscilla</u> (priskillan) to *Prisca* (*priskan*). [spell]

4   Who have for my life laid down their own necks: unto whom not only I give thanks, but also all the churches of the Gentiles.

5   Likewise *greet* the church that is in their house. Salute my wellbeloved Epaenetus, who is the firstfruits of <u>Achaia</u>[1] unto Christ.

6   Greet **<u>Mary</u>**[2], who bestowed much labour on **<u>us</u>**[3].

7   Salute Andronicus and Junia, my kinsmen, and my fellowprisoners, who are of note among the apostles, who also were in Christ before me.

8   Greet **<u>Amplias</u>**[4] my beloved in the Lord.

9   Salute Urbane, our helper in Christ, and Stachys my beloved.

10 Salute Apelles approved in Christ. Salute them which are of Aristobulus' *household.*

11 Salute Herodion my kinsman. Greet them that be of the *household* of Narcissus, which are in the Lord.

12 Salute Tryphena and Tryphosa, who labour in the Lord. Salute the beloved Persis, which laboured much in the Lord.

13 Salute Rufus chosen in the Lord, and his mother and mine.

14 Salute Asyncritus, Phlegon, **<u>Hermas</u>**[5], Patrobas, **<u>Hermes</u>**[6], and the brethren which are with them.

15 Salute Philologus, and Julia, Nereus, and his sister, and Olympas, and all the saints which are with them.

16 Salute one another with an holy kiss. The churches of Christ [∧**all**][7] salute you.

17 Now I beseech you, brethren, mark them which cause divisions and offences contrary to the doctrine which ye have learned; and avoid them.

18 For they that are such

---

[1] WH changed <u>Achai</u>a (<u>acai</u>as) to *Asia* (*asias*).
[2] WH changed <u>Mary</u> (<u>mari</u>am) to *Mary* (*marian*). [spell]
[3] WH changed **<u>us</u>** ([h]<u>Amas</u>) to *you* ([h]*umas*). [person]
[4] WH changed <u>Amplias</u> (amplian) to *Ampliatus* (*ampliaton*). Both Acc Masc Sing. [spell]

[5] WH changed *Hermas* ([h]er-man) to *Hermas* ([h]ermAn). Both Acc Masc Sing. [spell]
[6] WH changed <u>Hermes</u> ([h]er-mAn) to *Hermes* ([h]erman). Both Acc Masc Sing. [spell]
[7] WH added *all* (*pasai*).

serve not our Lord ~~Jesus~~[1] Christ, but their own belly; and by good words and fair speeches deceive the hearts of the simple.

19 For your obedience is come abroad unto all *men*. <u>**I am glad therefore**</u>[2] **[the]**[3] on your behalf: but yet I would have you wise unto that which is good, and simple concerning evil.

20 And the God of peace shall bruise Satan under your feet shortly. The grace of our Lord Jesus Christ *be* with you. ~~**Amen**~~[4]. <u>**[The grace of our Lord Jesus Christ** *be* **with you all. Amen.]**</u>[5]

21 Timotheus my workfellow, and Lucius, and Jason, and Sosipater, my kinsmen,

<u>**salute**</u>[6] you.

22 I Tertius, who wrote *this* epistle, salute you in the Lord.

23 Gaius mine host, and of the whole <u>**church**</u>[7], saluteth you. Erastus the chamberlain of the city saluteth you, and Quartus a brother.

~~**24 The grace of our Lord Jesus Christ** *be* **with you all. Amen.**~~[8]

<u>**25 Now to him that is of power to stablish you according to my gospel, and the preaching of Jesus Christ, according to the revelation of the mystery, which was kept secret since the world began,**</u>

<u>**26 But now is made**</u>

---

[1] WH omitted <u>Jesus</u> (<u>iASou</u>).
[2] WH changed the word order from <u>I AM GLAD THEREFORE</u> **the** <u>upon</u> <u>you</u> to *upon you THEREFORE I AM GLAD*.
[3] WH omitted the untranslated <u>the</u> (<u>to</u>).
[4] WH omitted <u>Amen</u> (<u>amAn</u>).
[5] In their margin, WH omitted the words of Romans 16:24--<u>the</u> <u>grace</u> of <u>our</u> <u>Lord</u> <u>Jesus</u> <u>Christ</u> [be] <u>with</u> <u>you</u> <u>all</u>. <u>Amen</u> (^h<u>A</u> <u>caris</u> <u>tou</u> <u>kuriou</u> ^h<u>amOn</u> <u>iasou</u> <u>cristou</u> <u>meta</u> <u>pantOn</u> ^h<u>umOn</u> <u>amAn</u>).

[6] WH changed **<u>they</u>** <u>greet</u> (<u>aspazontai</u>) to *he greets* (*aspazetai*). Pres M/P-D Ind 3rd **<u>Plur</u>** to Pres Mid Ind 3rd *Sing* [number].
[7] WH changed the word order from <u>OF THE</u> <u>CHURCH</u> of <u>whole</u> to *of whole OF THE CHURCH*.
[8] WH omitted all of Romans 16:24—<u>the</u> <u>grace</u> of <u>our</u> <u>Lord</u> <u>Jesus</u> <u>Christ</u> [be] <u>with</u> <u>you</u> <u>all</u>. <u>Amen</u> (^h<u>A</u> <u>caris</u> <u>tou</u> <u>kuriou</u> ^h<u>amOn</u> <u>iasou</u> <u>cristou</u> <u>meta</u> <u>pantOn</u> ^h<u>umOn</u> <u>amAn</u>). Their margin omitted these words from verse 20.

manifest, and by the scriptures of the prophets, according to the command-
ment of the everlasting
God, made known to all nations for the obedience of
faith:

27 To God only wise, *be*
glory through Jesus Christ
[ʌto whom][1]   for ever.
Amen.[2]

---

[1] WH added *to whom* (ʰ*O*),
making their text read
through Jesus Christ *to
whom* the glory.
[2] In their margin, WH omitted all of Romans 16:25-27
here. Their margin inserted
Romans 16:25-27 at the end
of Romans chapter 14.

1 CORINTHIANS

CHAPTER 1

1   Paul, called *to be* an apostle of Jesus Christ through the will of God, and Sosthenes *our* brother,

2   Unto the church of God which is at Corinth, to them that are sanctified in Christ Jesus, called *to be* saints, with all that in every place call upon the name of Jesus Christ our Lord, ~~both~~[1] theirs and ours:

3   Grace *be* unto you, and peace, from God our Father, and *from* the Lord Jesus Christ.

4   I thank **my**[2] God always on your behalf, for the grace of God which is given you by Jesus Christ;

5   That in every thing ye are enriched by him, in all utterance, and *in* all knowledge;

6   Even as the testimony of Christ was confirmed in you:

7   So that ye come behind in no gift; waiting for the coming of our Lord Jesus Christ:

8   Who shall also confirm you unto the end, *that ye may be* blameless in the day of our Lord Jesus Christ.

9   God *is* faithful, by whom ye were called unto the fellowship of his Son Jesus Christ our Lord.

10 Now I beseech you, brethren, by the name of our Lord Jesus Christ, that ye all speak the same thing, and *that* there be no divisions among you; but *that* ye be perfectly joined together in the same mind and in the same judgment.

11 For it hath been declared unto me of you, my brethren, by them *which are of the house* of Chloe, that there are contentions among you.

12 Now this I say, that every one of you saith, I am of Paul; and I of Apollos; and I of Cephas; and I of Christ.

13 Is Christ divided? was Paul crucified for you? or were ye baptized in the name of Paul?

14 I thank **God**[3] that I baptized none of you, but Crispus and Gaius;

15 Lest any should say

---

[1] WH omitted <u>both</u> (<u>te</u>).
[2] In their margin, WH omitted <u>of me</u> (<u>mou</u>) <u>from the God of me</u>.

[3] In their margin, WH omitted <u>the God</u> (<u>tO theO</u>).

that **I had baptized**[1] in mine own name.

16 And I baptized also the household of Stephanas: besides, I know not whether I baptized any other.

17 For Christ sent me not to baptize, but to preach the gospel: not with wisdom of words, lest the cross of Christ should be made of none effect.

18 For the preaching of the cross is to them that perish foolishness; but unto us which are saved it is the power of God.

19 For it is written, I will destroy the wisdom of the wise, and will bring to nothing the understanding of the prudent.

20 Where *is* the wise? where *is* the scribe? where *is* the disputer of this world? hath not God made foolish the wisdom of **this**[2] world?

21 For after that in the wisdom of God the world by wisdom knew not God, it pleased God by the foolish-

ness of preaching to save them that believe.

22 For the Jews require **a sign**[3], and the Greeks seek after wisdom:

23 But we preach Christ crucified, unto the Jews a stumblingblock, and unto the **Greeks**[4] foolishness;

24 But unto them which are called, both Jews and Greeks, Christ the power of God, and the wisdom of God.

25 Because the foolishness of God is wiser than men; and the weakness of God is stronger than men.

26 For ye see your calling, brethren, how that not many wise men after the flesh, not many mighty, not many noble, *are called*:

27 But God hath chosen the foolish things of the world **to confound**[5] the wise; and God hath chosen the weak things of the world to

---

[1] WH changed **I baptized** (ebaptisa) to *we baptized* (ebaptis**th**Ate). Both Aor Act Ind. **1**ˢᵗ **Sing** to *2ⁿᵈ Plur*. [person & number]

[2] WH omitted this (toutou) from of the world this.

[3] WH changed a sign (sAmeion) to *signs* (sAmeia). Acc Neut **Sing** to Acc Neut *Plur*. [number]

[4] WH changed **Greeks** (ʰel-lAsi) to *Gentiles* (e**th**nesi). [syn]

[5] WH changed the word order from the wise TO CONFOUND to *TO CONFOUND the wise*.

confound the things which are mighty;

28 And base things of the world, and things which are despised, hath God chosen, *yea*, **and**[1] things which are not, to bring to nought things that are:

29 That no flesh should glory in **his**[2] presence.

30 But of him are ye in Christ Jesus, who of God is made unto us **wisdom**[3], and righteousness, and sanctification, and redemption:

31 That, according as it is written, He that glorieth, let him glory in the Lord.

CHAPTER 2

1 And I, brethren, when I came to you, came not with excellency of speech or of wisdom, declaring unto you the **testimony**[4] of God.

2 For I determined not **[the]**[5] to know any thing among you, save Jesus Christ, and him crucified.

3 And I was with you in weakness, and in fear, and in much trembling.

4 And my speech and my preaching *was* not with enticing words of **man's**[6] wisdom, but in demonstration of the Spirit and of power:

5 That your faith should not stand in the wisdom of men, but in the power of God.

6 Howbeit we speak wisdom among them that are perfect: yet not the wisdom of this world, nor of the princes of this world, that come to nought:

7 But we speak the **wisdom**[7] of God in a mystery, *even* the hidden *wisdom*, which God ordained before the world unto our glory:

8 Which none of the princes of this world knew: for had they known *it*, they would not have crucified the

---

[1] In their margin, WH omitted and (kai).
[2] WH change **of him** (**aut**ou) to *of the God* (*tou* ~~th~~*eou*).
[3] WH changed the word order from unto us WISDOM to *WISDOM unto us*.
[4] WH changed **testimony** (**martu**rion) to *mystery* (*mustArion*) in their text but retained marturion in their margin.

---

[5] WH omitted the untranslated the (tou).
[6] WH omitted man's (an~~th~~rOpinAs).
[7] WH changed the word order from WISDOM of God to *of God WISDOM*.

Lord of glory.

9   But as it is written, Eye hath not seen, nor ear heard, neither have entered into the heart of man, the things **which**[1] God hath prepared for them that love him.

10 **But**[2] **God**[3] hath revealed *them* unto us by ~~his~~[4] Spirit: for the Spirit searcheth all things, yea, the deep things of God.

11 For what man knoweth the things of a man, save the spirit of man which is in him? even so the things of God **knoweth**[5] no man, but the Spirit of God.

12 Now we have received, not the spirit of the world, but the spirit which is of God; that we might know the things that are freely given to us of God.

13 Which things also we speak, not in the words which man's wisdom teacheth, but which the ~~Holy~~[6] Ghost teacheth; comparing spiritual things with spiritual.

14 But the natural man receiveth not the things of the Spirit of God: for they are foolishness unto him: neither can he know *them*, because they are spiritually discerned.

15 But he that is spiritual judgeth all things, yet he himself is judged of no man.

16 For who hath known the mind of the Lord, that he may instruct him? But we have the mind of Christ.

CHAPTER 3

1   And I, brethren, could not speak unto you as unto spiritual, but as unto **carnal**[7], *even* as unto babes in Christ.

2   I have fed you with milk, ~~and~~[8] not with meat: for hitherto ye were not able *to*

---

[1] WH changed which (^h**a**) to *which* (^h*osa*). Both Acc Neut Plur. **Relative** to *Correlative*.
[2] WH changed **but** (**de**) to *for* (*gar*).
[3] WH changed the word order from THE GOD hath revealed to *hath revealed* THE GOD.
[4] WH omitted of him (autou) from the spirit of him.
[5] WH changed has known (**oiden**) to *has known* (*egnOken*). Both Pf Act Ind. [syn]

[6] WH omitted holy (^hagiou).
[7] WH changed fleshly— **belonging** to the flesh (sarkikois) to *fleshly— consisting of the flesh* (*sarkinois*). Both Dat Masc Plur. [syn]
[8] WH omitted and (kai).

bear it, **neither**[1] yet now are ye able.

3   For ye are yet carnal: for whereas *there is* among you envying, and strife, ~~and divisions~~[2], are ye not carnal, and walk as men?

4   For while one saith, I am of Paul; and another, I *am* of Apollos; are ye **not**[3] **carnal**[4]?

5   **Who**[5] then is **Paul**[6], and **who**[7] [∧is][8] *is* **Apollos**, ~~but~~ [even][9] ministers by whom ye believed, even as the Lord gave to every man?

---

[1] WH changed <u>but not **also**</u> (<u>alla</u> <u>oute</u>) to *but not **and*** (*alla oude*).

[2] WH omitted <u>and divisions</u> (<u>kai dicostasiai</u>).

[3] WH changed <u>not</u> (<u>ouci</u>) to *not* (*ouk*). [**Emphatic** to *Regular* form of <u>ou</u>]

[4] WH changed **carnal** (**sarkikoi**) to *men* (*an*t͟hr*Opoi*).

[5] WH changed <u>who</u> (<u>tis</u>) to *what* (*ti*).

[6] WH changed the word order from <u>PAUL</u> . . . <u>Apollos</u> to *Apollos* . . . <u>PAUL</u>.

[7] WH changed <u>who</u> (<u>tis</u>) to *what* (*ti*).

[8] WH added *is* (*esti*) where the KJV supplied it.

[9] WH omitted <u>but</u> (<u>alla</u>) and the untranslated <u>even</u> (^h<u>A</u>).

6   I have planted, Apollos watered; but God gave the increase.

7   So then neither is he that planteth any thing, neither he that watereth; but God that giveth the increase.

8   Now he that planteth and he that watereth are one: and every man shall receive his own reward according to his own labour.

9   For we are labourers together with God: ye are God's husbandry, *ye are* God's building.

10   According to the grace of God which is given unto me, as a wise masterbuilder, **I have laid**[10] the foundation, and another buildeth thereon. But let every man take heed how he buildeth thereupon.

11   For other foundation can no man lay than that is laid, which is Jesus [~~the~~][11] Christ.

12   Now if any man build upon   ~~this~~[12]   foundation

---

[10] WH changed <u>I **have** laid</u> (<u>te</u>t͟h<u>eika</u>) to *I laid* (*e*t͟h*Aka*). **Pf** Act Ind to *Aor* Act Ind. [tense]

[11] WH omitted the untranslated <u>the</u> (^h<u>o</u>).

[12] WH omitted <u>this</u> (<u>touton</u>) from <u>the</u> <u>foundation</u> <u>this</u>.

gold[1], **silver**[2], precious stones, wood, hay, stubble;

13 Every man's work shall be made manifest: for the day shall declare it, because it shall be revealed by fire; and the fire [ʌ**itself**][3] shall try every man's work of what sort it is.

14 If any man's work abide which he hath built thereupon, he shall receive a reward.

15 If any man's work shall be burned, he shall suffer loss: but he himself shall be saved; yet so as by fire.

16 Know ye not that ye are the temple of God, and *that* the Spirit of God dwelleth in you?

17 If any man defile the temple of God, him shall God destroy; for the temple of God is holy, which *temple* ye are.

18 Let no man deceive himself. If any man among you seemeth to be wise in this world, let him become a fool, that he may be wise.

19 For the wisdom of this world is foolishness with God. For it is written, He taketh the wise in their own craftiness.

20 And again, The Lord knoweth the thoughts of the wise, that they are vain.

21 Therefore let no man glory in men. For all things are yours;

22 Whether Paul, or Apollos, or Cephas, or the world, or life, or death, or things present, or things to come; all **are**[4] yours;

23 And ye are Christ's; and Christ *is* God's.

CHAPTER 4

1 Let a man so account of us, as of the ministers of Christ, and stewards of the mysteries of God.

2 ~~**Moreover**~~[5] it is required in stewards, that a man be found faithful.

3 But with me it is a very small thing that I should be judged of you, or of man's judgment: yea, I judge not mine own self.

4 For I know nothing by myself; yet am I not hereby

---

[1] WH changed gold (cruson) to *gold* (*crusion*). [syn]
[2] WH changed silver (arguron) to *silver* (*argurion*). [syn]
[3] WH added *itself* (*auto*).

[4] WH omitted are (estin).
[5] WH changed but the rest (ʰO de loipon) to *but the rest* (ʰ*Ode loipon*). [3 words to 2]

justified: but he that judgeth me is the Lord.

5   Therefore judge nothing before the time, until the Lord come, who both will bring to light the hidden things of darkness, and will make manifest the counsels of the hearts: and then shall every man have praise of God.

6   And these things, brethren, I have in a figure transferred to myself and *to* Apollos for your sakes; that ye might learn in us not ~~to think~~[1] *of men* above **that which**[2] is written, that no one of you be puffed up for one against another.

7   For who maketh thee to differ *from another*? and what hast thou that thou didst not receive? now if thou didst receive *it*, why dost thou glory, as if thou hadst not received *it*?

8   Now ye are full, now ye are rich, ye have reigned as kings without us: and I would to God ye did reign, that we also might reign with you.

9   For I think ~~that~~[3] God hath set forth us the apostles last, as it were appointed to death: for we are made a spectacle unto the world, and to angels, and to men.

10   We *are* fools for Christ's sake, but ye *are* wise in Christ; we *are* weak, but ye *are* strong; ye *are* honourable, but we *are* despised.

11   Even unto this present hour we both hunger, and thirst, and are naked, and are buffeted, and have no certain dwellingplace;

12   And labour, working with our own hands: being reviled, we bless; being persecuted, we suffer it:

13   **Being defamed**[4], we intreat: we are made as the filth of the world, *and are* the offscouring of all things unto this day.

14   I write not these things to shame you, but as my beloved sons **I warn**[5] *you*.

15   For though ye have ten

---

[1] WH omitted <u>to think</u> (<u>fronein</u>).
[2] WH changed <u>that</u> {thing} <u>which</u> (<u>^ho</u>) to *those* {thing**s**} *which* (<u>["]A</u>). **Sing** to *Plur*. [number]

[3] WH omitted <u>that</u> (^h<u>oti</u>).
[4] WH changed <u>being **blasphem**ed</u> (**bla**sfAmoumenoi) to *being **defam**ed* (**dusf**A-moumenoi). Both Pres Pass Part. [syn]
[5] WH changed <u>I warn</u> (nou~~th~~etO) to *warning* (nou~~th~~etO**n**). Pres Act **Ind** to Pres Act *Part*. [mood]

thousand instructors in Christ, yet *have ye* not many fathers: for in Christ Jesus I have begotten you through the gospel.

16 Wherefore I beseech you, be ye followers of me.

17 For this cause have I sent unto you Timotheus, who is my beloved **son**[1], and faithful in the Lord, who shall bring you into remembrance of my ways which be in Christ, as I teach every where in every church.

18 Now some are puffed up, as though I would not come to you.

19 But I will come to you shortly, if the Lord will, and will know, not the speech of them which are puffed up, but the power.

20 For the kingdom of God *is* not in word, but in power.

21 What will ye? shall I come unto you with a rod, or in love, and *in* the spirit of meekness?

CHAPTER 5

1 It is reported commonly *that there is* fornication among you, and such fornication as ~~is~~ not so much as **named**[2] among the Gentiles, that one should have his father's wife.

2 And ye are puffed up, and have not rather mourned, that he that hath done this deed **might be taken away**[3] from among you.

3 For I verily, **as**[4] absent in body, but present in spirit, have judged already, as though I were present, *concerning* him that hath so done this deed,

4 In the name of our Lord Jesus ~~Christ~~[5], when ye are gathered together, and my spirit, with the power of our Lord Jesus ~~Christ~~[6],

5 To deliver such an one unto Satan for the destruction of the flesh, that the spirit may be saved in the day of the Lord **Jesus**[7].

---

[1] WH change the word order from SON of me to *of me SON.*

[2] WH omitted is named (onomazetai)

[3] WH changed **might be taken away** (**exarthA**) to *might be taken* (*arthA*). Both Aor Pass Sub. [prefix dropped]

[4] WH omitted as ([h]Os).

[5] WH omitted Christ (cristou).

[6] WH omitted Christ (cristou).

[7] In their margin, WH omitted Jesus (iAsou).

6   Your glorying *is* not good. Know ye not that a little leaven leaveneth the whole lump?

7   Purge out **therefore**[1] the old leaven, that ye may be a new lump, as ye are unleavened. For even Christ our passover **is sacrificed**[2] **for us**[3]:

8   Therefore let us keep the feast, not with old leaven, neither with the leaven of malice and wickedness; but with the unleavened *bread* of sincerity and truth.

9   I wrote unto you in an epistle not to company with fornicators:

10   **Yet**[4] not altogether with the fornicators of this world, or with the covetous, **or**[5] extortioners, or with idolaters; for then **must ye needs**[6] go out of the world.

11   But now I have written unto you not to keep company, if any man that is called a brother be a fornicator, or covetous, or an idolater, or a railer, or a drunkard, or an extortioner; with such an one no not to eat.

12   For what have I to do to judge them **also**[7] that are without? do not ye judge them that are within?

13   But them that are without God judgeth. **Therefore**[8] **put away**[9] from among yourselves that wicked person.

CHAPTER 6

1   Dare any of you, having a matter against another, go to law before the unjust, and not before the saints?

2   Do ye [∧**the**][10] not know that the saints shall judge the world? and if the world shall be judged by you, are ye unworthy to judge the

---

[1] WH omitted <u>therefore</u> (<u>oun</u>).
[2] WH changed <u>was sacrificed</u> (<u>eth</u>uth<u>An</u>) to *was sacrificed* (*etuthA*). Both Aor **Pass** Ind *3rd* **Sing**. [spell]
[3] WH omitted <u>for us</u> (^h<u>uper</u> ^hAOn).
[4] WH omitted <u>yet</u> (<u>kai</u>).
[5] WH changed **<u>or</u>** (**<u>A</u>**) to *and* (*kai*).
[6] WH changed <u>ye need to</u> (<u>ofeilete</u>) *ye* **were** *needing to*

(*Ofeilete*). **Pres** Act Ind to *Impf* Act Ind. [tense]
[7] WH omitted <u>also</u> (<u>kai</u>).
[8] WH omitted <u>therefore</u> (<u>kai</u>).
[9] WH changed <u>you^p</u> **will** <u>put away</u> (<u>exareite</u>) to *put you^p away* (*exarate*). **Fut** Act **Ind** to *Aor* Act *Imp*. [tense & mood]
[10] WH added *the* (^hA).

smallest matters?

3   Know ye not that we shall judge angels? how much more things that pertain to this life?

4   If then ye have judgments of things pertaining to this life, set them to judge who are least esteemed in the church.

5   I speak to your shame. Is it so, that **there is**[1] **not a wise man**[2] among you? no, not one that shall be able to judge between his brethren?

6   But brother goeth to law with brother, and that before the unbelievers.

7   Now therefore there is utterly a fault ~~among~~[3] you, because ye go to law one with another. Why do ye not rather take wrong? why do ye not rather *suffer yourselves to* be defrauded?

8   Nay, ye do wrong, and defraud, and **that**[4] *your* brethren.

9   Know ye not that the unrighteous shall not inherit **the kingdom**[5] of God? Be not deceived: neither fornicators, nor idolaters, nor adulterers, nor effeminate, nor abusers of themselves with mankind,

10   Nor thieves, nor covetous, **nor**[6] drunkards, nor revilers, nor extortioners, shall **[~~not~~]**[7] inherit the kingdom of God.

11   And such were some of you: but ye are washed, but ye are sanctified, but ye are justified in the name of the Lord Jesus [Λ**Christ**][8], and by the Spirit of our God.

12   All things are lawful unto me, but all things are not expedient: all things are

---

[1] WH changed there **is** (estin) to *there **exists*** (eni). Both Pres Ind. [syn

[2] WH changed not a wise {man} by combining not-but one (oude eis) into *not-but-one* (oudeis) and by changing the word order from WISE not-but one to *not-but-one WISE*.

[3] WH omitted among (en), forcing the dative case to supply the preposition.

[4] WH changed these (tauta) to *this* (touto). Nom Neut **Plur** to Nom Neut *Sing*. [number]

[5] WH changed the word order from KINGDOM of God to *of God KINGDOM*.

[6] WH changed not **and** (oute) to *not* (ou).

[7] WH omitted the untranslated [and negative strengthening] not (ou).

[8] WH added *Christ* (cristou).

lawful for me, but I will not be brought under the power of any.

13 Meats for the belly, and the belly for meats: but God shall destroy both it and them. Now the body *is* not for fornication, but for the Lord; and the Lord for the body.

14 And God hath both raised up the Lord, and will also raise up us by his own power.

15 Know ye not that your bodies are the members of Christ? shall I then take the members of Christ, and make *them* the members of an harlot? God forbid.

16 What? know ye not that he which is joined to an harlot is one body? for two, saith he, shall be one flesh.

17 But he that is joined unto the Lord is one spirit.

18 Flee fornication. Every sin that a man doeth is without the body; but he that committeth fornication sinneth against his own body.

19 What? know ye not that your body is the temple of the Holy Ghost *which is* in you, which ye have of God, and ye are not your own?

20 For ye are bought with a price: therefore glorify God in your body, ~~and in your spirit, which are God's~~[1].

CHAPTER 7

1 Now concerning the things whereof ye wrote ~~unto me~~[2]: *It is* good for a man not to touch a woman.

2 Nevertheless, *to avoid* fornication, let every man have his own wife, and let every woman have her own husband.

3 Let the husband render unto the wife **due benevolence**[3]: and likewise also the wife unto the husband.

4 The wife hath not power of her own body, but the husband: and likewise also the husband hath not power of his own body, but the wife.

5 Defraud ye not one the other, except *it be* with consent for a time, that **ye may**

---

[1] WH omitted <u>and in the spirit of you which are of the God</u> (<u>kai en tO pneumati ^humOn ^hatina esti tou theou</u>).
[2] WH omitted <u>unto me</u> (<u>moi</u>).
[3] WH changed **the being owed good attitude** (tAn ofeilomenAn **eunoian**) to *the debt* (*tAn ofeilAn*)

~~give yourselves~~[1] ~~to fasting and~~[2] prayer; and **come**[3] together again, that Satan tempt you not for your incontinency.

6 But I speak this by permission, *and* not of commandment.

7 **For**[4] I would that all men were even as I myself. But every man hath his proper **gift**[5] of God, **one**[6] after this manner, and **another**[7] after that.

8 I say therefore to the unmarried and widows, ~~It is~~[8] good for them if they abide even as I.

9 But if they cannot contain, let them marry: for it is better to marry than to burn.

10 And unto the married I command, *yet* not I, but the Lord, Let not the wife depart from *her* husband:

11 But and if she depart, let her remain unmarried, or be reconciled to *her* husband: and let not the husband put away *his* wife.

12 But to the rest **[myself]**[9] speak I, not the Lord: If any brother hath a wife that believeth not, and she be pleased to dwell with him, let him not put her away.

13 And the woman which hath an husband that believeth not, and **if he**[10] be pleased to dwell with her, let her not leave him.

14 For the unbelieving husband is sanctified by the wife, and the unbelieving wife

---

[1] WH changed ye **may** give yourselves (scolazAte) to *ye might give yourselves* (scolasAte). **Pres** Act Sub to *Aor* Act Sub. [tense]

[2] WH omitted to fasting and (tan Asteia kai), forcing the dative case to supply the preposition.

[3] WH changed **come** {with} (**sunercAsthe**) to *be* (*Ate*).

[4] WH changed **for** (**gar**) to *but* (*de*) in their text, but retained gar in their margin.

[5] WH changed the word order from GIFT hath to *hath GIFT*.

[6] WH changed **one** (ʰos) to *the* {one} (ʰo). **Rel Pro** to *Def Art*.

[7] WH changed **one** (ʰos) to *the* {one} (ʰo). **Rel Pro** to *Def Art*.

[8] WH omitted it is (estin).

[9] WH changed the word order from MYSELF speak I to *speak I MYSELF*

[10] WH changed {if} **he** (**autos**) to {if} *this* {one} (ʰoutos). **Pers** Pro to Dem Pro.

is sanctified by the **husband**[1]: else were your children unclean; but now are they holy.

15 But if the unbelieving depart, let him depart. A brother or a sister is not under bondage in such *cases*: but God hath called **u͟s**[2] to peace.

16 For what knowest thou, O wife, whether thou shalt save *thy* husband? or how knowest thou, O man, whether thou shalt save *thy* wife?

17 But as **God**[3] **hath distributed**[4] to every man, as the **Lord**[5] hath called every one, so let him walk. And so ordain I in all churches.

18 Is any man called being circumcised? let him not become uncircumcised. **I͟s a͟n͟y**[6]

called[7] in uncircumcision? let him not be circumcised.

19 Circumcision is nothing, and uncircumcision is nothing, but the keeping of the commandments of God.

20 Let every man abide in the same calling wherein he was called.

21 Art thou called *being* a servant? care not for it: but if thou mayest be made free, use *it* rather.

22 For he that is called in the Lord, *being* a servant, is the Lord's freeman: likewise ~~also~~[8] he that is called, *being* free, is Christ's servant.

23 Ye are bought with a price; be not ye the servants of men.

24 Brethren, let every man, wherein he is called, therein abide with [~~the~~][9] God.

25 Now concerning virgins I have no commandment of the Lord: yet I give my judgment, as one that hath obtained mercy of the Lord

---

[1] WH changed **husband** (**andri**) to *brother* (*adelfO*).
[2] In their margin, WH changed **us** (**ʰAmas**) to *you*[p] (*ʰumas*).
[3] WH changed the **God** (ʰo t͟heos) to *the Lord* (*ʰo kurios*).
[4] WH changed **distributed** (emerisen) to *has distributed* (*memeriken*). **Aor** Act Ind to *Pf* Act Ind. [tense]
[5] WH changed **Lord** (**kuri**os) to *God* (*t͟heos*).
[6] WH changed the word or-

der from A͟N͟Y **was called** to *has been called A͟N͟Y*.
[7] WH changed **was called** (eklAt͟hA) to *has been called* (*keklAtai*). **Aor** Pass Ind to *Pf* Pass Ind. [tense]
[8] WH omitted a͟l͟s͟o (kai).
[9] WH omitted the untranslated t͟h͟e (tO).

to be faithful.

26 I suppose therefore that this is good for the present distress, *I say*, that *it is* good for a man so to be.

27 Art thou bound unto a wife? seek not to be loosed. Art thou loosed from a wife? seek not a wife.

28 But and if thou marry, thou hast not sinned; and if a virgin marry, she hath not sinned. Nevertheless such shall have trouble in the flesh: but I spare you.

29 But this I say, brethren, the time *is* short: **it re-maineth**[1], that both they that have wives be as though they had none;

30 And they that weep, as though they wept not; and they that rejoice, as though they rejoiced not; and they that buy, as though they possessed not;

31 And they that use ~~this~~[2] **[the]** **world**[3], as not abusing *it*: for the fashion of this world passeth away.

---

[1] WH changed the word order from the rest IS to *IS the rest*.

[2] WH omitted this (toutO) from the world this.

[3] WH changed the world (t**O** kosm**O**) to *the world* (*ton kosmon*). **Dat** to *Acc*. [case]

32 But I would have you without carefulness. He that is unmarried careth for the things that belong to the Lord, how **he may please**[4] the Lord:

33 But he that is married careth for the things that are of the world, how **he may please**[5] his wife.

34 [∧**and**][6] There is differ-ence ∧*also*[7] between a wife and a virgin. **The unmarried woman**[8] careth for the things of the Lord, that she may be holy both in [∧**the**][9] body and in [∧**the**][10] spirit: but she that is married careth for the things of the world, how **she**

---

[4] WH changed he **will** please (aresei) to *he **might** please* (apesA). **Fut** Act **Ind** to *Aor* Act *Sub*. [tense & voice]

[5] WH changed he **will** please (aresei) to *he **might** please* (apesA). **Fut** Act **Ind** to *Aor* Act *Sub*. [tense & voice]

[6] WH added *and* (kai).

[7] WH added *also* (kai) where the KJV supplied it.

[8] In their margin, WH changed the word order from and the virgin THE UNMARRIED {female} to *THE UNMARRIED {female} and the virgin*.

[9] WH added *the* (tO).

[10] WH added *the* (tO).

may please[1] *her* husband.

35 And this I speak for your own **profit**[2]; not that I may cast a snare upon you, but for that which is comely, and **that ye may attend upon**[3] the Lord without distraction.

36 But if any man think that he behaveth himself uncomely toward his virgin, if she pass the flower of *her* age, and need so require, let him do what he will, he sinneth not: let them marry.

37 Nevertheless he that standeth **stedfast**[4] in ~~his~~[5] heart, having no necessity, but hath power over his own will, and hath so decreed in

his[6] [∧**his own**][7] **heart**[8] that he will **[the]**[9] keep his virgin, **doeth**[10] well.

38 So then **he that giveth *her* in marriage**[11] doeth well [∧**the virgin of himself]**[12]; **but**[13] **he that giveth *her*** not **in marriage**[14] **doeth**[15] better.

---

[6] WH omitted of him (autou) from the heart of him (tA kardia **autou**).

[7] WH added *his own* (idia) before heart.

[8] WH changed the word order from the HEART **of him** to *the **his own** HEART*.

[9] WH omitted the untranslated the (tou).

[10] WH changed does (poiei) to *will do* (poiAsei). **Pres** Act Ind to *Fut* Act Ind. [tense]

[11] WH changed he that giveth [her] {**out**} in marriage (**ek**-gamizOn) to *he that giveth [her] in marriage* (gamizOn). [prefix dropped]

[12] WH added *the virgin of himself* (tAn parthenon heautou).

[13] WH changed **but** (**de**) to *and* (kai).

[14] WH changed he that giveth [her] {**out**} in marriage (**ek**-gamizOn) to *he that giveth [her] in marriage* (gamizOn). [prefix dropped]

[15] WH changed does (poiei) to *will do* (poiAsei). **Pres** Act Ind to *Fut* Act Ind. [tense]

---

[1] WH changed she **will** please (are**sei**) to *she **might** please* (aresA). **Fut** Act **Ind** to *Aor* Act **Sub**. [tense & voice]

[2] WH changed profit**ing** (sum**f**eron) to *profitable* (sum**f**oron). **Verbal** (benefit-**ing**) to *Adj* (benefi**c**ial).

[3] WH changed devoted **toward** (eu**pros**edron) to *devoted to* (eu**par**edron). Both Acc Neut Sing Adj. [prefix changed]

[4] WH changed the word order from STEADFAST in the heart to *in the heart **of him** STEADFAST*.

[5] WH omitted of him (autou) from the heart of him.

39 The wife is bound ~~by the law~~[1] as long as ~~her~~[2] husband liveth; but if her husband be dead, she is at liberty to be married to whom she will; only in the Lord.

40 But she is happier if she so abide, after my judgment: and I think also that I have the Spirit of God.

CHAPTER 8

1 Now as touching things offered unto idols, we know that we all have knowledge. Knowledge puffeth up, but charity edifieth.

2 ~~And~~[3] if any man think **that he knoweth**[4] any thing, he **knoweth**[5] **nothing**[6] ~~yet~~[7]

as he ought to know.

3 But if any man love God, the same is known of him.

4 As concerning therefore the eating of those things that are offered in sacrifice unto idols, we know that an idol *is* nothing in the world, and that *there is* none ~~other~~[8] God but one.

5 For though there be that are called gods, whether in heaven or in ~~[the]~~[9] earth, (as there be gods many, and lords many,)

6 But to us *there is but* one God, the Father, of whom *are* all things, and we in him; and one Lord Jesus Christ, by whom *are* all things, and we by him.

7 Howbeit *there is* not in every man that knowledge: for some with **conscience**[10] **of the idol**[11] unto this hour eat *it* as a thing offered unto

---

[1] WH omitted <u>by the law</u> (<u>nomO</u>).
[2] WH omitted <u>of her</u> (<u>autAs</u>) from <u>the husband of her</u>.
[3] WH omitted <u>and</u> (<u>de</u>).
[4] WH changed <u>to have known</u> (<u>eidenai</u>) to *to have known* (*egnOkenai*). Both Pf Act Inf. <u>oida</u> to *ginOskO*. [syn]
[5] WH changed <u>he **has known**</u> (<u>egnOke</u>) to *he knew* (*egnO*). **Pf** Act Ind to *Aor* Act Ind. [tense]
[6] WH changed <u>not **but** as</u> (<u>oudepO</u>) to *not as* (*oupO*).
[7] WH omitted <u>yet</u> (<u>ouden</u>).

[8] WH omitted <u>other</u> {of a different kind} (<u>heteros</u>).
[9] WH omitted <u>the</u> untranslated <u>the</u> (<u>tAs</u>).
[10] WH changed **conscience** (<u>suneidAsei</u>) to *custom* (*sunA theia*).
[11] WH changed the word order from <u>OF THE IDOL</u> until <u>now</u> to *until now OF THE IDOL*.

an idol; and their conscience being weak is defiled.

8 But meat **commendeth**[1] us not to God: ~~for~~[2] neither, if we eat, **are we the better**[3]; neither, if **we eat not**, **are we the worse**[4].

9 But take heed lest by any means this liberty of yours become a stumblingblock to them **that are weak**[5].

10 For if any man see thee which hast knowledge sit at meat in the idol's temple, shall not the conscience of him which is weak be emboldened to eat those things which are offered to idols;

11 **And**[6] **through**[7] thy knowledge **shall** the weak [∧**the**][8] **brother**[9] **perish**[10], for whom Christ died?

12 But when ye sin so against the brethren, and wound their weak conscience, ye sin against Christ.

13 Wherefore, if meat make my brother to offend, I will eat no flesh while the world standeth, lest I make my brother to offend.

CHAPTER 9

1 Am I not an apostle?

---

[1] WH changed <u>commends</u> (*paristAsi*) to *will commend* (*parastAsei*). **Pres** Act Ind to **Fut** Act Ind. [tense]

[2] WH omitted <u>for</u> (*gar*).

[3] WH changed <u>are we the better</u> (*perisseuomen*) to *are we being the better* (*perisseume~~th~~a*). Pres Act **Ind** to Pres *Pass* Ind. [voice]

[4] WH changed the word order from <u>neither</u> if <u>we eat</u> <u>are we the better</u> <u>neither</u> if <u>NOT WE EAT ARE WE THE WORSE</u> to *neither if NOT WE EAT ARE WE THE WORSE neither if we eat are we the better*.

[5] WH changed <u>the **being** weak</u> {ones} (*tois as~~th~~enousin*) to *the weak {ones}* (*tois as~~th~~enesin*). Pres Act **Part** to *Adj*.

[6] WH changed **and** (**kai**) to *for* (*gar*) and made this conjunction the second word in the verse.

[7] WH changed **upon** (**epi**) to *in* (*en*).

[8] WH added *the* (*[h]o*).

[9] WH changed the word order from <u>the weak</u> BROTHER **upon** the of you knowledge to *the weak **in** the of you knowledge THE BROTHER*.

[10] WH changed **shall perish** (*apoleitai*) to *is being destroyed* (*apollutai*). **Fut Mid** Ind to *Pres Pass* Ind. [tense & voice]

am I not **free**[1]? have I not seen Jesus ~~Christ~~[2] our Lord? are not ye my work in the Lord?

2   If I be not an apostle unto others, yet doubtless I am to you: for the seal **[the]**[3] of **mine**[4] apostleship are ye in the Lord.

3   Mine answer to them that do examine me is **this**[5],

4   Have we not power to eat and to drink?

5   Have we not power to lead about a sister, a wife, as well as other apostles, and *as* the brethren of the Lord, and Cephas?

6   Or I only and Barnabas, have not we power **[the]**[6] to forbear working?

7   Who goeth a warfare any time at his own charges? who planteth a vineyard, and

eateth not ~~of~~[7] **the fruit**[8] thereof? or who feedeth a flock, and eateth not of the milk of the flock?

8   Say I these things as a man? or saith [9]**not**[10] the law the same also?

9   For it is written in the law of Moses, Thou shalt not muzzle the mouth of the ox that treadeth out the corn. Doth God take care for oxen?

10   Or saith he *it* altogether for our sakes? For our sakes, no doubt, *this* is written: that he that ploweth **should**[11] plow in hope; and that he that thresheth in hope [∧the][12] **should be partaker**[13] ~~of his~~

---

[1] WH changed the word order from <u>not</u> <u>I am</u> <u>apostle</u> <u>not I am</u> FREE to *not I am FREE not I am apostle.*

[2] WH omitted <u>Christ</u> (<u>cris-ton</u>).

[3] WH changed the word order from THE <u>my</u> <u>apostleship</u> to *of me* THE *apostleship.*

[4] WH changed <u>my</u> (**emAs**) to *of me* (**mou**)

[5] WH changed the word order from THIS <u>is</u> to *is THIS.*

[6] WH omitted the untranslated <u>the</u> (<u>tou</u>).

[7] WH omitted <u>of</u> (<u>ek</u>).

[8] WH changed <u>the</u> <u>fruit</u> (<u>tou karpou</u>) to *the fruit* (*ton karpon*). **Gen** to *Acc.* [case]

[9] WH changed the word order from **NOT** <u>also</u> <u>the</u> <u>law</u> <u>these</u> {things} to *the law also these* {things} *NOT.* [*2 Gk letters dropped]

[10] WH changed <u>not</u> (<u>ouci</u>—emphatic of <u>ou</u>) to *not* (*ou*)

[11] WH changed the word order from <u>upon</u> <u>hope</u> OUGHT to *OUGHT upon hope.*

[12] WH added *the* (*tou*).

[13] WH changed the word order from **of the** **hope** **of him** TO BE SHARING <u>upon</u> <u>hope</u> to *upon hope **the** TO BE SHARING.*

~~hope~~[1].

11 If we have sown unto you spiritual things, *is it* a great thing if we shall reap your carnal things?

12 If others be partakers of *this* **power**[2] over you, *are* not we rather? Nevertheless we have not used this power; but suffer all things, lest we should **hinder**[3] the gospel of Christ.

13 Do ye not know that they which minister about [∧**the**][4] holy things live *of the things* of the temple? and they which **wait at**[5] the altar are partakers with the altar?

14 Even so hath the Lord ordained that they which preach the gospel should live of the gospel.

15 But I [∧**not**][6] **have used**[7] **none**[8] of these things: neither have I written these things, that it should be so done unto me: for *it were* better for me to die, than ~~that~~[9] **any man**[10] **should make** my glorying **void**[11].

16 For though I preach the gospel, I have nothing to glory of: for necessity is laid upon me; **yea**[12], woe is unto me, if I preach not the gospel!

17 For if I do this thing willingly, I have a reward: but if against my will, a dispensation *of the gospel* is committed unto me.

---

[1] WH omitted of the hope of him (tAs elpidos outou),

[2] WH changed the word order from POWER over you to *over you POWER*.

[3] WH changed the word order from HINDRANCE anyone we give to *anyone HINDRANCE we give*.

[4] WH added *the (ta)*.

[5] WH changed serving **near** (**pros**edreuontes) to *serving beside* (*par*edreuontes). Both Pres Act Part. [prefix changed]

[6] WH added *not (ou)*.

[7] WH changed the word order from NONE have used to *not have used NONE*.

[8] WH changed used (ecrAsamAn) to *have used* (kecrAmai). **Aor Act-D** Ind (used) to *Pf Mid* Ind. [tense & voice]

[9] WH omitted **that** ([h]ina).

[10] WH changed **any** one (**tis**) to *no one* (*oudeis*).

[11] WH changed **might** make void (kenOsA) to *will make void* (*kenOsei*). **Aor** Act **Sub** to *Fut* Act **Ind**. [tense & mood]

[12] WH changed **yea** (**de**) to *for* (*gar*).

18 What is my reward then? *Verily* that, when I preach the gospel, I may make the gospel of [the] ~~Christ~~[1] without charge, that I abuse not my power in the gospel.

19 For though I be free from all *men*, yet have I made myself servant unto all, that I might gain the more.

20 And unto the Jews I became as a Jew, that I might gain the Jews; to them that are under the law, as under the law, [ʌ**not as myself under law**][2] that I might gain them that are under the law;

21 To them that are without law, as without law, (being not without law **to God**[3], but under the law **to Christ**[4],) that **I might gain**[5] them that are without law.

---

[1] WH omitted the Christ (tou cristou).

[2] WH added not as myself under law (mA On autos ᶜupo nomon).

[3] WH changed **to** God (~~the~~O) to *of God* (~~th~~eou). **Dat** to **Gen**. [case]

[4] WH changed **to** Christ (cristO) to *of Christ* (cris-tou). **Dat** to **Gen**. [case]

[5] WH changed I might gain (kerd**As**O) to *I might gain* (kerd*an*O). Both Aor Act Sub. [spell]

22 To the weak became I ~~as~~[6] weak, that I might gain the weak: I am made all things to [the][7] all *men*, that I might by all means save some.

23 And **this**[8] I do for the gospel's sake, that I might be partaker thereof with *you*.

24 Know ye not that they which run in a race run all, but one receiveth the prize? So run, that ye may obtain.

25 And every man that striveth for the mastery is temperate in all things. Now they *do it* to obtain a corruptible crown; but we an incorruptible.

26 I therefore so run, not as uncertainly; so fight I, not as one that beateth the air:

27 But I keep under my body, and bring *it* into subjection: lest that by any means, when I have preached to others, I myself should be a castaway.

CHAPTER 10

1   **Moreover**[9], brethren, I

---

[6] WH omitted as (ᶜOs).

[7] WH omitted the (ta).

[8] WH changed **this** {thing} (**touto**) to *all* {things} (*panta*). **Sing** to **Plur**. [number]

[9] WH changed **moreover** (**de**) to *for* (*gar*).

would not that ye should be ignorant, how that all our fathers were under the cloud, and all passed through the sea;

2   And were all baptized unto Moses in the cloud and in the sea;

3   And did all eat the same spiritual meat;

4   And did all drink the same spiritual drink: for they drank of that spiritual Rock that followed them: and that Rock was Christ.

5   But with many of them God was not well pleased: for they were overthrown in the wilderness.

6   Now these things were our examples, to the intent we should not lust after evil things, as they also lusted.

7   Neither be ye idolaters, as *were* some of them; **as**[1] it is written, The people sat down to eat and drink, and rose up to play.

8   Neither let us commit fornication, as some of them committed, and fell in one day three and twenty thousand.

9   Neither let us tempt **Christ**[2], as some of them

~~also~~[3] tempted, and **were destroyed**[4] of serpents.

10   Neither murmur ye, **as**[5] some of them ~~also~~[6] murmured, and were destroyed of the destroyer.

11   Now ~~all~~[7] these things happened unto them **for ensamples**[8]: and they are written for our admonition, upon whom the ends of the world **are come**[9].

12   Wherefore let him that thinketh he standeth take heed lest he fall.

13   There hath no temptation taken you but such as is common to man: but God *is*

---

ton) to **Lord** (**kurion**) in their text, but retained Christ (criston) in their margin.

[3] WH omitted also (kai).

[4] WH changed were destroyed (apOlonto) to *were being destroyed* (apOllunto). **Aor Mid** Ind to *Impf Pass* Ind. [tense & voice]

[5] WH changed as (^hOsper) to *as* (*ka*￼*haper*). [syn]

[6] WH omitted also (kai).

[7] WH omitted all (panta).

[8] WH changed patterns (tupoi) to *as patterns* (tupikOs). **Pro** to *Adv*.

[9] WH changed came (katAntAsen) to *have come* (katAntAken). **Aor** Act Ind to *Pf* Act Ind. [tense]

---

[1] WH changed as (^hOs) to *just as* (^hOsper).

[2] WH changed **Christ** (cris-

faithful, who will not suffer you to be tempted above that ye are able; but will with the temptation also make a way to escape, that ye [~~your-selves~~][1], may be able to bear *it*.

14 Wherefore, my dearly beloved, flee from idolatry.

15 I speak as to wise men; judge ye what I say.

16 The cup of blessing which we bless, is it not the communion of the blood of Christ? The bread which we break, is it not the communion of the body of Christ?

17 For we *being* many are one bread, *and* one body: for we are all partakers of that one bread.

18 Behold Israel after the flesh: are not they which eat of the sacrifices partakers of the altar?

19 What say I then? that **the idol**[2] is any thing, or that which is offered in sacrifice to idols is any thing?

20 But I *say*, that the things which the Gentiles sacrifice, they sacrifice to devils, and not to God: and I would not that ye should have fellowship with devils.

21 Ye cannot drink the cup of the Lord, and the cup of devils: ye cannot be partakers of the Lord's table, and of the table of devils.

22 Do we provoke the Lord to jealousy? are we stronger than he?

23 All things are lawful **~~for me~~**[3], but all things are not expedient: all things are lawful **~~for me~~**[4], but all things edify not.

24 Let no man seek his own, but **~~every man~~**[5] another's *wealth*.

25 Whatsoever is sold in the shambles, *that* eat, asking no question for conscience sake:

26 For the earth *is* the Lord's, and the fulness thereof.

27 [~~but~~][6] If any of them that believe not bid you *to a feast*, and ye be disposed to

---

[1] WH omitted the untranslated intensive <u>yourselves</u> (^h<u>umas</u>).

[2] WH changed the word order from <u>that</u> <u>IDOL</u> <u>anything</u> <u>is</u> <u>or</u> <u>that</u> <u>sacrificed to idols</u> <u>anything</u> <u>is</u> to *that sacrificed to idols anything is or that* IDOL *anything is*.

[3] WH omitted <u>for me</u> (<u>moi</u>).

[4] WH omitted <u>for me</u> (<u>moi</u>).

[5] WH omitted <u>every man</u> (<u>ekastos</u>—every one).

[6] WH omitted the untranslated <u>but</u> (<u>de</u>).

go; whatsoever is set before you, eat, asking no question for conscience sake.

28 But if any man say unto you, This is **offered in sacrifice unto idols**[1], eat not for his sake that shewed it, and for conscience sake: ~~for the earth *is* the Lord's, and the fulness thereof~~[2]:

29 Conscience, I say, not thine own, but of the other: for why is my liberty judged of another *man's* conscience?

30 ~~For~~[3] if I by grace be a partaker, why am I evil spoken of for that for which I give thanks?

31 Whether therefore ye eat, or drink, or whatsoever ye do, do all to the glory of God.

32 **Give**[4] none offence,

neither to the Jews, nor to the Gentiles, nor to the church of God:

33 Even as I please all *men* in all *things*, not seeking mine own profit, but the *profit* of many, that they may be saved.

CHAPTER 11

1 Be ye followers of me, even as I also *am* of Christ.

2 Now I praise you, ~~brethren~~[5], that ye remember me in all things, and keep the ordinances, as I delivered *them* to you.

3 But I would have you know, that the head of every man is Christ; and the head of the woman *is* the man; and ʌ**the**[6] head of Christ *is* God.

4 Every man praying or prophesying, having *his* head covered, dishonoureth his head.

5 But every woman that prayeth or prophesieth with *her* head uncovered dishonoureth **her**[7] head: for that is

---

[1] WH changed <u>offered **to idols**</u> (**eidOlothuton**) to *offered in sacrifice* (**ʰierothuton**). Both Nom Neut Sing Adj.

[2] WH omitted <u>for the earth</u> [is] <u>the Lord's and the fullness thereof</u> (<u>tou gar kuriou ʰA gA kai to plArOma autAs</u>).

[3] WH omitted <u>for</u> (<u>de</u>).

[4] WH changed the word order from <u>inoffensive</u> BECOME YE <u>also</u> to Jews to *inoffensive also to Jews* BECOME YE.

[5] WH omitted <u>brethren</u> (<u>adelfoi</u>).

[6] WH added *he* (*tou*) as the KJV supplied it.

[7] WH changed <u>of herself</u> (**ʰeautAs**) to *of her* (*autAs*). **Refl** Pro to **Pers** Pro.

even all one as if she were shaven.

6   For if the woman be not covered, let her also be shorn: but if it be a shame for a woman to be shorn or shaven, let her be covered.

7   For a man indeed ought not to cover *his* head, forasmuch as he is the image and glory of God: but ∧**the**[1] woman is the glory of the man.

8   For the man is not of the woman; but the woman of the man.

9   Neither was the man created for the woman; but the woman for the man.

10   For this cause ought the woman to have power on *her* head because of the angels.

11   Nevertheless neither is the man without the woman, **neither the woman without the man**[2], in the Lord.

12   For as the woman *is* of the man, even so *is* the man also by the woman; but all

things of God.

13   Judge in yourselves: is it comely that a woman pray unto God uncovered?

14   [~~or~~][3] Doth not even nature **itself**[4] teach you, that, if a man have long hair, it is a shame unto him?

15   But if a woman have long hair, it is a glory to her: for *her* hair is given her for a covering.

16   But if any man seem to be contentious, we have no such custom, neither the churches of God.

17   Now in this that I declare *unto you* I praise *you* not, that ye come together not for the better, but for the worse.

18   For first of all, when ye come together in ~~the~~[5] church, I hear that there be divisions among you; and I partly believe it.

19   For there must be also heresies among you, that they which are approved may be made manifest among you.

20   When ye come together therefore into one place, *this*

---

[1] WH added *the* (ʰA) as the KJV supplied it.
[2] WH changed the word order from <u>neither</u> <u>man</u> <u>without</u> <u>woman</u> NEITHER WOMAN WITHOUT MAN to *NEITHER WOMAN WITHOUT MAN* neither *man without woman.*

[3] WH omitted the untranslated <u>or</u> (ʰA).
[4] WH changed the word order from <u>ITSELF</u> <u>the</u> <u>nature</u> to *the nature ITSELF.*
[5] WH omitted <u>the</u> (tA).

is not to eat the Lord's supper.

21 For in eating every one taketh before *other* his own supper: and one is hungry, and another is drunken.

22 What? have ye not houses to eat and to drink in? or despise ye the church of God, and shame them that have not? What shall I say **to you**[1]? shall I praise you in this? I praise *you* not.

23 For I have received of the Lord that which also I delivered unto you, That the Lord Jesus the *same* night in which he was betrayed took bread:

24 And when he had given thanks, he brake *it*, and said, ~~Take, eat~~[2]: this is my body, which is ~~broken~~[3] for you: this do in remembrance of me.

25 After the same manner also *he took* the cup, when he had supped, saying, This cup is the new testament in my blood: this do ye, as oft as ye drink *it*, in remembrance of me.

26 For as often as ye eat this bread, and drink **this**[4] cup, ye do shew the Lord's death till he come.

27 Wherefore whosoever shall eat **this**[5] bread, and drink *this* cup of the Lord, unworthily, shall be guilty of the body and [∧**of the**][6] blood of the Lord.

28 But let a man examine himself, and so let him eat of *that* bread, and drink of *that* cup.

29 For he that eateth and drinketh ~~unworthily~~[7], eateth and drinketh damnation to himself, not discerning the ~~Lord's~~[8] body.

30 For this cause many *are* weak and sickly among you, and many sleep.

31 **For**[9] if we would judge ourselves, we should not be

---

[1] WH changed the word order from <u>what</u> TO YOU <u>might I say</u> to *what might I say TO YOU.*

[2] WH omitted <u>take eat</u> (<u>labete fagete</u>).

[3] WH omitted <u>broken</u> (<u>klOmenon</u>).

[4] WH omitted <u>this</u> (<u>touto</u>) from <u>the cup this</u>.

[5] WH omited <u>this</u> (<u>touton</u>) from <u>the bread this</u>.

[6] WH added *of the* (*tou*).

[7] WH omitted <u>unworthily</u> (<u>anaxiOs</u>).

[8] WH omitted <u>of the Lord</u> (<u>tou kuriou</u>) from <u>the body of the Lord</u>.

[9] WH changed **for** (**gar**) to *but* (*de*).

judged.

32 But when we are judged, we are chastened of the Lord, that we should not be condemned with the world.

33 Wherefore, my brethren, when ye come together to eat, tarry one for another.

34 ~~And~~[1] if any man hunger, let him eat at home; that ye come not together unto condemnation. And the rest will I set in order when I come.

CHAPTER 12

1 Now concerning spiritual *gifts*, brethren, I would not have you ignorant.

2 Ye know that [ʌ**when**][2] ye were Gentiles, carried away unto these dumb idols, even as ye were led.

3 Wherefore I give you to understand, that no man speaking by the Spirit of God calleth **Jesus**[3] accursed: and *that* no man can say that **Je-sus** is the **Lord**[4], but by the

Holy Ghost.

4 Now there are diversities of gifts, but the same Spirit.

5 And there are differences of administrations, but the same Lord.

6 And there are diversities of operations, but ~~it is~~[5] the same God which worketh all in all.

7 But the manifestation of the Spirit is given to every man to profit withal.

8 For to one is given by the Spirit the word of wisdom; to another the word of knowledge by the same Spirit;

9 [~~but~~][6] To another faith by the same Spirit; to another the gifts of healing by the **same**[7] Spirit;

10 To another the working of miracles; to another prophecy; to another discerning of spirits; [~~but~~][8] to another *divers* kinds of tongues; to another the interpretation

---

[1] WH omitted <u>and</u> (<u>de</u>).

[2] WH added *when* (*ʰote*).

[3] WH changed <u>Jesus</u> (<u>iAsoun</u>) to *Jesus* (*iAsous*). **Acc** to *Nom*. [case]

[4] WH changed <u>Jesus</u> [is the] <u>Lord</u> (<u>kurion iAsoun</u>) to *Je-sus* [is the] *Lord* (*kurios iAsous*). **Acc** to *Nom*. [case]

[5] WH omitted <u>there is</u> (<u>esti</u>).

[6] WH omittted the untranslated <u>but</u> (<u>de</u>).

[7] WH changed **same** (**autO**) to *one* (*ʰeni*).

[8] WH omitted the untranslated <u>but</u> (<u>de</u>).

of tongues:

11 But all these worketh that one and the selfsame Spirit, dividing to every man severally as he will.

12 For as the body is one, and hath **many**[1] members, and all the members of that ~~one~~[2] body, being many, are one body: so also *is* Christ.

13 For by one Spirit are we all baptized into one body, whether *we be* Jews or Gentiles, whether *we be* bond or free; and have been all made to drink ~~into~~[3] one Spirit.

14 For the body is not one member, but many.

15 If the foot shall say, Because I am not the hand, I am not of the body; is it therefore not of the body?

16 And if the ear shall say, Because I am not the eye, I am not of the body; is it therefore not of the body?

17 If the whole body *were* an eye, where *were* the hearing? If the whole *were* hearing, where *were* the smelling?

18 But **now**[4] hath God set the members every one of them in the body, as it hath pleased him.

19 And if they were all one member, where *were* the body?

20 But now *are they* many members, yet but one body.

21 And ∧**the**[5] eye cannot say unto the hand, I have no need of thee: nor again the head to the feet, I have no need of you.

22 Nay, much more those members of the body, which seem to be more feeble, are necessary:

23 And those *members* of the body, which we think to be less honourable, upon these we bestow more abundant honour; and our uncomely *parts* have more abundant comeliness.

24 For our comely *parts* have no need: but God hath tempered the body together, having given more abundant honour to that *part* **which lacked**[6]:

---

[1] WH changed the word order from <u>having</u> MANY to *MANY having.*

[2] WH omitted <u>of the</u> <u>one</u> (<u>tou</u> [h]<u>enos</u>) from <u>the</u> <u>members</u> <u>of</u> <u>the body</u> <u>of</u> <u>the</u> <u>one.</u>

[3] WH omitted <u>into</u> (<u>eis</u>).

[4] WH changed <u>now</u> (<u>nuni</u>) to

now (*nun*). **Empahtic** form to *Regular* form.

[5] WH added *the* ([h]*o*) as the KJV supplied it.

[6] WH changed <u>being in need</u> ([h]<u>usterou**nti**</u>) to *being in need* ([h]<u>usteroumen**O**</u>). Both Pres Pass Part Dat Masc Sing. [spell]

25 That there should be no schism in the body; but *that* the members should have the same care one for another.

26 And whether one member suffer, all the members suffer with it; or ~~one~~[1] member be honoured, all the members rejoice with it.

27 Now ye are the body of Christ, and members in particular.

28 And God hath set some in the church, first apostles, secondarily prophets, thirdly teachers, after that miracles, **then**[2] gifts of healings, helps, governments, diversities of tongues.

29 *Are* all apostles? *are* all prophets? *are* all teachers? *are* all workers of miracles?

30 Have all the gifts of healing? do all speak with tongues? do all interpret?

31 But covet earnestly the **best**[3] gifts: and yet shew I unto you a more excellent way.

CHAPTER 13

1 Though I speak with the tongues of men and of angels, and have not charity, I am become *as* sounding brass, or a tinkling cymbal.

2 And though I have *the gift of* prophecy, and understand all mysteries, and all knowledge; and though I have all faith, so that I could remove mountains, and have not charity, I am nothing.

3 And though I bestow all my goods to feed *the poor*, and though I give my body **to be burned**[4], and have not charity, it profiteth me nothing.

4 Charity suffereth long, *and* is kind; charity envieth not; charity vaunteth not itself, is not puffed up,

5 Doth not behave itself unseemly, seeketh not her own, is not easily provoked, thinketh no evil;

6 Rejoiceth not in iniquity, but rejoiceth in the truth;

7 Beareth all things, believeth all things, hopeth all

---

[1] WH omitted <u>one</u> (^hen).
[2] WH changed <u>then</u> (*eita*) to *then* (*epeita*). [prefix added]
[3] WH changed **best** (**kreittona**) to *greater* (*meizona*).

[4] In their margin, WH changed <u>in order that</u> I **shall be burned** (^hina kau<del>th</del>AsOmai) to *in order that I* **might boast** (^hina kaucAsOmai). **Fut Pass** Sub to *Aor Mid* Sub. [tense & mood & root]

things, endureth all things.

8   Charity never **faileth**[1]: but whether *there be* prophecies, they shall fail; whether *there be* tongues, they shall cease; whether *there be* knowledge, it shall vanish away.

9   For we know in part, and we prophesy in part.

10 But when that which is perfect is come, ~~then~~[2] that which is in part shall be done away.

11 When I was a child, I spake **as a child**[3], I understood as a child, I thought as a child: ~~but~~[4] when I became a man, I put away childish things.

12 For now we see through a glass, darkly; but then face to face: now I know in part; but then shall I know even as also I am known.

13 And now abideth faith, hope, charity, these three; but the greatest of these *is* charity.

CHAPTER 14

1   Follow after charity, and desire spiritual *gifts*, but rather that ye may prophesy.

2   For he that speaketh in an *unknown* tongue speaketh not unto men, but unto **[the]**[5] God: for no man understandeth *him*; howbeit in the spirit he speaketh mysteries.

3   But he that prophesieth speaketh unto men *to* edification, and exhortation, and comfort.

4   He that speaketh in an *unknown* tongue edifieth himself; but he that prophesieth edifieth the church.

5   I would that ye all spake with tongues, but rather that ye prophesied: **for**[6] greater *is* he that prophesieth than he that speaketh with tongues, except he interpret, that the church may receive edifying.

6   **Now**[7], brethren, if I

---

[1] WH changed <u>falls **out**</u> (**ek-piptei**) to *falls* (*piptei*). [prefix dropped]

[2] WH omitted <u>then</u> (<u>tote</u>).

[3] WH changed the word order from <u>AS CHILD</u> <u>I spoke</u> <u>as child</u> <u>I understood</u> <u>as child</u> <u>I thought</u> to *I spoke as child I understood as child I thought AS CHILD.*

[4] WH omitted <u>but</u> (<u>de</u>).

[5] WH omitted the untranslated <u>the</u> (<u>tO</u>).

[6] WH changed **for** (**gar**) to *but* (*de*).

[7] WH changed <u>now</u> (<u>nuni</u>) to *now* (*nun*). **Empahtic** form to *Regular* form.

come unto you speaking with tongues, what shall I profit you, except I shall speak to you either by revelation, or by knowledge, or by prophesying, or by doctrine?

7   And even things without life giving sound, whether pipe or harp, except they give a distinction in the sounds, how shall it be known what is piped or harped?

8   For if the trumpet give an uncertain sound, who shall prepare himself to the battle?

9   So likewise ye, except ye utter by the tongue words easy to be understood, how shall it be known what is spoken? for ye shall speak into the air.

10   **There are**[1], it may be, so many kinds of voices in the world, and none of them *is* without signification.

11   Therefore if I know not the meaning of the voice, I shall be unto him that speaketh a barbarian, and he that speaketh *shall be* a barbarian unto me.

12   Even so ye, forasmuch as ye are zealous of spiritual *gifts*, seek that ye may excel to the edifying of the church.

13   **Wherefore**[2] let him that speaketh in an *unknown* tongue pray that he may interpret.

14   For if I pray in an *unknown* tongue, my spirit prayeth, but my understanding is unfruitful.

15   What is it then? I will pray with the spirit, and I will pray with the understanding also: I will sing with the spirit, and I will sing with the understanding also.

16   Else when **thou shalt bless**[3] with ~~the~~[4] spirit, how shall he that occupieth the room of the unlearned say Amen at thy giving of thanks, seeing he understandeth not what thou sayest?

17   For thou verily givest thanks well, but the other is not edified.

18   I thank ~~my~~[5] God, **I**

---

[1] WH changed **it is** (estin) to *they are* (eisin). 3rd **Sing** to 3rd *Plur*. [number]

[2] WH changed wherefore (dio**per**) to *wherefore* (dio). **Empahtic** form to *Regular* form. [suffix dropped]

[3] WH changed thou **might** bless (eulogAs**As**) to *thou may bless* (eulogAs). **Aor** Act Sub to *Pres* Act Sub. [tense]

[4] WH omitted the (tO).

[5] WH omitted of me (mou) from the God of me.

speak[1] with tongues more than ye all:

19 Yet in the church I had rather speak five words ~~with~~[2] my **understanding**[3], that *by my voice* I might teach others also, than ten thousand words in an *unknown* tongue.

20 Brethren, be not children in understanding: howbeit in malice be ye children, but in understanding be men.

21 In the law it is written, With *men of* other tongues and **other**[4] lips will I speak unto this people; and yet for all that will they not hear me, saith the Lord.

22 Wherefore tongues are for a sign, not to them that believe, but to them that believe not: but prophesying *serveth* not for them that believe not, but for them which believe.

23 If therefore the whole church be come together into one place, and all **speak**[5] with tongues, and there come in *those that are* unlearned, or unbelievers, will they not say that ye are mad?

24 But if all prophesy, and there come in one that believeth not, or *one* unlearned, he is convinced of all, he is judged of all:

25 ~~And thus~~[6] are the secrets of his heart made manifest; and so falling down on *his* face he will worship God, and report that **God**[7] is in you of a truth.

26 How is it then, brethren? when ye come together, every one ~~of you~~[8] hath a psalm, hath a doctrine, **hath a tongue**[9], hath a revelation,

---

[1] WH change speak**ing** (lal**On**) to *I speak* (lalO). Pres Act **Part** to Pres Act *Ind*. [mood]

[2] WH omitted with (dia) and forced the noun case to supply the preposition.

[3] WH changed understanding (n**oos**) to *understanding* (n**oi**). **Genitive** to *Dative*. [case]

[4] WH changed other ([h]et**erois**) to *other* ([h]eter**On**). **Dat Neut** Plur to *Gen Masc* Plur. [case & gender]

[5] WH changed the word order from with tongues SPEAK to *SPEAK with tongues*.

[6] WH omitted and thus (kai [h]oupO).

[7] WH changed the word order from THE GOD of a truth in you is to *of a truth THE GOD in you is*.

[8] WH omitted of you ([h]umOn).

[9] WH changed the word order from TONGUE HAS revelation has to *revelation TONGUE HAS*.

hath an interpretation. **Let** all things **be done**[1] unto edifying.

27 If any man speak in an *unknown* tongue, *let it be* by two, or at the most *by* three, and *that* by course; and let one interpret.

28 But if there be no interpreter, let him keep silence in the church; and let him speak to himself, and to God.

29 Let the prophets speak two or three, and let the other judge.

30 If *any thing* be revealed to another that sitteth by, let the first hold his peace.

31 For ye may all prophesy one by one, that all may learn, and all may be comforted.

32 And the spirits of the prophets are subject to the prophets.

33 For God is not *the author* of confusion, but of peace, as in all churches of the saints.

34 Let ~~your~~[2] women keep silence in the churches: for **it is** not **permitted**[3] unto them

to speak; but *they are commanded* **to be under obedience**[4], as also saith the law.

35 And if they will learn any thing, let them ask their husbands at home: for it is a shame for **women**[5] **to speak**[6] in the church.

36 What? came the word of God out from you? or came it unto you only?

37 If any man think himself to be a prophet, or spiritual, let him acknowledge that the things that I write unto you **are** the **commandments**[7] of **the**[8] Lord.

---

permitted (<u>epitetraptai</u>) to *it is being* permitted (*epitrepetai*). **Pf** Pass Ind to **Pres** Pass Ind. [tense]

[4] WH changed <u>to be under obedience</u> (^hupotassesthai) to *let them be being under obedience* (^hupotassesthOsan). Pres **Mid Inf** to Pres *Pass Imp* 3rd Plur. [voice & mood]

[5] WH changed <u>women</u> (<u>gunaixin</u>) to *woman* (*gunaiki*). **Plur** to *Sing*. [number]

[6] WH changed the word order from <u>women</u> in <u>assembly</u> TO BE SPEAKING to *woman TO BE SPEAKING in assembly.*

[7] WH changed <u>are</u> <u>commandments</u> (<u>eisin entolai</u>) to *is commandment* (*estin entolA*). **Plur** to **Sing**. [number]

[8] WH omitted <u>the</u> (<u>tou</u>).

---

[1] WH changed <u>let be done</u> (<u>genesthO</u>) to *be letting be done* (*ginesthO*). **Aor** Mid Imp to *Pres* Mid Imp. [tense]

[2] WH omitted the <u>of you</u> (^hu-mOn) from <u>the women of</u> <u>you</u>.

[3] WH changed <u>it **has been**</u>

38 But if any man be ignorant, **let him be ignorant**[1].

39 Wherefore,   brethren
[∧**of me]**[2], covet to prophesy,
and forbid not to speak **with
tongues**[3].

40 [∧**but]**[4] Let all things
be done decently and in order.

CHAPTER 15

1 Moreover, brethren, I
declare unto you the gospel
which I preached unto you,
which also ye have received,
and wherein ye stand;

2 By which also ye are
saved, if ye keep in memory
what I preached unto you,
unless ye have believed in
vain.

3 For I delivered unto
you first of all that which I
also received, how that Christ

died for our sins according to
the scriptures;

4 And that he was buried,
and that he rose again the
third **day**[5] according to the
scriptures:

5 And that he was seen
of Cephas, then of the
twelve:

6 After that, he was seen
of above five hundred brethren at once; of whom the
greater part remain unto this
present, but [also]⁶ some are
fallen asleep.

7 After that, he was seen
of James; then of all the apostles.

8 And last of all he was
seen of me also, as of one
born out of due time.

9 For I am the least of
the apostles, that am not
meet to be called an apostle,
because I persecuted the
church of God.

10 But by the grace of
God I am what I am: and his
grace which *was bestowed*
upon me was not in vain; but
I laboured more abundantly
than they all: yet not I, but

---

[1] In their margin, WH
changed **let him be** ignorant
(*agnoeitO*) to *he is being* ig-
norant (*agnoeitai*). Pres **Act
Imp** to Pres *Pass Ind*. [voice
& mood]
[2] WH added *of me* (*mou*).
[3] WH changed the word order from to speak WITH
TONGUES not forbid to *to
speak fobid not WITH
TONGUEs*.
[4] WH added *but* (*de*).

[5] WH changed the word order from the third DAY to *DAY
the third*.
[6] WH omitted the untranslated also (kai).

the grace of God ~~which~~[1] was with me.

11 Therefore whether *it were* I or they, so we preach, and so ye believed.

12 Now if Christ be preached that he rose from the dead, how say **some**[2] among you that there is no resurrection of the dead?

13 But if there be no resurrection of the dead, then is Christ not risen:

14 And if Christ be not risen, then *is* our preaching vain, ~~and~~[3] **your**[4] faith *is* also vain.

15 Yea, and we are found false witnesses of God; because we have testified of God that he raised up Christ: whom he raised not up, if so be that the dead rise not.

16 For if the dead rise not, then is not Christ raised:

17 And if Christ be not raised, your faith *is* vain; ye are yet in your sins.

18 Then they also which are fallen asleep in Christ are perished.

19 If in this life only we have hope **in Christ**[5], we are of all men most miserable.

20 But now is Christ risen from the dead, *and* ~~become~~[6] the firstfruits of them that slept.

21 For since by man *came* **[the]**[7] death, by man *came* also the resurrection of the dead.

22 For as in Adam all die, even so in Christ shall all be made alive.

23 But every man in his own order: Christ the firstfruits; afterward they that are **[ʌthe]**[8] Christ's at his coming.

24 Then *cometh* the end, when **he shall have delivered up**[9] the kingdom to

---

[1] WH omitted which (ʰA).
[2] WH changed the word order from <u>SOME</u> among <u>you</u> to *among you SOME.*
[3] WH omitted <u>and</u> (de).
[4] In their margin, WH changed of **you** (ʰumOn) to *of **us*** (ʰAmOn). **2**ⁿᵈ Plur to **1**ʳˢᵗ Plur. [person]

[5] WH changed the word order from <u>hope we have</u> IN CHRIST to *IN CHRIST hope we have.*
[6] WH omitted <u>become</u> (egeneto).
[7] WH omitted the untranslated <u>the</u> (ʰo).
[8] WH added *the* (tou) making their text say *the* {ones} *of the Christ* instead of <u>the</u> {ones} <u>of Christ</u>.
[9] WH changed he **might** deliver up (paradO) to *he **may** deliver up (paradidoi).* **Aor** Act Sub to **Pres** Act Sub [tense]

God, even the Father; when he shall have put down all rule and all authority and power.

25 For he must reign, till [ever]¹ he hath put all enemies under his feet.

26 The last enemy *that* shall be destroyed *is* death.

27 For he hath put all things under his feet. But when he saith all things are put under *him, it is* manifest that he is excepted, which did put all things under him.

28 And when all things shall be subdued unto him, then shall the Son also himself be subject unto him that put all things under him, that God may be [the]² all in all.

29 Else what shall they do which are baptized for the dead, if the dead rise not at all? why are they then baptized for **the dead**³?

30 And why stand we in jeopardy every hour?

31 I protest by your rejoicing [∧brethren]⁴ which I

have in Christ Jesus our Lord, I die daily.

32 If after the manner of men I have fought with beasts at Ephesus, what advantageth it me, if the dead rise not? let us eat and drink; for to morrow we die.

33 Be not deceived: evil communications corrupt good manners.

34 Awake to righteousness, and sin not; for some have not the knowledge of God: **I speak**⁵ *this* to your shame.

35 But some *man* will say, How are the dead raised up? and with what body do they come?

36 *Thou* **fool**⁶, that which thou sowest is not quickened, except it die:

37 And that which thou sowest, thou sowest not that body that shall be, but bare grain, it may chance of wheat, or of some other *grain*:

---

¹ WH omitted the untranslated <u>ever</u> (<u>an</u>).
² WH omitted the untranslated <u>the</u> (<u>ta</u>).
³ WH changed **the dead** (**tOn nekrOn**) to *them* (**aut**On).
⁴ WH added *brethren* (*adel-*

foi).
⁵ WH changed <u>I speak</u> (**legO**) to *I speak* (**lalO**). Both Pres Act Ind. [syn]
⁶ WH changed <u>fool</u> (<u>afron</u>) to ***thou art a fool*** (*afrOn*). **Adj** Voc Masc to *Verb* Pres Act Ind

38 But God giveth it[1] a body as it hath pleased him, and to every seed [~~the~~][2] his own body.

39 All flesh *is* not the same flesh: but *there is* one *kind of* **flesh**[3] of men, another flesh of beasts, another [ᴧflesh][4] of **fishes**, *and* another of **birds**[5].

40 *There are* also celestial bodies, and bodies terrestrial: but the glory of the celestial *is* one, and the *glory* of the terrestrial *is* another.

41 *There is* one glory of the sun, and another glory of the moon, and another glory of the stars: for *one* star differeth from *another* star in glory.

42 So also *is* the resurrection of the dead. It is sown in corruption; it is raised in incorruption:

43 It is sown in dishonour; it is raised in glory: it is sown in weakness; it is raised in power:

44 It is sown a natural body; it is raised a spiritual body. [ᴧif][6] There is a natural body, **and**[7] there is a spiritual ~~body~~[8].

45 And so it is written, The first man Adam was made a living soul; the last Adam *was made* a quickening spirit.

46 Howbeit that *was* not first which is spiritual, but that which is natural; and afterward that which is spiritual.

47 The first man *is* of the earth, earthy: the second man *is* ~~the Lord~~[9] from heaven.

48 As *is* the earthy, such *are* they also that are earthy: and as *is* the heavenly, such *are* they also that are heavenly.

49 And as we have borne the image of the earthy, **we shall** also **bear**[10] the image of

---

[1] WH changed the word order from <u>God</u> ɪᴛ <u>gives</u> to *God gives ɪᴛ.*

[2] WH omitted the untranslated <u>the</u> (<u>to</u>).

[3] WH omitted <u>flesh</u> (<u>sarx</u>).

[4] WH added *flesh* (*sarx*).

[5] WH changed the word order from ᴏꜰ ꜰɪꜱʜ <u>but</u> <u>another</u> ᴏꜰ ʙɪʀᴅꜱ to *ᴏꜰ ʙɪʀᴅꜱ but another ᴏꜰ ꜰɪꜱʜ.*

[6] WH added *if* (*ei*).

[7] WH changed the word order from ᴀɴᴅ <u>there is</u> to *there is ᴀɴᴅ* {i.e. ᴀʟꜱᴏ}.

[8] WH omitted <u>body</u> (<u>sOma</u>).

[9] WH omitted <u>the Lord</u> (^h<u>o kurios</u>).

[10] In their margin, WH changed <u>we **shall** bear</u> (*foresomen*) to *we **might** bear* (*foresOmen*). **Fut Ind** to *Aor Sub*. [tense & mood]

the heavenly.

50 Now this I say, brethren, that flesh and blood cannot inherit the kingdom of God; neither doth corruption inherit incorruption.

51 Behold, I shew you a mystery; **[indeed]**[1] We shall not all sleep, but we shall all be changed,

52 In a moment, in the twinkling of an eye, at the last trump: for the trumpet shall sound, and the dead shall be raised incorruptible, and we shall be changed.

53 For this corruptible must put on incorruption, and this mortal *must* put on immortality.

54 So when **this corruptible shall have put on incorruption, and**[2] this mortal shall have put on immortality, then shall be brought to pass the saying that is written, Death is swallowed up in victory.

55 O death, where *is* thy **sting**? O **grave**[3], where *is* thy **victory**[4]?

56 The sting of death *is* sin; and the strength of sin *is* the law.

57 But thanks *be* to God, which giveth us the victory through our Lord Jesus Christ.

58 Therefore, my beloved brethren, be ye stedfast, unmoveable, always abounding in the work of the Lord, forasmuch as ye know that your labour is not in vain in the Lord.

CHAPTER 16

1 Now concerning the collection for the saints, as I have given order to the churches of Galatia, even so do ye.

2 Upon the first *day* **of the week**[5] let every one of you lay by him in store, as *God* hath prospered him, that there be no gatherings when I

---

[1] WH omitted the untranslated indeed (men).

[2] In their margin, WH omitted this corruptible shall have put on incorruption and (to ftharton touto endusAtai aftharsian kai).

[3] WH changed **grave** (^{h}AdA) to *death* (thanate).

[4] WH changed the word order from O DEATH where is thy sting O grave where is thy VICTORY to *O death where is thy VICTORY O death where is thy STING.*

[5] WH changed of sabbaths (sabbatOn) to *of sabbath* (*sabbatou*). **Plur** to *Sing*. [number]

come.

3   And when I come, whomsoever ye shall approve by *your* letters, them will I send to bring your liberality unto Jerusalem.

4   And if it be **meet**[1] that I go also, they shall go with me.

5   Now I will come unto you, when I shall pass through Macedonia: for I do pass through Macedonia.

6   And it may be that I will abide, yea, and winter with you, that ye may bring me on my journey whithersoever I go.

7   For I will not see you now by the way; **but**[2] I trust to tarry a while with you, if the Lord **permit**[3].

8   But I will tarry at Ephesus until Pentecost.

9   For a great door and effectual is opened unto me, and *there are* many adversaries.

10   Now if Timotheus come, see that he may be with you without fear: for he worketh the work of the Lord, as I also *do*.

11   Let no man therefore despise him: but conduct him forth in peace, that he may come unto me: for I look for him with the brethren.

12   As touching *our* brother Apollos, I greatly desired him to come unto you with the brethren: but his will was not at all to come at this time; but he will come when he shall have convenient time.

13   Watch ye, stand fast in the faith, quit you like men, be strong.

14   Let all your things be done with charity.

15   I beseech you, brethren, (ye know the house of Stephanas, that it is the firstfruits of Achaia, and *that* they have addicted themselves to the ministry of the saints,)

16   That ye submit yourselves unto such, and to every one that helpeth with *us*, and laboureth.

17   I am glad of the coming of Stephanas and **Fortunatus**[4] and Achaicus: for that

---

[1] WH changed the word order from it be MEET to MEET it be.

[2] WH changed **but** (**de**) to *for* (*gar*).

[3] WH changed **may** permit (epitrepA) to *might permit* (*epitreʃA*). **Pres** Act Sub to *Aor* Act Sub. **pi** for *psi* (1 letter to different 1 letter) [tense]

[4] WH changed Fortunatus (fourtounatou) to *Fortunatus* (*fortounatou*). [spell]

which was lacking on your part they have supplied.

18 For they have refreshed my spirit and yours: therefore acknowledge ye them that are such.

19 The churches of Asia **salute**[1] you. Aquila and **Priscilla**[2] salute you much in the Lord, with the church that is in their house.

20 All the brethren greet you. Greet ye one another with an holy kiss.

21 The salutation of *me* Paul with mine own hand.

22 If any man love not the Lord ~~Jesus Christ~~[3], let him be Anathema Maranatha.

23 The grace of our Lord Jesus Christ *be* with you.

24 My love *be* with you all in Christ Jesus. Amen.

---

[1] WH changed **they** greet (aspa**zon**tai) to *it greets* (*as-pazetai*). 3rd **Plur** to 3rd *Sing*. [number]

[2] WH changed Pris**cill**a (priskilla) to *Priska* (*priska*). [spell]

[3] WH omitted Jesus Christ (iAsoun criston).

2 CORINTHIANS

CHAPTER 1

1   Paul, an apostle of Jesus **Christ**[1] by the will of God, and Timothy *our* brother, unto the church of God which is at Corinth, with all the saints which are in all Achaia:

2   Grace *be* to you and peace from God our Father, and *from* the Lord Jesus Christ.

3   Blessed *be* God, even the Father of our Lord Jesus Christ, the Father of mercies, and the God of all comfort;

4   Who comforteth us in all our tribulation, that we may be able to comfort them which are in any trouble, by the comfort wherewith we ourselves are comforted of God.

5   For as the sufferings of [ʌ**the**][2] Christ abound in us, so our consolation also aboundeth by Christ.

6   And whether we be afflicted, *it is* for your consolation and salvation, which is effectual in the enduring of the same sufferings which we also suffer: **or whether we be comforted, *it is* for your consolation and salvation**[3].

7   And our hope of you *is* stedfast, knowing, that **as**[4] ye are partakers of the sufferings, so *shall ye be* also of the consolation.

8   For we would not, brethren, have you ignorant **of**[5] our trouble which came ~~to us~~[6] in Asia, that **we were pressed**[7] out of measure, above strength, insomuch

---

[1] WH changed the word order from Jesus CHRIST to *CHRIST Jesus*.

[2] WH added *the* (*tou*).

[3] WH changed the word order from which is effectual in the enduring of the same sufferings which also we suffer OR WHETHER WE BE COMFORTED [it is] FOR THE OF YOU CONSOLATION AND SALVATION to *OR WHETHER WE BE COMFORTED* [it is] *FOR THE OF YOU CONSOLATON AND SALVATION which is effectual in the enduring of the same sufferings which also we suffer*.

[4] WH changed **just** as (ʰOs-**per**) to *as* (ʰ*Os*).

[5] WH changed **of** (ʰ**uper**) to *about* (*peri*).

[6] WH omitted to us (ʰAmin).

[7] WH changed the word order from WE WERE PRESSED above measure to *above measure WE WERE PRESSED*.

that we despaired even of life:

9 But we had the sentence of death in ourselves, that we should not trust in ourselves, but in God which raiseth the dead:

10 Who delivered us from so great a death, and **doth deliver**[1]: in whom we trust **that**[2] he will yet deliver *us*;

11 Ye also helping together by prayer for us, that for the gift *bestowed* upon us by the means of many persons thanks may be given by many on our behalf.

12 For our rejoicing is this, the testimony of our conscience, that in **simplicity**[3] and godly sincerity, not with fleshly wisdom, but by the grace of God, we have had our conversation in the world, and more abundantly to you-ward.

13 For we write none other things unto you, than what ye read or acknowl-

edge; and I trust ye shall acknowledge ~~even~~[4] to the end;

14 As also ye have acknowledged us in part, that we are your rejoicing, even as ye also *are* ours in the day of the Lord [∧of us][5] Jesus.

15 And in this confidence I was minded to come unto you **before**[6], that **ye might have**[7] a second **benefit**[8];

16 And to pass by you into Macedonia, and to come again out of Macedonia unto you, and of you to be brought on my way toward Judaea.

17 **When I** therefore **was** thus **minded**[9], did I use lightness? or the things that I

---

[4] WH omitted even (kai).

[5] WH added *of us* (*ʰAmOn*).

[6] WH changed the word order from unto you come BEFORE to *BEFORE unto you come*.

[7] WH changed ye **may** have (ecAte) to *ye might have (scAte)*. **Pres** Act Sub to *Aor* Act Sub. [tense]

[8] In their margin, WH changed benefit (carin) to *benefit (caran)*. Acc Sing from caris (**grace**) to Acc Sing from *cara* (**joy**).

[9] WH changed planning (bouleuomenos) to *planning (boulomenos)*. Both Pres Part. bouleuomai to *boulomai*. [spell]

---

[1] WH changed **does** deliver (*ʰruetai*) to *delivered (*ʰrusetai*). **Pres** M/P Ind-D to *Aor* Mid Ind.

[2] In their margin, WH omitted that (*ʰoti*).

[3] WH changed simplicity (*ʰaplotAti*) to *holiness (*ʰagiotAti*).

purpose, do I purpose according to the flesh, that with me there should be yea yea, and nay nay?

18 But *as* God *is* true, our word toward you **was**[1] not yea and nay.

19 **For**[2] the Son of God, Jesus Christ, who was preached among you by us, *even* by me and Silvanus and Timotheus, was not yea and nay, but in him was yea.

20 For all the promises of God in him *are* yea, [ʌ**therefore**][3] and **in**[4] **him**[5] Amen, unto the glory of God by us.

21 Now he which stablisheth us with you in Christ, and hath anointed us, *is* God;

22 ~~Who~~[6] hath also sealed

us, and given the earnest of the Spirit in our hearts.

23 Moreover I call God for a record upon my soul, that to spare you I came not as yet unto Corinth.

24 Not for that we have dominion over your faith, but are helpers of your joy: for by faith ye stand.

CHAPTER 2

1 **But**[7] I determined this with myself, that I would not **come**[8] again to you in heaviness.

2 For if I make you sorry, who ~~is~~[9] he then that maketh me glad, but the same which is made sorry by me?

3 And I wrote this same ~~unto you~~[10], lest, when I came, **I should have**[11] sorrow

---

[1] WH changed **became** (**egeneto**) to *is* (**esti**). **Aor** Mid-D Ind of **giniomai** to *Pres* NV Ind of *eimi*. [tense & syn]

[2] WH changed the word order from the FOR of the God son to *the of the God FOR son*.

[3] WH added *therefore* (*dio*).

[4] WH changed **in** (**en**) to *through* (*di'*). [prep]

[5] WH changed him (aut**O**) to *him* (*autou*). **Dat** to *Gen*. [case]

[6] WH omitted who ([h]o).

---

[7] In their margin, WH changed **but** (**de**) to *for* (*gar*). [prep]

[8] WH changed the word order from COME in heaviness to you to *in heaviness to you COME*.

[9] WH omitted is (estin).

[10] WH omitted unto you ([h]umin).

[11] WH changed I **may** have (ec**O**) to *I might* have (sc**O**). **Pres** Act Sub to *Aor* Act Sub. [tense]

from them of whom I ought to rejoice; having confidence in you all, that my joy is *the joy* of you all.

4   For out of much affliction and anguish of heart I wrote unto you with many tears; not that ye should be grieved, but that ye might know the love which I have more abundantly unto you.

5   But if any have caused grief, he hath not grieved me, but in part: that I may not overcharge you all.

6   Sufficient to such a man *is* this punishment, which *was inflicted* of many.

7   So that contrariwise ye *ought* **rather**[1] to forgive *him*, and comfort *him*, lest perhaps such a one should be swallowed up with overmuch sorrow.

8   Wherefore I beseech you that ye would confirm *your* love toward him.

9   For to this end also did I write, that I might know the proof of you, **whether**[2] ye be obedient in all things.

10   To whom ye forgive any thing, I *forgive* also: for if I forgave any thing, **to whom**[3] **I forgave**[4] *it,* for your sakes *forgave I it* in the person of Christ;

11   Lest Satan should get an advantage of us: for we are not ignorant of his devices.

12   Furthermore, when I came to Troas to *preach* Christ's gospel, and a door was opened unto me of the Lord,

13   I had no rest in my spirit, because I found not Titus my brother: but taking my leave of them, I went from thence into Macedonia.

14   Now thanks *be* unto God, which always causeth us to triumph in Christ, and maketh manifest the savour of his knowledge by us in every place.

15   For we are unto God a sweet savour of Christ, in them that are saved, and in them that perish:

16   To the one *we are* the

---

[1] In their margin, WH omitted rather (mallon).

[2] In their margin, WH changed **whether** (**ei**) to *who* (**[h]A**).

[3] WH changed **to whom** ([h]O) to *it* ([h]o). **Dat Masc** Sing to *Acc Neut* Sing. [case & gender]

[4] WH changed the word order from if I forgave any thing **TO WHOM** I FORGAVE to *IT I FORGAVE* if *I forgave any thing.*

savour [ᴧ**out of**]¹ of death unto death; and to the other the savour of life unto life. And who *is* sufficient for these things?

17 For we are not as many, which corrupt the word of God: but as of sincerity, but as of God, **in the sight of**² [**the**]³ God speak we in Christ.

CHAPTER 3

1 Do we begin again to commend ourselves? or need we, as some *others*, epistles of commendation to you, or *letters* ~~of commendation~~⁴ from you?

2 Ye are our epistle written in our hearts, known and read of all men:

3 *Forasmuch as ye are* manifestly declared to be the epistle of Christ ministered by

us, written not with ink, but with the Spirit of the living God; not in tables of stone, but in fleshy tables **of the heart**⁵.

4 And such trust have we through Christ to God-ward:

5 Not that we are sufficient **of ourselves**⁶ to think any thing as of ourselves; but our sufficiency *is* of God;

6 Who also hath made us able ministers of the new testament; not of the letter, but of the spirit: for the letter killeth, but the spirit giveth life.

7 But if the ministration of death, written *and* engraven ~~in~~⁷ stones, was glorious, so that the children of Israel could not stedfastly behold the face of Moses for the glory of his countenance; which *glory* was to be done away:

8 How shall not the ministration of the spirit be rather

---

¹ WH added *out of* (*ek*) relieving the Genitive of <u>death</u> from the burden of supplying the preposition.
² WH changed <u>in the sight of</u> (katen**Opion**) to *in the sight of* (*katenanti*). **Prep** to *Adv.* [syn]
³ WH omitted the untranslated <u>the</u> (tou).
⁴ WH omitted <u>of commendation</u> (sustatikOn).

---

⁵ WH changed <u>of heart</u> (<u>kardias</u>) to *of hearts* (*kardiais*). **<u>Sing</u>** to ***Plur***. [number]
⁶ WH changed the word order from <u>sufficient</u> <u>we are</u> <u>OF</u> <u>OURSELVES</u> to *OF OURSELVES sufficient we are.*
⁷ WH omitted <u>in</u> (<u>en</u>) requiring the case of <u>stones</u> to supply the prepositon.

glorious?

9 For if __the ministra-tion__[1] of condemnation _be_ glory, much more doth the ministration of righteousness exceed ~~in~~[2] glory.

10 For even that which was made glorious had __no__[3] glory in this respect, by reason of the glory that excelleth.

11 For if that which is done away _was_ glorious, much more that which remaineth _is_ glorious.

12 Seeing then that we have such hope, we use great plainness of speech:

13 And not as Moses, _which_ put a vail over __his__[4] face, that the children of Israel could not stedfastly look to the end of that which is abolished:

14 But their minds were blinded: for until this day [∧__of day__][5] remaineth the same vail untaken away in the reading of the old testament; __which__[6] _vail_ is done away in Christ.

15 But even unto this day, when Moses [∧__ever__][7] __is read__[8], the vail is upon their heart.

16 Nevertheless when it shall turn to the Lord, the vail shall be taken away.

17 Now the Lord is that Spirit: and where the Spirit of the Lord _is_, ~~there~~[9] _is_ liberty.

18 But we all, with open face beholding as in a glass the glory of the Lord, are changed into the same image from glory to glory, _even_ as by the Spirit of the Lord.

CHAPTER 4

1 Therefore seeing we

---

[1] In their margin, WH changed the ministration (ʰA diakonia) to _the ministration_ (_tA diakonia_). __Nom__ Fem Sing to __Dat__ Fem Sing. [case]

[2] WH omitted in (en), requiring the case of glory to supply the preposition.

[3] WH changed no (oude) to _no_ (_ou_).

[4] WH changed of himself (ʰeautou) to _of him_ (_autou_) in the phrase the face of himself. __Refl__ Pro to __Pers__ Pro

[5] WH added _of day_ (ʰAmeras).

[6] WH changed __which__ (ʰo ti) to __that__ (ʰoti). __Two__ words to __One__ word.

[7] WH added _ever_ (_an_).

[8] WH changed __is being read__ (anaginOsketai) to __may be being read__ (anaginOskAtai). Pres Pass __Ind__ to Pres Pass __Sub__. [mood]

[9] WH omitted there (ekei).

have this ministry, as we have received mercy, **we faint**[1] not;

2   But have renounced the hidden things of dishonesty, not walking in craftiness, nor handling the word of God deceitfully; but by manifestation of the truth commending ourselves to every man's conscience in the sight of God.

3   But if our gospel be hid, it is hid to them that are lost:

4   In whom the god of this world hath blinded the minds of them which believe not, lest the light of the glorious gospel of Christ, who is the image of God, should shine ~~unto them~~[2].

5   For we preach not ourselves, but Christ Jesus the Lord; and ourselves your servants for **Jesus'**[3] sake.

6   For God, who commanded the light **to shine**[4]

out of darkness, hath shined in our hearts, to *give* the light of the knowledge of the glory of God in the face of Jesus Christ.

7   But we have this treasure in earthen vessels, that the excellency of the power may be of God, and not of us.

8   *We are* troubled on every side, yet not distressed; *we are* perplexed, but not in despair;

9   Persecuted, but not forsaken; cast down, but not destroyed;

10   Always bearing about in the body the dying of the ~~Lord~~[5] Jesus, that the life also of Jesus might be made manifest in our body.

11   For we which live are alway delivered unto death for Jesus' sake, that the life also of Jesus might be made manifest in our mortal flesh.

12   So   ~~then~~[6]   death worketh in us, but life in you.

13   We having the same spirit of faith, according as it is written, I believed, and therefore have I spoken; we also believe, and therefore speak;

---

[1] WH changed <u>we faint</u> (<u>ek-kakoumen</u>) to *we faint* (*eg-kakoumen*). Both Pres Act Ind. [spell]
[2] WH omitted <u>unto them</u> (<u>autois</u>).
[3] In their margin, WH changed <u>Jesus'</u> (<u>iAsoun</u>) to *Jesus'* (*iAsou*). [spell]
[4] WH changed **to** <u>shine</u> (lamşai) to *he will shine*

(*lamşei*). **Aor** Act **Inf** to *Fut* Act *Ind*. [tense & mood]
[5] WH omitted <u>Lord</u> (<u>kuriou</u>).
[6] WH omitted <u>then</u> (<u>men</u>).

14 Knowing that he which raised up the **Lord**[1] Jesus shall raise up us also **by**[2] Jesus, and shall present *us* with you.

15 For all things *are* for your sakes, that the abundant grace might through the thanksgiving of many redound to the glory of God.

16 For which cause **we faint**[3] not; but though our outward man perish, yet the **inward *man***[4] [∧**of us**][5] is renewed day by day.

17 For our light affliction, which is but for a moment, worketh for us a far more exceeding *and* eternal weight of glory;

18 While we look not at the things which are seen, but at the things which are not seen: for the things which are seen *are* temporal; but the things which are not seen *are* eternal.

---

[1] In their margin, WH omitted Lord (kurion).
[2] WH changed **by** (**dia**) to *with* (*sun*). [prep]
[3] WH changed we faint (ek-kakoumen) to *we faint* (*egkakoumen*). [spell]
[4] WH changed inner [man] (esOthen) to *inner* [man] (*esO*). [syn]
[5] WH added *of us* (*ʰAmOn*).

CHAPTER 5

1 For we know that if our earthly house of *this* tabernacle were dissolved, we have a building of God, an house not made with hands, eternal in the heavens.

2 For in this we groan, earnestly desiring to be clothed upon with our house which is from heaven:

3 If so be that being clothed we shall not be found naked.

4 For we that are in *this* tabernacle do groan, being burdened: not for that we would be unclothed, but clothed upon, that mortality might be swallowed up of life.

5 Now he that hath wrought us for the selfsame thing *is* God, who ~~also~~[6] hath given unto us the earnest of the Spirit.

6 Therefore *we are* always confident, knowing that, whilst we are at home in the body, we are absent from the Lord:

7 (For we walk by faith, not by sight:)

8 We are confident, *I say*, and willing rather to be absent from the body, and to

---

[6] WH omitted also (kai).

be present with the Lord.

9 Wherefore we labour, that, whether present or absent, we may be accepted of him.

10 For we must all appear before the judgment seat of Christ; that every one may receive the things *done* in *his* body, according to that he hath done, whether *it be* good or **bad**[1].

11 Knowing therefore the terror of the Lord, we persuade men; but we are made manifest unto God; and I trust also are made manifest in your consciences.

12 ~~For~~[2] we commend not ourselves again unto you, but give you occasion to glory on our behalf, that ye may have somewhat to *answer* them which glory in appearance, and **not**[3] ∧**in**[4] heart.

13 For whether we be beside ourselves, *it is* to God: or whether we be sober, *it is* for your cause.

14 For the love of Christ constraineth us; because we thus judge, that ~~if~~[5] one died for all, then were all dead:

15 And *that* he died for all, that they which live should not henceforth live unto themselves, but unto him which died for them, and rose again.

16 Wherefore henceforth know we no man after the flesh: yea, **[but]**[6] though we have known Christ after the flesh, yet now henceforth know we *him* no more.

17 Therefore if any man *be* in Christ, *he is* a new creature: old things are passed away; behold, ~~all things~~[7] are become new.

18 And all things *are* of God, who hath reconciled us to himself by ~~Jesus~~[8] Christ, and hath given to us the ministry of reconciliation;

19 To wit, that God was in Christ, reconciling the world unto himself, not imputing their trespasses unto them; and hath committed unto us the word of reconciliation.

20 Now then we are ambassadors for Christ, as

---

[1] WH changed bad (**kakon**) to bad (*faulon*). [syn]

[2] WH omitted for (*gar*).

[3] WH changed not (**ou**) to not (*mA*). [syn]

[4] WH added *in* (*en*) instead of letting the dative case supply the in as the KJV did.

[5] WH omitted if (*ei*).

[6] WH omitted the untranslated but (*de*).

[7] WH omitted the all {things} (*ta panta*).

[8] WH omitted Jesus (*iAsou*).

though God did beseech *you* by us: we pray *you* in Christ's stead, be ye reconciled to God.

21 ~~For~~[1] he hath made him *to be* sin for us, who knew no sin; that we **might be made**[2] the righteousness of God in him.

CHAPTER 6

1 We then, *as* workers together *with him*, beseech *you* also that ye receive not the grace of God in vain.

2 (For he saith, I have heard thee in a time accepted, and in the day of salvation have I succoured thee: behold, now *is* the accepted time; behold, now *is* the day of salvation.)

3 Giving no offence in any thing, that the ministry be not blamed:

4 But in all *things* approving ourselves as the ministers of God, in much patience, in afflictions, in necessities, in distresses,

5 In stripes, in imprisonments, in tumults, in labours, in watchings, in fastings;

6 By pureness, by knowledge, by longsuffering, by kindness, by the Holy Ghost, by love unfeigned,

7 By the word of truth, by the power of God, by the armour of righteousness on the right hand and on the left,

8 By honour and dishonour, by evil report and good report: as deceivers, and *yet* true;

9 As unknown, and *yet* well known; as dying, and, behold, we live; as chastened, and not killed;

10 As sorrowful, yet alway rejoicing; as poor, yet making many rich; as having nothing, and *yet* possessing all things.

11 O *ye* Corinthians, our mouth is open unto you, our heart is enlarged.

12 Ye are not straitened in us, but ye are straitened in your own bowels.

13 Now for a recompence in the same, (I speak as unto *my* children,) be ye also enlarged.

14 Be ye not unequally yoked together with unbelievers: **for**[3] what fellowship hath righteousness with unrighteousness? and what

---

[1] WH omitted <u>for</u> (gar).
[2] WH changed **may** be made (ginOme*th*a) to *might be made* (genOme*th*a). **Pres** M/P-D Sub to *Aor* Mid Sub. [tense]

[3] WH changed <u>for</u> (**de**) to *or* (*A*). [conj]

communion hath light with darkness?

15 And what concord hath **Christ**[1] with **Belial**[2]? or what part hath he that believeth with an infidel?

16 And what agreement hath the temple of God with idols? for **ye are**[3] the temple of the living God; as God hath said, I will dwell in them, and walk in *them*; and I will be their God, and they shall be **my**[4] people.

17 Wherefore come out from among them, and be ye separate, saith the Lord, and touch not the unclean *thing*; and I will receive you,

18 And will be a Father unto you, and ye shall be my sons and daughters, saith the Lord Almighty.

---

[1] WH changed <u>Christ</u> (<u>crist**O**</u>) to *Christ* (*crist**ou***). **Dat** to *Gen*. [case]

[2] In their margin, WH changed <u>Belial</u> (<u>belial</u>) to *Be-liar* (*beliar*). [spell]

[3] WH changed **your**<u>selves</u> <u>ye</u> <u>are</u> ([h]<u>umeis</u> + <u>este</u>) to ***our-selves we are*** (*[h]ameis* + *es-men*). **2**[nd] Plur to *1*[rst] Plur. [person]

[4] WH changed **to** me (<u>moi</u>) to *of me* (*mou*). **Dat** to *Gen*. [case]

CHAPTER 7

1 Having therefore these promises, dearly beloved, let us cleanse ourselves from all filthiness of the flesh and spirit, perfecting holiness in the fear of God.

2 Receive us; we have wronged no man, we have corrupted no man, we have defrauded no man.

3 I speak **not**[5] *this* to condemn *you*: for I have said before, that ye are in our hearts to die and live with *you*.

4 Great *is* my boldness of speech toward you, great *is* my glorying of you: I am filled with comfort, I am ex-ceeding joyful in all our tribu-lation.

5 For, when we were come into Macedonia, our flesh had no rest, but we were troubled on every side; without *were* fightings, within *were* fears.

6 Nevertheless God, that comforteth those that are cast down, comforted us by the coming of Titus;

7 And not by his coming

---

[5] WH changed the word or-der from <u>NOT</u> <u>toward</u> <u>con-demnation</u> to *toward con-demnation* NOT.

only, but by the consolation wherewith he was comforted in you, when he told us your earnest desire, your mourning, your fervent mind toward me; so that I rejoiced the more.

8   For though I made you sorry with a letter, I do not repent, though I did repent: **for**[1] I perceive that the same epistle hath made you sorry, though *it were* but for a season.

9   Now I rejoice, not that ye were made sorry, but that ye sorrowed to repentance: for ye were made sorry after a godly manner, that ye might receive damage by us in nothing.

10 For   godly   sorrow **worketh**[2] repentance to salvation not to be repented of: but the sorrow of the world worketh death.

11 For behold this selfsame   thing,   that   ye [~~yourseves~~][3] sorrowed after a godly sort, what carefulness it wrought in you, yea, *what* clearing of yourselves, yea, *what* indignation, yea, *what* fear, yea, *what* vehement desire, yea, *what* zeal, yea, *what* revenge! In all *things* ye have approved   yourselves   to   be clear ~~in~~[4] this matter.

12 Wherefore,   though   I wrote unto you, *I did it* not for his cause that had done the wrong, nor for his cause that suffered wrong, but that **our** care for **you**[5] in the sight of   God   might   appear   unto you.

13 Therefore   we   were comforted [∧**then**][6] in **your**[7] comfort: ~~yea, and~~[8] exceedingly the more joyed we for the joy of Titus, because his spirit was refreshed by you all.

14 For if I have boasted any thing to him of you, I am

---

[1] In their margin, WH omitted for (gar).
[2] WH changed works {**down**} (**kat**ergazetai) to works (ergazetai). [prefix dropped]
[3] WH omitted the untranslated intensive pronoun yourselves (ʰumas).

[4] WH omitted in (en) and forced the dative case to supply the preposition.
[5] WH changed the word order from the care of US the for YOU to *the care of YOU the for* US.
[6] WH added then (de).
[7] WH changed of **you** (ʰu-mOn) to of *us* (ʰAmOn) in the comfort of you. [person]
[8] WH omitted yea and (de).

not ashamed; but as we spake all things to you in truth, even so our boasting, which *I made* before Titus, is found a truth.

15 And his inward affection is more abundant toward you, whilst he remembereth the obedience of you all, how with fear and trembling ye received him.

16 I rejoice **therefore**[1] that I have confidence in you in all *things*.

CHAPTER 8

1 Moreover, brethren, we do you to wit of the grace of God bestowed on the churches of Macedonia;

2 How that in a great trial of affliction the abundance of their joy and their deep poverty abounded unto **the riches**[2] of their liberality.

3 For to *their* power, I bear record, yea, and **beyond**[3] *their* power *they were* willing of themselves;

4 Praying us with much intreaty that ~~we would re-eeive~~[4] the gift, and *take upon us* the fellowship of the ministering to the saints.

5 And *this they did*, not as we hoped, but first gave their own selves to the Lord, and unto us by the will of God.

6 Insomuch that we desired Titus, that as he had begun, so he would also finish in you the same grace also.

7 Therefore, as ye abound in every *thing, in* faith, and utterance, and knowl-edge, and *in* all diligence, and *in* **your** love to **us**[5], *see* that ye abound in this grace also.

8 I speak not by commandment, but by occasion of the forwardness of others, and to prove the sincerity of your love.

9 For ye know the grace of our Lord Jesus Christ, that, though he was rich, yet for your sakes he became poor, that ye through his

---

[1] WH omitted therefore (oun).

[2] WH changed the riches (to**n** plouto**n**) to *the riches* (*to ploutos*). Acc **Masc** Sing to Acc *Neut* Sing. [gender]

[3] WH changed **beyond** (**ʰu-per**) to *above* (*para*). [syn]

[4] WH omitted we would receive ourselves (dexas~~t~~hai ʰAmas).

[5] In their margin, WH changed the word order from the out of YOU in US love to *the out of US in YOU love*.

poverty might be rich.

10 And herein I give *my* advice: for this is expedient for you, who have begun before, not only to do, but also to be forward a year ago.

11 Now therefore perform the doing *of it*; that as *there was* a readiness to will, so *there may be* a performance also out of that which ye have.

12 For if there be first a willing mind, *it is* accepted according to that ~~a man~~[1] hath, *and* not according to that he hath not.

13 For *I mean* not that other men be eased, ~~and~~[2] ye burdened:

14 But by an equality, *that* now at this time your abundance *may be a supply* for their want, that their abundance also may be *a supply* for your want: that there may be equality:

15 As it is written, He that *had gathered* much had nothing over; and he that *had gathered* little had no lack.

16 But thanks *be* to God, which put the same earnest care into the heart of Titus for you.

17 For indeed he accepted the exhortation; but being more forward, of his own accord he went unto you.

18 And we have sent **with him**[3] the brother, whose praise *is* in the gospel throughout all the churches;

19 And not *that* only, but who was also chosen of the churches to travel with us **with**[4] this grace, which is administered by us to the glory of ~~the same~~[5] Lord, and *declaration of* **your**[6] ready mind:

20 Avoiding this, that no man should blame us in this abundance which is administered by us:

21 **Providing for**[7] [∧**for**][8]

---

[1] WH omitted a man (tis) and forced the verb to supply the subject *he*.

[2] WH omitted and (de).

[3] WH changed the word order from WITH HIM the brother to *the brother* WITH HIM.

[4] WH changed from **with** (**sun**) to *in* (*en*). [prep]

[5] WH omitted the same (autou).

[6] WH changed of you (ʰu-mOn) to *of us* (ʰAmOn). [person]

[7] WH changed providing for (pronooumenoi) to *we provide* (pronooumen). Pres **Mid Part** to Pres *Act Ind*. [voice & mood]

[8] WH added *for* (gar) instead of letting the verb supply the *for*.

honest things, not only in the sight of the Lord, but also in the sight of men.

22 And we have sent with them our brother, whom we have oftentimes proved diligent in many things, but now much more diligent, upon the great confidence which *I have* in you.

23 Whether *any do enquire* of Titus, *he is* my partner and fellowhelper concerning you: or our brethren *be enquired of, they are* the messengers of the churches, *and* the glory of Christ.

24 Wherefore shew ye to them, and before the churches, the proof of your love, ~~and~~[1] of our boasting on your behalf.

CHAPTER 9

1 For as touching the ministering to the saints, it is superfluous for me to write to you:

2 For I know the forwardness of your mind, for which I boast of you to them of Macedonia, that Achaia was ready a year ago; and [~~out of~~][2] your zeal hath pro-

voked very many.

3 Yet have I sent the brethren, lest our boasting of you should be in vain in this behalf; that, as I said, ye may be ready:

4 Lest haply if they of Macedonia come with me, and find you unprepared, we (that we say not, ye) should be ashamed in this same confident ~~boasting~~[3].

5 Therefore I thought it necessary to exhort the brethren, that they would go before unto you, and make up beforehand your bounty, **whereof ye had notice before**[4], that the same might be ready, as *a matter of* bounty, and not **as**[5] *of* covetousness.

6 But this *I say*, He which soweth sparingly shall reap also sparingly; and he which soweth bountifully

---

out of you zeal (kai [h]o ex [h]umOn zAlos).
[3] WH omitted boasting (kaucAseOs) and left *in this same confidence.*
[4] WH changed whereof ye had notice before (pro-**kat**AggelmenAn) to *whereof ye had notice before (proe-pAggelmenAn).* Both Pf Pass Part. [Prefix changed]
[5] WH changed **just as** ([h]Os-**per**) to *as* ([h]Os).

---

[1] WH omitted and (kai).
[2] WH omitted the untranslated out of (ex) from and the

shall reap also bountifully.

7 Every man according as **he purposeth**[1] in his heart, *so let him give*; not grudgingly, or of necessity: for God loveth a cheerful giver.

8 And God *is* **able**[2] to make all grace abound toward you; that ye, always having all sufficiency in all *things*, may abound to every good work:

9 (As it is written, He hath dispersed abroad; he hath given to the poor: his righteousness remaineth for ever.

10 Now he that ministereth seed to the sower both **minister**[3] bread for *your* food, and **multiply**[4] your

seed sown, and **increase**[5] the fruits of your righteousness;)

11 Being enriched in every thing to all bountifulness, which causeth through us thanksgiving to God.

12 For the administration of this service not only supplieth the want of the saints, but is abundant also by many thanksgivings unto God;

13 Whiles by the experiment of this ministration they glorify God for your professed subjection unto the gospel of Christ, and for *your* liberal distribution unto them, and unto all *men*;

14 And by their prayer for you, which long after you for the exceeding grace of God in you.

15 [~~but~~][6] Thanks *be* unto God for his unspeakable gift.

CHAPTER 10

1 Now I Paul myself beseech you by the meekness and gentleness of Christ, who in presence *am* base among

---

[1] WH changed he purposes (proaireitai) to *he has purposed* (proArAtai). **Pres** M/P Ind-D to *Pf* Mid Ind. [tense]

[2] WH changed able (dunatos) to *is able* (dunatei). **Adj** to *Verb* Pres Act Ind.

[3] WH changed **should** minister (corAgAsai) to *is ministering* (corAgAsei). **Aor** Act **Opt** to *Pres* Act *Ind*. [tense & mood]

[4] WH changed **should** multiply (plA*th*unai) to *will multiply* (plA*th*unei). **Aor** Act **Opt** to *Fut* Act *Ind*. [tense & mood]

[5] WH changed **should** increase (auxAsai) to *will increase* (auxAsei). **Aor** Act **Opt** to *Fut* Act *Ind*. [tense & mood]

[6] WH omitted the untranslated but (de).

you, but being absent am bold toward you:

2   But I beseech *you*, that I may not be bold when I am present with that confidence, wherewith I think to be bold against some, which think of us as if we walked according to the flesh.

3   For though we walk in the flesh, we do not war after the flesh:

4   (For the weapons of our warfare *are* not carnal, but mighty through God to the pulling down of strong holds;)

5   Casting down imaginations, and every high thing that exalteth itself against the knowledge of God, and bringing into captivity every thought to the obedience of Christ;

6   And having in a readiness to revenge all disobedience, when your obedience is fulfilled.

7   Do ye look on things after the outward appearance? If any man trust to himself that he is Christ's, let him **of**[1] himself think this again, that, as he *is* Christ's, even so *are* we ~~Christ's~~[2].

8   For though [~~also~~][3] I should boast somewhat more of our authority, which the Lord hath given ~~us~~[4] for edification, and not for your destruction, I should not be ashamed:

9   That I may not seem as if I would terrify you by letters.

10   For *his* letters, say they, *are* weighty and powerful; but *his* bodily presence *is* weak, and *his* speech contemptible.

11   Let such an one think this, that, such as we are in word by letters when we are absent, such *will we be* also in deed when we are present.

12   For we dare not make ourselves of the number, or compare ourselves with some that commend themselves: but they measuring themselves by themselves, and comparing themselves among themselves, are not wise.

13   But we will not boast of things without *our* measure, but according to the measure of the rule which God hath distributed to us, a measure to reach even unto

---

[1] WH change **from (af́)** to *upon* (*ef́*).

[2] WH omitted Christ's (cris-

tou).

[3] WH omitted the untranslated also (kai).

[4] WH omitted us (ʰAmin).

you.

14 For we stretch not ourselves beyond *our measure*, as though we reached not unto you: for we are come as far as to you also in *preaching* the gospel of Christ:

15 Not boasting of things without *our* measure, *that is,* of other men's labours; but having hope, when your faith is increased, that we shall be enlarged by you according to our rule abundantly,

16 To preach the gospel in the *regions* beyond you, *and* not to boast in another man's line of things made ready to our hand.

17 But he that glorieth, let him glory in the Lord.

18 For not he that commendeth himself is approved, but whom the Lord commendeth.

CHAPTER 11

1   Would to God ye could bear with me a little **in** *my*[1] **folly**[2]: and indeed bear with me.

2   For I am jealous over you with godly jealousy: for I have espoused you to one husband, that I may present *you as* a chaste virgin to Christ.

3   But I fear, lest by any means, as the serpent beguiled **Eve**[3] through his subtilty, **so**[4] your minds should be corrupted from the simplicity [∧**and the purity**][5] that is in Christ.

4   For if he that cometh preacheth another Jesus, whom we have not preached, or *if* ye receive another spirit, which ye have not received, or another gospel, which ye have not accepted, **ye might** well **bear with**[6] *him.*

5   For I suppose I was not a whit behind the very chiefest apostles.

6   But though *I be* rude in speech, yet not in knowledge; but **we have been throughly**

---

[1] WH omitted the (tA) from the phrase [in] the folly.
[2] WH changed {**in**} folly (af-rosunA) to {**of**} *folly* (*afro-sunAs*). **Dat** to *Gen.* [case]

[3] WH changed the word order from EVE beguiled to *beguiled EVE.*
[4] WH omitted so ([h]outO).
[5] WH added *and the purity* (*kai tAs* [h]*agnotAtos*).
[6] WH changed you[p] **were** bearing with (Aneicesthe) to *you[p] are bearing with* (*an-ecethe*). **Impf** M/P Ind-D to *Pres* Mid Ind. [tense]

made manifest[1] among you in all things.

7 Have I committed an offence in abasing myself that ye might be exalted, because I have preached to you the gospel of God freely?

8 I robbed other churches, taking wages *of them*, to do you service.

9 And when I was present with you, and wanted, I was chargeable to no man: for that which was lacking to me the brethren which came from Macedonia supplied: and in all *things* I have kept **myself**[2] from being burdensome unto you, and *so* will I keep *myself*.

10 As the truth of Christ is in me, no man shall stop me of this boasting in the regions of Achaia.

11 Wherefore? because I love you not? God knoweth.

12 But what I do, that I will do, that I may cut off occasion from them which desire occasion; that wherein they glory, they may be found even as we.

13 For such *are* false apostles, deceitful workers, transforming themselves into the apostles of Christ.

14 And no **marvel**[3]; for Satan himself is transformed into an angel of light.

15 Therefore *it is* no great thing if his ministers also be transformed as the ministers of righteousness; whose end shall be according to their works.

16 I say again, Let no man think me a fool; if otherwise, yet as a fool receive me, that I may boast **myself a little [something]**[4].

17 That which I speak, I speak *it* not after **the Lord**[5], but as it were foolishly, in this confidence of boasting.

---

[1] WH changed <u>we **were** throughly made manifest</u> (fanerO~~th~~entes) to *we throughly made manifest* (*fanerOsantes*). Aor **Pass** Part to Aor *Act* Part. [voice]

[2] WH changed the word order from <u>unto you</u> MYSELF to *MYSELF unto you.*

[3] WH changed <u>marvel**ous**</u> {thing} (~~th~~aumaston) to *marvel* (~~th~~auma). **Adj** to ***Noun***.

[4] WH changed the word order from that A LITTLE SOMETHING MYSELF I may boast to *that MYSELF A LITTLE SOMETHING I may boast.*

[5] WH changed the word order from <u>I speak</u> <u>according to</u> <u>LORD</u> to *according to LORD I speak.*

18 Seeing that many glory after the flesh, I will glory also.

19 For ye suffer fools gladly, seeing ye *yourselves* are wise.

20 For ye suffer, if a man bring you into bondage, if a man devour *you*, if a man take *of you*, if a man exalt himself, if a man smite **you**[1] on the face.

21 I speak as concerning reproach, as though we **had been weak**[2]. Howbeit whereinsoever any is bold, (I speak foolishly,) I am bold also.

22 Are they Hebrews? so *am* I. Are they Israelites? so *am* I. Are they the seed of Abraham? so *am* I.

23 Are they ministers of Christ? (I speak as a fool) I *am* more; in labours more abundant, **in stripes above measure**[3], in prisons more

frequent, in deaths oft.

24 Of the Jews five times received I forty *stripes* save one.

25 Thrice was I beaten with rods, once was I stoned, thrice I suffered shipwreck, a night and a day I have been in the deep;

26 *In* journeyings often, *in* perils of waters, *in* perils of robbers, *in* perils by *mine own* countrymen, *in* perils by the heathen, *in* perils in the city, *in* perils in the wilderness, *in* perils in the sea, *in* perils among false brethren;

27 ~~In~~[4] weariness and painfulness, in watchings often, in hunger and thirst, in fastings often, in cold and nakedness.

28 Beside those things that are without, that **which cometh upon**[5] **me**[6] daily, the care of all the churches.

29 Who is weak, and I am not weak? who is offended, and I burn not?

---

[1] WH changed the word order from <u>YOU</u> on <u>face</u> to *on face YOU*.

[2] WH changed <u>became weak</u> (As~~th~~enAsamen) to *had become weak* (As~~th~~enAkamen). **Aor** Act Ind to *Pf* Act Ind. [tense]

[3] WH changed the word order from <u>IN</u> <u>STRIPES</u> <u>ABOVE</u> <u>MEASURE</u> <u>in</u> <u>prisons</u> <u>more</u>

frequent to *in prisons more frequent IN STRIPES ABOVE MEASURE*.

[4] WH omitted <u>in</u> (<u>en</u>).

[5] WH changed <u>which cometh upon</u> (epi<u>su</u>stasis) to *which cometh upon* (epistasis). Both Noun Nom Fem Sing.

[6] WH changed <u>me</u> (m<u>ou</u>) to *me* (m<u>oi</u>). **Gen** to *Dat*. [case]

30 If I must needs glory, I will glory of the things which concern mine infirmities.

31 The God and Father of ~~our~~[1] Lord Jesus ~~Christ~~[2], which is blessed for evermore, knoweth that I lie not.

32 In Damascus the governor under Aretas the king kept the city of the Damascenes with a garrison, ~~desirous~~[3] to apprehend me:

33 And through a window in a basket was I let down by the wall, and escaped his hands.

CHAPTER 12

1 **It is** not **expedient**[4] **for me**[5] **doubtless**[6] to glory. **[for]**[7] I will come to visions and revelations of the Lord.

2 I knew a man in Christ above fourteen years ago, (whether in the body, I cannot tell; or whether out of the body, I cannot tell: God knoweth;) such an one caught up to the third heaven.

3 And I knew such a man, (whether in the body, or **out of**[8] the body, I cannot tell: God knoweth;)

4 How that he was caught up into paradise, and heard unspeakable words, which it is not lawful for a man to utter.

5 Of such an one will I glory: yet of myself I will not glory, but in ~~mine~~[9] infirmities.

6 For though I would desire to glory, I shall not be a fool; for I will say the truth: but *now* I forbear, lest any man should think of me above that which he seeth me *to be*, or ~~that~~[10] he heareth of me.

7 And lest I should be exalted above measure

---

[1] WH omitted of us (ʰamOn) from the Lord of us.

[2] WH omitted Christ (cristou).

[3] WH omitted desirous (thelOn).

[4] WH changed **it is** expedient (sumferei) to *being* expedient (sumferon). Pres Act **Ind** to Pres Act *Part*. [mood]

[5] WH changed **for me** (moi) to *then* (men).

[6] WH changed **doubtless** (dA) to *it is necessary* (dei). **Particle** to *Participle*.

[7] WH changed the untranslated **for** (gar) to *but* (de).

[8] WH changed out of (**ektos**) to *out of* (**cOris**). [syn]

[9] WH omitted of me (mou) from the weaknesses of me.

[10] WH omitted that (ti-- what).

through the abundance of the revelations, **[ₐtherefore]**[1] there was given to me a thorn in the flesh, the messenger of Satan to buffet me, lest I should be exalted above measure.

8 For this thing I besought the Lord thrice, that it might depart from me.

9 And he said unto me, My grace is sufficient for thee: for ~~my~~[2] strength **is made perfect**[3] in weakness. Most gladly therefore will I rather glory in my infirmities, that the power of Christ may rest upon me.

10 Therefore I take pleasure in infirmities, in reproaches, in necessities, in persecutions, in distresses for Christ's sake: for when I am weak, then am I strong.

11 I am become a fool ~~in glorying~~[4]; ye have compelled me: for I ought to have been commended of you: for in nothing am I behind the very chiefest apostles, though I be nothing.

12 Truly the signs of an apostle were wrought among you in all patience, ~~in~~[5] signs **[ₐboth]**[6], and wonders, and mighty deeds.

13 For what is it wherein ye were inferior to other churches, except *it be* that I myself was not burdensome to you? forgive me this wrong.

14 Behold, the third **[ₐthis]**[7] time I am ready to come to you; and I will not be burdensome ~~to you~~[8]: for I seek not yours, but you: for the children ought not to lay up for the parents, but the parents for the children.

15 And I will very gladly spend and be spent for you; though **[also]**[9] the more abundantly **I love**[10] you, the less I be loved.

---

[5] WH omitted <u>in</u> (*en*).
[6] WH added *both* (*te*).
[7] WH added *this* (*touto*) making their text read *behold this third time*.
[8] WH omitted <u>to you</u> (<u>ʰu-mOn</u>).
[9] WH omitted the untranslated <u>also</u> (<u>kai</u>).
[10] WH change <u>loving</u> (aga-p<u>On</u>) to *I love* (*agapO*). Pres Act **Part** to Pres Act *Ind*. [mood]

---

[1] WH added *therefore* (*dio*).
[2] WH omitted <u>of me</u> (<u>mou</u>) from <u>the strength of me</u>.
[3] WH changed <u>is made perfect</u> (<u>teleioutai</u>) to *is made perfect* (*teleitai*). Pres Pass Ind of <u>teleioO</u> to Pres Pass Ind of *teleO*.
[4] WH omitted <u>in glorying</u> (<u>kaucOmenos</u>).

16 But be it so, I did not burden you: nevertheless, being crafty, I caught you with guile.

17 Did I make a gain of you by any of them whom I sent unto you?

18 I desired Titus, and with *him* I sent a brother. Did Titus make a gain of you? walked we not in the same spirit? *walked we* not in the same steps?

19 **Again**[1], think ye that we excuse ourselves unto you? we speak **before**[2] God in Christ: but *we do* all things, dearly beloved, for your edifying.

20 For I fear, lest, when I come, I shall not find you such as I would, and *that* I shall be found unto you such as ye would not: lest *there be* **debates**[3], **envyings**[4], wraths, strifes, backbitings, whisperings, swellings, tumults:

21 *And* lest, <u>when **I come**</u>[5] again, my God will humble ∧**me**[6] among you, and *that* I shall bewail many which have sinned already, and have not repented of the uncleanness and fornication and lasciviousness which they have committed.

CHAPTER 13

1 This *is* the third *time* I am coming to you. In the mouth of two or three witnesses shall every word be established.

2 I told you before, and foretell you, as if I were present, the second time; and being absent now ~~I write~~[7] to them which heretofore have sinned, and to all other, that, if I come again, I will not spare:

3 Since ye seek a proof of Christ speaking in me, which to you-ward is not weak, but is mighty in you.

---

[1] WH changed **again** (pal**in**) to *formerly* (*palai*).

[2] WH changed before (katen**Opion**) to *before* (*katenanti*). **Prep** to *Adv*. [syn]

[3] WH changed debates (er**ei**s) to *debate* (*eris*). **Plur** to *Sing*. [number]

[4] WH changed envyings (**z**Alo**i**) to *envying* (*zAlos*). **Plur** to *Sing*. [number]

[5] WH changed <u>when I come</u> {<u>myself</u>} (el**th**onta <u>me</u>) to *when I come {myself}* (*elthontos mou*). Both Aor Act Part. **Acc** to *Gen*. [case]

[6] WH added *me* (*me*) as the KJV did.

[7] WH omitted <u>I write</u> (graf**O**).

4   For ~~though~~[1] he was crucified through weakness, yet he liveth by the power of God. For [~~even~~][2] we also are weak **in**[3] him, but **we shall live**[4] with him by the power of God toward you.

5   Examine yourselves, whether ye be in the faith; prove your own selves. Know ye not your own selves, how that Jesus Christ is in you, except ye be reprobates?

6   But I trust that ye shall know that we are not reprobates.

7   Now **I pray**[5] to God that ye do no evil; not that we should appear approved, but that ye should do that which is honest, though we be as reprobates.

8   For we can do nothing against the truth, but for the truth.

9   For we are glad, when we are weak, and ye are strong: ~~and~~[6] this also we wish, _even_ your perfection.

10   Therefore I write these things being absent, lest being present I should use sharpness, according to the power which **the Lord**[7] hath given me to edification, and not to destruction.

11   Finally, brethren, farewell. Be perfect, be of good comfort, be of one mind, live in peace; and the God of love and peace shall be with you.

12   Greet one another with an holy kiss.

13   All the saints salute you.

14   The grace of the Lord Jesus Christ, and the love of God, and the communion of the Holy Ghost, _be_ with you all. ~~Amen~~[8].

---

[1] WH omitted <u>though</u> (<u>ei</u>).

[2] WH omitted the untranslated <u>even</u> (<u>kai</u>).

[3] In their margin, WH changed **in** (<u>en</u>) to _with_ (_sun_).

[4] WH changed <u>we shall live</u> (<u>zAsome**tha**</u>) to _we shall live_ (_zAsome**n**_). Fut **Mid**-D Ind to Fut _Act_ Ind. [voice]

[5] WH changed **I pray** (<u>eucomai</u>) to _we pray_ (_eucome**tha**_). Both Pres Ind. First **Sing** to First _Plur_. [number]

[6] WH omitted <u>and</u> (<u>de</u>).

[7] WH changed the word order from <u>hath given me</u> THE LORD to _THE LORD hath given me._

[8] WH omitted <u>amen</u> (<u>amAn</u>).

GALATIANS

CHAPTER 1

1 Paul, an apostle, (not of men, neither by man, but by Jesus Christ, and God the Father, who raised him from the dead;)

2 And all the brethren which are with me, unto the churches of Galatia:

3 Grace *be* to you and peace from God the Father [**of us**][1], and *from* **our**[2] Lord Jesus Christ,

4 Who gave himself for our sins, that he might deliver us from **this present**[3] evil [∧**the**][4] world, according to the will of God and our Father:

5 To whom *be* glory for ever and ever. Amen.

6 I marvel that ye are so soon removed from him that called you into the grace of Christ unto another gospel:

7 Which is not another; but there be some that trouble you, and would pervert the gospel of Christ.

8 But though we, or an angel from heaven, **preach any other gospel**[5] **unto you**[6] than that which we have preached unto you, let him be accursed.

9 As we said before, so say I now again, If any *man* preach any other gospel unto you than that ye have received, let him be accursed.

10 For do I now persuade men, or God? or do I seek to please men? **for**[7] if I yet pleased men, I should not be the servant of Christ.

11 **But**[8] I certify you, brethren, that the gospel which was preached of me is not after man.

12 For I neither received it of man, neither was I taught *it*, but by the revelation of Jesus Christ.

---

[1] In their margin, WH added *of us* ([h]*AmOn*).

[2] In their margin, WH omitted of us ([h]AmOn) from Lord of us.

[3] WH changed the word order from from THE PRESENT age evil to *from* **the** *age* THE PRESENT *evil*.

[4] WH added *the* (*tou*).

[5] WH changed **may** preach any other gospel (*euaggeli-z*Atai) to **might** *preach any other gospel* (*euaggelisAtai*). **Pres** Mid Sub to *Aor* Mid Sub. [tense]

[6] In their margin, WH omitted unto you ([h]*umin*).

[7] WH omitted for (gar).

[8] WH changed **but** (**de**) to *for* (*gar*).

13 For ye have heard of my conversation in time past in the Jews' religion, how that beyond measure I persecuted the church of God, and wasted it:

14 And profited in the Jews' religion above many my equals in mine own nation, being more exceedingly zealous of the traditions of my fathers.

15 But when it pleased God, who separated me from my mother's womb, and called *me* by his grace,

16 To reveal his Son in me, that I might preach him among the heathen; immediately I conferred not with flesh and blood:

17 Neither went I up to Jerusalem to them which were apostles before me; but I went into Arabia, and returned again unto Damascus.

18 Then after three years I went up to Jerusalem to see **Peter**[1], and abode with him fifteen days.

19 But other of the apostles saw I none, save James the Lord's brother.

20 Now the things which I write unto you, behold, before God, I lie not.

21 Afterwards I came into the regions of Syria and Cilicia;

22 And was unknown by face unto the churches of Judaea which were in Christ:

23 But they had heard only, That he which persecuted us in times past now preacheth the faith which once he destroyed.

24 And they glorified God in me.

CHAPTER 2

1 Then fourteen years after I went up again to Jerusalem with Barnabas, and took Titus with *me* also.

2 And I went up by revelation, and communicated unto them that gospel which I preach among the Gentiles, but privately to them which were of reputation, lest by any means I should run, or had run, in vain.

3 But neither Titus, who was with me, being a Greek, was compelled to be circumcised:

4 And that because of false brethren unawares brought in, who came in privily to spy out our liberty which we have in Christ Jesus, that **they might bring** us

---

[1] WH changed **Peter** (**petron**) to *Cephas* (*kAfan*).

<u>**into bondage**</u>[1]:

5 To whom we gave place by subjection, no, not for an hour; that the truth of the gospel might continue with you.

6 But of these who seemed to be somewhat, (whatsoever they were, it maketh no matter to me: God accepteth no man's person:) for they who seemed *to be somewhat* in conference added nothing to me:

7 But contrariwise, when they saw that the gospel of the uncircumcision was committed unto me, as *the gospel* of the circumcision *was* unto Peter;

8 (For he that wrought effectually in Peter to the apostleship of the circumcision, the same was mighty in me toward the Gentiles:)

9 And when James, Cephas, and John, who seemed to be pillars, perceived the grace that was given unto me, they gave to me and Barnabas the right hands of fellowship; that we *should go* unto the heathen, and they unto the circumcision.

10 Only *they would* that we should remember the poor; the same which I also was forward to do.

11 But when <u>**Peter**</u>[2] was come to Antioch, I withstood him to the face, because he was to be blamed.

12 For before that certain came from James, he did eat with the Gentiles: but when they were come, he withdrew and separated himself, fearing them which were of the circumcision.

13 And the other Jews dissembled likewise with him; insomuch that Barnabas also was carried away with their dissimulation.

14 But when I saw that they walked not uprightly according to the truth of the gospel, I said unto <u>**Peter**</u>[3] before *them* all, If thou, being a Jew, livest after the manner of Gentiles, and not as do the Jews, <u>**why**</u>[4] compellest thou

---

[1] WH changed <u>they **might** bring into bondage</u> (*katdou-*<u>l**Os**</u>*Ontai*) to *they **will** bring into bondage* (*katadou-lOsousin*). <u>**Aor** **Mid** **Sub**</u> to *Fut Act Ind.* [tense, voice, & mood]

[2] WH changed <u>**Peter**</u> (<u>**petros**</u>) to *Cephas* (*kAfas*).

[3] WH changed <u>**Peter**</u> (*petrO*) to *Cephas* (*kAfa*).

[4] WH changed <u>**why**</u> (<u>**ti**</u>) to *how* (*pOs*).

the Gentiles to live as do the Jews?

15 We *who are* Jews by nature, and not sinners of the Gentiles,

16 [∧and]¹ Knowing that a man is not justified by the works of the law, but by the faith of Jesus Christ, even we have believed in Jesus Christ, that we might be justified by the faith of Christ, and not by the works of the law: for by the works of the law shall no flesh be justified.

17 But if, while we seek to be justified by Christ, we ourselves also are found sinners, *is* therefore Christ the minister of sin? God forbid.

18 For if I build again the things which I destroyed, I make myself a transgressor.

19 For I through the law am dead to the law, that I might live unto God.

20 I am crucified with Christ: nevertheless I live; yet not I, but Christ liveth in me: and the life which I now live in the flesh I live by the faith of the Son of God, who loved me, and gave himself for me.

21 I do not frustrate the grace of God: for if righteousness *come* by the law, then Christ is dead in vain.

---

¹ WH added *and* (*de*).

CHAPTER 3

1 O foolish Galatians, who hath bewitched you, ~~that ye should not obey the truth~~², before whose eyes Jesus Christ hath been evidently set forth, crucified ~~among you~~³?

2 This only would I learn of you, Received ye the Spirit by the works of the law, or by the hearing of faith?

3 Are ye so foolish? having begun in the Spirit, are ye now made perfect by the flesh?

4 Have ye suffered so many things in vain? if *it be* yet in vain.

5 He therefore that ministereth to you the Spirit, and worketh miracles among you, *doeth he it* by the works of the law, or by the hearing of faith?

6 Even as Abraham believed God, and it was accounted to him for righteousness.

7 Know ye therefore that they which are of faith, the

---

² WH omitted <u>the truth not to obey</u> (tA alAtheia mA peithesthai).
³ WH omitted <u>among you</u> (en ʰumin).

same are the children of Abraham.

8   And the scripture, fore-seeing that God would justify the heathen through faith, preached before the gospel unto Abraham, _saying_, In thee **shall** all nations **be blessed**[1].

9   So then they which be of faith are blessed with faithful Abraham.

10   For as many as are of the works of the law are under the curse: for it is written, [∧**that**][2] Cursed _is_ every one that continueth not in all things which are written in the book of the law to do them.

11   But that no man is justified by the law in the sight of God, _it is_ evident: for, The just shall live by faith.

12   And the law is not of faith: but, The ~~man~~[3] that doeth them shall live in them.

13   Christ hath redeemed us from the curse of the law,

being made a curse for us: **for**[4] **it is written**[5], Cursed _is_ every one that hangeth on a tree:

14   That the blessing of Abraham might come on the Gentiles through Jesus Christ; that we might receive the promise of the Spirit through faith.

15   Brethren, I speak after the manner of men; Though _it be_ but a man's covenant, yet _if it be_ confirmed, no man disannulleth, or addeth thereto.

16   Now to Abraham and his seed were the promises made. He saith not, And to seeds, as of many; but as of one, And to thy seed, which is Christ.

17   And this I say, _that_ the covenant, that was confirmed before of God ~~in Christ~~[6], the law, which was four hundred and thirty **years**[7] after, cannot

---

[1] WH changed shall be blessed (eulogAthAsontai) to _shall be blessed {in}_ (_eneulogAthAsontai_). [prefix added]

[2] WH added _that_ (ʰoti).

[3] WH omitted man (anthropos) and forced the to supply the subject _one_.

[4] WH changed **for** (**gar**) to _that_ (ʰoti).

[5] WH changed the word order from IT IS WRITTEN **for** to _that_ IT IS WRITTEN.

[6] WH omitted in Christ (eis criston).

[7] WH changed the word order from YEARS four hundred and thirty to _four hundred and thirty_ YEARS.

disannul, that it should make the promise of none effect.

18 For if the inheritance *be* of the law, *it is* no more of promise: but God gave *it* to Abraham by promise.

19 Wherefore then *serveth* the law? It was added because of transgressions, till the seed should come to whom the promise was made; *and it was* ordained by angels in the hand of a mediator.

20 Now a mediator is not *a mediator* of one, but God is one.

21 *Is* the law then against the promises of God? God forbid: for if there had been a law given which could have given life, verily righteousness should have been by the law.

22 But the scripture hath concluded all under sin, that the promise by faith of Jesus Christ might be given to them that believe.

23 But before faith came, we were kept under the law, **shut up**[1] unto the faith which should afterwards be revealed.

24 Wherefore the law was our schoolmaster *to bring us* unto Christ, that we might be justified by faith.

25 But after that faith is come, we are no longer under a schoolmaster.

26 For ye are all the children of God by faith in Christ Jesus.

27 For as many of you as have been baptized into Christ have put on Christ.

28 There is neither Jew nor Greek, there is neither bond nor free, there is neither male nor female: for ye are all one in Christ Jesus.

29 And if ye *be* Christ's, then are ye Abraham's seed, ~~**and**~~[2] heirs according to the promise.

CHAPTER 4

1 Now I say, *That* the heir, as long as he is a child, differeth nothing from a servant, though he be lord of all;

2 But is under tutors and governors until the time appointed of the father.

3 Even so we, when we were children, were in bondage under the elements of the world:

4 But when the fulness of

---

[1] WH changed shut up (sug-kekleismenoi) to *they will be shut up* (sugkleiomenoi). **Pf** Pass **Part** to *Fut* Pass *Ind.* [tense & mood]

[2] WH omitted and (kai).

the time was come, God sent forth his Son, made of a woman, made under the law,

5 To redeem them that were under the law, that we might receive the adoption of sons.

6 And because ye are sons, God hath sent forth the Spirit of his Son into **your**[1] hearts, crying, Abba, Father.

7 Wherefore thou art no more a servant, but a son; and if a son, then an heir of God **through**[2] ~~Christ~~[3].

8 Howbeit then, when ye knew not God, ye did service unto them which by nature are **no**[4] gods.

9 But now, after that ye have known God, or rather are known of God, how turn ye again to the weak and beggarly elements, whereunto ye desire again to be in bondage?

10 Ye observe days, and months, and times, and years.

11 I am afraid of you, lest I have bestowed upon you labour in vain.

12 Brethren, I beseech you, be as I *am*; for I *am* as ye *are*: ye have not injured me at all.

13 Ye know how through infirmity of the flesh I preached the gospel unto you at the first.

14 And **my**[5] temptation ~~which was~~[6] in my flesh ye despised not, nor rejected; but received me as an angel of God, *even* as Christ Jesus.

15 **Where**[7] ~~is~~[8] then the blessedness ye spake of? for I bear you record, that, if *it had been* possible, ye ~~would have~~[9] plucked out your own eyes, and have given them to me.

16 Am I therefore become your enemy, because I tell

---

[1] WH changed <u>of **you**</u> (^hu-mOn) to *of **us*** (^hAmOn) in <u>the hearts of you</u>. [person]

[2] WH changed the word order from <u>of God</u> THROUGH **Christ** to *THROUGH God.*

[3] WH omitted <u>Christ</u> (cris-tou).

[4] WH changed the word order from NOT <u>by nature</u> to *by nature NOT.*

[5] WH changed <u>of **me**</u> (**mou**) to *of **you*** (^h**umOn**) from <u>the temptation of me</u>. [number & person]

[6] WH omitted <u>the</u> {one} (ton).

[7] WH changed **where** (**tis**) to *where* (*pou*). [syn]

[8] WH omitted <u>is</u> (An--was).

[9] WH omitted the contingency laden particle (<u>an</u>) that required <u>would have.</u>

you the truth?

17 They zealously affect you, *but* not well; yea, they would exclude you, that ye might affect them.

18 But *it is* good [the][1] to be zealously affected always in *a* good *thing*, and not only when I am present with you.

19 My little children, of whom I travail in birth again until Christ be formed in you,

20 I desire to be present with you now, and to change my voice; for I stand in doubt of you.

21 Tell me, ye that desire to be under the law, do ye not hear the law?

22 For it is written, that Abraham had two sons, the one by a bondmaid, the other by a freewoman.

23 But he *who was* of the bondwoman was born after the flesh; but he of the free-woman *was* **by**[2] [the][3] promise.

24 Which things are an allegory: for these are the[4] two covenants; the one from the mount Sinai, which gendereth to bondage, which is Agar.

25 **For**[5] this **Agar**[6] is mount Sinai in Arabia, and answereth to Jerusalem which now is, **and**[7] is in bondage with her children.

26 But Jerusalem which is above is free, which is the mother of us all[8].

27 For it is written, Rejoice, *thou* barren that bearest not; break forth and cry, thou that travailest not: for the desolate hath many more children than she which hath an husband.

28 Now **we**[9] brethren, as Isaac was, **are**[10] the children of promise.

29 But as then he that was born after the flesh persecuted him *that was born* after the Spirit, even so *it is* now.

---

[1] WH omitted the untranslated the (to).

[2] WH changed by (dia) to *by* (*di'*). **Regular** form to *Contracted* form.

[3] WH omitted the untranslated the (tAs).

[4] WH omitted the (ai).

[5] WH changed **for** (gar) to *but* (*de*) in their text but retained for (gar) in their margin.

[6] In their margin, WH omitted Agar (agar).

[7] WH changed **and** (**de**) to *for* (*gar*).

[8] WH omitted all (pantOn).

[9] In their margin, WH changed **we** (*h*Ameis) to *you* (*h*umeis). [person]

[10] In their margin, WH changed **we** are (esmen) to *you are* (*este*). [person]

30 Nevertheless what saith the scripture? Cast out the bondwoman and her son: for the son of the bondwoman shall not be heir with the son of the freewoman.

31 So **then**[1], brethren, we are not children of the bondwoman, but of the free.

CHAPTER 5

1 Stand fast **therefore**[2] in **the**[3] liberty wherewith **Christ**[4] hath made us free, and be not entangled again with the yoke of bondage.

2 Behold, I Paul say unto you, that if ye be circumcised, Christ shall profit you nothing.

3 For I testify again to every man that is circumcised, that he is a debtor to do the whole law.

---

[1] WH changed then (**ara**) to *then* (**dio**).

[2] WH changed the word order from in the liberty THEREFORE with which Christ us set free stand fast to *in the liberty with which Christ us set free stand fast THEREFORE.*

[3] WH omitted the (A).

[4] WH changed the word order from CHRIST us to *us CHRIST.*

4 Christ is become of no effect unto you, whosoever of you are justified by the law; ye are fallen from grace.

5 For we through the Spirit wait for the hope of righteousness by faith.

6 For in Jesus Christ neither circumcision availeth any thing, nor uncircumcision; but faith which worketh by love.

7 Ye did run well; who **did hinder**[5] you that ye should not obey the truth?

8 This persuasion cometh not of him that calleth you.

9 A little leaven leaveneth the whole lump.

10 I have confidence in you through the Lord, that ye will be none otherwise minded: but he that troubleth you shall bear his judgment, whosoever he be.

11 And I, brethren, if I yet preach circumcision, why do I yet suffer persecution? then is the offence of the cross ceased.

12 I would they were even cut off which trouble you.

13 For, brethren, ye have been called unto liberty; only

---

[5] WH changed did hinder (**anekoşe**) to *did hinder* (**enekoşe**). Both Aor Act Ind. [spell]

use not liberty for an occasion to the flesh, but by love serve one another.

14 For all the law **is fulfilled**[1] in one word, *even* in this; Thou shalt love thy neighbour as **thyself**[2].

15 But if ye bite and devour one another, take heed that ye be not consumed one of another.

16 *This* I say then, Walk in the Spirit, and ye shall not fulfil the lust of the flesh.

17 For the flesh lusteth against the Spirit, and the Spirit against the flesh: **and**[3] these **are contrary**[4] the one to the other: so that ye cannot do the things that ye would.

18 But if ye be led of the Spirit, ye are not under the law.

---

[1] WH changed **is being fulfilled** (plAroutai) to *has been fulfilled* (*peplArOtai*). **Pres** Pass Ind to *Pf* Pass Ind. [tense]

[2] WH changed thyself (ᵇeauton) to *thyself* (*seauton*). [syn]

[3] WH changed **and** (**de**) to *for* (*gar*).

[4] WH the word order from ARE CONTRARY one to the other to *one to the other* ARE CONTRARY.

19 Now the works of the flesh are manifest, which are *these*; ~~Adultery~~[5], fornication, uncleanness, lasciviousness,

20 Idolatry, witchcraft, hatred, **variance**[6], emulations, wrath, strife, seditions, heresies,

21 Envyings, ~~murders~~[7], drunkenness, revellings, and such like: of the which I tell you before, as I have ~~also~~[8] told *you* in time past, that they which do such things shall not inherit the kingdom of God.

22 But the fruit of the Spirit is love, joy, peace, longsuffering, gentleness, goodness, faith,

23 Meekness, temperance: against such there is no law.

24 And they that are Christ's [ᴧ**Jesus**][9] have crucified the flesh with the affections and lusts.

25 If we live in the Spirit,

---

[5] WH omitted adultery (moiceia).

[6] WH changed divisions (ereis) to *division* (*eris*). **Plur** to *Sing*. [number]

[7] WH omitted murders (fonoi).

[8] WH omitted also (kai).

[9] WH added Jesus (iAsou) and made their text read *Christ Jesus's*.

let us also walk in the Spirit.

26 Let us not be desirous of vain glory, provoking one another, envying one another.

CHAPTER 6

1 Brethren, if a man be overtaken in a fault, ye which are spiritual, restore such an one in the spirit of meekness; considering thyself, lest thou also be tempted.

2 Bear ye one another's burdens, and so fulfil the law of Christ.

3 For if a man think himself to be something, when he is nothing, he deceiveth **himself**[1].

4 But let every man prove his own work, and then shall he have rejoicing in himself alone, and not in another.

5 For every man shall bear his own burden.

6 Let him that is taught in the word communicate unto him that teacheth in all good things.

7 Be not deceived; God is not mocked: for whatso-ever a man soweth, that shall he also reap.

8 For he that soweth to his flesh shall of the flesh reap corruption; but he that soweth to the Spirit shall of the Spirit reap life everlasting.

9 And **let us** not **be weary**[2] in well doing: for in due season we shall reap, if we faint not.

10 As we have therefore opportunity, let us do good unto all *men*, especially unto them who are of the household of faith.

11 Ye see how large a letter I have written unto you with mine own hand.

12 As many as desire to make a fair shew in the flesh, they constrain you to be circumcised; only **lest**[3] they should suffer persecution for the cross of Christ.

---

[1] WH changed the word order from HIMSELF he de-ceiveth to he deceiveth HIMSELF.

[2] WH changed <u>let us be weary</u> (ekkakOmen) to *let us be weary* (egkakOmen). Both Pres Act Sub. [spell]

[3] WH changed the word order from <u>only</u> <u>in order that</u> <u>NOT</u> {for} <u>the</u> <u>cross</u> {of} <u>the</u> <u>Christ</u> <u>they should suffer per-secution</u> to *only in order that* {for} *the cross* {of} *the Christ NOT they should suffer persecution*.

13 For neither they themselves **who are circumcised**[1] keep the law; but desire to have you circumcised, that they may glory in your flesh.

14 But God forbid that I should glory, save in the cross of our Lord Jesus Christ, by whom the world is crucified unto me, and I unto **the**[2] world.

15 **For** ~~in Christ Jesus~~[3] neither circumcision **availeth**[4] any thing, nor un-circumcision, but a new creature.

16 And as many as walk according to this rule, peace *be* on them, and mercy, and upon the Israel of God.

17 From henceforth let no man trouble me: for I bear in my body the marks of the ~~Lord~~[5] Jesus.

18 Brethren, the grace of our Lord Jesus Christ *be* with your spirit. Amen.

---

[1] In their margin, WH changed **to** be circumcised (peritem**n**omenoi) to *having been circumcised* (*peritet-mAmenoi*). **Pres** Pass **Inf** to *Pf* Pass *Part.* [tense & mood]

[2] WH omitted the (tO).

[3] WH omitted in Christ Jesus (en cristO iAsou) and forced a word order change from FOR neither to *neither FOR.*

[4] WH changed **availeth** (**is-cuei**) to *is* (*estin*).

[5] WH omitted Lord (kuriou).

EPHESIANS

CHAPTER 1

1   Paul, an apostle of **Je-sus**[1] Christ by the will of God, to the saints which are **at Ephesus**[2], and to the faithful in Christ Jesus:

2   Grace *be* to you, and peace, from God our Father, and *from* the Lord Jesus Christ.

3   Blessed *be* the God and Father of our Lord Jesus Christ, who hath blessed us with all spiritual blessings in heavenly *places* in Christ:

4   According as he hath chosen us in him before the foundation of the world, that we should be holy and without blame before him in love:

5   Having predestinated us unto the adoption of children by Jesus Christ to himself, according to the good pleasure of his will,

6   To the praise of the glory of his grace, **wherein**[3]

7   In whom we have redemption through his blood, the forgiveness of sins, according to **the riches**[4] of his grace;

8   Wherein he hath abounded toward us in all wisdom and prudence;

9   Having made known unto us the mystery of his will, according to his good pleasure which he hath purposed in himself:

10   That in the dispensation of the fulness of times he might gather together in one all things in Christ, **both**[5] which are **in**[6] heaven, and which are on earth; *even* in him:

11   In whom also we have obtained an inheritance, being predestinated according to the purpose of him who worketh all things after the counsel of his own will:

12   That we should be to

---

[1] WH changed the word order from JESUS Christ to *Christ JESUS.*

[2] In their margin, WH omitted at Ephesus (en efesO).

[3] WH omitted in (en) and changed **in** which (en A) to {**of**} which (*As*). **Dat** to *Gen.* [case]

[4] WH changed the riches (**to**n plouto**n**) to *the riches* (*to ploutos*). **Masc** to *Neut.* [gender]

[5] WH omitted both (te).

[6] WH changed **in** (**en**) to *upon* (*epi*).

the praise of ~~his~~[1] glory, who first trusted in Christ.

13 In whom ye also *trusted*, after that ye heard the word of truth, the gospel of your salvation: in whom also after that ye believed, ye were sealed with that holy Spirit of promise,

14 **Which**[2] is the earnest of our inheritance until the redemption of the purchased possession, unto the praise of his glory.

15 Wherefore I also, after I heard of your faith in the Lord Jesus, and ~~love~~[3] unto all the saints,

16 Cease not to give thanks for you, making mention ~~of you~~[4] in my prayers;

17 That the God of our Lord Jesus Christ, the Father of glory, may give unto you the spirit of wisdom and revelation in the knowledge of him:

18 The eyes of your **un-derstanding**[5] being enlightened; that ye may know what is the hope of his calling, ~~and~~[6] what the riches of the glory of his inheritance in the saints,

19 And what *is* the exceeding greatness of his power to us-ward who believe, according to the working of his mighty power,

20 Which he wrought in Christ, when he raised him from the dead, and **set**[7] *him* at his own right hand in the heavenly *places*,

21 Far above all principality, and power, and might, and dominion, and every name that is named, not only in this world, but also in that which is to come:

22 And hath put all *things* under his feet, and gave him *to be* the head over all *things* to the church,

23 Which is his body, the fulness of him that filleth [∧the][8] all in all.

---

[1] WH omitted <u>the</u> (<u>tAs</u>) from <u>the glory of him</u>.

[2] WH change <u>who</u> (^h<u>os</u>) to *which* (^h*o*). **Masc** to *Neut.* [gender]

[3] WH omitted {<u>the</u>} <u>love</u> (<u>tAn</u> <u>agapAn</u>) in their text, but retained it in their margin.

[4] WH omitted **of you** (^h<u>u-mOn</u>).

[5] WH changed **understand-ing** (**dianoias**) to *heart* (*kardias*).

[6] WH omitted <u>and</u> (<u>kai</u>).

[7] WH changed **he set** (**ekathisen**) to *having set* (*kathisas*). Aor Act **Ind** to Aor Act *Part.* [mood]

[8] WH added <u>the</u> (<u>ta</u>).

CHAPTER 2

1   And you *hath he quickened,* who were dead in trespasses and sins [∧**of you**][1];

2   Wherein in time past ye walked according to the course of this world, according to the prince of the power of the air, the spirit that now worketh in the children of disobedience:

3   Among whom also we all had our conversation in times past in the lusts of our flesh, fulfilling the desires of the flesh and of the mind; and **were**[2] by nature the children of wrath, even as others.

4   But God, who is rich in mercy, for his great love wherewith he loved us,

5   Even when we were dead in sins, hath quickened us together with Christ, (by grace ye are saved;)

6   And hath raised *us* up together, and made *us* sit together in heavenly *places* in Christ Jesus:

7   That in the ages to come he might shew **the exceeding**[3] **riches**[4] of his grace in *his* kindness toward us through Christ Jesus.

8   For by grace are ye saved through **[the]**[5] faith; and that not of yourselves: *it is* the gift of God:

9   Not of works, lest any man should boast.

10   For we are his workmanship, created in Christ Jesus unto good works, which God hath before ordained that we should walk in them.

11   Wherefore   remember, that **ye**[6] *being* in time past Gentiles in the flesh, who are called Uncircumcision by that which is called the Circumcision in the flesh made by hands;

12   That **at**[7] that time ye

---

[1] WH added *of you* (*ʰumOn*).

[2] WH changed were begin (Ame**n**) to *were being* (*Ame**th**a*). Both Impf NV Ind. [spell]

[3] WH changed surpassing (ʰuperballonta) to *surpassing* (*ʰuperballon*). Both Pres Act Part. Acc **Masc** Sing to Acc *Neut* Sing [gender]

[4] WH changed the riches (to**n** plouto**n**) to *the riches* (*to ploutos*). Acc **Masc** Sing to Acc *Neut* Sing [gender]

[5] WH omitted the untranslated the (tAs).

[6] WH changed the word order from YE in time past to *in time past YE.*

[7] WH omitted at (en) and forced the dative case to supply the preposition.

were without Christ, being aliens from the common-wealth of Israel, and strangers from the covenants of promise, having no hope, and without God in the world:

13 But now in Christ Jesus ye who sometimes were far off are made **nigh**[1] by the blood of Christ.

14 For he is our peace, who hath made both one, and hath broken down the middle wall of partition *between us*;

15 Having abolished in his flesh the enmity, *even* the law of commandments *contained* in ordinances; for to make in **himself**[2] of twain one new man, *so* making peace;

16 And that he might reconcile both unto God in one body by the cross, having slain the enmity thereby:

17 And came and preached peace to you which were afar off, and [ʌ**peace**][3] to them that were nigh.

18 For through him we both have access by one Spirit unto the Father.

19 Now therefore ye are no more strangers and foreigners, but [ʌ**ye are**][4] fellowcitizens with the saints, and of the household of God;

20 And are built upon the foundation of the apostles and prophets, **Jesus**[5] Christ himself being the chief corner *stone*;

21 In whom all **the**[6] building fitly framed together groweth unto an holy temple in the Lord:

22 In whom ye also are builded together for an habitation of God through the Spirit.

CHAPTER 3

1 For this cause I Paul, the prisoner of Jesus Christ for you Gentiles,

2 If ye have heard of the dispensation of the grace of God which is given me to you-ward:

3 How that by revelation **he made known**[7] unto me

---

[1] WH changed the word order from NEAR are made to *are made* NEAR.

[2] WH changed **himself** (ʰ**eautO**) to *him* (*autO*). **Refl** pronoun to *Pers* pronoun.

[3] WH added *peace* (*ei-rAnAn*).

[4] WH added *ye are* (*este*).

[5] WH changed the word order from JESUS Christ to *Christ* JESUS.

[6] WH omitted the (A).

[7] WH changed he made known (egnOrise) to *he was made known* (egnOris**thA**). Aor **Act** Ind to Aor **Pass** Ind. [voice]

the mystery; (as I wrote afore in few words,

4   Whereby, when ye read, ye may understand my knowledge in the mystery of Christ)

5   Which ~~in~~[1] other ages was not made known unto the sons of men, as it is now revealed unto his holy apostles and prophets by the Spirit;

6   That the Gentiles should be fellowheirs, and of the same body, and partakers of ~~his~~[2] promise in **[the]**[3] [∧Jesus][4] Christ by the gospel:

7   Whereof **I was made**[5] a minister, according to the gift of the grace of God **given**[6] unto me by the effec-

tual working of his power.

8   Unto me, who am less than the least of all **[the]**[7] saints, is this grace given, that I should preach ~~among~~[8] the Gentiles **the**[9] unsearchable **riches**[10] of Christ;

9   And to make ~~all men~~[11] see what *is* the **fellowship**[12] of the mystery, which from the beginning of the world hath been hid in God, who created all things ~~by Jesus Christ~~[13]:

10   To the intent that now unto the principalities and powers in heavenly *places* might be known by the church the manifold wisdom

---

[1] WH omitted in (en) and forced the dative case to supply the preposition.

[2] WH omitted of him (autou) from the promise of him.

[3] WH omitted the untranslated the (tO).

[4] WH added *Jesus* (iAsou).

[5] WH changed I became (egenomAn) to *I was become* (egenAthAn). Aor **Mid-D** Ind to Aor *Pass* Ind. [voice]

[6] WH changed given (tAn dotheisan) to *given* (tAs dotheisAs). Both Aor Pass Part. **Acc** to **Gen**. [case]

[7] WH omitted the untranslated the (tOn).

[8] WH omitted among (en) and forced the dative case to supply the preposition.

[9] WH changed the (ton) to *the* (to). Acc **Masc** Sing to Acc *Neut* Sing. [gender]

[10] WH changed riches (plouton) to *riches* (ploutos). Acc **Masc** Sing to Acc *Neut* Sing. [gender]

[11] WH omitted all [men] (pantas).

[12] WH changed **fellow**ship (koinOnia) to *stewardship* (oikonomia).

[13] WH omitted by Jesus Christ (dia iAsou cristou).

of God,

11 According to the eternal purpose which he purposed in [ₐthe][1] Christ Jesus our Lord:

12 In whom we have boldness and [~~the~~][2] access with confidence by the faith of him.

13 Wherefore I desire **that ye faint**[3] not at my tribulations for you, which is your glory.

14 For this cause I bow my knees unto the Father ~~of our Lord Jesus Christ~~[4],

15 Of whom the whole family in heaven and earth is named,

16 That **he would grant**[5] you, according to **the riches**[6]

---

[1] WH added *the* (*tO*).
[2] WH omitted the untranslated the (tAn).
[3] WH changed to be fainting (ekkakein) to *to be fainting* (egkakein). Both Pres Act Inf. [spell]
[4] WH omitted of the Lord of us Jesus Christ (tou kuriou ʰAmOn iAsou cristou).
[5] WH changed he might grant (dOA) to *he might grant* (dO). Both Aor Act Sub. [spell]
[6] WH changed the riches (ton plouton) *to the riches (to ploutos)*. **Masc** Acc Sing to

of his glory, to be strengthened with might by his Spirit in the inner man;

17 That Christ may dwell in your hearts by faith; that ye, being rooted and grounded in love,

18 May be able to comprehend with all saints what *is* the **breadth**, and **length**[7], and depth, and height;

19 And to know the love of Christ, which passeth knowledge, that ye might be filled with all the fulness of God.

20 Now unto him that is able to do exceeding abundantly above all that we ask or think, according to the power that worketh in us,

21 Unto him *be* glory in the church [ₐeven][8] by Christ Jesus throughout all ages, world without end. Amen.

CHAPTER 4

1 I therefore, the prisoner of the Lord, beseech you that ye walk worthy of the vocation wherewith ye are called,

---

Neut Acc Sing. [gender]
[7] WH changed the word order from BREADTH and LENGTH to *LENGTH and BREADTH*.
[8] WH added *even* (*kai*).

2   With all lowliness and meekness, with longsuffering, forbearing one another in love;

3   Endeavouring to keep the unity of the Spirit in the bond of peace.

4   *There is* one body, and one Spirit, even as ye are called in one hope of your calling;

5   One Lord, one faith, one baptism,

6   One God and Father of all, who *is* above all, and through all, and in ~~you~~[1] all.

7   But unto every one of us is given grace according to the measure of the gift of Christ.

8   Wherefore he saith, When he ascended up on high, he led captivity captive, and gave gifts unto men.

9   (Now that he ascended, what is it but that he also descended ~~first~~[2] into the lower parts of the earth?

10   He that descended is the same also that ascended up far above all heavens, that he might fill all things.)

11   And he gave some, apostles; and some, prophets; and some, evangelists; and some, pastors and teachers;

12   For the perfecting of the saints, for the work of the ministry, for the edifying of the body of Christ:

13   Till we all come in the unity of the faith, and of the knowledge of the Son of God, unto a perfect man, unto the measure of the stature of the fulness of Christ:

14   That we *henceforth* be no more children, tossed to and fro, and carried about with every wind of doctrine, by the sleight of men, *and* cunning craftiness, whereby they lie in wait to deceive;

15   But speaking the truth in love, may grow up into him in all things, which is the head, *even* [~~the~~][3] Christ:

16   From whom the whole body fitly joined together and compacted by that which every joint supplieth, according to the effectual working in the measure of every part, maketh increase of the body unto the edifying of itself in love.

17   This I say therefore, and testify in the Lord, that ye henceforth walk not as

---

[1] WH omitted <u>you</u> (^h<u>umin</u>).

[2] WH omitted <u>first</u> (<u>proton</u>) in their text, but retained it in their margin.

[3] WH omitted the untranslated <u>the</u> (^h<u>o</u>).

~~other~~[1] Gentiles walk, in the vanity of their mind,

18 Having the understanding darkened, being alienated from the life of God through the ignorance that is in them, because of the blindness of their heart:

19 Who being past feeling have given themselves over unto lasciviousness, to work all uncleanness with greediness.

20 But ye have not so learned Christ;

21 If so be that ye have heard him, and have been taught by him, as the truth is in Jesus:

22 That ye put off concerning the former conversation the old man, which is corrupt according to the deceitful lusts;

23 And be renewed in the spirit of your mind;

24 And that ye put on the new man, which after God is created in righteousness and true holiness.

25 Wherefore putting away lying, speak every man truth with his neighbour: for we are members one of another.

26 Be ye angry, and sin not: let not the sun go down upon ~~your~~[2] wrath:

27 **Neither**[3] give place to the devil.

28 Let him that stole steal no more: but rather let him labour, working with *his* hands the thing which is good, that he may have to give to him that needeth.

29 Let no corrupt communication proceed out of your mouth, but that which is good to the use of edifying, that it may minister grace unto the hearers.

30 And grieve not the holy Spirit of God, whereby ye are sealed unto the day of redemption.

31 Let all bitterness, and wrath, and anger, and clamour, and evil speaking, be put away from you, with all malice:

32 And be ye kind one to another, tenderhearted, forgiving one another, even as God for Christ's sake hath forgiven ~~you~~[4].

CHAPTER 5

1 Be ye therefore followers of God, as dear children;

---

[1] WH omitted <u>other</u> (<u>loipa</u>).
[2] WH omitted <u>the</u> (<u>tO</u>) from the <u>wrath</u> of you.
[3] WH changed <u>neither</u> (<u>mAte</u>) to *neither* (*mAde*). [syn]
[4] WH omitted <u>you</u> (<u>humin</u>).

2   And walk in love, as Christ also hath loved **us**[1], and hath given himself for **us**[2] an offering and a sacrifice to God for a sweetsmelling savour.

3   But fornication, and **all**[3] uncleanness, or covetousness, let it not be once named among you, as becometh saints;

4   Neither filthiness, nor foolish talking, nor jesting, which are not convenient: but rather giving of thanks.

5   For this **ye know**[4], that no whoremonger, nor unclean person, nor covetous man, **who**[5] is an idolater, hath any inheritance in the king-dom of Christ and of God.

6   Let no man deceive you with vain words: for because of these things cometh the wrath of God upon the children of disobedience.

7   Be not ye therefore partakers with them.

8   For ye were sometimes darkness, but now *are ye* light in the Lord: walk as children of light:

9   (For the fruit of the **Spirit**[6] *is* in all goodness and righteousness and truth;)

10   Proving what is acceptable unto the Lord.

11   And have no fellowship with the unfruitful works of darkness, but rather reprove *them.*

12   For it is a shame even to speak of those things which are done of them in secret.

13   But all things that are reproved are made manifest by the light: for whatsoever doth make manifest is light.

14   Wherefore he saith, Awake thou that sleepest, and arise from the dead, and Christ shall give thee light.

15   See then that ye walk

---

[1] WH changed **us** (ᵸ**Amas**) to *you* (ᵸ*umas*). [person]

[2] In their margin, WH changed **us** (ᵸ**AmOn**) to *you* (ᵸ*umOn*). [person]

[3] WH changed the word order from ALL uncleanness to *uncleanness ALL.*

[4] WH changed ye **are** knowing (este ginOskontes) to *know ye knowing* (*iste ginOskontes*). **Pres** NV **Ind** & Pres Act Part to *Pf* Act *Imp* & Pres Act Part. [tense & mood]

[5] WH changed **who** (ᵸos) to *which* (ᵸo). Nom **Masc** Sing to Nom *Neut* Sing. [gender]

[6] WH changed **Spirit** (**pneumatos**) to *light* (*fOtos*).

circumspectly[1], not as fools, but as wise,

16 Redeeming the time, because the days are evil.

17 Wherefore be ye not unwise, but **understanding**[2] what the will of the Lord _is_.

18 And be not drunk with wine, wherein is excess; but be filled with the Spirit;

19 Speaking to yourselves in psalms and hymns and spiritual songs, singing and making melody ~~in~~[3] your heart to the Lord;

20 Giving thanks always for all things unto God and the Father in the name of our Lord Jesus Christ;

21 Submitting yourselves one to another in the fear **of God**[4].

22 Wives, ~~submit your-selves~~[5] unto your own husbands, as unto the Lord.

23 For ~~the~~[6] husband is the head of the wife, even as Christ is the head of the church: ~~and~~[7] he ~~is~~[8] the saviour of the body.

24 Therefore **as**[9] the church is subject unto Christ, so _let_ the wives _be_ to ~~their own~~[10] husbands in every thing.

25 Husbands, love ~~your~~[11] wives, even as Christ also loved the church, and gave himself for it;

26 That he might sanctify and cleanse it with the washing of water by the word,

27 That he might present **it**[12] to himself a glorious church, not having spot, or wrinkle, or any such thing; but that it should be holy and

---

[1] WH changed the word order from HOW carefully to _carefully_ HOW.

[2] WH changed understand**ing** (sunientes) to _understand ye_ (suniete). Pres Act **Part** to Pres Act _Imp_. [mood]

[3] WH omitted in (en) and forced the dative case to supply the preposition.

[4] WH changed of **God** (~~th~~eou) to of _Christ_ (cristou).

[5] WH omitted submit your-selves ([h]upotassesthe).

[6] WH omitted the ([h]o).

[7] WH omitted and (kai).

[8] WH omitted is (esti).

[9] WH changed **just** as ([h]Os-**per**) to _as_ ([h]Os).

[10] WH omitted their own (idios) from the husbands their own.

[11] WH omitted of themselves ([h]eautOn) from the wives of themselves.

[12] WH changed **her** (autAn) to _him_ (autos). **Acc Fem** Sing to _Nom Masc_ Sing. [case & gender]

without blemish.

28 So ought [ˌalso][1] men to love their wives as their own bodies. He that loveth his wife loveth himself.

29 For no man ever yet hated his own flesh; but nourisheth and cherisheth it, even as the **Lord**[2] the church:

30 For we are members of his body, ~~of his flesh, and of his bones~~[3].

31 For this cause shall a man leave ~~his~~[4] father and mother, and shall be joined unto his wife, and they two shall be one flesh.

32 This is a great mystery: but I speak concerning Christ and the church.

33 Nevertheless let every one of you in particular so love his wife even as himself; and the wife *see* that she reverence *her* husband.

CHAPTER 6

1   Children,   obey   your parents in the Lord: for this is right.

2   Honour thy father and mother; (which is the first commandment with promise;)

3   That it may be well with thee, and thou mayest live long on the earth.

4   And, ye fathers, provoke not your children to wrath: but bring them up in the nurture and admonition of the Lord.

5   Servants, be obedient to them that are *your* **masters**[5] according to the flesh, with fear and trembling, in singleness of your heart, as unto Christ;

6   Not with eyeservice, as menpleasers; but as the servants of Christ, doing the will of God from the heart;

7   With good will doing service, as to the Lord, and not to men:

8   Knowing that whatsoever good ~~thing~~[6] **any man**[7]

---

[1] WH added *also* (*kai*).
[2] WH changed **Lord** (**kuri**os) to **Christ** (**cristos**).
[3] WH omitted out of the flesh of him and out of the bones of him (ek tAs sarkos autou kai ek tOn osteOn autou).
[4] WH omitted of him (autou) from the father of him.

[5] WH changed the word order from MASTERS according to flesh to *according to flesh MASTERS*.
[6] WH omitted thing (ti).
[7] WH changed the word order from what ever **thing** EVERY {ONE} does good to *EVERY {ONE} what ever does good*.

doeth, the same shall he receive of ~~the~~[1] Lord, whether *he be* bond or free.

9   And, ye masters, do the same things unto them, forbearing threatening: knowing that **your**[2] [∧**and**][3] [their] Master also is in heaven; neither is there respect of persons with him.

10 **Finally**[4], ~~my breth-ren~~[5], be strong in the Lord, and in the power of his might.

11 Put on the whole armour of God, that ye may be able to stand against the wiles of the devil.

12 For we wrestle not against flesh and blood, but against principalities, against powers, against the rulers of the darkness ~~of~~ this ~~world~~[6],

against spiritual wickedness in high *places.*

13 Wherefore take unto you the whole armour of God, that ye may be able to withstand in the evil day, and having done all, to stand.

14 Stand therefore, having your loins girt about with truth, and having on the breastplate of righteousness;

15 And your feet shod with the preparation of the gospel of peace;

16 **Above**[7] all, taking the shield of faith, wherewith ye shall be able to quench all the fiery darts of the wicked.

17 And take the helmet of salvation, and the sword of the Spirit, which is the word of God:

18 Praying always with all prayer and supplication in the Spirit, and watching ~~there-unto~~[8] with all perseverance and supplication for all saints;

19 And for me, that utterance **may be given**[9] unto me, that I may open my mouth

---

[1] WH omitted <u>the</u> (<u>tou</u>).
[2] WH changed the word order from <u>knowing</u> <u>that</u> <u>also</u> <u>OF YOU</u> <u>of them</u> <u>the</u> <u>master</u> to *knowing that also of them and OF YOU the master.*
[3] WH added *and* (*kai*) to separate <u>of you</u> (^h<u>umOn</u>) from the untranslated <u>of them</u> (<u>autOn</u>).
[4] WH changed <u>finally</u> (<u>to loi-pon</u>) to *finally* (*tou loipou*). Adj **Nom** Neut to Adj *Gen* Neut. [case]
[5] WH omitted <u>my</u> brethren (<u>adelfoi</u> <u>mou</u>).
[6] WH omitted <u>of the world</u>

(<u>tou aiOnos</u>).
[7] WH changed **above** (**epi**) to *in* (*en*).
[8] WH omitted <u>this</u> (<u>touto</u>) from <u>into</u> <u>this</u> <u>same.</u>
[9] WH changed **should** <u>be</u> <u>given</u> (<u>dotheiA</u>) to *might be given* (*dothA*). Aor Pass **Opt** to Aor Pass *Sub.* [mood]

boldly, to make known the mystery of the gospel,

20 For which I am an ambassador in bonds: that therein I may speak boldly, as I ought to speak.

21 But that **ye**[1] also may know my affairs, _and_ how I do, Tychicus, a beloved brother and faithful minister in the Lord, shall make known to you all things:

22 Whom I have sent unto you for the same purpose, that ye might know our affairs, and _that_ he might comfort your hearts.

23 Peace _be_ to the brethren, and love with faith, from God the Father and the Lord Jesus Christ.

24 Grace _be_ with all them that love our Lord Jesus Christ in sincerity. Amen.

---

[1] WH changed the word order from YE may know to may know YE.

PHILIPPIANS

CHAPTER 1

1   Paul and Timotheus, the servants of Jesus Christ, to all the saints in **Christ**[1] Jesus which are at Philippi, with the bishops and deacons:

2   Grace *be* unto you, and peace, from God our Father, and *from* the Lord Jesus Christ.

3   I thank my God upon every remembrance of you,

4   Always in every prayer of mine for you all making request with joy,

5   For your fellowship in the gospel from ʌ**the**[2] first day until now;

6   Being confident of this very thing, that he which hath begun a good work in you will perform *it* until the day of Jesus Christ:

7   Even as it is meet for me to think this of you all, because I have you in my heart; inasmuch as both in my bonds, and ʌ**in**[3] the defence and confirmation of the gospel, ye all are partakers of my grace.

8   For God i̶s̶[4] my record, how greatly I long after you all in the bowels of **Jesus**[5] Christ.

9   And this I pray, that your love may abound yet more and more in knowledge and *in* all judgment;

10   That ye may approve things that are excellent; that ye may be sincere and without offence till the day of Christ;

11   Being filled with the **fruits**[6] of righteousness, **which are**[7] by Jesus Christ, unto the glory and praise of God.

12   But I would ye should understand, brethren, that the things *which happened* unto me have fallen out rather unto the furtherance of the

---

[1] WH changed the word order from C̲H̲R̲I̲S̲T̲ J̲e̲s̲u̲s̲ to *Je-sus CHRIST*.

[2] WH added *the* (*tАs*) as the KJV supplied.

[3] WH added *in* (*en*) as the KJV supplied.

[4] WH omitted i̲s̲ (estin).

[5] WH changed the word order from J̲E̲S̲U̲S̲ C̲h̲r̲i̲s̲t̲ to *Christ JESUS*.

[6] WH changed f̲r̲u̲i̲t̲s̲ (kar-p**O**n) to *fruit* (*karpon*). **Gen** Masc **Plur** to *Acc* Masc *Sing*. [case & number]

[7] WH changed w̲h̲i̲c̲h̲ {are} (t**O**n) to *which* {**is**} (*ton*). **Gen** Masc **Plur** to *Acc* Masc *Sing*. [case & number]

gospel;

13 So that my bonds in Christ are manifest in all the palace, and in all other *places*;

14 And many of the brethren in the Lord, waxing confident by my bonds, are much more bold to speak the word [∧**of the God**][1] without fear.

15 Some indeed preach Christ even of envy and strife; and some also of good will:

16 The one **preach Christ of contention, not sincerely, supposing to add affliction to my bonds:**

17 But the other **of love, knowing that I am set for the defence of the gospel**.[2]

18 What then? Notwithstanding [∧**that**][3], every way, whether in pretence, or in truth, Christ is preached; and I therein do rejoice, yea, and will rejoice.

19 For I know that this shall turn to my salvation through your prayer, and the supply of the Spirit of Jesus Christ,

20 According to my earnest expectation and *my* hope, that in nothing I shall be ashamed, but *that* with all boldness, as always, *so* now also Christ shall be magnified in my body, whether *it be* by life, or by death.

21 For to me to live *is* Christ, and to die *is* gain.

22 But if I live in the flesh, this *is* the fruit of my labour: yet what I shall choose I wot not.

23 **For**[4] I am in a strait betwixt two, having a desire to depart, and to be with Christ; [∧**for**][5] which is far better:

24 Nevertheless to abide ~~in~~[6] the flesh *is* more needful for you.

25 And having this confidence, I know that I shall

---

[1] WH added *of the God* (*tou* ~~th~~*eou*).

[2] WH changed the word order from the way it is in the KJV to The one *of love, knowing that I am set for the defence of the gospel*: but the other *preach Christ of contention, not sincerely, supposing to add affliction to my bonds.* [The words in verse 1:16 changed places with the words in verse 1:17.]

[3] WH added *that* (*[h]oti*).

[4] WH changed **for** (**gar**) to *but* (*de*).

[5] WH added *for* (*gar*).

[6] WH omitted in (en) and forced the dative case to supply the preposition.

abide and **continue with**[1] you all for your furtherance and joy of faith;

26 That your rejoicing may be more abundant in Jesus Christ for me by my coming to you again.

27 Only let your conversation be as it becometh the gospel of Christ: that whether I come and see you, or else be absent, I may hear of your affairs, that ye stand fast in one spirit, with one mind striving together for the faith of the gospel;

28 And in nothing terrified by your adversaries: which [on the one hand][2] **is**[3] to them an evident token of perdition, but **to you**[4] of salvation, and that of God.

29 For unto you it is given in the behalf of Christ, not only to believe on him, but also to suffer for his sake;

30 Having the same con-flict which ye saw in me, and now hear *to be* in me.

CHAPTER 2

1 If *there be* therefore any consolation in Christ, if any comfort of love, if any fellowship of the Spirit, if **any**[5] bowels and mercies,

2 Fulfil ye my joy, that ye be likeminded, having the same love, *being* of one accord, of **one**[6] mind.

3 *Let* nothing *be done* through strife **or**[7] vainglory; but in lowliness of mind let each esteem other better than themselves.

4 **Look** not **every man**[8] **on**[9] his own things, but **every**

---

[1] WH changed continue **with** (**sum**paramenO) to *continue* (*paramenO*). [prefix dropped]

[2] WH omitted the untranslated on the one hand (men).

[3] WH changed the word order from to them **on the one hand** IS to *IS to them.*

[4] WH changed **to you** (ʰumin) to *of you* (ʰumOn). **Dative** Plur to *Genitive* Plur. [case]

[5] WH changed any (**tina**) to *any* (*tis*). **Pro** Nom **Neut Plur** to *Adj* Nom *Fem/Masc Sing.* [gender & number & part of sp]

[6] In their margin, WH changed **one** (ʰ**en**) to *same* (*auto*).

[7] WH changed **or** (**A**) to *through* (*mAde kata*).

[8] WH changed **every** {man} (ʰekasto**s**) to *all* {men} (ʰekasto**i**). Adj **Sing** to Adj *Plur.* [number]

[9] WH changed look on (skopeite) to *looking on* (*skopountes*). Pres Act **Imp** to Pres Act *Part.* [mood]

man[1] also on the things of others.

5 **[for]**[2] **Let this mind be**[3] in you, which was also in Christ Jesus:

6 Who, being in the form of God, thought it not robbery to be equal with God:

7 But made himself of no reputation, and took upon him the form of a servant, and was made in the likeness of men:

8 And being found in fashion as a man, he humbled himself, and became obedient unto death, even the death of the cross.

9 Wherefore God also hath highly exalted him, and given him **[ʌthe]**[4] a name which is above every name:

10 That at the name of Jesus every knee should bow,

of *things* in heaven, and *things* in earth, and *things* under the earth;

11 And *that* every tongue should confess that Jesus Christ *is* Lord, to the glory of God the Father.

12 Wherefore, my beloved, as ye have always obeyed, not **as**[5] in my presence only, but now much more in my absence, work out your own salvation with fear and trembling.

13 For it is **[the]**[6] God which worketh in you both to will and to do of *his* good pleasure.

14 Do all things without murmurings and disputings:

15 That ye may be blameless and harmless, the sons of God, **without rebuke**[7], **in the midst of**[8] a crooked and perverse nation, among whom ye shine as lights in the

---

[1] WH changed **every** {man} (ʰekastos) to *all* {men} (ʰekaastoi). Adj **Sing** to Adj *Plur*. [number]

[2] WH omitted the untranslated for (gar).

[3] WH changed **let this mind be** (froneisthO) to *have ye this mind* (froneite). Pres **Pass** Imp **3ʳᵈ Sing** to Pres *Act* Imp *2ⁿᵈ Plur*. [voice, person & number]

[4] WH added the definite article *the* (to).

[5] In their margin, WH omitted as (ʰOs).

[6] WH omitted the untranslated the (ʰo).

[7] WH changed without rebuke (amOmAta) to *without rebuke* (amOma). Both Nom Neut Plur. amOmAtos to *amOmos*. [syn]

[8] WH changed in the midst of (en mesO) to *in the midst of* (meson).

world;

16 Holding forth the word of life; that I may rejoice in the day of Christ, that I have not run in vain, neither laboured in vain.

17 Yea, and if I be offered upon the sacrifice and service of your faith, I joy, and rejoice with you all.

18 For the same cause also do ye joy, and rejoice with me.

19 But I trust in the Lord Jesus to send Timotheus shortly unto you, that I also may be of good comfort, when I know your state.

20 For I have no man likeminded, who will naturally care for your state.

21 For all seek their own, not the things which are **Jesus**[1] Christ's.

22 But ye know the proof of him, that, as a son with the father, he hath served with me in the gospel.

23 Him therefore I hope to send presently, so soon as I shall see how it will go with me.

24 But I trust in the Lord that I also myself shall come shortly.

25 Yet I supposed it necessary to send to you Epaphroditus, my brother, and companion in labour, and fellowsoldier, but your messenger, and he that ministered to my wants.

26 For he longed after you all **[to see]**[2], and was full of heaviness, because that ye had heard that he had been sick.

27 For indeed he was sick nigh unto death: but God had mercy on him; and not on him only, but on me also, lest I should have sorrow upon **sorrow**[3].

28 I sent him therefore the more carefully, that, when ye see him again, ye may rejoice, and that I may be the less sorrowful.

29 Receive him therefore in the Lord with all gladness; and hold such in reputation:

30 Because for the work of **[the]**[4] **Christ**[5] he was nigh

---

[1] WH changed the word order from of the Christ JESUS to *of the JESUS Christ.*

[2] In their margin, WH added *to see* (*idein*).

[3] WH changed sorrow (lupA) to *sorrow* (*lupAn*). **Dat** Fem Sing to *Acc* Fem Sing. [case]

[4] In their margin, WH omitted the untranslated the (tou).

[5] In their margin, WH changed **Christ** (**crist**ou) to **Lord** (*kuriou*).

unto death, **not regarding**[1] his life, to supply your lack of service toward me.

CHAPTER 3

1 Finally, my brethren, rejoice in the Lord. To write the same things to you, to me indeed *is* not grievous, but for you *it is* safe.

2 Beware of dogs, beware of evil workers, beware of the concision.

3 For we are the circumcision, which worship **God**[2] in the spirit, and rejoice in Christ Jesus, and have no confidence in the flesh.

4 Though I might also have confidence in the flesh. If any other man thinketh that he hath whereof he might trust in the flesh, I more:

5 **Circumcised**[3] the

eighth day, of the stock of Israel, *of* the tribe of Benjamin, an Hebrew of the Hebrews; as touching the law, a Pharisee;

6 Concerning **zeal**[4], persecuting the church; touching the righteousness which is in the law, blameless.

7 But what things were gain to me, those I counted loss for Christ.

8 Yea doubtless, and I count all things *but* loss for the excellency of the knowledge of Christ Jesus my Lord: for whom I have suffered the loss of all things, and do count them *but* dung [to be][5], that I may win Christ,

9 And be found in him, not having mine own righteousness, which is of the law, but that which is through the faith of Christ, the righteousness which is of God by faith:

10 That I may know him, and the power of his

---

[1] WH changed having **disregarded** (parabouleusamenos) to *having* **risked** (*paraboleusamenos*). Both Aor Mid Part Nom Masc Sing. [spell]
[2] WH changed God (theO) to *of God* (*theou*). Worship the {**in**} spirit God to *worship the spirit* {**of**} *God*. **Dative** to *Genitive*. [case]
[3] WH changed circumcized (peritomA) to *circumcized* (*peritomA*--with an iota sub-

script under the *A*). **Nom** Fem Sing to *Dat* Fem Sing. [case]
[4] WH changed zeal (zAlon) to *zeal* (*zAlos*). Acc **Masc** Sing to Acc *Neut* Sing. [gender]
[5] WH omitted the untranslated to be (einai).

resurrection, and ~~the~~[1] fellowship of his sufferings, **being
made conformable unto**[2] his
death;

11 If by any means I might
attain unto the resurrection **of
the**[3] [∧**out of**][4] dead.

12 Not as though I had already attained, either were already perfect: but I follow after, if that I may apprehend
that for which also I am apprehended of [~~the~~][5] Christ Jesus.

13 Brethren, I count **not**[6]
myself to have apprehended:
but _this_ one thing _I do_, for-
getting those things which are
behind, and reaching forth
unto those things which are
before,

14 I press toward the mark
for[7] the prize of the high calling of God in Christ Jesus.

15 Let us therefore, as
many as be perfect, be thus
minded: and if in any thing ye
be otherwise minded, God
shall reveal even this unto
you.

16 Nevertheless, whereto
we have already attained, let
us walk by the same **rule, let
us mind the same thing**[8].

17 Brethren, be followers
together of me, and mark
them which walk so as ye
have us for an ensample.

18 (For many walk, of
whom I have told you often,
and now tell you even weeping, _that they are_ the enemies
of the cross of Christ:

19 Whose end _is_ destruction, whose God _is their_
belly, and _whose_ glory _is_ in
their shame, who mind
earthly things.)

20 For our conversation is
in heaven; from whence also
we look for the Saviour, the
Lord Jesus Christ:

21 Who shall change our

---

[1] WH omitted the (tAn).
[2] WH changed being made
conformable unto (summor-
fo**u**menos) to _being made
conformable unto_ (summor-
fizomenos). Both Pres **Pass**
Part. [spell]
[3] WH changed of the (tOn)
to _the_ (tAn). **Gen Masc Plur**
to _Acc Fem Sing_. [case,
gender, number]
[4] WH added _out of_ (ek).
[5] WH omitted the untranslated the (tou).
[6] WH changed not (ou) to
not (oupO), but retained ou
in their margin.

---

[7] WH changed **upon** (epi) to
into (eis).
[8] WH omitted rule let us
mind the same {thing} (ka-
noni to auto fronein).

vile body, ~~that it may be~~[1] fashioned like unto his glorious body, according to the working whereby he is able even to subdue all things **unto himself**[2].

CHAPTER 4

1   Therefore, my brethren dearly beloved and longed for, my joy and crown, so stand fast in the Lord, *my* dearly beloved.

2   I beseech Euodias, and beseech Syntyche, that they be of the same mind in the Lord.

3   **And**[3] I intreat thee also, **true**[4] yokefellow, help those women which laboured with me in the gospel, with Clement also, and *with* other my fellowlabourers, whose names *are* in the book of life.

4   Rejoice in the Lord alway: *and* again I say, Rejoice.

5   Let your moderation be known unto all men. The Lord *is* at hand.

6   Be careful for nothing; but in every thing by prayer and supplication with thanksgiving let your requests be made known unto God.

7   And the peace of God, which passeth all understanding, shall keep your hearts and minds through Christ Jesus.

8   Finally, brethren, whatsoever things are true, whatsoever things *are* honest, whatsoever things *are* just, whatsoever things *are* pure, whatsoever things *are* lovely, whatsoever things *are* of good report; if *there be* any virtue, and if *there be* any praise, think on these things.

9   Those things, which ye have both learned, and received, and heard, and seen in me, do: and the God of peace shall be with you.

10   But I rejoiced in the Lord greatly, that now at the last your care of me hath flourished again; wherein ye were also careful, but ye lacked opportunity.

11   Not that I speak in respect of want: for I have learned, in whatsoever state I am, *therewith* to be content.

12   I know both how to be

---

[1] WH omitted <u>unto</u> <u>the</u> <u>to</u> <u>become</u> <u>it</u> (<u>eis</u> <u>to</u> genes~~t~~hai auto).

[2] WH changed {unto} **himself** ([h]eautO) to {unto} *him* (*autO*). **Refl** pro to **Pers** pro.

[3] WH changed **and** (<u>kai</u>) to *yes* (*nai*).

[4] WH changed the word order from <u>yokefellow</u> TRUE to *TRUE yokefellow*.

abased, and I know how to abound: every where and in all things I am instructed both to be full and to be hungry, both to abound and to suffer need.

13 I can do all things through ~~Christ~~[1] which strengtheneth me.

14 Notwithstanding ye have well done, that ye did communicate with my affliction.

15 Now ye Philippians know also, that in the beginning of the gospel, when I departed from Macedonia, no church communicated with me as concerning giving and receiving, but ye only.

16 For even in Thessalonica ye sent once and again unto my necessity.

17 Not because I desire a gift: but I desire fruit that may abound to your account.

18 But I have all, and abound: I am full, having received of Epaphroditus the things *which were sent* from you, an odour of a sweet smell, a sacrifice acceptable, wellpleasing to God.

19 But my God shall supply all your need according to his **riches**[2] in glory by Christ

Jesus.

20 Now unto God and our Father *be* glory for ever and ever. Amen.

21 Salute every saint in Christ Jesus. The brethren which are with me greet you.

22 All the saints salute you, chiefly they that are of Caesar's household.

23 The grace of ~~our~~[3] Lord Jesus Christ *be* with you **<u>all</u>**[4]. ~~Amen~~[5].

---

plouto**n**) to *the riches* (*to ploutos*) in <u>the</u> <u>riches</u> <u>of him</u>. Acc **Masc** Sing to Acc *Neut* Sing. [gender]

[3] WH omitted <u>of us</u> ([h]AmOn) from <u>of the</u> <u>Lord</u> <u>of us</u>.

[4] WH changed <u>with</u> **<u>all</u>** <u>of you</u> (meta **pantOn** [h]umOn) to *with* **the spirit** *of you* (*meta tou pneumatos* [h]*umOn*).

[5] WH omitted <u>amen</u> (amAn).

---

[1] WH omitted <u>Christ</u> (<u>cristO</u>).

[2] WH changed <u>the</u> <u>riches</u> (**to n**

COLOSSIANS

CHAPTER 1

1   Paul, an apostle of **Je-sus**[1] Christ by the will of God, and Timotheus *our* brother,

2   To the saints and faithful brethren in Christ which are at Colosse: Grace *be* unto you, and peace, from God our Father ~~and the Lord Je-sus Christ~~[2].

3   We give thanks to God **and**[3] the Father of our Lord Jesus Christ, praying always for you,

4   Since we heard of your faith in Christ Jesus, and of the love **_which_**[4] ∧*ye have*[5] to all the saints,

5   For the hope which is laid up for you in heaven, whereof ye heard before in the word of the truth of the gospel;

6   Which is come unto you, as *it is* in all the world; **and**[6] bringeth forth fruit **[**∧**and increasing]**[7], as *it* doth also in you, since the day ye heard *of it*, and knew the grace of God in truth:

7   As ye ~~also~~[8] learned of Epaphras our dear fellowservant, who is for **_you_**[9] a faithful minister of Christ;

8   Who also declared unto us your love in the Spirit.

9   For this cause we also, since the day we heard *it*, do not cease to pray for you, and to desire that ye might be filled with the knowledge of his will in all wisdom and spiritual understanding;

10 That ye **[**~~yourselves~~**]**[10] might walk worthy of the Lord unto all pleasing, being fruitful in every good work, and increasing ~~in~~[11] **the**

---

[1] WH changed the word order from JESUS Christ to *Christ JESUS.*

[2] WH omitted <u>and Lord Jesus Christ</u> (<u>kai kuriou iasou cristou</u>).

[3] WH omitted <u>and</u> (<u>kai</u>).

[4] WH changed **the** (**t**An) to *which* (*An*).

[5] WH added *ye have* (*ecete*) exactly as the KJV supplied in italics.

[6] WH omitted <u>and</u> (<u>kai</u>).

[7] WH added and *increasing* (*kai auxanomenon*).

[8] WH omitted <u>also</u> (<u>kai</u>).

[9] WH changed **you** (^humOn) to *us* (^hAmOn) in their text, but retained <u>you</u> (^humOn) in their margin. [person]

[10] WH omitted the untranslated intensive <u>yourselves</u> (^humas).

[11] WH omitted <u>in</u> (<u>eis</u>) and forced the new dative case to supply the preposition.

knowledge[1] of God;

11 Strengthened with all might, according to his glorious power, unto all patience and longsuffering with joyfulness;

12 Giving thanks unto the Father, which hath made **us**[2] meet to be partakers of the inheritance of the saints in light:

13 Who hath delivered us from the power of darkness, and hath translated *us* into the kingdom of his dear Son:

14 In whom we have redemption ~~through his blood~~[3], *even* the forgiveness of sins:

15 Who is the image of the invisible God, the firstborn of every creature:

16 For by him were all things created, ~~that are~~[4] in heaven, and ~~that are~~[5] in earth, visible and invisible, whether *they be* thrones, or dominions, or principalities, or powers: all things were created by him, and for him:

17 And he is before all things, and by him all things consist.

18 And he is the head of the body, the church: who is the beginning, the firstborn from the dead; that in all *things* he might have the preeminence.

19 For it pleased *the Father* that in him should all fulness dwell;

20 And, having made peace through the blood of his cross, by him to reconcile all things unto himself; by him, *I say*, whether *they be* things in earth, or things in heaven. 21 And you, that were sometime alienated and enemies in *your* mind by wicked works, yet now **hath he reconciled**[6]

---

[1] WH changed <u>the knowledge</u> (<u>tAn</u> epign<u>Osin</u>) to *the knowledge* (*tA epignOsei*). **Acc** to ***Dat***. [case]

[2] In their margin, WH changed **us** (^h<u>A</u>mas) to **you** (^h*umas*). [person]

[3] WH omitted <u>through the blood</u> of him (<u>dia tou</u> ^h<u>aimatos autou</u>).

[4] WH omitted <u>that</u> {are} (<u>ta</u>—the {things}).

[5] WH omitted <u>that</u> {are} (<u>ta</u>—the {things}).

[6] In their margin, WH changed **he reconciled** (<u>apokatAllaxen</u>) to *ye were reconciled* (*apokatAllagAte*). Aor **Act** Ind **3rd Sing** to Aor *Pass* Ind *2nd Plur*. [voice, person, & number]

22 In the body of his flesh through death, to present you holy and unblameable and unreproveable in his sight:

23 If ye continue in the faith grounded and settled, and *be* not moved away from the hope of the gospel, which ye have heard, *and* which was preached to every [the][1] creature which is under heaven; whereof I Paul am made a minister;

24 ~~Who~~[2] now rejoice in ~~my~~[3] sufferings for you, and fill up that which is behind of the afflictions of Christ in my flesh for his body's sake, which is the church:

25 Whereof I am made a minister, according to the dispensation of God which is given to me for you, to fulfil the word of God;

26 *Even* the mystery which hath been hid from ages and from generations, but **now**[4] is made manifest to his saints:

27 To whom God would make known **what** *is* **the**[5]

riches of the glory of this mystery among the Gentiles; **which**[6] is Christ in you, the hope of glory:

28 Whom we preach, warning every man, and teaching every man in all wisdom; that we may present every man perfect in Christ ~~Jesus~~[7]:

29 Whereunto I also labour, striving according to his working, which worketh in me mightily.

CHAPTER 2

1 For I would that ye knew what great conflict I have **for**[8] you, and *for* them at Laodicea, and *for* as many as have not seen my face in the flesh;

2 That their hearts might be comforted, **being knit together**[9] in love, and unto **all**

---

[1] WH omitted the untranslated the (tA).

[2] WH omitted who ([h]os).

[3] WH omitted of me (mou) from the sufferings of me.

[4] WH changed now (nuni) to now (nun). **Emphatic** form to *Regular* form of nun.

[5] WH changed who the (tis

[h]o) to *what the* (*ti to*). Nom **Masc** Sing to Nom *Neut* Sing. [gender]

[6] WH changed who ([h]os) to which ([h]o). Nom **Masc** Sing to Nom *Neut* Sing. [gender]

[7] WH omitted Jesus (iAsou).

[8] WH changed for (**peri**) to *for* ([h]**uper**).

[9] WH changed being knit together (sumbibas~~th~~entOn) to *being knit together* (*sumbibas~~th~~entes*). Both Aor Pass Part. **Gen** Masc Plur to *Nom* Masc Plur. [case]

riches[1] of the full assurance of understanding, to the acknowledgement of the mystery of God, ~~and of the Father, and of~~ [the][2] Christ;

3   In whom are hid all the treasures of wisdom and [the][3] knowledge.

4   ~~And~~[4] this I say, **lest any man**[5] should beguile you with enticing words.

5   For though I be absent in the flesh, yet am I with you in the spirit, joying and beholding your order, and the stedfastness of your faith in Christ.

6   As ye have therefore received Christ Jesus the Lord, *so* walk ye in him:

7   Rooted and built up in him, and stablished ~~in~~[6] the faith, as ye have been taught, abounding ~~therein~~[7] with thanksgiving.

8   Beware lest any man spoil you through philosophy and vain deceit, after the tradition of men, after the rudiments of the world, and not after Christ.

9   For in him dwelleth all the fulness of the Godhead bodily.

10 And ye are complete in him, which is the head of all principality and power:

11 In whom also ye are circumcised with the circumcision made without hands, in putting off the body ~~of the sins~~[8] of the flesh by the circumcision of Christ:

12 Buried with him in baptism, wherein also ye are risen with *him* through the faith of the operation of God, who hath raised him from the dead.

13 And you, being dead

---

[1] WH changed <u>all</u> <u>riches</u> (<u>panta</u> <u>plouton</u>) to *all riches* (*pan ploutos*). Acc **Masc** Sing to Acc *Neut* Sing. [gender]

[2] WH omitted <u>and</u> {of} <u>father</u> <u>and</u> {of} <u>the</u> (<u>kai</u> <u>patros</u> <u>kai</u> <u>tou</u>). In their margin, WH state that ancient authorities vary much.

[3] WH omitted the untranslated <u>the</u> (<u>tAs</u>).

[4] WH omitted <u>and</u> (<u>de</u>).

[5] WH changed <u>that</u> **not** **any** one (<u>h</u><u>ina</u> <u>mA</u> <u>tis</u>) to *that noone* (*[h]ina mAdeis*).

[6] WH omitted <u>in</u> (<u>en</u>) and forced the dative case to supply the preposition.

[7] WH omitted <u>in</u> <u>it</u> (<u>en</u> <u>autA</u>) in their text, but retained these words in their margin.

[8] WH omitted <u>of the</u> <u>sins</u> (<u>tOn</u> <u>[h]amartiOn</u>).

in[1] your sins and the uncircumcision of your flesh, hath he quickened **[∧you]**[2] together with him, having forgiven **you**[3] all trespasses;

14 Blotting out the handwriting of ordinances that was against us, which was contrary to us, and took it out of the way, nailing it to his cross;

15 _And_ having spoiled principalities and powers, he made a shew of them openly, triumphing over them in it.

16 Let no man therefore judge you in meat, or in drink, or in respect of an holyday, or of the new moon, or of the sabbath _days_:

17 Which are a shadow of things to come; but the body _is_ of Christ.

18 Let no man beguile you of your reward in a voluntary humility and worshipping of angels, intruding into those things which he hath **not**[4] seen, vainly puffed up by his fleshly mind,

19 And not holding the Head, from which all the body by joints and bands having nourishment ministered, and knit together, increaseth with the increase of God.

20 ~~Wherefore~~[5] if ye be dead with **[the]**[6] Christ from the rudiments of the world, why, as though living in the world, are ye subject to ordinances,

21 (Touch not; taste not; handle not;

22 Which all are to perish with the using;) after the commandments and doctrines of men?

23 Which things have indeed a shew of wisdom in will worship, and humility, and neglecting of the body; not in any honour to the satisfying of the flesh.

CHAPTER 3

1 If ye then be risen with Christ, seek those things which are above, where Christ sitteth on the right hand of God.

2 Set your affection on

---

[1] WH omitted in (en) and forced the dative case to supply the prepositon.
[2] WH added _you_ (_h_umas).
[3] WH changed **you** (_h_umin) to _us_ (_h_Amin). [person]
[4] WH omitted not (mA) in their text, but retained it in their margin.

[5] WH omitted wherefore (oun).
[6] WH omitted the untranslated the (tO).

things above, not on things on the earth.

3 For ye are dead, and your life is hid with Christ in God.

4 When Christ, *who is* our[1] life, shall appear, then shall ye also appear with him in glory.

5 Mortify therefore ~~your~~[2] members which are upon the earth; fornication, uncleanness, inordinate affection, evil concupiscence, and covetousness, which is idolatry:

6 For which things' sake the wrath of God cometh **on the children of disobedience**[3]:

7 In the which ye also walked some time, when ye lived in **them**[4].

8 But now ye also put off all these; anger, wrath, malice, blasphemy, filthy communication out of your mouth.

9 Lie not one to another, seeing that ye have put off the old man with his deeds;

10 And have put on the new *man*, which is renewed in knowledge after the image of him that created him:

11 Where there is neither Greek nor Jew, circumcision nor uncircumcision, barbarian, Scythian, bond *nor* free: but Christ *is* all, and in all.

12 Put on therefore, as the elect of God, holy and beloved, bowels **of mercies**[5], kindness, humbleness of mind, meekness, longsuffering;

13 Forbearing one another, and forgiving one another, if any man have a quarrel against any: even as **Christ**[6] forgave you, so also *do* ye.

14 And above all these

---

[1] In their margin, WH changed of **us** (*h*AmOn) to *of you* (*h*umOn) in the life of us. [person]

[2] WH omitted of you (*h*umOn) from the members of you.

[3] In their margin, WH omitted on the children of the disobedience (epi tous *h*uios tAs apeitheias).

[4] WH changed them (autois) to *these* (toutois). Both Dat Neut Plur. **Pers** pro to *Dem* pro.

[5] WH changed of mercies (oiktirmOn) to *of mercy* (oiktirmou). **Plur** to *Sing*. [number]

[6] WH changed the **Christ** (tou **cristou**) to *the Lord* (tou **kurios**) in their text; but retained the Christ (tou cristou) in their margin.

things *put on* charity, **which**[1] is the bond of perfectness.

15 And let the peace of **God**[2] rule in your hearts, to the which also ye are called in one body; and be ye thankful.

16 Let the word of **Christ**[3] dwell in you richly in all wisdom; teaching and admonishing one another in psalms ~~and~~[4] hymns ~~and~~[5] spiritual songs, singing with grace in **your hearts**[6] to the **Lord**[7].

17 And whatsoever ye do in word or deed, *do* all in the name of the Lord Jesus, giving thanks to God ~~and~~[8] the

Father by him.

18 Wives, submit your-selves unto ~~your own~~[9] hus-bands, as it is fit in the Lord.

19 Husbands, love *your* wives, and be not bitter against them.

20 Children, obey *your* parents in all things: for this **is**[10] well pleasing **unto the**[11] Lord.

21 Fathers, provoke not your children *to anger*, lest they be discouraged.

22 Servants, obey in all things *your* masters accord-ing to the flesh; not with eyeservice, as menpleasers; but in singleness of heart, fearing **God**[12]:

23 ~~And~~ **whatsoever**[13] ye do, do *it* heartily, as to the

---

[1] WH changed <u>which</u> (^h**Atis**) to *which* (^h*o*). Nom **Fem** Sing to Nom *Neut* Sing. [gender & root]

[2] WH changed **God** (~~th~~eou) to *Christ* (*cristou*).

[3] In their margin, WH changed **Christ** (**crist**ou) to *Lord* (*kuriou*) or *God* (~~th~~*eou*).

[4] WH omitted <u>and</u> (<u>kai</u>).

[5] WH omitted <u>and</u> (<u>kai</u>).

[6] WH changed <u>the</u> <u>heart</u> <u>of</u> <u>you</u> (t<u>A</u> <u>kardia</u> ^h<u>umOn</u>) to *the hearts of you* (*tais kardiais* ^h*umOn*). **Sing** to *Plur*. [num-ber]

[7] WH changed **Lord** (**kuriO**) to *God* (~~th~~*eO*).

[8] WH omitted <u>and</u> (<u>kai</u>).

---

[9] WH omitted <u>your own</u> (<u>idiois</u>) from <u>the</u> <u>your own</u> <u>husbands</u>.

[10] WH changed the word or-der form <u>is</u> <u>well-pleasing</u> to *well-pleasing is*.

[11] WH changed **unto the** (*tO*) to *in* (*en*).

[12] WH changed <u>the</u> **God** (<u>ton</u> ~~th~~<u>eon</u>) to *the Lord* (*ton ku-rion*).

[13] WH omitted <u>and</u> <u>all</u> <u>which</u> (<u>kai</u> <u>pan</u> <u>ti</u>) and retained <u>what</u> (^h<u>o</u>) and <u>ever</u> (<u>ean</u>) from <u>and</u> <u>whatsoever</u> (<u>kai</u> <u>pan</u> ^h<u>o</u> <u>ti</u> <u>ean</u>).

Lord, and not unto men;

24 Knowing that of the Lord ye shall receive the reward of the inheritance: **for**[1] ye serve the Lord Christ.

25 **But**[2] he that doeth wrong shall receive for the wrong which he hath done: and there is no respect of persons.

CHAPTER 4

1 Masters, give unto *your* servants that which is just and equal; knowing that ye also have a Master in **heaven**[3].

2 Continue in prayer, and watch in the same with thanksgiving;

3 Withal praying also for us, that God would open unto us a door of utterance, to speak the mystery of Christ, for which I am also in bonds:

4 That I may make it manifest, as I ought to speak.

5 Walk in wisdom toward them that are without, redeeming the time.

6 Let your speech *be* al-way with grace, seasoned with salt, that ye may know how ye ought to answer every man.

7 All my state shall Tychicus declare unto you, *who is* a beloved brother, and a faithful minister and fellowservant in the Lord:

8 Whom I have sent unto you for the same purpose, that **he might know**[4] **your**[5] estate, and comfort your hearts;

9 With Onesimus, a faithful and beloved brother, who is *one* of you. They shall make known unto you all things which *are done* here.

10 Aristarchus my fellowprisoner saluteth you, and Marcus, sister's son to **Barnabas**[6], (touching whom

---

[1] WH omitted <u>for</u> (<u>gar</u>).

[2] WH changed **but** (*de*) to *for* (*gar*).

[3] WH changed <u>heavens</u> (<u>ouranois</u>) to *heaven* (*ouranO*). Dat Masc **Plur** to Dat Masc *Sing*. [number]

[4] WH change <u>I might know</u> (<u>gnO</u>) to *ye might know* (*gnOte*). Both Aor Act Sub. **1**[ˢᵗ] **Sing** to **2**[ⁿᵈ] **Plur**. [person & number]

[5] WH changed <u>the</u> concerning **you** {things} (<u>ta peri</u> [ʰ]<u>u-mOn</u>) to *the concerning us* {things} (*ta peri* [ʰ]*AmOn*). [person]

[6] WH changed <u>Barnabas</u> (<u>ba-rnaba</u>) to *Barnabas* (*ba-rnaba*). WH dropped the iota subscript from the spelling of the last letter in <u>barnaba</u>. [spell]

ye received commandments: if he come unto you, receive him;)

11 And Jesus, which is called Justus, who are of the circumcision. These only *are my* fellowworkers unto the kingdom of God, which have been a comfort unto me.

12 Epaphras, who is *one* of you, a servant of Christ [∧**Jesus**][1], saluteth you, always labouring fervently for you in prayers, that ye may stand perfect and **complete**[2] in all the will of God.

13 For I bear him record, that he hath a **great**[3] **zeal**[4] for you, and them *that are* in Laodicea, and them in Hierapolis.

14 Luke, the beloved physician, and Demas, greet you.

15 Salute the brethren which are in Laodicea, and Nymphas, and the church which is in **his**[5] house.

16 And when this epistle is read among you, cause that it be read also in the church of the Laodiceans; and that ye likewise read the *epistle* from Laodicea.

17 And say to Archippus, Take heed to the ministry which thou hast received in the Lord, that thou fulfil it.

18 The salutation by the hand of me Paul. Remember my bonds. Grace *be* with you. ~~**Amen**~~[6].

---

[1] WH added *Jesus* (*iAsou*).
[2] WH changed complete (*peplArOmenoi*) to *complete* (*peplAroforAmenoi*). Both Pf Pass Part Nom Masc Plur. plAroO to *plAroforeO*. [syn]
[3] WH changed the word order from GREAT **zeal** to *suffering* GREAT.
[4] WH changed **zeal** (**zAl**on) to *suffering* (*ponon*).

---

[5] WH changed of him (aut**ou**) to *of them* (*aut**On***) in the phrase the house of him. **Sing** to *Plur*. [number] In their margin, WH retained of him (aut**ou**).
[6] WH omitted Amen (amAn).

1 THESSALONIANS

CHAPTER 1

1 Paul, and Silvanus, and
Timotheus, unto the church
of the Thessalonians *which is*
in God the Father and *in* the
Lord Jesus Christ: Grace *be*
unto you, and peace, ~~**from
God our Father, and the
Lord Jesus Christ**~~[1].
2 We give thanks to God
always for you all, making
mention ~~**of you**~~[2] in our
prayers;
3 Remembering without
ceasing your work of faith,
and labour of love, and patience of hope in our Lord
Jesus Christ, in the sight of
God and our Father;
4 Knowing, brethren be-
loved, your election of God.
5 For our gospel came
not unto you in word only,
but also in power, and in the
Holy Ghost, and ~~**in**~~[3] much assurance; as ye know what
manner of men we were
~~**among**~~[4] you for your sake.
6 And ye became follow-
ers of us, and of the Lord,
having received the word in
much affliction, with joy of
the Holy Ghost:
7 So that ye were **en-
samples**[5] to all that believe in
Macedonia and **[^in]**[6]
Achaia.
8 For from you sounded
out the word of the Lord not
only in Macedonia and
Achaia, **but**[7] ~~**also**~~[8] in every
place your faith to God-ward
is spread abroad; so that **we**[9]
need not to speak any thing.
9 For they themselves
shew of us what manner of
entering in we had unto you,
and how ye turned to God
from idols to serve the living
and true God;
10 And to wait for his Son
from heaven, whom he raised

---

[1] WH omitted from God Father of us and Lord Jesus Christ (apo theou patros [h]AmOn kai kuriou iAsou cristou).

[2] WH omitted of you ([h]umOn).

[3] WH omitted in (en) and forced the dative case to supply the preposition.

[4] WH omitted among (en).

[5] WH changed examples (tupous) to ***an*** *example* (*tupon*). **Plur** to ***Sing***. [number]

[6] WH added *in* (*en*).

[7] WH changed but (alla) to *but* (*all'*).

[8] WH omitted also (kai)

[9] WH changed the word order from need US to have to *need to have US*

from ˄**the**[1] dead, *even* Jesus, which delivered us **from**[2] the wrath to come.

CHAPTER 2

1   For yourselves, brethren, know our entrance in unto you, that it was not in vain:

2   But ~~even~~[3] after that we had suffered before, and were shamefully entreated, as ye know, at Philippi, we were bold in our God to speak unto you the gospel of God with much contention.

3   For our exhortation *was* not of deceit, nor of uncleanness, **nor**[4] in guile:

4   But as we were allowed of God to be put in trust with the gospel, even so we speak; not as pleasing men, but **[the]**[5] God, which trieth our hearts.

5   For neither at any time used we flattering words, as ye know, nor a cloke of covetousness; God *is* witness:

6   Nor of men sought we glory, neither of you, nor *yet* of others, when we might have been burdensome, as the apostles of Christ.

7   But we were **gentle**[6] among you, even as a nurse cherisheth her children:

8   So **being affectionately desirous**[7] of you, we were willing to have imparted unto you, not the gospel of God only, but also our own souls, because **ye were**[8] dear unto us.

9   For ye remember, brethren, our labour and travail: ~~for~~[9] labouring night and day, because we would not be chargeable unto any of you, we preached unto you the gospel of God.

10   Ye *are* witnesses, and

---

[1] WH added *the* (*tOn*) as the KJV did.
[2] WH changed **from** (**apo**) to *out of* (**ek**).
[3] WH omitted even (kai).
[4] WH changed nor (oute) to nor (oude).
[5] WH omitted the untranslated the (tO).
[6] In their margin, WH changed **gentle** (Apioi) to *innocent* (nApios).
[7] WH changed being affectionately *desirous* (ʰimeiromenoi) *to being affectionately desirous* (ʰomeiromenoi). Both Pres Mid Part. [spell]
[8] WH changed ye **had been** (gegenAsͭͪͤe) to *ye were* (egenAͭͪͤAte). **Pf** Pass Ind to *Aor* Pass Ind. [tense]
[9] WH omitted for (gar).

God *also*, how holily and justly and unblameably we behaved ourselves among you that believe:

11 As ye know how we exhorted and comforted and **charged**[1] every one of you, as a father doth his children,

12 That **ye would walk**[2] worthy of God, who **hath called**[3] you unto his kingdom and glory.

13 [∧**and**][4] For this cause also thank we God without ceasing, because, when ye received the word of God which ye heard of us, ye received *it* not *as* the word of men, but as it is in truth, the word of God, which effectually worketh also in you that believe.

14 For ye, brethren, became followers of the churches of God which in Judaea are in Christ Jesus: for ye also have suffered **like things**[5] of your own countrymen, even as they *have* of the Jews:

15 Who both killed the Lord Jesus, and ~~their own~~[6] prophets, and have persecuted us; and they please not God, and are contrary to all men:

16 Forbidding us to speak to the Gentiles that they might be saved, to fill up their sins alway: for the wrath is come upon them to the uttermost.

17 But we, brethren, being taken from you for a short time in presence, not in heart, endeavoured the more abundantly to see your face with great desire.

18 **Wherefore**[7] we would have come unto you, even I Paul, once and again; but Satan hindered us.

19 For what *is* our hope, or joy, or crown of rejoicing?

---

[1] WH changed <u>charged</u> (<u>mar-turou</u>menoi) to *charged* (*marturomenoi*). Both Pres Mid Part. [spell]

[2] WH changed <u>to walk</u> (<u>peri-pat**Asi**</u>) to *to be walking* (*peripatein*). **Aor** Act Inf to *Pres* Act Inf. [tense]

[3] In their margin, WH changed <u>call**ing**</u> (<u>kalou</u>ntos) to *having called* (*kalesantos*). **Pres** Act Part to *Aor* Act Part. [tense]

[4] WH added *and* (*kai*).

[5] WH changed **these** {things} (tauta) to *the same* {things} (*ta auta*).

[6] WH omitted <u>their own</u> (<u>idi-ous</u>) from <u>the</u> <u>their own prophets</u>.

[7] WH changed <u>wherefore</u> (<u>dio</u>) to *wherefore* (*dioti*).

Are not even ye in the presence of our Lord Jesus ~~Christ~~[1] at his coming?

20 For ye are our glory and joy.

CHAPTER 3

1 Wherefore when we could no longer forbear, we thought it good to be left at Athens alone;

2 And sent Timotheus, our brother, and **minister**[2] of God, ~~and our fellowlabourer~~[3] in the gospel of Christ, to establish you, and to comfort ~~you~~[4] **concerning**[5] your faith:

3 **That**[6] no man should be moved by these afflictions: for yourselves know that we

---

[1] WH omitted Christ (cristou).

[2] In their margin, WH changed **server** (**diakon**on) to *fellow-worker* (*sunergon*).

[3] WH omitted and our fellow-labourer (kai sunergon [h]AmOn).

[4] WH omitted you ([h]umas).

[5] WH changed **concerning** (**peri**) to *for* ([h]*uper*).

[6] WH changed {**to**} the (t**O**) to *the* (*to*). **Dat Masc** Sing to *Acc Neut* Sing. [case & gender]

are appointed thereunto.

4 For verily, when we were with you, we told you before that we should suffer tribulation; even as it came to pass, and ye know.

5 For this cause, when I could no longer forbear, I sent to know your faith, lest by some means the tempter have tempted you, and our labour be in vain.

6 But now when Timotheus came from you unto us, and brought us good tidings of your faith and charity, and that ye have good remembrance of us always, desiring greatly to see us, as we also *to see* you:

7 Therefore, brethren, we were comforted over you in all our **affliction** and **distress**[7] by your faith:

8 For now we live, if ye stand fast in the Lord.

9 For what thanks can we render to God again for you, for all the joy wherewith we joy for your sakes before our God;

10 Night and day praying exceedingly that we might see your face, and might perfect that which is lacking in your faith?

---

[7] WH changed the word order from AFFLICTION and DISTRESS to *DISTRESS and AFFLICTION*.

11 Now God himself and our Father, and our Lord Jesus ~~Christ~~[1], direct our way unto you.

12 And the Lord make you to increase and abound in love one toward another, and toward all *men*, even as we *do* toward you:

13 To the end he may stablish your hearts unblameable in holiness before God, even our Father, at the coming of our Lord Jesus ~~Christ~~[2] with all his saints. [__Amen__][3]

CHAPTER 4

1 ~~Furthermore~~[4] then we beseech you, brethren, and exhort *you* by the Lord Jesus, ∧__that__[5] as ye have received of us how ye ought to walk and to please God, [∧__just as also ye walk__][6] *so* ye would abound more and more.

2 For ye know what commandments we gave you by the Lord Jesus.

3 For this is the will of God, *even* your sanctification, that ye should abstain from fornication:

4 That every one of you should know how to possess his vessel in sanctification and honour;

5 Not in the lust of concupiscence, even as the Gentiles which know not God:

6 That no *man* go beyond and defraud his brother in *any* matter: because that ~~the~~[7] Lord *is* the avenger of all such, as we also have forewarned you and testified.

7 For God hath not called us unto uncleanness, but unto holiness.

8 He therefore that despiseth, despiseth not man, but God, who __hath__ ~~also~~[8] __given__[9] unto __us__[10] his holy Spirit.

---

[1] WH omitted Christ (cris-tos).

[2] WH omitted Christ (cris-tou).

[3] In their margin, WH added *Amen* (*amAn*).

[4] WH omitted the (to) from the rest (to loipon).

[5] WH added *that* (*ʰina*) just as the KJV did.

[6] WH added *just as also ye walk* (*katʰOs kai peripateite*).

[7] WH omitted the (ʰo).

[8] WH omitted also (kai).

[9] WH changed __having__ given (donta) to *giving* (*didonta*). __Aor__ Act Part to *Pres* Act Part. [tense]

[10] WH changed __us__ (ʰAmas) to *you* (*ʰumas*). [person]

9   But as touching brotherly love ye need not that I write unto you: for ye yourselves are taught of God to love one another.

10   And indeed ye do it toward all the brethren which are in all Macedonia: but we beseech you, brethren, that ye increase more and more;

11   And that ye study to be quiet, and to do your own business, and to work with ~~your own~~[1] hands, as we commanded you;

12   That ye may walk honestly toward them that are without, and *that* ye may have lack of nothing.

13   But **I would** not **have**[2] you to be ignorant, brethren, concerning them **which are asleep**[3], that ye sorrow not, even as others which have no hope.

---

[1] WH omitted your own (*idiais*) from the your own hands.
[2] WH changed **I will** (~~the~~**O**) to *we will* (~~the~~*lomen*). Both Pres Act Ind. 1rst **Sing** to 1rst *Plur* (**we** will). [number]
[3] WH changed which **have been a**sleeep (*kekoimA-menOn*) to *which are sleeping* (*koimOmenOn*). **Pf Pass** Part to *Pres Mid* Part. [tense & voice]

14   For if we believe that Jesus died and rose again, even so them also which sleep in Jesus will God bring with him.

15   For this we say unto you by the word of the Lord, that we which are alive *and* remain unto the coming of the Lord shall not prevent them which are asleep.

16   For the Lord himself shall descend from heaven with a shout, with the voice of the archangel, and with the trump of God: and the dead in Christ shall rise first:

17   Then we which are alive *and* remain shall be caught up together with them in the clouds, to meet the Lord in the air: and so shall we ever be with the Lord.

18   Wherefore comfort one another with these words.

CHAPTER 5

1   But of the times and the seasons, brethren, ye have no need that I write unto you.

2   For yourselves know perfectly that **the**[4] day of the Lord so cometh as a thief in the night.

3   ~~For~~[5] when they shall

---

[4] WH omitted the ([h]A).
[5] WH omitted for (*gar*).

say, Peace and safety; then sudden destruction cometh upon them, as travail upon a woman with child; and they shall not escape.

4   But ye, brethren, are not in darkness, that that day should overtake you as <u>a</u> <u>thief</u>[1].

5   [∧for][2] Ye are all the children of light, and the children of the day: we are not of the night, nor of darkness.

6   Therefore let us not sleep, as [~~also~~][3] *do* others; but let us watch and be sober.

7   For they that sleep sleep in the night; and they that be drunken are drunken in the night.

8   But let us, who are of the day, be sober, putting on the breastplate of faith and love; and for an helmet, the hope of salvaion.

9   For God hath not appointed us to wrath, but to obtain salvation by our Lord Jesus Christ,

10   Who died for us, that,

whether we wake or sleep, we should live together with him.

11   Wherefore comfort yourselves together, and edify one another, even as also ye do.

12   And we beseech you, brethren, to know them which labour among you, and are over you in the Lord, and admonish you;

13   And to esteem them very highly in love for their work's sake. *And* be at peace among yourselves.

14   Now we exhort you, brethren, warn them that are unruly, comfort the feeble-minded, support the weak, be patient toward all *men*.

15   See that none render evil for evil unto any *man*; but ever follow that which is good, ~~both~~[4] among yourselves, and to all *men*.

16   Rejoice evermore.

17   Pray without ceasing.

18   In every thing give thanks: for this is the will of God in Christ Jesus concerning you.

19   Quench not the Spirit.

20   Despise not prophesyings.

21   [∧but][5]   Prove   all

---

[1] In their margin, WH changed <u>a thief</u> (<u>keptAs</u>) to *thieves* (*kleptas*). Nom Masc **Sing** to Nom Masc *Plur*. [number]

[2] WH added *for* (*gar*).

[3] WH omitted the untranslated <u>also</u> (<u>kai</u>).

[4] WH omitted <u>both</u> (<u>kai</u>).

[5] WH added *but* (*de*).

things; hold fast that which is good.

22 Abstain from all appearance of evil.

23 And the very God of peace sanctify you wholly; and *I pray God* your whole spirit and soul and body be preserved blameless unto the coming of our Lord Jesus Christ.

24 Faithful *is* he that calleth you, who also will do *it*.

25 Brethren, pray **[∧also]**[1] for us.

26 Greet all the brethren with an holy kiss.

27 **I charge**[2] you by the Lord that this epistle be read unto all the ~~holy~~[3] brethren.

28 The grace of our Lord Jesus Christ *be* with you. ~~Amen~~[4].

---

[1] WH added *also* (*kai*).
[2] WH changed I charge (ᵸorkizO) to *I charge* {**in**} (*enorkizO*). Both Pres Act Ind. [prefix added]
[3] WH omitted holy (ᵸagiois) in their text, but retained it in their margin.
[4] WH omitted Amen (amAn).

2 THESSALONIANS

CHAPTER 1

1   Paul, and Silvanus, and Timotheus, unto the church of the Thessalonians in God our Father and the Lord Jesus Christ:

2   Grace unto you, and peace, from God ~~our~~[1] Father and the Lord Jesus Christ.

3   We are bound to thank God always for you, brethren, as it is meet, because that your faith groweth exceedingly, and the charity of every one of you all toward each other aboundeth;

4   So that we ourselves **glory**[2] in you in the churches of God for your patience and faith in all your persecutions and tribulations that ye endure:

5   *Which is* a manifest token of the righteous judgment of God, that ye may be counted worthy of the kingdom of God, for which ye also suffer:

6   Seeing *it is* a righteous thing with God to recompense tribulation to them that trouble you;

7   And to you who are troubled rest with us, when the Lord Jesus shall be revealed from heaven with his mighty angels,

8   In flaming fire taking vengeance on them that know not God, and that obey not the gospel of our Lord Jesus ~~Christ~~[3]:

9   Who shall be punished with everlasting destruction from the presence of the Lord, and from the glory of his power;

10   When he shall come to be glorified in his saints, and to be admired in all them **that believe**[4] (because our testimony among you was believed) in that day.

11   Wherefore also we pray always for you, that our God would count you worthy of *this* calling, and fulfil all the good pleasure of *his* goodness, and the work of faith with power:

12   That the name of our Lord Jesus Christ may be

---

[1] WH omitted <u>our</u> (^hAmOn).
[2] WH changed <u>boast</u> (<u>kaucasthai</u>) to *boast out* (*egkaucasthai*). Both Pres Mid Inf. [prefix added]

[3] WH omitted <u>Christ</u> (<u>cristou</u>).
[4] WH changed <u>believing</u> (<u>pisteuousin</u>) to *having believed* (*pisteusasin*). **Pres** Act Part to *Aor* Act Part. [tense]

glorified in you, and ye in him, according to the grace of our God and the Lord Jesus ~~Christ~~[1].

CHAPTER 2

1   Now we beseech you, brethren, by the coming of our Lord Jesus Christ, and *by* our gathering together unto him,

2   That ye be not soon shaken in mind, **or**[2] be troubled, neither by spirit, nor by word, nor by letter as from us, as that the day of **Christ**[3] is at hand.

3   Let no man deceive you by any means: for *that day shall not come*, except there come a falling away first, and that man of **sin**[4] be revealed, the son of perdition;

4   Who opposeth and exalteth himself above **all**[5] **that**[6]

is called God, or that is worshipped; so that he ~~as God~~[7] sitteth in the temple of God, shewing himself that he is God.

5   Remember ye not, that, when I was yet with you, I told you these things?

6   And now ye know what withholdeth that he might be revealed in **his**[8] time.

7   For the mystery of iniquity doth already work: only he who now letteth *will let*, until he be taken out of the way.

8   And then shall that Wicked be revealed, whom the Lord [˄Jesus][9] **shall consume**[10] with the spirit of his mouth, and shall destroy with

---

[1] WH omitted Christ (cristou).

[2] WH changed or (mAte) to or (mAde). [syn]

[3] WH changed the **Christ** (tou **crisou**) to the **Lord** (tou **kuriou**).

[4] In their margin, WH changed sin (ʰamartias) to *lawlessness* (*anomias*).

[5] WH changed all (pan) to all {things} (panta). **Sing** to *Plur*. [number]

---

[6] WH omitted that (to) after all. WH, then, changed all **that** (pan **to**) to all {**things**} (*panta*).

[7] WH omitted as God (ʰOs theon).

[8] WH changed his {own} (ʰeautou) to his (autou). **Inten** pro to *Pers* pro.

[9] WH added *Jesus* (iasous) in their text, but not in their margin.

[10] WH changed shall consume (analOsei) to *shall consume* (anelei). Both Fut Act Ind. [syn] WH retained analOsei in their margin.

the brightness of his coming:

9 *Even him*, whose coming is after the working of Satan with all power and signs and lying wonders,

10 And with all deceivableness of [the][1] unrighteousness in[2] them that perish; because they received not the love of the truth, that they might be saved.

11 And for this cause God **shall send**[3] them strong delusion, that they should believe a lie:

12 That they all might be damned who believed not the truth, but had pleasure in[4] unrighteousness.

13 But we are bound to give thanks alway to God for you, brethren beloved of the Lord, because God hath **from the beginning**[5] chosen you

to salvation through sanctification of the Spirit and belief of the truth:

14 Whereunto he called you by our gospel, to the obtaining of the glory of our Lord Jesus Christ.

15 Therefore, brethren, stand fast, and hold the traditions which ye have been taught, whether by word, or our epistle.

16 Now our Lord Jesus Christ himself, and God, **even**[6] our Father, which hath loved us, and hath given *us* everlasting consolation and good hope through grace,

17 Comfort your hearts, and stablish ~~you~~[7] in every good **word** and **work**[8].

CHAPTER 3

1 Finally, brethren, pray for us, that the word of the Lord may have *free* course,

---

[1] WH omitted the untranslated the (tAs).

[2] WH omitted in (en) and forced the dative case to supply the preposition.

[3] WH changed **shall** send (pemŞei) to *is sending* (*pempei*). **Fut** Act Ind to *Pres* Act Ind. The letter **psi** to the letter *pi*. [tense]

[4] WH omitted in (en) and forced the dative case to supply the preposition.

[5] In their margin, WH

changed from beginning (ap' arcAs) to *from beginning* (*aparcAn*). **Gen** Fem Sing to *Acc* Fem Sing. **2** words to *1* word. [case]

[6] WH changed **even** (**kai**) to *the* ([h]*o*).

[7] WH omitted you ([h]umas).

[8] WH changed the word order from WORD and WORK to *WORK and WORD*.

and be glorified, even as *it is* with you:

2   And that we may be delivered from unreasonable and wicked men: for all *men* have not faith.

3   But the Lord is faithful, who shall stablish you, and keep *you* from evil.

4   And we have confidence in the Lord touching you, that ye both do and will do the things which we command **you**[1].

5   And the Lord direct your hearts into the love of God, and into the patient waiting for Christ.

6   Now we command you, brethren, in the name of our Lord Jesus Christ, that ye withdraw yourselves from every brother that walketh disorderly, and not after the tradition which **he received**[2] of us.

7   For yourselves know how ye ought to follow us: for we behaved not ourselves disorderly among you;

8   Neither did we eat any man's bread for nought; but wrought with labour and travail **night** and **day**[3], that we might not be chargeable to any of you:

9   Not because we have not power, but to make ourselves an ensample unto you to follow us.

10   For even when we were with you, this we commanded you, that if any would not work, neither should he eat.

11   For we hear that there are some which walk among you disorderly, working not at all, but are busybodies.

12   Now them that are such we command and exhort **by**[4]   ~~our~~[5]   **Lord   Jesus   Christ**[6], that with quietness they work, and eat their own bread.

13   But ye, brethren, **be**

---

[1] WH omitted you (ʰumin).

[2] WH changed **he received** (parelabe) to *they received* (*parelabosan*). Both Aor Act Ind. 3ʳᵈ **Sing** to 3ʳᵈ **Plur**. [number] (In their margin, WH had *parelabete.*)

[3] WH changed NIGHT and DAY to *DAY and NIGHT*.

[4] WH changed **by** (**dia**) to *in* (*en*).

[5] WH omitted the (tou) and of us (ʰAmOn) from the Lord of us.

[6] WH changed Lord Jesus Christ (kuriou iAsou cristou) to *Lord Jesus Christ* (*kuriO iAsou cristO*). **Dative** to *Genitive*. [case]

not **weary**[1] in well doing.

14 And if any man obey not our word by this epistle, note that man, **and**[2] **have** no **company with**[3] with him, that he may be ashamed.

15 Yet count *him* not as an enemy, but admonish *him* as a brother.

16 Now the Lord of peace himself give you peace always by all means. The Lord *be* with you all.

17 The salutation of Paul with mine own hand, which is the token in every epistle: so I write.

18 The grace of our Lord Jesus Christ *be* with you all. **Amen**[4].

---

[1] WH changed <u>might be weary</u> (<u>ekkakAsAte</u>) to *might be weary* (*egkakAsAte*). Both Aor Act Sub. [spell]

[2] WH omitted <u>and</u> (<u>kai</u>).

[3] WH changed <u>have company with</u> (<u>sunanamignusthe</u>) to *to have company with* (*sunanamignusthai*). Pres Mid **Imp** to Pres M/P *Inf.* [mood]

[4] WH omitted <u>Amen</u> (<u>amAn</u>).

1 TIMOTHY

CHAPTER 1

1　Paul, an apostle of Jesus ~~Christ~~[1] by the commandment of God our Saviour, and ~~Lord~~[2] **Jesus**[3] Christ, *which is* our hope;

2　Unto Timothy, *my* own son in the faith: Grace, mercy, *and* peace, from God ~~our~~[4] Father and Jesus Christ our Lord.

3　As I besought thee to abide still at Ephesus, when I went into Macedonia, that thou mightest charge some that they teach no other doctrine,

4　Neither give heed to fables and endless genealogies, which minister **questions**[5], rather than godly **edifying**[6] which is in faith: *so do.*

5　Now the end of the commandment is charity out of a pure heart, and *of* a good conscience, and *of* faith unfeigned:

6　From which some having swerved have turned aside unto vain jangling;

7　Desiring to be teachers of the law; understanding neither what they say, nor whereof they affirm.

8　But we know that the law *is* good, if a man use it lawfully;

9　Knowing this, that the law is not made for a righteous man, but for the lawless and disobedient, for the ungodly and for sinners, for unholy and profane, for murderers of fathers and murderers of mothers, for manslayers,

10　For whoremongers, for them that defile themselves with mankind, for menstealers, for liars, for perjured persons, and if there be any other thing that is contrary to sound doctrine;

11　According to the glorious gospel of the blessed God, which was committed to my trust.

---

[1] WH omitted <u>Christ</u> (<u>cristou</u>).

[2] WH omitted <u>Lord</u> (<u>kuriou</u>).

[3] WH changed the word order from <u>Jesus</u> Christ to *Christ Jesus*.

[4] WH omitted <u>our</u> (<u>[h]AmOn</u>— of us).

[5] WH changed <u>questions</u> (<u>zAtAseis</u>) to *questions* (***ekzAtAseis***). [prefix added]

[6] WH changed **edifying** (<u>oiko</u>domian—house **build-** ing) to *stewardship* (*oiko-nomian*—house **law**).

12 ~~And~~[1] I thank Christ Jesus our Lord, who **hath enabled**[2] me, for that he counted me faithful, putting me into the ministry;

13 Who was **[the]**[3] before a blasphemer, and a persecutor, and injurious: but I obtained mercy, because I did *it* ignorantly in unbelief.

14 And the grace of our Lord was exceeding abundant with faith and love which is in Christ Jesus.

15 This *is* a faithful saying, and worthy of all acceptation, that Christ Jesus came into the world to save sinners; of whom I am chief.

16 Howbeit for this cause I obtained mercy, that in me first Jesus Christ might shew forth **all**[4] longsuffering, for a pattern to them which should hereafter believe on him to life everlasting.

17 Now unto the King eternal, immortal, invisible, the only ~~wise~~[5] God, *be* honour and glory for ever and ever. Amen.

18 This charge I commit unto thee, son Timothy, according to the prophecies which went before on thee, that thou by them mightest war a good warfare;

19 Holding faith, and a good conscience; which some having put away concerning faith have made shipwreck:

20 Of whom is Hymenaeus and Alexander; whom I have delivered unto Satan, that they may learn not to blaspheme.

CHAPTER 2

1 I exhort therefore, that, first of all, supplications, prayers, intercessions, *and* giving of thanks, be made for all men;

2 For kings, and *for* all that are in authority; that we may lead a quiet and peaceable life in all godliness and honesty.

3 ~~For~~[6] this *is* good and acceptable in the sight of God our Saviour;

4 Who will have all men to be saved, and to come

---

[1] WH omitted <u>and</u> (<u>kai</u>).

[2] In their margin, WH changed **having** enable**d** (<u>endunamOsa</u>nti) to *enabling* (*endunamounti*). **Aor** Act Part to *Pres* Act Part. [tense]

[3] WH omitted the untranslated <u>the</u> (<u>ton</u>).

[4] WH changed <u>all</u> (<u>pasan</u>) to *all* (^h*apasan*). [prefix added]

[5] WH omitted <u>wise</u> (<u>sofO</u>).

[6] WH omitted <u>for</u> (<u>gar</u>).

unto the knowledge of the truth.

5   For *there is* one God, and one mediator between God and men, the man Christ Jesus;

6   Who gave himself a ransom for all, to be testified in due time.

7   Whereunto I am ordained a preacher, and an apostle, (I speak the truth ~~in Christ~~[1], *and* lie not;) a teacher of the Gentiles in faith and verity.

8   I will therefore that men pray every where, lifting up holy hands, without wrath and doubting.

9   In like manner ~~also, that~~[2] women adorn themselves in modest apparel, with shamefacedness and sobriety; not with broided hair, ~~or~~[3] **gold**[4], or pearls, or costly array;

10   But (which becometh women professing godliness) with good works.

11   Let the woman learn in silence with all subjection.

12   But I suffer not a woman **to teach**[5], nor to usurp authority over the man, but to be in silence.

13   For Adam was first formed, then Eve.

14   And Adam was not deceived, but the woman **being deceived**[6] was in the transgression.

15   Notwithstanding she shall be saved in childbearing, if they continue in faith and charity and holiness with sobriety.

CHAPTER 3

1   This *is* a true saying, If a man desire the office of a bishop, he desireth a good work.

2   A bishop then must be blameless, the husband of one

---

[1] WH omitted in Christ (en cristO).
[2] WH omitted also that (kai tas—also the).
[3] WH changed or (**A**) to *and* (*kai*).
[4] WH changed gold (crusO) to *gold* (*crusiO*). Dat **Masc** Sing from krusos to Dat *Neut* Sing from *krusion*. [gender & syn]

[5] WH changed the word order from but woman TO TEACH to *but TO TEACH woman*.
[6] WH changed having been led away (apatAtheisa) to *having been led away out* (*exapatA theisa*). Both Aor **Pass** Part Nom Fem Sing. [prefix added]

wife, vigilant, sober, of good behaviour, given to hospitality, apt to teach;

3   Not given to wine, no striker, ~~not greedy of filthy lucre~~[1]; but patient, not a brawler, not covetous;

4   One that ruleth well his own house, having his children in subjection with all gravity;

5   (For if a man know not how to rule his own house, how shall he take care of the church of God?)

6   Not a novice, lest being lifted up with pride he fall into the condemnation of the devil.

7   Moreover **he**[2] must have a good report of them which are without; lest he fall into reproach and the snare of the devil.

8   Likewise *must* the deacons *be* grave, not double-tongued, not given to much wine, not greedy of filthy lucre;

9   Holding the mystery of the faith in a pure conscience.

10 And let these also first be proved; then let them use the office of a deacon, being *found* blameless.

11 Even so *must their* wives *be* grave, not slanderers, sober, faithful in all things.

12 Let the deacons be the husbands of one wife, ruling their children and their own houses well.

13 For they that have used the office of a deacon well purchase to themselves a good degree, and great boldness in the faith which is in Christ Jesus.

14 These things write I unto thee, hoping to come unto thee **shortly**[3]:

15 But if I tarry long, that thou mayest know how thou oughtest to behave thyself in the house of God, which is the church of the living God, the pillar and ground of the truth.

16 And without controversy great is the mystery of godliness: **God**[4] was manifest

---

[1] WH omitted <u>not greedy of filthy lucre</u> (mA ais-crokerdA).

[2] WH omitted <u>he</u> (auton).

[3] WH changed **shortly** (ta<u>cion</u>) to *in haste* (en ta-cei). **Adverb** to *Prep + Noun*.

[4] WH changed **God** (<s>th</s>eos) to *who* (*[h]os*) in their text. In their margin, they had *the* {one} (*[h]o*) with the note that "<s>th</s>eos [God] rests on no sufficient ancient evidence."

in the flesh, justified in the Spirit, seen of angels, preached unto the Gentiles, believed on in the world, received up into glory.

CHAPTER 4

1   Now the Spirit speaketh expressly, that in the latter times some shall depart from the faith, giving heed to seducing spirits, and doctrines of devils;

2   Speaking lies in hypocrisy; having their conscience seared with a hot iron;

3   Forbidding to marry, *and commanding* to abstain from meats, which God hath created to be received with thanksgiving of them which believe and know the truth.

4   For every creature of God *is* good, and nothing to be refused, if it be received with thanksgiving:

5   For it is sanctified by the word of God and prayer.

6   If thou put the brethren in remembrance of these things, thou shalt be a good minister of **Jesus**[1] Christ, nourished up in the words of faith and of good doctrine,

whereunto thou hast attained.

7   But refuse profane and old wives' fables, and exercise thyself *rather* unto godliness.

8   For bodily exercise profiteth little: but godliness is profitable unto all things, having promise of the life that now is, and of that which is to come.

9   This *is* a faithful saying and worthy of all acceptation.

10 For therefore we ~~both~~[2] labour and **suffer reproach**[3], because we trust in the living God, who is the Saviour of all men, specially of those that believe.

11 These things command and teach.

12 Let no man despise thy youth; but be thou an example of the believers, in word, in conversation, in charity, ~~in spirit~~[4], in faith, in purity.

13 Till I come, give attendance to reading, to exhortation, to doctrine.

14 Neglect not the gift

---

[1] WH changed the word order from JESUS Christ to *Christ JESUS.*

[2] WH omitted <u>also</u> (<u>kai</u>).

[3] WH changed **suffer reproach** (**oneid**izome~~th~~a) to *strugggle* (*agOnizome~~th~~a*). Pres **Pass** Ind of **oneid**iz**O** to Pres *Mid* Ind of *agOnizomai.* [voice & verb]

[4] WH omitted <u>in</u> <u>spirit</u> (<u>en</u> <u>pneumati</u>).

that is in thee, which was given thee by prophecy, with the laying on of the hands of the presbytery.

15 Meditate upon these things; give thyself wholly to them; that thy profiting may appear **to**[1] all.

16 Take heed unto thyself, and unto the doctrine; continue in them: for in doing this thou shalt both save thyself, and them that hear thee.

CHAPTER 5

1 Rebuke not an elder, but intreat *him* as a father; *and* the younger men as brethren;

2 The elder women as mothers; the younger as sisters, with all purity.

3 Honour widows that are widows indeed.

4 But if any widow have children or nephews, let them learn first to shew piety at home, and to requite their parents: for that is **good and**[2] acceptable before God.

5 Now she that is a widow indeed, and desolate,

trusteth in **[the]**[3] God, and continueth in supplications and prayers night and day.

6 But she that liveth in pleasure is dead while she liveth.

7 And these things give in charge, that they may be blameless.

8 But if any provide not for his own, and specially for **those of his own**[4] house, he hath denied the faith, and is worse than an infidel.

9 Let not a widow be taken into the number under threescore years old, having been the wife of one man,

10 Well reported of for good works; if she have brought up children, if she have lodged strangers, if she have washed the saints' feet, if she have relieved the afflicted, if she have diligently followed every good work.

11 But the younger widows refuse: for when they have begun to wax wanton against Christ, they will marry;

---

[1] WH omitted to (en) and forced the dative case to supply the prepositon.
[2] WH omitted good and (kalon kai).

[3] WH omitted the untranslated the (ton).
[4] WH omitted those of his own (tOn) from those of his own house (tOn oikeiOn— the household or family members).

12 Having damnation, because they have cast off their first faith.

13 And withal they learn *to be* idle, wandering about from house to house; and not only idle, but tattlers also and busybodies, speaking things which they ought not.

14 I will therefore that the younger women marry, bear children, guide the house, give none occasion to the adversary to speak reproachfully.

15 For some are already turned aside after Satan.

16 If any man or woman [**faithful**] **that**[1] believeth have widows, let them relieve them, and let not the church be charged; that it may relieve them that are widows indeed.

17 Let the elders that rule well be counted worthy of double honour, especially they who labour in the word and doctrine.

18 For the scripture saith, Thou shalt not muzzle the ox that treadeth out the corn. And, The labourer *is* worthy of his reward.

19 Against an elder receive not an accusation, but before two or three witnesses.

20 Them that sin rebuke before all, that others also may fear.

21 I charge *thee* before God, and the ~~Lord~~[2] **Jesus**[3] Christ, and the elect angels, that thou observe these things without preferring one before another, doing nothing by partiality.

22 Lay hands suddenly on no man, neither be partaker of other men's sins: keep thyself pure.

23 Drink no longer water, but use a little wine for ~~thy~~[4] stomach's sake and thine often infirmities.

24 Some men's sins are open beforehand, going before to judgment; and some *men* they follow after.

25 Likewise also **the good**[5] [ʌ**the**][6] works *of some*

---

[2] WH omitted <u>Lord</u> (<u>kuriou</u>)

[3] WH changed the word order from <u>JESUS</u> <u>Christ</u> to *Christ JESUS*.

[4] WH omitted <u>of thee</u> (<u>sou</u>) from <u>the</u> <u>stomach</u> <u>of thee</u>.

[5] WH changed the word order from <u>THE</u> <u>GOOD</u> <u>works</u> to *the works THE GOOD*.

[6] WH added *the* (*ta*)

---

[1] WH omitted the untranslated <u>faithful</u> (<u>pistos</u>) & <u>the</u> (<u>A</u>).

~~are~~[1] manifest beforehand; and they that are otherwise cannot be hid.

CHAPTER 6

1   Let as many servants as are under the yoke count their own masters worthy of all honour, that the name of God and *his* doctrine be not blasphemed.

2   And they that have believing masters, let them not despise *them*, because they are brethren; but rather do *them* service, because they are faithful and beloved, partakers of the benefit. These things teach and exhort.

3   If any man teach otherwise, and consent not to wholesome words, *even* the words of our Lord Jesus Christ, and to the doctrine which is according to godliness;

4   He is proud, knowing nothing, but doting about questions and strifes of words, whereof cometh envy, strife, railings, evil surmisings,

5   **Perverse   disputings**[2]

of men of corrupt minds, and destitute of the truth, supposing that gain is godliness: ~~from such withdraw thyself~~[3].

6   But godliness with contentment is great gain.

7   For we brought nothing into *this* world, *and it is* ~~certain~~[4] we can carry nothing out.

8   And having food and raiment let us be therewith content.

9   But they that will be rich fall into temptation and a snare, and *into* many foolish and hurtful lusts, which drown men in destruction and perdition.

10   For the love of money is the root of all evil: which while some coveted after, they have erred from the faith, and pierced themselves through with many sorrows.

11   But thou, O man of [the][5] God, flee these things; and follow after righteousness,

---

added]
[3] WH omitted withdraw thyself from the such like (afistaso apo tOn toioutOn).
[4] WH omitted [and it is] certain (dAlon).
[5] WH omitted the untranslated the (tou).

---

[1] WH omitted are (esti).
[2] WH changed perverse disputings (**paradia**tribai) to *completely* pervese disputings (*diaparatribai*). [prefix

godliness, faith, love, patience, **meekness**[1].

12 Fight the good fight of faith, lay hold on eternal life, whereunto thou art ~~also~~[2] called, and hast professed a good profession before many witnesses.

13 I give thee charge in the sight of God, who **quickeneth**[3] all things, and *before* Christ Jesus, who before Pontius Pilate witnessed a good confession;

14 That thou keep *this* commandment without spot, unrebukeable, until the appearing of our Lord Jesus Christ:

15 Which in his times he shall shew, *who is* the blessed and only Potentate, the King of kings, and Lord of lords;

16 Who only hath immortality, dwelling in the light which no man can approach unto; whom no man hath seen, nor can see: to whom *be* honour and power ever-

lasting. Amen.

17 Charge them that are rich in this world, that they be not highminded, nor trust in uncertain riches, but **in**[4] ~~the~~[5] ~~living~~[6] God, who giveth us **richly**[7] all things to enjoy;

18 That they do good, that they be rich in good works, ready to distribute, willing to communicate;

19 Laying up in store for themselves a good foundation against the time to come, that they may lay hold on **eternal**[8] life.

20 O Timothy, keep that **which is committed to**[9] thy trust, avoiding profane *and* vain babblings, and oppositions of science falsely so called:

---

[1] WH changed meekness (pra**ot**A**ta**) to *meekness* (*praupa**th**eian*). [syn]
[2] WH omitted also (kai).
[3] WH changed quickeneth (z**Oo**poiountos) to *quickenth* (*z**Oo**gonountos*). Both Pres Act Part. z**Oo**-**poie**O to *z**Oo**-goneO*. [syn]

[4] WH changed **in** (en) to *on* (*epi*).
[5] WH omitted the (t**O**).
[6] WH omitted the living (t**O** z**O**nti).
[7] WH changed the word order from RICHLY all {things} to *all* {things} *RICHLY*.
[8] WH changed **eternal** (**aiOniou**) to *real* (*ontOs*).
[9] WH changed which is committed to (para-kata**th**AkAn) to *which is committed to* (*para**th**AkAn*). Both noun Acc Fem Sing. [prefix dropped]

21 Which some professing
have erred concerning the
faith. Grace *be* **with thee**[1].
~~**Amen**~~[2].

---

[1] WH changed <u>with</u> **thee**
(<u>me</u>**ta** <u>**sou**</u>) to *with you*
(*me* ~~*th*~~*'* *ⁿumOn*). **Sing** to
Plur. [number]
[2] WH omitted <u>Amen</u> (<u>amAn</u>).

2 TIMOTHY

CHAPTER 1

1   Paul, an apostle of **Je-sus**[1] Christ by the will of God, according to the promise of life which is in Christ Jesus,

2   To Timothy, *my* dearly beloved son: Grace, mercy, *and* peace, from God the Father and Christ Jesus our Lord.

3   I thank God, whom I serve from *my* forefathers with pure conscience, that without ceasing I have remembrance of thee in my prayers night and day;

4   Greatly desiring to see thee, being mindful of thy tears, that I may be filled with joy;

5   **When I call**[2] to remembrance the unfeigned faith that is in thee, which dwelt first in thy grandmother Lois, and thy mother Eunice; and I am persuaded that in thee also.

6   Wherefore I put thee in remembrance that thou stir up the gift of God, which is in thee by the putting on of my hands.

7   For God hath not given us the spirit of fear; but of power, and of love, and of a sound mind.

8   Be not thou therefore ashamed of the testimony of our Lord, nor of me his prisoner: but be thou partaker of the afflictions of the gospel according to the power of God;

9   Who hath saved us, and called *us* with an holy calling, not according to our works, but according to his own purpose and grace, which was given us in Christ Jesus before the world began,

10   But is now made manifest by the appearing of our Saviour **Jesus**[3] Christ, who hath abolished death, and hath brought life and immortality to light through the gospel:

11   Whereunto I am appointed a preacher, and an apostle, and a teacher ~~of the Gentiles~~[4].

---

[1] WH changed the word order from J̲E̲S̲U̲S̲ Christ to *Christ J̲E̲S̲U̲S̲*

[2] WH changed **call**ing (lam-banOn) to *having called* (*la-bOn*). **Pres** Act Part to *Aor* Act Part. [tense]

[3] WH changed the word order from J̲E̲S̲U̲S̲ Christ to *Christ J̲E̲S̲U̲S̲.*

[4] WH omitted of nations (ethnOn).

12 For the which cause I also suffer these things: nevertheless I am not ashamed: for I know whom I have believed, and am persuaded that he is able to keep that which I have committed unto him against that day.

13 Hold fast the form of sound words, which thou hast heard of me, in faith and love which is in Christ Jesus.

14 That good thing **which was committed**[1] unto thee keep by the Holy Ghost which dwelleth in us.

15 This thou knowest, that all they which are in Asia be turned away from me; of whom are **Phygellus**[2] and Hermogenes.

16 The Lord give mercy unto the house of Onesiphorus; for he oft refreshed me, and was not ashamed of my chain:

17 But, when he was in Rome, he sought me out **very diligently**[3], and found *me*.

18 The Lord grant unto him that he may find mercy of the Lord in that day: and in how many things he ministered unto me at Ephesus, thou knowest very well.

CHAPTER 2

1 Thou therefore, my son, be strong in the grace that is in Christ Jesus.

2 And the things that thou hast heard of me among many witnesses, the same commit thou to faithful men, who shall be able to teach others also.

3 ~~Thou therefore~~[4] **endure hardness**[5], as a good soldier of **Jesus**[6] Christ.

4 No man that warreth entangleth himself with the affairs of *this* life; that he may please him who hath chosen him to be a soldier.

---

[1] WH changed which was committed **down** (para-kata**th**AkAn) to *which was committed* (*para**th**AkAn*). [prefix dropped]
[2] WH changed fugellos (fugellos) to *fugelos* (*fuge-los*). [spell]
[3] WH changed **more** earnest

[4] WH omitted thou therefore (ou oun).
[5] WH changed endure hardness (kakopath**Ason**) to *endure hardness **together*** (*sugkakopath**Ason***). Both Aor Act Imp. [prefix added]
[6] WH changed the word order from JESUS Christ to *Christ JESUS*.

5　And if a man also strive for masteries, *yet* is he not crowned, except he strive lawfully.

6　The husbandman that laboureth must be first partaker of the fruits.

7　Consider **what**[1] I say; and the Lord **give**[2] thee understanding in all things.

8　Remember that Jesus Christ of the seed of David was raised from the dead according to my gospel:

9　Wherein I suffer trouble, as an evil doer, *even* unto bonds; but the word of God is not bound.

10　Therefore I endure all things for the elect's sakes, that they may also obtain the salvation which is in Christ Jesus with eternal glory.

11　*It is* a faithful saying: For if we be dead with *him*, we shall also live with *him*:

12　If we suffer, we shall also reign with *him*: if **we deny**[3] *him*, he also will deny us:

13　If we believe not, *yet* he abideth faithful: [**ʌfor**][4] he cannot deny himself.

14　Of these things put *them* in remembrance, charging *them* before the **Lord**[5] that they strive not about words **to**[6] no profit, *but* to the subverting of the hearers.

15　Study to shew thyself approved unto God, a workman that needeth not to be ashamed, rightly dividing the word of truth.

16　But shun profane *and* vain babblings: for they will increase unto more ungodliness.

17　And their word will eat as doth a canker: of whom is Hymenaeus and Philetus;

18　Who concerning the truth have erred, saying that **the**[7] resurrection is past already; and overthrow the faith of some.

19　Nevertheless the foundation of God standeth

---

[1] WH changed <u>what</u> (^h**A**) to *what* (^h*o*).
[2] WH changed **should** give (d**OA**) to *will* give (*dOsei*). **Aor** Act **Opt** to *Fut* Act *Ind*. [tense & mood]
[3] WH changed <u>we deny</u> (ar-noumetha) to *we will deny* (*arnAsometha*). **Pres** M/P

Ind to *Fut* Mid Ind. [tense]
[4] WH added <u>for</u> (<u>gar</u>).
[5] In their margin, WH changed **Lord** (**kuri**ou) to *God* (*theou*).
[6] WH changed **into** (**eis**) to *upon* (*ep'*).
[7] In their margin, WH omitted <u>the</u> (t**An**).

623

sure, having this seal, The Lord knoweth them that are his. And, Let every one that nameth the name of **Christ**[1] depart from iniquity.

20 But in a great house there are not only vessels of gold and of silver, but also of wood and of earth; and some to honour, and some to dishonour.

21 If a man therefore purge himself from these, he shall be a vessel unto honour, sanctified, ~~and~~[2] meet for the master's use, *and* prepared unto every good work.

22 Flee also youthful lusts: but follow righteousness, faith, charity, peace, with them that call on the Lord out of a pure heart.

23 But foolish and unlearned questions avoid, knowing that they do gender strifes.

24 And the servant of the Lord must not strive; but be gentle unto all *men*, apt to teach, patient,

25 In meekness instructing those that oppose themselves; if God peradventure **will give**[3] them repentance to the acknowledging of the truth;

26 And *that* they may recover themselves out of the snare of the devil, who are taken captive by him at his will.

CHAPTER 3

1 This know also, that in the last days perilous times shall come.

2 For men shall be lovers of their own selves, covetous, boasters, proud, blasphemers, disobedient to parents, unthankful, unholy,

3 Without natural affection, trucebreakers, false accusers, incontinent, fierce, despisers of those that are good,

4 Traitors, heady, highminded, lovers of pleasures more than lovers of God;

5 Having a form of godliness, but denying the power thereof: from such turn away.

6 For of this sort are they which creep into houses, and **lead captive**[4] [~~the~~][5] silly

---

[1] WH changed **Christ** (**cristou**) to *Lord* (*kuriou*).
[2] WH omitted <u>and</u> (<u>kai</u>).
[3] WH changed **might** give (<u>dO</u>) to **should** *give* (*dOA*). Aor Act **Sub** to Aor Act *Opt*.

[mood]
[4] WH changed <u>leading captive</u> (<u>aicmalOteuontes</u>) to *leading captive* (*aicmalOtizontes*). Both Pres Act Part. <u>AicmalOteuO</u> to *aicmalOtizO*. [syn]
[5] WH omitted the untranslated <u>the</u> (<u>ta</u>).

women laden with sins, led away with divers lusts,

7 Ever learning, and never able to come to the knowledge of the truth.

8 Now as Jannes and Jambres withstood Moses, so do these also resist the truth: men of corrupt minds, reprobate concerning the faith.

9 But they shall proceed no further: for their folly shall be manifest unto all *men*, as theirs also was.

10 But thou **hast fully known**[1] my doctrine, manner of life, purpose, faith, longsuffering, charity, patience,

11 Persecutions, afflictions, which came unto me at Antioch, at Iconium, at Lystra; what persecutions I endured: but out of *them* all the Lord delivered me.

12 Yea, and all that will live godly in Christ Jesus shall suffer persecution.

13 But evil men and seducers shall wax worse and worse, deceiving, and being deceived.

14 But continue thou in the things which thou hast learned and hast been assured of, knowing of **whom**[2] thou hast learned *them*;

15 And that from a child thou hast known **the**[3] holy scriptures, which are able to make thee wise unto salvation through faith which is in Christ Jesus.

16 All scripture *is* given by inspiration of God, and *is* profitable for doctrine, for **reproof**[4], for correction, for instruction in righteousness:

17 That the man of God may be perfect, throughly furnished unto all good works.

CHAPTER 4

1 I charge *thee* [~~myself~~][5]

---

[1] WH changed {you^s} **have fully known** (parAko-louth Akas) to {you^s} *fully knew* (parAkolouth Asas). **Pf** Act Ind to *Aor* Act Ind. [tense]

[2] WH changed whom (tinos) to *whom* (tin**On**). Gen Masc **Sing** to Gen Masc *Plur*. [number]

[3] WH omitted the (ta).

[4] WH changed reproof (eleg-con) to *reproof* (elegmon). Both Acc Masc Sing. Verification, certainty to *refutation of error*.

[5] WH omitted the untranslated intensive myself (egO).

~~**therefore**~~[1] before God, and the Lord **Jesus**[2] Christ, who shall judge the quick and the dead **at**[3] his appearing and his kingdom;

2   Preach the word; be instant in season, out of season; reprove, rebuke, exhort with all longsuffering and doctrine.

3   For the time will come when they will not endure sound doctrine; but after their own lusts shall they heap to themselves teachers, having itching ears;

4   And they shall turn away *their* ears from the truth, and shall be turned unto fables.

5   But watch thou in all things, endure afflictions, do the work of an evangelist, make full proof of thy ministry.

6   For I am now ready to be offered, and the time of my departure is at hand.

7   I have fought a good fight, I have finished *my* course, I have kept the faith:

8   Henceforth there is laid up for me a crown of right-eousness, which the Lord, the righteous judge, shall give me at that day: and not to me only, but unto all them also that love his appearing.

9   Do thy diligence to come shortly unto me:

10   For Demas hath forsaken me, having loved this present world, and is departed unto Thessalonica; Crescens to Galatia, Titus unto Dalmatia.

11   Only Luke is with me. Take Mark, and bring him with thee: for he is profitable to me for the ministry.

12   And Tychicus have I sent to Ephesus.

13   The cloke that I left at Troas with Carpus, when thou comest, bring *with thee*, and the books, *but* especially the parchments.

14   Alexander the coppersmith did me much evil: the Lord **reward**[4] him according to his works:

15   Of whom be thou ware also; for **he hath** greatly **withstood**[5] our words.

---

[1] WH omitted therefore (oun).

[2] WH changed the word order from JESUS Christ to *Christ **Jesus***.

[3] WH changed **at** (kata) to *and* (*kai*).

[4] WH changed **should** reward (**apodOA**) to *will reward* (*apodOsei*). **Aor** Act **Opt** to *Fut* Act *Ind*. [tense & mood]

[5] WH changed he **has** withstood (ant̲h̲estAke) to *he withstood* (*antestA*). **Pf** Act Ind to *Aor* Act Ind. [tense]

16 At my first answer no man **stood with**[1] me, but all _men_ forsook me: _I_ pray _God_ that it may not be laid to their charge.

17 Notwithstanding the Lord stood with me, and strengthened me; that by me the preaching might be fully known, and _that_ all the Gentiles might hear: and I was delivered out of the mouth of the lion.

18 ~~And~~[2] the Lord shall deliver me from every evil work, and will preserve _me_ unto his heavenly kingdom: to whom _be_ glory for ever and ever. Amen.

19 Salute Prisca and Aquila, and the household of Onesiphorus.

20 Erastus abode at Corinth: but Trophimus have I left at Miletum sick.

21 Do thy diligence to come before winter. Eubulus greeteth thee, and Pudens, and Linus, and Claudia, and all the brethren.

22 The Lord ~~Jesus Christ~~[3] _be_ with thy spirit.

Grace _be_ with you. ~~Amen~~[4].

---

[1] WH changed <u>stood **with**</u> (**sum**<u>paregeneto</u>) to _stood_ (_paregeneto_). Both Aor Mid Ind. [prefix dropped]

[2] WH omitted <u>and</u> (<u>kai</u>).

[3] WH omitted <u>Jesus Christ</u> (<u>iAsous</u> <u>cristos</u>).

[4] WH omitted <u>Amen</u> (<u>amAn</u>).

TITUS

CHAPTER 1

1   Paul, a servant of God, and an apostle of Jesus Christ, according to the faith of God's elect, and the acknowledging of the truth which is after godliness;

2   In hope of eternal life, which God, that cannot lie, promised before the world began;

3   But hath in due times manifested his word through preaching, which is committed unto me according to the commandment of God our Saviour;

4   To Titus, *mine* own son after the common faith: Grace, ~~mercy~~[1], ∧*and*[2] peace, from God the Father and the ~~Lord~~[3] **Jesus**[4] Christ our Saviour.

5   For this cause **left I**[5]

---

[1] WH omitted <u>mercy</u> (<u>eleos</u>).
[2] WH added *and* (*kai*) as the KJV supplied it.
[3] WH omitted <u>Lord</u> (<u>kuriou</u>).
[4] WH changed the word order from Jesus <u>Christ</u> to *Christ Jesus.*
[5] WH changed <u>I left</u> **down** (**kat**<u>elipon</u>) to *I left from* (*apelipon*). Both Aor Act Ind. [prefix changed]

thee in Crete, that thou shouldest set in order the things that are wanting, and ordain elders in every city, as I had appointed thee:

6   If any be blameless, the husband of one wife, having faithful children not accused of riot or unruly.

7   For a bishop must be blameless, as the steward of God; not selfwilled, not soon angry, not given to wine, no striker, not given to filthy lucre;

8   But a lover of hospitality, a lover of good men, sober, just, holy, temperate;

9   Holding fast the faithful word as he hath been taught, that he may be able by sound doctrine both to exhort and to convince the gainsayers.

10   For there are many **[and]**[6] unruly and vain talkers and deceivers, specially they of the circumcision:

11   Whose mouths must be stopped, who subvert whole houses, teaching things which they ought not, for filthy lucre's sake.

12   One of themselves, *even* a prophet of their own, said, The Cretians *are* alway liars, evil beasts, slow bellies.

---

[6] WH omitted the untranslated <u>and</u> (<u>kai</u>).

13 This witness is true. Wherefore rebuke them sharply, that they may be sound in the faith;

14 Not giving heed to Jewish fables, and commandments of men, that turn from the truth.

15 Unto the pure all things [~~then~~][1] _are_ pure: but unto them that are defiled and unbelieving _is_ nothing pure; but even their mind and conscience is defiled.

16 They profess that they know God; but in works they deny _him_, being abominable, and disobedient, and unto every good work reprobate.

CHAPTER 2

1 But speak thou the things which become sound doctrine:

2 That the aged men be sober, grave, temperate, sound in faith, in charity, in patience.

3 The aged women likewise, that _they be_ in behaviour as becometh holiness, not false accusers, **not**[2] given to much wine, teachers of good things;

4 That they may teach the young women to be sober, to love their husbands, to love their children,

5 _To be_ discreet, chaste, **keepers at home**[3], good, obedient to their own husbands, that the word of God be not blasphemed.

6 Young men likewise exhort to be sober minded.

7 In all things shewing thyself a pattern of good works: in doctrine _shewing_ **uncorruptness**[4], gravity, ~~sincerity~~[5],

8 Sound speech, that cannot be condemned; that he that is of the contrary part may be ashamed, having no evil thing **to say**[6] of you.

9 _Exhort_ servants to be obedient unto their own masters, _and_ to please _them_ well

---

[1] WH omitted the untranslated then (men).

[2] WH changed not (mA) to **and** _not_ (mAde).

[3] WH changed **keep**ers at home (oikourous) to **workers** _at home_ (oikourgous).

[4] WH changed uncorruptness (**adia**fthorian—**completely** without corruption) to _uncorruptness_ (afthorian—without corruption). [prefix dropped]

[5] WH omitted sincerity (aftharsian).

[6] WH changed the word order from of you TO SAY to _TO SAY of you._

in all *things*; not answering again;

10 Not purloining, but shewing **all**[1] good fidelity; that they may adorn the doctrine [∧**the**][2] of God our Saviour in all things.

11 For the grace of God **that**[3] bringeth salvation hath appeared to all men,

12 Teaching us that, denying ungodliness and worldly lusts, we should live soberly, righteously, and godly, in this present world;

13 Looking for that blessed hope, and the glorious appearing of the great God and our Saviour Jesus Christ;

14 Who gave himself for us, that he might redeem us from all iniquity, and purify unto himself a peculiar people, zealous of good works.

15 These things speak, and exhort, and rebuke with all authority. Let no man despise thee.

CHAPTER 3

1 Put them in mind to be subject to principalities **and**[4] powers, to obey magistrates, to be ready to every good work,

2 To speak evil of no man, to be no brawlers, *but* gentle, shewing all meekness unto all men.

3 For we ourselves also were sometimes foolish, disobedient, deceived, serving divers lusts and pleasures, living in malice and envy, hateful, *and* hating one another.

4 But after that the kindness and love of God our Saviour toward man appeared,

5 Not by works of righteousness **which**[5] we have done, but according to [**the**][6] his **mercy**[7] he saved us, by the washing of regeneration, and renewing of the Holy Ghost;

6 Which he shed on us

---

[1] WH changed the word order from faith ALL showing to *ALL faith showing.*
[2] WH added *the* (*tAn*).
[3] WH omitted that (*ʰA*).

[4] WH omitted and (kai).
[5] WH changed which (*ʰOn*) to *which* (*ʰA*). **Gen** Neut Plur. to *Acc* Neut Plur. [case]
[6] WH changed the untranslated the (ton) to *the* (*to*). Acc **Masc** Sing to Acc *Neut* Sing. [gender]
[7] WH changed mercy (eleon) to *mercy* (**eleos**). Acc **Masc** Sing to Acc *Neut* Sing. [gender]

abundantly through Jesus Christ our Saviour;

7   That being justified by his grace, **we should be made**[1] heirs according to the hope of eternal life.

8   *This is* a faithful saying, and these things I will that thou affirm constantly, that they which have believed in [**the**][2] God might be careful to maintain good works. These things are [**the**][3] good and profitable unto men.

9   But avoid foolish questions, and genealogies, and contentions, and strivings about the law; for they are unprofitable and vain.

10   A man that is an heretick after the first and second admonition reject;

11   Knowing that he that is such is subverted, and sinneth, being condemned of himself.

12   When I shall send Artemas unto thee, or Tychicus, be diligent to come unto me to Nicopolis: for I have determined there to winter.

13   Bring Zenas the lawyer and Apollos on their journey diligently, that nothing be wanting unto them.

14   And let ours also learn to maintain good works for necessary uses, that they be not unfruitful.

15   All that are with me salute thee. Greet them that love us in the faith. Grace *be* with you all. **Amen**[4].

---

[1] WH changed we **might** be made (genOmetha) to *we may* be made (genAthOmen). Aor M/P Sub to Aor Pass Sub.

[2] WH omitted the untranslated the (tO).

[3] WH omitted the untranslated the (ta).

---

[4] WH omitted Amen (amAn).

PHILEMON

CHAPTER 1

1   Paul, a prisoner of Jesus Christ, and Timothy *our* brother, unto Philemon our **dearly beloved**[1], and fellow-labourer,

2   And to *our* beloved Apphia, and Archippus our fellowsoldier, and to the church in thy house:

3   Grace to you, and peace, from God our Father and the Lord Jesus Christ.

4   I thank my God, making mention of thee always in my prayers,

5   Hearing of thy love and faith, which thou hast toward the Lord Jesus, and toward all saints;

6   That the communication of thy faith may become effectual by the acknowledging of every good thing which is in **you**[2] in Christ ~~Jesus~~[3].

7   For **we have**[4] **great**[5]

joy and consolation in thy love, because the bowels of the saints are refreshed by thee, brother.

8   Wherefore, though I might be much bold in Christ to enjoin thee that which is convenient,

9   Yet for love's sake I rather beseech *thee*, being such an one as Paul the aged, and now also a prisoner of **Jesus**[6] Christ.

10   I beseech thee for my son Onesimus, whom I have begotten in ~~my~~[7] bonds:

11   Which in time past was to thee unprofitable, but now profitable to thee and to me:

12   Whom I have sent again: **thou**[8] ~~therefore~~[9] ~~receive~~[10] him, that is, mine own

---

Pres Act Ind 1[rst] **Plur** to *Aor* Act Ind 1[rst] *Sing*. [tense & number]

[5] WH changed the word order from **we have** GREAT to GREAT *I had*.

[6] WH changed the word order from JESUS Christ to *Christ JESUS*.

[7] WH omitted of me (mou) from the bonds of me.

[8] WH changed thou (su) to *thou* (*soi*). **Nom** Sing to *Dat* Sing. [case]

[9] WH omitted therefore (de).

[10] WH omitted receive (proslabou).

---

[1] WH changed **dearly beloved** (**agapAtA**) to *sister* (*adelfA*).

[2] WH changed you ([h]umin) to *us* (*[h]Amin*). [person]

[3] WH omitted Jesus (iasoun).

[4] WH changed **we have** (ecomen) to *I had*. (*escon*).

632

bowels:

13 Whom I would have re-
tained with me, that in thy
stead he might have ministered **unto me**[1] in the bonds
of the gospel:

14 But without thy mind
would I do nothing; that thy
benefit should not be as it were
of necessity, but willingly.

15 For perhaps he there-
fore departed for a season,
that thou shouldest receive
him for ever;

16 Not now as a servant,
but above a servant, a brother
beloved, specially to me, but
how much more unto thee,
both in the flesh, and in the
Lord?

17 If thou count **me**[2]
therefore a partner, receive
him as myself.

18 If he hath wronged
thee, or oweth *thee* ought,
put that **on mine account**[3];

19 I Paul have written *it*
with mine own hand, I will
repay *it*: albeit I do not say to
thee how thou owest unto me
even thine own self besides.

20 Yea, brother, let me
have joy of thee in the Lord:
refresh my bowels in **the
Lord**[4].

21 Having confidence in
thy obedience I wrote unto
thee, knowing that thou wilt
also do more **than**[5] I say.

22 But withal prepare me
also a lodging: for I trust that
through your prayers I shall
be given unto you.

23 There **salute**[6] thee
Epaphras, my fellowprisoner
in Christ Jesus;

24 Marcus, Aristarchus,
Demas, Lucas, my fellowlabourers.

25 The grace of **our**[7] Lord
Jesus Christ *be* with your
spirit. **Amen**[8].

---

[1] WH changed the word order from he might have ministered UNTO ME to *UNTO ME
he might have ministered.*

[2] WH changed me (**eme**) to
me (*me*). Both Acc Sing.
[spell]

[3] WH changed put on mine
account (ellog**ei**) to *put on
mine account* (*elloga*). Both
Pres Act Imp. [spell]

[4] WH changed **the Lord** (**kuriO**) to *Christ* (*cristO*).

[5] WH changed than (*[h]o*) to
than (*[h]a*). Acc Neut **Sing** to
Acc Neut *Plur*. [number]

[6] WH changed salute {**ye**}
(aspaz**on**tai) to *salute* {**thou**}
(*aspazetai*). Pres M/P Ind 3rd
Plur to Pres Mid Ind 3rd
Sing. [number]

[7] In their margin, WH omitted of us ([h]AmOn) from the
Lord of us.

[8] In their margin, WH omitted Amen (amAn).

HEBREWS

CHAPTER 1

1   God, who at sundry times and in divers manners spake in time past unto the fathers by the prophets,

2   Hath in **these last days**[1] spoken unto us by *his* Son, whom he hath appointed heir of all things, by whom also **he made**[2] the worlds;

3   Who being the brightness of *his* glory, and the express image of his person, and upholding all things by the word of his power, ~~when he had~~[3] ~~by himself~~[4] purged ~~our~~[5] sins, sat down on the right hand of the Majesty on high;

4   Being made so much better than the angels, as he hath by inheritance obtained a more excellent name than they.

5   For unto which of the angels said he at any time, Thou art my Son, this day have I begotten thee? And again, I will be to him a Father, and he shall be to me a Son?

6   And again, when he bringeth in the firstbegotten into the world, he saith, And let all the angels of God worship him.

7   And of the angels he saith, Who maketh his angels spirits, and his ministers a flame of fire.

8   But unto the Son *he saith*, Thy throne, O God, *is* for ever and ever: [ᴧ**and the**][6] a sceptre [ᴧ**the**][7] of righteousness *is* ~~**the**~~[8] sceptre of **thy**[9] kingdom.

9   Thou hast loved righteousness, and hated iniquity; therefore God, *even* thy God,

---

[1] WH changed <u>these last days</u> (escat**On**) to *this last day* (*escatou*). Gen **Fem Plur** to Gen *Neut Sing*. [gender & number]

[2] WH changed the word order from <u>the ages</u> ʜᴇ ᴍᴀᴅᴇ to *ʜᴇ ᴍᴀᴅᴇ the ages*.

[3] WH omitted <u>when he had</u> (<u>poiAsamenos</u>).

[4] WH omitted <u>by himself</u> (di' ʰeautou).

[5] WH omitted <u>of us</u> (ʰAmOn) from <u>the sins of us</u>.

[6] WH added *and the* (kai ʰA) to read *and the* <u>sceptre</u>.

[7] WH added *the* (tAn) to read *and the* <u>sceptre</u> *the* {one} <u>of righteousness</u>.

[8] WH omitted <u>the</u> (ʰA).

[9] In their margin, WH changed <u>of **thine**</u> (<u>sou</u>) to *of him* (*autou*) in the phrase <u>the kingdom of thine</u>. [person]

hath anointed thee with the oil of gladness above thy fellows.

10 And, Thou, Lord, in the beginning hast laid the foundation of the earth; and the heavens are the works of thine hands:

11 They shall perish; but thou remainest; and they all shall wax old as doth a garment;

12 And as a vesture shalt thou fold them up [ʌ**as a garment]**[1], and they shall be changed: but thou art the same, and thy years shall not fail.

13 But to which of the angels said he at any time, Sit on my right hand, until I make thine enemies thy footstool?

14 Are they not all ministering spirits, sent forth to minister for them who shall be heirs of salvation?

CHAPTER 2

1 Therefore **we**[2] ought to give the more earnest heed to the things which we have

heard, lest at any time we should let _them_ slip.

2 For if the word spoken by angels was stedfast, and every transgression and disobedience received a just recompence of reward;

3 How shall we escape, if we neglect so great salvation; which at the first began to be spoken by the Lord, and was confirmed unto us by them that heard _him_;

4 God also bearing _them_ witness, both with signs and wonders, and with divers miracles, and gifts of the Holy Ghost, according to his own will?

5 For unto the angels hath he not put in subjection the world to come, whereof we speak.

6 But one in a certain place testified, saying, What is man, that thou art mindful of him? or the son of man, that thou visitest him?

7 Thou madest him a little lower than the angels; thou crownedst him with glory and honour, **and didst set him over the works of thy hands**[3]:

---

[1] WH added _as a garment_ (ʰ_Os_ ʰ_imation_).

[2] WH changed the word order from WE to give the more earnest heed to _to give the more earnest heed_ WE.

[3] In their margin, WH omitted and didst set him over the works of the hands of thee (kai katestAsas auton epi ta erga tOn ceirOn sou).

8   Thou hast put all things in subjection under his feet. **For**[1] in that he put all in subjection under him, he left nothing _that is_ not put under him. But now we see not yet all things put under him.

9   But we see Jesus, who was made a little lower than the angels for the suffering of death, crowned with glory and honour; that he by the grace of God should taste death for every man.

10   For it became him, for whom _are_ all things, and by whom _are_ all things, in bringing many sons unto glory, to make the captain of their salvation perfect through sufferings.

11   For both he that sanctifieth and they who are sanctified _are_ all of one: for which cause he is not ashamed to call them brethren,

12   Saying, I will declare thy name unto my brethren, in the midst of the church will I sing praise unto thee.

13   And again, I will put my trust in him. And again, Behold I and the children which God hath given me.

14   Forasmuch then as the children are partakers of **flesh** and **blood**[2], he also himself likewise took part of the same; that through death he might destroy him that had the power of death, that is, the devil;

15   And deliver them who through fear of death were all their lifetime subject to bondage.

16   For verily he took not on _him the nature of_ angels; but he took on _him_ the seed of Abraham.

17   Wherefore in all things it behoved him to be made like unto _his_ brethren, that he might be a merciful and faithful high priest in things _pertaining_ to God, to make reconciliation for the sins of the people.

18   For in that he himself hath suffered being tempted, he is able to succour them that are tempted.

CHAPTER 3

1   Wherefore, holy brethren, partakers of the heavenly calling, consider the Apostle and High Priest of our profession, ~~**Christ**~~[3] Jesus;

---

[1] WH changed the word order from FOR in that to _in FOR that_.

[2] WH changed the word order from FLESH and BLOOD to _BLOOD and FLESH._

[3] WH omitted Christ (cris-ton).

2   Who was faithful to him that appointed him, as also Moses *was faithful* in all his house.

3   For this *man* was counted worthy of more **glory**[1] than Moses, inasmuch as he who hath builded the house hath more honour than the house.

4   For every house is builded by some *man*; but he that built **[the]**[2] all things *is* God.

5   And Moses verily *was* faithful in all his house, as a servant, for a testimony of those things which were to be spoken after;

6   But Christ as a son over his own house; whose house are we, **if [only]**[3] we hold fast the confidence and the rejoicing of the hope firm unto the end.

7   Wherefore (as the Holy Ghost saith, To day if ye will hear his voice,

8   Harden not your hearts, as in the provocation, in the day of temptation in the wilderness:

derness:

9   When your fathers tempted ~~me~~[4], **proved**[5] ~~me~~[6], and saw my works forty years.

10   Wherefore I was grieved with **that**[7] generation, and said, They do alway err in *their* heart; and they have not known my ways.

11   So I sware in my wrath, They shall not enter into my rest.)

12   Take heed, brethren, lest there be in any of you an evil heart of unbelief, in departing from the living God.

13   But exhort one another daily, while it is called To day; lest any of you be hardened through the deceitfulness of sin.

14   For **we are made**[8] partakers of Christ, if we hold

---

[1] WH changed the word order from GLORY this {one} to *this* {one} GLORY.
[2] WH omitted the untranslated the (ta).
[3] WH changed if only (ean-per) to *if* (*ean*).

[4] WH omitted me (me).
[5] WH changed **proved** (edokimasan) to *in testing* (*en dokimasia*). **1** word to **2** words. **Verb** to *Preposition + Noun*.
[6] WH omitted me (me).
[7] WH changed that (ekeinA) to *this* (*tautA*).
[8] WH changed the word order from partakers WE ARE MADE of the Christ to *partakers of the Christ* WE ARE MADE.

the beginning of our confidence stedfast unto the end;

15 While it is said, To day if ye will hear his voice, harden not your hearts, as in the provocation.

16 For some, when they had heard, did provoke: howbeit not all that came out of Egypt by Moses.

17 But with whom was he grieved forty years? *was it* not with them that had sinned, whose carcases fell in the wilderness?

18 And to whom sware he that they should not enter into his rest, but to them that believed not?

19 So we see that they could not enter in because of unbelief.

CHAPTER 4

1 Let us therefore fear, lest, a promise being left *us* of entering into his rest, any of you should seem to come short of it.

2 For unto us was the gospel preached, as well as unto them: but the word preached did not profit them, not **being mixed with**[1] faith

in them that heard *it*.

3 **For**[2] we which have believed do enter into rest, as he said, As I have sworn in my wrath, if they shall enter into my rest: although the works were finished from the foundation of the world.

4 For he spake in a certain place of the seventh *day* on this wise, And God did rest the seventh day from all his works.

5 And in this *place* again, If they shall enter into my rest.

6 Seeing therefore it remaineth that some must enter therein, and they to whom it was first preached entered not in because of unbelief:

7 Again, he limiteth a certain day, saying in David, To day, after so long a time; as **it is said**[3], To day if ye

---

[1] WH changed having been mixed with (sugkekramenos) to *having been mixed with*

(*sugkekerasmenous*) in their text. Both Pf Pass Part. **Nom** Masc **Sing** to *Acc* Masc *Plur*. [case & number] In their margin, WH retained sugkekramenos.

[2] In their margin, WH changed for (**gar**) to *therefore* (*oun*).

[3] WH changed it is said (eirAtai) to *it is said in advance* (*proeirAtai*). Both Pf Pass Ind. [prefix added]

will hear his voice, harden not your hearts.

8   For if Jesus had given them rest, then would he not afterward have spoken of another day.

9   There remaineth therefore a rest to the people of God.

10 For he that is entered into his rest, he also hath ceased from his own works, as God *did* from his.

11 Let us labour therefore to enter into that rest, lest any man fall after the same example of unbelief.

12 For the word of God *is* quick, and powerful, and sharper than any twoedged sword, piercing even to the dividing asunder of soul [both]¹ and spirit, and of the joints and marrow, and *is* a discerner of the thoughts and intents of the heart.

13 Neither is there any creature that is not manifest in his sight: but all things *are* naked and opened unto the eyes of him with whom we have to do.

14 Seeing then that we have a great high priest, that is passed into the heavens, Jesus the Son of God, let us

hold fast *our* profession.

15 For we have not an high priest which cannot be touched with the feeling of our infirmities; but was in all points tempted like as *we are, yet* without sin.

16 Let us therefore come boldly unto the throne of grace, that we may obtain **mercy**², and find grace to help in time of need.

CHAPTER 5

1   For every high priest taken from among men is ordained for men in things *pertaining* to God, that he may offer both gifts and sacrifices for sins:

2   Who can have compassion on the ignorant, and on them that are out of the way; for that he himself also is compassed with infirmity.

3   And **by reason hereof**³ he ought, as for the people, so also for himself, to offer

---

¹ WH omitted the untranslated <u>both</u> (<u>te</u>).

² WH changed <u>mercy</u> (<u>eleon</u>) to *mercy* (*eleos*). Acc **Masc** Sing to Acc *Neut* Sing. [gender]

³ WH changed <u>by reason of</u> **<u>this</u>** (<u>dia</u> <u>tautAn</u>) to *by reason of it* (*di' autAn*). **Demonstrative** pronoun to *Personal* pronoun.

for[1] sins.

4   And no man taketh this honour unto himself, but **he**[2] that is called of God, **as**[3] *was* **[the]**[4] Aaron.

5   So also Christ glorified not himself to be made an high priest; but he that said unto him, Thou art my Son, to day have I begotten thee.

6   As he saith also in another *place*, Thou *art* a priest for ever after the order of Melchisedec.

7   Who in the days of his flesh, when he had offered up prayers and supplications with strong crying and tears unto him that was able to save him from death, and was heard in that he feared;

8   Though he were a Son, yet learned he obedience by the things which he suffered;

9   And being made perfect, he became the author of eternal salvation **unto all**[5] them that obey him;

10   Called of God an high priest after the order of Melchisedec.

11   Of whom we have many things to say, and hard to be uttered, seeing ye are dull of hearing.

12   For when for the time ye ought to be teachers, ye have need that one teach you again which *be* the first principles of the oracles of God; and are become such as have need of milk, and not of strong meat.

13   For every one that useth milk *is* unskilful in the word of righteousness: for he is a babe.

14   But strong meat belongeth to them that are of full age, *even* those who by reason of use have their senses exercised to discern both good and evil.

CHAPTER 6

1   Therefore leaving the principles of the doctrine of Christ, let us go on unto perfection; not laying again the foundation of repentance from dead works, and of faith toward God,

2   **Of the doctrine**[6] of

---

[1] WH changed **for** (**^huper**) to *for* (***peri***).
[2] WH omitted <u>he</u> (^ho—the).
[3] WH changed <u>as</u> (<u>kathaper</u>) to *as* (*ka<s>th</s>Osper*). [syn]
[4] WH omitted the untranslated <u>the</u> (^ho).
[5] WH changed the word order from <u>the</u> {ones} <u>obeying</u> <u>him</u> unto all to *unto all* *the* {ones} *obeying him*.

[6] In their margin, WH changed **of** the doctrine (<u>didacAs</u>) to *the doctrine* (*didacAn*). **Gen** Fem Sing to *Acc* Fem Sing. [case]

baptisms, and of laying on of hands, and of resurrection of the dead, and of eternal judgment.

3   And this will we do, if God permit.

4   For *it is* impossible for those who were once enlightened, and have tasted of the heavenly gift, and were made partakers of the Holy Ghost,

5   And have tasted the good word of God, and the powers of the world to come,

6   If they shall fall away, to renew them again unto repentance; seeing they crucify to themselves the Son of God afresh, and put *him* to an open shame.

7   For the earth which drinketh in the rain that cometh **oft**[1] upon it, and bringeth forth herbs meet for them by whom it is dressed, receiveth blessing from God:

8   But that which beareth thorns and briers *is* rejected, and *is* nigh unto cursing; whose end *is* to be burned.

9   But, beloved, we are persuaded better things of you, and things that accompany salvation, though we thus speak.

10   For God *is* not unrighteous to forget your work and ~~labour~~[2] of love, which ye have shewed toward his name, in that ye have ministered to the saints, and do minister.

11   And we desire that every one of you do shew the same diligence to the full assurance of hope unto the end:

12   That ye be not slothful, but followers of them who through faith and patience inherit the promises.

13   For when God made promise to Abraham, because he could swear by no greater, he sware by himself,

14   Saying, **Surely**[3] blessing I will bless thee, and multiplying I will multiply thee.

15   And so, after he had patiently endured, he obtained the promise.

16   For men **[then]**[4] verily swear by the greater: and an oath for confirmation *is* to them an end of all strife.

17   Wherein God, willing more abundantly to shew unto the heirs of promise the

---

[1] WH changed the word order from OFT cometh to *cometh OFT.*

[2] WH omitted the labour (tou kopou).
[3] WH changed **even** (**A**) to *if* (*ei*) in even not [i.e. Surely].
[4] WH omitted the untranslated then (men).

immutability of his counsel, confirmed *it* by an oath:

18 That by two immutable things, in which *it was* impossible for God to lie, we might have a strong consolation, who have fled for refuge to lay hold upon the hope set before us:

19 Which *hope* we have as an anchor of the soul, both sure and stedfast, and which entereth into that within the veil;

20 Whither the forerunner is for us entered, *even* Jesus, made an high priest for ever after the order of Melchisedec.

CHAPTER 7

1 For this Melchisedec, king of Salem, priest of the most high God, who met Abraham returning from the slaughter of the kings, and blessed him;

2 To whom also Abraham gave a tenth part of all; first being by interpretation King of righteousness, and after that also King of Salem, which is, King of peace;

3 Without father, without mother, without descent, having neither beginning of days, nor end of life; but made like unto the Son of God; abideth a priest con-

tinually.

4 Now consider how great this man *was*, unto whom **even**[1] the patriarch Abraham gave the tenth of the spoils.

5 And verily they that are of the sons of Levi, who receive the office of the priesthood, have a commandment to take tithes of the people according to the law, that is, of their brethren, though they come out of the loins of Abraham:

6 But he whose descent is not counted from them received tithes of **[the]**[2] Abraham, and blessed him that had the promises.

7 And without all contradiction the less is blessed of the better.

8 And here men that die receive tithes; but there he receiveth *them*, of whom it is witnessed that he liveth.

9 And as I may so say, Levi also, who receiveth tithes, payed tithes in Abraham.

10 For he was yet in the loins of his father, when **[the]**[3] Melchisedec met him.

---

[1] WH omitted <u>even</u> (<u>kai</u>).
[2] WH omitted the untranslated <u>the</u> (<u>ton</u>).
[3] WH omitted the untranslated <u>the</u> (<u>^{h}o</u>).

11 If therefore perfection were by the Levitical priest-hood, (for under **it**[1] the peo-ple **received the law**[2],) what further need *was there* that another priest should rise af-ter the order of Melchisedec, and not be called after the order of Aaron?

12 For the priesthood being changed, there is made of neces-sity a change also of the law.

13 For he of whom these things are spoken pertaineth to another tribe, of which no man gave attendance at the altar.

14 For *it is* evident that our Lord sprang out of Juda; of which tribe Moses spake **nothing**[3] concerning **priest-hood**[4].

15 And it is yet far more evident: for that after the si-militude of Melchisedec there ariseth another priest,

16 Who is made, not after the law of a **carnal**[5] com-mandment, but after the power of an endless life.

17 For **he testifieth**[6], Thou *art* a priest for ever af-ter the order of Melchisedec.

18 For there is verily a disannulling of the com-mandment going before for the weakness and unprofit-ableness thereof.

19 For the law made noth-ing perfect, but the bringing in of a better hope *did*; by the which we draw nigh unto God.

20 And inasmuch as not without an oath *he was made priest*:

21 (For those priests were made without an oath; but this with an oath by him that said unto him, The Lord sware and will not repent, Thou *art* a priest for ever **af-ter the order of Melchis-edec**[7]:)

---

[1] WH changed it (autA) to *it* (*autAs*). **Dat** Fem Sing to *Gen* Fem Sing. [case]

[2] WH changed **had received the law** (nenomoⱶhetAto) to *received the law* (*nenomoⱶhetAtai*). **PastPf** Pass Ind to *Pf* Pass Ind. [tense]

[3] WH changed the word or-der from NOTHING concern-ing **priesthood** to *concerning priests NOTHING*.

[4] WH changed **priesthood** (ʰierOsunAs) to *priests* (ʰiereOn).

[5] WH changed carnal (sarki-kAs) to *carnal* (*sarkinAs*). Both Gen Fem Sing. [spell]

[6] WH changed **he** testifies (marturei) to *it is being testi-fied* (*martureitai*). Pres **Act** Ind to Pres *Pass* Ind. [voice]

[7] WH omitted after the order of Melchisedec (kata tAn taxin melcisedek).

22 By so much [ʌalso][1] was Jesus made a surety of a better testament.

23 And they truly were many priests, because they were not suffered to continue by reason of death:

24 But this *man*, because he continueth ever, hath an unchangeable priesthood.

25 Wherefore he is able also to save them to the uttermost that come unto God by him, seeing he ever liveth to make intercession for them.

26 For such an high priest became us, *who is* holy, harmless, undefiled, separate from sinners, and made higher than the heavens;

27 Who needeth not daily, as those high priests, to offer up sacrifice, first for his own sins, and then for the people's: for this he did once, when he offered up himself.

28 For the law maketh men high priests which have infirmity; but the word of the oath, which was since the law, *maketh* the Son, who is consecrated for evermore.

CHAPTER 8

1 Now of the things

which we have spoken *this is* the sum: We have such an high priest, who is set on the right hand of the throne of the Majesty in the heavens;

2 A minister of the sanctuary, and of the true tabernacle, which the Lord pitched, ~~and~~[2] not man.

3 For every high priest is ordained to offer gifts and sacrifices: wherefore *it is* of necessity that this man have somewhat also to offer.

4 **For**[3] if he were on earth, he should not be a priest, seeing that there are ~~priests~~[4] that offer gifts according to **the**[5] law:

5 Who serve unto the example and shadow of heavenly things, as Moses was admonished of God when he was about to make the tabernacle: for, See, saith he, *that* **thou make**[6] all things according to the pattern shewed

---

[1] WH added *also* (*kai*).

[2] WH omitted and (kai).
[3] WH changed **for** (**gar**) to *therefore* (*oun*).
[4] WH omitted the priests (tOn ʰiereOn).
[5] WH omitted the (ton).
[6] WH changed youˢ **might make** (poiAsAs) to *youˢ will make* (*poiAseis*). **Aor** Act **Sub** to *Fut* Act *Ind*. [tense & mood]

to thee in the mount.

6 But now **hath he obtained**[1] a more excellent ministry, by how much also he is the mediator of a better covenant, which was established upon better promises.

7 For if that first *covenant* had been faultless, then should no place have been sought for the second.

8 For finding fault with them, he saith, Behold, the days come, saith the Lord, when I will make a new covenant with the house of Israel and with the house of Judah:

9 Not according to the covenant that I made with their fathers in the day when I took them by the hand to lead them out of the land of Egypt; because they continued not in my covenant, and I regarded them not, saith the Lord.

10 For this *is* the covenant that I will make with the house of Israel after those days, saith the Lord; I will put my laws into their mind, and write them in their hearts: and I will be to them a

God, and they shall be to me a people:

11 And they shall not teach every man his **neighbour**[2], and every man his brother, saying, Know the Lord: for all shall know me, from the least [~~of them~~][3] to the greatest.

12 For I will be merciful to their unrighteousness, and their sins ~~and their iniquities~~[4] will I remember no more.

13 In that he saith, A new *covenant*, he hath made the first old. Now that which decayeth and waxeth old *is* ready to vanish away.

CHAPTER 9

1 Then verily the first *covenant* had also ordinances of divine service, and a worldly sanctuary.

---

[1] WH changed hath he obtained (tet**e**uce) to *hath he obtained* (*tetuce*). Both Pf Act Ind. [spell]

[2] WH changed neighbor (**plAsion**) to *neighbor* (*politAn*). Fellow **man** to *fellow citizen*.
[3] WH omitted the untranslated of them (autOn) after least, apparently thinking that the untranslated of them after greatest was sufficient.
[4] WH omitted and the iniquities of them (kai tOn anomiOn autOn).

2 For there was a tabernacle made; the first, wherein *was* the candlestick, and the table, and the shewbread; which is called the sanctuary.

3 And after the second veil, the tabernacle which is called the Holiest of all;

4 Which had the golden censer, and the ark of the covenant overlaid round about with gold, wherein *was* the golden pot that had manna, and Aaron's rod that budded, and the tables of the covenant;

5 And over it the cherubims of glory shadowing the mercyseat; of which we cannot now speak particularly.

6 Now when these things were thus ordained, the priests went always into the first tabernacle, accomplishing the service *of God*.

7 But into the second *went* the high priest alone once every year, not without blood, which he offered for himself, and *for* the errors of the people:

8 The Holy Ghost this signifying, that the way into the holiest of all was not yet made manifest, while as the first tabernacle was yet standing:

9 Which *was* a figure for the time then present, **in which**[1] were offered both gifts and sacrifices, that could not make him that did the service perfect, as pertaining to the conscience;

10 *Which stood* only in meats and drinks, and divers washings, ~~and~~[2] carnal **ordinances**[3], imposed *on them* until the time of reformation.

11 But Christ being come an high priest of good things **to come**[4], by a greater and more perfect tabernacle, not made with hands, that is to say, not of this building;

12 Neither by the blood of goats and calves, but by his own blood he entered in once into the holy place, having obtained eternal redemption

---

[1] WH changed in which (ʰon) to *in whom* (ʰAn). Acc **Masc** Sing to Acc *Fem* Sing. [gender]

[2] WH omitted and (kai).

[3] WH changed ordinances (dikaiOmasi) to *ordinances* (dikaiOmata). **Dat** Neut Plur to *Nom* Neut Plur. [case]

[4] In their margin, WH changed **com**ing (**mellont**On) to *to having become* (**genomen**On). **Pres Act** Part of **mellO** to *Aor Mid* Part of *ginomai*. [tense & voice & root]

for us.

13 For if the blood **of bulls** and **of goats**[1], and the ashes of an heifer sprinkling the unclean, sanctifieth to the purifying of the flesh:

14 How much more shall the blood of Christ, who through the eternal Spirit offered himself without spot to God, purge **your**[2] conscience from dead works to serve the living God?

15 And for this cause he is the mediator of the new testament, that by means of death, for the redemption of the transgressions *that were* under the first testament, they which are called might receive the promise of eternal inheritance.

16 For where a testament *is*, there must also of necessity be the death of the testator.

17 For a testament *is* of force after men are dead: otherwise it is of no strength at all while the testator liveth.

18 Whereupon neither the first *testament* was dedicated without blood.

19 For when Moses had spoken every precept to all the people according to ∧**the**[3] law, he took the blood of calves and of [∧**the**][4] goats, with water, and scarlet wool, and hyssop, and sprinkled both the book, and all the people,

20 Saying, This *is* the blood of the testament which God hath enjoined unto you.

21 Moreover he sprinkled with blood both the tabernacle, and all the vessels of the ministry.

22 And almost all things are by the law purged with blood; and without shedding of blood is no remission.

23 *It was* therefore necessary that the patterns of things in the heavens should be purified with these; but the heavenly things themselves with better sacrifices than these.

24 For [**the**][5] Christ is not entered into the holy places

---

[1] WH changed the word order from <u>blood</u> OF BULLS <u>and</u> OF GOATS to *blood OF GOATS and OF BULLS.*

[2] In their margin, WH changed <u>of **you**</u> (^humOn) to *of* ***us*** (^hAmOn) in the phrase <u>the</u> <u>conscience</u> <u>of you.</u> [person]

[3] WH added *the* (*ton*) as the KJV supplied it.

[4] WH added *the* (*tOn*).

[5] WH omitted the untranslated <u>the</u> (^ho).

made with hands, *which are* the figures of the true; but into heaven itself, now to appear in the presence of God for us:

25 Nor yet that he should offer himself often, as the high priest entereth into the holy place every year with blood of others;

26 For then must he often have suffered since the foundation of the world: but **now**[1] once in the end of the world hath he appeared to put away sin by the sacrifice of himself.

27 And as it is appointed unto men once to die, but after this the judgment:

28 So Christ [ʌ**also**][2] was once offered to bear the sins of many; and unto them that look for him shall he appear the second time without sin unto salvation.

CHAPTER 10

1 For the law having a shadow of good things to come, *and* not the very image of the things, **can**[3] never with

those sacrifices which they offered year by year continually make the comers thereunto perfect.

2 For then would they not have ceased to be offered? because that the worshippers once **purged**[4] should have had no more conscience of sins.

3 But in those *sacrifices there is* a remembrance again *made* of sins every year.

4 For *it is* not possible that the blood of bulls and of goats should take away sins.

5 Wherefore when he cometh into the world, he saith, Sacrifice and offering thou wouldest not, but a body hast thou prepared me:

6 In burnt offerings and *sacrifices* for sin thou hast had no pleasure.

7 Then said I, Lo, I come (in the volume of the book it is written of me,) to do thy will, O God.

Both Pres Mid Ind. 3rd **Sing** to 3rd *Plur*. [number] WH retained dunatai in their margin.
[4] WH changed to purge (kekatharmenous) to *having been* purged (kekatharismenous). **Pres Act Inf** to *Pf Pass Part*. [tense, voice, & mood]

---

[1] WH changed now (nun) to *now* (nuni). **Regular** form to *Emphatic* form.
[2] WH added *also* (kai).
[3] WH changed {**it**} can (dunatai) {**they**} *can* (dunantai).

8 Above when he said, **Sacrifice**[1] and **offering**[2] and burnt offerings and *offering* for sin thou wouldest not, neither hadst pleasure *therein*; which are offered by ~~the~~[3] law;

9 Then said he, Lo, I come to do thy will, ~~O God~~[4]. He taketh away the first, that he may establish the second.

10 By the which will we are sanctified through the offering of the body of [~~the~~][5] Jesus Christ once *for all*.

11 And every **priest**[6] standeth daily ministering and offering oftentimes the same sacrifices, which can never take away sins:

12 But **this man**[7], after he had offered one sacrifice for sins for ever, sat down on the right hand of God;

13 From henceforth expecting till his enemies be made his footstool.

14 For by one offering he hath perfected for ever them that are sanctified.

15 *Whereof* the Holy Ghost also is a witness to us: for after that he had **said before**[8],

16 This *is* the covenant that I will make with them after those days, saith the Lord, I will put my laws into their hearts, and in their **minds**[9] will I write them;

17 And their sins and iniquities **will I remember**[10] no more.

---

[1] WH changed <u>sacrifice</u> (~~th~~usian) to *sacrifices* (~~th~~usias). Acc Fem **Sing** to Acc Fem ***Plur***. [number]

[2] WH changed <u>offering</u> (prosforan) to *offerings* (prosforas). Acc Fem **Sing** to Acc Fem ***Plur***. [number]

[3] WH omitted <u>the</u> (ton).

[4] WH omitted <u>O God</u> (^ho ~~th~~eos).

[5] WH omitted the untranslated <u>the</u> (tou).

[6] In their margin, WH changed <u>priest</u> (^hiereus) to *highpriest* (*arciereus*).

[7] WH changed **he-himself** (autos) to *this* {one} (*outos*).

Both Nom Masc Sing. **Pers** pro to ***Dem*** pro.

[8] WH changed <u>said before</u> (**pro**eirAkenai) to *said* (*eirAkenai*). Both Pf Act Inf. [prefix dropped]

[9] WH changed <u>the minds</u> (tOn dianoiOn) to *the mind* (*tAn dianoian*). **Gen** Fem **Plur** to *Acc* Fem ***Sing***. [case & number]

[10] WH changed I **might** be remembered (mnAs~~th~~O) to *I **will** be remembered* (*mnAs~~th~~Asomai*). **Aor** Pass **Sub** to ***Fut*** Pass ***Ind***. [tense & mood]

18 Now where remission of these *is, there is* no more offering for sin.

19 Having therefore, brethren, boldness to enter into the holiest by the blood of Jesus,

20 By a new and living way, which he hath consecrated for us, through the veil, that is to say, his flesh;

21 And *having* an high priest over the house of God;

22 Let us draw near with a true heart in full assurance of faith, having our hearts sprinkled from an evil conscience, and our bodies washed with pure water.

23 Let us hold fast the profession of *our* faith without wavering; (for he *is* faithful that promised;)

24 And let us consider one another to provoke unto love and to good works:

25 Not forsaking the assembling of ourselves together, as the manner of some *is*; but exhorting *one another*: and so much the more, as ye see the day approaching.

26 For if we sin wilfully after that we have received the knowledge of the truth, there remaineth no more sacrifice for sins,

27 But a certain fearful looking for of judgment and fiery indignation, which shall devour the adversaries.

28 He that despised Moses' law died without mercy under two or three witnesses:

29 Of how much sorer punishment, suppose ye, shall he be thought worthy, who hath trodden under foot the Son of God, and hath counted the blood of the covenant, wherewith he was sanctified, an unholy thing, and hath done despite unto the Spirit of grace?

30 For we know him that hath said, Vengeance *belongeth* unto me, I will recompense, ~~saith the Lord~~[1]. And again, The Lord **shall judge**[2] his people.

31 *It is* a fearful thing to fall into the hands of the living God.

32 But call to remembrance the former days, in which, after ye were illuminated, ye endured a great fight of afflictions;

33 Partly, whilst ye were made a gazingstock both by reproaches and afflictions;

---

[1] WH omitted <u>saith</u> {the} <u>Lord</u> (<u>legei</u> <u>kurios</u>).
[2] WH changed the word order from <u>Lord</u> SHALL JUDGE to *SHALL JUDGE Lord.*

and partly, whilst ye became companions of them that were so used.

34 For ye had compassion of me **in** ~~my~~[1] **bonds**[2], and took joyfully the spoiling of your goods, knowing ~~in~~[3] **yourselves**[4] that ye have ~~in heaven~~[5] a better and an enduring substance.

35 Cast not away therefore your confidence, which hath **great**[6] recompence of reward.

36 For ye have need of patience, that, after ye have done the will of God, ye might receive the promise.

37 For yet a little while, and he that shall come will come, and will not tarry.

38 Now the just [∧**of me**][7]

---

[1] WH omitted of me (mou) from the bonds of me.
[2] WH changed **in the bonds** (tois desmois) to **with** *the* **prisoners** (*tois desmiois*).
[3] WH omitted in (en).
[4] WH changed yourselves ([h]eauto**is**) to *yourselves* ([h]*eauto**us***). **Dat** Masc Plur to **Acc** Masc Plur. [case] In their margin, WH retained [h]eauto**is**.
[5] WH omitted in heaven (en ouranois).
[6] WH changed the word order from reward GREAT to *GREAT reward*.
[7] WH added of me (mou) in

shall live by faith: but if *any man* draw back, my soul shall have no pleasure in him.

39 But we are not of them who draw back unto perdition; but of them that believe to the saving of the soul.

CHAPTER 11

1 Now faith is the substance of things hoped for, the evidence of things not seen.

2 For by it the elders obtained a good report.

3 Through faith we understand that the worlds were framed by the word of God, so that **things which are seen**[8] were not made of things which do appear.

4 By faith Abel offered unto God a more excellent sacrifice than Cain, by which he obtained witness that he was righteous, **God**[9] testifying

---

their text but not in their margin.
[8] WH changed things which are seen (ta blepomena) to *the* thing which *is* seen (*to blepomenon*). Both Pres Pass Part. **Nom** Neut **Plur** to *Acc* Neut *Sing*. [case & number]
[9] In their margin, WH noted the uncertainty of the reading [God (tou ~~theou~~)]. They preferred to let the verb supply the subject *he*.

of his gifts: and by it he being dead yet speaketh.

5 By faith Enoch was translated that he should not see death; and was not found, because God had translated him: for before ~~his~~[1] translation he had this testimony, that he pleased God.

6 But without faith *it is* impossible to please *him*: for he that cometh to God must believe that he is, and *that* he is a rewarder of them that diligently seek him.

7 By faith Noah, being warned of God of things not seen as yet, moved with fear, prepared an ark to the saving of his house; by the which he condemned the world, and became heir of the righteousness which is by faith.

8 By faith Abraham, when he was called to go out into [the][2] a place which he should after receive for an inheritance, obeyed; and he went out, not knowing whither he went.

9 By faith he sojourned in **the**[3] land of promise, as *in a* strange country, dwelling in tabernacles with Isaac and Jacob, the heirs with him of the same promise:

10 For he looked for a city which hath foundations, whose builder and maker *is* God.

11 Through faith also Sara herself received strength to conceive seed, and ~~was delivered~~[4] of a child when she was past age, because she judged him faithful who had promised.

12 Therefore sprang there even of one, and him as good as dead, *so many* as the stars of the sky in multitude, and **as**[5] the sand which is by the sea shore innumerable.

13 These all died in faith, not **having received**[6] the promises, but having seen them afar off, ~~and were persuaded of *them*~~[7], and embraced *them*, and confessed

---

[1] WH omitted <u>of him</u> (<u>autou</u>) from <u>the</u> <u>translation</u> <u>of him</u>.
[2] WH omitted the untranslated <u>the</u> (<u>ton</u>) before <u>place</u>.
[3] WH omitted <u>the</u> (<u>tAn</u>) before <u>land</u>.

[4] WH omitted <u>was delivered</u> (<u>eteken</u>).
[5] WH changed <u>as</u> (^hOsei) to *as the* (^hOs ^h**A**).
[6] WH changed **having** re<u>ceiv</u>**ed** (**labontes**) to *will be receiving* (**komisamenoi**). **Aor** **Act** Part to *Fut Mid* Part. [tense & voice]
[7] WH omitted <u>and</u> <u>were persuaded</u> (<u>kai peisthentes</u>).

that they were strangers and pilgrims on the earth.

14 For they that say such things declare plainly that they seek a country.

15 And truly, if they had been mindful of that *country* from whence **they came out**[1], they might have had opportunity to have returned.

16 But **now**[2] they desire a better *country*, that is, an heavenly: wherefore God is not ashamed to be called their God: for he hath prepared for them a city.

17 By faith Abraham, when he was tried, offered up Isaac: and he that had received the promises offered up his only begotten *son*,

18 Of whom it was said, That in Isaac shall thy seed be called:

19 Accounting that God *was* able to raise *him* up, even from the dead; from whence also he received him in a figure.

20 By faith Isaac blessed

Jacob and Esau concerning things to come.

21 By faith Jacob, when he was a dying, blessed both the sons of Joseph; and worshipped, *leaning* upon the top of his staff.

22 By faith [^also][3] Joseph, when he died, made mention of the departing of the children of Israel; and gave commandment concerning his bones.

23 By faith Moses, when he was born, was hid three months of his parents, because they saw *he was* a proper child; and they were not afraid of the king's commandment.

24 By faith Moses, when he was come to years, refused to be called the son of Pharaoh's daughter;

25 Choosing rather to suffer affliction with the people of God, than to enjoy the pleasures of sin for a season;

26 Esteeming the reproach of Christ greater riches than the treasures ~~in~~[4] **Egypt**[5]: for

---

[1] WH changed they came out (exAlthon) to *they came out* (exebAsan). Both Aor Act Ind. **exercomai** to *ekbainO*. [syn]

[2] WH change from now (nuni) to *now* (nun). **Emphatic** form to *Regular* form.

[3] WH added *also* (kai) after faith.

[4] WH omitted in (en) and forced the case of Egypt to supply the preposition.

[5] WH changed Egypt (aiguptO) to (*of*) *Egypt* (aiguptou). **Dat** to **Gen**. [case]

he had respect unto the recompence of the reward.

27 By faith he forsook Egypt, not fearing the wrath of the king: for he endured, as seeing him who is invisible.

28 Through faith he kept the passover, and the sprinkling of blood, lest he that destroyed the firstborn should touch them.

29 By faith they passed through the Red sea as by dry ∧*land*¹: which the Egyptians assaying to do were drowned.

30 By faith the walls of Jericho **fell down**², after they were compassed about seven days.

31 By faith the harlot Rahab perished not with them that believed not, when she had received the spies with peace.

32 And what shall I more say? **for**³ the time would fail me to tell of Gedeon, and *of*

Barak, **[then]**⁴ ~~and~~⁵ *of* Samson, **and**⁶ *of* Jephthae; *of* David also, and Samuel, and *of* the prophets:

33 Who through faith subdued kingdoms, wrought righteousness, obtained promises, stopped the mouths of lions,

34 Quenched the violence of fire, escaped the edge of the sword, out of weakness **were made strong**⁷, waxed valiant in fight, turned to flight the armies of the aliens.

35 Women received their dead raised to life again: and others were tortured, not accepting deliverance; that they might obtain a better resurrection:

36 And others had trial of *cruel* mockings and scourgings, yea, moreover of bonds and imprisonment:

37 They were stoned, they were sawn asunder, were tempted, were slain with the

---

¹ WH added *land* (*gAs*) as the KJV supplied it.
² WH changed {**it**} fell down (epese) to {**they**} *fell down* (*epesan*). Both Aor Act Ind. 3ʳᵈ **Sing** to 3ʳᵈ *Plur.* [number]
³ WH changed the word order from FOR would fail me to *would fail FOR me.*

⁴ WH omitted the untranslated then (te).
⁵ WH omitted and (kai).
⁶ WH omitted and (kai).
⁷ WH changed were made strong **in** (**enedu**namOthAsan) to *were made strong* (*edunamOthAsan*). Both Aor Pass Ind. [prefix dropped]

sword: they wandered about in sheepskins and goatskins; being destitute, afflicted, tormented;

38 (Of whom the world was not worthy:) they wandered **in**[1] deserts, and *in* mountains, and *in* dens and caves of the earth.

39 And these all, having obtained a good report through faith, received not the promise:

40 God having provided some better thing for us, that they without us should not be made perfect.

CHAPTER 12

1 Wherefore seeing we also are compassed about with so great a cloud of witnesses, let us lay aside every weight, and the sin which doth so easily beset *us*, and let us run with patience the race that is set before us,

2 Looking unto Jesus the author and finisher of *our* faith; who for the joy that was set before him endured the cross, despising the shame, and **is set down**[2] at

the right hand of the throne of God.

3 For consider him that endured such contradiction of sinners against **himself**[3], lest ye be wearied and faint in your minds.

4 Ye have not yet resisted unto blood, striving against sin.

5 And ye have forgotten the exhortation which speaketh unto you as unto children, My son, despise not thou the chastening of the Lord, nor faint when thou art rebuked of him:

6 For whom the Lord loveth he chasteneth, and scourgeth every son whom he receiveth.

7 **If**[4] ye endure chastening, God dealeth with you as with sons; for what son **is**[5] he whom the father chasteneth not?

8 But if ye be without

---

[1] WH changed **in** (**en**) to *upon* (**epi**).

[2] WH changed sat down (ekaťhisen) to *has sat down* (kekaťhiken). **Aor** Act Ind to *Pf* Act Ind. [tense]

[3] WH changed **him**self (auton) to *themselves* (ʰeautous). **Sing Pers** pro to *Plur Refl* pro. [number & pro] In their margin, WH had *himself* (ʰeauton).

[4] WH changed if (ei) to *if* (eis). [spell]

[5] WH omitted is (este).

chastisement, whereof all are partakers, then **are ye**[1] bastards, and not sons.

9 Furthermore we have had fathers of our flesh which corrected *us*, and we gave *them* reverence: shall we not **much**[2] rather be in subjection unto the Father of spirits, and live?

10 For they verily for a few days chastened *us* after their own pleasure; but he for *our* profit, that *we* might be partakers of his holiness.

11 **Now**[3] no chastening for the present seemeth to be joyous, but grievous: nevertheless afterward it yieldeth the peaceable fruit of righteousness unto them which are exercised thereby.

12 Wherefore lift up the hands which hang down, and the feeble knees;

13 And make straight paths for your feet, lest that which is lame be turned out of the way; but let it rather be healed.

14 Follow peace with all *men*, and holiness, without which no man shall see the Lord:

15 Looking diligently lest any man fail of the grace of God; lest any root of bitterness springing up trouble *you*, and thereby [ʌ**the**][4] many be defiled;

16 Lest there *be* any fornicator, or profane person, as Esau, who for one morsel of meat sold **his**[5] birthright.

17 For ye know how that afterward, when he would have inherited the blessing, he was rejected: for he found no place of repentance, though he sought it carefully with tears.

18 For ye are not come unto ~~the mount~~[6] that might be touched, and that burned with fire, nor unto blackness, and **darkness**[7], and tempest,

19 And the sound of a

---

[1] WH changed the word order from ARE YE and not sons to *and not sons ARE YE.*

[2] WH changed much (poll**O**) to *much (pol**u**)*. **Dat** Neut Sing to *Acc* Neut Sing. [case]

[3] WH changed **now** (**de**) to *then* (*men*).

[4] WH added *the* ([h]*oi*) before many.

[5] WH changed of him (autou) to *of himself* ([h]*eautou*) in the birthright of him. **Pers** pro to *Refl* pro.

[6] WH omitted {the} mount (orei).

[7] WH changed **darkness** (skot**O**) to *gloom (zopA)*. Both Dat Masc Sing. [syn]

trumpet, and the voice of words; which *voice* they that heard intreated that the word should not be spoken to them any more:

20 (For they could not endure that which was commanded, And if so much as a beast touch the mountain, it shall be stoned, or ~~thrust through with a dart~~[1]:

21 And so terrible was the sight, *that* Moses said, I exceedingly fear and quake:)

22 But ye are come unto mount Sion, and unto the city of the living God, the heavenly Jerusalem, and to an innumerable company of angels,

23 To the general assembly and church of the firstborn, **which are written**[2] in heaven, and to God the Judge of all, and to the spirits of just men made perfect,

24 And to Jesus the mediator of the new covenant, and to the blood of sprinkling, that speaketh **better**[3]

things than *that of* [**the**][4] Abel.

25 See that ye refuse not him that speaketh. For if they **escaped**[5] not who refused ∧**him**[6] that spake [**the**][7] on [**the**][8] earth, **much**[9] more *shall not* we *escape*, if we turn away from him that *speaketh* from heaven:

26 Whose voice then shook the earth: but now he hath promised, saying, Yet once more I **shake**[10] not the earth only, but also heaven.

Acc Neut **Plur** to Acc Neut *Sing* [number]
[4] WH changed the untranslated <u>the</u> (<u>to</u>) to *the* (*to***n**).
Acc **Neut** Sing to Acc *Masc* Sing. [gender]
[5] WH changed <u>escaped</u> (<u>efugon</u>) to *escaped* {**out**} (*exefugon*). [prefix added]
[6] WH added *the* {**one**} (*ton*) after <u>refused</u> where the KJV has <u>him</u>.
[7] WH omitted <u>who</u> (<u>ton</u>—the {one}) before <u>on</u> (<u>epi</u>).
[8] WH omitted the untranslated <u>the</u> (<u>tAs</u>) before <u>on</u> (epi).
[9] WH changed <u>much</u> (<u>pollO</u>) to *much* (*polu*). **Dat** Neut Sing to *Acc* Neut Sing. [case]
[10] WH changed <u>shake</u> (<u>seiO</u>) to *will shake* (*seisO*). **Pres** Act Ind to **Fut** Act Ind. [tense]

---

[1] WH omitted <u>with the dart thrust through</u> (<u>A bolidi katatoxeuthAsetai</u>).
[2] WH changed the word order from <u>in heaven</u> WHICH ARE WRITTEN to *WHICH ARE WRITTEN in heaven*.
[3] WH changed <u>better</u> (<u>kreittona</u>) to *better* (*kreitton*).

27 And this *word*, Yet once more, signifieth the removing **of those things**[1] that are shaken, as of things that are made, that those things which cannot be shaken may remain.

28 Wherefore we receiving a kingdom which cannot be moved, let us have grace, whereby we may serve God acceptably with **reverence**[2] **and godly fear**[3]:

29 For our God *is* a consuming fire.

CHAPTER 13

1 Let brotherly love continue.

2 Be not forgetful to entertain strangers: for thereby some have entertained angels unawares.

3 Remember them that are in bonds, as bound with them; *and* them which suffer adversity, as being yourselves also in the body.

4 Marriage *is* honourable in all, and the bed undefiled: **but**[4] whoremongers and adulterers God will judge.

5 *Let your* conversation *be* without covetousness; *and be* content with such things as ye have: for he hath said, I will never leave thee, nor forsake thee.

6 So that we may boldly say, The Lord *is* my helper, **and**[5] I will not fear what man shall do unto me.

7 Remember them which have the rule over you, who have spoken unto you the word of God: whose faith follow, considering the end of *their* conversation.

8 Jesus Christ the same **yesterday**[6], and to day, and for ever.

9 **Be** not **carried about**[7]

---

[1] WH changed the word order from OF THE {THINGS} being shaken the to *the OF THE* {THINGS} *being shaken.*

[2] WH changed **reverence** (**ai-d**ous) to *awe* (*deous*). [syn]

[3] WH changed the word order from **reverence** AND GODLY FEAR to from GODLY FEAR AND **awe.**

[4] WH changed **but** (**de**) to *for* (*gar*).

[5] WH omitted and (kai).

[6] WH changed yesterday (c~~t~~hes) to *yesterday* (ec~~th~~es). [spell]

[7] WH changed be carried **around** (periferes~~th~~e) to *be carried* **beside** (*paraf-eres~~th~~e*). Both Pres Pass Imp. periferO to *paraferO*. [prefix changed]

with divers and strange doctrines. For *it is* a good thing that the heart be established with grace; not with meats, which have not profited them that have been occupied therein.

10 We have an altar, whereof they have no right to eat which serve the tabernacle.

11 For the bodies of those beasts, whose blood is brought into the sanctuary by the high priest for sin, are burned without the camp.

12 Wherefore Jesus also, that he might sanctify the people with his own blood, suffered without the gate.

13 Let us go forth therefore unto him without the camp, bearing his reproach.

14 For here have we no continuing city, but we seek one to come.

15 By him **therefore**[1] let us offer the sacrifice of praise to God continually, that is, the fruit of *our* lips giving thanks to his name.

16 But to do good and to communicate forget not: for with such sacrifices God is well pleased.

17 Obey them that have the rule over you, and submit yourselves: for they watch for your souls, as they that must give account, that they may do it with joy, and not with grief: for that *is* unprofitable for you.

18 Pray for us: for **we trust**[2] we have a good conscience, in all things willing to live honestly.

19 But I beseech *you* the rather to do this, that I may be restored to you the sooner.

20 Now the God of peace, that brought again from the dead our Lord Jesus, that great shepherd of the sheep, through the blood of the everlasting covenant,

21 Make you perfect in every good **work**[3] to do his will, working in **you**[4] that which is wellpleasing in his sight, through Jesus Christ; to

---

[1] In their margin, WH omitted therefore (oun).

[2] WH changed we **have** trusted (**pepoithamen**) to *we are being* trusted (*peithometha*). **Pf Act** Ind to *Pres Pass* Ind. [tense & voice]

[3] WH omitted work (ergO) in their text but not in their margin.

[4] WH changed **you** (humin) to *us* (hAmin) in their text but not in their margin. [person]

whom *be* glory for ever and ever. Amen.

22 And I beseech you, brethren, suffer the word of exhortation: for I have written a letter unto you in few words.

23 Know ye that ∧*our*[1] brother Timothy is set at liberty; with whom, if he come shortly, I will see you.

24 Salute all them that have the rule over you, and all the saints. They of Italy salute you.

25 Grace *be* with you all. Amen.

---

[1] WH added *our* (*ʰAmOn*) as the KJV supplied it.

JAMES

CHAPTER 1

1 James, a servant of God and of the Lord Jesus Christ, to the twelve tribes which are scattered abroad, greeting.

2 My brethren, count it all joy when ye fall into divers temptations;

3 Knowing *this*, that the trying of your faith worketh patience.

4 But let patience have *her* perfect work, that ye may be perfect and entire, wanting nothing.

5 If any of you lack wisdom, let him ask of God, that giveth to all *men* liberally, and upbraideth not; and it shall be given him.

6 But let him ask in faith, nothing wavering. For he that wavereth is like a wave of the sea driven with the wind and tossed.

7 For let not that man think that he shall receive any thing of the Lord.

8 A double minded man *is* unstable in all his ways.

9 Let the brother of low degree rejoice in that he is exalted:

10 But the rich, in that he is made low: because as the flower of the grass he shall pass away.

11 For the sun is no sooner risen with a burning heat, but it withereth the grass, and the flower thereof falleth, and the grace of the fashion of it perisheth: so also shall the rich man fade away in his ways.

12 Blessed *is* the man that endureth temptation: for when he is tried, he shall receive the crown of life, which ~~the Lord~~[1] hath promised to them that love him.

13 Let no man say when he is tempted, I am tempted of God: for God cannot be tempted with evil, neither tempteth he any man:

14 But every man is tempted, when he is drawn away of his own lust, and enticed.

15 Then when lust hath conceived, it bringeth forth sin: and sin, when it is finished, bringeth forth death.

16 Do not err, my beloved brethren.

17 Every good gift and every perfect gift is from above, and cometh down from the Father of lights,

---

[1] WH omitted the Lord (^{h}o kurios) and forced the verb to supply the subject *he*.

with whom is no variableness, neither shadow of turning.

18 Of his own will begat he us with the word of truth, that we should be a kind of firstfruits of his creatures.

19 **Wherefore**[1], my beloved brethren, [∧**then**][2] let every man be swift to hear, slow to speak, slow to wrath:

20 For the wrath of man **worketh**[3] **not**[4] the righteousness of God.

21 Wherefore lay apart all filthiness and superfluity of naughtiness, and receive with meekness the engrafted word, which is able to save your souls.

22 But be ye doers of the word, and not hearers only, deceiving your own selves.

23 For if any be a hearer of the word, and not a doer, he is like unto a man beholding his natural face in a glass:

24 For he beholdeth himself, and goeth his way, and straightway forgetteth what manner of man he was.

25 But whoso looketh into the perfect law of liberty, and continueth *therein,* ~~he~~[5] being not a forgetful hearer, but a doer of the work, this man shall be blessed in his deed.

26 If any man ~~among you~~[6] seem to be religious, and bridleth not his tongue, but deceiveth his own heart, this man's religion *is* vain.

27 Pure religion and undefiled before God and the Father is this, To visit the fatherless and widows in their affliction, *and* to keep himself unspotted from the world.

CHAPTER 2

1 My brethren, have not the faith of our Lord Jesus Christ, *the Lord* of glory, with respect of persons.

2 For if there come unto your [~~the~~][7] assembly a man with a gold ring, in goodly apparel, and there come in also a poor man in vile raiment;

---

[1] WH changed **wherefore** (^h**O**ste) to *behold* (*iste*). **Conj** to *Verb* (Pf Act Imp).

[2] WH added *then* (*de*).

[3] WH changed works **down** (**kat**ergazetai) to *works* (*ouk ergazetai*). [prefix dropped]

[4] WH changed not (ou) to *not* (*ouk*). [spell]

[5] WH omitted he (^houtos).

[6] WH omitted among you (en ^humin).

[7] WH omitted the untranslated the (tAn) from the assembly of you.

3　And ye have respect to him that weareth the gay clothing, and say ~~unto him~~[1], Sit thou here in a good place; and say to the poor, Stand thou there, or sit ~~here~~[2] under my footstool:

4　Are ye not ~~then~~[3] partial in yourselves, and are become judges of evil thoughts?

5　Hearken, my beloved brethren, hath not God chosen the poor **of** ~~this~~[4] **world**[5] rich in faith, and heirs of the kingdom which he hath promised to them that love him?

6　But ye have despised the poor. Do not rich men oppress you, and draw you before the judgment seats?

7　Do not they blaspheme that worthy name by the which ye are called?

8　If ye fulfil the royal law according to the scripture, Thou shalt love thy neighbour as thyself, ye do well:

9　But if ye have respect to persons, ye commit sin, and are convinced of the law as transgressors.

10　For whosoever **shall keep**[6] the whole law, and yet **offend**[7] in one *point*, he is guilty of all.

11　For he that said, Do not commit adultery, said also, Do not kill. Now if **thou commit** no **adultery**[8], yet if **thou kill**[9], thou art become a transgressor of the law.

12　So speak ye, and so do, as they that shall be judged by the law of liberty.

13　For he shall have judgment without mercy, that

---

[1] WH omitted unto him (autO).

[2] WH omitted here (ʰOde).

[3] WH omitted then (kai).

[4] WH omitted this (toutou) from the world this {one}.

[5] WH changed **of the** world (**tou** kosmou) to *in the* world (*tO kosmO*). **Gen** to *Dat*. [case]

[6] WH changed **shall** keep (tArAsei) to *might keep* (*tArAsA*). **Fut** Act **Ind** to *Aor* Act *Sub*. [tense & mood]

[7] WH changed **shall** offend (ptaisei) to *might offend* (*ptaisA*). **Fut** Act **Ind** to *Aor* Act *Sub*. [tense & mood]

[8] WH changed youˢ **will** commit adultery (moiceuseis) to *youˢ* *are committing adultery* (*moiceueis*). **Fut** Act Ind to *Pres* Act Ind. [tense]

[9] WH changed youˢ **will** murder (foneuseis) to *youˢ* *are murdering* (*foneueis*). **Fut** Act Ind to *Pres* Act Ind. [tense]

hath shewed no mercy; ~~and~~[1] mercy rejoiceth against judgment.

14 What *doth it* profit, my brethren, though a man say he hath faith, and have not works? can faith save him?

15 [~~but~~][2] If a brother or sister be naked, and [~~be~~][3] destitute of daily food,

16 And one of you say unto them, Depart in peace, be *ye* warmed and filled; notwithstanding ye give them not those things which are needful to the body; what *doth it* profit?

17 Even so faith, if it hath not **works**[4], is dead, being alone.

18 Yea, a man may say, Thou hast faith, and I have works: shew me thy faith without ~~thy~~[5] works, and I will shew thee ~~my~~[6] faith by my works.

19 Thou believest that there is one **God**[7]; thou doest well: the devils also believe, and tremble.

20 But wilt thou know, O vain man, that faith without works is **dead**[8]?

21 Was not Abraham our father justified by works, when he had offered Isaac his son upon the altar?

22 Seest thou how faith wrought with his works, and by works was faith made perfect?

23 And the scripture was fulfilled which saith, Abraham believed God, and it was imputed unto him for righteousness: and he was called the Friend of God.

24 Ye see ~~then~~[9] how that by works a man is justified, and not by faith only.

25 Likewise also was not Rahab the harlot justified by works, when she had received the messengers, and had sent *them* out another way?

26 For as the body without the spirit is dead, so faith

---

[1] WH omitted <u>and</u> (<u>kai</u>).

[2] WH omitted the untranslated <u>but</u> (<u>de</u>).

[3] WH omitted the untranslated <u>be</u> (<u>ʰOsi</u>).

[4] WH changed the word order from <u>not</u> WORKS <u>it has</u> to *not it has* WORKS.

[5] WH omitted <u>of thee</u> (<u>sou</u>) from <u>the works of thee</u>.

[6] WH omitted <u>of me</u> (<u>mou</u>) from <u>the faith of me</u>.

[7] WH changed the word order from <u>THE</u> <u>GOD</u> <u>one</u> <u>is</u> to *one is* *THE GOD*. In their margin they had *one* GOD *is*.

[8] WH changed **dead** (**nekra**) to *useless* (*argA*).

[9] WH omitted <u>then</u> (<u>toinun</u>).

without [the][1] works is dead also.

CHAPTER 3

1   My brethren, be not many masters, knowing that we shall receive the greater condemnation.

2   For in many things we offend all. If any man offend not in word, the same *is* a perfect man, *and* able also to bridle the whole body.

3   **Behold**[2], we put bits in the horses' mouths, **that**[3] they may obey us; and we turn about their whole body.

4   Behold also the ships, which though *they be* so great, and *are* driven of fierce winds, yet are they turned about with a very small helm, whither~~soever~~[4] the governor **listeth**[5].

5   Even so the tongue is a little member, and **boasteth great things**[6]. Behold, how great a matter **a little**[7] fire kindleth!

6   And the tongue *is* a fire, a world of iniquity: ~~so~~[8] is the tongue among our members, that it defileth the whole body, and setteth on fire the course of nature; and it is set on fire of hell.

7   For every kind of beasts, and of birds, and of serpents, and of things in the sea, is tamed, and hath been tamed of mankind:

8   But the tongue can no man tame; *it is* an **unruly**[9] evil, full of deadly poison.

9   Therewith bless we **God**[10], even the Father; and therewith curse we men,

---

[1] WH omitted the untranslated the (tOn).
[2] WH changed **behold** (**idou**) to *but if* (*ei de*).
[3] WH changed **toward** (**pros**) to *unto* (*eis*).
[4] WH omitted -soever (an) from wither-soever.
[5] WH changed **may** will (boulAtai) to *wills* (*bouletai*). Pres M/P **Sub** to Pres Mid *Ind*. [mood]

[6] WH changed boasts great things (megalaucei) to *boasts great things* (*megala aucei*). **Verb** Pres Act Ind to *Adj* + *Verb* Pres Act Ind.
[7] WH changed a **little** (ologon) to *how small a* (*ʰAlikon*).
[8] WH omitted so (ʰoutOs).
[9] WH changed un**controll**able (akatasceton) to *unstable* (*akatastaton*). Both Nom Neut Sing. [spell]
[10] WH changed the **God** (ton ~~the~~on) to *the* **Lord** (ton **ku-rion**).

which are made after the similitude of God.

10 Out of the same mouth proceedeth blessing and cursing. My brethren, these things ought not so to be.

11 Doth a fountain send forth at the same place sweet *water* and bitter?

12 Can the fig tree, my brethren, bear olive berries? either a vine, figs? ~~so~~[1] *can* **no**[2] ~~fountain~~[3] ~~both~~[4] yield salt water and fresh.

13 Who *is* a wise man and endued with knowledge among you? let him shew out of a good conversation his works with meekness of wisdom.

14 But if ye have bitter envying and strife in your hearts, glory not, and lie not against the truth.

15 This wisdom descendeth not from above, but *is* earthly, sensual, devilish.

16 For where envying and strife *is*, there *is* confusion and every evil work.

17 But the wisdom that is from above is first pure, then peaceable, gentle, *and* easy to be intreated, full of mercy and good fruits, without partiality, ~~and~~[5] without hypocrisy.

18 And the fruit of righteousness is sown in peace of them that make peace.

CHAPTER 4

1 From whence *come* wars and [∧**from whence**][6] fightings among you? *come they* not hence, *even* of your lusts that war in your members?

2 Ye lust, and have not: ye kill, and desire to have, and cannot obtain: ye fight and war, ~~yet~~[7] ye have not, because ye ask not.

3 Ye ask, and receive not, because ye ask amiss, that ye may consume *it* upon your lusts.

4 ~~Ye adulterers and~~[8] adulteresses, know ye not that the friendship of the world is enmity with God? whosoever therefore will be a

---

[1] WH omitted **so** ([h]outOs).
[2] WH changed **no** (**oudemia**) to n**either** (*oute*).
[3] WH omitted fountain (pAgA).
[4] WH omitted both (kai).

[5] WH omitted and (kai) before without hypocrisy.
[6] WH added *from whence* (po~~th~~en).
[7] WH omitted yet (de).
[8] WH omitted ye adulterers and (moicoi kai).

666

friend of the world is the enemy of God.

5   Do ye think that the scripture saith in vain, The spirit that **dwelleth**[1] in us lusteth to envy?

6   But he giveth more grace. Wherefore he saith, God resisteth the proud, but giveth grace unto the humble.

7   Submit yourselves therefore to God. Resist [∧**then**][2] the devil, and he will flee from you.

8   Draw nigh to God, and he will draw nigh to you. Cleanse *your* hands, *ye* sinners; and purify *your* hearts, *ye* double minded.

9   Be afflicted, and mourn, and weep: let your laughter be turned to mourning, and *your* joy to heaviness.

10 Humble yourselves in the sight of the Lord, and he shall lift you up.

11 Speak not evil one of another, brethren. He that speaketh evil of *his* brother, **and**[3] judgeth his brother,

speaketh evil of the law, and judgeth the law: but if thou judge the law, thou art not a doer of the law, but a judge.

12 There is one lawgiver [∧**and judge**][4], who is able to save and to destroy: [∧**but**][5] who art thou **that judgest**[6] **another**[7]?

13 Go to now, ye that say, To day or to morrow we will go into such a city, and continue there [~~one~~][8] a year, and buy and sell, and get gain:

14 Whereas ye know not what *shall be* on the morrow. ~~For~~[9] what *is* your life? **It is**[10] even a vapour, that appeareth for a little time, **and**[11] then

---

[4] WH added *and judge* (*kai kritAs*).

[5] WH added *but* (*de*).

[6] WH changed **who** judges (^hos krin**eis**) to **the** {one} jud**ging** (^ho krin**On**). Pres Act **Ind** to Pres Act *Part*. [mood]

[7] WH changed the **different** {one} (ton ^h**eteron**) to *the* **neighbor** (*ton plAsion*).

[8] WH omitted the untranslated one (^hena).

[9] WH omitted for (gar).

[10] WH changed **it is** (estin) to *ye are* (este). Pres Ind **3rd Sing** to Pres Ind *2nd Plur*. [person & number]

[11] WH changed and (**de**) to *and* (*kai*).

---

[1] WH changed dwelled (ka-tOk**A**sen) to *dwelled* (ka-tOk**i**sen). Both Aor Act Ind. katoik**e**O to *katoikizO*. [syn]

[2] WH added *then* (*de*).

[3] WH changed **and** (**kai**) to *or* (*A*).

vanisheth away.

15 For that ye *ought* to say, If the Lord will, we shall live, and do this, or that.

16 But now ye rejoice in your boastings: all such rejoicing is evil.

17 Therefore to him that knoweth to do good, and doeth *it* not, to him it is sin.

CHAPTER 5

1 Go to now, *ye* rich men, weep and howl for your miseries that shall come upon *you*.

2 Your riches are corrupted, and your garments are motheaten.

3 Your gold and silver is cankered; and the rust of them shall be a witness against you, and shall eat your flesh as it were fire. Ye have heaped treasure together for the last days.

4 Behold, the hire of the labourers who have reaped down your fields, which is of you kept back by fraud, crieth: and the cries of them which have reaped are entered into the ears of the Lord of sabaoth.

5 Ye have lived in pleasure on the earth, and been wanton; ye have nourished your hearts, as¹ in a day of

slaughter.

6 Ye have condemned *and* killed the just; *and* he doth not resist you.

7 Be patient therefore, brethren, unto the coming of the Lord. Behold, the husbandman waiteth for the precious fruit of the earth, and hath long patience for it, until [~~ever~~]² he receive the early and latter rain.

8 Be ye also patient; stablish your hearts: for the coming of the Lord draweth nigh.

9 Grudge not one against another, **brethren**³, lest **ye be condemned**⁴: behold, the judge standeth before the door.

10 Take, ~~my~~⁵ **brethren**⁶, the prophets, who have spoken

---

¹ WH omitted as (ʰOs).

² WH omitted the untranslated ever (an).
³ WH changed the word order from against one another BRETHREN to *BRETHREN against one another*.
⁴ WH changed ye be judged **against** (**kata**krithAte) to *ye be judged (krithAte)*. [prefix dropped]
⁵ WH omitted of me (mou) from the brethren of me.
⁶ WH changed the word order from of the suffering affliction BRETHREN **of me** to *BRETHREN of the suffering affliction*.

ʌ**in**[1] the name of the Lord, for an example of suffering affliction, and of patience.

11 Behold, we count them happy which **endure**[2]. Ye have heard of the patience of Job, and have seen the end of the Lord; that the Lord is very pitiful, and of tender mercy.

12 But above all things, my brethren, swear not, neither by heaven, neither by the earth, neither by any other oath: but let your yea be yea; and *your* nay, nay; lest ye fall into condemnation.

13 Is any among you afflicted? let him pray. Is any merry? let him sing psalms.

14 Is any sick among you? let him call for the elders of the church; and let them pray over him, anointing him with oil in the name of the Lord:

15 And the prayer of faith shall save the sick, and the Lord shall raise him up; and if he have committed sins, they shall be forgiven him.

16 Confess [ʌ**therefore**][3]

your **faults**[4] one to another, and pray one for another, that ye may be healed. The effectual fervent prayer of a righteous man availeth much.

17 Elias was a man subject to like passions as we are, and he prayed earnestly that it might not rain: and it rained not on the earth by the space of three years and six months.

18 And he prayed again, and the heaven gave rain, and the earth brought forth her fruit.

19 Brethren [ʌ**of me**][5] , if any of you do err from the truth, and one convert him;

20 **Let him know**[6], that he which converteth the sinner from the error of his way shall save a soul from death, and shall hide a multitude of sins.

---

[1] WH added <u>in</u> (<u>en</u>) as the KJV supplied it.

[2] WH changed <u>enduring</u> ([h]u-pomenontas) to *having en-dured* ([h]upomeinantas). **Pres** Act Part to *Aor* Act Part. [tense]

[3] WH added *therefore* (*oun*).

[4] WH changed <u>the</u> **faults** (<u>ta</u> **paraptOmata**) to *the sins* (*tas* [h]*amartias*).

[5] WH added *of me* (*mou*) after <u>brethren</u>.

[6] In their margin, WH changed **let him** <u>know</u> (<u>gi-nOsketO</u>) to *know ye* (*gi-nOskete*). Both Pres Act Imp. **3**[rd] **Sing** to *2*[nd] *Plur*. [person & number]

1 PETER

CHAPTER 1

1   Peter, an apostle of Jesus Christ, to the strangers scattered throughout Pontus, Galatia, Cappadocia, Asia, and Bithynia,

2   Elect according to the foreknow-ledge of God the Father, through sanctification of the Spirit, unto obedience and sprinkling of the blood of Jesus Christ: Grace unto you, and peace, be multiplied.

3   Blessed *be* the God and Father of our Lord Jesus Christ, which according to his abundant mercy hath begotten us again unto a lively hope by the resurrection of Jesus Christ from the dead,

4   To an inheritance incorruptible, and undefiled, and that fadeth not away, reserved in heaven for you,

5   Who are kept by the power of God through faith unto salvation ready to be revealed in the last time.

6   Wherein ye greatly rejoice, though now for a season, if need be, ye are in heaviness through manifold temptations:

7   That the trial of your faith, being **much more precious**[1] than of gold that per-

isheth, though it be tried with fire, might be found unto praise and **honour** and **glory**[2] at the appearing of Jesus Christ:

8   Whom having not seen, ye love; in whom, though now ye see *him* not, yet believing, ye rejoice with joy unspeakable and full of glory:

9   Receiving the end of your faith, *even* the salvation of *your* souls.

10 Of which salvation the prophets have enquired and searched diligently, who prophesied of the grace *that should come* unto you:

11 Searching what, or what manner of time the Spirit of Christ which was in them did signify, when it testified beforehand the sufferings of Christ, and the glory that should follow.

12 Unto whom it was revealed, that not unto themselves, but unto **us**[3] they did minister the things, which are

---

precious (polu timiOteron) to *far more valuable* (*polu-timoteron*). Both Nom Neut Sing. polu timios to *polu+timos.* [syn]

[2] WH changed the word order from HONOR and GLORY to *GLORY and HONOUR.*

[3] WH changed **us** (^hAmin) to *you* (^humin). [person]

---

[1] WH changed **much** more

now reported unto you by them that have preached the gospel unto you with the Holy Ghost sent down from heaven; which things the angels desire to look into.

13 Wherefore gird up the loins of your mind, be sober, and hope to the end for the grace that is to be brought unto you at the revelation of Jesus Christ;

14 As obedient children, not fashioning yourselves according to the former lusts in your ignorance:

15 But as he which hath called you is holy, so be ye holy in all manner of conversation;

16 Because it is written, **Be ye**[1] holy; for I **am**[2] holy.

17 And if ye call on the Father, who without respect of persons judgeth according to every man's work, pass the time of your sojourning _here_ in fear:

18 Forasmuch as ye know that ye were not redeemed with corruptible things, _as_ silver and gold, from your vain conversation _received_ by tradition from your fathers;

19 But with the precious blood of Christ, as of a lamb without blemish and without spot:

20 Who verily was foreordained before the foundation of the world, but was manifest in these **last**[3] times for you,

21 Who by him **do believe**[4] in God, that raised him up from the dead, and gave him glory; that your faith and hope might be in God.

22 Seeing ye have purified your souls in obeying the truth ~~through the Spirit~~[5] unto unfeigned love of the brethren, _see that ye_ love one another with a ~~pure~~[6] heart fervently:

---

[1] WH changed **become** ye (**gen**es~~the~~) to _ye will be_ (_eses~~the~~_). **Aor** Mid **Imp** to _Fut_ Mid _Ind_. [tense & mood]

[2] WH omitted am (eimi) after I.

[3] WH changed last (escat**On**) to _last_ (_escatou_). Gen Masc **Plur** to Gen Masc _Sing_. [number]

[4] WH changed believing (**piste**uontas) to believing (_pistous_). **Verbal**: Pres Act Part Acc Masc Plur (believing) to _Adjective_: Acc Masc Plur (_believing_).

[5] WH omitted through {the} Spirit (dia pneumatos).

[6] WH omitted pure (katharas) in their text, but retained it in their margin.

23 Being born again, not of corruptible seed, but of incorruptible, by the word of God, which liveth and abideth ~~for ever~~[1].

24 For all flesh *is* as grass, and all the glory **of man**[2] as the flower of grass. The grass withereth, and the flower ~~thereof~~[3] falleth away:

25 But the word of the Lord endureth for ever. And this is the word which by the gospel is preached unto you.

CHAPTER 2

1 Wherefore laying aside all malice, and all guile, and hypocrisies, and envies, and all evil speakings,

2 As newborn babes, desire the sincere milk of the word, that ye may grow [∧**into salvation**][4] thereby:

3 **If so be**[5] ye have tasted that the Lord *is* gracious.

4 To whom coming, *as unto* a living stone, disallowed indeed of men, but chosen of God, *and* precious,

5 Ye also, as lively stones, are built up a spiritual house [∧**into**][6], an holy priesthood, to offer up spiritual sacrifices, acceptable to [~~the~~][7] God by Jesus Christ.

6 **Wherefore also**[8] it is contained in ~~the~~[9] scripture, Behold, I lay in Sion a chief corner stone, elect, precious: and he that believeth on him shall not be confounded.

7 Unto you therefore which believe *he is* precious: but **unto them which be disobedient**[10], **the stone**[11]

---

[1] WH omitted <u>into the ages</u> (<u>eis ton aiOna</u>).

[2] WH changed <u>of **man**</u> (**anthrOpou**) to *of it* (*autAs*).

[3] WH omitted <u>thereof</u> (<u>autou</u>) after <u>flower</u>.

[4] WH added *into salvation* (*eis sOtArian*) after <u>ye may grow</u>.

[5] WH changed <u>if **so be**</u> (<u>eiper</u>) to *if* (*ei*).

[6] WH added *into* (*eis*) after <u>house</u> <u>spiritual</u>.

[7] WH omitted the untranslated <u>the</u> (<u>tO</u>) before <u>God</u>.

[8] WH changed <u>wherefore</u> **also** (<u>dio **kai**</u>) to *wherefore then* (*dioti*).

[9] WH omitted <u>the</u> (<u>tA</u>) before <u>scripture</u>.

[10] WH changed <u>unto them which be **disobedient**</u> (*apeithousi*) to *unto them which be **unfaithful*** (*apistousi*). Both Pres Act Part. <u>a-peitheO</u> to *a-pisteO*.

[11] WH changed <u>the stone</u> (<u>lithon</u>) to *the stone* (*lithos*). **Acc** Masc Sing to **Nom** Masc Sing. [case]

672

which the builders disallowed, the same is made the head of the corner,

8 And a stone of stumbling, and a rock of offence, *even to them* which stumble at the word, being disobedient: whereunto also they were appointed.

9 But ye *are* a chosen generation, a royal priesthood, an holy nation, a peculiar people; that ye should shew forth the praises of him who hath called you out of darkness into his marvellous light:

10 Which in time past *were* not a people, but *are* now the people of God: which had not obtained mercy, but now have obtained mercy.

11 Dearly beloved, I beseech *you* as strangers and pilgrims, abstain from fleshly lusts, which war against the soul;

12 Having your conversation honest among the Gentiles: that, whereas they speak against you as evildoers, they may by *your* good works, **which they shall behold**[1],

glorify God in the day of visitation.

13 Submit yourselves **[therefore]**[2] to every ordinance of man for the Lord's sake: whether it be to the king, as supreme;

14 Or unto governors, as unto them that are sent by him for the punishment **[on the one hand]**[3] of evildoers, and for the praise of them that do well.

15 For so is the will of God, that with well doing ye may put to silence the ignorance of foolish men:

16 As free, and not using *your* liberty for a cloke of maliciousness, but as the servants of God.

17 Honour all *men*. Love the brotherhood. Fear God. Honour the king.

18 Servants, *be* subject to *your* masters with all fear; not only to the good and gentle, but also to the froward.

19 For this *is* thankworthy, if a man for conscience toward God endure grief, suffering wrongfully.

---

[1] WH changed **having** beheld (epopteusantes) to *beholding* (epopteuontes). **Aor** Act Part to *Pres* Act Part. [tense]

[2] WH omitted the untranslated therefore (oun) after submit yourselves.
[3] WH omitted the untranslated on the one hand (men) after punishment.

20 For what glory *is it*, if, when ye be buffeted for your faults, ye shall take it patiently? but if, when ye do well, and suffer *for it*, ye take it patiently, this *is* acceptable with God.

21 For even hereunto were ye called: because Christ also suffered for **us**[1], leaving **us**[2] an example, that ye should follow his steps:

22 Who did no sin, neither was guile found in his mouth:

23 Who, when he was reviled, reviled not again; when he suffered, he threatened not; but committed *himself* to him that judgeth righteously:

24 Who his own self bare our sins in his own body on the tree, that we, being dead to sins, should live unto righteousness: by ~~whose~~[3] stripes ye were healed.

25 For ye were as sheep **going astray**[4]; but are now returned unto the Shepherd and bishop of your souls.

CHAPTER 3

1 Likewise, **ye**[5] wives, *be* in subjection to your own husbands; that, if any obey not the word, **they** also **may** without the word **be won**[6] by the conversation of the wives;

2 While they behold your chaste conversation *coupled* with fear.

3 Whose adorning let it not be that outward *adorning* of plaiting the hair, and of wearing of gold, or of putting on of apparel;

4 But *let it be* the hidden man of the heart, in that which is not corruptible, *even the ornament* of a meek and quiet spirit, which is in the sight of God of great price.

5 For after this manner in the old time the holy women also, who trusted **in**[7]

---

[1] WH changed **us** (^hAmOn) to *you* (^humOn). [person]

[2] WH changed **us** (^hAmin) to *you* (^humin). [person]

[3] WH omitted of him (autou) from the stripes of him.

[4] WH changed going astray (planOmena) to *going astray* (planOmenoi). Both Pres Pass Part. Nom **Neut** Plur to Nom *Masc* Plur. [gender]

[5] WH omitted ye (ai--the) before wives.

[6] WH changed they **might** be won (kerdAthAsOntai) to *they will* be won (kerdAthAsontai). **Aor** Pass **Sub** to *Fut* Pass **Ind**. [tense & mood]

[7] WH changed **in** (eis) to *on* (epi).

[the][1] God, adorned themselves, being in subjection unto their own husbands:

6 Even as Sara obeyed Abraham, calling him lord: whose daughters ye are, as long as ye do well, and are not afraid with any amazement.

7 Likewise, ye husbands, dwell with _them_ according to knowledge, giving honour unto the wife, as unto the weaker vessel, and as being heirs together of the grace of life; that your prayers **be not hindered**[2].

8 Finally, _be ye_ all of one mind, having compassion one of another, love as brethren, _be_ pitiful, **_be courteous_**[3]:

9 Not rendering evil for evil, or railing for railing: but contrariwise blessing; **knowing**[4] that ye are thereunto called, that ye should inherit a blessing.

10 For he that will love life, and see good days, let him refrain **his**[5] tongue from evil, and **his**[6] lips that they speak no guile:

11 **[ʌbut]**[7] Let him eschew evil, and do good; let him seek peace, and ensue it.

12 For **the**[8] eyes of the Lord _are_ over the righteous, and his ears _are open_ unto their prayers: but the face of the Lord _is_ against them that do evil.

13 And who _is_ he that will harm you, if ye be **followers**[9] of that which is good?

14 But and if ye suffer for righteousness' sake, happy _are ye_: and be not afraid of their terror, neither be troubled;

15 But sanctify the Lord **God**[10] in your hearts:

---

[1] WH omitted the untranslated <u>the</u> (<u>ton</u>) before <u>God</u>.
[2] WH changed <u>be not hindered</u> (<u>ekkoptesthai</u>) to _be not hindered_ (_egkoptesthai_). Both Pres Pass Inf. [spell]
[3] WH changed [be] **courteous** (**fiofrones**) to [be] **_humble-minded_** (_tapeinofrones_). Both Adjective: Nom Masc Plur.
[4] WH omitted <u>knowing</u> (<u>eidotes</u>) before <u>that</u>.

[5] WH omitted <u>of him</u> (<u>autou</u>) from <u>the</u> tongue <u>of him</u>.
[6] WH omitted <u>of him</u> (<u>autou</u>) from <u>the</u> lips <u>of him</u>.
[7] WH added _but_ (_de_) to go before <u>Let him eschew</u>.
[8] WH omitted <u>the</u> (<u>oi</u>) before <u>eyes</u>.
[9] WH changed **followers** (**mimAtai**) to _zealots_ (_zAlOtai_).
[10] WH changed **God** (**theon**) to **_Christ_** (_criston_).

~~and~~[1] *be* ready always to *give* an answer to every man that asketh you a reason of the hope that is in you [∧**but**][2] with meekness and fear:

16 Having a good conscience; that, whereas **they speak evil**[3] ~~of you, as of evildoers~~[4], they may be ashamed that falsely accuse your good conversation in Christ.

17 For *it is* better, if the will of God **be so**[5], that ye suffer for well doing, than for evil doing.

18 For Christ also **hath** once **suffered**[6] for sins, the just for the unjust, that he might bring us to God, being put to death in the flesh, but quickened by ~~the~~[7] Spirit:

19 By which also he went and preached unto the spirits in prison;

20 Which sometime were disobedient, when ~~once~~[8] the longsuffering of God **waited**[9] in the days of Noah, while the ark was a preparing, wherein **few**[10], that is, eight souls were saved by water.

21 The like figure **whereunto**[11] *even* baptism doth

---

[1] WH omitted <u>and</u> (<u>de</u>) that went before [<u>be</u>] <u>ready</u>.

[2] WH added *but* (*alla*) to go after <u>concerning</u> the <u>in</u> <u>you</u> <u>hope</u>.

[3] WH changed <u>they **might** speak evil against</u> (<u>katalalOsin</u>) to *we are being* sp*oken* evil **against** (*katalaleisthe*). Pres **Act** **Sub** 3rd Plur to Pres *Pass Ind* 2nd Plur. [voice, mood, & person]

[4] WH omitted <u>of you</u> <u>as of evildoers</u> (<u>ʰumOn</u> <u>ʰOs kakopoiOn</u>).

[5] WH changed <u>wills</u> (<u>thelei</u>) to *should* will (*theloi*). Pres Act **Ind** to Pres Act *Opt*. [mood]

[6] In their margin, WH changed <u>has suffered</u> (<u>epathe</u>) to *has suffered* (*apethane*). Both Aor Act Ind. **pascO** to *apothnAskO*. [syn]

[7] WH omitted <u>the</u> (<u>tO</u>) before <u>Spirit</u>.

[8] WH omitted <u>once</u> (^hapax) after <u>when</u>.

[9] WH changed <u>waited</u> (<u>exedeceto</u>) to *waited* (*apexedeceto*). Both Impf M/P-D Ind. [prefix added]

[10] WH changed <u>few</u> (^holigai) to *few* (^holigoi). Nom **Fem** Plur to Nom *Masc* Plur. [gender]

[11] WH changed <u>whereunto</u> (^h**O**) to *whereunto* (^h*o*). **Dat** Neut Sing to *Nom* Neut Sing. [case]

also now save **us**[1] (not the putting away of the filth of the flesh, but the answer of a good conscience toward God,) by the resurrection of Jesus Christ:

22 Who is gone into heaven, and is on the right hand of God; angels and authorities and powers being made subject unto him.

CHAPTER 4

1 Forasmuch then as Christ hath suffered ~~for us~~[2] in the flesh, arm yourselves likewise with the same mind: for he that hath suffered ~~in~~[3] the flesh hath ceased from **sin**[4];

2 That he no longer should live the rest of *his* time in the flesh to the lusts of men, but to the will of God.

3 For the time past ~~of~~

~~our~~ life[5] may suffice **us**[6] **to have wrought**[7] the **will**[8] of the Gentiles, when we walked in lasciviousness, lusts, excess of wine, revellings, banquetings, and abominable idolatries:

4 Wherein they think it strange that ye run not with *them* to the same excess of riot, speaking evil of *you*:

5 Who shall give account to him that is ready to judge the quick and the dead.

6 For for this cause was the gospel preached also to them that are dead, that they might be judged according to men in the flesh, but live according to God in the spirit.

7 But the end of all things is at hand: be ye therefore sober, and watch unto [~~the~~][9] prayer.

8 ~~And~~[10] above all things

---

[1] WH changed **us** (^{h}Amas) to *you* (^{h}umas). [person]
[2] WH omitted for us (^{h}uper ^{h}AmOn) after suffered.
[3] WH omitted in (en) before flesh.
[4] In their margin, WH changed sin (^{h}amartias) to *sins* (^{h}amartiais). **Gen** Fem **Sing** to *Dat* Fem ***Plur***. [case & number]

[5] WH omitted of [our] life (tou biou).
[6] WH omitted us (^{h}amin).
[7] WH changed to work (katergasasthai) to *to have worked* (kateirgas*th*ai). **Aor** Mid Inf to *Pf* Mid Inf. [tense]
[8] WH changed will (**the**lAma) to *will* (**boul**Ama). [syn]
[9] WH omitted the untranslated the (tas) before prayer.
[10] WH omitted and (de).

have fervent charity among yourselves: for charity **shall cover**[1] the multitude of sins.

9 Use hospitality one to another without **grudging**[2].

10 As every man hath received the gift, *even so* minister the same one to another, as good stewards of the manifold grace of God.

11 If any man speak, *let him speak* as the oracles of God; if any man minister, *let him do it* as of the ability which God giveth: that God in all things may be glorified through Jesus Christ, to whom be praise and dominion for ever and ever. Amen.

12 Beloved, think it not strange concerning the fiery trial which is to try you, as though some strange thing happened unto you:

13 But rejoice, inasmuch as ye are partakers of Christ's sufferings; that, when his glory shall be revealed, ye may be glad also with exceeding joy.

14 If ye be reproached for the name of Christ, happy *are ye*; for the spirit of glory and of God resteth upon you: ~~on their part he is evil spoken of, but on your part he is glorified~~[3].

15 But let none of you suffer as a murderer, or *as* a thief, or *as* an evildoer, or as a busybody in other men's matters.

16 Yet if *any man suffer* as a Christian, let him not be ashamed; but let him glorify God on this **behalf**[4].

17 For the time *is come* that judgment must begin at the house of God: and if *it* first *begin* at us, what shall the end *be* of them that obey not the gospel of God?

18 And if the righteous scarcely be saved, where shall the ungodly and the sinner appear?

19 Wherefore let them that suffer according to the will of God commit the keeping of

---

[1] WH changed **shall** cover (kaluṩei) to *covers* (*kaluptei*). **Fut** Act Ind to *Pres* Act Ind. [tense]

[2] WH changed grudgings (goggusm**On**) to *grudging* (*goggusmou*). Gen Masc **Plur** to Gen Masc *Sing*. [number]

[3] WH omitted according to them then he is evil spoken of but according to you he is glorified (kata men autous blasfAmeitai kata de [h]umas doxazetai).

[4] WH change **part** (**merei**) to *name* (*onomati*).

their[1] souls *to him* in well doing, ~~as~~[2] unto a faithful Creator.

CHAPTER 5

1   The elders **which**[3] are among you I exhort, who am also an elder, and a witness of the sufferings of Christ, and also a partaker of the glory that shall be revealed:

2   Feed the flock of God which is among you, **taking the oversight**[4] *thereof*, not by constraint, but willingly [∧**according to God**][5] ; not for filthy lucre, but of a ready mind;

3   Neither as being lords over *God's* heritage, but being ensamples to the flock.

4   And when the chief Shepherd shall appear, ye shall receive a crown of glory that fadeth not away.

5   Likewise, ye younger, submit yourselves unto the elder. Yea, all *of you* ~~be subject~~[6] one to another, and be clothed with humility: for God resisteth the proud, and giveth grace to the humble.

6   Humble   yourselves therefore under the mighty hand of God, that he may exalt you in due time:

7   Casting all your care upon him; for he careth for you.

8   Be sober, be vigilant; ~~because~~[7] your adversary the devil, as a roaring lion, walketh about, seeking whom **he may devour**[8]:

9   Whom resist stedfast in the faith, knowing that the same afflictions are accomplished in your brethren that are in the world.

10   But the God of all grace, who hath called **us**[9] unto his eternal glory by

---

[1] WH changed of them**selves** (**ʰ**eautOn) to *of them* (*autOn*) in the phrase the keeping of the souls of themselves. **Refl** pro to *Pers* pronoun.

[2] WH omitted as (ʰOs)

[3] WH changed **which** (**tous**) to *therefore* (*oun*).

[4] In their margin, WH omitted taking the oversight (episkopountes).

[5] WH added *according to God (kata ~~th~~eon)* after willingly. They did not make this addition in their margin, however.

[6] WH omitted be subject (ʰu-potassomenoi).

[7] WH omitted because (ʰoti).

[8] WH changed **he might** devour (katapiA) to *to devour* (*katapiein*). Aor Act **Sub** to Aor Act *Inf.* [mood]

[9] WH changed **us** (ʰAmas) to *you* (ʰumas). [person]

Christ **Jesus**[1], after that ye have suffered a while, **make you**[2] **perfect**[3], **stablish**[4], **strengthen**[5], settle *you*.

11 To him *be* **glory and**[6] dominion for ever and ever. Amen.

12 By Silvanus, a faithful brother unto you, as I suppose, I have written briefly, exhorting, and testifying that this is the true grace of God wherein **ye stand**[7].

13 The *church that is* at Babylon, elected together with *you*, saluteth you; and *so* doth Marcus my son.

14 Greet ye one another with a kiss of charity. Peace *be* with you all that are in Christ **Jesus**[8]. **Amen**[9].

---

[1] WH omitted <u>Jesus</u> (<u>iAsou</u>).

[2] WH omitted <u>you</u> (^h<u>umas</u>).

[3] WH changed **should** <u>make perfect</u> (<u>katartisai</u>) to *will make perfect* (*katartisei*). **Aor** Act **Opt** to *Fut* Act *Ind*. [tense & mood]

[4] WH changed **should** <u>stablish</u> (<u>st̶henOsai</u>) to *will stablish* (*st̶henOsei*). **Aor** Act **Opt** to *Fut* Act *Ind*. [tense & mood]

[5] WH omitted <u>strengthen</u> (<u>t̶hemeliOsai</u>). In their margin, they changed **should** <u>strengthen</u> (<u>t̶hemeliOsai</u>) to *will strengthen* (*t̶hemeliOsei*). **Aor** Act **Opt** to *Fut* Act *Ind*. [tense & mood]

[6] WH omitted <u>the glory</u> <u>and</u> (^h<u>A</u> <u>doxa</u> <u>kai</u>) before <u>dominion</u>.

[7] WH changed **ye have** <u>stood</u> (^h<u>estAkate</u>) to *stand ye*

(*stAte*). **Pf** Act **Ind** to *Aor* Act *Imp*. [tense & mood]

[8] WH omitted <u>Jesus</u> (<u>isou</u>).

[9] WH omitted <u>Amen</u> (<u>amAn</u>).

2 PETER

CHAPTER 1

1   **Simon**[1] Peter, a servant and an apostle of Jesus Christ, to them that have obtained like precious faith with us through the righteousness of God and ~~our~~[2] Saviour Jesus Christ:

2   Grace and peace be multiplied unto you through the knowledge of God, and of Jesus our Lord,

3   According as his divine power hath given unto us all things that *pertain* unto life and godliness, through the knowledge of him that hath called us ~~to~~[3] [ᴧ**his own**][4] **glory** and **virtue**[5]:

4   Whereby are given unto us exceeding great **and** **precious**[6] promises: that by these ye might be partakers of the divine nature, having escaped the corruption that is in ᴧ**the**[7] world through lust.

5   And beside this, giving all diligence, add to your faith virtue; and to virtue knowledge;

6   And to knowledge temperance; and to temperance patience; and to patience godliness;

7   And to godliness brotherly kindness; and to brotherly kindness charity.

8   For if these things be in you, and abound, they make *you that ye shall* neither *be* barren nor unfruitful in the knowledge of our Lord Jesus Christ.

9   But he that lacketh these things is blind, and cannot see afar off, and hath forgotten that he was purged from his old sins.

10   Wherefore the rather, brethren, give diligence to make your calling and election sure: for if ye do these things, ye shall never fall:

---

[1] In their margin, WH changed Simon (zimOn) to *Simeon* (*zumeOn*). [spell]

[2] WH omitted of us (ʰAmOn) from the Saviour of us.

[3] WH omitted to (dia) and forced the dative case to supply the preposition.

[4] WH added *his own* (*idia*) before glory.

[5] WH changed glory and virtue (doxAs kai aretAs) to *glory and virtue* (*dixA kai aretA*). **Gen** to **Dat**. [case]

[6] WH changed the word order from great unto us AND PRECIOUS to *PRECIOUS unto us AND great*.

[7] WH added the (tO) after in as the KJV supplied.

681

11 For so an entrance shall be ministered unto you abundantly into the everlasting kingdom of our Lord and Saviour Jesus Christ.

12 Wherefore **I will** ~~not~~[1] **be negligent**[2] to put you **always**[3] in remembrance of these things, though ye know *them*, and be established in the present truth.

13 Yea, I think it meet, as long as I am in this tabernacle, to stir you up by putting *you* in remembrance;

14 Knowing that shortly I must put off *this* my tabernacle, even as our Lord Jesus Christ hath shewed me.

15 Moreover I will endeavour that ye may be able after my decease to have these things always in remembrance.

16 For we have not followed cunningly devised fables, when we made known unto you the power and coming of our Lord Jesus Christ, but were eyewitnesses of his majesty.

17 For he received from God the Father honour and glory, when there came such a voice to him from the excellent glory, This is my beloved Son, in whom I am well pleased.

18 And this voice which came from heaven we heard, when we were with him in the holy mount.

19 We have also a more sure word of prophecy; whereunto ye do well that ye take heed, as unto a light that shineth in a dark place, until the day dawn, and the day star arise in your hearts:

20 Knowing this first, that no prophecy of the scripture is of any private interpretation.

21 For the prophecy came not **in old time**[4] by the will of man: but **holy**[5] men of God spake *as they were* moved by the Holy Ghost.

CHAPTER 2

1 But there were false

---

[1] WH omitted <u>not</u> (<u>ouk</u>).
[2] WH changed <u>I will **be negligent**</u> (<u>amelAsO</u>) to *I will **intend*** (*mellAsO*). Both Fut Act Ind. **a**meleO to mellO. [prefix dropped & spell]
[3] WH changed the word order from <u>you</u> <u>ALWAYS</u> to *ALWAYS you*.

[4] WH changed the word order from <u>IN OLD TIME</u> <u>prophecy</u> to *prophecy IN OLD TIME*.
[5] WH changed **holy** (^h<u>agioi</u>) to ***from*** (*apa*).

prophets also among the people, even as there shall be false teachers among you, who privily shall bring in damnable heresies, even denying the Lord that bought them, and bring upon themselves swift destruction.

2   And many shall follow their **pernicious ways**[1]; by reason of whom the way of truth shall be evil spoken of.

3   And through covetousness shall they with feigned words make merchandise of you: whose judgment now of a long time lingereth not, and their damnation slumbereth not.

4   For if God spared not the angels that sinned, but cast *them* down to hell, and delivered *them* into **chains**[2] of darkness, **to be reserved**[3]

unto judgment;

5   And spared not the old world, but saved Noah the eighth *person*, a preacher of righteousness, bringing in the flood upon the world of the ungodly;

6   And turning the cities of Sodom and Gomorrha into ashes condemned *them* with an overthrow, making *them* an ensample unto those that after should live ungodly;

7   And delivered just Lot, vexed with the filthy conversation of the wicked:

8   (For that righteous man dwelling among them, in seeing and hearing, vexed *his* righteous soul from day to day with *their* unlawful deeds;)

9   The Lord knoweth how to deliver the godly out of **temptations**[4], and to reserve the unjust unto the day of judgment to be punished:

10   But chiefly them that walk after the flesh in the lust of uncleanness, and despise government. Presumptuous *are they*, selfwilled, they are not afraid to speak evil of

---

[1] WH changed **pernicious ways** (**apOleiais**) to *indecent ways* (*aselgeiais*). **apOleia** (destruction) to *aselgeia* (*sensuality*).

[2] WH changed chains (seirais) to *chains* (*seirois*). Dat **Fem** Plur to Dat *Masc* Plur. [gender]

[3] WH changed **having been** reserved (**tetArAmenous**) to *being reserved* (*tAroumenous*). Both Acc Masc Plur. **Pf** Pass Part to

---

Pres Pass Part. [tense]

[4] WH changed temptations (peirasmOn) to *temptation* (*peirasmou*). Gen Masc **Plur** to Gen Masc *Sing*. [number]

dignities.

11 Whereas angels, which are greater in power and might, bring not railing accusation against them before the Lord.

12 But these, as **natural**[1] brute beasts, **made**[2] to be taken and destroyed, speak evil of the things that they understand not; ∧and[3] **shall utterly perish**[4] in their own corruption;

13 **And shall receive**[5] the reward of unrighteousness, *as* they that count it pleasure to riot in the day time. Spots *they are* and blemishes,

sporting themselves with their own **deceivings**[6] while they feast with you;

14 Having eyes full of adultery, and that cannot cease from sin; beguiling unstable souls: an heart they have exercised with **covetous practices**[7]; cursed children:

15 **Which have forsaken**[8] **the**[9] right way, and are gone astray, following the way of Balaam *the son* of **Bosor**[10], who loved the wages of unrighteousness;

16 But was rebuked for his iniquity: the dumb ass speaking with man's voice

---

[1] WH changed the word order from NATURAL made to *made NATURAL.*

[2] WH changed made (gegenAmena) to *made* (*gegennAmena*). Both Pf Pass Part. [spell]

[3] WH added *and* (*kai*) as the KJV supplied.

[4] WH changed shall **utterly** perish (**katafth**arAsontai) to *shall perish* (*ftharAsontai*). Both Fut Pass Ind. [prefix dropped]

[5] WH changed {and} **shall receive** (**komi**oumenoi) to {and} *being guilty of* (*adikoumenoi*). **Fut** Mid Part of **komizO** to *Pres* M/P Part of *adikeO*. [tense]

[6] WH changed **deceivings** (apatais) to *seductions* (*agapais*). In their margin, WH retained deceivings (apatais).

[7] WH changed covetous practices (pleonexiais) to *covetous practice* (*pleonexias*). **Dat** Fem **Plur** to *Gen* Fem **Sing**. [case & number]

[8] WH changed **having** forsaken (katalipontes) to *forsaking* (*kataleipontes*). **Aor** Act Part to *Pres* Act Part. [tense]

[9] WH omitted the (tAn) before right.

[10] WH changed Bosor (**bosor**) to *Beor* (*beOr*). In their margin, they retained Bosor (**bosor**). [spell]

forbad the madness of the prophet.

17 These are wells without water, **[ᴧand]**[1] **clouds**[2] that are carried with a tempest; to whom the mist of darkness is reserved ~~for ever~~[3].

18 For when they speak great swelling *words* of vanity, they allure through the lusts of the flesh, ~~*through*~~[4] *much* wantonness, those **that were clean**[5] **escaped**[6] from them who live in error.

19 While they promise them liberty, they themselves are the servants of corruption: for of whom a man is overcome, of the same is he brought in bondage.

20 For if after they have escaped the pollutions of the world through the knowledge

of the Lord **[ᴧof us]**[7] and Saviour Jesus Christ, they are again entangled therein, and overcome, the latter end is worse with them than the beginning.

21 For it had been better for them not to have known the way of righteousness, than, after they have known *it*, **to turn**[8] from the holy commandment delivered unto them.

22 ~~**But**~~[9] it is happened unto them according to the true proverb, The dog *is* turned to his own vomit again; and the sow that was washed to her wallowing in the mire.

CHAPTER 3

1 This second epistle, beloved, I now write unto you; in *both* which I stir up your pure minds by way of remembrance:

2 That ye may be mindful of the words which were spoken before by the holy

---

[1] WH added *and* (*kai*) before clouds.
[2] WH changed **clouds** (*nefelai*) to *mists* (*ouiclai*).
[3] WH omitted for ever (*eis aiOna*).
[4] WH omitted the through (*en*) that the KJV supplied.
[5] WH changed {that were} **clean** (*ontOs*--really) to {*that were*} *barely* (*ʰoligOs*).
[6] WH changed escap**ed** (*apofugontas*) to *escaping* (*apofeugontas*). **Aor** Act Part to *Pres* Act Part. [tense]

[7] WH added *of us* (*ʰAmOn*) after Lord.
[8] WH changed to turn **on** (*epi*streṣai) to *to turn by* (*ʰu-postreṣai*). Both Aor Act Inf. [prefix changed]
[9] WH omitted but (*de*).

prophets, and of the commandment **of us**[1] the apostles of the Lord and Saviour:

3   Knowing this first, that there shall come in **the last days**[2] scoffers, walking after their own **lusts**[3],

4   And saying, Where is the promise of his coming? for since the fathers fell asleep, all things continue as *they were* from the beginning of the creation.

5   For this they willingly are ignorant of, that by the word of God the heavens were of old, and the earth standing out of the water and in the water:

6   Whereby the world that then was, being overflowed with water, perished:

7   But the heavens and the earth, which are now, by the same word are kept in store, reserved unto fire against the day of judgment and perdition of ungodly men.

8   But, beloved, be not ignorant of this one thing, that one day *is* with the Lord as a thousand years, and a thousand years as one day.

9   The Lord is not slack concerning his promise, as some men count slackness; but is longsuffering to **us-ward**[4], not willing that any should perish, but that all should come to repentance.

10 But the day of **the**[5] Lord will come as a thief ~~in the night~~[6]; in the which the heavens shall pass away with a great noise, and the elements **shall melt**[7] with fervent heat, the earth also and the works that are therein **shall be burned up**[8].

---

[1] WH changed **of us** (^hAmOn) to *of you* (^humOn). [person]
[2] WH changed {the} last day (escatou) to {the} *last days* (escatOn). Gen **Neut Sing** to Gen *Fem Plur*. [gender & number]
[3] WH changed the word order from their own of them LUSTS to *their own LUSTS of them.*

[4] WH changed **us**-ward (^hAmas) to *you-ward* (^humas). [person]
[5] WH omitted the (^hA) before Lord.
[6] WH omitted in {the} night (en nukti).
[7] WH changed **they** will be loosed (luthAsontai) to *it will be loosed* (luthAsetai). Both Fut Pass Ind. 3rd **Plur** to 3rd *Sing*. [number]
[8] In their margin, WH changed shall be **burned up** (katakaAsetai) to *shall be discovered* (eurethAsetai). Both Fut Pass Ind. **katakaiO** to ^heuriskO.

11 *Seeing* **then**[1] *that* all these things shall be dissolved, what manner *of persons* ought ye to be in *all* holy conversation and godliness,

12 Looking for and hasting unto the coming of the day of God, wherein the heavens being on fire shall be dissolved, and the elements shall melt with fervent heat?

13 Nevertheless we, according to his promise, look for new heavens and a new earth, wherein dwelleth righteousness.

14 Wherefore, beloved, seeing that ye look for such things, be diligent that ye may be found of him in peace, without spot, and blameless.

15 And account *that* the longsuffering of our Lord *is* salvation; even as our beloved brother Paul also according to the wisdom given unto him hath written unto you;

16 As also in all *his*[2] epistles, speaking in them of these things; in **which**[3] are some things hard to be understood, which they that are unlearned and unstable wrest, as *they do* also the other scriptures, unto their own destruction.

17 Ye therefore, beloved, seeing ye know *these things* before, beware lest ye also, being led away with the error of the wicked, fall from your own stedfastness.

18 But grow in grace, and *in* the knowledge of our Lord and Saviour Jesus Christ. To him *be* glory both now and for ever. Amen.

---

[1] WH changed **then** (<u>oun</u>) to *so* (*^houtOs*).

[2] WH omitted <u>the</u> (<u>tais</u>) before <u>epistles</u>.

[3] WH changed <u>which</u> (<u>ois</u>) to *which* (*ais*). Dat **Masc** Plur to Dat **Fem** Plur. [gender]

1 JOHN

CHAPTER 1

1   That which was from the beginning, which we have heard, which we have seen with our eyes, which we have looked upon, and our hands have handled, of the Word of life;

2   (For the life was manifested, and we have seen *it*, and bear witness, and shew unto you that eternal life, which was with the Father, and was manifested unto us;)

3   That which we have seen and heard declare we [ʌ**also**]¹ unto you, that ye also may have fellowship with us: and truly our fellowship *is* with the Father, and with his Son Jesus Christ.

4   And these things write we **unto you**², that **your**³ joy

---

¹ WH added *also* (*kai*) before unto you.

² WH changed **unto you** (ʰ**umin**) to *we* (ʰ*Ameis*). **Dat** Plur (write we **unto you**) to *Nom* Plur (write we *ourselves*). [case & person]

³ WH changed of **you** (ʰ**u-mOn**) to *of us* (ʰ*AmOn*) in the phrase the joy of you. In their margin, they retained of you (ʰumOn). [person]

---

may be full.

5   This then is the message which we have heard of him, and declare unto you, that God is light, and in him is no darkness at all.

6   If we say that we have fellowship with him, and walk in darkness, we lie, and do not the truth:

7   But if we walk in the light, as he is in the light, we have fellowship one with another, and the blood of Jesus ~~Christ~~⁴ his Son cleanseth us from all sin.

8   If we say that we have no sin, we deceive ourselves, and the truth is not in us.

9   If we confess our sins, he is faithful and just to forgive us *our* sins, and to cleanse us from all unrighteousness.

10   If we say that we have not sinned, we make him a liar, and his word is not in us.

CHAPTER 2

1   My little children, these things write I unto you, that ye sin not. And if any man sin, we have an advocate with the Father, Jesus Christ the righteous:

---

⁴ WH omitted Christ (cristou) after Jesus.

2 And he is the propitiation for our sins: and not for ours only, but also for *the sins of* the whole world.
3 And hereby we do know that we know him, if we keep his commandments.
4 He that saith **[^that]**[1]**,** I know him, and keepeth not his commandments, is a liar, and the truth is not in him.
5 But whoso keepeth his word, in him verily is the love of God perfected: hereby know we that we are in him.
6 He that saith he abideth in him ought himself also ~~**so**~~[2] to walk, even as he walked.
7 **Brethren**[3], I write no new commandment unto you, but an old commandment which ye had from the beginning. The old commandment is the word which ye have heard ~~**from the beginning**~~[4].
8 Again, a new commandment I write unto you, which thing is true in him and in you: because the darkness is past, and the true light now shineth.
9 He that saith he is in the light, and hateth his brother, is in darkness even until now.
10 He that loveth his brother abideth in the light, and there is none occasion of stumbling in him.
11 But he that hateth his brother is in darkness, and walketh in darkness, and knoweth not whither he goeth, because that darkness hath blinded his eyes.
12 I write unto you, little children, because your sins are forgiven you for his name's sake.
13 I write unto you, fathers, because ye have known him *that is* from the beginning. I write unto you, young men, because ye have overcome the wicked one. **I write**[5] unto you, little children, because ye have known the Father.
14 I have written unto you, fathers, because ye have known him *that is* from the beginning. I have written unto you, young men, because ye are strong, and the word of God abideth in you,

---

[1] WH added *that* (*^{h}oti*) after saith.
[2] WH omitted so (^{h}outO) before to walk.
[3] WH changed **brethren** (**adelf**oi) to ***beloved*** (***aga-pA****toi*).
[4] WH omitted from {the} beginning (ap' arcAs).

[5] WH changed I wr**i**te (graf**O**) to *I wrote* (*egra**ŝa***). **Pres** Act Sing to ***Aor*** Act Ind. [tense]

and ye have overcome the wicked one.

15 Love not the world, neither the things *that are* in the world. If any man love the world, the love of the Father is not in him.

16 For all that *is* in the world, the lust of the flesh, and the lust of the eyes, and the pride of life, is not of the Father, but is of the world.

17 And the world passeth away, and the lust thereof: but he that doeth the will of God abideth for ever.

18 Little children, it is the last time: and as ye have heard that [the]¹ antichrist shall come, even now are there many antichrists; whereby we know that it is the last time.

19 They went out from us, but they were not of us; for if they had been of us, they would *no doubt* have continued with us: but *they went out*, that they might be made manifest that they were not all of us.

20 But ye have an unction from the Holy One, and ye know **all things**².

21 I have not written unto you because ye know not the truth, but because ye know it, and that no lie is of the truth.

22 Who is a liar but he that denieth that Jesus is the Christ? He is antichrist, that denieth the Father and the Son.

23 Whosoever denieth the Son, the same hath not the Father: *(but) he that acknowledgeth the Son hath the Father also.*

24 Let that **therefore**³ abide in you, which ye have heard from the beginning. If that which ye have heard from the beginning shall remain in you, ye also shall continue in the Son, and in the Father.

25 And this is the promise that he hath promised **us**⁴, *even* eternal life.

26 These *things* have I written unto you concerning them that seduce you.

27 But the anointing

---

¹ WH omitted the untranslated <u>the</u> (ʰ<u>o</u>) before <u>anti-christ</u>.
² In their margin, WH changed <u>all</u> {things} (<u>panta</u>) to *all* (*pantes*). **Acc Neut** Plur (ye know <u>all</u> [things]) to *Nom Masc* Plur (ye *all* know). [case & gender]
³ WH omitted <u>therefore</u> (<u>oun</u>).
⁴ In their margin, WH changed <u>us</u> (ʰ<u>Amin</u>) to *you* (ʰ*umin*). [person]

which ye have received of him **abideth**[1] in you, and ye need not that any man teach you: but as the **same**[2] anointing teacheth you of all things, and is truth, and is no lie, and even as it hath taught you, **ye shall abide**[3] in him.

28 And now, little children, abide in him; that, **when**[4] he shall appear, **we may have**[5] confidence, and not be ashamed before him at his coming.

29 If ye know that he is righteous, ye know that [∧**also**][6] every one that doeth righteousness is born of him.

---

[1] WH changed the word order from in you ABIDES to *ABIDES in you.*

[2] WH changed **same** (auto) to *of him* (*autou*). **Nom Neut** Sing to *Gen Masc* Sing. [case & gender]

[3] WH changed ye **shall** abide (mene**i**te) to *ye abide* (*menete*). **Fut** Act Ind to *Pres* Act Ind. [tense]

[4] WH changed when ([h]otan) to *if* (*ean*).

[5] WH changed we **may** have (ecOmen) to *we **might** have* (*scOmen*). **Pres** Act Sub to *Aor* Act Sub. [tense]

[6] WH added *also* (*kai*) after that.

CHAPTER 3

1 Behold, what manner of love the Father hath bestowed upon us, that we should be called [∧**and we are**][7] the sons of God: therefore the world knoweth us not, because it knew him not.

2 Beloved, now are we the sons of God, and it doth not yet appear what we shall be: ~~but~~[8] we know that, when he shall appear, we shall be like him; for we shall see him as he is.

3 And every man that hath this hope in him purifieth himself, even as he is pure.

4 Whosoever committeth sin transgresseth also the law: for sin is the transgression of the law.

5 And ye know that he was manifested to take away ~~our~~[9] sins; and in him is no sin.

6 Whosoever abideth in him sinneth not: whosoever sinneth hath not seen him, neither known him.

---

[7] WH added *and we are* (*kai esmen*) after we should be called.

[8] WH omitted but (*de*) before we know.

[9] WH omitted of us ([h]AmOn) from the sins of us.

7   Little children, let no man deceive you: he that doeth righteousness is righteous, even as he is righteous.

8   He that committeth sin is of the devil; for the devil sinneth from the beginning. For this purpose the Son of God was manifested, that he might destroy the works of the devil.

9   Whosoever is born of God doth not commit sin; for his seed remaineth in him: and he cannot sin, because he is born of God.

10 In this the children of God are manifest, and the children of the devil: whosoever doeth not righteousness is not of God, neither he that loveth not his brother.

11 For this is the message that ye heard from the beginning, that we should love one another.

12 Not as Cain, *who* was of that wicked one, and slew his brother. And wherefore slew he him? Because his own works were evil, and his brother's righteous.

13 Marvel not, ~~my~~[1] brethren, if the world hate you.

14 We know that we have passed from death unto life, because we love **the breth-ren**[2]. He that loveth not *his* brother abideth in death.

15 Whosoever hateth his brother is a murderer: and ye know that no murderer hath eternal life abiding in him.

16 Hereby perceive we the love ~~of God~~[3], because he laid down his life for us: and we ought **to lay down**[4] *our* lives for the brethren.

17 But whoso hath this world's good, and seeth his brother have need, and shutteth up his bowels *of compassion* from him, how dwelleth the love of God in him?

18 ~~My~~[5] little children, let us not love in word, neither in [∧**the**][6] tongue; but ∧**in**[7] deed and in truth.

---

[1] WH omitted <u>of me</u> (<u>mou</u>) from <u>the</u> <u>brethren</u> <u>of me</u>.

[2] WH omitted <u>the</u> <u>brethren</u> (<u>ton</u> <u>adelfon</u>) after <u>we love</u>.

[3] WH omitted <u>of the</u> <u>God</u> (<u>tou</u> <u>theou</u>) after <u>the</u> <u>love</u>.

[4] WH changed <u>to</u> **<u>be laying</u> <u>down</u>** (**<u>tith</u>**enai) to *to lay down (**th**einai)*. **Pres** Act Inf to ***Aor*** Act Inf. [tense]

[5] WH omitted <u>of me</u> (<u>mou</u>) from <u>the</u> <u>little children</u> <u>of me</u>.

[6] WH added *the* (*tA*) before <u>tongue</u>.

[7] WH added *in* (*en*) before <u>deed</u> as the KJV supplied from the dative case.

19 ~~And~~[1] hereby **we know**[2] that we are of the truth, and shall assure our **hearts**[3] before him.

20 **For**[4] if our heart condemn us, God is greater than our heart, and knoweth all things.

21 Beloved, if ~~our~~[5] heart condemn us not, *then* have we confidence toward God.

22 And whatsoever we ask, we receive **of**[6] him, because we keep his commandments, and do those things that are pleasing in his sight.

23 And this is his commandment, That we should

believe on the name of his Son Jesus Christ, and love one another, as he gave us commandment.

24 And he that keepeth his commandments dwelleth in him, and he in him. And hereby we know that he abideth in us, by the Spirit which he hath given us.

CHAPTER 4

1 Beloved, believe not every spirit, but try the spirits whether they are of God: because many false prophets are gone out into the world.

2 Hereby know ye the Spirit of God: Every spirit that confesseth that Jesus Christ is come in the flesh is of God:

3 And every spirit that **confesseth not**[7] that Jesus ~~Christ is come in the flesh~~[8] is not of God: and this is that *spirit* of antichrist, whereof ye have heard that it should come; and even now already

---

[1] WH omitted and (kai) before hereby.

[2] WH changed **we are** knowing (ginOskomen) to we *will know* (gnOsome*tha*). **Pres Act** Ind to *Fut Mid* Ind. [tense & voice]

[3] WH changed the hearts (**tas** kardias) to *the heart* (*tAn kardian*) in the phrase the hearts of us. Acc Fem **Plur** to Acc Fem *Sing*. [number]

[4] WH changed for (^h oti) to *for* (^h o ti). **One** word to *Two* words.

[5] WH omitted of us (^h AmOn) from the heart of us.

[6] WH changed **of** (**par'**) to **from** (*apo*).

[7] In their margin, WH changed **confesses** **not** (**mA** ^h omologei) to *destroys* (*luei*). Both Pres Act Ind 3rd Sing. ^h omologeO to *luO*.

[8] WH omitted Christ in {the} flesh is come (criston en sarki elAlu*th*onta).

is it in the world.

4 Ye are of God, little children, and have overcome them: because greater is he that is in you, than he that is in the world.

5 They are of the world: therefore speak they of the world, and the world heareth them.

6 We are of God: he that knoweth God heareth us; he that is not of God heareth not us. Hereby know we the spirit of truth, and the spirit of error.

7 Beloved, let us love one another: for love is of God; and every one that loveth is born of God, and knoweth God.

8 He that loveth not knoweth not God; for God is love.

9 In this was manifested the love of God toward us, because that God sent his only begotten Son into the world, that we might live through him.

10 Herein is love, not that we loved God, but that he loved us, and sent his Son *to be* the propitiation for our sins.

11 Beloved, if God so loved us, we ought also to love one another.

12 No man hath seen God at any time. If we love one another, God dwelleth in us, and his love is perfected in us.

13 Hereby know we that we dwell in him, and he in us, because he hath given us of his Spirit.

14 And we have seen and do testify that the Father sent the Son *to be* the Saviour of the world.

15 Whosoever shall confess that Jesus is the Son of God, God dwelleth in him, and he in God.

16 And we have known and believed the love that God hath to us. God is love; and he that dwelleth in love dwelleth in God, and God in him [˄dwelleth][1].

17 Herein is our love made perfect, that we may have boldness in the day of judgment: because as he is, so are we in this world.

18 There is no fear in love; but perfect love casteth out fear: because fear hath torment. He that feareth is not made perfect in love.

19 We love **him**[2], because he first loved us.

---

[1] WH added *dwelleth* (*menei*) after in him.
[2] WH omitted him (*auton*) after love.

20 If a man say, I love God, and hateth his brother, he is a liar: for he that loveth not his brother whom he hath seen, **how**¹ can he love God whom he hath not seen?

21 And this commandment have we from him, That he who loveth God love his brother also.

CHAPTER 5

1 Whosoever believeth that Jesus is the Christ is born of God: and every one that loveth him that begat loveth him also that is begotten of him.

2 By this we know that we love the children of God, when we love God, and **keep**² his commandments.

3 For this is the love of God, that we keep his commandments: and his commandments are not grievous.

4 For whatsoever is born of God overcometh the world: and this is the victory that overcometh the world,

even our faith.

5 [ʌ**but**]³ Who is he that overcometh the world, but he that believeth that Jesus is the Son of God?

6 This is he that came by water and blood, *even* Jesus [**the**]⁴ Christ; not by water only, but by water and [ʌ**in**]⁵ blood. And it is the Spirit that beareth witness, because the Spirit is truth.

7 For there are three that bear record ~~in heaven, the Father, the Word, and the Holy Ghost: and these three are one.~~

8 ~~And there are three that bear witness in earth~~⁶, the Spirit, and the water, and the blood: and these three agree in one.

---

¹ WH changed **how** (**pOs**) to *not* (*ou*) in their text, but not in their margin.

² WH changed **may keep** (**tArOmen**) to *may do* (*poiOmen*). Both Pres Act Sub. **tAreO** to **poieO**.

³ WH added *but* (*de*) to come before <u>who</u>.

⁴ WH omitted the untranslated <u>the</u> (ʰ<u>o</u>) before <u>Christ</u>.

⁵ WH added *in* (*en*) before <u>blood</u>.

⁶ WH omitted <u>in the heaven the father the word and the holy spirit and these the three one are and three are the witnessing {ones} in the earth</u> (en tO ouranO ʰo patAr ʰo logos kai to ʰagion pneuma kai outoi ʰoi treis ʰen eisi kai treis eisin ʰoi marturountes en tA gA).

9   If we receive the witness of men, the witness of God is greater: for this is the witness of God **which**[1] he hath testified of his Son.

10 He that believeth on the Son of God hath the witness in **himself**[2]: he that believeth not God hath made him a liar; because he believeth not the record that God gave of his Son.

11 And this is the record, that God hath given to us eternal life, and this life is in his Son.

12 He that hath the Son hath life; *and* he that hath not the Son of God hath not life.

13 These things have I written unto you ~~that believe on the name of the Son of God~~[3]; that ye may know that ye have eternal life, ~~and~~[4] **that ye may believe**[5] on the name

of the Son of God.

14 And this is the confidence that we have in him, that, if we ask any thing according to his will, he heareth us:

15 And if we know that he hear us, whatsoever we ask, we know that we have the petitions that we desired of him.

16 If any man see his brother sin a sin *which is* not unto death, he shall ask, and he shall give him life for them that sin not unto death. There is a sin unto death: I do not say that he shall pray for it.

17 All unrighteousness is sin: and there is a sin not unto death.

18 We know that whosoever is born of God sinneth not; but he that is begotten of God keepeth **himself**[6], and that wicked one toucheth him not.

19 *And* we know that we are of God, and the whole world lieth in wickedness.

20 And we know that the

---

[1] WH changed **which** (ʰAn) to *that* (ʰoti).

[2] WH changed him**self** (ʰeautO) to *him* (autO). **Refl** pro to ***Pers*** pro.

[3] WH omitted the {ones} believing on the name of the Son of the God (tois pisteuousin eis to onoma tou ʰuiou tou theou).

[4] WH omitted and (kai) before that.

[5] WH changed **that ye may**

believe (ʰina pisteuAte) to *to the* {ones} *believing* (*tois pisteuousin*). Pres Act **Sub** to Pres Act *Part*. [mood]

[6] WH changed him**self** (ʰeauton) to *him* (auton). **Refl** pro to ***Pers*** pro.

Son of God is come, and hath given us an understanding, that **we may know**[1] him that is true, and we are in him that is true, *even* in his Son Jesus Christ. This is the true God, and [~~the~~][2] eternal life.

21 Little children, keep **yourselves**[3] from idols. ~~**Amen**~~[4].

---

[1] WH changed <u>we **may** know</u> (<u>ginOsk**O**men</u>) to *we know* (*ginOskomen*). Pres Act **Sub** to Pres Act ***Ind***. [mood]

[2] WH omitted the untranslated <u>the</u> ([h]A) before <u>life</u> <u>eternal</u>.

[3] WH changed **your**selves ([h]eaut**ous**) to ***itselves*** ([h]*eauta*). Acc **Masc** Plur to Acc ***Neut*** Plur. [gender]

[4] WH omitted <u>Amen</u> (<u>amAn</u>) after <u>idols</u>.

2 JOHN

CHAPTER 1

1　The elder unto the elect lady and her children, whom I love in the truth; and not I only, but also all they that have known the truth;

2　For the truth's sake, which dwelleth in us, and shall be with us for ever.

3　Grace be with **you**[1], mercy, *and* peace, from God the Father, and from the ~~Lord~~[2] Jesus Christ, the Son of the Father, in truth and love.

4　I rejoiced greatly that I found of thy children walking in truth, as we have received a commandment from the Father.

5　And now I beseech thee, lady, not as though I wrote a new commandment unto thee, but that which we had from the beginning, that we love one another.

6　And this is love, that we walk after his commandments. This **is**[3] the com-

mandment, That, as ye have heard from the beginning, ye should walk in it.

7　For many deceivers **are entered**[4] into the world, who confess not that Jesus Christ is come in the flesh. This is a deceiver and an antichrist.

8　Look to yourselves, that **we lose**[5] not those things which **we have wrought**[6], but that **we receive**[7] a full reward.

9　Whosoever **transgresseth**[8], and abideth not in the

---

[1] WH changed **you** ([h]**umOn**) to *us* ([h]*AmOn*). [person]

[2] WH omitted Lord (kuriou) before Jesus.

[3] WH changed the word order from this IS the commandment to *this the commandment IS.*

[4] WH changed went **into** (eisAlthon) to *went out* (*exAlthon*). Both Aor Act Ind. [prefix changed]

[5] WH changed **we** might lose (apoles**Omen**) to *ye might lose* (*apolesAte*). Both Aor Act Sub. **1**[rs] Plur to **2**[nd] Plur. [person]

[6] In their margin, WH changed we have wrought (eirgasametha) to *we have wrought* (*eirgasasthe*). Both Aor Mid Ind. [spell]

[7] WH changed **we** might receive (apolab**Omen**) to *ye might receive* (*apolabAte*). Both Aor Act Sub. **1**[st] Plur to **2**[nd] Plur. [person]

[8] WH changed going **along side of** (**parabain**On) to *going ahead* (*proagOn*). Both Pres Act Part. [prefix changed]

doctrine of Christ, hath not God. He that abideth in the doctrine ~~of Christ~~[1], he hath both the Father and the Son.

10 If there come any unto you, and bring not this doctrine, receive him not into *your* house, neither bid him God speed:

11 For he that biddeth him God speed is partaker of his evil deeds.

12 Having many things to write unto you, I would not *write* with paper and ink: but I trust **to come**[2] unto you, and speak face to face, that **our**[3] joy may be full.

13 The children of thy elect sister greet thee. ~~Amen~~[4].

---

[1] WH omitted <u>of the</u> <u>Christ</u> (<u>tou</u> <u>cristou</u>) after <u>doctrine</u>.

[2] WH changed <u>to come</u> (**el~~th~~ein**) to *to become* (**genes~~th~~ai**). Aor **Act** Inf of **erc**omai to Aor ***Mid*** Inf of **gin**omai. [voice & syn]

[3] WH changed <u>of **us**</u> ([h]**AmOn**) to *of you* ([h]**umOn**) in the phrase <u>the</u> <u>joy</u> <u>of us</u>. [person]

[4] WH omitted <u>Amen</u> (<u>amAn</u>) after <u>thee</u>.

3 JOHN

CHAPTER 1

1   The elder unto the wellbeloved Gaius, whom I love in the truth.

2   Beloved, I wish above all things that thou mayest prosper and be in health, even as thy soul prospereth.

3   For I rejoiced greatly, when the brethren came and testified of the truth that is in thee, even as thou walkest in the truth.

4   I have no greater **joy**[1] than to hear that my children walk in [∧**the**][2] truth.

5   Beloved, thou doest faithfully whatsoever thou doest to the brethren, and **to**[3] strangers;

6   Which have borne witness of thy charity before the church: whom if thou bring forward on their journey after a godly sort, thou shalt do well:

7   Because that for **his**[4]

name's sake they went forth, taking nothing of the **Gentiles**[5].

8   We therefore ought **to receive**[6] such, that we might be fellowhelpers to the truth.

9   I wrote [∧**something**][7] unto the church: but Diotrephes, who loveth to have the preeminence among them, receiveth us not.

10   Wherefore, if I come, I will remember his deeds which he doeth, prating against us with malicious words: and not content therewith, neither doth he himself receive the brethren, and forbiddeth them that would, and casteth *them* out of the church.

11   Beloved, follow not that which is evil, but that which is good. He that doeth good is of God: **but**[8] he that

---

[1] In their margin, WH changed **joy** (<u>caran</u>) to *grace* (*carin*).

[2] WH added *the* (*tA*) before <u>truth</u>.

[3] WH changed <u>into</u> <u>the</u> (**<u>eis</u> <u>tous</u>**) to *this* (*touto*).

[4] WH omitted <u>of him</u> (<u>autou</u>)

from <u>for</u> <u>the sake of</u> <u>the</u> <u>name of him</u>.

[5] WH changed <u>Gentiles</u> (<u>eth̶nOn</u>) to *Gentiles* (*e th̶nikOn*). Gen **Neut** Plur to Gen *Masc* Plur. [gender]

[6] WH changed <u>to receive</u> **from** (<u>apolambanein</u>) to *to receive* ***by*** (*[h]upolambanein*). [prefix changed]

[7] WH added *something* (*ti*) after <u>wrote</u>.

[8] WH omitted <u>but</u> (<u>de</u>).

doeth evil hath not seen God.

12 Demetrius hath good report of all *men*, and of the truth itself: yea, and we *also* bear record; and **ye know**[1] that our record is true.

13 I had many things **to write**[2] [∧**to thee**][3], but I will not with ink and pen **write**[4] unto thee:

14 But I trust I shall shortly see thee, and we shall speak face to face. Peace *be* to thee. *Our* friends salute thee. Greet the friends by name.

---

[1] WH changed **you**[p] <u>have known</u> (oida**te**) to *you*[s] *have known* (oida**s**). Both Pf Act Ind. 2nd **Plur** to 2nd *Sing*. [number]

[2] WH changed <u>to write</u> (<u>grafein</u>) to *to be writing* (*gra𝔰ai*). **Aor** Act Inf to *Pres* Act Inf. [tense]

[3] WH added <u>to thee</u> (<u>soi</u>) after <u>write</u>.

[4] WH changed <u>to write</u> (<u>gra𝔰 ai</u>) to *to be writing* (*grafein*). **Aor** Act Inf to *Pres* Act Inf. [tense]

JUDE

CHAPTER 1

1 Jude, the servant of Jesus Christ, and brother of James, to them **that are sanctified**[1] by God the Father, and preserved in Jesus Christ, *and* called:

2 Mercy unto you, and peace, and love, be multiplied.

3 Beloved, when I gave all diligence to write unto you of the common [∧**of us]**[2] salvation, it was needful for me to write unto you, and exhort *you* that ye should earnestly contend for the faith which was once delivered unto the saints.

4 For there are certain men crept in unawares, who were before of old ordained to this condemnation, ungodly men, turning the grace of our God into lasciviousness, and denying the only Lord ~~God~~[3], and our Lord Je-

sus Christ.

5 I will therefore put you in remembrance, though **ye**[4] once knew **this**[5], how that the **Lord**[6], having saved the people out of the land of Egypt, afterward destroyed them that believed not.

6 And the angels which kept not their first estate, but left their own habitation, he hath reserved in everlasting chains under darkness unto the judgment of the great day.

7 Even as Sodom and Gomorrha, and the cities about them in like **manner**[7], giving themselves over to fornication, and going after strange flesh, are set forth for an example, suffering the vengeance of eternal fire.

8 Likewise also these *filthy* dreamers defile the flesh, despise dominion, and

---

[1] WH changed that are **sanctified** ([h]Agiasmenois) to *that are loved* (*Agapamenois*). Pf Pass Part of [h]**agiazO** to Pf Pass Part of *agapaO*.

[2] WH added *of us* ([h]*AmOn*) after common.

[3] WH omitted God (~~theon~~)

after Lord.

[4] WH omitted ye ([h]umas) after the Gk participle having known (eidontas).

[5] WH changed **this** (**touto**) to *all* (*panta*).

[6] In their margin, WH changed **Lord** (**kurios**) to *Jesus* (*iAsous*).

[7] WH changed the word order from like MANNER to *MANNER like*.

702

speak evil of dignities.

9   Yet Michael the arch-angel, when contending with the devil he disputed about the body of Moses, durst not bring against him a railing ac-cusation, but said, The Lord rebuke thee.

10 But these speak evil of those things which they know not: but what they know naturally, as brute beasts, in those things they corrupt themselves.

11 Woe unto them! for they have gone in the way of Cain, and ran greedily after the error of Balaam for re-ward, and perished in the gainsaying of Core.

12 These are [∧the]¹ spots in your feasts of charity, when they feast ~~with you~~², feeding themselves without fear: clouds *they are* without water, **carried about**³ of winds; trees whose fruit withereth, without fruit, twice dead, plucked up by the roots;

13 Raging waves of the sea, foaming out their own shame; wandering stars, to whom is reserved the black-ness of darkness for [~~the~~]⁴ ever.

14 And Enoch also, the seventh from Adam, prophe-sied of these, saying, Behold, the Lord cometh with **ten thousands**⁵ of his saints,

15 To execute judgment upon all, and **to convince**⁶ all that ˏare ungodly ~~among them~~⁷ of all their ungodly deeds which they have un-godly committed, and of all their hard *speeches* which ungodly sinners have spoken against him.

16 These are murmurers, complainers, walking after their own lusts; and their mouth speaketh great swell-ing *words*, having men's per-sons in admiration because of

---

¹ WH added *the* (*ʰoi*) after are.

² WH omitted with you (*ʰumin*) after when they feast.

³ WH changed carried **about** (periferomenai) to *carried* **along** (paraferomenai). [pre-fix changed]

⁴ WH omitted the untrans-lated the (ton) in the phrase unto the age.

⁵ WH changed the word or-der from TEN THOUSANDS holy {ones} of him to *holy* {ones} TEN THOUSANDS *of him.*

⁶ WH changed to convince (**exelegxai**) to *to convince* (*elegxai*). Both Aor Act Inf. [prefix dropped]

⁷ WH omitted among them (autОn) after ungodly.

advantage.

17 But, beloved, remember ye the words which were spoken before of the apostles of our Lord Jesus Christ;

18 How that they told you [~~that~~][1] there should be mockers **in** **the last time**[2], who should walk after their own ungodly lusts.

19 These be they who separate ~~themselves~~[3], sensual, having not the Spirit.

20 But ye, beloved, **building up yourselves**[4] on your most holy faith, praying in the Holy Ghost,

21 Keep yourselves in the love of God, looking for the mercy of our Lord Jesus Christ unto eternal life.

22 And of some **have**

compassion[5], **making a difference**[6]:

23 And others save **with fear**[7], pulling *them* out of ~~the~~[8] fire [ʌ**but therefore have compassion**][9]; hating even the garment spotted by the flesh.

24 Now unto him that is able to keep you from falling, and to present *you* faultless before the presence of his glory with exceeding joy,

---

[1] WH omitted the untranslated <u>that</u> (ʰ<u>oti</u>) after <u>you</u>.

[2] WH changed <u>in</u> {the} <u>last</u> time (<u>en escatO cronO</u>) to *on* {the} *last time* (*ep' escatou cronou*). **Dat** to *Gen*. [case]

[3] WH omitted <u>themselves</u> (ʰ<u>eautous</u>) after <u>separate</u>.

[4] WH changed the word order from <u>on your</u> <u>most holy</u> <u>faith</u> BUILDING UP YOURSELVES to *BUILDING YOURSELVES UP on your most holy faith*.

[5] WH changed <u>be having compassion</u> (<u>eleeite</u>) to *be having compassion* (*eleate*). Pres Act Imp of <u>eleeO</u> to Pres Act Imp of *eleaO*. [spell]

[6] WH changed <u>making a difference</u> (<u>diakrinomenoi</u>) to *making a difference* (*diakrinomenous*). Both Pres Mid Part. **Nom** Masc Plur to *Acc* Masc Plur. [case]

[7] WH changed the word order from <u>and others</u> WITH FEAR <u>save out of</u> **the** <u>fire</u> <u>pulling</u> to *and others save pulling out of fire* **but therefore have compassion** WITH FEAR.

[8] WH omitted <u>the</u> (<u>tou</u>) before <u>fire</u>.

[9] WH added <u>but therefore have compassion</u> (<u>de ous eleate</u>).

704

25 To the only ~~wise~~[1] God
our Saviour [ₐ**through Jesus
Christ the Lord of us**][2], *be*
glory ~~and~~[3] majesty, dominion
and power [ₐ**before every
the age**][4], both now and ever.
Amen.

---

[1] WH omitted <u>wise</u> (sofO)
before <u>God</u>.
[2] WH added *through Jesus
Christ the Lord of us* (*dia
iAsou cristou tou kuriou
*ʰ*AmOn*).
[3] WH omitted <u>and</u> (<u>kai</u>) after
<u>glory</u>.
[4] WH added *before every the
age* (*pro pantos tou aiOnos*)
after <u>power</u>.

REVELATION

CHAPTER 1

1   The Revelation of Jesus Christ, which God gave unto him, to shew unto his servants things which must shortly come to pass; and he sent and signified *it* by his angel unto his servant John:

2   Who bare record of the word of God, and of the testimony of Jesus Christ, ~~and~~[1] of all things that he saw.

3   Blessed *is* he that readeth, and they that hear the words of this prophecy, and keep those things which are written therein: for the time *is* at hand.

4   John to the seven churches which are in Asia: Grace *be* unto you, and peace, from ~~him~~[2] which is, and which was, and which is to come; and from the seven Spirits which ~~are~~[3] before his throne;

5   And from Jesus Christ, *who is* the faithful witness, *and* the first begotten ~~of~~[4] the

dead, and the prince of the kings of the earth. Unto him **that loved**[5] us, and **washed**[6] us **from**[7] our sins in his own blood,

6   And hath made us **kings**[8] ~~and~~[9] priests unto God and his Father; to him *be* glory and dominion for ever **and ever**[10]. Amen.

7   Behold, he cometh with clouds; and every eye shall see him, and they *also* which pierced him: and all kindreds

---

[1] WH omitted <u>and</u> (<u>te</u>).

[2] WH omitted <u>him</u> (<u>tou</u>—"the {one}") after <u>from</u>.

[3] WH omitted <u>are</u> (<u>estin</u>) after <u>which</u>.

[4] WH omitted <u>of</u> (<u>ek</u>—"out

of") and forced the case of <u>the</u> <u>dead</u> to supply the preposition.

[5] WH changed **having** loved (<u>agap**A**santi</u>) to *loving* (*agapOnti*). **Aor** Act Part to ***Pres*** Act Part. [tense]

[6] WH changed **washed** (<u>lousanti</u>) to *loosed* (*lusanti*). Both Aor Act Part. **louO** to *luO*. In their margin, they retained <u>washed</u> (<u>lousanti</u>).

[7] WH changed **from** (**apo**) to *out of* (*ek*).

[8] WH changed <u>kings</u> (<u>basileis</u>) to *kingdom* (*basileian*).

[9] WH omitted <u>and</u> (<u>kai</u>) before <u>priests</u>.

[10] In their margin, WH omitted <u>and ever</u> (<u>tOn aiOnOn</u>—"of the ages") from <u>for ever and ever</u> ("<u>unto</u> <u>the</u> <u>ages of the ages</u>").

of the earth shall wail because of him. Even so, Amen.

8   I am Alpha and Omega, ~~the beginning and the ending~~[1], saith ~~the~~[2] Lord [ᴧthe God][3], which is, and which was, and which is to come, the Almighty.

9   I John, who ~~also~~[4] am your brother, and companion in tribulation, and ~~in the~~[5] kingdom and patience [ᴧin][6] of Jesus ~~Christ~~[7], was in the isle that is called Patmos, for the word of God, and ~~for~~[8] the testimony of Jesus ~~Christ~~[9].

10   I was in the Spirit on the Lord's day, and heard behind me a great voice, as of a trumpet,

11   Saying, ~~I am Alpha and Omega, the first and the last: and~~[10], What thou seest, write in a book, and send *it* unto the seven churches ~~which are in Asia~~[11]; unto Ephesus, and unto Smyrna, and unto Pergamos, and unto Thyatira, and unto Sardis, and unto Philadelphia, and unto Laodicea.

12   And I turned to see the voice that **spake**[12] with me. And being turned, I saw seven golden candlesticks;

13   And in the midst of the ~~seven~~[13] candlesticks *one* like unto the Son of man, clothed with a garment down to the foot, and girt about the paps with a golden girdle.

14   His head and *his* hairs

---

[1] WH omitted {the} <u>beginning</u> <u>and</u> {the} <u>ending</u> (<u>arcA</u> <u>kai</u> <u>telos</u>).

[2] WH omitted <u>the</u> (^h<u>o</u>) before <u>Lord</u>.

[3] WH added *the God* (^h*o* *θeos*) after <u>Lord</u>.

[4] WH omitted <u>also</u> (<u>kai</u>).

[5] WH omited <u>in the</u> (<u>en</u> <u>tA</u>) before <u>kingdom</u>.

[6] WH added *in* (<u>en</u>) before <u>Jesus</u> and forced the Genitive supplied <u>of</u> to drop out.

[7] WH omitted <u>Christ</u> (<u>cristou</u>) after <u>Jesus</u>.

[8] WH omitted <u>for</u> (<u>dia</u>) before <u>the</u> <u>testimony</u>.

[9] WH omitted <u>Christ</u> (<u>cristou</u>) once again after <u>Jesus</u>.

[10] WH omitted <u>myself</u> <u>I am</u> <u>the</u> <u>Alpha</u> <u>and</u> <u>the</u> <u>Omega</u> <u>the</u> <u>first</u> <u>and</u> <u>the</u> <u>last</u> <u>and</u> (<u>egO</u> <u>eimi</u> <u>to</u> <u>a</u> <u>kai</u> <u>to</u> <u>O</u> ^h<u>o</u> <u>prOtos</u> <u>kai</u> ^h<u>o</u> <u>eskatos</u> <u>kai</u>).

[11] WH omitted <u>the</u> {ones} <u>in</u> <u>Asia</u> (<u>tais</u> <u>en</u> <u>asia</u>).

[12] WH changed <u>spoke</u> (<u>ela-lAse</u>) to *was speaking* (*elalei*). **Aor** Act Ind to *Impf* Act Ind. [tense]

[13] WH omitted <u>seven</u> (^h<u>epta</u>) before <u>candlesticks</u>.

were white **like**¹ wool, as white as snow; and his eyes *were* as a flame of fire;

15 And his feet like unto fine brass, as if **they burned**² in a furnace; and his voice as the sound of many waters.

16 And he had in his right **hand**³ seven stars: and out of his mouth went a sharp twoedged sword: and his countenance *was* as the sun shineth in his strength.

17 And when I saw him, I fell at his feet as dead. And **he laid**⁴ his right **hand**⁵ upon me, saying **unto me**⁶, Fear not; I am the first and the

last:

18 I *am* he that liveth, and was dead; and, behold, I am alive for evermore, ~~Amen~~⁷; and have the keys of **hell** and of **death**⁸.

19 Write [ʌ**therefore**]⁹ the things which thou hast seen, and the things which are, and the things which shall be hereafter;

20 The mystery of the seven stars **which**¹⁰ thou sawest in my right hand, and the seven golden candle-sticks. The seven stars are the angels of the seven churches: and the **seven**¹¹ [ʌ**the**]¹² can-dlesticks ~~which   thou sawest~~¹³ are the seven churches.

---

¹ WH changed <u>like</u> (ʰ<u>Osei</u>) to *like* (ʰ*Os*).

² WH changed **they** <u>had been burned</u> (<u>pepurOmenoi</u>) to *she had been burned* (*pepurOme-nAs*). Both Pf Pass Part. **Nom Masc Plur** to *Gen Fem Sing*. [case, gender, number]

³ WH changed the word order from <u>the</u> <u>right</u> <u>of him</u> <small>HAND</small> to *the right* <small>HAND</small> *of him*.

⁴ WH changed <u>he laid</u> {**upon**} (<u>epethAke</u>) to *he laid* (*ethAke*). **epit**<u>ithAmi</u> to *tithAmi*. [prefix dropped]

⁵ WH omitted <u>hand</u> (<u>ceira</u>) before <u>upon</u> <u>me</u>.

⁶ WH omitted <u>unto me</u> (<u>moi</u>) after <u>saying</u>.

---

⁷ WH omitted <u>Amen</u> (<u>amAn</u>).

⁸ WH changed the word order from <u>of the</u> <small>HELL</small> <u>and of the</u> <small>DEATH</small> to *of the* <small>DEATH</small> *and of the* <small>HELL</small>.

⁹ WH added *therefore* (*oun*) after <u>write</u>.

¹⁰ WH changed <u>which</u> (ʰ<u>On</u>) to *which* (*ous*). **Gen** Masc Plur to *Acc* Masc Plur. [case]

¹¹ WH changed the word order from <u>the</u> <small>SEVEN</small> <u>candle-sticks</u> to *the candlesticks the* <small>SEVEN</small>.

¹² WH added *the* (ʰ*ai*) before <u>candlesticks</u>.

¹³ WH omitted <u>which</u> <u>thou sawest</u> (ʰ<u>as eides</u>).

CHAPTER 2

1   Unto the angel **of the**[1] church [∧**in**][2] of **Ephesus**[3] write; These things saith he that holdeth the seven stars in his right hand, who walketh in the midst of the seven golden candlesticks;

2   I know thy works, and ~~thy~~[4] labour, and thy patience, and how thou canst not bear them which are evil: and **thou hast tried**[5] them **which say they are**[6] apostles, and are not, and hast found them

liars:

3   And **hast borne, and**[7] hast patience, ~~and~~[8] for my name's sake **hast laboured**[9], and ~~hast~~ not **fainted**[10].

4   Nevertheless I have _somewhat_ against thee, because thou hast left thy first love.

5   Remember therefore from whence **thou art fallen**[11], and repent, and do the first works; or else I will come unto thee ~~quickly~~[12], and will remove thy candlestick out of his place, except thou repent.

6   But this thou hast, that thou hatest the deeds of the Nicolaitans, which I also

---

[1] WH changed **of the** (tAs) to **in the** (tO). **Gen** to _Dat._ [case]

[2] WH added _in_ (_en_) and forced the Genitive supplied of to drop out.

[3] WH changed Ephesus (ef-esinAs) to _Ephesus_ (_efesO_). [case & spell] They changed, then, from **of the** Ephesus church to _in the in Ephesus church_.

[4] WH omitted of thee (sou) from the labour of thee.

[5] WH changed you[s] tried {**for yourself**} (epeirasO) to _you[s] tried_ (_epeirasas_). Aor **Mid** Ind to Aor _Act_ Ind. [voice]

[6] WH changed **which say they are** (**faskontas einai**) to _claiming themselves_ (_legontas_ [h]_eautous_).

[7] WH changed the word order from CARRIED AND patience has to _patience has AND CARRIED._

[8] WH omitted and (kai) after patience.

[9] WH changed the word order from HAST LABOURED and not **hast fainted** to _and not HAST LABOURED._

[10] WH omitted hast fainted (kekmAkas).

[11] WH changed thou art fallen {**out**} (**ekpeptOkas**) to _thou art fallen_ (_peptOkas_). [prefix dropped]

[12] WH omitted quickly (tacu) after to you.

hate.

7   He that hath an ear, let him hear what the Spirit saith unto the churches; To him that overcometh will I give to eat of the tree of life, which is in ~~the midst~~[1] **of the para-dise**[2] of God.

8   And unto the angel **of the church in Smyrna**[3] write; These things saith the first and the last, which was dead, and is alive;

9   I know thy ~~works, and~~[4] tribulation, and poverty, (**but**[5] thou art **rich**[6]) and *I know* the blasphemy [ʌout

of][7] of them which say they are Jews, and are not, but *are* the synagogue of Satan.

10   Fear **none**[8] of those things which thou shalt suffer: behold, **the devil**[9] shall **cast**[10] *some* of you into prison, that ye may be tried; and y̲e̲ ̲s̲h̲a̲l̲l̲ ̲h̲a̲v̲e̲[11] tribulation ten days: be thou faithful unto death, and I will give thee a crown of life.

11   He that hath an ear, let him hear what the Spirit saith unto the churches; He that overcometh shall not be hurt of the second death.

12   And to the angel of the church in Pergamos write; These things saith he which

---

[1] WH omitted the midst (mesO) after in.

[2] WH changed **of** the paradise (**tou** paradeisou) to *the paradise* (*tO paradeisO*). **Gen** to *Dat*. [case]

[3] WH changed **of** the church in Smyrna (t**As** ekklAsias zmurn**aiOn**) to *to the in Smyrna church* (*tO en zmurnA ekklAsias*). **Gen** to *Dat*. [case & word order]

[4] WH omitted {the} works and (ta erga kai) before tribu-lation.

[5] WH changed but (**de**) for *but* (*alla*).

[6] WH changed the word or-der from RICH but to *but RICH*.

[7] WH added *out of* (*ek*) after blasphemy and forced the Genitive supplied of to drop off.

[8] WH changed none (**mAden**) to *not* (*mA*).

[9] WH changed the word or-der from of you THE DEVIL to *THE DEVIL of you*.

[10] WH changed to cast (bal-ein) to *to* **be** *casting* (*ballein*). **Aor** Act Inf to *Pres* Act Inf. [tense]

[11] In their margin, WH changed ye **shall** have (**h**exete) to *ye* **may** *have* (*ecAte*). **Fut** Act **Ind** to *Pres* Act **Sub**. [tense & mood]

hath the sharp sword with two edges;

13 I know ~~thy works, and~~[1] where thou dwellest, *even* where Satan's seat *is*: and thou holdest fast my name, and hast not denied my faith, even in those days ~~wherein~~[2] Antipas *was* my faithful [∧**of me**][3] martyr, who was slain among you, where Satan **dwelleth**[4].

14 But I have a few things against thee, because thou hast there them that hold the doctrine of Balaam, who taught [**the**][5] Balac to cast a stumblingblock before the children of Israel, to eat things sacrificed unto idols, and to commit fornication.

15 So hast thou also them

that hold the doctrine of **the**[6] Nicolaitans, **which thing I hate**[7].

16 Repent [∧**therefore**][8]; or else I will come unto thee quickly, and will fight against them with the sword of my mouth.

17 He that hath an ear, let him hear what the Spirit saith unto the churches; To him that overcometh will I give ~~to eat of~~[9] the hidden manna, and will give him a white stone, and in the stone a new name written, which no man **knoweth**[10] saving he that receiveth *it*.

18 And unto the angel of the church in Thyatira write; These things saith the Son of God, who hath his eyes like unto a flame of fire, and his feet *are* like fine brass;

19 I know thy works, and

---

[1] WH omitted the works of thee and (ta erga sou kai).

[2] WH omitted wherein (en ais) before Antipas.

[3] WH added *of me* (*mou*) after faithful. The result is *the martyr of me the faithful of me*.

[4] WH changed the word order from where DWELLETH the Satan to *where the Satan* DWELLETH.

[5] WH changed the untranslated the (ton) to {to} *the* (tO) before Balac. **Acc** Masc Sing to *Dat* Masc Sing. [case]

[6] WH omitted the (tOn) before Nicolaitans.

[7] WH changed **which things I hate** ([h]o misO) to *too* ([h]omoiOs).

[8] WH added *therefore* (*oun*) after repent.

[9] WH omitted to eat of (fagein apo) after I give.

[10] WH changed knew (**egnO**) to *has known* (*oiden*). **Aor** Act Ind of **ginOskO** to *Pf* Act Ind of *oida*.

charity, and **service**, and **faith**[1], and thy patience, and thy works; **and**[2] the last *to be* more than the first.

20 Notwithstanding I have **a few things**[3] against thee, because **thou sufferest**[4] that woman **[of thee]**[5] **Jezebel**[6], **which calleth** herself a prophetess, **[∧and]**[8] **to teach**[9]

---

[1] WH changed the word order from <u>the SERVICE and the FAITH</u> to *the FAITH and the SERVICE*.

[2] WH omitted <u>and</u> (kai) after <u>works</u>.

[3] WH omitted {a} <u>few</u> {things} (<u>oliga</u>).

[4] WH changed <u>you</u>^s <u>are permitting</u> (<u>eas</u>) to *you*^s *are permitting* (*afeis*). Both Pres Act Ind. **eaO** to *afiAmi*. [syn]

[5] In their margin, WH added *of thee* (*sou*) after <u>woman</u>.

[6] WH changed <u>Jezebel</u> (<u>iezabAl</u>) to *Jezebel* (*iezabel*). [spell]

[7] WH changed <u>which calls</u> (**tAn** <u>legousan</u>) to *which calls* (*ʰa legousa*). Both Pres Act Part. **Acc** Fem Sing to *Nom* Fem Sing. [case]

[8] WH added *and* (*kai*) after <u>prophetess</u>.

[9] WH changed **to be teaching** (<u>didaskein</u>) to *she teaches* (*didaskei*). Pres Act **Inf** to Pres Act *Ind*. [mood]

and **to seduce**[10] **[∧the]**[11] my servants to commit fornication, and **to eat**[12] things sacrificed unto idols.

21 And I gave her space to repent **of her fornication**[13]; and **[∧she is willing]**[14] **she repented**[15] not.

22 Behold, I **[myself]**[16] will cast her into a bed, and them that commit adultery with her into great tribulation, except they repent of

---

[10] WH changed **to be seduced** (<u>planasthai</u>) to *she seduces* (*plana*). Pres **Pass Inf** to Pres *Act Ind*. [voice & mood]

[11] WH added *the* (*tous*) before <u>my</u> <u>servants</u>.

[12] WH changed the word order from <u>things sacrificed unto idols</u> TO EAT to *TO EAT things sacrificed unto idols*.

[13] WH changed the word order from <u>OF THE FORNICATION OF HER</u> and <u>not she repented</u> to *and not she is willing to repent OF THE FORNICATION OF HER*.

[14] WH added *she is willing* (*thelei*).

[15] WH changed <u>she repented</u> (<u>metenoAsen</u>) to *to repent* (*metanoAsai*). Aor Act **Ind** to Aor Act *Inf*. [mood]

[16] WH omitted the untranslated <u>myself</u> before <u>will cast</u>.

their[1] deeds.

23 And I will kill her children with death; and all the churches shall know that I am he which searcheth the reins and hearts: and I will give unto every one of you according to your works.

24 But unto you I say, **and**[2] unto the rest in Thyatira, as many as have not this doctrine, and which have not known the **depths**[3] of Satan, as they speak; **I will put**[4] upon you none other burden.

25 But that which ye have *already* hold fast till I come.

26 And he that overcometh, and keepeth my works unto the end, to him will I give power over the nations:

27 And he shall rule them

with a rod of iron; as the vessels of a potter shall they be broken to shivers: even as I received of my Father.

28 And I will give him the morning star.

29 He that hath an ear, let him hear what the Spirit saith unto the churches.

CHAPTER 3

1 And unto the angel of the church in Sardis write; These things saith he that hath the seven Spirits of God, and the seven stars; I know thy works, that thou hast **[the]**[5] a name that thou livest, and art dead.

2 Be watchful, and strengthen the things which remain, that **are ready**[6] to die: for I have not found **thy**[7] works perfect before God **[∧of me]**[8].

---

[1] WH changed of **them** (aut**On**) to of **her** (aut**As**) in the phrase the deeds of them. **Plur** to *Sing*. [number] In their margin, they retained of them (autOn).

[2] WH omitted and (kai) after I say.

[3] WH changed dep**ths** (bath**A**) to *deep secrets* (*bathea*). bat**hos** to *bathus*.

[4] WH changed I **will** put (balO) to *I am putting* (*ballO*). **Fut** Act Ind to *Pres* Act Ind. [tense]

[5] WH omitted the untranslated the (to) before name.

[6] WH changed **it is** being ready (mell**ei**) to *they were being ready* (*emellon*). **Pres** Act Ind 3rd **Sing** to *Impf* Act Ind 3rd *Plur*. [tense & number]

[7] WH omitted the (ta) from the works of thee.

[8] WH added *of me* (*mou*) after God.

3 Remember therefore how thou hast received and heard, and hold fast, and repent. If therefore thou shalt not watch, I will come ~~on thee~~[1] as a thief, and thou shalt not know what hour I will come upon thee.

4 [∧**but**][2] Thou hast a few names ~~even~~[3] in Sardis which have not defiled their garments; and they shall walk with me in white: for they are worthy.

5 He that overcometh, **the same**[4] shall be clothed in white raiment; and I will not blot out his name out of the book of life, but **I will confess**[5] his name before my Father, and before his angels.

6 He that hath an ear, let him hear what the Spirit saith unto the churches.

7 And to the angel of the church in Philadelphia write; These things saith he that is holy, he that is true, he that hath the **key**[6] of [**the**][7] David, he that openeth, and no man **shutteth**[8]; and **shutteth**[9], and no man openeth;

8 I know thy works: behold, I have set before thee an open door, **and**[10] no man can shut it: for thou hast a little strength, and hast kept my word, and hast not denied my name.

9 Behold, **I will make**[11] them of the synagogue of Satan, which say they are Jews, and are not, but do lie; behold, I will make them to

---

[1] WH omitted on thee (epi se) after I will come.

[2] WH added *but* (*alla*) before thou hast.

[3] WH omitted even (kai) after names.

[4] WH changed **this** {one} ([h]outos) to *in this manner* ([h]outOs). **Pro** to *Adv*.

[5] WH changed I will confess {out} (**ex**omolog**A**s**o**mai) to *I will confess* ([h]omolog**A**s**O**). Fut **Mid** Ind to Fut *Act* Ind. [voice & prefix dropped]

[6] WH changed key (klei**da**) to *key* (klei**n**). Both Acc Fem Sing. [spell]

[7] WH omitted the untranslated the (tou) before David.

[8] WH changed shuts (kleiei) to *will shut* (kleisei). **Pres** Act Ind to *Fut* Act Ind. [tense]

[9] WH changed shutt**eth** (kleiei) to *shutting* (klei**On**). Pres Act **Ind** to Pres Act *Part*. [mood]

[10] WH changed **and** (**kai**) to *which* ([h]An).

[11] WH changed I **will** make (did**Omi**) to *I may make* (did**O**). **Fut** Act **Ind** to Pres Act *Sub*. [mood]

come[1] and **worship**[2] before thy feet, and to know that I have loved thee.

10 Because thou hast kept the word of my patience, I also will keep thee from the hour of temptation, which shall come upon all the world, to try them that dwell upon the earth.

11 ~~Behold~~[3], I come quickly: hold that fast which thou hast, that no man take thy crown.

12 Him that overcometh will I make a pillar in the temple of my God, and he shall go no more out: and I will write upon him the name of my God, and the name of the city of my God, *which is* new Jerusalem, which **cometh down**[4] out of heaven

from my God: and *I will write upon him* my new name.

13 He that hath an ear, let him hear what the Spirit saith unto the churches.

14 And unto the angel of the **church**[5] [∧in][6] **of the Laodiceans**[7] write; These things saith the Amen, the faithful and true witness, the beginning of the creation of God;

15 I know thy works, that thou art neither cold nor hot: I would **thou wert**[8] cold or hot.

16 So then because thou art lukewarm, and neither **cold** nor **hot**[9], I will spue thee out of my mouth.

17 Because thou sayest, I

---

[1] WH changed **might** come (ʰAx**O**si) to *will come* (ʰ*Axousi*). **Aor** Act **Sub** to *Fut* Act *Ind*. [tense & mood]

[2] WH changed **might** worship (proskunAs**O**sin) to *will worship* (*proskunAsousin*). **Aor** Act **Sub** to *Fut* Act *Ind*. [tense & mood]

[3] WH omitted behold before I.

[4] WH changed comes down (*katabainei*) to *coming down* (*katabainousa*). Pres Act **Ind** to Pres Act *Part*. [mood]

[5] WH changed the word order from the CHURCH **of** Laodiceans to *the in Laodicea CHURCH*.

[6] WH added *in* (*en*).

[7] WH changed of {the} Laodiceans (laodike**O**n) to in Laodicia (en laodikeia). **Gen** to *Dat* w/ prep.

[8] WH changed you[s] **should** be (**ei**As) to *you[s] were being*. (*As*). **Pres** NV **Opt** to *Impf* Act *Ind*. [tense & mood]

[9] WH changed the word order from COLD nor HOT to *HOT nor COLD*.

am rich, and increased with goods, and have need of **nothing**[1]; and knowest not that thou art wretched, and miserable, and poor, and blind, and naked:

18 I counsel thee to buy of me gold tried in the fire, that thou mayest be rich; and white raiment, that thou mayest be clothed, and *that* the shame of thy nakedness do not appear; and **anoint**[2] thine eyes with eyesalve, that thou mayest see.

19 As many as I love, I rebuke and chasten: **be zealous**[3] therefore, and repent.

20 Behold, I stand at the door, and knock: if any man hear my voice, and open the door, I will come in to him, and will sup with him, and he with me.

21 To him that overcometh will I grant to sit with me in my throne, even as I also overcame, and am set down with my Father in his throne.

22 He that hath an ear, let him hear what the Spirit saith unto the churches.

CHAPTER 4

1 After this I looked, and, behold, a door *was* opened in heaven: and the first voice which I heard *was* as it were of a trumpet talking with me; **which said**[4], Come up hither, and I will shew thee things which must be hereafter.

2 **And**[5] immediately I was in the spirit: and, behold, a throne was set in heaven, and *one* sat on **the throne**[6].

3 And he that sat ~~was~~[7] to look upon like a jasper and a

---

[1] WH changed nothing (oudenos) to *nothing* (*ouden*). **Adj**: Gen Neut to **Pro**: Acc Neut Sing. [syn]

[2] WH changed anoint (egcrison) to *to anoint* (*egcrisai*). Aor Act **Imp** to Aor Act *Inf*. [mood]

[3] WH change be zealous (zAlOson) to *be being zealous* (*zAleue*). **Aor** Act Imp to Pres Act Imp. [tense]

[4] WH changed saying (legousa) to *saying* (*legOn*). Both Pres Act Part. Nom **Fem** Sing to Nom *Masc* Sing. [gender]

[5] WH omitted and (kai) before immediately.

[6] WH changed the throne (tou thronou) to *the throne* (*ton thronon*). **Gen** to *Acc*. [case]

[7] WH omitted was (An).

sardine[1] stone: and *there was* a rainbow round about the throne, in sight like unto an emerald.

4   And round about the throne *were* four ~~and~~[2] twenty seats: and upon the seats ~~I saw~~ **[the]**[3] four ~~and~~[4] twenty elders sitting, clothed in white raiment; and ~~they had~~[5] on their heads crowns of gold.

5   And out of the throne proceeded lightnings and **thunderings** and **voices**[6]: and *there were* seven lamps of fire burning before the throne, which are the seven Spirits of God.

6   And before the throne *there was* [∧**as**][7] a sea of glass like unto crystal: and in the midst of the throne, and round about the throne, *were* four beasts full of eyes before and behind.

7   And the first beast *was* like a lion, and the second beast like a calf, and the third beast **had**[8] a face as **a man**[9], and the fourth beast *was* like a **flying**[10] eagle.

8   And ∧**the**[11] four beasts **had**[12] **each** [∧**one**][13] **of**

---

[1] WH changed sardine (sardinO) to *sardine* (*sardiO*). Dat **Masc** Sing to Dat *Neut* Sing. [gender]
[2] WH omitted and (kai) between twenty and four.
[3] WH omitted I saw (eidon) and the untranslated the (tous) after seats.
[4] WH omitted and (kai) between twenty and four.
[5] WH omitted they had (escon) before on.
[6] WH changed the word order from THUNDERINGS and VOICES to *VOICES and THUNDERINGS*.

[7] WH added *as* (*ʰOs*) before sea.
[8] WH changed it had (econ) to *he had* (*ecOn*). Both Pres Act Part. Nom **Neut** Sing to Nom *Masc* Sing. [gender]
[9] WH changed a man (anthrOpos) to {of} *a man* (*anthrOpou*). **Nom** to *Gen*. [case]
[10] WH changed flying (petOmenO) to *flying* (*petomenO*). Both Pres Mid Part Dat Masc Sing. [spell]
[11] WH added *the* (*ta*) before four as the KJV supplied.
[12] WH changed {they} were having (eicon) to {it} *having* (*ecOn*). **Impf** Act **Ind Plur** to *Pres* Act *Part*). [tense, mood, & number]
[13] WH added *one* (*ʰen*) before **of them**.

them[1] six wings about *him*; and *they were* **full**[2] of eyes within: and they rest not day and night, **saying**[3], Holy, holy, holy, Lord God Almighty, which was, and is, and is to come.

9   And when those beasts give glory and honour and thanks to him that sat on the throne, who liveth for ever and ever,

10 The four ~~and~~[4] twenty elders fall down before him that sat on the throne, and **worship**[5] him that liveth for

ever and ever, and **cast**[6] their crowns before the throne, saying,

11 Thou art worthy, [∧the][7] **O Lord**[8], [∧**even the God of us**][9] to receive glory and honour and power: for thou hast created all things, and for thy pleasure they ~~are~~[10] and were created.

CHAPTER 5

1   And I saw in the right hand of him that sat on the throne a book written within and on the backside, sealed with seven seals.

2   And I saw a strong angel proclaiming ∧**with**[11] a

---

[1] WH changed **itself** ([h]eauto) to *of them* (*autOn*). As a result, WH changed one according to **itself** ([h]en ka[th]' [h]eauto) to *one according to one of them* ([h]en ka[th]' [h]en autOn).

[2] WH changed **being** full (gemo[n]ta) to *they are full* (*gemousin*). Pres Act **Part** to Pres Act **Ind**. [mood]

[3] WH changed saying (le-gonta) to *saying* (*legontes*). Both Pres Act Part. **Acc** Masc **Sing** to *Nom* Masc **Plur**. [case & number]

[4] WH omitted and (kai) between twenty and four.

[5] WH changed worship (proskunousi) to *will worship* (*proskunAsousi*). **Pres** Act Ind to *Fut* Act Ind. [tense]

[6] WH changed cast (ballousi) to *will cast* (*balousi*). **Pres** Act Ind to *Fut* Act Ind. [tense]

[7] WH added *the* ([h]o) before Lord.

[8] WH changed O Lord (ku-rie) to *Lord* (*kurios*). **Voc** Masc Sing to *Nom* Masc Sing. [case]

[9] WH added *even the God of us* (kai [h]o [th]eos [h]AmOn) after Lord.

[10] WH omitted are (eisi).

[11] WH added *with* (en) after proclaiming as the KJV supplied.

loud voice, Who **is**[1] worthy to open the book, and to loose the seals thereof?

3   And no man in heaven, nor in earth, neither under the earth, was able to open the book, **neither**[2] to look thereon.

4   And I wept **much**[3], because no man was found worthy to open **and to read**[4] the book, neither to look thereon.

5   And one of the elders saith unto me, Weep not: behold, the Lion [**being**][5] of the tribe of Juda, the Root of David, hath prevailed to open the book, and **to loose**[6] the seven seals thereof.

6   And I beheld, **and, lo**[7],

in the midst of the throne and of the four beasts, and in the midst of the elders, stood a Lamb as it had been slain, **having**[8] seven horns and seven eyes, which are the **seven**[9] **Spirits**[10] of God [**the**][11] **sent forth**[12] into all the earth.

7   And he came and took **the book**[13] out of the right hand of him that sat upon the throne.

8   And when he had taken the book, the four beasts and four *and* twenty elders fell

---

idou) after I beheld.

[8] WH changed {**it**} having (econ) to {**he**} *having* (ecOn). Both Pres Act Part. Nom **Neut** Sing to Nom *Masc* Sing. [gender]

[9] WH omitted seven ([h]epta) after the.

[10] WH changed the word order from the **seven** of the God SPIRITS to *the SPIRITS of the God.*

[11] WH omitted the untranslated the (ta) before sent forth.

[12] WH changed sent forth (apestalmena) to *sent forth* (apestalmenoi). Both Pf Pass Part. Nom **Neut** Plur to Nom *Masc* Plur. [gender]

[13] WH omitted the book (to biblion) after took.

---

[1] WH omitted is (estin) after who.

[2] WH changed neither (oude) to *neither* (oute). [syn]

[3] WH changed much (po**ll**a) to *much* (pol**u**). Acc Neut **Plur** to Acc Neut **Sing**. [number]

[4] WH omitted and to read (kai anaknOnai) after to open.

[5] WH omitted the untranslated being (On) after the Lion the.

[6] WH omitted to loose (lusai) before the seven.

[7] WH omitted and lo (kai

down before the Lamb, having every one of them **harps**[1], and golden vials full of odours, which are the prayers of saints.

9 And they sung a new song, saying, Thou art worthy to take the book, and to open the seals thereof: for thou wast slain, and hast redeemed **us**[2] to God by thy blood out of every kindred, and tongue, and people, and nation;

10 And hast made **us**[3] unto our God **kings**[4] and priests: and **we shall reign**[5] on the earth.

11 And I beheld, and I heard the voice of many angels round about the throne and the beasts and the elders: and the number of them was ten thousand times ten thousand, and thousands of thousands;

12 Saying with a loud voice, Worthy is the Lamb that was slain to receive power, and riches, and wisdom, and strength, and honour, and glory, and blessing.

13 And every creature which ~~is~~[6] in heaven, and ~~on~~[7] ~~**the earth**~~[8], and under the earth, and ~~such as~~[9] are in the sea, and all that are in them, heard I saying, Blessing, and honour, and glory, and power, *be* unto him that sitteth upon the throne, and unto the Lamb for ever and ever.

14 And the four beasts said, Amen. And the ~~four~~ ~~*and twenty*~~[10] elders fell down and worshipped ~~him~~ ~~that liveth for ever and ever~~[11].

---

[1] WH changed harps (ki**th**aras) to *harp* (ki**th**aran). Acc Fem **Plur** to Acc Fem ***Sing***. [number]

[2] WH omitted us ([h]Amas) after hast redeemed.

[3] WH omitted us ([h]Amas) after hast made.

[4] WH changed kings (basileis) to *a kingdom* (basilei**an**).

[5] WH changed **we shall reign** (basileus**omen**) to *they shall reign* (basileu**ousin**). Both Fut Act Ind. **1**[st] Plur to *3*[rd] Plur. [person]

[6] WH omitted is (estin) after which.

[7] WH changed **in** (**in**) to ***upon*** (*epi*).

[8] WH changed the earth (tA gA) to *the earth* (tAs gAs). **Dat** to ***Gen***. [case]

[9] WH omitted such as ([h]a) before are.

[10] WH omitted four [and] twenty before elders.

[11] WH omitted {one} living unto the ages of the ages (zOnti eis tous aiOnas tOn aiOnOn).

CHAPTER 6

1   And I saw when the Lamb opened one of the [ʌseven][1] seals, and I heard, as it were the **noise**[2] of thunder, one of the four beasts saying, Come ~~and see~~[3].

2   And I saw, and behold a white horse: and he that sat on **him**[4] had a bow; and a crown was given unto him: and he went forth conquering, and to conquer.

3   And when he had opened the second [ʌthe][5] **seal**[6], I heard the second beast say, Come ~~and see~~[7].

4   And there went out another horse *that was* red: and *power* was given to him that sat **there**on[8] to take peace **from**[9] the earth, and that **they should kill**[10] one another: and there was given unto him a great sword.

5   And when he had opened the **third** [ʌthe][11] **seal**[12], I heard the third beast say, Come ~~and see~~[13]. And I beheld, and lo a black horse; and he that sat on **him**[14] had a pair of balances in his hand.

6   And I heard [ʌas][15] a voice in the midst of the four

---

[8] WH omitted it (autO) from thereon.
[9] WH changed **from** (**apo**) to *out of* (*ek*) in their text, but omitted it from their margin.
[10] WH changed they **might** kill (sfaxOsi) to *they will kill* (*sfaxousi*). **Aor** Act **Sub** to *Fut* Act *Ind*. [tense & mood]
[11] WH added *the* (*tAn*) before seal.
[12] WH changed the word order from the third SEAL to *the SEAL the third*.
[13] WH omitted and see (kai blepe) after come.
[14] WH changed him (autO) to *him* (*auton*). **Dat** Masc Sing to *Acc* Masc Sing. [case]
[15] WH added as (ʰOs) after heard.

---

[1] WH added *seven* (ʰepta) before seals.
[2] WH changed noise (fOnAs) to *noise* (*fOnA*). **Gen** Fem Sing *Nom* Fem Sing. [case]
[3] WH omitted and see (kai blepte) in their text, but retained these words in their margin.
[4] WH changed him (autO) to *him* (*auton*). **Dat** Masc Sing to *Acc* Masc Sing. [case]
[5] WH added *the* (*tAn*) before seal.
[6] WH changed the word order from the second SEAL to *the SEAL the second*.
[7] WH omitted and see (kai blepe) after come.

beasts say, A measure of wheat for a penny, and three measures **of barley**[1] for a penny; and *see* thou hurt not the oil and the wine.

7 And when he had opened the fourth seal, I heard the voice of the fourth beast **say**[2], Come **and see**[3].

8 And I looked, and behold a pale horse: and his name that sat on him was Death, and Hell **followed**[4] with him. And power was given unto them over the fourth part of the earth, **to kill**[5] with sword, and with

hunger, and with death, and with the beasts of the earth.

9 And when he had opened the fifth seal, I saw under the altar the souls of them that were slain for the word of God, and for the testimony which they held:

10 And **they cried**[6] with a loud voice, saying, How long, O Lord, holy and **[the]**[7] true, dost thou not judge and avenge our blood **on**[8] them that dwell on the earth?

11 And **white robes**[9] **were given**[10] **unto every one**[11] **of**

---

[1] WH changed of barley (krith**As**) to *of barley* (*krithOn*). Gen Fem **Sing** to Gen Fem **Plur**. [number]
[2] WH changed saying (legou-san) to *saying* (*legontos*). Both Pres Act Part. **Acc Fem** Sing to **Gen Neut** Sing. [case & gender]
[3] WH omitted and see (kai blepe) after come.
[4] WH changed **are** following (akolouthei) to *were following* (*Akolouthai*). **Pres** Act Ind to *Impf* Act Ind. [tense]
[5] WH changed the word order from TO KILL over the fourth {part} of the earth to *over the fourth {part} of the earth TO KILL.*

[6] WH changed they were cry-ing (ekrazon) to *they cried* (*ekraxan*). **Impf** Act Ind to *Aor* Act Ind. [tense]
[7] WH omitted the untrans-lated the ([h]o) before true.
[8] WH changed **on** (**apo**) to *out of* (*ek*).
[9] WH changed white robes (stolai leukai) to *a white robe* (*stolA leukA*). **Plur** to *Sing*. [number]
[10] WH changed **they were** given (edoth**A**san) to *it was given* (*edothA*). Both Aor pass Ind. 3rd **Plur** to 3rd *Sing*. [number]
[11] WH changed from unto every one ([h]ekast**ois**) to *unto every one* ([h]ekast**O**). Dat Masc **Plur** to Dat Masc *Sing*. [number]

ᴧ**them**[1]; and it was said unto them, that they should rest yet for a little season, until [**not**][2] their fellowservants also and their brethren, that should be killed as they *were*, **should be fulfilled**[3].

12 And I beheld when he had opened the sixth seal, and, l̶o̶[4], there was a great earthquake; and the sun became black as sackcloth of hair, and the [ᴧ**whole**][5] moon became as blood;

13 And the stars of heaven fell unto the earth, even as a fig tree casteth her untimely figs, when she is shaken of a mighty wind.

14 And ᴧ**the**[6] heaven departed as a scroll when it is rolled together; and every mountain and island were moved out of their places.

15 And the kings of the earth, and the great men, and the rich men, and **the chief captains**[7], and the **mighty men**[8], and every bondman, and e̶v̶e̶r̶y̶[9] free man, hid themselves in the dens and in the rocks of the mountains;

16 And said to the mountains and rocks, Fall on us, and hide us from the face of him that sitteth on the throne, and from the wrath of the Lamb:

17 For the great day of **his**[10] wrath is come; and who shall be able to stand?

---

[1] WH added *them* as the KJV supplied, but changed it from of them (implied) to *to them* (*autois*). **Implied Gen** to *Dative*. The result was a change from white robes **were** given to each to *a white* robe *was given* **to them** each.

[2] WH omitted the untranslated not (ou) after until.

[3] WH changed **will fulfill** (plArOs**ontai**) to *might be fulfilled* (plArO*th*Osi) in their text. **Fut** **Mid** **Ind** to *Aor Pass Sub*. [tense, voice, & mood] In their margin, WH had *plArOsOsai*.

[4] WH omitted lo (idou) after and.

[5] WH added *whole* (*ʰolA*) after the.

[6] WH added *the* (*ʰo*) before heaven as the KJB supplied.

[7] WH changed the word order from the rich men and THE CHIEF CAPTAINS to *THE CHIEF CAPTAINS and the rich men.*

[8] WH changed **mighty** men (**dunat**oi) to *strong men* (*is-curoi*). [syn]

[9] WH omitted every (pas) before free man.

[10] WH changed of **him** (aut**ou**) to *of them* (*autOn*) in the phrase the wrath of him. **Sing** to *Plur*. [number]

CHAPTER 7

1   ~~And~~[1]   after   **these things**[2]   I saw four angels standing on the four corners of the earth, holding the four winds of the earth, that the wind should not blow on the earth, nor on the sea, nor on **any**[3] tree.

2   And I saw another angel ascending from the east, having the seal of the living God: and he cried with a loud voice to the four angels, to whom it was given to hurt the earth and the sea,

3   Saying, Hurt not the earth, neither the sea, nor the trees, till **[not]**[4] we have sealed the servants of our God in their foreheads.

4   And I heard the number of them which were sealed: *and there were* sealed an hundred *and* forty *and* four thou-

thousand of all the tribes of the children of Israel.

5   Of the tribe of Juda *were* sealed twelve thousand. Of the tribe of Reuben *were* ~~sealed~~[5] twelve thousand. Of the tribe of Gad *were* ~~sealed~~[6] twelve thousand.

6   Of the tribe of Aser *were* ~~sealed~~[7] twelve thousand. Of the tribe of Nepthalim *were* ~~sealed~~[8] twelve thousand. Of the tribe of Manasses *were* ~~sealed~~[9] twelve thousand.

7   Of the tribe of Simeon *were* ~~sealed~~[10] twelve thousand. Of the tribe of Levi *were* ~~sealed~~[11] twelve thousand. Of the tribe of **Issachar**[12]

---

[1] WH omitted <u>and</u> (<u>kai</u>) before <u>after</u>.

[2] WH changed <u>these things</u> (<u>tauta</u>) to *this thing* (*touto*). Acc Neut **Plur** to Acc Neut *Sing*. [number]

[3] WH changed <u>any</u> (**pan**) to *any* (*ti*).

[4] WH omitted the untranslated <u>not</u> (<u>ou</u>). They changed until **not** (<u>acris</u> **ou**) to *until* (*acri*).

[5] WH omitted <u>sealed</u> (<u>esfragismenoi</u>).

[6] WH omitted <u>sealed</u> (<u>esfragismenoi</u>).

[7] WH omitted <u>sealed</u> (<u>esfragismenoi</u>).

[8] WH omitted <u>sealed</u> (<u>esfragismenoi</u>).

[9] WH omitted <u>sealed</u> (<u>esfragismenoi</u>).

[10] WH omitted <u>sealed</u> (<u>esfragismenoi</u>).

[11] WH omitted <u>sealed</u> (<u>esfragismenoi</u>).

[12] WH changed <u>Isachar</u> (<u>isacar</u>) to *Issachar* (*issacar*). [spell]

were **sealed**[1] twelve thou-sand.

8   Of the tribe of Zabulon *were* **sealed**[2] twelve thou-sand. Of the tribe of Joseph *were* sealed twelve thousand. Of the tribe of Benjamin *were* sealed twelve thousand.

9   After this I beheld, and, lo, a great multitude, which no man could number, of all nations, and kindreds, and people, and tongues, stood before the throne, and before the Lamb, **clothed**[3] with white robes, and palms in their hands;

10   And **cried**[4] with a loud voice, saying, Salvation to our God which sitteth upon the throne, and unto the Lamb.

11   And all the angels stood round about the throne,

and *about* the elders and the four beasts, and fell before the throne on [∧**the**][5] their **faces**[6], and worshipped God,

12   Saying, Amen: Bless-ing, and glory, and wisdom, and thanksgiving, and hon-our, and power, and might, *be* unto our God for ever and ever. Amen.

13   And one of the elders answered, saying unto me, What are these which are ar-rayed in white robes? and whence came they?

14   And I said unto him, Sir [∧**of me**][7], thou knowest. And he said to me, These are they which came out of great tribulation, and have washed their robes, and made them white in the blood of the Lamb.

15   Therefore are they be-fore the throne of God, and serve him day and night in his temple: and he that sitteth on the throne shall dwell among

---

[1] WH omitted sealed (es-fragismenoi).

[2] WH omitted sealed (es-fragismenoi).

[3] WH changed **were** clothed (peribeblAmenoi) to *having clothed themselves* (*peribe-blAmenous*). Pf **Pass** Part *Nom* to Pf *Mid* Part *Acc*. [voice & case]

[4] WH changed **crying** (kra-zontes) to *they cried* (*kra-zousi*). Pres Act **Part** to Pres Act *Ind*. [mood]

[5] WH added *the* (*ta*) after on (epi).

[6] WH changed face (pro-sOpon) to *faces* (*prosOpa*). Acc Neut **Sing** to Acc Neut *Plur*. [number] The result changed on face of them to *on the faces of them*.

[7] WH added *of me* (*mou*) af-ter Sir.

them.

16 They shall hunger no more, neither thirst any more; neither shall the sun light on them, nor any heat.

17 For the Lamb which is in the midst of the throne shall feed them, and shall lead them unto **living**[1] fountains of waters: and God shall wipe away all tears **from**[2] their eyes.

CHAPTER 8

1 And **when**[3] he had opened the seventh seal, there was silence in heaven about the space of half an hour.

2 And I saw the seven angels which stood before God; and to them were given seven trumpets.

3 And another angel came and stood at **the altar**[4],

having a golden censer; and there was given unto him much incense, that **he should offer**[5] *it* with the prayers of all saints upon the golden altar which was before the throne.

4 And the smoke of the incense, *which came* with the prayers of the saints, ascended up before God out of the angel's hand.

5 And the angel took the censer, and filled it with fire of the altar, and cast *it* into the earth: and there were **voices**, and **thunderings**[6], and lightnings, and an earthquake.

6 And the seven angels which had the seven trumpets prepared **themselves**[7] to sound.

7 The first **angel**[8] sounded, and there followed

---

[1] WH changed <u>living</u> (<u>zOsas</u>) to *living* (*zOAs*). **Verbal**: Pres Act Part **Plur** to **Noun**: Gen Fem *Sing*. [number & part of sp]

[2] WH changed **from** (**apo**) to *out of* (*ek*).

[3] WH changed <u>when</u> ([h]<u>ote</u>) to *when* ([h]*otan*). [**Adv** to *Conj*]

[4] WH changed <u>the</u> <u>altar</u> (<u>to thusiastArion</u>) to *the altar* (*tou thusiastAriou*). **Acc** Neut Sing to *Gen* Neut Sing.

[case]

[5] WH changed <u>he **might** offer</u> (<u>dOsA</u>) to *he **will** offer* (*dOsei*). **Aor** Act **Sub** to *Fut* Act *Ind*. [tense & mood]

[6] WH changed the word order from <u>VOICES and THUNDERINGS</u> to *THUNDERINGS and VOICES*.

[7] WH changed <u>them**selves**</u> ([h]*eautous*) to *them* (*autous*). **Refl** pro to *Pers* pro.

[8] WH omitted <u>angel</u> (<u>aggelos</u>) after <u>first</u>.

hail and fire mingled ᴧwith[1] blood, and they were cast upon the earth [ᴧand the third {part} of the earth was burned up][2]: and the third part of trees was burnt up, and all green grass was burnt up.

8   And the second angel sounded, and as it were a great mountain burning with fire was cast into the sea: and the third part of the sea became blood;

9   And the third part of the creatures which were in the sea, and had life, died; and the third part of the ships were destroyed[3].

10 And the third angel sounded, and there fell a great star from heaven, burning as it were a lamp, and it fell upon the third part of the rivers, and upon the fountains of [ᴧthe][4] waters;

11 And the name of the star is called [ᴧthe][5] Wormwood: and the third part of the waters **became**[6] wormwood; and many [ᴧof the][7] men died of the waters, because they were made bitter.

12 And the fourth angel sounded, and the third part of the sun was smitten, and the third part of the moon, and the third part of the stars; so as the third part of them was darkened, and the day **shone**[8] not for a third part of it, and the night likewise.

13 And I beheld, and heard an **angel**[9] **flying**[10] through the midst of heaven, saying with a loud voice,

---

[1] WH added *with* (*en*) after mingled as the KJV supplied.
[2] WH added *and the third {part} of the earth was burned up* (*kai to triton tAs gAs katekaA*).
[3] WH changed **it was de-stroyed** (*dief̶t̶harA*) to *they were destroyed* (*dief̶t̶harAsan*). Both Aor Pass Ind. 3ʳᵈ **Sing** to 3ʳᵈ *Plur*. [number]
[4] WH added *the* (*tOn*) before

waters.
[5] WH added *the* (*ʰo*) before wormwood.
[6] WH changed **becomes** (**gi-netai**) to *became* (*egeneto*). **Pres** M/P Ind to *Aor* Mid Ind. [tense]
[7] WH added *of the* (*tOn*) before men.
[8] WH changed **may** shine (**fainA**) to **might** shine (*fanA*). **Pres** Act Sub to Aor *Act* Sub. [tense]
[9] WH changed **angel** (**agge-lou**) to *eagle* (*aetou*).
[10] WH changed **flying** (**pe-tOmenou**) to *flying* (*peto-menou*). Pres **M/P** Part to Pres **M/P** Part. [spell]

Woe, woe, woe, **to the in-habiters**[1] of the earth by rea-son of the other voices of the trumpet of the three angels, which are yet to sound!

CHAPTER 9

1   And   the   fifth   angel sounded, and I saw a star fall from heaven unto the earth: and to him was given the key of the bottomless pit.

2   And he opened the bot-tomless pit; and there arose a smoke out of the pit, as the smoke of a great furnace; and the sun and the air were dark-ened by reason of the smoke of the pit.

3   And there came out of the smoke locusts upon the earth: and unto them was given power, as the scorpions of the earth have power.

4   And it was commanded them that they should not hurt the grass of the earth, neither any green thing, nei-ther any tree; but ~~only~~[2] those men which have not the seal

of God in ~~their~~[3] foreheads.

5   And to them it was given that they should not kill them, but that **they should be tormented**[4] five months: and their tormen _was_ as the torment of a scorpion, when he striketh a man.

6   And in those days shall men seek death, and **shall not**[5] [∧**not**][6] **find**[7] it; and shall desire to die, and death **shall flee**[8] from them.

7   And the shapes of the locusts _were_ like unto horses prepared unto battle; and on their heads _were_ as it were

---

[3] WH omitted of them (autOn) from the foreheads of them.

[4] WH changed they **might** be tormented (basanisthOsi) to _they **will** be tormented_ (_basanisthAsontai_). **Aor** Pass **Sub** to **Fut** Pass _Ind_. [tense & mood]

[5] WH changed not (ouc) to _not (ou)._ [spell]

[6] WH added _not (mA)_ to strengthen the negative.

[7] WH changed **shall** find (eurAsousin) to _found (eurOsin)._ **Fut** Act Ind to _Aor_ Act Ind. [tense]

[8] WH changed **shall** flee (feuxetai) to _flees (feugei)._ **Fut** Mid Ind-D to _Pres_ Act Ind. [tense]

---

[1] WH changed **to** the inhabit-ers (to**is** katoikous**in**) to _the inhabiters (tous katoikoun-tas)._ Both Pres Act Part. **Dat** Masc Plur to _Acc_ Masc Plur. [case]

[2] WH omitted only (monous).

crowns like gold, and their faces *were* as the faces of men.

8   And they had hair as the hair of women, and their teeth were as *the teeth* of lions.

9   And they had breastplates, as it were breastplates of iron; and the sound of their wings *was* as the sound of chariots of many horses running to battle.

10   And they had tails like unto scorpions, and there **were**[1] stings in their tails: **and**[2] their power *was* to hurt men five months.

11   **And**[3] they had a king over them, *which is* the angel of the bottomless pit, whose name in the Hebrew tongue *is* Abaddon, but in the Greek tongue hath *his* name Apollyon.

12   One woe is past; *and*, behold, **there come**[4] two woes more hereafter.

13   And the sixth angel sounded, and I heard a voice from the **four**[5] horns of the golden altar which is before God,

14   **Saying**[6] to the sixth angel **which had**[7] the trumpet, Loose the four angels which are bound in the great river Euphrates.

15   And the four angels were loosed, which were prepared for an hour, and a day, and a month, and a year, for to slay the third part of men.

16   And the number of ^**the**[8] army of the horsemen *were* two hundred thousand thousand: **and**[9] I heard the number of them.

17   And thus I saw the

---

[1] WH changed **were** (**An**) to *and* (*kai*).

[2] WH omitted *and* (*kai*) before the power of them.

[3] WH omitted *and* (*kai*) at the beginning of verse eleven.

[4] WH changed **they** come (**ercon**tai) to *it comes* (*ercetai*). Both Pres Mid Ind. 3rd **Plur** to 3rd *Sing*. [number]

[5] WH omitted *four* (*tessarOn*) before horns.

[6] WH changed saying (**legousan**) to *saying* (*legonta*). Both Pres Act Part. Acc **Fem** Sing to Acc *Masc* Sing. [gender]

[7] WH changed **which was** having (ʰos eice) to *the* {**one**} *having* (ʰo ecOn). **Impf** Act **Ind** to *Pres* Act *Part*. [tense & mood]

[8] WH added *the* (*tOn*) before armies as the KJV supplied.

[9] WH omitted *and* (*kai*) before I heard.

horses in the vision, and them that sat on them, having breastplates of fire, and of jacinth, and brimstone: and the heads of the horses *were* as the heads of lions; and out of their mouths issued fire and smoke and brimstone.

18 **By**[1] these three **[ᴧplagues]**[2] was the third part of men killed, by the fire, and ~~by~~[3] the smoke, and ~~by~~[4] the brimstone, which issued out of their mouths.

19 For **their**[5] power is in their mouth, and in their tails: for their tails *were* like unto serpents, and had heads, and with them they do hurt.

20 And the rest of the men which were not killed by these plagues yet repented not of the works of their hands, that they **should** not **worship**[6] devils, and **[ᴧthe]**[7]

idols of gold, and silver, and brass, and stone, and of wood: which neither **can**[8] see, nor hear, nor walk:

21 Neither repented they of their murders, nor of their **sorceries**[9], nor of their fornication, nor of their thefts.

CHAPTER 10

1 And I saw another mighty angel come down from heaven, clothed with a cloud: and **[ᴧthe]**[10] a rainbow *was* upon **his head**[11] **[ᴧof**

---

[1] WH changed **by** (ʰ**upo**) to *from* (*apo*).

[2] WH added *plagues* (*plAgOn*) after three.

[3] WH omitted by (ek) before the smoke.

[4] WH omitted by (ek) before the brimstone.

[5] WH changed of **them** (**autOn**) to *of the horse* (*tOn* ʰ*ippOn*) in the phrase the power of them.

[6] WH changed **might** wor-

ship (proskunAsOsi) to *will worship* (*proskunAsousi*). **Aor** Act **Sub** to *Fut* Act *Ind*. [tense & mood]

[7] WH added *the* (*ta*) before idols.

[8] WH changed **they are able** (dunatai) to *it is able* (*dunantai*). Both Pres Mid Ind. 3rd **Plur** to 3rd *Sing*. [number]

[9] WH changed **sorceries** (farmakeiOn) to *magic potions* (*farmakOn*). Gen **Fem** Plur to Gen *Neut* Plur. farmakeia to *farmakon*. [gender]

[10] WH added *the* (ʰ*A*) before rainbow.

[11] WH changed the head (tAs kefalAs) to *the head* (*tAn kefalAn*). **Gen** Fem Sing to *Acc* Fem Sing. [case]

him]¹, and his face _was_ as it were the sun, and his feet as pillars of fire:

2   And **he had**² in his hand a little book open: and he set his right foot upon **the sea**³, and _his_ left _foot_ on **the earth**⁴,

3   And cried with a loud voice, as _when_ a lion roareth: and when he had cried, seven thunders uttered their voices.

4   And when the seven thunders had uttered **their voices**⁵, I was about to write: and I heard a voice from heaven saying **unto me**⁶, Seal up those things which the seven thunders uttered, and

write **them**⁷ not.

5   And the angel which I saw stand upon the sea and upon the earth lifted up his hand [ˇ**the right**]⁸ to heaven,

6   And sware by him that liveth for ever and ever, who created heaven, and the things that therein are, and the earth, and the things that therein are, ~~and the sea, and the things which are therein~~⁹, that **there should be**¹⁰ time **no longer**¹¹:

7   But in the days of the voice of the seventh angel, when he shall begin to sound, the mystery of God **should be finished**¹², as he hath

---

¹ WH added _of him_ (_autou_) after <u>the head</u>.

² WH changed **he was** <u>having</u> (_eicen_) to _having_ (_ecOn_). **Impf** Act **Ind** to _Pres_ Act _Part_. [tense & mood]

³ WH changed <u>the sea</u> (_tAn thalassan_) to _the sea_ (_tAs thalassAs_). **Acc** Fem Sing to _Gen_ Fem Sing. [case]

⁴ WH changed <u>the earth</u> (_tAn gAn_) to _the earth_ (_tAs gAs_). **Acc** Fem Sing _Gen_ Fem Sing. [case]

⁵ WH omitted <u>their voices</u> (_tas fOnas_ ʰ_eautOn_).

⁶ WH omitted <u>unto me</u> (_moi_) after <u>saying</u>.

⁷ WH omitted <u>them</u> (_tauta_— "these {things}").

⁸ WH added _the right_ (_tAn dexian_) after <u>the hand</u>.

⁹ WH omitted <u>and the sea and the {things} in it</u> (_kai tAn thalassan kai ta en autA_).

¹⁰ WH changed the word order from <u>time no will be longer</u> to _time no longer will be_.

¹¹ WH changed <u>no longer</u> (_ouk eti_) to _no longer_ (_ouketi_). **Two** words to _One_ word.

¹² WH changed **might be finished** (_telesthA_) to _was finished_ (_etelesthA_). Aor Pass **Sub** to Aor Pass _Ind_ [mood]

declared **to his servants the prophets**[1].

8   And the voice which I heard from heaven **spake**[2] unto me again, and **said**[3], Go *and* take the **little book**[4] which is open in the hand of ∧**the**[5] angel which standeth upon the sea and upon the earth.

9   And I went unto the angel, and said unto him, **Give**[6] me the little book. And he said unto me, Take *it*, and eat it up; and it shall make thy belly bitter, but it shall be in thy mouth sweet as honey.

10 And I took the little book out of the angel's hand, and ate it up; and it was in my mouth sweet as honey: and as soon as I had eaten it, my belly was bitter.

11 And **he said**[7] unto me, Thou must prophesy again before many peoples, and nations, and tongues, and kings.

CHAPTER 11

1   And there was given me a reed like unto a rod: ~~and the angel stood~~[8], saying, Rise, and measure the temple of God, and the altar, and them that worship therein.

2   But the court which is without the temple leave **out**[9], and measure it not; for it is given unto the Gentiles: and the holy city shall they tread under foot forty *and*

---

[1] WH changed to the of himself servants the prophets (to**is** ^h^eautou doulo**is** to**is** profAt**ais**) to *to the of himself servants the prophets* (*to**us** ^h^eautou doulo**us** tous profAt**as**)*. **Dat** to *Acc*. [case]

[2] WH changed speaking (lalousa) to *speaking* (*lalousan*). Both Pres Act Part. **Nom** Fem Sing to *Acc* Fem Sing. [case]

[3] WH changed saying (legousa) to *saying* (*legousan*). Both Pres Act Part. **Nom** Fem Sing to *Acc* Fem Sing. [case]

[4] WH changed **little** book (bibl**arid**ion) to *book* (*biblion*).

[5] WH added *the* (*tou*) before angel as the KJV supplied.

[6] WH changed give (dos) to *to give* (*dounai*). Aor Act **Imp** to Aor Act *Inf*. [mood]

[7] WH changed **he says** (legei) to *they say* (*legousi*). Both Pres Act Ind. 3rd **Sing** to 3rd *Plur*. [number]

[8] WH omitted and the angel stood (kai ^h^o aggelos eistA-kei).

[9] WH changed out (exO) to *outside* (^h^exO~~th~~en).

two months.

3   And I will give *power* unto my two witnesses, and they shall prophesy a thousand two hundred *and* threescore days, clothed in sackcloth.

4   These are the two olive trees, and the two candlesticks **standing**[1] before the **God**[2] of the earth.

5   And if any man **will**[3] hurt them, fire proceedeth out of their mouth, and devoureth their enemies: and if any man **will**[4] hurt **them**[5], he must in this manner be killed.

6   These have [∧the][6]

power to shut heaven, that **it rain**[7] not ~~in~~[8] ∧the[9] **days**[10] of **their**[11] prophecy: and have power over waters to turn them to blood, and to smite the earth ∧**with**[12] all plagues, as often as they will.

7   And when they shall have finished their testimony, the beast that ascendeth out of the bottomless pit shall make **war**[13] against them, and shall overcome them, and kill them.

8   And their **dead bodies**[14] *shall lie* in the street of

---

[1] WH changed having stood (^hestOsai) to *having stood* (^hestOtes). Both Pf Act Part. Nom **Fem** Plur to Nom *Masc* Plur. [gender]

[2] WH changed **God** (~~the~~ou) to *Lord* (*kuriou*).

[3] WH changed **may** will (~~the~~lA) to *wills* (~~the~~lei). Pres Act **Sub** to Pres Act *Ind*. [mood]

[4] WH changed **may** will (~~the~~lA) to *might will* (~~the~~lAsA). **Pres** Act Sub to *Aor* Act Sub. [tense]

[5] WH changed the word order from THEM **may** will to hurt to *might will* THEM to hurt.

[6] WH added *the* (*tAn*) before power.

[7] WH changed the word order from IT RAIN rain to *rain IT RAIN*.

[8] WH omitted in (en).

[9] WH added *the* (*tas*) before days as the KJV supplied.

[10] WH changed days (^hAmerais) to *days* (^hAmeras). **Dat** Fem Plur to *Acc* Fem Plur. [case]

[11] WH changed the word order from OF THEM of the prophecy to *of the prophecy OF THEM*.

[12] WH added *with* (*en*) as the KJV supplied.

[13] WH changed the word order from shall make WAR against them to *shall make against them WAR*.

[14] WH changed the dead bodies (ta ptOmata) to *the dead body* (*to ptOma*). Nom Neut **Plur** to Nom Neut *Sing*. [number]

the great [ᴧ**the**]¹ city, which spiritually is called Sodom and Egypt, where also **our**² Lord was crucified.

9   And **they** of the people and kindreds and tongues and nations **shall see**³ their **dead bodies**⁴ three days and an half, and **shall** not **suffer**⁵ their dead bodies to be put in **graves**⁶.

10   And they that dwell upon the earth **shall rejoice**⁷

over   them,   and   **make merry**⁸, and shall send gifts one to another; because these two prophets tormented them that dwelt on the earth.

11   And after three days and an half the Spirit of life from   God   entered   **into them**⁹, and they stood upon their feet; and great fear **fell**¹⁰ upon them which saw them.

12   And they heard **a great voice**¹¹ from heaven **saying**¹²

---

¹ WH added *the* (*tAs*) before city.
² WH changed of us (ʰ*amOn*) to *of them* (*autOn*) in the phrase the Lord of us. [person]
³ WH changed they **shall** see (ble$ousin) to *they see* (*blepousin*). **Fut** Act Ind to ***Pres*** Act Ind. [tense]
⁴ WH changed the dead bodies (**ta** ptOmata) to *the dead body* (*to ptOma*). Acc Neut **Plur** to Acc Neut ***Sing***. [number]
⁵ WH changed **shall** suffer (af**A**sousi) to *suffer* (*afiousi*). **Fut** Act Ind to ***Pres*** Act Ind. [tense]
⁶ WH changed graves (mnAmata) to *grave* (*mnAma*). Acc Neut **Plur** to Acc Neut ***Sing***. [number]
⁷ WH changed **shall** rejoice (carousin) to *rejoices*

(*cairousin*). **Fut** Act Ind to ***Pres*** Act Ind. [tense]
⁸ WH changed **will be** gladdened (eufran**th**Asontai) to *is being gladdened* (*eufrainontai*). **Fut** Pass Ind to ***Pres*** Pass Ind. [tense]
⁹ WH changed **upon** them (ep' **autous**) to *in them* (*en autois*). [prep & case]
¹⁰ WH changed fell (epesen) to *fell* **upon** (*epepesen*). Both Aor Act Ind. piptO to *epipiptO*. [prefix added]
¹¹ WH changed a great voice (fOnAn *megalAn*) to *a great voice* (*fOnAs megalAs*). **Acc** Fem Sing to ***Gen*** Fem Sing. [case]
¹² WH changed saying (legousan) to *saying* (*legousAs*). Both Pres Act Part. **Acc** Fem Sing to ***Gen*** Fem Sing. [case]

unto them, **Come up**[1] hither. And they ascended up to heaven in a cloud; and their enemies beheld them.

13 And the same hour was there a great earthquake, and the tenth part of the city fell, and in the earthquake were slain of men seven thousand: and the remnant were affrighted, and gave glory to the God of heaven.

14 The second woe is past; ~~and~~[2], behold, the third woe cometh quickly.

15 And the seventh angel sounded; and there were great voices in heaven, **saying**[3], **The kingdoms**[4] of this world **are become**[5] *the king-*

doms of our Lord, and of his Christ; and he shall reign for ever and ever.

16 And the four ~~and~~[6] twenty elders, ~~which~~[7] **sat**[8] before God on their seats, fell upon their faces, and worshipped God,

17 Saying, We give thee thanks, O Lord God Almighty, which art, and wast, ~~and art to come~~[9]; because thou hast taken to thee thy great power, and hast reigned.

18 And the nations were angry, and thy wrath is come, and the time of the dead, that they should be judged, and that thou shouldest give reward unto thy servants the prophets, and to the saints, and them that fear thy name, **small**[10]

---

[1] WH changed <u>come up</u> (ana-bAte) to *come up* (*anabate*). Both Aor Act Imp 2nd Plur. [spell]

[2] WH omitted <u>and</u> (<u>kai</u>).

[3] WH changed <u>saying</u> (<u>le-gousai</u>) to *saying* (*legontes*). Both Pres Act Part. Nom **Fem** Plur to Nom *Masc* Plur. [gender]

[4] WH changed <u>the kingdoms</u> (<u>hai basileiai</u>) to *the kingdom* (*hA Basileia*). Nom Fem **Plur** to Nom Fem *Sing*. [number]

[5] WH changed **are** <u>become</u> (<u>egenonto</u>) to *is become* (*egeneto*). Both Aor Mid Ind. 3rd **Plur** to 3rd *Sing*. [number]

[6] WH omitted <u>and</u> (<u>kai</u>) between <u>twenty</u> and <u>four</u>.

[7] WH omitted <u>which</u> (<u>hoi</u>) after <u>elders</u>.

[8] WH changed **sitting** (<u>kathAmenoi</u>) to *he sat* (*kathAntai*). Pres M/P **Part**-D to Pres Mid *Ind*. [mood]

[9] WH omitted <u>and</u> <u>the</u> {one} <u>coming</u> (<u>kai ho ercomenos</u>).

[10] WH changed **to the** <u>small</u> (<u>tois mikrois</u>) to *the small* (*tous mikrous*). **Dat** Plur to *Acc* Plur. [case]

and **great**[1]; and shouldest destroy them which destroy the earth.

19 And the temple of God was opened [∧**the**][2] in heaven, and there was seen in his temple the ark of his testament: and there were lightnings, and voices, and thunderings, and an earthquake, and great hail.

CHAPTER 12

1 And there appeared a great wonder in heaven; a woman clothed with the sun, and the moon under her feet, and upon her head a crown of twelve stars:

2 And she being with child [∧**and**][3] cried, travailing in birth, and pained to be delivered.

3 And there appeared another wonder in heaven; and behold a great **red**[4]

dragon, having seven heads and ten horns, and seven **crowns**[5] upon his heads.

4 And his tail drew the third part of the stars of heaven, and did cast them to the earth: and the dragon **stood**[6] before the woman which was ready to be delivered, for to devour her child as soon as it was born.

5 And she brought forth **a man**[7] child, who was to rule all nations with a rod of iron: and her child was caught up unto God, and ∧*to*[8] his throne.

6 And the woman fled into the wilderness, where she hath [∧**there**][9] a place

---

[1] WH changed **to** the great (**tois** megalois) to *the great* (*tous megalous*). **Dat** Plur to *Acc* Plur. [case]

[2] WH added *the* (*ʰo*) before in the heaven and after of the God.

[3] WH added *and* (*kai*) after and in womb having.

[4] WH changed the word order from great RED to *RED great*.

[5] WH changed the word order from CROWNS seven to *seven CROWNS*.

[6] WH changed **was standing** (*ʰestAken*) to *has stood* (*estAken*). **Impf** Act Ind to *Pf* Act Ind. [tense]

[7] WH changed a man child (*ʰuion* arrena—"son male") to *a man child* (*ʰuion arsen*—"son male"). **Noun**: Acc **Masc** Sing to *Adj*: Acc **Neut** Sing. [part of speech & gender]

[8] WH added *to* (*pros*) as the KJV supplied.

[9] WH added *there* (*ekei*) after she hath.

prepared of God, that they should feed her there a thousand two hundred *and* three-score days.

7   And there was war in heaven: Michael and his angels [ʌthe]¹ **fought**² **against**³ the dragon; and the dragon fought and his angels,

8   And prevailed not; **neither**⁴ was their place found any more in heaven.

9   And the great dragon was cast out, that old serpent, called the Devil, and Satan, which deceiveth the whole world: he was cast out into the earth, and his angels were cast out with him.

10 And I heard a loud voice **saying**⁵ in heaven, Now is come salvation, and strength, and the kingdom of our God, and the power of

his Christ: for the accuser of our brethren **is cast down**⁶, which accused them before our God day and night.

11 And they overcame him by the blood of the Lamb, and by the word of their testimony; and they loved not their lives unto the death.

12 Therefore rejoice, ~~ye~~⁷ heavens, and ye that dwell in them. Woe ~~to the inhabiters of~~⁸ the earth and of the sea! for the devil is come down unto you, having great wrath, because he knoweth that he hath but a short time.

13 And when the dragon saw that he was cast unto the earth, he persecuted the woman which brought forth the man *child.*

14 And to the woman were given [ʌthe]⁹ two wings of a great eagle, that she might fly into the wilderness, into her place, where she is nourished for a time, and

---

¹ WH added *the* (*tou*) before fought.
² WH changed **they fought** (**epolemAsan**) to *to fight* (*polemAsai*). Aor Act **Ind** to Aor Act *Inf.* [mood]
³ WH changed **against** (**kata**) to *with* (*meta*). [prep]
⁴ WH changed neither (oute) to *neither* (*oude*).
⁵ WH changed the word order from SAYING in the heaven to *in the heaven* SAYING.

⁶ WH changed was cast **down** (**kat**eblA~~th~~A) to *was cast* (*eblAtA*). Both Aor Pass Ind. [prefix dropped]
⁷ WH omitted the (ʰoi) which the KJV supplied as *ye.*
⁸ WH omitted to the inhabiters of (tois katoikousi).
⁹ WH added *the* (ʰai) before two wings.

times, and half a time, from the face of the serpent.

15 And the serpent cast out of his mouth water as a flood **after** **the** **woman**[1], that he might cause **her**[2] to be carried away of the flood.

16 And the earth helped the woman, and the earth opened her mouth, and swallowed up the flood which the dragon cast out of his mouth.

17 And the dragon was wroth with the woman, and went to make war with the remnant of her seed, which keep the commandments of God, and have the testimony of **[the]**[3] Jesus ~~Christ~~[4].

CHAPTER 13

1 And **I stood**[5] upon the

sand of the sea, and saw a beast rise up out of the sea, having **seven** **heads** and **ten** **horns**[6], and upon his horns ten crowns, and upon his heads **the name**[7] of blasphemy.

2 And the beast which I saw was like unto a leopard, and his feet were as _the feet_ of **a bear**[8], and his mouth as the mouth of a lion: and the dragon gave him his power, and his seat, and great authority.

3 And ~~I saw~~[9] one ∧of[10] his heads as it were wounded to death; and his deadly wound was healed: and all

---

[1] WH changed the word order from AFTER THE WOMAN out of the mouth of him to _out of the mouth of him AFTER THE WOMAN._

[2] WH changed **this** (one) (**tautAn**) to _her (autAn)._ **Dem** pro to _Pers_ pro.

[3] WH omitted the untranslated the (tou) before Jesus.

[4] WH omitted Christ (cristou) after Jesus.

[5] WH changed **I stood** (estath̄An) to _he stood_ (estath̄A). Both Aor Pass

Ind. **1**[rst] Sing to _3_[rd] Sing. [number]

[6] WH changed the word order from HEADS SEVEN and HORNS TEN to _HORNS TEN and HEADS SEVEN._

[7] WH changed the name (onoma) to _names (onomata)._ **Nom** Neut **Sing** to _Acc_ Neut _Plur._ [case & number]

[8] WH changed bear (arktou) to _bear (arkou)._ Both Gen Fem Sing. [spell]

[9] WH omitted I saw (eidon) before one.

[10] WH added of (ek) after one to replace the KJV genitive supplied of.

the world wondered after the beast.

4   And they worshipped **the dragon**[1] **which**[2] gave [ʌ**the**][3] power unto the beast: and they worshipped **the beast**[4], saying, Who _is_ like unto the beast? [ʌ**and**][5] who is able to make war with him?

5   And there was given unto him a mouth speaking great things and blasphemies; and power was given unto him to continue forty _and_ two months.

6   And he opened his mouth in **blasphemy**[6] against God, to blaspheme his name,

and his tabernacle, **~~and~~**[7] them that dwell in heaven.

7   **And it was given unto him to make war**[8] **with the saints, and to overcome them**[9]: and power was given him over all kindreds, [ʌ**and people**][10] and tongues, and nations.

8   And all that dwell upon the earth shall worship **him**[11], **whose**[12] **names**[13] [ʌof him][14]

---

[7] WH omitted <u>and</u> (<u>kai</u>) after <u>tabernacle</u>.
[8] WH changed the word order from WAR <u>to make</u> to _to make_ WAR.
[9] In their margin, WH omitted <u>and it was given</u> <u>unto him</u> <u>to make war</u> <u>with</u> <u>the</u> <u>saints</u> <u>and</u> <u>to over-come</u> <u>them</u> (<u>kai edotha autO po-lemon poiasai meta tOn ʰagiOn kai nikAsai autous</u>).
[10] WH added _and people_ (_kai laon_) after <u>kindreds</u>.
[11] WH changed <u>him</u> (<u>autO</u>) to _him_ (_auton_). **Dat** **Neut** Sing to _Acc Masc_ Sing. [case & gender]
[12] WH changed <u>whose</u> (ʰ**On**) to _whose_ (ʰ**ou**). Gen Masc **Plur** to Gen Masc _Sing_. [number]
[13] WH changed <u>the names</u> (<u>ta onomata</u>) to _the name_ (_to onoma_). Nom Neut **Plur** to Nom Neut _Sing_. [number]
[14] WH added _of him_ (_autou_) after <u>names</u>.

---

[1] WH changed <u>the dragon</u> (<u>ton</u> <u>drakonta</u>) to _the dragon_ (_tO drakonti_). **Acc** Masc Sing to _Dat_ Masc Sing. [case]
[2] WH changed **which** (ʰos) to _that_ (ʰoti). **Relative pronoun** to _Subordinating conjunction_.
[3] WH added _the_ (_tAn_) before <u>power</u>.
[4] WH changed <u>the beast</u> (**to** **thArion**) to _the beast_ (_tO thAriO_). **Acc** Neut Sing to _Dat_ Neut Sing. [case]
[5] WH added _and_ (_kai_) after <u>beast</u>.
[6] WH changed <u>blasphemy</u> (<u>blasfAmian</u>) to _blasphemies_ (_blasfAmias_). Acc Fem **Sing** to Acc Fem _Plur_. [number]

739

are not written in **the book**[1] of life of the Lamb [∧the {one}][2] slain from the foundation of the world.

9　If any man have an ear, let him hear.

10　He that ~~leadeth~~[3] ∧into[4] captivity shall go into captivity: he that killeth with the sword must be killed with the sword. Here is the patience and the faith of the saints.

11　And I beheld another beast coming up out of the earth; and he had two horns like a lamb, and he spake as a dragon.

12　And he exerciseth all the power of the first beast before him, and causeth the earth and them which **dwell**[5] therein to **worship**[6] the first

beast, whose deadly wound was healed.

13　And he doeth great wonders, so that he maketh fire **come down**[7] from heaven on the earth in the sight of men,

14　And deceiveth them that dwell on the earth by *the means of* those miracles which he had power to do in the sight of the beast; saying to them that dwell on the earth, that they should make an image to the beast, **which**[8] had the wound by a sword, and did live.

15　And **he**[9] had power to give life unto the image of the beast, that the image of the

---

[1] WH change the book (t**a** biblO) to *the* {**little**} *book* (*tO bibliO*). Dat **Fem** Sing of bibl**os** to Dat *Neut* Sing of *biblion*. [gender &]
[2] WH added *the* {one} (*tou*) before slain.
[3] WH omitted leadeth (sunagei). Their margin notes the uncertainty of the reading.
[4] WH added *into* (*eis*) as the KJV supplied.
[5] WH changed the word order from DWELL in it to *in it DWELL*.
[6] WH changed they **might**

worship (*proskunAsOsi*) to *they will worship* (*proskunAsousi*). **Aor** Act **Sub** to *Fut* Act *Ind*. [tense & mood]
[7] WH changed the word order from TO COME DOWN from the heaven to *from the heaven* TO COME DOWN.
[8] WH changed which (ᵸo) to *which* (ᵸos). Nom **Neut** Sing to Nom *Masc* Sing. [gender]
[9] WH changed to him (autO) to *to him* (*autA*) in the expression and it was given **to him** (kai edo~~th~~A autO) [*loosely rendered in KJV* and he had power]. Dat **Neut** Sing to Dat *Fem* Sing. [gender]

beast should both speak, and **cause**[1] ∧**that**[2] as many as **[ever]**[3] would not worship **the image**[4] of the beast **[that]**[5] should be killed.

16 And he causeth all, both small and great, rich and poor, free and bond, to **receive**[6] a mark in their right hand, or in their **foreheads**[7]:

17 And that no man might buy or sell, save he that had

---

[1] In their margin, WH changed **might** cause (poi-AsA) to *will cause* (*poiAsei*). **Aor** Act **Sub** to *Fut* Act *Ind*. [tense & mood]

[2] WH added *that* (*[h]ina*) as the KJV supplied after cause.

[3] WH changed the untranslated ever (an) to *ever* (*ean*).

[4] WH changed the image (t**An** eikona) to *the image* (*tA eikoni*). **Acc** Fem Sing to *Dat* Fem Sing. [case]

[5] WH omitted *that* (*[h]ina*) after beast.

[6] WH changed **he** might receive (d**Os**A) to *they might receive* (*dOsin*). Both Aor Act Sub. 3rd **Sing** to 3rd *Plur*. [number]

[7] WH changed the foreheads (t**On** met**O**p**O**n) to *the forehead* (*to metOpon*) in the phrase the foreheads of them. **Gen** Neut **Plur** to *Acc* Neut *Sing*. [case & number]

---

the mark, ~~or~~[8] the name of the beast, or the number of his name.

18 Here is wisdom. Let him that hath **[the]**[9] understanding count the number of the beast: for it is the number of a man; and his number *is* Six hundred threescore *and* six[10].

CHAPTER 14

1 And I looked, and, lo, [∧**the**][11] a Lamb stood on the mount Sion, and with him an hundred forty *and* four thousand, having his Father's name [∧**of him and the name**][12] written in their

---

[8] WH omitted or ([h]A) after mark.

[9] WH omitted the untranslated the (ton) before understanding.

[10] In their margin, WH changed 666 (c-**x**-s) to 6 (c-**i**-s). [c-i-s is not used in any computerized NT Greek text or in the LXX. 6 (ex) is used by the modern critical text in Rev 13:18]

[11] WH added *the* (*to*) before lamb.

[12] WH added *of him and the name* (*autou kai to onoma*) after name. The result was having the name *of him and the name* of the father of him.

---

foreheads.

2   And I heard a voice from heaven, as the voice of many waters, and as the voice of a great thunder: and I heard ∧the[1] **voice**[2] [∧**which**][3] [∧**as**][4] of harpers harping with their harps:

3   And they sung as it were a new song before the throne, and before the four beasts, and the elders: and no man could learn that song but the hundred *and* forty *and* four thousand, which were redeemed from the earth.

4   These are they which were not defiled with women; for they are virgins. These **are**[5] they which follow the Lamb whithersoever he goeth. These were redeemed from among men, *being* the firstfruits unto God and to the Lamb.

5   And in their mouth was found no **guile**[6]: ~~for~~[7] they are without fault ~~before the throne of God~~[8].

6   And I saw another angel **fly**[9] in the midst of heaven, having the everlasting gospel to preach ∧unto[10] them **that dwell**[11] on the earth, and ∧to[12] every nation, and kindred, and tongue, and people,

7   **Saying**[13] with a loud

---

[1] WH added *the* (ʰA) before voice as the KJV supplied.

[2] WH changed voice (fOnAn) to *voice* (fOnA). **Acc** Fem Sing to *Nom* Sing Fem. [case]

[3] WH added *which* (ʰAn) after voice and before I heard. The result was a change from voice I heard to *the* voice *which* I heard.

[4] WH added *as* (ʰOs) before of harpers.

[5] WH omitted are (eisin) after these.

[6] WH changed **guile** (dolos) to *lying* (seudos).

[7] WH omitted for (gar).

[8] WH omitted before the thrown of the God (enOpion tou thronou tou theou).

[9] WH changed flying (petO-menon) to *flying* (petome-non). Both Pres M/P-D Part. [spell]

[10] WH added *unto* (epi) after to preach as the KJV supplied.

[11] WH changed settling down (katoikountas) to *sitting down* (kathAmenous). Both Pres Act Part. katoikeO to kathAmai. [syn]

[12] WH added *to* (epi) before every nation as the KJV supplied.

[13] WH changed saying (le-gonta) to *saying* (legOn). Both Pres Act Part. **Acc** Masc Sing to *Nom* Masc Sing. [case]

voice, Fear God, and give glory to him; for the hour of his judgment is come: and worship him that made heaven, and earth, and the sea, and the fountains of waters.

8   And there followed another angel, saying, Babylon is fallen, is fallen, that great ~~city~~[1], **because**[2] she made all [∧**the**][3] nations drink of the wine of the wrath of her fornication.

9   And [∧**another**][4] the third **angel**[5] followed them, saying with a loud voice, If any man **worship**[6] the beast and his image, and receive *his* mark in his forehead, or in his hand,

10   The same shall drink of the wine of the wrath of God, which is poured out without mixture into the cup of his indignation; and he shall be tormented with fire and brimstone in the presence of **the**[7] holy **angels**[8], and in the presence of the Lamb:

11   And the smoke of their torment **ascendeth up**[9] for ever and ever: and they have no rest day nor night, who worship the beast and his image, and whosoever receiveth the mark of his name.

12   Here is ∧**the**[10] patience of the saints: ~~here~~[11] *are* they that keep the commandments of God, and the faith of Jesus.

13   And I heard a voice from heaven saying ~~unto me~~[12], Write, Blessed *are* the dead which die in the Lord from henceforth: yea, saith the Spirit, that **they may**

---

[1] WH omitted <u>the</u> <u>city</u> (ʰA polis).

[2] WH changed **because** (ʰ**oti**) to *which* (ʰ*A*).

[3] WH added *the* (*ta*) before <u>nations</u>.

[4] WH added *another* (*allos*).

[5] WH changed the word order from <u>third</u> ANGEL to ANGEL *third*.

[6] WH changed the word order from <u>the</u> <u>beast</u> WORSHIP to WORSHIP <u>the</u> <u>beast</u>.

[7] WH omitted <u>the</u> (tOn) before <u>holy</u> <u>angels</u>.

[8] WH changed the word order from <u>holy</u> ANGELS to ANGELS *holy*.

[9] WH changed the word order from ASCENDS UP <u>unto</u> <u>ages</u> <u>of ages</u> to *unto ages of ages ASCENDS UP*.

[10] WH added *the* (*A*) before <u>patience</u>.

[11] WH omitted <u>here</u> (ʰOde).

[12] WH omitted <u>unto me</u> (moi) after <u>saying</u>.

rest[1] from their labours; **and**[2] their works do follow them.

14 And I looked, and behold a white cloud, and upon the cloud *one* **sat like unto**[3] **the Son**[4] of man, having on his head a golden crown, and in his hand a sharp sickle.

15 And another angel came out of the temple, crying with a loud voice to him that sat on the cloud, Thrust in thy sickle, and reap: for the time is come ~~for thee~~[5] [the][6] to reap; for the harvest of the earth is ripe.

16 And he that sat on **the**

cloud[7] thrust in his sickle on the earth; and the earth was reaped.

17 And another angel came out of the temple which is in heaven, he also having a sharp sickle.

18 And another angel came out from the altar, ˄**which**[8] had power over fire; and cried with a loud **cry**[9] to him that had the sharp sickle, saying, Thrust in thy sharp sickle, and gather the clusters of the vine of the earth; for her grapes are fully ripe.

19 And the angel thrust in his sickle into the earth, and gathered the vine of the earth, and cast *it* into the great winepress of the wrath of God.

20 And the winepress was trodden **without**[10] the city, and blood came out of the winepress, even unto the horse bridles, by the space of

---

[1] WH changed they **might** rest (anapausOntai) to *they will rest* (anapaAsontai). **Aor Mid Sub** to *Fut Pass Ind*. [tense, voice & mood]
[2] WH changed **and** (**de**) to *for* (*gar*).
[3] WH changed sitting like unto (kathAmenos ʰomois) to *sitting like unto* (*kathAmenon* ʰomoion). Pres M/P Part **Nom** Masc Sing to Pres M/P Part *Acc* Masc Sing. [case]
[4] WH changed son (ʰuiO) to *son* (ʰuion). **Dat** Masc Sing to *Acc* Masc Sing. [case]
[5] WH omitted for thee (soi) after is come.
[6] WH omitted the untraslated the (tou) before to reap.

[7] WH changed the cloud (tAn nefelAn) to *the cloud* (*tAs nefelAs*). **Acc** Fem Sing to *Gen* Fem Sing. [case]
[8] WH added *which* (ʰo—"the {one}") as the KJV supplied it.
[9] WH changed **cry** (**kraugA**) to *voice* (*fOnA*).
[10] WH changed outside (exO) to *outside* (exOthen). [syn]

a thousand *and* six hundred furlongs.

CHAPTER 15

1   And I saw another sign in heaven, great and marvellous, seven angels having the seven last plagues; for in them is filled up the wrath of God.

2   And I saw as it were a sea of glass mingled with fire: and them that had gotten the victory over the beast, and over his image, and ~~over his mark~~[1], *and* over the number of his name, stand on the sea of glass, having the harps of God.

3   And they sing the song of Moses the servant of God, and the song of the Lamb, saying, Great and marvellous *are* thy works, Lord God Almighty; just and true *are* thy ways, thou King of **saints**[2].

4   Who   shall   not   fear **thee**[3], O Lord, and **glorify**[4] thy name? for *thou* only *art* holy: for all nations shall come and worship before thee; for thy judgments are made manifest.

5   And after that I looked, and, ~~behold~~[5], the temple of the tabernacle of the testimony in heaven was opened:

6   And the seven angels came out of the temple, [ʌ**the {ones}**][6] having the seven plagues, clothed in pure **and**[7] white **linen**[8], and having their breasts girded with golden girdles.

7   And one of the four beasts gave unto the seven angels seven golden vials full of the wrath of God, who liveth for ever and ever.

8   And the temple was

---

[1] WH omitted <u>over</u> <u>the</u> <u>mark</u> <u>of him</u> (<u>ek</u> <u>tou</u> <u>caragmatos</u> <u>autou</u>).

[2] WH changed <u>the</u> **saints** (<u>tOn</u> ^h**agiOn**) to *the ages* (*tOn aiOnOn*). In their margin, WH suggested *the nations* (*tOn e†hnOn*).

[3] WH omitted <u>thee</u> (<u>se</u>) after <u>fear</u>.

[4] WH changed **might** <u>glorify</u> (<u>doxasA</u>) to *will glorify* (*doxasei*). **Aor** Act **Sub** to *Fut* Act *Ind*. [tense & mood]

[5] WH omitted <u>behold</u> (<u>idou</u>).

[6] WH added *the {ones}* before *having*.

[7] WH omitted <u>and</u> (<u>kai</u>) between <u>pure</u> and <u>white</u>.

[8] WH changed **linen** (<u>linon</u>) to *stone* (*li†hon*) in their text, but retained <u>linon</u> in their margin.

745

filled with smoke from the glory of God, and from his power; and no man was able to enter into the temple, till the seven plagues of the seven angels were fulfilled.

CHAPTER 16

1   And I heard a great voice out of the temple saying to the seven angels, Go your ways, and pour out the [∧**seven**][1] vials of the wrath of God upon the earth.

2   And the first went, and poured out his vial **upon**[2] the earth; and there fell a noisome and grievous sore **upon**[3] the men which had the mark of the beast, and *upon* them which **worshipped**[4] his image.

3   And the second **angel**[5] poured out his vial upon the sea; and it became as the blood of a dead *man*: and every **living**[6] soul died in the sea.

4   And the third **angel**[7] poured out his vial upon the rivers and [**into**][8] fountains of waters; and **they became**[9] blood.

5   And I heard the angel of the waters say, Thou art righteous, **O Lord**[10], which art, and wast, **and**[11] **shalt be**[12], because thou hast judged thus.

6   For they have shed the blood of saints and prophets,

---

[1] WH added *seven* (*ʰepta*) before vials.
[2] WH changed **upon** (**epi**) to *into* (*eis*).
[3] WH changed **into** (**eis**) to *upon* (*epi*).
[4] WH changed the word order from the image of him WORSHIPPED to *WORSHIPPED the image of him*.
[5] WH omitted angel (aggelos) after second.

[6] WH changed living (zOsa) to *living* (zOAs). **Verb**: Pres Act Part **Nom** Fem Sing to *Noun*: *Gen* Fem Sing. [part of speech & case]
[7] WH omitted angel (aggelos) after third.
[8] WH omitted the untranslated into (eis) before fountains.
[9] In their margin, WH changed **it became** (egeneto) to *they became* (egenonto). Both Aor Mid Ind. 3rd **Sing** to 3rd **Plur**. [number]
[10] WH omitted O Lord (kurie) after righteous.
[11] WH omitted and (kai) after wast.
[12] WH changed **shalt be** (**esomenos**) to *holy* (ʰosios). **Verbal** to *Adj*.

and **thou hast given**[1] them blood to drink; ~~for~~[2] they are worthy.

7   And I heard ~~another out of~~[3] the altar say, Even so, Lord God Almighty, true and righteous *are* thy judgments.

8   And the fourth **angel**[4] poured out his vial upon the sun; and power was given unto him to scorch men with fire.

9   And men were scorched with great heat, and blasphemed the name of God, which hath [ʌ**the**][5] power over these plagues: and they repented not to give him glory.

10   And the fifth **angel**[6] poured out his vial upon the seat of the beast; and his kingdom was full of darkness; and they gnawed their tongues for pain,

11   And blasphemed the God of heaven because of their pains and their sores, and repented not of their deeds.

12   And the sixth **angel**[7] poured out his vial upon the great river Euphrates; and the water thereof was dried up, that the way of the kings of the east might be prepared.

13   And I saw three unclean spirits **like**[8] **frogs**[9] *come* out of the mouth of the dragon, and out of the mouth of the beast, and out of the mouth of the false prophet.

14   For they are the spirits **of devils**[10], working miracles, *which* go forth unto the kings ~~of the earth and~~[11] of the whole world, to gather them

---

[1] WH changed you[s] gave (edOkas) to *you[s] have given* (*dedOkas*). **Aor** Act Ind to *Pf* Act Ind. [tense]

[2] WH omitted for (gar).

[3] WH omitted another out of (allou ek) after I heard.

[4] WH omitted angel (aggelos) after fourth.

[5] WH added *the* (*tAn*) before power.

[6] WH omitted angel (aggelos) after fifth.

[7] WH omitted angel (aggelos) after sixth.

[8] WH changed **like** ([h]omoia) to *as* ([h]Os). **Adj**: Acc Neut Plur to **Sub Conj**. [part of sp]

[9] WH changed frogs (batracois) to *frogs* (*batracoi*). **Dat** Masc Plur to *Nom* Masc Plur. [case]

[10] WH changed of demons (daimonOn) to *of demons* (*daimoniOn*). Gen **Masc** Plur to Gen *Neut* Plur. [gender]

[11] WH omitted of the earth and (tAs gAs kai) after kings.

to the battle of ~~that~~[1] great day of God Almighty.

15 Behold, I come as a thief. Blessed *is* he that watcheth, and keepeth his garments, lest he walk naked, and they see his shame.

16 And he gathered them together into a place called in the Hebrew tongue **Armageddon**[2].

17 And the seventh ~~angel~~[3] poured out his vial **into**[4] the air; and there came a great voice **out of**[5] the temple ~~of heaven~~[6], from the throne, saying, It is done.

18 And there were voices, and thunders, **and lightnings**[7]; and there was a great earthquake, such as was not since ~~[the]~~[8] **men were**[9] upon the earth, so mighty an earthquake, *and* so great.

19 And the great city was divided into three parts, and the cities of the nations fell: and great Babylon came in remembrance before God, to give unto her the cup of the wine of the fierceness of his wrath.

20 And every island fled away, and the mountains were not found.

21 And there fell upon men a great hail out of heaven, *every stone* about the weight of a talent: and men blasphemed God because of the plague of the hail; for the plague thereof was exceeding great.

CHAPTER 17

1 And there came one of

---

[1] WH omitted that (ekeinAs) from the day that {one} of the great the God the Almighty.

[2] WH changed Armageddon ([h]armageddOn) to *Armagedon* ([h]armagedOn). **Nom** Neut Sing to *Acc* Neut Sing. [case]

[3] WH omitted angel (aggelos) after seventh.

[4] WH changed **into** (e**is**) to ***upon*** (e**pi**). [prep]

[5] WH changed **from** (**apo**) to **out of** (*ek*). [prep]

[6] WH omitted of the heaven (tou ouranou) after temple.

[7] WH changed the word or-

---

der from voices and thunders AND LIGHTNINGS to *LIGHTNINGS AND voices and thunders*.

[8] WH omitted the untranslated the (oi) before men.

[9] In their margin, WH changed **men were** (an[th]ropoi egenonto) to ***man was*** (*an[th]ropos egeneto*). **Plur** to ***Sing***. [number]

the seven angels which had the seven vials, and talked with me, saying **unto me**[1], Come hither; I will shew unto thee the judgment of the great whore that sitteth upon **[the]**[2] many **[the]**[3] waters:

2   With whom the kings of the earth have committed fornication, and **the inhabitants of the earth**[4] have been made drunk with the wine of her fornication.

3   So he carried me away in the spirit into the wilderness: and I saw a woman sit upon a scarlet coloured beast, **full**[5] **of names**[6] of blasphemy,

having seven heads and ten horns.

4   And the woman was arrayed in **purple**[7] and **scarlet colour**[8], and decked with **gold**[9] and precious stones and pearls, having a golden **cup**[10] in her hand full of abominations and **[∧the]**[11] **filthiness**[12]

---

[1] WH omitted <u>unto me</u> (<u>moi</u>) after <u>saying</u>.
[2] WH omitted the untranslated <u>the</u> (<u>tOn</u>) before <u>many</u>.
[3] WH omitted the untranslated <u>the</u> (<u>tOn</u>) before <u>waters</u>.
[4] WH changed the word order from <u>have been made drunk with the wine of the fornication of her</u> THE INHABITANTS OF THE EARTH to *have been made drunk* THE INHABITANTS OF THE EARTH *with the wine of the fornication of her*.
[5] WH changed {**he**} <u>being full</u> (<u>gemon</u>) to {**they**} *being full* (*gemonta*). Both Pres Act Part. Acc Neut **Sing** to Acc Neut *Plur*. [number]

[6] WH changed <u>of names</u> (<u>onomatOna</u>) to *of names* (*onomata*). **Gen** Neut Plur to *Acc* Neut Plur. [case]
[7] WH changed <u>purple **cloth**</u> (<u>porfura</u>) to purple {**thing**} (*porfuroun*). **Noun**: **Dat Fem** Sing to *Adj*: *Acc Neut* Sing. [part of sp, case, & gender]
[8] WH changed <u>scarlet colour</u> (<u>kokinO</u>) to *scarlet colour* (*kokinon*). **Dat** Neut Sing to *Acc* Neut Sing. [case]
[9] WH changed <u>gold</u> (<u>crusO</u>) to *gold* (*crusiO*). Dat **Masc** Sing of <u>crusos</u> to Dat *Neut* Sing of *crusion*. [case & syn]
[10] WH changed the word order from <u>golden</u> CUP to CUP *golden*.
[11] WH added *the* (*ta*) before <u>filthiness</u>.
[12] WH changed <u>filthiness</u> (<u>akathartAtos</u>) to *unclean* {*things*} (*akatharta*). **Noun**: **Gen Fem Sing** to *Adj*: *Acc Neut Plur*. [part of sp, case, gender, & number]

of her [∧**the**]¹ fornication:

5   And upon her forehead
was a name written,
MYSTERY, BABYLON
THE GREAT, THE
MOTHER OF harlots AND
abominations OF THE
EARTH.

6   And I saw the woman
drunken with the blood of the
saints, and with the blood of
the martyrs of Jesus: and
when I saw her, I wondered
with great admiration.

7   And the angel said unto
me, Wherefore didst thou
marvel? I will tell **thee**² the
mystery of the woman, and of
the beast that carrieth her,
which hath the seven heads
and ten horns.

8   The beast that thou
sawest was, and is not; and
shall ascend out of the bottomless pit, and **go**³ into perdition: and they that dwell on
the earth shall wonder, whose

names⁴ were not written in
the book of life from the
foundation of the world,
when they behold⁵ the beast
that⁶ was, and is not, **and
yet**⁷ **is**⁸.

9   And here _is_ the mind
which hath wisdom. The
seven heads are **seven**⁹
mountains, on which the
woman sitteth.

10 And there are seven
kings: five are fallen, **and**¹⁰

---

¹ WH added _the_ (_ta_) before
fornication in of fornication
of her.
² WH changed the word or-
der from myself THEE I will
tell to _myself I will tell_ THEE.
³ In their margin, WH
changed **to be** going (ʰu-
pagein) to _he is going_ (ʰu-
pagei). Pres Act **Inf** to Pres
Act _Ind_. [mood]

---

⁴ WH changed the names (**ta**
onoma**ta**) to _the name_ (_to
onoma_). Nom Neut **Plur** to
Nom Neut _Sing_. [number]
⁵ WH changed beholding
(ble_pont_es) to _beholding_
(_blepontOn_). Both Pres Act
Part (beholding). **Nom** Masc
Plur to _Gen_ Masc Plur. [case]
⁶ WH changed that (ʰo ti) to
that (ʰoti). [2-word to 1-
word]
⁷ WH changed and **yet**
(kai_per_) to _and_ (_kai_). [suffix
dropped]
⁸ WH changed **is** (est_in_) to
will be (_parestai_). **Pres** Ind
to _Fut_ Mid Ind. [prefix added
& tense] The result changes
and **yet is** to _and will be_.
⁹ WH changed the word or-
der from mountains are
SEVEN to _SEVEN mountains
are_.
¹⁰ WH omitted _and_ (kai) before the one.

one is, _and_ the other is not yet come; and when he cometh, he must continue a short space.

11 And the beast that was, and is not, even he is the eighth, and is of the seven, and goeth into perdition.

12 And the ten horns which thou sawest are ten kings, which have received no kingdom as yet; but receive power as kings one hour with the beast.

13 These have one mind, and **shall give**[1] **their**[2] power and [~~the~~][3] strength unto the beast.

14 These shall make war with the Lamb, and the Lamb shall overcome them: for he is Lord of lords, and King of kings: and they that are with him _are_ called, and chosen, and faithful.

15 And he saith unto me,

The waters which thou sawest, where the whore sitteth, are peoples, and multitudes, and nations, and tongues.

16 And the ten horns which thou sawest **upon**[4] the beast, these shall hate the whore, and shall make her desolate and naked, and shall eat her flesh, and burn her with fire.

17 For God hath put in their hearts to fulfil his will, and to agree, and give their kingdom unto the beast, until **the words**[5] of God **shall be fulfilled**[6].

18 And the woman which thou sawest is that great city, which reigneth over the kings of the earth.

CHAPTER 18

1   ~~And~~[7] after these things

---

[1] WH changed <u>give</u> {**through**} (**dia**did**Osou**sin) to _give_ (_didoasin_). Both Pres Act Ind 3rd Plur. [prefix dropped]

[2] WH changed <u>of them**selves**</u> (**ʰeaut**On) to _of them_ (_autOn_) in the phrase <u>the power and the strength of them**selves**</u>. **Refl** pro to **Pers** pro.

[3] WH omitted the untranslated <u>the</u> (<u>tAn</u>) before <u>strength</u>.

[4] WH changed **upon** (**epi**) to _and_ (_kai_).

[5] WH changed <u>the words</u> (**tA** **ʰrAmata**) to _the words_ (_ʰoi logoi_). [syn]

[6] WH changed **it was** <u>fulfilled</u> (teles**th**A) to **they shall be** _fulfilled_ (teles**th**Asontai). **Aor** Pass **Sub** 3rd **Sing** to **Fut** Pass _Ind_ 3rd **Plur**. [tense, mood, & number]

[7] WH omitted <u>and</u> (<u>kai</u>) before <u>after</u>.

I saw another angel come down from heaven, having great power; and the earth was lightened with his glory.

2   And he cried **mightily**[1] with ~~a strong~~[2] voice, saying, Babylon the great is fallen, is fallen, and is become the habitation **of devils**[3], and the hold of every foul spirit, and a cage of every unclean and hateful bird.

3   For all nations **have drunk**[4] **of the wine**[5] of the wrath of her fornication, and the kings of the earth have committed fornication with her, and the merchants of the earth are waxed rich through the abundance of her delicacies.

4   And I heard another voice from heaven, saying, Come **out of her**[6], my people, that ye be not partakers of her sins, and **that ye receive not**[7] of her plagues.

5   For her sins have reached unto heaven, and God hath remembered her iniquities.

6   Reward her even as she rewarded **~~you~~**[8], and double **~~unto her~~**[9] [∧the][10] double according to her works: in the cup which she hath filled fill to her double.

7   How much she hath

---

[1] WH changed <u>might</u> (<u>iscui</u>) to *mighty* (*iscura*). **Noun** to **Adjective**.

[2] WH omitted <u>strong</u> (<u>megalA</u>). As a result they changed <u>mightily</u> <u>with a</u> **strong** voice (<u>en</u> <u>iscui</u> <u>fOnA</u> **megalA**) to *with a **mighty** voice* (*en iscura fOnA*).

[3] WH changed <u>of demons</u> (<u>daimonOn</u>) to *of demons* (*daimoniOn*). Gen **Masc** Plur of <u>daimOn</u> to Gen *Neut* Plur of *daimonion*. [gender & syn]

[4] WH changed **it has** <u>drunk</u> (<u>pepOke</u>) to *they have drunk* (*peptOkan*) in their text but retained <u>pepOke</u> in their margin. Both Pf Act Ind. 3rd **Sing** to 3rd *Plur* [number]

[5] In their margin, WH omitted <u>of the wine</u> (<u>tou oinou</u>).

[6] WH changed the word order from <u>come</u> <u>OUT OF</u> <u>HER</u> <u>the</u> <u>people</u> <u>of me</u> to *come the people of me OUT OF HER.*

[7] WH changed the word order from <u>THAT</u> <u>NOT</u> <u>YE</u> <u>RECEIVE</u> of the <u>plagues</u> <u>of her</u> to *of the plagues of her THAT NOT YE RECEIVE.*

[8] WH omitted <u>you</u> (<u>humin</u>) after <u>rewarded</u>.

[9] WH omitted <u>unto her</u> (<u>autA</u>).

[10] WH added *the* (*ta*) before <u>double</u>.

glorified **herself**[1], and lived deliciously, so much torment and sorrow give her: for she saith in her heart, [ʌ**that**][2] I sit a queen, and am no widow, and shall see no sorrow.

8 Therefore shall her plagues come in one day, death, and mourning, and famine; and she shall be utterly burned with fire: for strong *is* the **Lord**[3] God who **judgeth**[4] her.

9 And the kings of the earth, who have committed fornication and lived deliciously with her, shall bewail **her**[5], and lament for **her**[6], when they shall see the smoke of her burning,

10 Standing afar off for the fear of her torment, saying, Alas, alas, that great city Babylon, that mighty city! for **in**[7] one hour is thy judgment come.

11 And the merchants of the earth shall weep and mourn over **her**[8]; for no man buyeth their merchandise any more:

12 The merchandise of gold, and silver, and precious stones, and **of pearls**[9], and **fine linen**[10], and purple, and **silk**[11], and scarlet, and all thyine wood, and all manner vessels of ivory, and all manner vessels of most precious wood, and of brass, and iron, and marble,

---

[1] WH changed herself (ʰeautAn) to *her* (autAn). **Refl** pro to **Pers** pro.

[2] WH added *that* (ʰoti) before I sit.

[3] In their margin, WH omitted Lord (kurios).

[4] WH changed judging (krinOn) to *having judged* (krinas). **Pres** Act Part to *Aor* Act Part. [tense]

[5] WH omitted her (autAn).

[6] WH omitted her (autA) after bewail.

[7] WH omitted in (en) and forced the case to supply the preposition.

[8] WH changed her (autA) to *her* (autAn). **Dat** Fem Sing to *Acc* Fem Sing. [case]

[9] WH changed pearl (margaritou) to *pearls* (margaritOn). Gen Masc **Sing** to Gen Masc *Plur*. [number]

[10] WH changed fine linen (bussou) to *made of fine linen* (bussinou). Gen **Fem** Sing of bussos to Gen *Neut* Sing of bussinos. [gender & syn]

[11] WH changed silk (sArikou) to *silk* (sirikou). Both Gen Neut Sing. [spell]

13 And **cinnamon**[1], [∧**and spice**][2] and odours, and ointments, and frankincense, and wine, and oil, and fine flour, and wheat, and beasts, and sheep, and horses, and chariots, and slaves, and souls of men.

14 And the fruits that **thy**[3] soul lusted after are departed from thee, and all things which were dainty and goodly **are departed**[4] from thee, and **thou shalt find them**[6] no more at all.

15 The merchants of these things, which were made rich by her, shall stand afar off for the fear of her torment, weeping and wailing,

16 ~~**And**~~[7] saying, Alas, alas, that great city, that was clothed in fine linen, and purple, and scarlet, and decked ~~**with**~~[8] **gold**[9], and precious stones, and **pearls**[10]!

17 For in one hour so great riches is come to nought. And every shipmaster, and all **the company in ships**[11], and sailors, and as

---

[1] WH changed <u>cinnamon</u> (<u>kinamOmon</u>) to *cinnamon* (*kinnamOmon*). [spell]
[2] WH added *and spice* (*kai amOmon*) after <u>cinnamon</u>.
[3] WH changed the word order from <u>the</u> <u>fruit</u> <u>of the</u> <u>lust</u> <u>of the</u> <u>soul</u> OF THEE to *the fruit OF THEE of the lust of the soul*.
[4] WH changed <u>did</u> **depart** (<u>apAlthen</u>) to *did pass away* (*apOleto*). Both Aor Act Ind. <u>ap</u><u>ercomai</u> to *apollumi*. [syn]
[5] WH changed **you**s **might find** (<u>eurAsAs</u>) to *they will find* (*eurAsousin*). **Aor** Act **Sub 2**nd **Sing** to *Fut Act Ind 3*rd *Plur*. [tense, mood, person, & number]
[6] WH changed the word order from <u>no more</u> <u>not</u> <u>ever</u> <u>thou found</u> THEM to *no more*

THEM not ever **they shall find**.
[7] WH omitted <u>and</u> (<u>kai</u>) before <u>saying</u>.
[8] WH omitted <u>with</u> (<u>en</u>) before <u>gold</u> and forced the dative case to supply the preposition.
[9] WH changed <u>gold</u> (<u>krusO</u>) to *gold* (*krusiO*). Dat **Masc** Sing of <u>krusos</u> to Dat *Neut* Sing of *krusion*. [gender & syn]
[10] WH changed <u>pearls</u> (<u>margaritais</u>) to *pearl* (*margaritA*). Dat Masc **Plur** to Dat Masc *Sing*. [number]
[11] WH changed <u>the</u> **company in ships** (<u>epi</u> **tOn** <u>ploiOn</u> ^h<u>o</u> ^h**omilos**) to *the* {one} *in place of ships* (^h*o epi* **topon** *pleOn*).

many as trade by sea, stood afar off,

18 And **cried**[1] **when they saw**[2] the smoke of her burning, saying, What *city is* like unto this great city!

19 And they cast dust on their heads, and **cried**[3], weeping and wailing, saying, Alas, alas, that great city, wherein were made rich all that had [ʌthe][4] ships in the sea by reason of her costliness! for in one hour is she made desolate.

20 Rejoice over **her**[5], *thou* heaven, and *ye* holy [ʌand the][6] apostles and prophets;

---

[1] WH changed they **were** crying (ekrazon) to *they cried* (*ekraxan*). **Impf** Act Ind to *Aor* Act Ind. [tense]

[2] WH changed seeing (ʰorOntes) to *seeing* (*blepontes*). Both Pres Act Part Nom Masc Plur. ʰoraO to *blepO*. [syn]

[3] WH changed they **were** crying (ekrazon) to *they cried* (*ekraxan*). **Impf** Act Ind to *Aor* Act Ind. [tense]

[4] WH added *the* (*ta*) before ships.

[5] WH changed her (autAn) to *her* (*autA*). **Acc** Fem Sing to *Dat* Fem Sing. [case]

[6] WH added *and the* (*kai* ʰ*oi*) before apostles.

for God hath avenged you on her.

21 And a mighty angel took up a stone like a great **millstone**[7], and cast *it* into the sea, saying, Thus with violence shall that great city Babylon be thrown down, and shall be found no more at all.

22 And the voice of harpers, and musicians, and of pipers, and trumpeters, shall be heard no more at all in thee; and no craftsman, ~~of whatsoever craft *he be*~~[8], shall be found any more in thee; and the sound of a millstone shall be heard no more at all in thee;

23 And the light of a candle shall shine no more at all in thee; and the voice of the bridegroom and of the bride shall be heard no more at all in thee: for thy merchants were the great men of the earth; for by thy sorceries were all nations deceived.

24 And in her was found

---

[7] WH changed millstone (mulon) to *mill stone* (*mulinon*). **Noun** of mulon to *Adj* of *mulinos*.

[8] WH omitted of whatsoever craft (pasAs tecnAs) after craftsman.

the blood[1] of prophets, and of saints, and of all that were slain upon the earth.

CHAPTER 19

1   ~~And~~[2] after these things I heard [∧as][3] a **great**[4] voice of much people in heaven, **saying**[5], Alleluia; Salvation, and glory, ~~and honour~~[6], and power, unto ~~the Lord~~[7] our **God**[8]:

---

[1] WH changed <u>blood</u> ([h]*aima*) to *bloods* ([h]*aimata*). Acc Neut **Sing** to Acc Neut *Plur*. [number]

[2] WH omitted <u>and</u> (<u>kai</u>) before <u>after</u>.

[3] WH added *as* ([h]*Os*) after <u>heard</u>.

[4] WH changed the word order from <u>voice</u> <u>of many</u> <u>people</u> GREAT to *voice GREAT of many people*.

[5] WH changed <u>saying</u> (<u>legontos</u>) to *saying* (*legontOn*). Both Pres Act Part. Gen Masc **Sing** to Gen Masc *Plur*. [number]

[6] WH omitted <u>and the honour</u> (<u>kai</u> [h]<u>A</u> <u>timA</u>) after <u>glory</u>.

[7] WH omitted <u>Lord</u> (<u>kuriO</u>) before <u>the God of us</u>.

[8] WH changed <u>the God</u> (<u>tO theO</u>) to *the God* (*tou theou*) in the phrase <u>the God of us</u>. **Dat** Masc Sing to *Gen* Masc

2   For true and righteous *are* his judgments: for he hath judged the great whore, which did corrupt the earth with her fornication, and hath avenged the blood of his servants at her [**the**][9] hand.

3   And again they said, Alleluia. And her smoke rose up for ever and ever.

4   And the four ~~and~~[10] twenty elders and the four beasts fell down and worshipped God that sat on **the throne**[11], saying, Amen; Alleluia.

5   And a voice came **out of**[12] the throne, saying, Praise our **God**[13], all ye his servants, ~~and~~[14] ye that fear him, both

---

Sing. [case]

[9] WH omitted the untranslated <u>the</u> (<u>tAs</u>) in <u>the</u> <u>hand of</u> <u>her</u>.

[10] WH omitted the <u>and</u> (<u>kai</u>) between <u>twenty</u> and <u>four</u>.

[11] WH changed <u>the</u> <u>throne</u> (**tou** ~~th~~<u>ronou</u>) to *the throne* (*tO* ~~th~~*ronO*). **Gen** Masc Sing to *Dat* Masc Sing. [case]

[12] WH changed **out of** (**ek**) to *from* (*apo*). [prep]

[13] WH changed <u>the</u> <u>God</u> (<u>ton</u> ~~th~~<u>eon</u>) to *the God* (*tO theO*) in the phrase <u>the God of us</u>. **Acc** Masc Sing to *Dat* Masc Sing. [case]

[14] WH omitted <u>and</u> (<u>kai</u>).

small and great.

6   And I heard as it were the voice of a great multitude, and as the voice of many waters, and as the voice of mighty thunderings, **say-ing**[1], Alleluia: for the Lord God **[∧of us]**[2] omnipotent reigneth.

7   Let us be glad and **re-joice**[3], and give honour to him: for the marriage of the Lamb is come, and his wife hath made herself ready.

8   And to her was granted that she should be arrayed in fine linen, **clean** ~~and~~[4] **white**[5]: for the fine linen **is**[6] the right-

eousness of saints.

9   And he saith unto me, Write, Blessed *are* they which are called unto the marriage supper of the Lamb. And he saith unto me, These **are**[7] the true sayings of God.

10   And I fell at his feet to worship him. And he said unto me, See *thou do it* not: I am thy fellowservant, and of thy brethren that have the testimony of **[the]**[8] Jesus: worship God: for the testimony of **[the]**[9] Jesus is the spirit of prophecy.

11   And I saw heaven opened, and behold a white horse; and he that sat upon him *was* **called**[10] Faithful and True, and in righteousness he doth judge and make war.

12   His eyes *were* **as**[11] a flame of fire, and on his head *were* many crowns; and he

---

[1] WH changed saying (legontas) to *saying* (legontOn). Both Pres Act Part. **Acc** Masc Plur to **Gen** Masc Plur. [case]

[2] WH added *of us* (^hAmOn) after Lord the God.

[3] WH changed may rejoice (agalliOme~~tha~~) to *may re-joice* (agalliOmen). Pres **M/P-D** Sub to Pres **Act** Sub. [voice]

[4] WH omitted and (kai) between clean and white.

[5] WH changed the word order from CLEAN **and** WHITE to *WHITE CLEAN*

[6] WH changed the word order from the righteousness IS of the saints to *the righteous-*

ness of the saints IS.

[7] WH changed the word order from ARE of the God to *of the God ARE.*

[8] WH omitted the untranslated the (tou) before Jesus.

[9] WH omitted the untranslated the (tou) before Jesus.

[10] In their margin, WH omitted called (kaloumenos) before faithful.

[11] WH omitted as (^hOs) before flame.

had a name written, that no man knew, but he himself.

13 And he _was_ clothed with a vesture **dipped**[1] in blood: and his name **is called**[2] The Word of God.

14 And the armies _which were_ in heaven followed him upon white horses, clothed in fine linen, white ~~and~~[3] clean.

15 And out of his mouth goeth a sharp sword, that with it **he should smite**[4] the nations: and he shall rule them with a rod of iron: and he treadeth the winepress of the fierceness ~~and~~[5] wrath of Almighty God.

16 And he hath on _his_ vesture and on his thigh a name written, KING OF KINGS, AND LORD OF LORDS.

17 And I saw an angel standing in the sun; and he cried with a loud voice, saying to all the fowls that **fly**[6] in the midst of heaven, Come ~~and~~[7] **gather yourselves together**[8] unto the supper **of the great**[9] [∧**the**][10] God;

18 That ye may eat the flesh of kings, and the flesh of captains, and the flesh of mighty men, and the flesh of

---

[6] WH changed fly (pet**O**-menois) to _fly_ (pet_omenois_). Both Pres Mid Part.
[7] WH omitted and (kai) before gather yourselves together.
[8] WH changed **be** gather**ing** yourselves together (su-nagesth**e**) to _gather your-selves together_ (sunac**th**At**e**). **Pres** Pass Imp to **Aor** Pass Imp. [tense]
[9] WH changed of the great (to**u** megal**ou**) to _the great_ (_to mega_). **Gen Masc** Sing to _**Acc Neut**_ Sing. [case & gender]
[10] WH added _the_ (_tou_) before God. As a result, they changed the supper of **the great God** to _the great sup-per_ _of **the** God._

---

[1] WH changed **dipped** (**be-bam**menon) to _purified_ (**ʰ**_rerantis_menon) in their text, but retained bebam-menon in their margin. Both Pf Pass Part Acc Neut Sing. [syn]
[2] WH changed **he is being** called (**kalei**tai) to _he **has been** called_ (_kekl_A_tai_). **Pres** Pass Ind to _Pf_ Pass Ind. [tense]
[3] WH omitted and (kai) be-tween white and clean.
[4] WH changed he might smite (patass**A**) to _he might smite_ (_patax_A). Both Aor Act Sub 3ʳᵈ Sing. [spell]
[5] WH omitted and (kai) be-fore wrath.

horses, and of them that sit on **them**[1], and the flesh of all *men, both* free and bond, both small and great.

19 And I saw the beast, and the kings of the earth, and their armies, gathered together to make [∧**the**][2] war against him that sat on the horse, and against his army.

20 And the beast was taken, and **with**[3] **him**[4] the false prophet that wrought miracles before him, with which he deceived them that had received the mark of the beast, and them that worshipped his image. These both were cast alive into a lake of fire **burning**[5] with

[**the**][6] brimstone.

21 And the remnant were slain with the sword of him that sat upon the horse, which *sword* **proceeded out**[7] of his mouth: and all the fowls were filled with their flesh.

CHAPTER 20

1 And I saw an angel come down from heaven, having the **key**[8] of the bottomless pit and a great chain in his hand.

2 And he laid hold on the dragon, that old serpent, which is the Devil, and [∧**the**][9] Satan, and bound him a thousand years,

3 And cast him into the

---

[1] WH changed them (*autOn*) to *them* (*autous*). **Gen** Masc Plur to *Acc* Masc Plur. [case]
[2] WH added *the* (*ton*) before war.
[3] WH changed with (*meta*) to *with* (*met'*). **Full spell** to *Contraction*.
[4] WH changed **this** {one} (*toutou*) to *him* (*autou*). **Dem** pro to *Pers* pro.
[5] WH change the {one} burning (*tAn* kaiomenAn) to *the* {one} *burning* (*tAs kaiomenAs*). Both Pres Pass Part. **Acc** Fem Sing to *Gen* Fem Sing. [case]

[6] WH omitted the untranslated the (*tO*) before brimstone.
[7] WH changed proceeding out (*ekporeuomenA*) to *having proceeded out* (*exelthousa*). **Pres** M/P-D Part of ekporeuomai to *Aor* Act Part of *exercomai*. [tense & syn]
[8] WH changed key (kleida) to *key* (*klein*). Both Acc Fem Sing. [spell]
[9] WH added *the* (*ʰo*) before Satan.

bottomless pit, and shut ~~him~~[1] up, and set a seal upon him, that he should deceive the nations **no more**[2], till the thousand years should be fulfilled: ~~and~~[3] after that **he**[4] must be loosed a little season.

4   And I saw thrones, and they sat upon them, and judgment was given unto them: and _I saw_ the souls of them that were beheaded for the witness of Jesus, and for the word of God, and which had not worshipped **the beast**[5], **neither**[6] his image, neither had received _his_ mark upon ~~their~~[7] foreheads, or in their hands; and they lived and

and reigned with [ʌ**the**][8] Christ a thousand years.

5   ~~But~~[9] the rest of the dead **lived** not **again**[10] **until**[11] the thousand years were finished. This _is_ the first resurrection.

6   Blessed and holy _is_ he that hath part in the first resurrection: on such the second [~~the~~][12]   **death**[13]   hath   no power, but they shall be priests of God and of Christ, and shall reign with him [**the**][14] a thousand years.

7   And when the thousand years are expired, Satan shall be loosed out of his prison,

8   And shall go out to deceive the nations which are in the four quarters of the earth,

---

[1] WH omitted <u>him</u> (_auton_).
[2] WH changed the word order from <u>the</u> <u>nations</u> NO MORE to _NO MORE the nations_.
[3] WH omitted <u>and</u> (_kai_) before <u>after</u>.
[4] WH changed the word order from HIM <u>to be loosed</u> to _to be loosed HIM_.
[5] WH changed <u>the</u> <u>beast</u> (**tO thAriO**) to _the beast_ (_to thArion_). **Dat** Neut Sing to _Acc_ Neut Sing. [case]
[6] WH changed <u>neither</u> (**oute**) to _neither_ (_oude_).
[7] WH omitted <u>of them</u> (_autOn_) in <u>the</u> <u>foreheads</u> <u>of</u> <u>them</u>.

[8] WH added _the_ (_tou_) before <u>Christ</u>.
[9] WH omitted <u>but</u> (_de_).
[10] WH changed <u>lived</u> **again** (**an**ez_Asan_) to _lived_ (_ezAsan_). Both Aor Act Ind. [prefix dropped]
[11] WH changed <u>until</u> (^h**eOs**) to _until_ (_acri_). [syn]
[12] WH omitted the untranslated <u>the</u> (^h_o_) before <u>death</u>.
[13] WH changed the word order from <u>the</u> DEATH <u>the</u> second to _the second DEATH_.
[14] In their margin, WH added _the_ (_ta_) before <u>thousand</u>.

Gog and [~~the~~]¹ Magog, to gather them together to [ᴧthe]² battle: the number [ᴧof them]³ of whom *is* as the sand of the sea.

9   And they went up on the breadth of the earth, and **compassed** the camp of the saints **about**⁴, and the beloved city: and fire came down ~~from God~~⁵ out of heaven, and devoured them.

10   And the devil that deceived them was cast into the lake of fire and brimstone, where [ᴧalso]⁶ the beast and the false prophet *are*, and shall be tormented day and night for ever and ever.

11   And I saw a great

white⁷ throne, and him that sat on it, from whose [ᴧthe]⁸ face the earth and the heaven fled away; and there was found no place for them.

12   And I saw the dead, [ᴧthe]⁹ **small** and [ᴧthe]¹⁰ **great**¹¹, stand before **God**¹²; and the books **were opened**¹³: and another **book**¹⁴ **was opened**¹⁵, which

---

⁷ WH changed the word order from and I saw throne WHITE great to and *I saw throne great WHITE.*

⁸ WH added *the (tou)* before face.

⁹ WH added *the (tous)* before small.

¹⁰ WH added *the (tous)* before great.

¹¹ WH changed the word order from SMALL and GREAT to *the* GREAT *and the* SMALL.

¹² WH changed the **God** (tou ~~the~~ou) to *the* **throne** (tou ~~thr~~onou).

¹³ WH changed were opened (AneOc~~th~~Asan) to *were opened* (Anoic~~th~~Asan). Both Aor Pass Ind 3ʳᵈ Plur. [spell]

¹⁴ WH changed the word order from BOOK another was opened to *another* BOOK *was opened.*

¹⁵ WH changed was opened (AnOc~~th~~A) to *was opened* (Anoic~~th~~A). Both Aor Pass Ind 3ʳᵈ Sing. [spell]

---

¹ WH omitted the untranslated the (ton) before Magog.

² WH added *the (ton)* before battle.

³ WH added *of them (autOn)* after number to read *of whom the number of them.*

⁴ WH changed surrounded (ekuklOsan) to *surrounded (ekukleusan)*. Both Aor Act Ind. kukloO to *kukleuO.* [syn]

⁵ WH omitted from the God (apo tou ~~the~~ou) in their text, but retained these words in their margin.

⁶ WH added *also (kai)* after where.

is *the book* of life: and the dead were judged out of those things which were written in the books, according to their works.

13 And the sea gave up **the dead**[1] which were in it; and death and hell delivered up **the dead**[2] which were **in**[3] them: and they were judged every man according to their works.

14 And death and hell were cast into the lake of fire. This **is** **the** **second**[4] [∧**the**][5] death. [∧**the lake of the fire**][6]

15 And whosoever was not found written in the book of life was cast into the lake of fire.

---

[1] WH changed the word order from gave up the in it DEAD to *gave up* DEAD *the in it*.

[2] WH changed the word order from delivered up the in them DEAD to *delivered up* DEAD *the out of them*.

[3] WH changed **in** (**en**) to *out of* (*ek*). [prep]

[4] WH changed the word order from this IS THE SECOND death to *this* **the** *death* THE SECOND IS.

[5] WH added *the* (*^{h}o*) before death.

[6] WH added *the lake of the fire* (*^{h}A limnA tou puros*).

CHAPTER 21

1 And I saw a new heaven and a new earth: for the first heaven and the first earth **were passed away**[7]; and there was no more sea.

2 And **I** [**myself**] ~~John~~[8] **saw**[9] the holy city, new Jerusalem, coming down **from God**[10] out of heaven, prepared as a bride adorned for her husband.

3 And I heard a great voice out of **heaven**[11] saying, Behold, the tabernacle of

---

[7] WH changed **it** passed away (**parAl**~~t~~**he**) to *they passed away* (*apAl*~~t~~*hon*). Aor Act Ind 3rd **Sing** of **pa**rercomai to Aor Act Ind 3rd **Plur** of *apercomai*). [number & prefix changed]

[8] WH omitted the untranslated myself (egO) and John (iOannAs).

[9] WH changed the word order from and I **myself John** SAW the city the holy Jerusalem new to *and the city the holy Jerusalem new I* SAW.

[10] WH changed the word order from FROM THE GOD out of the heaven to *out of the heaven* FROM THE GOD.

[11] WH changed the **heaven** (tou **ouran**ou) to *the* **throne** (*tou* ~~t~~**hron**ou).

God *is* with men, and he will dwell with them, and they shall be his people, and God himself **shall be**[1] with them, *and be* **their God**[2].

4   And **~~God~~**[3] shall wipe away all tears **from**[4] their eyes; and there shall be no more death, neither sorrow, nor crying, neither shall there be any more pain: **~~for~~**[5] the former things are passed away.

5   And he that sat upon **the throne**[6] said, Behold, **I make**[7] all things new. And he said **~~unto me~~**[8], Write: for these words are **true** and **faithful**[9].

6   And he said unto me, **It is done**[10]. I **~~am~~**[11] Alpha and Omega, the beginning and the end. I will give unto him that is athirst of the fountain of the water of life freely.

7   He that overcometh shall inherit **all things**[12]; and I will be his God, and he shall be my **[~~the~~]**[13] son.

8   But ∧**the**[14] fearful, and unbelieving, and the abominable, and murderers, and whoremongers, and **sorcerers**[15], and idolaters, and all

---

[1] WH changed the word order from SHALL BE with them to *with them SHALL BE.*

[2] In their margin, WH omitted their God (theos autOn).

[3] WH omitted the God (ho theos) and forced the verb to supply the subject he.

[4] WH changed **from** (**apo**) to *out of* (*ek*).

[5] WH omitted for (hoti).

[6] WH changed the throne (tou thronou) to *the throne* (*tO thronO*). **Gen** Masc Sing to *Dat* Masc Sing. [case]

[7] WH changed the word order from new all {things} I MAKE to *new I MAKE all* {things}.

[8] WH omitted unto me (moi) after he said.

[9] WH changed the word order from TRUE and FAITHFUL to *FAITHFUL and TRUE.*

[10] WH changed it is done (gegone) to *they are done* (*gegonan*). Both Pf Act Ind. 3rd **Sing** to 3rd *Plur.* [number]

[11] WH omitted I am (eimi) after the intensive I (egO).

[12] WH changed **all** {things} (**pan**ta) to *these* {things} (*tauta*).

[13] WH omitted the untranslated the (ho) from the son of me.

[14] WH added *the* (*tois*) as the KJV supplied.

[15] WH changed sorcerers (farmak**eusi**) to *sorcerers* (*farmakois*). Both Dat Masc Plur. [spell]

liars, shall have their part in the lake which burneth with fire and brimstone: which is ∧the[1] **second** [∧the][2] **death**[3].

9   And there came ~~unto me~~[4] one [∧**out of**][5] of the seven angels which had the seven vials **full of**[6] the seven last plagues, and talked with me, saying, Come hither, I will shew thee the bride, the **Lamb's**[7] wife.

10   And he carried me away in the spirit to a great and high mountain, and shewed me that ~~great~~[8] city,

the holy Jerusalem, descending out of heaven from God,

11   Having the glory of God: ~~and~~[9] her light *was* like unto a stone most precious, even like a jasper stone, clear as crystal;

12   ~~And~~[10] **had**[11] a wall great and high, *and* **had**[12] twelve gates, and at the gates twelve angels, and names written thereon, which are *the names* of the twelve tribes of ~~the~~[13] children of Israel:

13   On the east three gates; [∧**and**][14] on the north three gates; [∧**and**][15] on the south three gates; and on the west three gates.

14   And the wall of the city

---

[1] WH added *the* (*ho*) before second as the KJV supplied.
[2] WH added *the* (*ho*) before death.
[3] WH changed the word order from SECOND DEATH to *the* DEATH *the* SECOND.
[4] WH omitted unto me (pros me) after came.
[5] WH added *out of* (*ek*) after one.
[6] WH changed the {ones} full of (**tas gemousas**) to *the* {ones} *full of* (*tOn gemontOn*). Both Pres Act Part. **Acc Fem** Plur to *Gen Neut* Plur. [case & gender]
[7] WH changed the word order from OF THE LAMB the wife to *the wife* OF THE LAMB.
[8] WH omitted the great (tAn megalAn).

[9] WH omitted and (kai) after God.
[10] WH omitted and (te).
[11] WH changed having (ecousan) to *having* (*ecousa*). Both Pres Act Part. **Acc** Fem Sing to *Nom* Fem Sing. [case]
[12] WH changed having (ecousan) to *having* (*ecousa*). Both Pres Act Part. **Acc** Fem Sing To *Nom* Fem Sing. [case]
[13] WH omitted the (tOn) before children.
[14] WH added *and* (kai).
[15] WH added *and* (kai).

had[1] twelve foundations, and in[2] them[3] the [∧twelve][4] names of the twelve apostles of the Lamb.

15 And he that talked with me had a golden [∧measure][5] reed to measure the city, and the gates thereof, and the wall thereof.

16 And the city lieth four-square, and the length ~~is as large~~[6] as the breadth: ~~and~~[7] he measured the city with the reed, twelve thousand fur-longs. The length and the breadth and the height of it are equal.

17 And he measured the wall thereof, an hundred *and* forty *and* four cubits, *according to* the measure of a man, that is, of the angel.

18 And the **building**[8] of the wall of it ~~was~~[9] *of* jasper: and the city *was* pure gold, **like unto**[10] clear glass.

19 ~~And~~[11] the foundations of the wall of the city *were* garnished with all manner of precious stones. The first foundation *was* jasper; the second, sapphire; the third, a chalcedony; the fourth, an emerald;

20 The fifth, sardonyx; the sixth, **sardius**[12]; the seventh, chrysolite; the eighth, beryl; the ninth, a topaz; the tenth, a chrysoprasus; the eleventh, a jacinth; the twelfth, an ame-thyst.

21 And the twelve gates *were* twelve pearls; every several gate was of one pearl: and the street of the city *was*

---

[1] WH changed having (econ) to *having* (ecOn). Both Pres Act Part. Nom **Neut** Sing to Nom *Masc* Sing. [gender]
[2] WH changed in (en) to *on* (ep'). [prep]
[3] WH changed them (autois) to *them* (autOn). **Dat** Masc Plur to *Gen* Masc Plur. [case]
[4] WH added *twelve* (dOdeka) before names.
[5] WH added *measure* (met-ron) before reed.
[6] WH omitted is as large (to-souton estin).
[7] WH omitted and (kai).

[8] WH changed building (en-domAsis) to *building* (en-dOmAsis). Both Nom Fem Sing. [spell]
[9] WH omitted was (An).
[10] WH changed like unto ([h]omoia) to *like unto* ([h]o-moion). Nom **Fem** Sing to Nom *Neut* Sing. [gender]
[11] WH omitted and (kai).
[12] WH changed sardius (sar-dios) to *sardios* (sardion). Nom **Masc** Sing to Nom *Neut* Sing. [gender]

pure gold, as it were **transparent**[1] glass.

22 And I saw no temple therein: for the Lord God Almighty and the Lamb are the temple of it.

23 And the city had no need of the sun, neither of the moon, to shine ~~in~~[2] it: for the glory of God did lighten it, and the Lamb *is* the light thereof.

24 And the nations ~~of them which are saved~~[3] **shall walk**[4] **in**[5] the light of it: and the kings of the earth do bring their glory ~~and honour~~[6] into it.

---

[1] WH changed transparent (dia**fan**As) to *transparent* (diaug*As*). Both Adj: Nom Masc Sing. [syn]

[2] WH omitted in (en) and forced the dative case to supply the preposition.

[3] WH omitted of them which are saved (tOn sOzomenOn).

[4] WH changed the word order from and the nations **of the** {ones} **being saved** in the light of it SHALL WALK to *SHALL WALK the nations **through** the light of it.*

[5] WH changed **in** (**en**) to *through (dia)*. [prep]

[6] WH omitted and the honour (kai tAn timAn) from do bring the glory and the hon-

25 And the gates of it shall not be shut at all by day: for there shall be no night there.

26 And they shall bring the glory and honour of the nations into it.

27 And there shall in no wise enter into it any thing **that defileth**[7], neither *whatsoever* **worketh**[8] abomination, or *maketh* a lie: but they which are written in the Lamb's book of life.

CHAPTER 22

1 And he shewed me a **pure**[9] river of water of life, clear as crystal, proceeding out of the throne of God and of the Lamb.

2 In the midst of the street of it, and on either side of the river, *was there* **[from**

---

our of them.

[7] WH changed that defile**s** (koinoun) to *defiled (koinon)*. **Verbal**: Pres Act Part Nom Neut Sing to *Adj*: Nom Neut Sing. [part of sp]

[8] WH changed work**s** (poioun) to *the* {one} *working* (*h*o poiOn). Both Pres Act Part. Nom **Neut** Sing to Nom *Masc* Sing.

[9] WH omitted pure (kat**h**aron) before river.

here][1] the tree of life, which bare twelve _manner of_ fruits, _and_ yielded her fruit ~~every~~[2] month: and the leaves of the tree _were_ for the healing of the nations.

3   And there shall be no more **curse**[3]: but the throne of God and of the Lamb shall be in it; and his servants shall serve him:

4   And they shall see his face; and his name _shall be_ in their foreheads.

5   And there shall be no night **there**[4]; and they need no [∧**light of**][5] candle, neither light of the sun; for the Lord God **giveth** [∧**upon**][6] them **light**[7]: and they shall reign for ever and ever.

6   And he said unto me, These sayings _are_ faithful and true: and ∧**the**[8] Lord God of the **holy**[9] prophets sent his angel to shew unto his servants the things which must shortly be done.

7   [∧**and**][10]   Behold, I come quickly: blessed _is_ he that keepeth the sayings of the prophecy of this book.

8   And I John **saw** these things, **and**[11] heard _them._ And when I had heard and seen, I fell down to worship before the feet of the angel which   shewed   me   these things.

9   Then saith he unto me, See _thou do it_ not: ~~for~~[12] I am thy fellowservant, and of thy brethren the prophets, and of

---

[1] WH changed the untraslated from here (**enteut~~h~~en**) to _from there_ (_ekei~~th~~en_).

[2] WH omitted one ([h]ena) from the Gk phrase according to month one each. (kata mAna [h]ena [h]ekaston).

[3] WH changed curse (katana~~th~~ema) to _curse_ (_kata~~th~~ema_). [spell]

[4] WH changed **there** (**ekei**) to _still_ (_eti_).

[5] WH added _light of_ (_fOtos_) before candle.

[6] WH added _upon_ (_ep'_) before them.

[7] WH changed gives light (fOti~~z~~ei) to _will give light_

(fOtisei). **Pres** Act Ind to _Fut_ Act Ind. [tense]

[8] WH added _the_ ([h]o) as the KJV supplied.

[9] WH changed **holy** ([h]agiOn) to _spirits of the_ (_pneumatOn tOn_).

[10] WH added _and_ (_kai_) before behold.

[11] WH changed the word order from seeing these {things} AND HEARING to _HEARING AND seeing these_ {things}

[12] WH omitted for (gar).

them which keep the sayings of this book: worship God.

10 And he saith unto me, Seal not the sayings of the prophecy of this book: **for**[1] the time is at hand.

11 He that **is unjust**[2], **let him be unjust**[3] still: and he which is filthy, let him be filthy still: and he that is righteous, **let him be righteous**[4] still: and he that is holy, let him be holy still.

12 ~~And~~[5], behold, I come quickly; and my reward *is* with me, to give every man

according as **his**[6] work **shall be**[7].

13 I ~~am~~[8] Alpha and Omega, the beginning and the end, **the first and the last**[9].

14 Blessed *are* they that **do**[10] his **commandments**[11], that they may have right to the tree of life, and may enter in through the gates into the city.

15 ~~For~~[12] without *are* dogs, and sorcerers, and whore-mongers, and murderers, and idolaters, and whosoever

---

[1] WH changed <u>for</u> (^hoti) to *for* (*gar*).

[2] WH changed <u>the</u> {one} **be-ing** <u>unjust</u> (^ho ^hrup**On**) to *the* {one} *unjust* (^ho ^hruparos*). **Verbal**: Pres Act Part Nom Masc Sing to *Adj*: Nom Masc Sing.

[3] WH changed <u>let him **do** in-justice</u> (^hrup**OsatO**) to *let him be unjust* (^hru-pan**thAtO**). Aor **Act** Imp to Aor *Pass* Imp. [voice]

[4] WH changed <u>let him **be** righteous</u> (dikai**OthAtO**) to *let him do righteousness* (*di-kaiosunAn poiAsatO*). Aor **Pass** Imp to Aor *Act* Imp + *noun*.

[5] WH omitted <u>and</u> (*kai*) be-fore <u>behold</u>.

[6] WH changed the word or-der from <u>OF HIM</u> **shall be** to *is OF HIM*.

[7] WH changed **shall be** (<u>estai</u>) to *is* (*estin*). **Fut** NV Ind to *Pres* Act Ind. [tense]

[8] WH omitted <u>I am</u> (*eimi*) be-fore <u>I myself</u> (*egO*).

[9] WH changed the word or-der from <u>the</u> beginning <u>and the end</u> THE FIRST AND THE LAST to *THE FIRST AND THE LAST the beginning and the end.*

[10] WH changed {are} **doing** (**poiou**ntes) to {are} *washing* (*plunontes*). Pres Act Part of poieO to Pres Act Part of *plunO*.

[11] WH changed **command-ments** (<u>ento</u>las) to *robes* (*stolas*).

[12] WH omitted <u>for</u> (*de*).

loveth and maketh a lie.

16 I Jesus have sent mine angel to testify unto you these things in the churches. I am the root and the offspring of [∧**the**]¹ David, *and* the bright ~~and~~² **morning**³ star.

17 And the Spirit and the bride say, **Come**⁴. And let him that heareth say, **Come**⁵. And let him that is athirst **come**⁶. ~~And~~⁷ whosoever will, **let him take**⁸ ~~the~~⁹ water of

life freely.

18 ~~**For**~~¹⁰ **I testify**¹¹ [∧**myself**]¹² unto every [∧**the**]¹³ man that heareth the words of the prophecy of this book, If any man **shall add**¹⁴ **unto**¹⁵ **these things**¹⁶, God shall add unto him the plagues that are written in this [∧**the**]¹⁷ book:

19 And if any man **shall take away**¹⁸ from the words

---

¹ WH added *the* (*tou*) before David.
² WH omitted and (kai) between bright and morning.
³ WH changed morning (**or~~th~~rinos**) to *morning* (*prO-inos*). Both Adj: Nom Masc Sing. [syn]
⁴ WH changed come (**el~~th~~e**) to *be coming* (**ercou**). **Aor Act** Imp to *Pres Mid* Imp. [tense & voice]
⁵ WH changed come (**el~~th~~e**) to *be coming* {**for yourself**} (**ercou**). **Aor Act** Imp to *Pres Mid* Imp. [tense & voice]
⁶ WH changed come (**el~~th~~etO**) to *be coming* {**for yourself**} (**erces~~th~~O**). **Aor Act** Imp to *Pres Mid* Imp. [tense & voice]
⁷ WH omitted and (kai).
⁸ WH changed let him **be taking** (**lambanetO**) to *let him take* (*labetO*). **Pres** Act Imp

⁹ WH omitted the (to) before water.
¹⁰ WH omitted for (gar).
¹¹ WH changed I testify (**sum**marturoumai) to *I testify* (*marturO*). Pres M/P Ind of **sum**martureO to Pres Act Ind of *martureO*.
¹² WH added *myself* (*egO*) after I testify.
¹³ WH added *the* (*tO*) before the Gk participle hearing.
¹⁴ WH changed he **may** add (epiti~~th~~A) to *he **might** add*. **Pres** Act Sub to *Aor* Act Sub. [tense]
¹⁵ WH changed **unto** (*pros*) to **upon** (*ep'*). [prep]
¹⁶ WH **these** {things} (**tauta**) to *them* (*auta*).
¹⁷ WH added *the* (*tO*) before book.
¹⁸ WH changed **may** take away (afaira) to ***might** take away* (*afelei*). **Pres** Act Sub to *Aor* Act Sub. [tense]

of ˄the[1] book of this prophecy, God **shall take away**[2] his part out of ˄the[3] **book**[4] of life, and out of the holy city, ~~and~~[5] *from* the things which are written in this [˄the][6] book.

20 He which testifieth these things saith, Surely I come quickly. Amen. ~~Even so~~[7], come, Lord Jesus.

21 The grace of ~~our~~[8] Lord Jesus ~~Christ~~[9] *be* with **you all**[10]. Amen.

---

[1] WH added *the* (*tou*) before book as the KJV supplied.

[2] WH changed shall take away (**afairAse**i) to *shall take away* (*afelei*). Both Fut Act Ind of afaireO.

[3] WH added *the* (*tou*) before book as the KJV supplied.

[4] WH changed **book** (**bibl**ou) to *tree* (*xulou*).

[5] WH omitted and (kai).

[6] WH added *the* (*tO*) before book.

[7] WH omitted even so (nai) after amen.

[8] WH omitted of us ([h]AmOn) from the Lord of us.

[9] WH omitted Christ (cristou) in their text, but retained it in their margin.

[10] WH changed **you all** (**pant**On [h]**um**On) to *the holy* {ones} (*tOn hagiOn*). In their margin, WH retained just *all* (*pantOn*).